JOSEPH BLENKINSOPP

EZRA-NEHEMIAH

THE OLD TESTAMENT LIBRARY

JOSEPH BLENKINSOPP

EZRA-NEHEMIAH

A Commentary

THE WESTMINSTER PRESS
PHILADELPHIA

First edition

Published by The Westminster Press®
Philadelphia, Pennsylvania

PRINTED IN THE UNITED STATES OF AMERICA

9 8 7 6 5 4 3 2 1

Library of Congress Cataloging-in-Publication Data

Blenkinsopp, Joseph, 1927–
   Ezra-Nehemiah : a commentary / Joseph Blenkinsopp.
      p.   cm. — (The Old Testament library)
   Bibliography: p.
   ISBN 0-664-22186-6 pbk

   1. Bible. O.T. Ezra—Commentaries. 2. Bible. O.T.
Nehemiah—Commentaries. I. Title. II. Series.
BS1355.3.B58 1988
222'.7077—dc19   88-14877
                                     CIP

In the vacant places
We will build with new bricks
There are hands and machines
And clay for new brick
And lime for new mortar
Where the bricks are fallen
We will build with new stone
Where the beams are rotten
We will build with new timbers
Where the word is unspoken
We will build with new speech.

T. S. Eliot, *The Rock*

Wer spricht von Siegen? Überstehn ist alles.

R. M. Rilke

CONTENTS

PREFACE

In writing this commentary over the last three years or so I have incurred many debts of gratitude: to my family for their patience, and to students and colleagues here and elsewhere for arguing points of interpretation or just listening politely. It is a pleasant duty to thank especially my assistants Mr. John Wright and Mr. Yun Chun Han for help with research, to graduate student Sister Catherine Cory for opportune help with a recalcitrant computer, to colleague Professor Gene Ulrich for supplying photographs of 4QEzra, and to Dr. Keith Crim for inviting me on behalf of The Westminster Press to write the commentary.

The translation offered is my own, and I have supplied it with what seemed the necessary minimum of textual notes. I have departed from scholarly orthopraxy in transliterating the sixth letter of the Hebrew alphabet as v instead of w, and have therefore written the Tetragrammaton YHVH rather than YHWH. Some may find this objectionable or merely annoying, but it has the advantage of alignment with current pronunciation, now that a command of modern Hebrew is a practical necessity in the study of the Hebrew Bible. For convenience of reference, works cited by author only will usually be found listed in the select bibliography at the head of each section. Works cited by author and year will be found in the general bibliography of "Works Consulted."

The commentary grew out of a long-standing interest in the religious history of the Second Temple period. Writing almost sixty years ago, Hans Heinrich Schaeder, author of an important monograph on Ezra, described what was then—and residually still is—the standard approach to postexilic Judaism in Christian scholarship, and concluded as follows: "This historical perspective, which sees Judaism as fulfilling its mission and then making way for the gospel and the Church, has an impressive inner consistency and spiritual allure; the only problem with it is the real history of Judaism" (*Esra der Schreiber,* Tübingen, 1930, 2). My hope is that the present commentary may make a modest contribution to recovering that history.

December 15, 1987   Joseph Blenkinsopp

ABBREVIATIONS

AASOR	Annual of the American Schools of Oriental Research
ABR	Australian Biblical Review
AfO	Archiv für Orientforschung
AI	R. de Vaux, *Ancient Israel: Its Life and Institutions,* London, 1961
AJBA	*Australian Journal of Biblical Archaeology*
AJSL	*American Journal of Semitic Languages and Literatures*
Akk.	Akkadian
ANEP	J. B. Pritchard (ed.), *The Ancient Near East in Pictures,* Princeton, 1954
ANET	J. B. Pritchard (ed.), *Ancient Near Eastern Texts,* Princeton, 1969³
Ant.	Josephus, *Antiquities*
AP	A. Cowley, *Aramaic Papyri of the Fifth Century B.C.,* Oxford, 1923
Arab.	Arabic version
Aram.	Aramaic
AUSS	*Andrews University Seminary Studies*
BA	*Biblical Archaeologist*
BAR	*Biblical Archaeology Review*
BASOR	*Bulletin of the American Schools of Oriental Research*
BDB	F. Brown, S. R. Driver, and C. A. Briggs, *Hebrew and English Lexicon of the Old Testament,* Oxford, 1907
Bib	*Biblica*
BeO	*Bibbia e Oriente*
BJPES	*Bulletin of the Jewish Palestine Exploration Society*
BM	*Beit Mikra*
BMAP	E. G. Kraeling, *The Brooklyn Museum Aramaic Papyri,* New Haven, 1953
BO	*Bibliotheca Orientalis*
BR	*Bible Review*
BSac	*Bibliotheca Sacra*

BSOAS	*Bulletin of the School of Oriental and African Studies*
BTB	*Biblical Theology Bulletin*
BZ	*Biblische Zeitschrift*
C	the Chronicler
CAD	*The Assyrian Dictionary of the Oriental Institute of the University of Chicago*
C. Apion	Josephus, *Contra Apion*
CBQ	*Catholic Biblical Quarterly*
CHJ	W. D. Davies and L. Finkelstein (eds.), *The Cambridge History of Judaism* I, Cambridge, 1984
cod.	codex
CTM	*Concordia Theological Monthly*
CV	*Communio Viatorum*
DBSup.	*Dictionnaire de la Bible. Supplément*
EAEHL	M. Avi-Yonah (ed.), *Encyclopedia of Archaeological Excavations in the Holy Land,* 4 vols., Jerusalem, 1975–78
EI	*Eretz Israel*
EM	Ezra Memoir
Eth.	Ethiopic version
ETL	*Ephemerides Theologicae Lovanienses*
Ep.	*Epistula*
EstBib	*Estudios Biblicos*
EvQ	*Evangelical Quarterly*
EvTh	*Evangelische Theologie*
ExpT	*Expository Times*
Gk.	Greek
GTT	*Gereformeerd Theologisch Tijdschrift*
Heb.	Hebrew
HB	Hebrew Bible
Hist. Eccl.	Eusebius, *Historia Ecclesiastica*
HJ	*Heythrop Journal*
HTR	*Harvard Theological Review*
HUCA	*Hebrew Union College Annual*
IB	*Interpreter's Bible*
IDB	G. A. Buttrick (ed.), *Interpreter's Dictionary of the Bible* 4 vols., Nashville, 1962
IDBSup.	K. Crim (ed.), *IDB Supplementary Volume,* Nashville, 1976
IEJ	*Israel Exploration Journal*
Int.	*Interpretation*
IR	*Iliff Review*
JAOS	*Journal of the American Oriental Society*
JBL	*Journal of Biblical Literature*
JEA	*Journal of Egyptian Archaeology*
JNES	*Journal of Near Eastern Studies*
JNSL	*Journal of Northwest Semitic Languages*

JJS	*Journal of Jewish Studies*
JPOS	*Journal of the Palestine Oriental Society*
JQR	*Jewish Quarterly Review*
JSJ	*Journal for the Study of Judaism in the Persian, Hellenistic and Roman Period*
JSOR	*Journal of the Society for Oriental Research*
JSOT	*Journal for the Study of the Old Testament*
JSS	*Journal of Semitic Studies*
JTS	*Journal of Theological Studies*
KS	A. Alt, *Kleine Schriften,* 3 vols., Munich, 1953–59
L	Lucianic recension of LXX
LXX	Septuagint, Greek translation of the OT (LXX^A = Codex Alexandrinus; LXX^B = Codex Vaticanus; LXX^L = Lucianic recension; LXX^S = Codex Sinaiticus)
MS(S)	Manuscript(s)
MT	Masoretic text
NAB	New American Bible
NEB	New English Bible
NM	Nehemiah Memoir
NTT	*Nieuw Theologisch Tijdschrift*
OG	Old Greek version
OLZ	*Orientalische Literaturzeitung*
OTS	*Oudtestamentische Studiën*
PEF	*Palestine Exploration Fund*
PEQ	*Palestine Exploration Quarterly*
PJB	*Palästina-Jahrbuch*
PTR	*Princeton Theological Review*
RA	*Revue d'Assyriologie et d'Archéologie Orientale*
RB	*Revue Biblique*
RevBibl	*Revista Biblica*
RGG	*Die Religion in Geschichte und Gegenwart*
RHP	*Revue de l'Histoire des Religions*
RHPR	*Revue d'Histoire et de Philosophie Religieuses*
RSV	Revised Standard Version
SEA	*Svensk Exegetisk Årsbok*
StTh	*Studia Theologica*
Syr	Syriac version
Targ	Targum
TDOT	G. T. Botterweck and H. Ringgren (eds.), *Theological Dictionary of the Old Testament,* Grand Rapids, 1977–
TLZ	*Theologische Literaturzeitung*
Ug.	Ugaritic
UM	C. H. Gordon, *Ugaritic Manual,* Rome 1955
US	M. Noth, *Überlieferungsgeschichtliche Studien,* Halle, 1943
VD	*Verbum Domini*
VT	*Vetus Testamentum*

VTSup.	Supplements to *Vetus Testamentum*
Vulg.	Vulgate edition
ZAW	*Zeitschrift für die alttestamentliche Wissenschaft*
ZDMG	*Zeitschrift für die deutsche Morgenländische Gesellschaft*
ZDPV	*Zeitschrift des deutschen Palästina-Vereins*
ZRGG	*Zeitschrift für Religions- und Geistesgeschichte*

Rabbinic and Qumranic texts

b.	Babylonian Talmud
j.	Jerusalem Talmud (Talmud of the Land of Israel)
m.	Mishnah
t.	Tosephta
Abot	The Sayings of the Fathers
B.B.	*Baba Batra*
Ber.	*Berakot*
B.K.	*Baba Kamma*
Cant Rab.	*Canticles Rabbah*
Erub.	*Erubin*
Gen. Rab.	*Genesis Rabbah*
Hor.	*Horayot*
Hull.	*Hullin*
Kidd.	*Kiddushin*
Lev. Rab.	*Leviticus Rabbah*
Makk.	*Makkot*
Meg.	*Megillah*
Pes.	*Pesahim*
Sanh.	*Sanhedrin*
Shabb.	*Shabbat*
Sukk.	*Sukkah*
Taan.	*Taanit*
Yeb.	*Yebamot*
CD	Damascus Document
4QDibHam[a]	Words of the Heavenly Luminaries from Cave 4 (see Baillet)
4QEzra	Ezra fragments from Cave 4
1QM	War Scroll from Cave 1
1QPs[a]	Psalms Scroll from Cave 1
1QS	Community Rule *(serek)* from Cave 1

WORKS CONSULTED

Ackroyd, P. R., 1958. "Two Old Testament Historical Problems of the Early Persian Period," *JNES* 17, 13–27.

———, 1968a. *Exile and Restoration,* London and Philadelphia.

———, 1968b. "Historians and Prophets," *SEA* 33, 18–54.

———, 1970. *Israel Under Babylon and Persia,* Oxford.

———, 1972. "The Temple Vessels—A Continuity Theme," *VTSup.* 23, 166–181.

———, 1973. *I & II Chronicles, Ezra, Nehemiah,* London.

———, 1976. "God and People in the Chronicler's Presentation of Ezra," in J. Coppens (ed.), *La notion biblique de Dieu,* Louvain, 145–162.

———, 1979a. "Faith and Its Reformulation in the Post-exilic Period," *Theology Digest* 27, 323–346.

———, 1979b. "The History of Israel in the Exilic and Post-exilic Periods," in G. W. Anderson (ed.), *Tradition and Interpretation,* Oxford, 328–342.

———, 1982. "Archaeology, Politics and Religion," *IR* 39, 11–13.

———, 1984. "The Jewish Community in Palestine in the Persian Period," *CHJ* I, 130–161.

———, 1985. "The Historical Literature," in D. A. Knight and G. M. Tucker (eds.), *The Hebrew Bible and Its Modern Interpreters,* Philadelphia, 297–324.

Aharoni, Y., 1962. *Excavations at Ramat Rahel (1959–1960),* Rome.

———, 1969. "The Israelite Sanctuary at Arad," in D. N. Freedman and J. C. Greenfield (eds.), *New Directions in Biblical Archaeology,* Garden City, 28–32.

———, 1970. "Three Hebrew Ostraca from Arad," *BASOR* 197, 16–28.

———, 1979. *The Land of the Bible* (2nd ed.), London.

Albright, W. F., 1921. "The Date and Personality of the Chronicler," *JBL* 40, 104–124.

———, 1953. "Dedan," in G. Ebeling (ed.), *Geschichte und Altes Testament,* Beiträge zur historischen Theologie, Tübingen, 1–12.

———, 1965. *The Biblical Period from Abraham to Ezra* (2nd ed.), New York, 81–96.

Alexander, P. S., 1978. "Remarks on Aramaic Epistolography in the Persian Period," *JSS* 23, 155–170.

Allan, N., 1982. "The Jerusalem Priesthood During the Exile," *HJ* 23, 259–269.

Allgeier, A., 1941. "Beobachtungen am LXX-Text der Bücher Esdras und Nehemias," *Bib* 22, 227–251.

Allrik, H. L., 1954a. "I Esdras According to Codex B and Codex A," *ZAW* 66, 272–292.

———, 1954b. "The Lists of Zerubbabel (Neh. 7 and Ezr. 2) and the Hebrew Numerical Notation," *BASOR* 136, 21–27.

Alt, A., 1928. "Das Taltor von Jerusalem," *PJB* 24, 74–98 (= Alt, *Kleine Schriften zur Geschichte des Volkes Israels* III, Munich, 1959, 326–347).

———, 1931. "Judas Nachbarn zur Zeit Nehemias," *PJB* 27, 58–74 (= *Kleine Schriften* II, 1953, 338–345).

———, 1934. "Die Rolle Samarias bei der Entstehung des Judentums," *Festschrift Otto Procksch zum 60. Geburtstag,* Leipzig, 5–28 (= *Kleine Schriften* II, 1953, 316–337).

———, 1935. "Zur Geschichte der Grenze zwischen Judäa und Samaria," *PJB* 31, 94–111 (= *Kleine Schriften* II, 1953, 346–362).

Andersen, F. I., 1958. "Who Built the Second Temple?" *ABR* 6, 1–35.

———, 1969. "Israelite Kinship Terminology and Social Structure," *Bible Translator* 20, 29–39.

Ararat, N., 1972. "Ezra and His Activity in the Biblical and Post-biblical Sources," *BM* 17, 451–492 (Heb.).

Auscher, D., 1967. "Les relations entre la Grèce et la Palestine avant la conquête d'Alexandre," *VT* 17, 8–30.

Avigad, N., 1970. "Excavations in the Jewish Quarter of the Old City of Jerusalem," *IEJ* 20, 129–140.

———, 1976. *Bullae and Seals from a Post-exilic Judaean Archive,* Qedem: Monographs of the Institute of Archaeology 4, Jerusalem.

———, 1980. *Discovering Jerusalem,* Nashville.

Avi-Yonah, M., 1954. "The Walls of Nehemiah—A Minimalist View," *IEJ* 4, 239–248.

———, 1966. *The Holy Land from the Persian to the Arab Conquest,* Grand Rapids.

———, 1971. "The Newly-Found Wall of Jerusalem and Its Topographical Significance," *IEJ* 21, 168–169.

Baillet, M., 1961. "Un recueil liturgique de Qumran, Grotte 4: Les Paroles des Luminaires," *RB* 68, 1961, 195–250.

Baltzer, K., 1961. "Das Ende des Staates Juda und die Messiasfrage," in R. Rendtorff and K. Koch (eds.), *Studien zur Theologie der alttestamentlichen Überlieferungen,* Neukirchen, 33–44.

Barag, D., 1966. "The Effects of the Tennes Rebellion on Palestine," *BASOR* 183, 6–12.

Bartal, A., 1979. "Again—Who Was Sheshbazzar?" *BM* 24, 357–369 (Heb.).

Barthélemy, D., 1982. *Critique textuelle de l'Ancien Testament* I, Fribourg.

Batten, L. W., 1913. *A Critical and Exegetical Commentary on the Books of Ezra and Nehemiah,* Edinburgh.

Bayer, E., 1911. *Das dritte Buch Esdras und sein Verhältnis zu den Büchern Esra-Nehemia,* Freiburg-im-Breisgau.

Baynes, N. H., 1924. "Zerubbabel's Rebuilding of the Temple," *JTS* 25, 154–160.

Begrich, J., 1940. "Sōfēr und Mazkīr," *ZAW* 58, 1–29.

Bengtson, H., 1969. "Syria Under the Persians," *The Greeks and the Persians,* London, 386–401.

Bentzen, A., 1930. "Quelques remarques sur le mouvement messianique parmi les Juifs aux environs de l'an 520 avant Jésus-Christ," *RHPR* 10, 493–503.

———, 1930/31. "Priesterschaft und Laien in der jüdischen Gemeinde des fünften Jahrhunderts," *AfO* 6, 280–286.

———, 1950/51. "Sirach, der Chronist und Nehemia," *StTh* 3, 158–161.

Ben-Yashar, M., 1981. "On the Problem of Sheshbazzar and Zerubbabel," *BM* 27, 46–56 (Heb.).

Bertheau, E., and V. Ryssel, 1882. *Die Bücher Esra, Nehemia und Ester erklärt,* Leipzig.

Bertholet, A., 1902. *Die Bücher Esra und Nehemia,* Tübingen and Leipzig.

Betlyon, J. W., 1986. "The Provincial Government of Persian Period Judea and the Yehud Coins," *JBL* 105, 633–642.

Bewer, J. A., 1919. "The Gap Between Ezra Chapters 1 and 2," *AJSL* 36, 18–26.

———, 1922. *Der Text des Buches Esra,* Göttingen.

———, 1924. "Josephus' Accounts of Nehemiah," *JBL* 43, 226–227.

Beyse, K-M., 1971. *Serubbabel und die Königserwartungen der Propheten Haggai und Sacharja,* Berlin.

Bickerman, E. J., 1946. "The Edict of Cyrus in Ezra 1," *JBL* 65, 249–275 (= *Studies in Jewish and Christian History,* Leiden, 1976, 72–108).

———, 1948. "Viri magnae congregationis," *RB* 55, 397–402.

———, 1962. *From Ezra to the Last of the Maccabees,* New York.

———, 1981. "En marge de l'Ecriture. I. Le comput des années de règne des Achéménides (Néh. i,2; ii,1 et Thuc. viii,58)," *RB* 88, 19–23.

Bigwood, J. M., 1976. "Ctesias' Account of the Revolt of Inarus," *Phoenix* 30, 1–25.

Bossman, D., 1979. "Ezra's Marriage Reform: Israel Redefined," *BTB* 9, 32–38.

Bowman, J., 1975. *The Samaritan Problem: Studies in the Relationships of Samaritanism, Judaism and Early Christianity,* Pittsburgh.

———, 1977. *Samaritan Documents Relating to Their History, Religion and Life,* Pittsburgh.

Bowman, R. A., 1941. "An Aramaic Journal Page," *AJSL* 58, 302–313.

———, 1954. "Ezra and Nehemiah," *Interpreter's Bible* III, New York and Nashville, 551–819.

———, 1970. *Aramaic Ritual Texts from Persepolis,* Chicago.

Boyce, M., 1975–82. *A History of Zoroastrianism,* vols. I, II, Leiden.

———, 1984. "Persian Religion in the Achemenid Age," *CHJ* I, 279–307.

Braun, R. L., 1979. "Chronicles, Ezra and Nehemiah: Theology and Literary History," *VTSup.* 30, 52–64.

Bresciani, E., 1984. "Egypt, Persian Satrapy," *CHJ* I, 358–372.

Bright, J., 1981. *A History of Israel* (3rd ed.), Philadelphia.

Brindle, W. A., 1984. "The Origin and History of the Samaritans," *GTJ* 5, 47–75.

Brockington, L. H., 1969. *Ezra, Nehemiah and Esther,* London.

Broshi, M., 1974. "The Expansion of Jerusalem in the Reigns of Hezekiah and Manasseh," *IEJ* 24, 21–26.

Browne, L. E., 1916. "A Jewish Sanctuary in Babylon," *JTS* 17, 400–401.

————, 1962. "Ezra and Nehemiah," *Peake's Commentary on the Bible* (ed. M. Black and H. H. Rowley), London, 370–380.

Buis, P., 1967. "Notification de jugement et confession nationale," *BZ* n.F. 11, 193–205.

Cameron, G. G., 1941. "Darius and Xerxes in Babylonia," *AJSL* 58, 314–325.

————, 1943. "Darius, Egypt and the 'Lands Beyond the Sea,' " *JNES* 2, 307–313.

————, 1948. *Persepolis Treasury Tablets,* Chicago.

————, 1955. "Ancient Persia," in R. C. Dentan (ed.), *The Idea of History in the Ancient Near East,* New Haven, 79–97.

————, 1965. "New Tablets from the Persepolis Treasury," *JNES* 24, 167–192.

Cardascia, G., 1951. *Les Archives des Murašū: Une famille d'hommes d'affaires babyloniens à l'époque perse (455–403 av. J.-C.),* Paris.

Caro, J. M. S., 1985. "Esdras, Nehemias y los origenes del judaismo," *Salmanticensis* 32, 5–34.

Causse, A., 1937. *Du groupe ethnique à la communauté religieuse,* Paris.

Cazelles, H., 1954. "La mission d'Esdras," *VT* 4, 113–140.

Clines, D. J. A., 1974. "The Evidence for an Autumnal New Year in Pre-exilic Israel Reconsidered," *JBL* 93, 22–40.

————, 1984. *Ezra, Nehemiah, Esther,* Grand Rapids.

Cody, A., 1969. *A History of Old Testament Priesthood,* Rome.

Cogan, M., 1979. "The Men of Nebo—Repatriated Reubenites," *IEJ* 29, 37–39.

Coggins, R. J., 1975. *Samaritans and Jews: The Origins of Samaritanism Reconsidered,* Atlanta.

————, 1976. *The Books of Ezra and Nehemiah,* Cambridge.

Coggins, R. J., and M. A. Knibb, 1979. *The First and Second Books of Esdras,* New York and London.

Cohn, H., 1973. "Legal Studies in the Book of Ezra," in *Zer li-Geburot* (Zalman Shazar Jubilee Volume), Jerusalem, 371–401 (Heb.).

Coogan, M. D., 1973. "Patterns in Jewish Personal Names in the Diaspora," *JSJ* 4, 184–191.

————, 1974. "Life in the Diaspora: Jews at Nippur in the Fifth Century B.C.," *BA* 37, 6–12.

————, 1976. *West Semitic Personal Names in the Murašû Documents,* Missoula.

Cook, J. M., 1983. *The Persian Empire,* London.

Cook, S. A., 1950. "The Age of Zerubbabel," in H. H. Rowley (ed.), *Studies in Old Testament Prophecy Presented to Theodore H. Robinson,* Edinburgh, 19–36.

Cowley, A., 1910. "Ezra's Recension of the Law," *JTS* 11, 542–545.

————, 1923. *Aramaic Papyri of the Fifth Century B.C.,* Oxford.

Cross, F. M., 1955. "Geshem the Arabian, Enemy of Nehemiah," *BA* 18, 46–47.

————, 1963. "The Discovery of the Samaria Papyri," *BA* 26, 110–121.

————, 1965. "The Aramaic Script of the Late Persian Empire and the Rise of the National Script," in G. E. Wright (ed.), *The Bible and the Ancient Near East: Essays in Honor of W. F. Albright,* Garden City, 174–213.

————, 1966. "Aspects of Samaritan and Jewish History in Late Persian and Hellenistic Times," *HTR* 59, 201–211.

————, 1969a. "Judean Stamps," *EI* 9, 20–27.

———, 1969b. "Papyri from the Fourth Century B.C. from Dâliyeh," in D. N. Freedman and J. C. Greenfield (eds.), *New Directions in Biblical Archaeology,* Garden City, 41–62.

———, 1973. "Notes on the Ammonite Inscription from Tell Sīrān," *BASOR* 212, 12–15.

———, 1974. "The Papyri and Their Historical Implications," *AASOR* 41, 17–29.

———, 1975. "A Reconstruction of the Judean Restoration," *JBL* 94, 4–18 (= *Int.* 29, 1975, 187–203).

Cullican, W., 1965. *The Medes and the Persians,* New York and Washington.

Dandamaev, M. A., 1976. *Persien unter den ersten Achämeniden,* Wiesbaden.

———, 1984. "Babylonia in the Persian Age," *CHJ* I, 326–342.

Delcor, M., 1962. "Hinweise auf das samaritanische Schisma im Alten Testament," *ZAW* 74, 281–291.

———, 1968. "Le Temple d'Onias en Egypt," *RB* 75, 188–203.

Dion, P-E., 1979. "Les types épistolaires hébréo-araméens jusqu'au temps de Bar-Kokhbah," *RB* 96, 544–579.

Dougherty, R. P., 1923. *The Shirkûtu of Babylonian Deities,* New Haven.

Driver, G. R., 1957. *Aramaic Documents of the Fifth Century B.C.,* London.

———, 1966. "Forgotten Hebrew Idioms," *ZAW* 78, 1–7.

Driver, S. R., 1897. *Introduction to the Literature of the Old Testament,* Edinburgh (repr. Cleveland and New York, 1956), 516–554.

Dumbrell, W. J., 1971. "The Tell el-Maskhuta Bowls and the 'Kingdom' of Qedar in the Persian Period," *BASOR* 203, 33–44.

Dunand, M., 1968. "La défense du front mediterranéan de l'empire Achéménide," in W. A. Ward (ed.), *The Role of the Phoenicians in the Interaction of Mediterranean Civilizations,* Beirut, 43–51.

Dupont-Sommer, A., 1979. "L'Inscription Araméenne," in H. Metzger et al., *Fouilles de Xanthos,* Paris, 129–178.

Ehrlich, A. B., 1914. *Randglossen zur hebräischen Bibel* VII, Leipzig.

Ehtecham, M., 1946. *L'Iran sous les Achéménides,* Fribourg.

Eilers, W., 1940. *Iranische Beamtennamen in der Keilschriftlichen Überlieferung,* Abhandlungen für die Kunde des Morgenlandes 25, Leipzig.

Eissfeldt, O., 1965. *The Old Testament: An Introduction,* Oxford, 541–557.

Ellis, R., 1968. *Foundation Deposits in Ancient Mesopotamia,* New Haven.

Ellison, H. L., 1981. "The Importance of Ezra," *EvQ* 53, 48–53.

Emerton, J. A., 1966. "Did Ezra Go to Jerusalem in 428 B.C.?" *JTS* 17, 1–19.

Epstein, L. M., 1942. *Marriage Laws in the Bible and Talmud,* Cambridge, Mass.

Eskenazi, T. C., 1986. "The Chronicler and the Composition of 1 Esdras," *CBQ* 48, 39–61.

Fennelly, J. M., 1980. "The Persepolis Ritual," *BA* 43, 135–162.

Fensham, F. C., 1975. "Mĕdînâ in Ezra and Nehemiah," *VT* 25, 795–797.

———, 1982. *The Books of Ezra and Nehemiah,* Grand Rapids.

———, 1983. "Some Theological and Religious Aspects in Ezra and Nehemiah," *JNSL* 11, 59–68.

Fernández, A., 1921. "Epoca de la Actividad de Esdras," *Bib* 2, 431–439.

———, 1950. *Esdras y Nehemias,* Madrid.

————, 1951. "Esdras y Nehemias," *Bib* 32, 196–218.

Fischer, J., 1903. *Die chronologische Fragen in den Büchern Esra-Nehemia,* Freiburg-im-Breisgau.

Fishbane, M., 1985. *Biblical Interpretation in Ancient Israel,* Oxford.

Fitzmyer, J. A., 1974. "Some Notes on Aramaic Epistolography," *JBL* 93, 201–225.

————, 1979. "Aramaic Epistolography," *A Wandering Aramean: Collected Aramaic Essays,* Missoula, 183–204.

Fraenkel, S., 1899. "Zum Buche Ezra," *ZAW* 19, 178–180.

Fraine, J. de, 1961. *Esdras en Nehemias,* Roermond.

Frame, G., 1984. "Neo-Babylonian and Achaemenid Economic Texts from the Sippar Collection of the British Museum," *JAOS* 104, 745–752.

Frei, P., and K. Koch, 1984. *Reichsidee und Reichsorganisation im Perserreich,* Freiburg and Göttingen.

Frye, R. N., 1976. *The Heritage of Persia,* London, 119–137.

————, 1984. *The History of Ancient Iran,* Munich, 87–135.

Galling, K., 1937a. "Kyrus-edikt und Tempelbau," *OLZ* 40, 473–478.

————, 1937b. "Der Tempelschatz nach Berichten und Urkunden im Buche Esra," *ZDPV* 60, 177–183.

————, 1938. "Denkmäler zur Geschichte Syriens und Palästinas unter der Herrschaft der Perser," *PJB* 34, 59–79.

————, 1950. "Königliche und nichtkönigliche Stifter beim Tempel in Jerusalem," *ZDPV* 68, 134–142.

————, 1952. "Die Exilwende in der Sicht des Propheten Sacharja," *VT* 2, 18–36.

————, 1953–54. "Von Naboned zu Darius," *ZDPV* 69, 1953, 46–64; 70, 1954, 4–32.

————, 1954. *Die Bücher der Chronik, Esra, Nehemia,* Göttingen.

————, 1961. "Serubbabel und der Wiederaufbau des Tempels in Jerusalem," in A. Kuschke (ed.), *Verbannung und Heimkehr,* Tübingen, 67–96.

————, 1964. *Studien zur Geschichte Israels im persischen Zeitalter,* Tübingen.

Gamoran, H., 1971/72. "The Biblical Law Against Loans on Interest," *JNES* 30, 1971/72, 127–134.

Gardner, A. E., 1986. "The Purpose and Date of I Esdras," *JJS* 37, 18–27.

Geissler, J., 1899. *Die literarischen Beziehungen der Esramemoiren insb. zur Chronik und den hexateuchischen Quellschriften,* Chemnitz.

Gelin, A., 1960. *Le Livre d'Esdras et Néhémie* (2nd ed.), Paris.

Gelston, A., 1966. "The Foundations of the Second Temple," *VT* 16, 232–235.

Gertner, M., 1962. "Terms of Scriptural Interpretation: A Study in Hebrew Semantics," *BSOAS* 25, 22–23.

Gese, H., 1963. "Zur Geschichte der Kultsänger am zweiten Tempel," in O. Betz (ed.), *Abraham unser Vater,* Leiden, 222–234.

Geva, H., 1979. "The Western Boundary of Jerusalem at the End of the Monarchy," *IEJ* 29, 84–91.

Ghirshman, R., 1954. *Iran,* Harmondsworth, 106–205.

Gilbert, M., 1981. "La place de la loi dans la prière de Néhémie 9," in M. Carrez et al. (eds.), *De la Tôrah au Messie,* Paris, 307–316.

Gillis, D., 1979. *Collaboration with the Persians,* Historia Einzelschrift 34, Wiesbaden.

Goldstein, J. A., 1983. *II Maccabees: A New Translation with Introduction and Commentary,* Garden City, 154–188.

Gotthard, H., 1958. *Der Text des Buches Nehemia,* Wiesbaden.

Grabbe, L. L., 1987. "The Jewish Theocracy from Cyrus to Titus: A Programmatic Essay," *JSOT* 37, 125–128.

Grafman, R., 1974. "Nehemiah's 'Broad Wall,' " *IEJ* 24, 50–51.

Grelot, P., 1954. "Etudes sur le 'Papyrus Pascal' d'Eléphantine,' " *VT* 4, 349–384.

——, 1955. "Le Papyrus Pascal d'Eléphantine et le problème du Pentateuque," *VT* 5, 250–265.

——, 1956. "La dernière étape de la rédaction sacerdotale," *VT* 6, 174–189.

——, 1967. "Le Papyrus Pascal d'Eléphantine: Essai de restauration," *VT* 17, 201–207.

——, 1972. *Documents araméens d'Egypt,* Paris.

Grosheide, H. H., 1950. "Een geschrift van Tabeël?" *GTT* 50, 71–79.

——, 1954a. "Juda als onderdeel van het Perzische Rijk," *GTT* 54, 65–76.

——, 1954b. "Twee Edicten van Cyrus ten gunste van de Joden," *GTT* 54, 1–12.

——, 1956. "Ezra de Schriftgeleerde," *GTT* 56, 84–88.

Gunneweg, A. H. J., 1965. *Leviten und Priester,* Göttingen.

——, 1981. "Zur Interpretation der Bücher Esra-Nehemia," *VTSup.* 32, 146–161.

——, 1982. "Die aramäische und die hebräische Erzählung über die nachexilische Restauration—ein Vergleich," *ZAW* 94, 299–302.

Hallock, R. T., 1969. *Persepolis Fortification Tablets,* Chicago.

Hanel, J., 1937. "Das Recht des Opferschlachtens in der chronistischen Literatur," *ZAW* 55, 46–67.

Hanhart, R., 1974. *Text und Textgeschichte des 1. Esrabuches,* Göttingen.

——, 1977. "Zu Text und Textgeschichte des ersten Esrabuches," *Proceedings of the Sixth World Congress of Jewish Studies,* Jerusalem, 201–212.

——, 1982, "Zu den ältesten Traditionen über das Samaritanische Schisma," *EI* 16, 106–115.

Haran, M., 1961. "The Gibeonites, the Nethinim and the Sons of Solomon's Servants," *VT* 11, 159–169.

——, 1961. "Studies in the Account of the Levitical Cities," *JBL* 80, 45–54, 156–165.

——, 1978. *Temples and Temple Service in Ancient Israel: An Inquiry Into the Character of Cult Phenomena and the Historical Setting of the Priestly School,* Oxford.

——, 1982. "Book Scrolls at the Beginning of the Second Temple Period," *EI* 16, 86–92.

——, 1985. "Book Size and the Device of Catch-Lines in the Biblical Canon," *JJS* 36, 1–11.

——, 1986. "Explaining the Identical Lines at the End of Chronicles and the Beginning of Ezra," *BR* 2.3, 18–20.

Harper, W., 1902. *Ezra, Nehemiah and Esther,* London.

Haupt, P., 1919. "Nehemiah's Night Ride," *JAOS* 39, 143.

Hawley, C. A., 1922. *A Critical Examination of the Peshitta Version of the Book of Ezra,* New York.

Heichelheim, F. M., 1951. "Ezra's Palestine and Periclean Athens," *ZRG* 3, 251–253.

Heinemann, I., 1947. "The Development of Technical Terms for the Interpretation of Scripture," *Leshonenu* 15, 108–115 (Heb.).

Heller, J., 1968. "Die abgeschlagene Mauer," *CV* 11, 175–178.

Heltzer, M., 1979. "A propos des banquets des rois achéménides et du retour d'Exil sous Zorobabel," *RB* 86, 102–106.

Hensley, L. V., 1977. "The Official Persian Documents in the Book of Ezra," Diss., University of Liverpool.

Herzfeld, E., 1936. "Die Religion der Achämeniden," *RHR* 1, 21–41.

——, 1968. *The Persian Empire*, Wiesbaden.

Hill, G. F., 1914. *Catalogue of the Greek Coins of Palestine*, London.

Hinz, W., 1976. *Darius und die Perser* I, Baden-Baden.

Höffken, P., 1975. "Warum schwieg Jesus Sirach über Esra?" *ZAW* 87, 184–201.

Hölscher, G., 1903. *Palästina in der persischen und hellenistischen Zeit*, Berlin.

——, 1923. *Die Bücher Esra und Nehemia* (ed. E. Kautzsch and A. Bertholet), Tübingen.

——, 1924. "Les origines de la communauté juive à l'époque perse," *RHPR* 6, 105–126.

Hoonacker, A. van, 1890. "Néhémie et Esdras: une nouvelle hypothèse sur la chronologie de l'époque de la restauration," *Le Muséon* 9, 151–184, 317–351, 389–401.

——, 1896. *Nouvelles études sur la restauration juive après l'exil de Babylone*, Paris.

——, 1901. "Notes sur l'histoire de la restauration juive après l'exil de Babylone," *RB* 10, 5–26, 175–199.

——, 1923–24. "La succession chronologique Néhémie-Esdras," *RB* 32, 1923, 481–494; 33, 1924, 33–64.

Houtman, C., 1981. "Ezra and the Law: Observations on the Supposed Relation Between Ezra and the Pentateuch," in A. S. van der Woude (ed.), *Remembering All the Way . . . ,* OTS 21, Leiden, 91–115.

Howorth, H. H., 1893a. "A Criticism of the Sources and the Relative Importance and Value of the Canonical Book of Ezra and the Apocryphal Book Known as Esdras 1," *Transactions of the Ninth International Congress of Orientalists* II, London, 68–85.

——, 1893b. "The Real Character and Importance of the First Book of Esdras," *Academy* 43, 13–14, 60, 106, 174–175, 326–327, 524.

——, 1901–03. "Some Unconventional Views on the Text of the Bible," *Proceedings of the Society of Biblical Archaeology* 23, 1901, 147–159; 24, 1902, 232–240; 25, 1903, 15–22, 90–98.

Hurwitz, A., 1974. "The Evidence of Language in Dating the Priestly Code: A Linguistic Study in Technical Idioms and Terminology," *RB* 81, 24–56.

In der Smitten, W. Th., 1971. "Der Tirschātā' in Esra-Nehemia," *VT* 21, 618–620.

——, 1972a. Die Gründe für die Aufnahme der Nehemiaschrift in das chronistische Geschichtswerk," *BZ* n.F. 16, 207–221.

——, 1972b. "Nehemias Parteigänger," *BO* 29, 155–157.

——, 1973a. *Esra Quellen, Überlieferung und Geschichte*, Assen.

————, 1973b. "Historische Probleme zum Kyrosedikt und zum Jerusalemer Tempelbau von 515," *Persica* 6, 167–178.

————, 1974. "Erwägungen zu Nehemias Davidizität," *JSJ* 5, 41–48.

Jahn, G., 1909. *Die Bücher Esra (A und B) und Nehemia*, Leiden.

James, M. R., 1917–18. "Ego Salathiel qui et Esdras," *JTS* 18, 1917, 167–169; 19, 1918, 347–349.

Janssen, E., 1956. *Juda in der Exilzeit. Ein Beitrag zur Frage der Entstehung des Judentums*, Göttingen.

Japhet, S., 1969. "The Supposed Common Authorship of Chronicles and Ezra-Nehemiah Investigated Anew," *VT* 18, 330–371.

————, 1977. *The Ideology of the Book of Chronicles and Its Place in Biblical Thought*, Jerusalem (Heb.).

————, 1982. "Sheshbazzar and Zerubbabel Against the Background of the Historical and Religious Tendencies of Ezra-Nehemiah," *ZAW* 94, 66–98.

Jepsen, A., 1929. "Zur Chronologie des Priesterkodex," *ZAW* 47, 1929, 251–255.

Johnson, J. H., 1974. "The Demotic Chronicle as an Historical Source," *Euchoria* 4, 1–19.

Jones, D. R., 1963. "The Cessation of Sacrifice After the Destruction of the Temple in 586 B.C.," *JTS* 14, 12–31.

Joüon, P., 1927. "Notes sur quelques versets araméens de Daniel et d'Esdras," *Bib* 8, 182–187.

————, 1931. "Notes philologiques sur le texte hébreu d'Esdras et de Néhémie," *Bib* 12, 85–89.

Junge, P. J., 1944. *Dareios I König der Perser*, Leipzig.

Kanael, B., 1963. "Ancient Jewish Coins and Their Historical Importance," *BA* 24, 38–62.

Kapelrud, A. S., 1944. *The Question of Authorship in the Ezra-Narrative*, Oslo.

————, 1963. "Temple Building: A Task for Gods and Kings," *Orientalia* 32, 56–62.

Kaufmann, Y., 1977. *History of the Religion of Israel*, IV, *From the Babylonian Captivity to the End of Prophecy*, New York.

Kegel, M., 1921. *Die Kultusreformation des Esra. Aussagen moderner Kritik über Neh 8–10 kritisch beleuchtet*, Gütersloh.

Keil, C. F., 1870. *Biblischer Commentar über die nachexilischen Geschichtsbücher: Chronik, Esra, Nehemia und Esther*, Leipzig.

Kellermann, U., 1966. "Die Listen in Nehemia 11 eine Dokumentation aus den letzten Jahren des Reiches Juda?" *ZDPV* 82, 209–227.

————, 1967. *Nehemia: Quellen, Überlieferung und Geschichte*, Berlin.

————, 1968. "Erwägungen zum Problem der Esradatierung," *ZAW* 80, 55–87.

Kent, R. G., 1938. "The Restoration of Order by Darius," *JAOS* 58, 112–121.

Kenyon, K. M., 1974. *Digging Up Jerusalem*, London & Tonbridge.

Kidner, F. D., 1979. *Ezra and Nehemiah: An Introduction and Commentary*, Downers Grove, Ill.

Kienitz, F. K., 1953. *Die politische Geschichte Ägyptens vom 7. bis zum 4. Jahrhundert vor der Zeitwende*, Berlin.

Kippenberg, H. G., 1978. *Religion und Klassenbildung im antiken Judäa*, Göttingen.

Klein, R. W., 1969. "Old Readings in 1 Esdras: The List of Returnees from Babylon," *HTR* 62, 99–107.

———, 1976. "Ezra and Nehemiah in Recent Studies," in F. M. Cross et al. (eds.), *Magnalia Dei: The Mighty Acts of God: Essays on the Bible and Archaeology in Memory of G. Ernest Wright,* Garden City, 361–376.

Knudtzon, J. A., 1907–15. *Die El-Amarna Tafeln,* Leipzig.

Koch, K., 1974. "Ezra and the Origins of Judaism," *JSS* 19, 173–197.

Kochavi, M. (ed.), 1972. *Judea, Samaria and the Golan: Archaeological Survey 1967–1968,* Jerusalem (Heb.).

Koopmans, J. J., 1955. "Die eerste Aramese deel van het Boek Ezra, 4:7–6:19," *GTT* 55, 142–160.

Kornfeld, W., 1978. *Onomastica aramaica aus Ägypten,* Vienna.

Kraeling, E. G., 1953. *The Brooklyn Museum Aramaic Papyri,* New Haven.

Kraus, H-J., 1972. "Zum Gesetzverständnis der nachprophetischen Zeit," in *Biblisch-theologische Aufsätze,* Neukirchen-Vluyn, 179–194.

Kreissig, H., 1973. *Die sozialökonomische Situation in Juda zur Achämenidenzeit,* Berlin.

Kuenen, A., 1894. "Die Chronologie des persischen Zeitalters der jüdischen Geschichte," in *Gesammelte Abhandlungen zur biblischen Wissenschaft,* Heidelberg, 212–251.

Kuhrt, A., 1983. "The Cyrus Cylinder and Achaemenid Imperial Policy," *JSOT* 25, 83–97.

Kuschke, A. (ed.), 1961. *Verbannung und Heimkehr,* Tübingen.

Lagrange, M. J., 1895. "Néhémie et Esdras," *RB* 4, 193–202.

Lambert, G., 1947. "La Restauration juive sous les rois Achéménides," *Cahiers Sion* 1, 314–337.

Landes, G. M., 1962. "Ammon," *IDB* I, 108–114.

Lapp, P. M., 1963a. "The Qasr el-'Abd: A Proposed Reconstruction," *BASOR* 171, 39–45.

———, 1963b. "The Second and Third Campaigns at 'Arâq el-Emîr," *BASOR* 171, 8–39.

Lapp, P. M., and Nancy Lapp, 1974. "Discoveries in the Wâdi ed-Dâliyeh," *AASOR* 41.

Leeseberg, M. W., 1962. "Ezra and Nehemiah: A Review of the Return and Reform," *CTM* 33, 79–90.

Lefèvre, A., 1960. "Néhémie et Esdras," *DBSup.* VI, Paris, 393–424.

Leuze, O., 1935. *Die Satrapieneinteilung in Syrien und im Zweistromlande von 520–330,* Halle.

Levine, B. A., 1963. "The Netînîm," *JBL* 82, 207–212.

———, 1969. "Notes on a Hebrew Ostracon from Arad," *IEJ* 19, 1969, 50–51.

Liver, J., 1971. "The Problem of the Order of the Kings of Persia in the Books of Ezra and Nehemiah" (Heb.), *Studies in the Bible and the Judean Desert Scrolls,* Jerusalem, 263–276.

Lloyd, A. B., 1982a. "The Inscription of Udjahorresnet: A Collaborator's Testament," *JEA* 68, 166–180.

———, 1982b. "Nationalist Propaganda in Ptolemaic Egypt," *Historia* 31, 41–45.

Luria, B. Z., 1979–81. "At the Time of the Return to Zion," *BM* 24, 1979, 127–139; 25, 1980, 99–113; 26, 1981, 358–361; 27, 1982, 3–14 (Heb.).

——, 1981. "The Temple Mount at the Time of the Return to Zion," *BM* 26, 206–216 (Heb.).

McCarthy, D. J., 1982. "Covenant and Law in Chronicles-Nehemiah," *CBQ* 44, 25–44.

McConville, J. G., 1985. *Ezra, Nehemiah, and Esther,* Edinburgh and Philadelphia.

——, 1986. "Ezra-Nehemiah and the Fulfillment of Prophecy," *VT* 36, 205–224.

McCown, C., 1957. "The 'Araq el-Emir and the Tobiads," *BA* 20, 63–76.

Macdonald J., 1964. *The Theology of the Samaritans,* Philadelphia.

——, 1976. "The Status and Role of the Na'ar in Israelite Society," *JNES* 35, 147–170.

McEvenue, S. E., 1981. "The Political Structure in Judah from Cyrus to Nehemiah," *CBQ* 43, 353–364.

Mallowan, M. E. L., 1972. "Cyrus the Great (558–529 B.C.)," *Iran* 10, 1–17.

Margalith, O., 1986. "The Political Role of Ezra as Persian Governor," *ZAW* 98, 110–112.

Marmorstein, A., and S. Zeitlin, 1919/20. "The Takkanot of Ezra," *JQR* 10, 367–371.

Mazar, B., 1957. "The Tobiads," *IEJ* 7, 137–145, 229–238.

——, 1975. *The Mountain of the Lord,* New York.

Meiggs, R., and D. M. Lewis, 1969. *A Selection of Greek Historical Inscriptions to the End of the Fifth Century B.C.,* Oxford.

Mendelsohn, I., 1940a. "Guilds in Ancient Palestine," *BASOR* 80, 17–21.

——, 1940b. "Guilds in Babylonia and Assyria," *JAOS* 60, 68–72.

Meshorer, Y., 1966. *Jewish Coins of the Second Temple Period,* Tel Aviv (Heb.).

Meyer, E., 1896. *Die Entstehung des Judentums,* Halle.

——, 1915. *"Ägyptische Dokumente aus der Perserzeit I,"* Sitzungs-berichte der Preussischen Akademie der Wissenschaften, Philosophisch-historische Klasse, 287–304.

Mezzacasa, F., 1961. "Esdras, Nehemias y el Año Sabático," *RevBibl* 23, 82–96.

Michaeli, F., 1967. *Les livres des Chroniques, d'Esdras et de Néhémie,* Neuchâtel.

Milgrom, J., 1970. *Studies in Levitical Terminology,* Berkeley.

——, 1983. *Studies in Cultic Theology and Terminology,* Leiden.

Möhlenbrink, K., 1934. "Die levitischen Überlieferungen des Alten Testaments," *ZAW* n.F. 11, 184–231.

Morgenstern, J., 1938. "A Chapter in the History of the High Priesthood," *AJSL* 55, 1–24, 183–197, 360–377.

——, 1956–60. "Jerusalem—485 B.C.," *HUCA* 27, 1956, 101–179; 28, 1957, 15–47; 31, 1960, 1–29.

——, 1962. "The Dates of Ezra and Nehemiah," *JSS* 7, 1–11.

Moss, C., 1933. "The Peshitta Version of Ezra," *Le Muséon* 46, 55–110.

Movers, F. C., 1834. *Kritische Untersuchungen über die biblische Chronik,* Bonn.

Mowinckel, S., 1923. "Die vorderasiatischen Königs- und Fürsteninschriften," in *Eucharisterion H. Gunkel zum 60. Geburtstage* I, Göttingen, 278–322.

——, 1960. "Erwägungen zum chronistischen Geschichtswerk," *TLZ* 85, 1–8.

————, 1961. " 'Ich' und 'Er' in der Esrageschichte," in A. Kuschke (ed.), *Verbannung und Heimkehr*, Tübingen, 211–233.

————, 1964–65. *Studien zu dem Buche Ezra-Nehemia*, 3 vols., Oslo.

Muffs, Y., 1973. *Studies in the Aramaic Legal Papyri from Elephantine*, New York.

Myers, J. M., 1965. *Ezra-Nehemiah*, Garden City.

————, 1971. "Edom and Judah in the Sixth-Fifth Centuries B.C.," in H. Goedicke (ed.), *Near Eastern Studies in Honor of W. F. Albright*, Baltimore and London, 377–392.

————, 1982. *I & II Esdras*, Garden City.

Nagah, R., 1980. "Why Is Ezra's Name Missing from the List of Those Who Signed the Covenant?" *BM* 25, 79–80 (Heb.).

Naveh, J., 1971. "Hebrew Texts in Aramaic Script in the Persian Period?" *BASOR* 203, 27–31.

————, 1973. "The Aramaic Ostraca," in Y. Aharoni (ed.), *Beer-Sheba I*, Tel Aviv, 79–82.

Naveh, J., and J. C. Greenfield, 1984. "Hebrew and Aramaic in the Persian Period," *CHJ* I, 115–129.

Newsome, J. D., 1975. "Toward a New Understanding of the Chronicler and His Purposes," *JBL* 94, 201–217.

Nikel, J., 1900. *Die Wiederherstellung des jüdischen Gemeinwesens nach dem babylonischen Exil*, Freiburg-im-Breisgau.

Noordtzij, A., 1951. *De Boeken Esra en Nehemiah*, Kampen.

North, F. S., 1954. "Aaron's Rise in Prestige," *ZAW* n.F. 25, 191–199.

North, R., 1968. "Ezra and Nehemiah," *The Jerome Biblical Commentary* (ed. R. E. Brown et al.), Englewood Cliffs, 426–438.

————, 1971. "Civil Authority in Ezra," *Studi in onore di Edoardo Volterra*, Milan, 377–404.

Noth, M., 1928. *Die israelitischen Personennamen im Rahmen der gemeinsemitischen Namengebung*, Stuttgart.

————, 1943. *Überlieferungsgeschichtliche Studien*, Halle.

————, 1960. *The History of Israel*, New York.

Olmstead, A. T., 1948. *History of the Persian Empire*, Chicago.

Orr, A., 1956. "The Seventy Years of Babylon," *VT* 6, 304–306.

Pardee, D., 1978. "An Overview of Ancient Hebrew Epistolography," *JBL* 97, 321–346.

Parker, R. A., 1941. "Darius and His Egyptian Campaign," *AJSL* 58, 373–377.

Parker, R. A., and W. Dubberstein, 1956. *Babylonian Chronology 626 B.C.–A.D. 45*, Providence, R.I.

Pavlovský, V., 1957. "Die Chronologie der Tätigkeit Esdras. Versuch einer neuen Lösung," *Bib* 38, 275–305, 428–456.

Pelaia, B. M., 1960. *Esdra e Neemia*, Turin.

Petersen, D. L., 1974. "Zerubbabel and Jerusalem Temple Reconstruction," *CBQ* 36, 366–372.

Petitjean, A., 1966. "La mission de Zorobabel et la reconstruction du Temple, Zach III,8–10," *ETL* 42, 40–71.

Pfeiffer, R. H., 1941. *Introduction to the Old Testament*, New York.

Ploeg, J. P. M. van der, 1972. "Slavery in the Old Testament," *VTSup.* 22, 72–87.

Plöger, O., 1957. "Reden und Gebete im deuteronomistischen und chronistischen Geschichtswerk," in W. Schneemelcher (ed.), *Festschrift für Günther Dehn*, Neukirchen, 35–49.

———, 1968. *Theocracy and Eschatology*, Atlanta.

Poebel, A., 1938. "Chronology of Darius' First Year of Reign," *AJSL* 55, 142–165, 285–314.

Pohlmann, K-F., 1970. *Studien zum Dritten Esra. Ein Beitrag zur Frage nach dem ursprünglichen Schluss des chronistischen Geschichtswerkes*, Göttingen.

———, 1980. *3. Esra-Buch*, Gütersloh.

Polzin, R., 1976. *Late Biblical Hebrew: Toward an Historical Typology of Biblical Hebrew Prose*, Missoula.

Porten, B., 1968. *Archives from Elephantine: The Life of an Ancient Jewish Military Colony*, Berkeley and Los Angeles.

———, 1978/79. "The Documents in the Book of Ezra and the Mission of Ezra," *Shnaton* 3, 174–196 (Heb.).

———, 1984. "The Jews in Egypt," *CHJ* I, 372–400.

Porten, B., and J. Greenfield, 1968. "The Aramaic Papyri from Hermopolis," *ZAW* 80, 216–231.

Posener, G., 1936. *La Première Domination perse en Egypte*, Cairo.

Purvis, J. D., 1968. *The Samaritan Pentateuch and the Origin of the Samaritan Schism*, Cambridge, Mass.

Rabinowitz, I., 1956. "Aramaic Inscriptions of the Fifth Century B.C.E. from a North-Arab Shrine in Egypt," *JNES* 15, 1–9.

Rad, G. von, 1930. *Das Geschichtsbild des chronistischen Werkes*, Stuttgart.

———, 1964. "Die Nehemia-Denkschrift," *ZAW* 76, 176–187.

Rahmani, L. Y., 1971. "Silver Coins of the Fourth Century B.C. from Tel Gamma," *IEJ* 21, 158–160.

Rainey, A. F., 1969. "The Satrapy 'Beyond the River,' *AJBA* 1, 51–78.

Ran, Z., 1982. "Remarks on Ezra and Nehemiah," *ZAW* 94, 296–298.

Rawlinson, G., 1891. *Ezra and Nehemiah*, New York.

Rehm, M., 1956. *Esra-Nehemia*, Würzburg.

Reich, N., 1933. "The Codification of the Egyptian Laws by Darius and the Origin of the 'Demotic Chronicle,'" *Mizraim* 1, 78–83.

Rendtorff, R., 1984. "Esra und das 'Gesetz,'" *ZAW* 96, 165–184.

Rost, L., "Erwägungen zum Kyroserlass," in A. Kuschke (ed.), *Verbannung und Heimkehr*, Tübingen, 1961, 301–307.

Rowley, H. H., 1948. "The Chronological Order of Ezra and Nehemiah," in S. Löwinger and J. Somogyi (eds.), *Ignace Goldziher Memorial Volume* I, Budapest, 117–149 (= Rowley, *The Servant of the Lord and Other Essays on the Old Testament*, London, 1965, 135–168).

———, 1954/55. "Nehemiah's Mission and Its Background," *BJRL* 37, 528–561 (= Rowley, *Men of God: Studies in Old Testament History and Prophecy*, London, 1963, 211–245).

———, 1955/56. "Sanballat and the Samaritan Temple," *BJRL* 38, 166–198 (= *Men of God*, 246–276).

———, 1962. "The Samaritan Schism in Legend and History," in B. W. Anderson and W. Harrelson (eds.), *Israel's Prophetic Heritage*, New York, 208–222.

Rudolph, W., 1949. *Esra und Nehemia samt 3. Esra,* Tübingen.

Ryle, H. E., 1897. *The Books of Ezra and Nehemiah,* Cambridge.

Saley, R. J., 1978. "The Date of Nehemiah Reconsidered," in G. A. Tuttle (ed.), *Biblical and Near Eastern Studies: Essays in Honor of William Sanford LaSor,* Grand Rapids, 151–165.

Schaeder, H. H., 1930a. *Esra der Schreiber,* Tübingen.

———, 1930b. *Iranische Beiträge* I, Halle, 197–296.

Schneider, H., 1959. *Die Bücher Esra und Nehemia* (2nd ed.), Bonn.

Schottroff, W., 1967. *"Gedenken" im alten Orient und im Alten Testament* (2nd ed.), Neukirchen.

———, 1982. "Zur Sozialgeschichte Israels in der Perserzeit," *Verkündigung und Forschung* 27.

Schreiner, J., 1981. *Das 4. Buch Esra,* Gütersloh.

Schultz, C., 1980. "The Political Tensions Reflected in Ezra-Nehemiah," in C. D. Evans et al. (eds.), *Scripture in Context: Essays on the Comparative Method,* Pittsburgh, 221–244.

Scott, W. M. F., 1946/47. "Nehemiah-Ezra?" *ExpT* 58, 263–267.

Segal, M. H., 1943. "The Books of Ezra-Nehemiah," *Tarbiz* 14, 81–103 (Heb.).

Sellin, E., 1942/43. "Noch einmal der Stein des Sacharja," *ZAW* n.F. 18, 59–77.

Selms, A. van, 1935. *Ezra en Nehemia,* Groningen.

Siegfried, D. C., 1901. *Esra, Nehemia und Esther,* Göttingen.

Simons, J., 1952. *Jerusalem in the Old Testament,* Leiden.

Smend, R., 1881. *Die Listen der Bücher Esra und Nehemia,* Basel.

———, 1882. "Über die Genesis des Judenthums," *ZAW* 2, 94–151.

Smith, M., 1971. *Palestinian Parties and Politics That Shaped the Old Testament,* New York and London.

———, 1972. "Ezra," in *Ex Orbe Religionum. Studia Geo. Widengren* I, Leiden, 141–143.

———, 1984. "Jewish Religious Life in the Persian Period," *CHJ* I, 219–278.

Snaith, N. H., 1951. "The Date of Ezra's Arrival in Jerusalem," *ZAW* 63, 53–66.

Snell, D. C., 1980. "Why Is There Aramaic in the Bible?" *JSOT* 18, 32–51.

Snijders, L. A., 1958. "Het 'volk des lands' in Juda," *NTT* 12, 241–256.

Soleh, M. Z., 1983/84. "The Festive Assembly on the First of the Seventh Month in the Time of Ezra and Nehemiah," *BM* 29, 381–383 (Heb.).

Speiser, E. A., 1963. "Unrecognized Dedication," *IEJ* 13, 69–73.

Spiegelberg, W., 1915. *Die sogenannte demotische Chronik des Pap. 215 der Bibliotèque Nationale zu Paris,* Leipzig.

Steck, O., 1968. "Das Problem theologischer Strömungen in nachexilischer Zeit," *EvTh* 28, 445–458.

Stern, E., 1982. *The Material Culture of the Land of the Bible in the Persian Period (538–332 B.C.E.),* Warminster.

———, 1984a. "The Archaeology of Persian Palestine," *CHJ* I, 88–114.

———, 1984b. "The Persian Empire and the Political and Social History of Palestine in the Persian Period," *CHJ* I, 70–87.

Stone, M. E., 1982. "The Metamorphosis of Ezra: Jewish Apocalyptic and Medieval Vision," *JTS* 33, 1–18.

————, 1983. "Greek Apocalypse of Ezra," in J. H. Charlesworth, *The Old Testament Pseudepigrapha* I, Garden City, 561–579.

Stronach, D., 1978. *Pasargadae,* Oxford.

Swete, H. B., 1902. *An Introduction to the Old Testament in Greek,* Cambridge.

Tadmor, H., 1964. "The Historical Background of the Edict of Cyrus," in *Jubilee Volume in Honor of David Ben-Gurion,* Jerusalem, 450–473 (Heb.).

Talmon, S., 1953. "The Sectarian YHD—a Biblical Noun," *VT* 3, 133–140.

————, 1973. "Biblical Tradition on the Early History of the Samaritans," *Eretz Shomron. The Thirtieth Archaeological Convention of the Israel Exploration Society,* Jerusalem, 19–33 (Heb.).

————, 1976. "Ezra and Nehemiah," *IDBSup.,* 317–318.

Teixidor, J., 1978. "The Aramaic Text in the Trilingual Stele from Xanthus," *JNES* 37, 181–185.

Thompson, A., 1931. "An Inquiry Concerning the Books of Ezra and Nehemiah," *AJSL* 68, 99–132.

Throntveit, M. A., 1982. "Linguistic Analysis and the Question of Authorship in Chronicles, Ezra and Nehemiah," *VT* 32, 201–216.

Torrey, C. C., 1895. *The Composition and Historical Value of Ezra-Nehemiah,* Giessen.

————, 1897. "The Missing Conclusion of Ezra 1," *JBL* 16, 166–170.

————, 1906. "Portions of First Esdras and Nehemiah in the Syro-hexaplar Version," *AJSL* 23, 65–74.

————, 1907a. "The First Chapter of Ezra in Its Original Form and Setting," *AJSL* 24, 7–33.

————, 1907b. "The Nature and Origin of First Esdras," *AJSL* 23, 116–141.

————, 1907/08. "The Aramaic Portions of Ezra," *AJSL* 24, 209–281.

————, 1908/09. "The Chronicler as Editor and as Independent Narrator," *AJSL* 25, 157–173, 188–217.

————, 1909. "The Ezra Story in Its Original Sequence," *AJSL* 25, 276–311.

————, 1910. *Ezra Studies,* Chicago (repr. New York, 1970).

————, 1928. "Sanballat the 'Horonite,' " *JBL* 47, 380–389.

————, 1945. "A Revised View of First Esdras," *Louis Ginzberg Jubilee Volume,* New York, 395–410.

————, 1954. *The Chronicler's History of Israel: Chronicles-Ezra-Nehemiah Restored to Its Original Form,* New Haven.

Touzard, J., 1915. "Les juifs au temps de la période persane," *RB* 12, 59–133.

Tuland, C. G., 1958. "Hanani-Hananiah," *JBL* 77, 157–161.

————, 1974. "Ezra-Nehemiah or Nehemiah-Ezra? An Investigation Into the Validity of the van Hoonacker Theory," *AUSS* 12, 47–62.

Tulli, A., 1941. *Il Naoforo Vaticano,* Rome.

Tushingham, A. D., 1979. "The Western Hill Under the Monarchy," *ZDPV* 95, 39–55.

Ungnad, A., 1940/41. "Keilinschriftliche Beiträge zum Buch Esra und Ester," *ZAW* 58, 240–244.

Vaux, R. de, 1937. "Les décrets de Cyrus et de Darius sur la reconstruction du Temple," *RB* 46, 29–57 (= de Vaux, *The Bible and the Ancient Near East,* Garden City, 1971, 63–96).

————, 1961. *Ancient Israel: Its Life and Institutions,* London, 1961.

————, "Israel (Histoire de)," *DBSup.* 4:729–777.

Vincent, A., 1937. *La religion des judéo-araméens d'Eléphantine,* Paris.

Vischer, W., 1971. "Nehemia und die Bedeutung der Befestigung Jerusalems für die biblische Geschichte und Theologie," *Probleme biblischer Theologie. Gerhard von Rad zum 70. Geburtstag,* Munich.

Vogt, H. C. M., 1966. *Studie zur nachexilischen Gemeinde in Esra-Nehemia,* Werl.

Walde, B., 1913. *Die Esrabücher der Septuaginta,* Freiburg-im-Breisgau.

Walser, G. (ed.), 1972. *Beiträge zur Achämenidengeschichte,* Wiesbaden.

Waterman, L., 1954. "The Camouflaged Purge of Three Messianic Conspirators," *JNES* 13, 73–79.

Weinberg (Vejnberg), J., 1972. "Demographische Notizen zur Geschichte der nachexilischen Gemeinde in Juda," *Klio* 54, 45–59.

————, 1973a. "Das Bēit 'ābōt im 6.–4. Jh. v.u.Z.," *VT* 23, 400–414.

————, 1973b. "Probleme der sozialökonomischen Struktur Judäas vom 6. Jahrhundert v.u.Z. bis zum 1. Jahrhundert u.Z.," *Jahrbuch für Wirtschaftsgeschichte,* 237–251.

————, 1976. "Die Agrarverhältnisse in der Bürger-Tempel-Gemeinde der Achämenidenzeit," in J. Harmatta and G. Komoróczy (eds.), *Wirtschaft und Gesellschaft im alten Vorderasien,* 473–486.

Weinberg, S. S., 1969. "Post-exilic Palestine: An Archaeological Report," *Israel Academy of Sciences and Humanities Proceedings* 4.5, Jerusalem.

Weisberg, D. B., 1967. *Guild Structure and Political Allegiance in Early Achaemenid Mesopotamia,* New Haven.

Welch, A. C., 1935. *Post-exilic Judaism,* Edinburgh and London.

Whitley, C. F., 1954. "The Term Seventy Years Captivity," *VT* 4, 60–72.

Widengren, G., 1969. "Israelite-Jewish Religion," in C. J. Bleeker and G. Widengren (eds.), *Historia Religionum* I, Leiden, 225–317.

————, 1977. "The Persian Period," in J. H. Hayes and J. M. Miller (eds.), *Israelite and Judaean History,* London and Philadelphia, 489–538.

Wiener, H. M., 1927. "The Relative Dates of Ezra and Nehemiah," *JPOS* 7, 145–158.

Williamson, H. G. M., 1977. *Israel in the Book of Chronicles,* Cambridge.

————, 1979. "The Origins of the Twenty-Four Priestly Courses," *VTSup.* 30, 251–268.

————, 1983. "The Composition of Ezra i–vi," *JTS* 33, 1–30.

————, 1984. "Nehemiah's Wall Revisited," *PEQ* 116, 81–88.

————, 1986. *Ezra, Nehemiah,* Waco, Tex.

Wilson, R. D., 1915. "Titles of the Persian Kings," *Festschrift Eduard Sachau,* Berlin, 179–207.

Wilson, R. R., 1977. *Genealogies and History in the Biblical World,* New Haven.

Witton Davies, T., 1909. *Ezra, Nehemiah and Esther,* Edinburgh.

Wood, C. T., 1947/48. "Nehemiah-Ezra," *ExpT* 59, 53–54.

Wright, G. E., 1962. "The Samaritans at Shechem," *HTR* 55, 366–377.

Wright, J. S., 1958a. *The Building of the Second Temple,* London.

————, 1958b. *The Date of Ezra's Coming to Jerusalem* (2nd ed.), London.

Yamauchi, E. M., 1980a. "The Archaeological Background of Ezra," *BSac* 137, 195–211.

———, 1980b. "The Archaeological Background of Nehemiah," *BSac* 137, 291–309.

———, 1980c. "The Reverse Order of Ezra/Nehemiah Reconsidered," *Themelios* 5, 7–13.

———, 1980d. "Was Nehemiah the Cupbearer a Eunuch?" *ZAW* 92, 132–142.

York, H. C., 1910. "The Latin Versions of First Esdras," *AJSL* 26, 253–302.

Zadok, R., 1980. "Notes on the Biblical and Non-Biblical Onomasticon," *JQR* 71, 107–117.

Zimmerli, W., 1968. "Planungen für den Wiederaufbau nach der Katastrophe von 587," *VT* 18, 229–255.

———, 1971. "Erstgeborene und Leviten: Ein Beitrag zur exilisch-nachexilischen Theologie," in H. Goedicke (ed.), *Near Eastern Studies in Honor of William Foxwell Albright*, Baltimore and London, 459–475.

Zunz, L., 1832. *Die gottesdienstliche Vorträge der Juden historisch entwickelt*, Berlin, 13–36.

INTRODUCTION

1. On Reading Ezra-Nehemiah

The composition which is the subject of this commentary is not one of the more popular biblical books. From the beginning of the historical-critical study of the Bible at the time of the Enlightenment it has routinely been dismissed as symptomatic of decline from the high level attained by prophetic religion. Together with other Second Temple compositions, Chronicles and Esther in particular, it has been used as evidence in the indictment of early Judaism as an illiberal religion dominated by legalism and ritualism, a religion looking inward rather than out into the world beyond its carefully guarded confines. This accusation of *amixia,* a routine item in anti-Jewish polemic in late antiquity (e.g., Josephus, *Ant.* 13.245; Tacitus, *Hist.* 5.5), acquired a specifically theological qualification in early Christianity, one which has proved to be very persistent. Even for the Christian reader deeply sympathetic with Judaism, the religious history recorded in Ezra-Nehemiah might seem to do nothing to discourage this kind of indictment.

Leaving aside specifically religious prejudices, the few biblical texts which have survived from the Persian period, of which this is the most important, seem to evince little interest in the expansive possibilities of cultural and intellectual life. In this respect the contrast with the Greek-speaking world during these centuries is quite remarkable. For this was the age of decisive advances in mathematics, geometry, astronomy, and cosmology; the age of Xenophanes, Heraclitus, the Eleatics and Sophists; the age of Socrates, a contemporary of Ezra. Granted that this state of affairs can be explained by the attainment, especially in Ionia and Magna Graecia, of a level of economic prosperity which permitted the emergence of a leisured class of lay thinkers, whereas in the province of Judah we hear much of economic distress exacerbated by the fiscal policy of the Persian overlord. The fact remains that these Judean writings seem to be dominated by the narrow concerns of a clerical order which had little interest in *litterae humaniores* and the creative activity of the mind. And even within the confines of the biblical canon these books might seem to be more of an appendix than an integral and essential component; an afterthought; like the Greek title of Chronicles, "things left over," a filling in of gaps largely with the help of genealogies and interminable lists of names.

This last point, the place of Ezra-Nehemiah in the collection, may nevertheless provide a useful point of departure for the reader of the book willing to risk discouragement and disillusionment. Together with Chronicles, Ezra-Nehemiah belongs to the second great historical corpus in the Hebrew Bible. The first consists in the books of Genesis to 2 Kings and covers the history from creation to the catastrophe of the destruction of Jerusalem and its temple followed by exile. It tells the story of a great possibility, implicit in the creation narrative and explicit in the promise to Abraham (Gen. 12:1–3), and the failure to grasp that possibility. The pattern is adumbrated in the early history of mankind in Gen. 1–11: settlement in a fertile and life-enhancing environment, a command essential for the preservation of the good order of creation, violation of the command and consequent disturbance of that order, exile progressively from Eden, the arable land, and then from the face of the earth with the deluge. Far from being mere coincidence, the correspondence between the narrative pattern in the history of humankind and that of the nation is a structural fact of the greatest importance. So, in spite of the faint glimmer of hope with which the latter concludes (2 Kings 25:27–30), the first great historical corpus narrates a history from creation to catastrophe.

The second historical corpus covers the same ground but continues beyond the point at which the first concludes to take in the constitution of a new community around a rebuilt sanctuary. It would, however, be erroneous to suppose that it reproduces more or less mechanically the first history, with some adjustments, omissions, and a chapter appended at the end. Taking over a narrative technique from the Priestly source (P), it extends the use of linear genealogies to cover the entire period from creation to the monarchy. This procedure does not imply lack of interest in the founding events recorded in the first seven books of the Bible. On the contrary, the authority of the Mosaic law is evident at every point. Moreover, what is omitted at the beginning—captivity in a land of exile, exodus, passover, settlement of the land, establishment of the sanctuary in it—is brought in at the end, precisely in Ezra-Nehemiah, thereby imposing a new, contemporary meaning on the history as a whole. What is implied is that the author was no longer content with the *literal* meaning of the events, especially the occupation of the land and treatment of its inhabitants, and therefore chose to interpret them *typologically* with reference to the possibilities and constraints of the new situation confronting his people. In this respect also he followed the lead of the Priestly tradent who omitted the conquest, passing at once to the setting up of the sanctuary in the land and distribution of the tribal territories (Josh. 18–19). He seems, in fact, to have appropriated the structure of the Priestly narrative as a whole, a narrative which hinges on creation of the world as a temple for the worship of God, the making of the sanctuary in accordance with specifications received at Sinai, and the setting up of that sanctuary in the promised land.

In keeping with this basic intention, the emphasis in the second great corpus is on those individuals who preserved the order established in creation by their active concern for worship. Hence the story of David is redesigned to depict him as the founder of the national cult, and those Judean kings are singled out for special attention who restore the cult after a dark period of disorder and neglect—Hezekiah following on Ahaz, Josiah following on Manasseh and Amon. The exile is reinterpreted as the sabbath rest of the land, and becomes only a temporary break of comparable length to the periods preceding the reforms just mentioned. Quite apart from the question of authorship, currently much in dispute, we can see how essential it is maintain the structural unity of Chronicles and Ezra-Nehemiah. It allows us to see what the story is really about. It is giving the people back their history, a usable past which will enable them to see that their lives have meaning even in an imperfect world, even in the absence of political autonomy.

The first requirement for the reader is, then, to place the book in the context of the biblical narrative as a whole, and therefore to read it as the furthest limit of the story, the gathering up of the past and reshaping it in such a way as to allow for a future. Those who did the reshaping, the Chronicler (as will be argued) and the scholiasts who completed his work, were concerned not so much to produce a polished and finished work (which Ezra-Nehemiah certainly is not) as to sustain the life and energy of the community to which they belonged.

One of the most positive aspects of Old Testament studies in recent decades is the renewal of interest in the religious history of the

Second Temple period. For anyone wishing to understand early
Christianity in relation to the varieties of Judaism in which it arose,
it is not enough to study contemporary Jewish "backgrounds," or
even the broader period between the Hasmonean principate and the
Mishnah. Most of the issues being debated and the battles being
fought then must be traced back to the formative period of the two
centuries of Persian rule; issues focusing on conflicting legal interpretations, the confessional status of certain beliefs and practices, relation to the outside world, proselytism, acceptance or nonacceptance
of the political status quo, tension between assimilationist and anti-
assimilationist tendencies, etc. With all of its problems, some insolu-
ble, Ezra-Nehemiah is the indispensable source for our knowledge of
that period which links the world of Israel with that of emergent
Judaism.

2. Ezra-Nehemiah in the Biblical Canon

In the Hebrew Bible Ezra and Nehemiah form one book: the verse
total (685) is given only after the last chapter of Nehemiah, and the
midpoint *(h ᵃṣî hassēper)* is marked between Neh. 3:31 and 3:32. In
thus presenting the work, the Masoretes followed ancient Jewish
tradition attested to by Melito of Sardis (Eusebius, *Hist. Eccl.* 4.26.14)
and deducible from Josephus' enumeration of the biblical books (*C.
Apion* 40). This arrangement can, in fact, be traced back to the
allusions in the text itself which link the work of the two men (Neh.
8:9; 12:26, 36). The subsequent division into two books—suggested
by the superscription of Nehemiah's memoir (Neh. 1:1)—is at least
as old as Origen (Eusebius, *Hist. Eccl.* 6.25.2) and is reproduced in
Jerome's Vulgate. It was adopted in the Hebrew Bible only with the
first printed editions in the fifteenth century. Since the titles of the
canonical books together with those of the apocryphal 1 Esdras and
the Ezra Apocalypse (apocryphal 2 Esdras) can be somewhat confusing, they are set out here for convenience:

MT	*LXX*	*Vulgate*	*Modern*
	Esdras alpha	III Esdras	1 Esdras
Ezra	Esdras beta	I Esdras	Ezra
Nehemiah	Esdras gamma	II Esdras	Nehemiah
		IV Esdras	2 Esdras

There is no uniformity in the canonical order of the books. In
LXX Ezra-Nehemiah follows Chronicles (Paralipomena) in accord
with the roughly chronological order of the historical books, some-

times with 1 Esdras in between. In MT it follows Daniel in the third section or Writings *(k^etûbîm),* presumably because both deal with events in the Persian period and chronicle the reestablishment of the cult after a period of adversity. It generally precedes Chronicles, which comes at the end of Writings—perhaps with a view to concluding on a hopeful note—but there are also MSS in which Chronicles stands at the beginning. In these instances it serves as an introduction to Psalms, since it presents David as founder of liturgical music and himself prophetic hymnographer. The view often expressed that Ezra-Nehemiah was "canonized" before Chronicles, since much of the latter reproduces the history in Samuel-Kings, is without foundation and therefore throws no light on the relative position of the two works in the canon.

In the previous section something was said about the significance of Ezra-Nehemiah's place in the canon, and the historical record in particular. The serious disturbances of an original order which most commentators have found in the book also draw attention, more acutely than in most other biblical books, to the theological significance of the final form in which the material has come down to us. This other aspect of canonicity, emphasized recently by B. S. Childs *(Introduction to the Old Testament as Scripture,* Philadelphia, 1979, 624–638), can more conveniently be addressed after surveying the contents of the book in its present order.

3. Contents

The story opens with the decree of Cyrus permitting the repatriation of Babylonian Jews and the rebuilding of the temple. The invitation was enthusiastically accepted, resulting in a return to the homeland of some 50,000 accompanied by Sheshbazzar bearing the temple vessels confiscated by Nebuchadnezzar and under the leadership of twelve men, prominent among whom were Zerubbabel and the high priest Jeshua. In the seventh month of the same year the altar was set up, the daily sacrifice resumed, and the feast of Booths celebrated. Preparations for the rebuilding of the temple got under way at once, and in the following year the foundations were laid with the appropriate liturgy. The rejection of an offer of help from neighboring people, descendants of deportees resettled by the Assyrians, though worshipers of YHVH, led to sustained opposition which continued throughout the reigns of Darius I, Xerxes, and Artaxerxes. The work progressed notwithstanding, thanks to confirmation of the original decree by Darius, and was completed under the leadership of Zerubbabel and Jeshua and with prophetic support in the sixth year of

Darius. The dedication of the completed building was duly solemnized and crowned with the celebration of Passover and Unleavened Bread (Ezra 1–6).

After the lapse of some time, the narrative resumes with the mission of Ezra, priest and scribe, who arrived from Babylon at the head of some 5,000 repatriates in the seventh year of Artaxerxes. Armed with a firman from the Persian king for the administration of justice according to the traditional laws, and weighed down with offerings for the temple, Ezra arrived safely and offered sacrifices in the Jerusalem temple. After four months he was confronted with the bad news that many in the province, including members of the civic and religious ruling caste, had contracted marriages with foreign women. After an initial reaction of mourning, fasting, etc., he recruited support from prominent laymen and a group of pietists and convoked a plenary assembly to solve the problem. After the meeting was rained out, the solution was entrusted to a committee of prominent laymen who reviewed cases submitted to them and completed their work in three months. The list of offenders is appended, and the impression is given that they signed an agreement to divorce their foreign wives (Ezra 7–10).

The scene now shifts to Susa, where the royal steward Nehemiah heard from his brother Hanani and other Jews that the walls and gates of Jerusalem had been destroyed. While serving at the royal table some three or four months later, he requested a leave of absence to go to Jerusalem. Permission was granted, Nehemiah made the journey with an armed escort, and shortly after arriving he made a nocturnal tour of the wall and confided his decision to rebuild it to the Jewish leadership. In spite of sustained opposition from Sanballat of Samaria and his allies, and a crisis of morale among the builders, the work went forward and was completed within fifty-two days. In the meantime, however, economic and social problems, exacerbated by a famine, had to be dealt with, in addition to several attempts by the opposition, which had close ties with the Judean aristocracy, to get rid of Nehemiah. Dispositions for the defense of the gates completed this phase of the work (Neh. 1:1–7:4).

Since Jerusalem was still relatively underpopulated, Nehemiah proposed a census for which the list of the first repatriates, here reproduced, was to serve as a basis. Before this project was begun, however, a plenary gathering was convened in Jerusalem for the purpose of reading and explaining the law under the leadership of Ezra, with Nehemiah the governor present. It was followed by the celebration of Booths and a penitential service in the seventh month. With their leaders lay and clerical, the people then entered into a binding agreement to keep the law, especially in the matter of foreign marriages and support of the cult. Only then did the transfer of a tenth of the population to Jerusalem take place, the list of the inhabitants of the city together with other lists of clergy being appended. The rebuilt wall was then solemnly dedicated in the presence of both Ezra and Nehemiah, provisions for the support of the clergy and proper functioning of the cult were made, and those foreigners who did not qualify for membership in the community were expelled. Various abuses which had arisen during Nehemiah's absence in the thirty-second year of Artaxerxes and for some time thereafter then called for action. On his return, Nehemiah expelled Tobiah from the temple precincts, saw to the payment of the Levitical tithe and the observance of sabbath, and took stern measures to deal with the problem of foreign marriages (Neh. 7:5–13:31).

Concern for what Childs calls the canonical shaping of the material requires that we try to understand the present order and arrangement before engaging in critical deconstruction and reconstruction. The story divides, then, into two sequences of unequal length, both resulting from royal decrees, of Cyrus and Artaxerxes respectively. They are separated by a period of about half a century which, following the pattern in Chronicles (see the following section), we must suppose was marked by failure. In both, events and personalities are telescoped. There is only one return following immediately and enthusiastically on the Cyrus rescript in which Sheshbazzar, Zerubbabel, and Jeshua participate. Opposition comes exclusively from external sources and is overcome with divine help mediated through the benevolence of the Persian kings, prophetic support, and inspired leadership. The project is brought to a successful completion with the dedication of the rebuilt temple and celebration of the festal liturgy. The second and longer sequence brings together the efforts of the two men (Neh. 8–12) who, in spite of external opposition, bring to a successful conclusion the task of unifying and purifying the community through the law publicly proclaimed and explained. It, too, ends with a service of dedication, that of the wall and, by implication, the city which it protects. The religious and civic foundations of the Jewish commonwealth are thus securely laid.

4. The Composition of Ezra-Nehemiah

It is important to bear in mind that the final or canonical form of the material, as set out in the previous section, is a theological or ideological construct. In other words, it is one possible interpretation of the events described and, whatever its authority, it is not immune to challenge by alternative explanations from a historical-critical perspective. One of the problems with "canonical criticism"—a term which, though sometimes disavowed, seems appropriate—is a tendency to circumvent the tension between confessional and critically reconstructed history. This tension seems to be inescapable, and it is difficult to see how theology can maintain its integrity, or avoid degenerating into ideology in the pejorative sense, if it is avoided. Hence the necessity of juxtaposing a critical reconstruction of a text like Ezra-Nehemiah with the form imposed on it by its successive authors or editors.

The most obvious literary characteristic of Ezra 1–6, the history from the Cyrus decree to the dedication of the temple (538–515), is the extensive use of source material. The sources quoted are: the Cyrus decree (1:2–4; cf. 6:3–5, an Aramaic version, and 5:13–15, a paraphrase); a list of temple vessels (1:9–11); the list of repatriates (2:1–67; cf. Neh. 7:6–68 [69]); Rehum's letter to Artaxerxes and the king's reply (4:7–22); Tattenai's letter to Darius and his reply (5:6–17; 6:6–12). The entire section 4:8–6:18 is in Aramaic, the diplomatic *lingua franca* of the Persian empire. The view that this entire section comprises one Aramaic source (the so-called Tabeel hypothesis) has not been sustained (see commentary on 4:7) and, in addition, the final paragraph (6:16–18) is clearly from the editor. Thus we have several distinct sources in Aramaic incorporated into a narrative which, as in Daniel (2:4–7:28), simply continues in that language. The narrative sequence is blurred by the tendency to foreshorten or telescope events, a procedure which has left its mark on the historiography of the Persian period down to rabbinic times. Hence the bringing together first of Sheshbazzar, Zerubbabel, and Jeshua, then of Ezra and Nehemiah. Hence also the direct genealogical connection between Ezra and Seraiah, last preexilic high priest (Ezra 7:1; cf. 2 Kings 25:18–21), leading to the curious rabbinic tradition that Ezra learned Torah from Baruch, secretary of Jeremiah (e.g., *Cant. Rab.* 2:12).

The account of the first return has drawn selectively on the Aramaic documents, especially with respect to the Cyrus edict (Ezra 1:2–4; cf. 6:3–5), the role of Sheshbazzar (1:7–11; cf. 5:14–15), and the laying of the foundations and preparations for the rebuilding (3:1–13; cf. 5:8, 16; 6:4). It also betrays familiarity with Haggai and Zechariah 1–8, though the messianic expectations focusing on Zerubbabel are passed over in silence. In the section 4:1–6:12 attention focuses on sustained opposition which had to be overcome before the project could be finished. The insertion of the passage 4:6–23, summarizing opposition during the two reigns subsequent to Darius I

(522–486)—i.e., Xerxes I (486–465) and Artaxerxes I (465–424)—is confusing for the modern reader, especially since it introduces the city wall in addition to the temple. But this compositional technique is by no means rare in ancient historiography, and the editor has alerted us to it by the resumptive verse 4:24, which reattaches the narrative sequence to the point just before the digression (i.e., 4:5). There is therefore no need to question the author's knowledge of the historical order of the early Persian kings. From this point the narrative proceeds smoothly to the completion and dedication of the temple and Passover, once the original building permit had been confirmed by Darius.

Williamson (1983, 1–30) has argued that Ezra 1–6 was composed subsequently to the combination of the Ezra and Nehemiah records, and that therefore it represents the final stage in the formation of the book. He believes that this conclusion gives the *coup de grâce* to the thesis of the common authorship of Chronicles and Ezra-Nehemiah. His main point is that the insertion of the repatriation list also takes in the narrative immediately following (Ezra 2:68–3:1 = Neh. 7:69[70]–8:1a), and that this narrative conclusion to the list is native to the Nehemiah context whence it has been imported into Ezra 1–6. The priority of the Nehemiah version of the list is, he believes, apparent from the allusion to the seventh month at Neh. 7:72b [73b], which is part of the larger Nehemiah context since it anticipates the dating of the public reading of the law in the same month (Neh. 8:2). The list of offerings in Ezra 2:68–69 also appears to be a summary of Neh. 7:68–70 [69–71] since it rounds out the figures given there. The subsequent narrative in Ezra 3, however, also refers to the seventh month, during which Sukkoth was celebrated (v. 6). Arguments from numbers can be rather slippery, due to textual variations. In any case, 61,000 gold darics is hardly a rounding out of the 41,000 in Nehemiah. The argument *could* hold for the quantity of silver minas (4,700 in Nehemiah, 5,000 in Ezra) and for vestments (97 in Nehemiah, 100 in Ezra), though it requires a textual emendation at Neh. 7:69 [70] which is possible but not compelling. Due weight must also be given to the narrative continuity before and after the list in Ezra, emphasized by the same terminology—"the house of YHVH which is in Jerusalem," "heads of ancestral houses," "votive offerings." The "treasury of the work" also continues the theme of temple endowment, especially in view of the allusion to priestly vestments. This theme remains totally unexplained in the Nehemiah context. That the list with its narrative sequel has been adapted to a new context in Nehemiah is also suggested by the syntactic awkwardness of Neh. 7:69 [70], which begins with the heads of ancestral houses, breaks off without giving their contributions, then begins again with a listing of donors in descending order of importance. Reference to months by numbers rather than by names is also characteristic of Ezra 1–6 (see Ezra 3:1, 6, 8; 6:19), the only exception being Adar at 6:15. In the Nehemiah memoir, on the other hand, months are invariably referred to by names (Neh. 1:1; 2:1; 6:15). The weight of evidence is therefore against Williamson's hypothesis, and to this we must add the indications of close linguistic, stylistic, thematic, and structural affinity between Chronicles and Ezra 1–6 to be considered in the following section of the Introduction.

That more than half a century (515–458) elapsed between the dedication of the temple and the arrival of Ezra (Ezra 7) emphasizes the beginning of a quite new and distinct phase. That the editor had some information on the interim period can be seen in the allusion to problems during the reign of Xerxes (4:6) and the exchange of correspondence with the court of Artaxerxes I (4:7–22). If Ezra 1–6 is read as the continuation of 1-2 Chronicles, this would be one of those low periods followed by a movement of restoration: Saul—David and Solomon; Ahaz—Hezekiah; Manasseh—Josiah; destruction of the temple and exile—return and rebuilding of the temple. Ezra 7–10 also makes use of an Aramaic source, the rescript of Artaxerxes authorizing the mission (7:12–26). Like other sources in the book, this one has been liberally edited (see commentary). The account of the mission combines narrative in the third person (Ezra 7:1–11; 10:1–44) and first person (7:27–9:15), which in places are closely parallel (especially 9:1–5; 10:1–6). The third-person narrative either derives from an independent source known to the editor (Ahlemann) or it represents a selective paraphrase of a personal memoir authored by Ezra (Rudolph 1949; Noth 1943). Other sources incorporated into the story are the list of families which made the journey (8:1–14) and the list of those who had contracted foreign marriages (10:18–43), perhaps also the confessional prayer attributed to Ezra (9:6–15). Beneath the surface we may perhaps discern vestiges of a version less favorable to Ezra (see commentary on Ezra 10:15 and 1 Esd. 9:14–16). The story ends very abruptly with a brief statement which is textually obscure. While the explanation for this unsatisfactory conclusion, so different from the conclusion to Ezra 1–6, is uncertain, it reinforces the impression that the mission was something less than an unqualified success.

Nehemiah 8 also belongs to the Ezra narrative, and its relocation at this point is generally attributed to an editor for whom Ezra and Nehemiah were simultaneously present and active in Jerusalem. While the reading of the law and celebration of Sukkoth have their chronological sequel in the ceremonies described in the following two chapters (Neh. 9–10), Ezra no longer appears in them, suggesting that the connection is editorial. The reading of the law is preceded by a version of the golah list practically identical with Ezra 2. The context (Neh. 7:4–5) suggests that the repetition of this list, surprising in a relatively succinct narrative, was meant to serve as the basis for an expanded census which would facilitate the transfer of people to Jerusalem. But it also serves to identify those who were to gather as one in Jerusalem, forming a community versed in and faithful to the law. The original location of Neh. 8 is debated. In 1 Esdras it follows the solution of the marriage crisis as the last incident recorded in the book. While some have accepted this as the original order, the reading of the law would more naturally precede than follow the application of a particular point of law—or, rather, of a particular interpretation of the law. A good parallel would be Neh. 13:1–3, where the public reading of a provision of Deuteronomic law is followed by its implementation. An original location after Ezra 8 also provides a more coherent chronology. Ezra arrived in the fifth month (Ezra 7:8), the law was read in the seventh (Neh. 7:72 [73]; 8:2), and the marriage crisis was dealt with in the ninth month (Ezra 10:9). To the extent that Neh. 8 records an actual event, which it clearly did in the intent of the author, it is also more likely that Ezra discharged his task with respect to the law shortly after his arrival rather than waiting twelve years to do so.

A final note on Neh. 8. It seems that here too vestiges of an alternative version, one in which Levites have a prominent role, shows through the surface of the narrative in the manner of a palimpsest (see commentary on Neh. 8:2–4). It may also be relevant to the compositional history of the book that the following chapters (9–10), though represented as a distinct liturgical event following on the celebration of Sukkoth, replicate the elements of Ezra's reforming activity: fasting and confession of sin, separation from foreigners, public reading of the law, and commitment to reform.

A great variety of opinion has been expressed on the origin of the Ezra first-person narrative. Its stylistic features require attribution to the author of Chronicles (Torrey 1910) or an author belonging to the Chronicler's circle (Kapelrud 1944, Noth 1943); the same conclusion follows from the quite different premise that Ezra himself authored Chronicles (Albright 1921); it comes from an unknown fourth-century B.C.E. author (Mowinckel 1961), in the form of a midrash on the Artaxerxes rescript (Kellermann 1967); it was written by Ezra in the form of a report addressed to the Persian court (Schaeder 1930a, Noth 1943, Koch 1974), mandated after the lapse of one year

(Williamson). While certainty is unattainable, we see no reason to reject the basic authenticity of the Ezra memorandum, though it has been extensively edited and has not been cited *in extenso*. Whether it was written in the form of a mandated report to the central government or as a personal apologia addressed to the author's contemporaries and to posterity cannot, however, be determined.

While chapters 9–10 of Nehemiah do not belong to the Ezra material, they may be conveniently considered here. The penitential service with collective confession of sin, attributed to Ezra in LXX, is related chronologically to the reading of the law and Sukkoth but serves more directly as preface to the binding agreement which follows. This final link in the narrative complex Neh. 7:5–10:40 [39] rounds it off and gives a semblance of unity to what in reality is an editorial construct put together out of disparate material. The entire section begins and ends with the law, and Nehemiah, the principal *dramatis persona*, is present at the beginning and the end (8:9; 10:2 [1]). In its final form, the covenant of Neh. 10 is probably the latest unit in the book. As will be argued in the commentary, the individual stipulations presuppose Nehemiah's measures described in chapter 13, and the list of names, which follows a different order from the introduction to the list (10:1 [9:38]), has also been subsequently added, especially since we would expect the list of signatories to follow rather than precede the stipulations which they agree to observe. We are therefore led to the conclusion that this long section (Neh. 7:5–10:40[39]) has been spliced into the Nehemiah memoir in which the issue of the repopulation of Jerusalem, broached in 7:4, is only resumed at 11:1. Though put together from diverse elements at different times, this insert has its own logic and preserves a kind of unity independently of its context.

In the remaining narrative in Nehemiah (1:1–7:5 and 11:1–13:31) we have a situation comparable to that noted in the Ezra material: the combination of a first-person narrative in which Nehemiah tells his own story (1:1–2:20; 3:33[4:1]–7:5; 12:31–43; 13:4–31) with a third-person account dealing with several of the same incidents (3:1–32; 11:1–2; 12:27–30, 44–47; 13:1–3). The combined narrative is likewise supplemented with lists and genealogies (11:3–12:26). This alternation of first and third person is therefore a prominent feature of the book as a whole. The first-person narrative has some features in common with those psalms in which an accused person rebuts the accusations of opponents (Kellermann 1967), and others which bring to mind certain royal inscriptions from the ancient Near East (Mowinckel 1923, 1964–65). The closest parallels, however, are with late Egyptian autobiographical votive texts addressed to a deity and deposited in a temple. These are clearly apologetic and deal with the difficulties encountered and overcome in the pursuit of the author's political and religious goals. In Nehemiah's case these goals were the rebuilding of the wall and securing the defenses of Jerusalem; its repopulation; the rectification of social abuses; the support and smooth functioning of the cult; the preservation of the community's identity threatened by foreign admixture; and, in general, its regulation by law. Coverage of these goals in the memoir is very uneven. The rebuilding of the wall occupies only fifty-two days out of more than twelve years (5:14; 6:15; 13:6), and yet it takes up half of the surviving text. This would most naturally suggest that only excerpts from a longer work have been preserved. (For a more complicated explanation, see Williamson 1986, xxv–xxviii.)

We have the same problem here as with the Ezra material, that of deciding whether the third-person component derives from a distinct source or represents an editor's paraphrase of the original memoir. The fact that this third-person strand more often than not parallels the memoir—the building of the wall, the repopulation of Jerusalem, the service of dedication, and dismissal from the community of those of foreign descent—would more naturally suggest the former alternative. But the issue cannot be decided beyond reasonable doubt.

Nehemiah's own account of his achievements (the designation "memoir," though not entirely appropriate, is retained for convenience) must have existed as a distinct source which has been excerpted, edited, and incorporated into the larger narrative. The title (1:1) was added, a prayer has been attributed to him (1:5–11a), and the account of the dedication of the wall has been expanded (12:27–29, 33–36, 41–42). The conclusion of this episode (12:43), strongly reminiscent of the Chronicler's style, sets up a conscious parallelism with the dedication of the temple at Ezra 3:13 and may well mark the conclusion of the Chronicler's history of the postexilic community. The process of literary growth did not, of course, end there. Additions continued to be made, including a further excerpt from the memoir detailing problems encountered and overcome in the final phase of Nehemiah's governorship of the province (13:4–31). For more detailed corroboration of these conclusions the reader is referred to the relevant sections of the commentary.

5. Ezra-Nehemiah and "the Chronicler"

By "the Chronicler" (hereafter C) is meant the author of 1-2 Chronicles. It may still be necessary to insist, especially with Bible readers from more traditionalist backgrounds, that modern ideas of book production are not necessarily valid for antiquity. In the modern sense a book is the production of one, less commonly more than one, author, which enjoys legal protection from subsequent intrusions well-meaning or otherwise. The earliest composition within the biblical area which might qualify under this definition is the Wisdom of Jesus the Son of Sirach, written early in the second century B.C.E., which comes with a commendatory prologue from his grandson and in which the author identifies himself by name (50:27). When, therefore, we designate the anonymous C as the author of Chronicles, we must leave open the possibility that "author" may stand for a plurality or school rather than an individual, that is, a group sharing the same concerns, convictions, and idiom, perhaps active over several generations (as, for example, in the critical reconstructions of D. N. Freedman, *CBQ* 23, 1961, 436–442, and F. M. Cross, *JBL* 94, 1975, 4–18). With this in mind we must now turn to the question, much discussed in recent years, whether Ezra-Nehemiah is essentially a continuation of 1-2 Chronicles or, to put it differently, whether C, so understood, had a decisive role in the production of our book. While it is always possible to interpret a text in and by itself, as a closed system, there are important levels of meaning which will emerge only when it is read within the larger literary context to which it belongs. If, therefore, Ezra-Nehemiah was conceived as part of a larger work which included 1-2 Chronicles—with whatever editorial modifications were subsequently added—this will be an important factor in its interpretation.

Though Chronicles and Ezra-Nehemiah are distinct books in the Hebrew Bible, they are brought into relationship with each other by the concluding verses of the former (2 Chron. 36:22–23), which are practically identical with the opening verses of the latter (Ezra 1:1–3a). Since a decree issued in the first year of the first reign of a new dynasty more appropriately marks a beginning than a conclusion, the verses were probably added at the end of C's history of the monarchy. There is nothing quite like this in the Hebrew Bible, though we detect some less obvious attempts at linkage, e.g., at the end of Genesis and beginning of Exodus, and between Numbers (36:13) and Deuteronomy (1:1, 5). It could have served simply to indicate where the reader must go for the next chapter of the history, but it is also possible that 1-2 Chronicles and Ezra-Nehemiah, or (following 1 Esdras) Ezra 1–10 with Neh. 8, or at least Ezra 1–6, were conceived as one segmented work, and that a break was made at this point to emphasize the new era which opened with the accession of Cyrus. The division into books in the Hebrew Bible does not necessarily correspond either to the logical structuring of the material (as, for example, the break between Samuel and Kings) or its original form. But even if the separation between Chronicles and Ezra-Nehemiah is original, it might still be possible to argue that they share the same authorship, understood in the sense outlined above. This has, in fact, been the critical consensus since the work of L. Zunz (1832) and F. C. Movers (1834), with only an occasional demurral (e.g., A. C. Welch 1935). In recent years, however, the debate has been reopened, with the Israeli scholar Sarah Japhet (1969), followed by H. G. M. Williamson (1977, 1986), marshaling an array of arguments aimed at proving the completely separate origin of the two books. Since the debate has important consequences for the interpretation of Ezra-Nehemiah, the arguments must be evaluated at the appropriate level of detail, even at the risk of severely testing the reader's patience.

The conclusion reached by Japhet and Williamson is based primarily on a study of the distinct linguistic and stylistic features of the two compositions. At the outset, the reader needs to be aware of the severe methodological problems besetting this kind of investigation. The most obvious of these is the extensive use of sources in Ezra-Nehemiah, constituting about 70 percent of the total narrative, which greatly reduces the data base on which such conclusions can be drawn. One must also bear in mind that different contexts, of the monarchy and the postexilic confessional community respectively, elicit different kinds of language. Japhet notes, for example, that in describing the preparation for ritual acts Chronicles favors the verb *qdš* while Ezra-Nehemiah uses *ṭhr* (both in Hithpael). But apart from the fact that the distinction is not absolute (see, e.g., 2 Chron. 30:18), there may be reasons why the same author would find *ṭhr* more appropriate to the postexilic context, especially in view of the danger of contamination from surrounding peoples. The distinction between *hakkōhēn hārō'š*, chief priest, and *hakkōhēn haggādôl*, high priest, the former characteristic of Chronicles, the latter of Ezra-Nehemiah, is equally ineffective. The terms are not identical; *hakkōhēn haggādôl*, which occurs only in the author's source material (Neh. 3:1, 20; 13:28), corresponds to postexilic usage, a conclusion confirmed by the allusion to Aaron as *hakkōhēn hārō'š* at Ezra 7:5. (Japhet attempts to avoid this conclusion by translating "first priest," but for this we should expect *ri'šôn* rather than *rō'š*.) Another example is the term *maḥlᵉqôt*, referring to the divisions of the clergy, deemed to be characteristic of Chronicles but not of Ezra-Nehemiah. Yet it occurs at Ezra 6:18 (Aramaic) and Neh. 11:36, and a comparison of the former with 2 Chron. 35:2–5, where the same term is used, illustrates the importance of taking context into account in this kind of lexicographical study:

2 Chron. 35:2–5	Ezra 6:18
He appointed the priests in their offices *(mišmᵉrôt)* and encouraged them in the service of the house of YHVH *('ᵃbôdat bêt* YHVH). . . . "Prepare yourselves . . . according to your sections *(mahlᵉqôt),* according to the direction of David king of Israel and of Solomon his son. Stand in the holy place according to the divisions *(pᵉluggôt)* of ancestral houses. . . .	They set up the priests in their divisions *(pᵉluggātᵉhôn)* and the Levites in their sections *(mahlᵉqātᵉhôn)* for the service of God *('abîdat ᵉlāhā')* who is in Jerusalem, according to what is written in the book of Moses.

There are other terms of a more or less technical nature which occur frequently in Ezra-Nehemiah—e.g., *nᵉtînîm* (temple servants), *mᵉdînāh* (province), *sᵉgānîm* (officials), *pehāh* (governor)—but which a historian of the monarchy would have little or no occasion to use. They therefore have no bearing on the issue of authorship.

On the other side of the ledger, it would be possible to draw up a list of equal length of expressions either characteristic of or exclusive to Chronicles and Ezra-Nehemiah taken together. Years ago S. R. Driver drew up such a list (1897, 535–540), which, though in need of pruning and updating, still retains its value. The following examples, not all in Driver's list, will suffice to make the point: the verb *hityahaś,* enroll in a genealogy (1 Chron. 4:33, etc.; Ezra 2:62; 8:1, 3; Neh. 7:5, 64); *hedvāh,* joy (1 Chron. 16:27; Ezra 6:16; Neh. 8:10); *hēᶜîr et-hārûah,* rouse the spirit (1 Chron. 5:26; 36:21; Ezra 1:1, 5); *'ᵃrûkāh,* healing, repair, used as a building term with the verb *'ālāh* (2 Chron. 24:13; Neh. 4:1 [7]); *hᵃzāq va'ᵃśēh,* act strongly (1 Chron. 28:10, 20; 2 Chron. 19:11; Ezra 10:4). In addition to these, all exclusive to Chronicles-Ezra-Nehemiah, there are many others which are characteristic of this corpus and of infrequent occurrence elsewhere; as, for example: *nᵉdābāh,* votive offering, and the related verb *hitnaddēb,* offer freely (1 Chron. 29:5; 2 Chron. 17:16; 31:14, etc.; Ezra 1:4, 6; 2:68; 3:5; 8:28; Neh. 11:2); *niš'ār,* survivor (1 Chron. 13:2, etc.; Ezra 1:4; 9:15; Neh. 1:2, 3); *maᶜal,* infidelity, with the corresponding verb (17 times in Chronicles, 7 times in Ezra-Nehemiah); *ha'ᵃbîr qôl,* send round a proclamation (2 Chron. 30:5; Ezra 1:1; 10:7; Neh. 8:15); *yôm bᵉyôm,* day by day (frequently in Chronicles; Ezra 3:4; 6:9; Neh. 8:18); the introductory formula *kᵉkallôt 'ēlleh,* when these things had been completed (2 Chron. 7:1; 20:23; 24:10, 14; 31:1; Ezra

9:1). This list, which is far from exhaustive, cannot be disposed of by appealing to the characteristics of late Hebrew, which are more a matter of grammatical and syntactic features than of vocabulary. It does not prove common authorship, but it at least greatly complicates the task of proving separate authorship.

The proponents of separate authorship have also made much of what appear to them distinct and contrasting themes in the two works. Thus, Chronicles gives pride of place to David, the account of whose reign occupies nineteen out of sixty-five chapters, while Ezra-Nehemiah evinces little interest in him. Conversely, the exodus and occupation theme, never far below the surface in Ezra-Nehemiah, is of little interest to the author of Chronicles. In this instance, however, appearances are deceptive. In Chronicles David is important less as a great political figure than as the founder of Jerusalem as the national cult center, the provider for the temple, and the organizer of the cult with special reference to liturgical music. But it is precisely *in this role* that he is referred to in Ezra-Nehemiah wherever the occasion offers (Ezra 3:10; 8:20; Neh. 11:23; 12:24, 36, 45–46). That this book is silent on the political aspirations associated with the native dynasty is hardly surprising in view of the situation of the province under Persian rule. It is also gratuitous to assume that the author of Chronicles had no interest in the early traditions. His purpose was to write the history from First to Second Temple, the latter anticipated in the final paragraph of Chronicles and narrated fully in Ezra 1–6. And, as observed earlier (sect. 1, above), what is omitted as literal event in the beginning is introduced typologically at the end, in the new exodus and settlement of the land of which Ezra-Nehemiah speaks.

An argument of a similar stripe runs as follows. The author of Chronicles omits whatever would tarnish the reputations of David and Solomon, and therefore passes over in silence the latter's addiction to foreign women which led him to introduce alien cults into Israel (1 Kings 11:1–4). It would therefore be inconceivable that the same author would allow Nehemiah to cite Solomon as an example of the evil consequences of foreign marriages (Neh. 13:26). As the context makes clear, however, the point is that if this happened to Solomon, greatest of kings and beloved of God, how much more would it be likely to happen to those less favored whom Nehemiah was addressing? The women referred to in the text cited, moreover, include natives of Egypt, Moab, Ammon, and Edom, precisely those countries whose inhabitants are the object of legislation in Deut. 23:4–9 [3–8], the text which provided the basis for Nehemiah's anti-assimilationist measures (Neh. 13:1–3). Even if 1 Kings 11:1–4 was not formulated as a postexilic exegetical expansion with reference to the Deuteronomic law (a plausible suggestion of Fishbane 1985, 125–126), it was clearly this connection which accounts for citing Solomon as a cautionary example, in spite of his acknowledged political and religious eminence.

It is also pointed out that Chronicles goes out of its way to present the northern tribes in as favorable a light as possible. It omits the overall condemnation of the "northerners" in 2 Kings 17:7–41 and describes efforts by Judean kings to bring them back into the fold (2 Chron. 30:1–22; 34:9). Ezra-Nehemiah, on the other hand, restricts the true Israel to the golah group in Judah and Benjamin and evinces such a negative attitude to the people of Samaria as to rule out the possibility of common authorship. A closer reading of the texts, however, reveals a rather more nuanced situation. The author of Chronicles condemns in no uncertain terms the cult set up in the Northern Kingdom and repudiates its clergy as illegitimate (2 Chron. 11:14–15; 13:8–12). On prophetic advice, Amaziah rejects military assistance from the north since "YHVH is not with Israel, with all these Ephraimites" (2 Chron. 25:6–10). The only offer extended to them comes from Hezekiah, who is attempting to win them back after the fall of the Northern Kingdom to the Assyrians. They are invited to participate in a Passover in Jerusalem, on condition of repentance, an offer which is greeted with derision (30:10–12). Some refugees do take part, however, after undergoing ritual purification (30:18, 25), a situation exactly parallel to the Passover following the dedication of the Second Temple (Ezra 6:21). In light of these considerations, it would be imprudent to make too much of the omission of 2 Kings 17:7–41, an omission susceptible of more than one explanation. Throughout Ezra-Nehemiah "Judah and Benjamin" describes the surviving embodiment of Israel (Ezra 4:1; 7:14; 10:9; Neh. 11:4), but the same term occurs at numerous points in Chronicles. Identity of viewpoint could not be more clearly stated than by the phrase "all Israel in Judah and Benjamin" added to 1 Kings 12:23 at 2 Chron. 11:3. Neither Chronicles (especially in 1 Chron. 1–9) nor Ezra-Nehemiah loses sight of the totality of Israel, the latter signaling its concern by repeated allusion to the number twelve (Ezra 2:2; 6:17; 8:24, 25; cf. 1 Chron. 25:9–21). At the same time, both assume that the contemporary Judean community is the only legitimate representative of an Israel now dispersed as a result of apostasy. It should be unnecessary to add that the negative attitude to Samaria in Ezra-Nehemiah is prompted by the opposition of the political leadership of that city to the resurgence of its southern neighbor.

A similar type of argument focuses on the contrast between the major role played by prophets in Chronicles and the relative absence of prophecy from Ezra-Nehemiah. But apart from the fact that the most significant event recorded in the latter, the rebuilding of the temple, was accomplished with prophetic backing (Ezra 5:1–2), the argument overlooks the fundamental change which prophecy underwent at the exile, a change of which the author was as aware as we are (cf. the substitution of "priests and Levites" at 2 Chron. 34:30 for "priests and prophets" at 2 Kings 23:2). Likewise, the claim that the theology of retribution, emphasized in Chronicles, is absent from Ezra-Nehemiah fails to take account of the lack of an adequate narrative base in the editorial framework for making a meaningful comparison.

On the positive side, indications that the two works share the same religious interests and ideology are numerous. While these will be noted in the commentary, the following examples will suffice to make the point:

1. Preparations for building the First and the Second Temple are described in parallel ways (Ezra 3:7; cf. 1 Chron. 22:2, 4, 15; 2 Chron. 2:9, 15–16).

2. In both instances the altar is set up *before* the temple is built, in order to ward off danger (Ezra 3:2; cf. 1 Chron. 21:18–22:1).

3. Both temples are endowed by the heads of ancestral houses (Ezra 2:68; 1 Chron. 26:26), whereas 2 Kings 12:18 speaks only of royal endowment.

4. Both show great interest in the sacred vessels (Ezra 1:7; 7:19; 8:25–30, 33–34; cf. 1 Chron. 28:13–19; 2 Chron. 5:1), and Chronicles omits 2 Kings 24:13—according to which the gold vessels were destroyed by the Babylonians—in anticipation of their restoration to the repatriated Jews.

5. Both the order of sacrifices (Ezra 3:4–6; cf. 2 Chron. 2:3; 8:13) and the enumeration of sacrificial materials (Ezra 6:9, 17; 7:22; 7:17–18; 8:35–36; cf. 1 Chron. 29:21; 2 Chron. 29:21, 32) are practically identical in the two works.

6. The descriptions of liturgical music and of musical instruments and who are to play them correspond closely (Ezra 3:10; Neh. 12:35; cf. 1 Chron. 15:19; 16:5–6; 25:1, 6; 2 Chron. 5:12–13).

7. The same holds for liturgical prayer: the antiphon "for he is good, for his loving-kindness endures for ever," of frequent occurrence in Chronicles, is slipped in at Ezra 3:11; the blessing form at Ezra 7:27–28 ("blessed be YHVH, God of our fathers"), and especially the confessional psalm beginning, exceptionally, with this type of formula at Neh. 9:5–6, is paralleled in 1 Chron. 29:10–19; (cf. also 2 Chron. 2:11; 6:4–11; 9:9; 20:5–12).

A final observation about structure, which will be developed in the commentary, points us in the same direction. The last part of Chronicles is ordered according to movements of renewal and reform following on periods of religious infidelity: Hezekiah after Ahaz, Josiah after Manasseh, both followed by celebration of Passover (2 Chron. 30; 35:1–19). This pattern continues into Ezra 1–6, where the renewal of the cult concludes with the celebration of the same festival (6:19–22). As at the time of Hezekiah, the priests and Levites prepared themselves by ritual purification (Ezra 6:20; cf. 2 Chron. 30:3, 15), the festival was celebrated with joy, outsiders were allowed to participate after suitable preparation, and a concern for a return of the dispersed to the land is expressed (2 Chron. 30:9). Another structural feature which binds the two works together is the retrospective comment accompanying the epoch-marking festivals throughout the work. At the celebration of Hezekiah's Passover we are told that "since the time of Solomon son of David king of Israel there had been nothing like this in Jerusalem" (2 Chron. 30:26). Of Josiah's celebration we hear that "no Passover like it had been kept in Israel since the days of Samuel the prophet" (2 Chron. 35:18), while the author says of the feast of Tabernacles celebrated at the time of Ezra that "from the days of Joshua son of Nun to that day the people of Israel had not done so" (Neh. 8:17). There is a progression here which is hardly accidental: the later the point in time, the further back the retrospective allusion goes. It would be difficult to find a clearer indication of unity of conception which binds together the two works into one history with its own distinctive point of view and purpose.

6. Ezra and Nehemiah in Jewish Tradition

It was practically inevitable that the contrasting roles of Ezra and Nehemiah, somewhat like those of Aaron and Moses, should be appealed to in the long struggle for self-definition in which Judaism was engaged throughout the remainder of the Second Temple period and beyond. This process, whose point of departure is the personal record left behind by both men, is already at work in the redaction of these records and the history which has been built around them. Their conflation into the narrative of a single event, in which both are active as contemporaries, was inspired (as I have argued) by the desire to give the priest and scribe, whose mission was not an unqualified success, his full due over against the layman whose political achievements were a matter of record. Polemical intent is also detectable in additions subsequently made to the book (for different estimates see In der Smitten 1973a, 68–69, and Kellermann 1967, 97–112), especially in regard to the role of the laity over against that of the temple clergy (e.g., Neh. 8), and respective roles and prerogatives within the clerical ranks (e.g., Neh. 10:39–40 [38–39]). Unfortunately, however, we know too little about the history of Judah in the late Persian and early Hellenistic periods to interpret these post-Chronistic additions in the context of the internal history of the province at that time.

The silence is first broken by the scribe Jesus son of Sirach writing in the early decades of the second century B.C.E. His book concludes with an encomium of the great figures of Israel's history, toward the end of which he makes honorable mention of Zerubbabel, Jeshua, and Nehemiah but passes over Ezra in silence (Sir. 49:11–13), an omission which has given rise to a great deal of discussion. If we could suppose that Jesus was unacquainted with the Ezra tradition (as K. F. Pohlmann 1970, 72–73), or knew it to be based on a fiction (as C. C. Torrey, *JAOS* 70, 1950, 118), an answer would lie ready at hand. But this seems to be highly unlikely, and the explanation that he had before him a separate Nehemiah memoir (M. Noth 1943, 155; G. Hölscher 1923, 496) is no more satisfactory, since we would still have to conclude that he was ignorant of a *separate* Ezra tradition. The author is clearly familiar with 1-2 Chronicles, which he follows in the special praise bestowed on David as liturgist (47:8–10) and on the great liturgical reformers Hezekiah and Josiah (48:17–25; 49:1–4). It is all the more improbable, therefore, that he was ignorant of the work of Ezra. Another solution is that Nehemiah was deliberately paired with Simon the high priest, one of whose achievements was to repair the temple and its walls (50:1–4; K. Galling 1964, 129 n. 3). This may be so, but it would still not explain the omission of Ezra, who could have been named before Nehemiah. Besides, the twinning of Nehemiah with Ezra would seem to be much more natural and would parallel the pairing of Zerubbabel and Jeshua immediately preceding.

The most probable explanation, therefore, is that the omission was deliberate and polemical. We can readily understand the inclusion of Nehemiah, the intransigent opponent of Tobiah the Ammonite, in light of Jesus ben Sirach's attachment to the Oniad priestly house and its contemporary representative Simon II, and in the context of the bitter Oniad-Tobiad rivalry under Ptolemaic and Seleucid rule. We may also suppose that Ezra's singleminded theocratic ideal was uncongenial to the author, who took political realities, and the possibility and desirability of political autonomy, seriously. Ezra's extreme integrationist position, exemplified in his marriage policy,

must for him have contrasted unfavorably with the political realism
of Nehemiah (In der Smitten 1973a, 69–74; Kellermann 1967, 112–
115). In this respect he may be seen to anticipate the Hasmonean
ideology which looked to Nehemiah as the real founder of the commonwealth and the ideal of political-religious leadership.

The Hasmoneans, who traced their ancestry through the priest
Joiarib of the first return (1 Chron. 9:10; Neh. 11:10; 12:6, 19; cf. 1
Chron. 24:7), seem to have cherished the memory of Nehemiah. He
features prominently in a letter prefixed to 2 Maccabees (1:10b–2:18)
which purports to have been written at the time of the purification
of the temple in 164 B.C.E. but was actually composed in the last
years of the second century B.C.E. or shortly thereafter. According
to the anonymous writer, an apologist for the Hasmoneans, it was
Nehemiah rather than Zerubbabel who rebuilt the altar and the
temple immediately after the first return. The author probably justified this boldly revisionist view on the grounds that Zerubbabel was
Nehemiah's Babylonian name, and that therefore the two men were
identical (cf. also *b. Sanh.* 38a). The legend of the spectacular dedication of the rebuilt temple may have drawn on a Nehemiah apocry-
phon then in circulation (Kellermann 1967, 124–128), though it is
just as likely that the author invented it. Divine approval was manifested by the spontaneous combustion of naphtha preserved from the
perpetual fire of the First Temple following instructions left behind
by Jeremiah. This fire festival, presented as the *hieros logos* of the
Second Temple, established a link of continuity with Solomon's temple and at the same time won the approval of the Zoroastrian Persians, who venerated fire. More important for the writer of the letter,
it provided a model for the Maccabean celebration of "Sukkoth in
Chislev," later Hanukkah, commemorating the reconsecration of the
temple desecrated by Antiochus Epiphanes.

In other respects, too, Nehemiah served as a role model for the
Hasmoneans. Like the Maccabee brothers he was a political leader,
a staunch defender of Jewish rights, and a man deeply concerned for
the law and the temple. Like Judah Maccabee, he collected the
writings which constituted the national heritage after they had been
dispersed or lost with the destruction of Jerusalem and ensuing exile
(2 Macc. 2:13–15). The portrait which emerges from this letter preserved by the epitomist of Jason's five-volume history (2 Macc. 2:23)
is therefore of Nehemiah as the real founder of the Second Commonwealth, the forerunner of those who had to repeat the task after the
lapse of more than three and a half centuries.

Unlike the allegorical allusion in *Enoch* 89:72–73, which speaks
of three sheep returning and rebuilding the ruined temple (Zerubba-

bel, Jeshua, Nehemiah?), the letter allows no other founding father
to share the honors with Nehemiah. A very different account of the
origins of the Second Commonwealth is presented in 1 Esdras, which
may be roughly contemporary with the letter. This Greek version of
events from Josiah to Ezra differs in two important respects from the
canonical book: it omits entirely the Nehemiah narrative and adds
a long novelistic account of how Zerubbabel obtained permission
from Darius to return and rebuild both the city and the temple (chs.
3–4). The author was familiar with a Nehemiah contemporary with
Zerubbabel, but he plays no important part in events, and his role
is further diminished by being linked with a certain Attharias or
Attharates, a fictitious name formed from the Persian loanword
hattiršātā', "the governor" (1 Esd. 5:40). It is this latter, not Nehemiah, who gives instructions to Ezra and his associates during the
solemn reading of the law (1 Esd. 9:49; cf. Neh. 8:9). On the assumption that 1 Esdras is a tendentious rewriting of the last section of C's
history, its intent appears to be to elevate Zerubbabel and Ezra as the
founding fathers at the expense of Nehemiah. And in that case it
could be plausibly read as countering the kind of pro-Hasmonean
propaganda represented by the letter.

With the ascendancy of Pharisaic rabbinism, after the suppression of the revolts against Rome, it was inevitable that Ezra the
scribe rather than Nehemiah the political activist should become
the model of leadership for the Jewish people. The controversial
note is, however, still faintly detectable in 2 Esdras (the Ezra
apocalypse), written toward the end of the first century C.E. Ezra
rather than Nehemiah (who is not mentioned) is backdated to the
period immediately following the fall of Jerusalem (3:1, 29), a move
which was no doubt inspired by the genealogy in Ezra 7:1–5, and
it is he rather than Nehemiah who restored the written records lost
during the destruction of city and temple (ch. 14). If the legend of
the fire on the altar is intended to recall the Elijah story, and therefore imply that Nehemiah was a prophetic figure of comparable
power, the parallelism would be even closer. For the author of 2
Esdras presents his hero as the only prophet left (12:42; cf. 1 Kings
19:10, 14) and anticipates that, like Elijah, he will be taken up into
heaven (8:19; 14:9).

2 Esdras transforms Ezra into prophet and apocalyptic seer after
the manner of Moses, who received both the Torah and esoteric
knowledge on Mount Sinai (14:3–6), a transformation which would
inspire a long series of apocalyptic and esoteric tracts down into the
Middle Ages (see M. E. Stone 1983, 561–579). In the space of forty
days, assisted by five scribes and fortified by a fiery liquid, he rewrote

the entire scriptures destined for public use and seventy books of
esoteric knowledge reserved to the initiated (14:19–48). He is thereby
identified as a second Moses much more clearly than in the canonical
book in which he merely promulgates, explains, and administers the
law. There is no overt connection between this composition and the
canonical book, except perhaps that it was the law rewritten by Ezra
under divine inspiration in the diaspora that he brought with him on
his mission to Jerusalem.

In the part of his *Antiquities* dealing with Ezra and Nehemiah
(11.120–183), Josephus for the most part follows 1 Esdras but betrays no hint of polemic. Unlike the canonical book, he keeps their
careers quite separate, placing Ezra's mission in the seventh and
Nehemiah's in the twenty-fifth year of Xerxes. This impossible chronology (Xerxes reigned for only twenty-one years) resulted from a
praiseworthy but misguided attempt to arrange the Persian kings in
their correct order. The Artaxerxes of 1 Esd. 2:16 (Ezra 4:7) is
changed to Cambyses (11.21, 26), and the Ahasuerus of the book of
Esther, which follows Ezra-Nehemiah in LXX, is identified with the
Artaxerxes who succeeded Xerxes (11.184).

Josephus describes Ezra as the leading priest *(prōtos hiereus)* in the
Babylonian diaspora (11.121), a position which he also holds in
rabbinic tradition; but he does not go so far as the author of 1 Esdras,
who elevates him to the high priesthood after his arrival in Jerusalem
(1 Esd. 9:39–40); he is content to describe him as "reader of the laws"
(anagnōstos tōn nomōn, 11.123, 127). He omits the detail about the
disquieting lack of Levites in Ezra's caravan and refers to foreign
marriages as a violation of the constitution *(politeia)* in force at that
time. His narrative ends with the death of Ezra at an advanced age
in Jerusalem (11.158). His account of Nehemiah's mission which
followed eighteen years later (11.159–183) contains several details
not in the canonical book. He is at pains to present him in as favorable a light as possible. He not only built houses in Jerusalem—a
detail perhaps taken from Sir. 49:13—but also completed the building of the temple. Allusions to internal difficulties and opposition are
passed over in silence. He too died at a ripe age in Jerusalem, honored
by all.

The many rabbinic traditions about Ezra, and the few about Nehemiah, collected in the now outdated work of L. Ginzberg (*The
Legends of the Jews,* Philadelphia, 1909–38) call for careful form-
critical analysis. Attention should also be paid to the work of the
medieval Jewish commentators, constituting an alternative exegetical tradition which is now only beginning to be rediscovered by
post-Enlightenment biblical scholarship. Unfortunately, however,

these tasks exceed the bounds of a simple commentary of this kind. The more significant of these traditions should, however, be at least briefly mentioned.

As the son of the high priest Seraiah, Ezra is backdated to the exilic period and yet presented as a contemporary of Zerubbabel and Jeshua (*Cant. Rab.* 5:5) and even identified with Malachi (*b. Meg.* 15a; Targ. on Mal. 1:1). He acquired legal expertise as a disciple of Baruch, Jeremiah's amanuensis, and refused to emigrate until after the death of his master, since Torah study is superior to temple worship (*b. Meg.* 16b). This tradition, probably dependent on the apocryphal book of Baruch, recalls 2 Macc. 2:2–3 in which Jeremiah entrusted the law to the departing exiles. There was much discussion among late third and early fourth century scholars about a dictum of R. Eleazar that "Ezra did not go up from Babylon until he had made it like pure sifted flour," that is, until he had screened out all of impure descent to take them with him, and thus ensured the ethnic purity of the Babylonian community (*b. Kidd.* 69a–b). This tradition evidently had its starting point in the list of immigrants of doubtful lineage in the census of the first return (Ezra 2:59–63). Ezra himself, naturally, made sure of his own lineage before departing (*b. B.B.* 15a).

It goes without saying that Ezra's principal achievement was to restore the Torah (*b. Sukk.* 20a), so that if Moses had not preceded him he would have received Torah directly from God himself (*b. Sanh.* 21b; *t. Sanh.* 4:7; *j. Meg.* 1:9). As the prototype of the sage (*j. Meg.* 4:1), he founded the first yeshiva (*b. B.B.* 21b–22a)—compare the Torah "seminar" of Neh. 8:13—presided over the men of the Great Assembly (*'anšê kᵉneset haggᵉdôlāh, b. Meg.* 18b), and issued the ten *taqqanot* (*b. B.K.* 82a–b) together with numerous other ethical and ritual ordinances. For good measure he also authored the targum (based on Neh. 8:8; *b. Meg.* 3a; *b. Sanh.* 21b), introduced the square or Assyrian script (cf. 2 Esd. 14:42), and was eventually transformed into the compiler of the Mishnah and the first of the Masoretes. He also authored Chronicles and the book which bears his name (*b. B.B.* 15a), though there existed an alternative opinion which held that Nehemiah authored the latter but did not get credit for it on account of vainglory and his habit of disparaging his predecessors (*b. Sanh.* 93b).

Nehemiah, understandably, received much less attention. He was a lesser figure in that first springtime of Judaism (*Cant. Rab.* 2:12) and his significance was even further diluted by identification with Zerubbabel (e.g., *b. Sanh.* 38a), an identification which we have seen was made long before the compilation of the Gemarah.

7. The Political and Social Context

Ezra-Nehemiah is our principal source of information on Judaism during the first century of Persian rule (538 to shortly after 432 B.C.E.), but it is far from being a straightforward, factual account of events during that century. Chronologically, it covers only the first and the last quarter century, leaving a large gap between the completion of the temple in 515 and the arrival of Ezra in 458, and providing only few and uncertain indications of what was happening during that half century. Geographically, the field of vision is restricted almost exclusively to Jerusalem and the surrounding region, an area of little more than twenty-five square miles, about half the size of Rhode Island. Many Jews lived elsewhere—in Samaria, the Galilee, the coastal region, Transjordan, Babylon, Egypt, and further afield, and the available literary and artifactual evidence reveals a quite different situation in these other regions. And even within the chronological and geographical limits of the book and the sources which it quotes, the events are refracted through several interpretative prisms. There are inner contradictions, foreshortenings, and idealizations which the historian must negotiate in order to attain even a partial view of the restoration and consolidation of the Jewish community in the homeland. The task of historical reconstruction must therefore be informed by an acute sense of the fragile and provisional nature of our knowledge of this obscure but crucial century.

The surviving kingdom of Judah passed under Babylonian control in 605 B.C.E., following which ill-advised rebellion led, in the early years of the sixth century, to the destruction of Jerusalem and its temple and successive deportations (598–582). The more conservative and probably more accurate estimate of the number of deportees provided in the biblical text is 4,600 (Jer. 52:28–30), though this figure probably included only adult males. Those who remained were for the most part the agrarian class, called "the poor of the land" (*dallat hā'āreṣ,* 2 Kings 24:14; 25:12), who were permitted, in the interest of maintaining the economy of the province, to take over holdings and estates of the deportees (Jer. 39:11). The ground was thus prepared for social conflict—of the kind which flared up as late as Nehemiah's administration (Neh. 5:1)—when Babylonian Jews began to trickle back in the early Persian period. The new owners justified the expropriation on the grounds that the deportees had, in effect, been expelled from the Yahvistic cult community and had therefore forfeited title to property (Ezek. 11:15–16), an argument which we may be sure persuaded few if any of the descendants of the former owners.

With the fall of the city of Babylon in October 539 the entire Babylonian empire, including Judah, passed under Persian control. Cyrus II (Kurush), head of the Achaemenid clan of the Pasargadae tribe in southern Iran, had by then united the Persian tribes, defeated the Medes, and won control of vast territories including the Kingdom of Lydia and much of the Greek-speaking Ionian littoral. From about the time of the capture of Sardis in 547 Jewish prophets were predicting the fall and destruction of Babylon (Isa. 47 and 13, though the latter may refer to the fate of the city at the hands of Xerxes more than half a century later). The Cyrus cylinder, inscribed in 538, informs us that the western provinces submitted at once (*ANET*, 316), but it seems that the changeover initially made little difference. Judah became part of a vast satrapy which included Babylon and the Trans-Euphrates region (Babili-Ebirnari), an administrative arrangement which seems to have remained in place until Xerxes made Babylon a separate satrapy after crushing rebellion there in the early years of his reign. The administrative relation between Judah and Samaria (corresponding to the Assyrian province of Samerina) has long been a subject of dispute. Albrecht Alt (*KS* 2:316–337) maintained that the Babylonians did not grant separate provincial status to Judah, but that it continued as an appendage to Samaria until Nehemiah established its separate identity. The issue continues to be argued, but the mention of governors who preceded Nehemiah in the biblical record (Ezra 5:14; Neh. 5:15; Hag. 1:1; Mal. 1:18), and perhaps elsewhere, though the dating of the material is disputed (see N. Avigad 1970, 26–36), must be given full weight, and the office may have been temporarily vacant at the time of Tattenai's inspection and Ezra's arrival (Ezra 5:3–5; 8:32–34; see further M. Smith 1971, 195–198). The governor of Samaria may have been charged with supervision of the province shortly before Nehemiah's arrival in 445, but this would have been an exceptional situation occasioned by the disturbances which led to Nehemiah's mission (Neh. 1:3; cf. Ezra 4:23).

After the destruction of Jerusalem the administrative center of the province was at Mizpah (Tell en-Nasbeh, Jer. 40–41), which retained its importance after the Persians took over (see Neh. 3:7). Some form of worship continued, at least for a time, on the site of the ruined temple (Jer. 41:4–5), but not of a kind to win the approval of the Babylonian Jews after their return. Cyrus' cylinder announced a policy of clemency to the peoples deported by the Babylonians and of appeasement of their deities who had been exiled with them. In general, the early Achaemenids respected local cults as a matter of political expediency. Cyrus claimed to have reestablished the Marduk cult in Babylon, neglected by Nabonidus, and to have returned the statues of deities to their original sites in Susa, Akkad, Uruk, and elsewhere. The edicts quoted in Ezra 1:1–4 and 6:1–5 (cf. the paraphrase in 5:13–15) allowed diaspora Jews to collect funds with a view to returning and building the temple, restored the sacred vessels confiscated by Nebuchadnezzar, and even decreed that the project should be financed out of the royal treasury. While these measures are consistent with the policy just mentioned, their authenticity cannot be taken for granted, certainly not in the precise form in which they are presented (see commentary). In any case, no substantial progress was made toward rebuilding the temple before the reign of Darius almost two decades later, as Hag. 2:15 explicitly attests. A governor with a Babylonian name, Sheshbazzar, was appointed by Cyrus (Ezra 5:16), and some deportees may have returned with him within a year of the fall of Babylon. Others may have accompanied Cambyses on his conquest of Egypt in 525—the staging area for the conquest appears to have been in or near Akko on the Mediterranean coast—but it is unlikely that there was any substantial influx from the Babylonian diaspora before the accession of Darius in 522 B.C.E.

Cyrus died fighting the Massagetai tribes east of the Caspian Sea in the summer of 530. He was succeeded without incident by Cambyses, who had been appointed ruler of Babylon after the capture of that city. In 525 Cambyses invaded Egypt, in an operation planned by his father, and incorporated it into the Persian empire as the satrapy of Mudriya, becoming himself successor to the pharaohs of the twenty-seventh dynasty. Cambyses' bad reputation with classical authors (e.g., Herodotus 3.1–38) is contradicted by Egyptian sources which testify to his respect for native customs and religion, though he did, with some justification, restrict the income of many of the wealthier temples and their clergy. Though Cambyses is not even mentioned in Ezra-Nehemiah, the conquest of Egypt may have brought with it a number of new settlers in Judah; the Udjahorresnet inscription says that many foreigners accompanied Cambyses on his campaign. From that time until the end of Achaemenid rule the policy of the central government with respect to this most recalcitrant part of the empire would necessarily have repercussions in the neighboring province of Judah.

One of the charges leveled against Cambyses was that of murdering his brother Bardiya (known to the Greeks as Smerdis), whom he suspected of designs on the throne. The story put out by Darius in his famous Behistun rock inscription, supported by the classical authors, is that a certain Gaumata passed himself off as Bardiya, claimed the throne, and won widespread support throughout the empire, especially after suspending taxes for three years (Herodotus 3.67). The truth of this item of Darius' propagandistic manifesto is still being debated (see the different assessments of J. M. Cook 1983, 49–55, and R. N. Frye 1984, 96–106). After the death of Cambyses in 522 on his way back from Egypt, Darius of the cadet branch of the Achaemenids killed the pretender and established himself in power after a hard struggle lasting almost two years. Though the Behistun inscription records no uprisings either in Egypt or the Syro-Palestinian area during this period, we know that Judean prophets were urging the rebuilding of the temple as a prelude to the restoration of the native dynasty in the person of Zerubbabel, governor of the province (Hag. 2:6–7, 20–23; Zech. 6:9–15). We do not know whether these prophetic urgings were acted on, or even whether they came to the attention of the Persian authorities, but it is significant that Zerubbabel had disappeared from the scene by the time of a tour of inspection carried out by Tattenai, governor of Abar-nahara (Ezra 5:3–5). About the same time (520 or 519) Darius had to deal with successive rebellions in Babylon led by Nidintu-Bel and Arakha respectively, both claiming descent from the Babylonian royal house. The suppression of these revolts and consequent economic hardship may have impelled other Babylonian Jews to take the prophet Zechariah's advice to "escape to Zion" (Zech. 2:10 [6]). The arrival of a new group of *ôlîm,* including wealthy members of the Babylonian community (Zech. 6:9–14), would have given additional impetus to the building program. Shortly afterward Darius came in person to settle affairs in Egypt. Though there is no evidence that he visited the province of Judah, he would have passed along the coastal route a few miles to the west, and it would be natural to assume that he would take the occasion to verify that all was well in the province. It may also have been at this time that he gave permission to rebuild the temple, which would not be inconsistent with the report that this permission was granted after the original edict of Cyrus was discovered in the archives at Ecbatana (Ezra 6:1–2). In any event, the temple was completed and dedicated by the sixth year of the reign, that is, by 516/515 B.C.E. (Ezra 6:15).

Nothing is known of affairs in Judah during the remaining twenty-five years of Darius' reign. The satrap of Babili-Ebirnari at that time was a certain Ushtani (Hystanes), and Tattenai served under him as governor of the Trans-Euphrates region (Ezra 5:3). Whether Zerubbabel was recalled and another governor of Judah appointed, one of those whose rapacity was condemned by Nehemiah (Neh. 5:15), we do not know. This was the time when Darius could at last turn to the reorganization of the empire badly shaken by the events of the previous four years. It is unlikely that this thorough shakeup left Judah untouched, especially in view of its proximity to Egypt, where unrest was endemic. The empire was divided into twenty satrapies for administrative and fiscal purposes. Judah belonged to the fifth of these together with the rest of the Syro-Palestinian region, Phoenicia, and Cyprus, assessed at three hundred and fifty talents of silver (Herodotus 3.89–94). The subdivision of the province into ten administrative units *(pᵉlākîm)*, each under an officer *(śar)* responsible to the governor, may also date to this time (see commentary on Neh. 3). An important aspect of Darius' new order was the collection, codification, and administration of local law codes, which were enforced together with Persian imperial law *(dātā'*; see commentary on Ezra 7:26). After Darius had suppressed the revolt of the Egyptian satrap Aryandes in 518, he ordered his successor Pharnadates to appoint a commission charged with the codification of traditional Egyptian law as an instrument of the *pax Persica* in that satrapy. The Demotic Chronicle informs us that this task lasted several years and that the final draft was written up in Aramaic and demotic Egyptian. While we have no evidence of similar activity in Judah, it would be reasonable to suppose that in this respect Persian policy contributed to the redaction of the laws which were to attain their final formulation in the Pentateuch.

By the time of Darius' death in 486 Egypt was once again in revolt under Khabasha, and it was left to his successor Xerxes (Khshayarsha, Ahasuerus in Ezra 4:6 and in Esther) to deal with the problem. After suppressing the revolt with great severity, Xerxes appointed his own brother Achaemenes as satrap. Then in 484 revolt broke out in Babylon instigated by Bel-shimanni and Shamash-eriba, who, like their predecessors thirty-six years earlier, claimed descent from the great Nebuchadnezzar. The ferocious suppression of this revolt led to the separation of Babylon from Abar-nahara and may well have driven other Babylonian Jews to emigrate to Judah. Ezra 4:6 has a brief and cryptic allusion to a complaint lodged against the people of Judah and Jerusalem at the beginning of the reign, occasioned, we must suppose, by real or alleged complicity in the revolts in either Egypt or Babylon. That is all we are told, and the notice provides insufficient grounds for theorizing a major catastrophe following on invasion of the province by its neighbors (J. Morgenstern 1956–60). For the remainder of the reign, which ended with the murder of Xerxes in 465, we have no information relevant to the history of the province. Preparations for the massive expedition against the mainland Greeks, which ended in total defeat at Salamis, Plataea, and Mykale (480–479), must have greatly exacerbated the burden of taxation and the economic misery of the mass of the population, especially in regions of subsistence economy like the Judean highlands (cf. the reference to the royal tax at Neh. 5:4).

Artaxerxes I (Artakhshassa) came to the throne after the murder of his father and the usual palace intrigue. The early years of a long reign (465–424) were full of unrest in different parts of the empire. After he had put down a revolt in Bactria instigated by his brother Hystaspes, a much more serious problem arose in Egypt with the rebellion of the Lybian Inaros supported by a large Athenian fleet. The Persian forces sent to quell the uprising were defeated and the satrap Achaemenes was killed in 459, at which time it must have seemed that Egypt and other western provinces might be lost to the empire. After four years of fighting, however, the Persian nobleman Megabyzus managed to trap and destroy the Athenian fleet sent by Pericles, with the result that by 454 Persian control was reestablished and a new satrap, Arsames, appointed. The peace of Kallias in 448, by which the Delian League and the Persian empire agreed on reciprocal noninterference, brought to an end a long period of overt hostility between the two powers which dated back to the reign of Darius. In the meantime, however, Megabyzus, now satrap of Abarnahara, himself revolted, defeated two expeditionary forces sent against him, and then apparently sought and obtained pardon of Artaxerxes, the least intransigent of the Achaemenid rulers. The details of this incident, for which we depend exclusively on Ctesias, are obscure; it seems to have taken place in the early years of the fourth decade of that century.

This straightforward summary of well-known political events during the first century of Persian rule is itself an interpretation, based on sources with their own interested points of view and providing only partial coverage of the period. Herodotus, for example, stops before the reign of Artaxerxes, leaving us at the mercy of the gossipy and unreliable Ctesias. It does not and cannot validate any particular reading of the biblical sources nor does it, taken by itself, prove the chronological priority of Ezra. The most that can be claimed is that the order defended in this commentary makes a reasonable fit with the outline of events as presented. It will be seen that Ezra's mission in 458 coincides with one of the gravest crises at the western end of the empire, and therefore it could be interpreted as an attempt on the part of the central government to assure stability in an area which was, in the circumstances of those years, strategically crucial. And though Ezra's law cannot simply be equated with the Pentateuch, the concern for the implementation of traditional Jewish law expressed in the rescript could be seen as a further stage in the formation of Pentateuchal law, following on what has been surmised about developments during the reign of Darius. There may, finally, be a connection between the short-lived revolt of Megabyzus and the allegations of Mithredath and Rehum (Ezra 4:7–23) leading to hostile intervention and thus to the mission of Nehemiah. All of these possibilities are discussed more fully at the relevant points in the commentary.

Something of the economic and social condition of the province during this century can be learned from allusions in the biblical sources taken in conjunction with the results garnered from archaeological sites with Persian remains. Here too, and here especially, the fragmentary and provisional nature of our information has to be kept in mind. We know the size of the province, less than nine hundred square miles, but not its population density. Attempts to determine the population of Judah during this period (e.g., Albright 1965, 87: about 20,000 at the beginning) must take into account the number of deportees as a percentage of the total population, the extent of physical destruction (to which the archaeological record certainly attests), the influx of outsiders between 586 and 538, and the dating and detailed interpretation of the various lists in Ezra-Nehemiah, especially the census of Ezra 2 and Neh. 7. There would appear to be too many imponderables here to make even an approximate guess worthwhile. We may take it that the bulk of the population which remained in the land was composed of the agrarian class (the *dallat ḥāʾāreṣ*), with their traditional holdings and those expropriated from the deportees. While these expropriations hardly amounted to a social revolution, as has been claimed, they inevitably contributed to social conflict indicated here and there in contemporary sources (Neh. 5; Zech. 8:10; Isa. 58:4; 59:7). The potential for unrest would also have been increased, especially among the subsistence farmers of the Judean highlands, by bad harvests and other calamities alluded to in the same sources (e.g., Neh. 5:3; Hag. 1:6, 10–11; 2:16–17; Joel). To these must be added the effects of the extensive destruction and depopulation during the Babylonian period: damage to trade following on the destruction of Jerusalem and most of the larger towns, loss of the skilled artisan class, and a decrease in productivity due to the disappearance or takeover of the larger holdings and estates.

The imperial policy of the Achaemenids is often taken to be more benign that that of their predecessors. They appear to have been well disposed toward their Jewish subjects, but their fiscal policy was every bit as harsh and unenlightened as that of the Assyrians and Babylonians. The point has been made that taxation was a severe burden which increased with the passage of time and contributed substantially to unrest and rebellion. The tendency to hoard bullion also left the provinces with inadequate resources for maintaining a flourishing or even viable economy. The practice of farming out the collection of taxes to large businesses (e.g., the Murashu house in Nippur and the Egibi in Babylon) or prominent members of local aristocracies was another factor creating disaffection and division. The impact of taxation was especially severe on a subsistence agrarian economy like that of Judah. Farmers would have had to produce a surplus in order to have the means to pay, especially after the introduction of coinage by Darius around 500 B.C.E. This in its turn forced many of them to borrow from loan sharks, at interest rates greatly in excess of what would be considered tolerable today, leading to the mortgaging of fields, vineyards, and olive orchards and, not infrequently, the reduction to slavery of the farmer and his children (e.g., Neh. 5:4–5). The traditional agrarian economy was thereby slowly undermined, holdings which had stayed in the same family for generations were enclosed, and we begin to see the emergence of the great estates which flourished during the Hellenistic period.

The political setup of Judah within the Persian empire was superimposed on a social organization based on tribe and phratry. The census list of Ezra 2 suggests that at the time of compilation there were seventeen of these large interrelated kinship groups with a considerable range in size but averaging about nine hundred members. J. Weinberg (1973a, 400–414) has argued that this agnatic unit or ancestral "house" *(bêt 'ābôt;* cf. the Greek *oikos),* though claiming genealogical descent from preexilic tribal units, represented a new form of social organization large enough to allow for the integration of immigrants with natives. The patriarchs or "heads of ancestral houses," no doubt identical with the elders (*z^eqēnîm,* Ezra 10:8, 14, 16) who were prominent in the diaspora and after the return, played an important part in the affairs of the province during the period in question (Ezra 4:3; 10:16), even the leading role during periods when the office of governor may have been vacant (Ezra 5:5, 9; 6:7, 14; "the governor of the Jews" at Ezra 6:7 has been added). Also playing an important role at the time of Nehemiah were those who claimed descent from the hereditary nobility under the monarchy. Most, perhaps all, of these were descendants of aristocratic deportees who had survived the execution squads after the fall of Jerusalem (Jer. 27:20; cf. 39:6). On more than one occasion these *ḥôrîm* found themselves at odds with Nehemiah. They were accused of oppressive measures, of distraining the persons and property of the agrarian poor (Neh. 5:7) and of violating the sabbath law in furtherance of their commercial interests (Neh. 13:17). Many of them were also in collusion with his enemies (Neh. 6:17). Also frequently mentioned are the *śārîm,* a term which can refer to military personnel (Neh. 2:9) and district administrators (Neh. 3:9, 12, 14–19). The distinction between *śārîm* and *s^{e}gānîm,* here translated "officials," is not entirely clear. Both categories share the blame for giving bad example in the matter of foreign marriages (Ezra 9:2), and the *s^{e}gānîm* come in for censure from Nehemiah also (Neh. 13:11).

Use of the term "Jews" *(y^{e}hûdîm)* in Ezra-Nehemiah is somewhat problematic. It can refer simply to the inhabitants of the province of Judah *(Y^{e}hûd,* Ezra 4:23; 5:1; Neh. 1:2, 3:33–34 [4:1–2]), though there were also Jews living elsewhere (Neh. 4:6 [12]; 5:8), and in a rather special sense to immigrants from Babylonia (Ezra 4:12 [18]). These latter seem to have retained their identity as an economically and socially higher stratum of the population, distinct from the *dallat hā'āreṣ,* who had never left the land (Neh. 5:1, 17; cf. 2:16). While Nehemiah drew much of his support from this segment of the population, he had to confront problems created by the disparity in economic status between them and the "natives." This division within the population of the province is the social reality behind the editorial emphasis on the golah group *(b^{e}nê haggôlāh;* see commentary on Ezra 1:5). Though C represents them occupying a land totally depopulated (2 Chron. 36:20–21), the idealistic and fictional nature of this representation soon becomes apparent. The religious differences between the two groups, with which the narrative is mainly concerned, are matched by an economic and social contrast which comes to clearest expression in the complaint of the common people and their wives against their "Jewish brethren" (Neh. 5). Most of those who returned must have been relatively well off by the very faċt of being able to return, and the sources themselves testify, though with exaggeration, to the wealth which they brought with them (e.g., Ezra 2:68–69; 8:26–27; Zech. 6:9–11).

Once rebuilt, the temple played an important role in the economic and social, not just the religious sphere. At the most obvious level, support of a large, tax-exempt (Ezra 7:24) clerical bureaucracy must have been a considerable burden. In Judah as elsewhere in the empire the tithe was collected like any other tax, in addition to an annual levy of one third of a shekel (Neh. 10:33 [32]). The sacrificial cult itself took a heavy toll of livestock, grain, and other commodities including wood (Neh. 10:35 [34]; 13:31). The cumulative weight of this burden can be gauged by frequent allusions in the sources to noncompliance (e.g., Neh. 13:10–11; Mal. 1:7–10, 13–14; 3:8–10). Within the clerical ranks themselves there was conflict of interest between the high levels of the priesthood, including the high-priestly family, and the Levites. The former aimed at complete control over the material and fiscal resources of the temple, and their alliances with the ruling families in Judah and neighboring lands were designed to further their own special interests (e.g., Neh. 10:39 [38]; 13:4–9, 28–29). Nehemiah's policies brought him into conflict with both the Judean aristocracy and the high priesthood, and there are indications that he sought to limit the latter's control over the temple resources. His appointment of a panel of temple treasurers which included his own representative and a Levite was clearly a move in this direction (Neh. 13:13). It is therefore not surprising that the Levites were among the staunchest supporters of his program.

The social rift between the indigenous population and the go-lah Jews was intensified by the initiative of the *bᵉnê haggôlāh* in rebuilding and establishing control of the temple. Comparison with other "temple communities" (Weinberg's "Bürger-Tempel-Gemeinde") throughout the empire, especially in Mesopotamia and Asia Minor, suggests that they thereby constituted themselves as a distinct entity within which participation in, and of course active support of, the cult were closely linked with social and economic status in the province. Effective control of the "redemptive media," in effect the sacrificial system, translated into social control, including the ability to dictate terms for qualification as members of this entity. It is this situation more than anything else which created the conditions for the emergence of sectarianism in the Second Temple period. The study of the social coordinates of Second Temple sectarianism still remains to be undertaken. It cannot be pursued here, but one illustration, discussed at greater length in the commentary, may be given. In his campaign to reverse the assimilationist trend, in which the priesthood took a prominent part (Ezra 9:1; 10:5; cf. Neh. 13:28–29), Ezra relied primarily on a group of those who trembled at the word of God (Ezra 9:4; 10:3). It is significant that a group bearing the same designation *(ḥᵃrēdîm)* are addressed by an anonymous seer in Isa. 66:5 in terms which make it clear that they have been "excommunicated" by their fellow Jews and are therefore excluded from the temple community by those then in control, including of course the temple priesthood. Control of and access to the temple would continue to be an important factor in the social and religious life of the Jewish community well beyond the Persian period.

8. Text and Versions

The Hebrew and Aramaic text of Ezra-Nehemiah has, by and large, been well transmitted with relatively few obscurities. Variations in lists of names and numbers, which can be documented in the two versions of the golah census (Ezra 2 and Nehemiah 7), are no more than expected. The existence of two Greek versions, Esdras alpha (1 Esdras) and Esdras beta, has given rise to a great deal of discussion since the end of the nineteenth century; this discussion has entered a new phase with the discovery of the Qumran scrolls, including three fragments of the Hebrew and Aramaic text of Ezra (4QEzra). Esdras beta, of which the principal witnesses are LXX^B and LXX^A, is a literal translation of the same Semitic *Vorlage* as the canonical book. Howorth's hypothesis that it represents the Theodotionic version of the second century C.E. rather than the Old Greek version, the surviving portion of which he identified with our 1 Esdras, has not enjoyed much success. Rudolph (1949, xx) lists twenty-five instances where Esdras beta has the correct reading over against MT; some of these will be noted in the commentary. Esdras alpha (1 Esdras) is a much freer translation in good Greek which, whatever its origin, was not a revision of Esdras beta nor a compilation based on it. There appears to be only one instance where 1 Esdras agrees with Esdras beta against the canonical text (1 Esd. 2:25; cf. Ezra 4:23). Since it was used by Josephus in the relevant part of his *Antiquities,* 1 Esdras must have been in existence by the end of the first century C.E. Since, however, detailed study has shown close affinity between its language and that of Sirach, Judith, Maccabees, and the Old Greek of Daniel, it probably dates from some time in the late second or early first century B.C.E.

1 Esdras is an alternative version of part of Ezra-Nehemiah but with some significant omissions, additions, and displacements. It begins with Josiah's Passover and narrates events from then until the exile, corresponding to 2 Chron. 35–36 with only minor variations. The incident under Artaxerxes in Ezra 4:7–24 is made to follow immediately after the return with Sheshbazzar (1 Esd. 2:16–30), after which a long account of a contest of wits at the court of Darius serves to introduce Zerubbabel and explain how he obtained permission to return and build the temple (3:1–5:3). The Ezra story runs its course as in the canonical book but ends with the reading of the law in Neh. 7:72b[73b]–8:13a (1 Esd. 9:37–55). The Nehemiah material is entirely omitted. Opinion is divided on the origin of 1 Esdras. Since the end of the last century the view has been defended that it reproduces in part a version of Chronicles-Ezra-Nehemiah earlier than the one

which forms the basis of the canonical text (Torrey 1907b, 1945, Hölscher 1923, Mowinckel 1964–65, Pohlmann 1970). If this were so, the importance of 1 Esdras for the history not only of the text but also of the early postexilic period would of course be greatly enhanced. This positive evaluation of the work seemed to be confirmed by the juxtaposition of different text types among the Qumran biblical manuscripts. According to Cross (1975), the Palestinian type represented by 4QEzra and MT is expansionist and conflate in contrast with the Egyptian text type, represented in this case by 1 Esdras, which is shorter and better, meaning that it represents an older version of the Chronicler's work. The same conclusions were reached by Klein (1969), a student of Cross, in his study of the census list in Ezra 2, Nehemiah 7 and 1 Esdras 5.

The debate on the relation between 1 Esdras and the canonical book, begun by Howorth in 1893 and still going on, is too complex to be dealt with exhaustively here. It can be said, however, that the hypothesis that 1 Esdras is an excerpt from an earlier version of Chronicles-Ezra-Nehemiah is weakened by the indications that it forms a clearly articulated and complete narrative dealing with the restoration of true worship by, successively, Josiah, Zerubbabel, and Ezra. It would theoretically still be possible to argue that such a work was put together with material drawn from a version different from the canonical books, but there is nothing in the text which obliges us to draw this conclusion and some indications which tell against it. Thus, the author appears to have tried to correct the chronology of the canonical Ezra but without understanding the rationale for the latter's ordering of the material. This is the case especially with the narrative in Ezra 4 dealing with opposition under the early Achaemenids. The resumptive verse 4:24, referring back to 4:5, is therefore brought in much later (1 Esd. 5:70), resulting in further chronological confusion. It is also arguable that the omission of the Nehemiah story was part of a deliberate aim to highlight the achievements of Zerubbabel and Ezra at the expense of Nehemiah, whose name is omitted from the account of the public reading of the law (1 Esd. 9:49; cf. Neh. 8:9). For these reasons the position is taken in this commentary that 1 Esdras is a work based on the canonical text or its *Vorlage* in the late second or early first century B.C.E., without independent value as a historical source though not without value as a textual witness. Rudolph (xvi) provides a list of better reading in 1 Esdras, some of which will be noted at the appropriate points in the commentary.

The three fragments from the fourth Qumran cave (4QEzra) correspond to Ezra 4:2–6 (= 1 Esd. 5:69–73) in Hebrew and Ezra

4:9–11; 5:17–6:5 (= 1 Esd. 2:17; 6:21–26) in Aramaic. They follow MT closely and diverge significantly from 1 Esdras. Comparison between these fragments and MT on the one hand and 1 Esdras on the other does not support Cross's theory of a corresponding contrast between a conflate Palestinian and a succinct Egyptian text of the book. Apart from the general objections which have been raised against this theory, the commentary and textual notes will provide several examples pointing in the opposite direction and confirm the impression that the author of 1 Esdras was working with essentially the same text as the canonical book.

With respect to the other ancient versions: the Syriac, which follows MT fairly closely, has a number of variant readings which may serve as a basis for emendation. The Vulgate, on the contrary, is fairly free and sometimes paraphrastic. Ezra-Nehemiah is the only biblical book—other than Daniel—without a targum.

COMMENTARY

I

EZRA 1–6

The Rescript of Cyrus (Ezra 1:1–4)

P. R. **Ackroyd,** "Two Old Testament Problems of the Early Persian Period," *JNES* 17, 1958, 23–27; P. S. **Alexander,** "Remarks on Aramaic Epistolography in the Persian Period," *JSS* 23, 1978, 155–170; D. K. **Andrews,** "Yahweh the God of the Heavens," in W. S. McCullough (ed.), *The Seed of Wisdom: Essays in Honor of T. J. Meek,* Toronto, 1964, 45–57; E. J. **Bickerman,** "The Edict of Cyrus in Ezra 1," *JBL* 65, 1946, 249–275; K. **Galling,** "Die Proklamation des Kyros in Esra 1," *Studien,* Tübingen, 1964, 61–77; H. L. **Ginsberg,** "Ezra 1,4," *JBL* 79, 1960, 167–169; M. D. **Goldman,** "The True Meaning of Ezra 1,4," *ABR* 1, 1951, 58; H. H. **Grosheide,** "Twee Edicten van Cyrus ten gunste van de Joden," *GTT* 54, 1954, 1–12; M. **Haran,** "Explaining the Identical Lines at the End of Chronicles and the Beginning of Ezra," *BR* 2.3, 1986, 18–20; A. **Kuhrt,** "The Cyrus Cylinder and Achaemenid Imperial Policy," *JSOT* 25, 1983, 83–97; J. **Liver,** "The Beginning of the Restoration of Zion," *Studies,* 249–262 (Heb.); L. **Rost,** "Erwägungen zum Kyroserlass," in A. Kuschke (ed.), *Verbannung und Heimkehr,* Tübingen, 1961, 301–307; H. **Tadmor,** "The Historical Background of the Edict of Cyrus" (Heb.), *Jubilee Volume in Honor of David Ben-Gurion,* Jerusalem, 1964, 450–473; C. C. **Torrey,** *Ezra Studies,* 115–139; R. **de Vaux,** "Les décrets de Cyrus et de Darius sur la reconstruction du temple," *RB* 46, 1937, 29–57 (= de Vaux, *The Bible and the Ancient Near East,* Garden City, 1971, 63–96); C. F. **Whitley,** "The Term 'Seventy Years Captivity,' " *VT* 4, 1954, 60–72; H. G. M. **Williamson,** "The Composition of Ezra i–vi," *JTS* n.s. 34, 1983, 1–30.

1:1 And in the first year of Cyrus king of Persia, in order to fulfill his word spoken by[a] Jeremiah, YHVH inspired Cyrus king of Persia, so that he issued a proclamation throughout his kingdom, and also set it down in writing:

2"Thus says Cyrus king of Persia: 'YHVH the God of heaven has delivered to me all the kingdoms of the earth, and he has commissioned me to build him a house in Jerusalem which is in Judah. ³If anyone among you belongs to his people, may his god be with him! Let him go up to Jerusalem which is in Judah to build the house of YHVH the God of Israel, that is, the God who is in Jerusalem. ⁴Let the people of the place where there is any Jew remaining, wherever he may reside, support him with silver, gold, goods, and cattle, together with votive offerings for the house of the God who is in Jerusalem.' "

a. Reading *bᵉpî* with 2 Chron. 36:22 (cf. 1 Esd. 2:1) for MT *mippî.*

The opening paragraph of Ezra overlaps with the last of 2 Chron. (36:22–23), the connecting link being the allusion to Jeremiah's prophecy, though in fact the turn of phrase used in this opening sentence suggests a conflation of Jeremiah and the exilic Isaiah (41:2, 25; 45:13). C's account of the exile as the sabbatical rest of the land, interpreting Jer. 29:10–14 (cf. 25:11–14) in light of Lev. 26:34–35, marked the conclusion of the history of the First Temple. It also allowed him to represent the return under Cyrus as a new beginning with a temple built by diaspora Jews in a depopulated land. While the decree authorizing the return and the rebuilding of the temple is in general consonant with early Achaemenid policy, the present version has the appearance of a free composition. It contradicts the Aramaic version at 6:3–5, which stipulates that the operation be financed by the Persian government; and this and other differences are not adequately explained by diversity of function (*pace* Bickerman). Internal indications suggest the same conclusion as, for example, the term "survivor" ("any Jew remaining," *niš'ār*) and the allusion to votive offering *(nᵉdābāh),* the latter characteristic of C.

[1:1] The first regnal year of Cyrus was 559/8 but his first year as ruler of Babylon was 538/7, the year of the well-known cylinder inscription (*ANET,* 315–316). The designation "king of Persia" does not occur in the Aramaic documents nor in Persian inscriptions during the period of Cyrus' reign subsequent to the conquest of Babylon. His measures on behalf of the diaspora community are ascribed directly to YHVH who "stirred up" *(hēʿîr)* his spirit. The same expression is used of Tiglath-pileser (1 Chron. 5:26) and of Philistines and Arabs (2 Chron. 21:16). Haggai (1:14) uses it of Zerubbabel and, more directly to the point, the exilic Isaiah speaks in the same terms of Cyrus himself. There is therefore perhaps implied a reading of the Isaiah Cyrus text as indicating the concrete fulfillment of the Jeremiah prophecy. The rescript marks therefore a very special moment of grace, the historical realization of a new dispensation brought about by divine agency in fulfillment of the prophecies. The Jeremian text predicted judgment on Babylon, return after seventy years, and the renewal of religious life. The seventy years cannot be taken literally since we know of no deportation in 608. (Following Dan. 1:1 the nearest would be 606/5, but in the absence of confirmation this must remain uncertain.) But the author may be looking forward to the completion of the temple in 516/15, almost exactly seventy years after the destruction of the First Temple in 586 (cf. Zech. 1:12; 7:5; perhaps also Hag. 1:2); and it may not be pure coincidence that Nehemiah arrived to complete the rebuilding program exactly seventy years later, in 445. The proclamation was originally oral, carried through the streamlined Persian courier network. It was then committed to writing, certainly in Aramaic, the diplomatic lingua franca of the Persian empire.

[2] While the opening formula follows the pattern of Achaemenid royal inscriptions (e.g., Behistun), it was also familiar to Jews of the province. The title "God of heaven" with reference to YHVH is used in official documents (7:12, 21, 23) and when Jews are dealing with Gentiles (5:12; Jonah 1:9; cf. *AP* 30:2, 15, 27–28). It corresponds to the title of the Zoroastrian deity Ahura Mazda, though it has not yet been established beyond doubt that Cyrus worshiped as a Zoroastrian. The attribution of his success to YHVH and the consequent need to restore his cult are historically plausible as a political adaptation of the language and ideology of the Cyrus cylinder, which credits the Babylonian imperial deity Marduk with his success; with which may be compared the inscribed brick from Ur reading "the great gods have delivered all the lands into my hands." C was surely familiar with the preaching of the exilic Isaiah, who interprets the success of Cyrus in the same way, and it is even possible that the same prophetic text had come to the attention of Cyrus himself, as claimed by Josephus (*Ant.* 11.6).

[3] The syntax of this verse is problematic, but MT is intelligible as it stands. The translation given above assumes that the firman was addressed to the public at large rather than exclusively to golah Jews. The title "the god who is in Jerusalem" is standard in the Aramaic section (4:24; 5:2, 16, 17; 6:3, 12, 18; 7:16, 17, 19), though it is not always clear whether the reference is to the deity or the temple. It may be compared with "Yahu the god who is in the fortress of Jeb" of the Elephantine papyri (e.g., *AP* 30:6).

[4] The command to provide material support is directed at the population as a whole, a requirement which is historically quite implausible. Most likely the author has in mind the exodus theme of the despoiling of the Egyptians (Ex. 3:21–22; 11:2; 12:35–36), the

first of many allusions to the early traditions which form a kind of deep structure to the history of this new beginning. The beneficiary is described as a "survivor" *(niš'ār)*, a term with theological resonance identifying the Babylonian golah as the prophetic remnant (see also 1 Chron. 13:2; 2 Chron. 30:6; 34:21; Neh. 1:2–3; Hag. 2:3). The same term is used of golah Jews at Lev. 26:36 immediately following the description of exile as the sabbath of the land, a text which, as we have seen, stands behind 2 Chron. 36:21. Such language would not, of course, be used in an imperial Persian edict. The votive offering (*nᵉdābāh;* cf. 2 Chron. 31:14; 35:8; Ezra 3:5) belongs to a special category since the donor is Jewish and the gift is specifically for the temple. The verb *hitnaddēb*, volunteer, give freely, and related forms are characteristic of C (1 Chron. 29:5, 6, 9, 14, 17; 2 Chron. 17:16; cf. Ezra 7:13, 15–16).

Response of the Diaspora to the Rescript (Ezra 1:5–11)

P. R. **Ackroyd**, "The Temple Vessels—A Continuity Theme," *VTSup.* 23, 1972, 166–181; W. F. **Albright**, "The Date and Personality of the Chronicler," *JBL* 40, 1921, 104–124; F. I. **Andersen**, "Israelite Kingship Terminology and Social Structure," *Bible Translator* 20, 1969, 29–39; A. **Bartal**, "Again—Who Was Sheshbazzar?" (Heb.), *BM* 24, 1979, 357–369; M. **Ben-Yashar**, "On the Problem of Sheshbazzar and Zerubbabel" (Heb.), *BM* 27, 1981, 46–56; P.-R. **Berger**, "Zu den Namen *ššbsr* und *šn'sr*," *ZAW* 83, 1971, 98–100; F. M. **Cross**, "A Reconstruction of the Judean Restoration," *JBL* 94, 1975, 4–18 (= *Int.* 29, 1975, 187–203); P. E. **Dion**, "*ššbsr* and *ssnwry*," *ZAW* 95, 1983, 111–112; D. N. **Freedman**, "The Chronicler's Purpose," *CBQ* 23, 1961, 436–442; K. **Galling**, "Der Tempelschatz nach Berichten und Urkunden im Buche Esra," *ZDPV* 60, 1937, 177–183; "Das Protokoll über die Rückgabe der Tempelgeräte," *Studien,* 78–88; W. Th. **In der Smitten**, "Historische Probleme zum Kyrosedikt und zum Jerusalemer Tempelbau," *Persica* 6, 1973, 167–178; S. **Japhet**, "Sheshbazzar and Zerubbabel Against the Background of the Historical and Religious Tendencies of Ezra-Nehemiah," *ZAW* 94, 1982, 66–98; C. C. **Torrey**, "The Chronicler's History of the Return Under Cyrus," *AJSL* 37, 1920/21, 81–100; J. **Weinberg**, "Das Bēit 'ābōt im 6.–4. Jh. v. u. Z.," *VT* 23, 1973, 400–414.

1:5 Whereupon the heads of ancestral houses of Judah and Benjamin, together with the priests and Levites—in short, all whom God had inspired to go up and build the house of YHVH in Jerusalem—prepared to leave. ⁶All their neighbors supported them in every way,[a] with silver, gold, goods, and cattle, and an abundance[b] of precious gifts, apart from what they gave of their own free will. ⁷King Cyrus, moreover, retrieved the vessels belonging to YHVH's house which Nebuchadnezzar had brought[c] from Jerusalem to place in the house of his god; [8]Cyrus king of Persia had them delivered into the keeping of Mithredath the treasurer, who counted them out to Sheshbazzar prince of Judah. [9]The total was: thirty gold basins, one thousand and twenty-nine assorted[d] silver basins, [10]thirty gold bowls, two thousand four hundred and ten[e] silver bowls, and a thousand other vessels. [11]All of the gold and silver vessels came to five thousand four hundred. Sheshbazzar took them[f] all up to Jerusalem when the exiles were brought back from Babylon to Jerusalem.

a. Reading *bakkōl* with 1 Esd. 2:6 and LXX for MT *biklê-kesep,* "with silver vessels."
b. Reading *lārōb* with LXX and Syr. for MT *l*ᵉ*bad.*
c. Reading *hēbî'* for *hôsî'* with 1 Esd. 2:10 and LXX.
d. This translation of *mah*ᵃ*lāpîm* (cf. NEB) is speculative, but no more so than the many other interpretations and emendations which have been suggested; e.g., a marginal note reading "to be changed" (Rudolph 1949, 5); "repaired" (Galling 1964, 83–85); "duplicates" (Williamson 1986, 4). Bewer 1922, 15–16, redivides *'lpym hlpym* and deletes the latter as dittographic.
e. Reading *š*ᵉ*nayim 'elep* for MT *mišnîm* with 1 Esd. 2:13.
f. Alternatively, "sent them" *(he'lāh).*

[1:5] As C would have it, the rescript evoked an immediate and enthusiastic response from the exiles, the surrounding Gentiles supporting them no less enthusiastically. Those who answered the call are presented as a well-organized community henceforth referred to as the golah (1:11; 2:1; 9:4; 10:6; Neh. 7:6), alternatively the golah assembly (*q*ᵉ*hal haggôlāh,* Ezra 10:8) or the golah group (*b*ᵉ*nê-haggôlāh,* Ezra 4:1; 6:19–20; 8:35; 10:7, 16; in Aramaic *b*ᵉ*nê-gālûtā',* Ezra 6:16). Civil leadership was exercised by the heads of the ancestral houses of Judah and Benjamin. The ancestral house *(bêt 'ābôt),* a basic social unity of the postexilic temple community, was a subdivision of the "family" or phratry *(mišpāḥāh),* itself a subdivision of the tribe *(šebet).* As an organizational unit perpetuating the old tribal structure, it seems to have played an important role during the Babylonian exile; and it is noteworthy that the term "heads of ancestral houses" *(rā'šê hā'ābôt,* short for *rā'šê bātê hā'ābôt)* is attested only in P, Chronicles, Ezra, and Nehemiah. The individual *bêt 'ābôt* preserved its claim to its own parcel of land *(naḥ*ᵃ*lāh, '*ᵃ*ḥuzzāh)* by genealogical descent, an issue with considerable potential for conflict after Babylonian Jews began to trickle back only to find their ancestral holdings expropriated (cf. Ezek. 11:15). The same term *(bêt* *'ābôt)* could also be applied to priests and Levites (Ex. 4:2; 6:25; 1 Chron. 15:2; 23:9, 24; 24:6, 31; 26:21; Neh. 12:21–23). The heads of these kinship units continued to play an important role in community affairs after the return (e.g., Ezra 1:5; 2:68; 4:2–3; 7:28; 10:16; Neh. 8:13). Use of the term "Judah and Benjamin," here and elsewhere in Ezra-Nehemiah, is appropriate since attention is focused on return of the Judean diaspora of which Benjaminites formed a substantial part (see on 2:20–35). It does not imply denial of authentic Israelite status to descendants of the ten tribes (as von Rad 1930, et al.); the pan-Israelite ideal is never lost sight of at any point in C's history (see Introduction, sect. 5).

[6] The distinction made here is between assistance mandated by the authorities and freewill or votive offerings for the temple, a favorite theme of C; witness the rather close parallelism with 1 Chron. 29:9, dealing with the support provided for the building of Solomon's temple.

[7] The return of the sacred vessels establishes a vital link of continuity between the First and the Second Temple (see also 5:13–15 and 6:3–5). According to C, David prepared the material for the manufacture of the vessels and the temple furniture (1 Chron. 28:13–19), and the vessels were subsequently deposited in the temple treasury by Solomon (2 Chron. 5:1). Omitting the notice that Nebuchadnezzar destroyed the gold vessels (2 Kings 24:13), C reports that *all* the temple vessels were taken to Babylon at the time of the first deportation (2 Chron. 36:10, 18). These same vessels were now restored by Cyrus in recognition of the legitimacy of the Judean sanctuary, in somewhat the same way in which he claimed on the Cyrus cylinder to have restored the gods to their shrines. The theme is carried over into Ezra's mission (7:19; 8:25–30, 33–34). We may detect here, too, an echo of the exilic Isaiah (see Isa. 52:11–12).

[8] For his account of the transfer and inventory the editor probably had access to an official document preserved in the temple archives (for the sanctuary at Elephantine see *AP* 61 and 63). The treasurer has a common Persian name meaning "gift of Mithra" (see also *AP* 26:2, 7; 80:7), and the word used for his office, *gizbār,* from the Old Persian *ganzabara,* occurs only here (Vulg. has "Mithradatis son of Gabazar," which last name was later modified to Caspar and assigned to one of the three kings of legend). The drawing up of a precise inventory indicates a concern for authenticity; and it should be noted that C has already informed us that the temple treasure must be counted each time it is taken out (1 Chron. 9:28).

Sheshbazzar's title has given rise to a great deal of speculation. The Aramaic source has it that he was appointed governor (*pehāh,* 5:14).

If this is so, he would have been responsible for the administration of the temple. It is tempting to conclude that "the prince of Judah" *(hannāśî' lîhûdāh)* must refer to a scion of the native dynasty in exile, and the temptation would be irresistible if Sheshbazzar could be identified with Shenazzar, fourth son of Jehoiachin in 1 Chron. 3:18. But the names, both of which are Babylonian, are not identical (see especially Berger), no Davidic ancestry is given, as we might expect, and elsewhere C follows established usage in applying the designation *nāśî'* to the tribal head (1 Chron. 2:10; 4:38; 5:6; 7:40) or the head of an ancestral house (2 Chron. 1:2; 5:2). There is therefore no connection with the Davidic dynasty or with usage in Ezekiel's temple law (Ezek. 44:3; 45:7–11, etc.). The other suggestion, that Sheshbazzar be identified with Zerubbabel, hinted at by Josephus *(Ant.* 11.13–14), first proposed in the modern period by Ewald, and still occasionally argued (e.g., by Bartal), is speculative and highly improbable. Both names are Babylonian (Sheshbazzar from *šamaš-aba-uṣur* rather than *šamaš-apla-uṣur* or *sin-ab-uṣur*), and the Aramaic source makes a clear distinction between them (Ezra 5:14–16).

[9–11] In both MT and LXX the grand total is 5,400 but in neither case does this tally with the sum of the individual items (2,499 or, amending v. 10 as suggested, 4,499 in MT; 2,289 in LXX). The total in 1 Esd. 2:9–11, 5,469, does represent the sum of the items listed. Not being a round number, it may bring us closer to the archival list, either in the temple or in Babylonian records, on which the different versions appear to be based. Josephus *(Ant.* 11.15) does not total his individual listings which, however, come to 5,220. It is unlikely that he had access to any source not known to us. The precise identity of some of the items is no longer clear. *'ᵃgarṭēl* (v. 9), probably "basin," is *hapax legomenon,* possibly a Persian loan-word; *kāpôr,* probably "bowl" (Akkadian *kaparu*), occurs also at Ezra 8:27 and 1 Chron. 28:17. Somewhat surprisingly, there is no account of the actual aliyah, as there is for that of Ezra (8:15–36) in which the transfer of the sacred vessels also occurs as an important theme.

On the historical issues connected with the rescript, the repatriation under Cyrus, and the role of Sheshbazzar see Introduction, sect. 7.

A Census of the Temple Community
(Ezra 2:1–67 = Neh. 7:6–68 [69])

Y. **Aharoni,** *The Land of the Bible,* 362–365; S. **Ahituv,** "Pashhur," *IEJ* 20, 1970, 95–96; W. F. **Albright,** *The Biblical Period,* 87–88, 110–111; L. **Allrik,** "I Esdras

According to Codex B and Codex A," *ZAW* 66, 1954, 272–292; "The Lists of Zerubbabel (Neh. 7 and Ezr. 2) and the Hebrew Numerical Notation," *BASOR* 136, 1954, 21–27; A. **Alt,** *KS* 2:316–337; J. **Blenkinsopp,** *Gibeon and Israel,* London, 1972, 106–108; J. **Bright,** *A History of Israel* (3rd ed.), 376–377; R. P. **Dougherty,** *The Shirkûtu of Babylonian Deities,* New Haven, 1923; F. C. **Fensham,** "Mĕdînâ in Ezra and Nehemiah," *VT* 25, 1975, 795–797; K. **Galling,** *RGG* (3rd ed.), 6:1193–1194; "The 'Gōlā-List' According to Ezra 2/Neh. 7," *JBL* 70, 1951, 149–158 (= Galling, *Studien,* 89–108); H. **Gese,** "Zur Geschichte der Kultsänger am Zweiten Tempel," in O. **Betz** (ed.), *Abraham unser Vater,* Leiden, 1963, 222–234; *Vom Sinai zum Zion,* Munich, 1974, 147–158; A. H. J. **Gunneweg,** "Zur Interpretation der Bücher Esra-Nehemia," *VTSup.* 32, 1981, 146–181; M. **Haran,** "The Gibeonites, the Nethinim and the Sons of Solomon's Servants," *VT* 11, 1961, 159–169; W. Th. **In der Smitten,** "Der Tirschātā' in Esra-Nehemia," *VT* 21, 1971, 618–620; R. W. **Klein,** "Old Readings in 1 Esdras: The List of Returnees from Babylon (Ezra 2/Nehemiah 7)," *HTR* 62, 1969, 99–107; B. A. **Levine,** "The Netînîm," *JBL* 82, 1963, 207–212; "Notes on a Hebrew Ostracon from Arad," *IEJ* 19, 1969, 50–51; J. **Maier,** *IDB* 4:739–740; I. **Mendelsohn,** "State Slavery in Ancient Palestine," *BASOR* 85, 1942, 14–15; E. **Meyer,** *Die Entstehung des Judentums,* 94–102, 190–198; S. **Mowinckel,** *Studien* I, 29–45; M. **Noth,** *US,* 124–128; K- F. **Pohlmann,** *Studien zum Dritten Esra,* 57–64; H. H. **Schaeder,** *Esra der Schreiber,* 15–20; R. **Smend,** *Die Listen der Bücher Esra und Nehemia,* Basel, 1881, 15–23; E. A. **Speiser,** "Unrecognized Dedication," *IEJ* 13, 1963, 69–73; C. C. **Torrey,** *The Composition and Historical Value of Ezra-Nehemiah,* Berlin, 1896, 39–50; H. C. M. **Vogt,** *Studie zur nachexilischen Gemeinde in Esra-Nehemia,* Werl, 1966, 118–148; J. P. **Weinberg,** "Demographische Notizen zur Geschichte der nachexilischen Gemeinde in Juda," *Klio* 54, 1972, 45–59; "Nᵉtînîm und 'Söhne der Sklaven Salomos' im 6.–4. Jh. v. u. Z.," *ZAW* 87, 1975, 355–371; H. G. M. **Williamson,** "The Composition of Ezra i–vi," *JTS* 33, 1983, 1–30; R. **Zadok,** "Notes on the Biblical and Extra-Biblical Onomasticon," *JQR* 71, 1980, 107–117.

2:1 These are the inhabitants of the province who came up from captivity in the diaspora, whom Nebuchadnezzar king of Babylon had taken into exile to Babylon. They returned to Jerusalem and Judah, each to his own town.

²They came with Zerubbabel, Jeshua, Nehemiah, Seraiah, Reelaiah, Nahamani, [a] Mordecai, Bilshan, Mispar, Bigvai, Rehum, Baanah.

The sum total of the men of the people of Israel:

³Descendants of Parosh, 2,172

⁴Descendants of Shephatiah, 372

⁵Descendants of Arah, 775

⁶Descendants of Pahath-moab, of the descendants of Jeshua, Joab, 2,812

⁷Descendants of Elam, 1,254

⁸Descendants of Zattu, 945

[9]Descendants of Zaccai, 760
[10]Descendants of Bani,[b] 642
[11]Descendants of Bebai, 623
[12]Descendants of Azgad, 1,222
[13]Descendants of Adonikam, 666
[14]Descendants of Bigvai, 2,056
[15]Descendants of Adin, 454
[16]Descendants of Ater, of Hezekiah, 98
[17]Descendants of Bezai,[c] 323
[18]Descendants of Jorah,[d] 112
[19]Descendants of Hashum, 223
[20]Descendants of Gibeon,[e] 95
[21]Descendants of Bethlehem, 123
[22]Men of Netophah, 56[f]
[23]Men of Anathoth, 128
[24]Descendants of Azmaveth,[g] 42
[25]Descendants of Kiriath-jearim,[h] Chephirah, and Beeroth, 743
[26]Descendants of Ramah and Geba, 621[i]
[27]Men of Michmas, 122
[28]Men of Bethel and Ai, 223
[29]Descendants of Nebo,[j] 52
[30]Descendants of Magbish, 156
[31]Descendants of the other Elam,[k] 1,254
[32]Descendants of Harim, 320
[33]Descendants of Lod, Hadid, and Ono, 725
[34]Descendants of Jericho, 345
[35]Descendants of Senaah, 3,630

[36]Priests: descendants of Jedaiah, of Jeshua's house, 973
[37]Descendants of Immer, 1,052
[38]Descendants of Pashhur, 1,247
[39]Descendants of Harim, 1,017.

[40]Levites: descendants of Jeshua and Kadmiel, of the descendants of Hodaviah, 74.

[41]Musicians: descendants of Asaph, 128.

[42]Gatekeepers:[l] descendants of Shallum, Ater, Talmon, Akkub, Hatita, and Shobai; in all: 139.

[43]Temple servants: descendants of Ziha, Hasupha, Tabbaoth, [44]Keros, Siaha, Padon, [45]Lebanah, Hagabah, Akkub, [46]Hagab, Shamlai, Hanan,

⁴⁷Giddel, Gahar, Reaiah,
⁴⁸Rezin, Nekoda, Gazzam,
⁴⁹Uzza, Paseah, Besai,
⁵⁰Asnah, Meunim, Nephisim,
⁵¹Bakbuk, Hakupha, Harhur,
⁵²Bazluth, Mehida, Harsha,
⁵³Barkos, Sisera, Temah,
⁵⁴Neziah, Hatipha.

⁵⁵Descendants of Solomon's slaves:
Descendants of Sotai, Hassophereth, Peruda,
⁵⁶Jaalah, Darkon, Giddel,
⁵⁷Shephatiah, Hattil, Pochereth-hazzebaim, Ami.
⁵⁸All the temple servants and descendants of Solomon's slaves came to 392.

⁵⁹These are the ones who came up from Tel Melah, Tel Harsha, Cherub, Addan, and Immer, but were unable to declare their ancestral house and descent, as to whether they belonged to Israel:
⁶⁰Descendants of Delaiah, Tobiah, Nekoda: 652.
⁶¹Of the priests:ᵐ descendants of Habaiah, Hakkoz, Barzillai (he had taken one of the daughters of Barzillai the Gileadite as his wife and was therefore named after them).
⁶²These looked up their registration in the official list but did not find it, and were therefore excluded from the priesthood.
⁶³His Excellency the governor ordered them not to partake of the consecrated food until there should be a priest to consult Urim and Thummim.
⁶⁴The sum total of the congregation: 42,360, ⁶⁵not counting their male and female slaves, who came to 7,337. They also had 200 male and female singers, ⁶⁶736 horses, 245 mules, ⁶⁷435 camels, and 6,720 donkeys.

a. Supplied from Neh. 7:7.
b. Or Binnui; cf. Neh. 7:15.
c. 1 Esd. 5:15–16 adds five names between Ater and Bezai.
d. Hariph at Neh. 7:24.
e. With Neh. 7:25; MT has Gibbar.
f. Bethlehem and Netophah are listed together at Neh. 7:26.
g. Beth-azmaveth at Neh. 7:28; cf. Bethasmoth, 1 Esd. 5:18.
h. With Neh. 7:29; MT has Kiriath-arim, cf. 1 Esd. 5:19.
i. 1 Esd. 5:20 has Chadasians and Ammidians between Beeroth and Ramah.
j. Neh. 7:33 has "the other Nebo."
k. 1 Esd. 5:22 adds "Ono."

l. Omit $b^e n\hat{e}$, "sons of," with Neh. 7:45 and 1 Esd. 5:28.
m. Reading $\hat{u}min$ for $\hat{u}mibb^e n\hat{e}$ with Neh. 7:39.

The alternative version in Neh. (7:5) identifies the list as "the book of the genealogy of the first '$\hat{o}l\hat{i}m$'" (literally, "those who went up at the beginning"), in spite of which there is no unanimity on either its date or its function. It is clearly not a pure fabrication, as Torrey believed, but equally clearly it is not a checklist of any one aliyah; the numbers involved (49,897 in Ezra, 49,942 in Neh.) are too high for that. It may have resulted from the combination of several repatriations in the early Achaemenid period, as the vague "at the beginning" at Neh. 7:5 suggests. More probably, however, it derives from a census record closer to the time of Nehemiah's mission toward the middle of the fifth century (as Albright, Bright). It was certainly compiled after the settlement since it names localities in which the immigrants settled. The same conclusion is suggested by the occurrence of several of the names in later lists (Ezra 8; Neh. 10), and a later date would more easily explain the size of the Bigvai group (2,056 or 2,067) in view of the Persian origin of this name. Hölscher's suggestion (1923) that it served as an official tax register is reasonable enough, since a census was generally taken for this purpose; the only problem is that clergy appear to have been exempt from taxation and therefore, on this showing, should not have been included. It may also have served in responses to such official inquiries as are addressed to the leadership in Ezra 5:3–4, 9–10. More basically, however, it established membership in good standing in the cult community (the $q\bar{a}h\bar{a}l$, 2:64) which, for C, is identical with the $b^e n\hat{e}$ $hagg\hat{o}l\bar{a}h$, the legitimate successors of ancient Israel. By the same token, it would have confirmed title to land which was contingent on participation in and, of course, support of the cult.

We have already attempted to show (Introduction, sect. 4) that this list, perhaps originally composite, was inserted into the account of the first return and then, with the fragmentary narrative following (2:68–3:1), spliced into the Nehemiah story immediately following the first long section of first-person narrative (Neh. 7:5). The reason for the insertion in Ezra 2 is to fill out the impression of a unified, full-scale response to the rescript. As the immediate context makes clear (Neh. 7:5), the list was reproduced to provide a basis for the transfer of one tenth of the population to Jerusalem. It also came to serve as an appropriate introduction to the reading of the law before the entire community (Neh. 8:1).

The clue to the theological significance of the list is to be sought in the parallelism with the occupation of the land in Joshua, which also makes extensive use of lists. More specifically, we are to think of the Priestly version of the distribution of land to the twelve tribes (cf. the twelve leaders, Ezra 2:2) under Joshua and Eleazar the priest (cf. Zerubbabel and Jeshua). A crucial point is that in both the occupation of the land is associated with the sanctuary to be erected on it (Josh. 18:1; 19:51). By virtue of this connection the land receives its specific religious qualification, as a fief of the sanctuary and in the gift of the deity who dwells in it. This indissoluble association with land remains a crucial and immensely problematic issue in Jewish self-understanding, and therefore also in Jewish-Christian relations.

[2:1–2a] The province *(m^edînāh)* is Judah not Babylon *(pace* Fensham; cf. 1 Esd. 5:1; Ezra 5:8). Judah *(Y^ehûd)* was a semiautonomous administrative unit in the satrapy first of Babylon, later—from the time of Xerxes—in the separate Trans-Euphrates satrapy *(Abarnahara).* Supplying Nahamani from Neh. 7:7 (Enenios at 1 Esd. 5:8), there are twelve leaders representing the Israel which came out of Egypt, that is, Babylon. Three of the names are Babylonian (Zerubbabel, Mordecai, Bilshan) and one Persian (Bigvai). Zerubbabel instead of the anticipated Sheshbazzar will be easier to accept if we assume a roster of community leaders throughout the Persian period. But we have also seen that C tends to collapse distinct events and movements together in this section of the history.

According to the Aramaic source (5:2), confirmed by Haggai and Zechariah, **Zerubbabel** was governor of the province for some time under Darius when he set up the first altar, laid the foundation of the temple, and took part in its rebuilding. He was a scion of the Davidic dynasty, grandson of Jehoiachin, his father being either the exiled king's first son Shealtiel (so Ezra; Neh. 12:1; Haggai) or his third son Pedaiah (so 1 Chron. 3:19). The harmonizing view that he was son of Pedaiah by levirate marriage with the widow of Shealtiel is pure speculation. Haggai and Zechariah attest that he became, perhaps unwittingly, the focus of messianic expectations during the troubled period following on the death of Cambyses in 522 B.C.E. He cannot be related to, much less identified with, Sheshbazzar, a much more shadowy figure, since the Aramaic source clearly distinguishes the two (Ezra 5:14, 16). As noted earlier, the chronological confusion results from a deliberate telescoping of events in the early Persian period, possibly compounded by a lack of precise information.

Jeshua *(y^ešûa'),* alternatively Joshua *(y^ehôšûa')* in Hag. and Zech. 1–8, descendant of the last preexilic chief priest Jozadak (1 Chron. 5:41), is generally associated with Zerubbabel and listed after him except in Ezra 3:2. Zech. 3:1–10 suggests that he was given the high priesthood after the return even though he or his "house" had been involved in apostasy or suspect religious practice. Later in the same prophetic text he is one of the two anointed, the other being Zerubbabel (4:11–14). Zech. 6:9–14 speaks of his coronation, but the passage must have referred originally to Zerubbabel, the Davidic "branch" who was to build the temple and stay on good terms with the priesthood. The supplanting of Zerubbabel by Joshua, whatever the circumstances by which it came about, reflects the ascendancy of the priesthood as compliant agents of Persian policy after the collapse of the messianic hopes to which Haggai attests.

While the name **Nehemiah** occurs elsewhere (Neh. 3:16 and in the Daliyeh papyri, see F. M. Cross 1963, 111–112), it is a curious coincidence that the following name in the Neh. version of the list, Azariah, is an alternative form of Ezra, and that the name corresponding to it in the Ezra version, namely, Seraiah, belongs to the father of Ezra (Ezra 7:1). Also, both Seraiah and Ezra occur in another list of the early repatriates (Neh. 12:2). **Reelaiah** (Raamiah at Neh. 7:7, Resaiah at 1 Esd. 5:8) is otherwise unattested. **Mordecai,** named for the Babylonian deity Marduk, and **Bilshan** are Babylonian diasporic names, and **Mispar** (Mispereth in the Neh. version) is otherwise unknown. **Bigvai,** alternatively Bagoas or Bagohi, is the name of the governor of Judah following on Nehemiah (*AP* 30 and 32). Hence the possibility, suggested earlier, that the author has prefaced his list with the names of prominent individuals from different periods after the settlement. **Rehum** (Nehum at Neh. 7:7) is also the name of a satrapy official who, together with others, wrote a letter of complaint to Artaxerxes (Ezra 4:7–24). It may be noted that five of these names also occur in the list of signatories to the covenant in Neh. 10.

[2b–35] The names of the laity are grouped some according to family or phratry, some according to locality (most of vs. 20–35). The fact that some are listed as "men of X" (22–23, 27–28) and some as "sons of X" (the others) does not seem to have any special significance. The list confirms their good standing in the cult community (*'am yiśrā'ēl,* 2b, identified with the golah group). The grand total is 24,141 (25,406 in the Nehemiah version), a not unreasonable total for the male population of the province in the fifth century, though of course those of Babylonian origin were not its only inhabitants. The numbers vary considerably in the three versions. Out of the thirty-seven listed only seven have identical numbers in Ezra, Neh. 7, and 1 Esd. 5, while Ezra agrees with Nehemiah only sixteen times. Since numerals were indicated by vertical and horizontal slashes (see Allrik), error could easily creep in. The attention of the scribe would also be more likely to wander while transcribing long lists of names and numbers. But it is doubtful whether one should follow Allrik in opting for the priority of the Nehemiah version, which tends to have higher figures, on the grounds that omitting slashes is more easily explained than adding them. It would be interesting to test this conclusion, but in any case eleven higher numbers in Nehemiah is hardly a decisive margin, especially since there are also seven lower. There may also be instances which cannot be explained purely on this basis.

[2b–19] Of the seventeen phratries (twenty-one in 1 Esd. 5) in this part of the list, fourteen appear as signatories of the binding agreement in Neh. 10, eleven are listed in Ezra's caravan (Ezra 8), and six in the list of those agreeing to divorce foreign wives (Ezra 10). Only two of the names—**Shephatiah** and **Adonikam** (= Adonijah, Neh. 10:17) are theophoric with YHVH, though others (**Zaccai, Bani**) may be hypocoristic. Others again appear to have originated as nicknames (**Parosh** = flea, **Jorah/Hariph** = wintry?), and some have a foreign sound (**Azgad, Bigvai, Ater, Elam**).

[20–35] These twenty-two names (twenty-one in Neh., eighteen in 1 Esd.) are arranged almost entirely according to locality outside of Jerusalem, which is conspicuous by its absence. Only two of the towns, Bethlehem and Netophah, lie south of Jerusalem, a circumstance probably to be explained by Edomite encroachments beginning in the late Babylonian period (see, e.g., Jer. 13:19). A high proportion—fourteen out of twenty-two—belonged originally to Benjamin, recalling the designation "Judah and Benjamin" (see on 1:5). Benjamin was, of course, closely linked with Judah from the time of the early monarchy. On settlement in Jerusalem see at 2:70.

Gibeon can be securely identified with el-Jîb about eight miles northwest of Jerusalem; the other three cities of the Gibeonite tetrapolis are listed together later (v. 25; cf. Josh. 18:25). C puts the Gibeonites at the end of his list of returning expatriates, linking them with the family of Saul (1 Chron. 9:35–44). The close association between this Hivite enclave and the n^{e}tînîm or temple servants was maintained into the postexilic period (see below). **Bethlehem,** five miles south of Jerusalem, is linked with **Netophah,** perhaps Khirbet Bedd Faluh near the spring Ain en-Natuf, which has preserved the name and which may also be identical with Nephtoah (Josh. 18:15). **Anathoth,** birthplace of Jeremiah, about three miles north of Jerusalem, is probably to be identified with Tell Ḥarrube near the present village of Anata, belonging to Benjamin. **Azmaveth,** or Beth-azmaveth (Neh. 7:28; cf. 12:29), perhaps Hizmeh five miles north of Jerusalem, is also Benjaminite. **Kiriath-jearim, Chephirah, Beeroth**

belonged to the Gibeonite-Hivite enclave northwest of Jerusalem. (For their location see Blenkinsopp, 1–13.) **Ramah,** probably er-Ram about five miles north of Jerusalem, and **Geba,** probably Jiba' a mile further north, were Benjaminite frontier towns (Josh. 18:24–25). **Michmas** is Mukhmas about seven miles north of Jerusalem. **Bethel** and **Ai,** linked in critical discussion of the conquest narrative in Joshua, were originally Ephraimite but are listed as Benjaminite at Josh. 18:22. They were absorbed into Judah as a result of Josiah's expansion northward. Bethel is identified with Beitin, about twelve miles north of Jerusalem, and Ai with et-Tell, two miles east-south-east of Bethel. **Nebo** ("the other Nebo" in Neh., absent from 1 Esd.) is perhaps identical with Nob, residence of the Elide priesthood after the destruction of Shiloh, also in Benjamin (1 Sam. 22:11). Its location was on Mount Scopus *(har haṣṣōpîm).*

Magbish (missing in Neh.; Niphis in 1 Esd.) is unidentified; it could be the same as Magpiash at Neh. 10:21 [20]. **The other Elam** has the same number as Elam (v. 7); it is attested as a personal name (Ezra 2:7 = Neh. 7:12; Ezra 8:7; 10:2, 26; Neh. 10:15 [14]) and may be out of place here. **Harim** is absent at the corresponding point in the Nehemiah version but is a priest's name in all three versions (also at 1 Chron. 24:8; Neh. 10:6 [5]; 12:15)—appropriately, in view of its meaning (= dedicated). The three towns next listed together marked the most western part of the province: **Lod** (= Lydda) in the Plain of Sharon belonged to Benjamin (1 Chron. 8:12); **Hadid** is perhaps el-Haditheh about four miles northeast of Lod, known as Adida in the Greco-Roman period (1 Macc. 12:38; 13:13; *Ant.* 13.203, 392; *War* 4.486). **Ono** is probably Kefr 'Ana in Wadi Mus-rara, the Vale of Ono (cf. Neh. 6:2). **Jericho,** originally Benjaminite, marked the furthest point east. **Senaah,** also with the article at Neh. 3:3, has easily the largest number of the list (even larger at Neh. 7:38), which has led to much speculation. Some have opted to read *śᵉnûāh* with the meaning "despised one" (fem.) or "despised ones" (fem. collective)—cf. 1 Chron. 9:7 and Neh. 11:9—and have referred it to the lowest class in that society or, alternatively, in Jerusalem. Others follow the safer option of identifying it with Magdal-sena'a about eight miles northeast of Jericho, but in that case the settlement of so many people in such a remote and inhospitable region remains unexplained.

There seems to be no clear topographical order in the listing of these place-names. They begin in the south, then go north, then northwest and southwest, concluding with the points furthest west and east.

[36–39] There follow the names of four priestly families. Three of them (Jedaiah, Pashhur, Immer) occur in C's list of repatriates who settled in Jerusalem (1 Chron. 9:10–13; cf. Neh. 11:10–14), Jedaiah being among the first six to arrive. Three also appear in the list of twenty-four priest courses *(mišmārôt, ma'ªmādôt)* in 1 Chron. 24:7–19, Pashhur being the one missing. This arrangement dates from the late Persian period (see Williamson 1979, 251–268), by which time the Pashhur group may have lost its priestly status; on the one hand it has the highest rate of exogamous marriage (Ezra 10:18–22), but on the other Pashhur signed the pledge in Neh. 10 (vs. 2–9 [1–8]). The high proportion of priests in the list—about 1:17 of the laity and 1:10 overall—is not historically implausible. Significantly, they are not called "sons of Aaron."

Jedaiah is presumably identical with the eponym of the second priestly course (1 Chron. 24:7); the Jedaiah who is said to have brought contributions from Babylon is not designated a priest (Zech. 6:10, 14). **Jeshua** the chief priest (see on 2:2) belonged to this group (cf. also 10:18). **Immer** is a name often attested in the postexilic period (1 Chron. 9:12; Ezra 10:2; Neh. 3:29; 11:13), perhaps having some connection with the Jewish settlement in Babylonia of that name (Ezra 2:59). Immer is also eponym of the sixteenth priestly course (1 Chron. 24:14). **Pashhur,** an Egyptian name (= "son of Horus"), is absent from the courses list. If the Pashhur ben Immer of Jer. 20:1–6 is the eponym of this group, it may have hived off from the Immer phratry during the exile. It is the largest of the four groups. **Harim** (see on 2:32) is the eponym of the third course (1 Chron. 24:8).

[40] The number of Levites is very low compared to priests: seventy-four against four thousand two hundred and eighty-nine. Ezra also had difficulty recruiting Levites for his mission. Either very few or none were in the original caravan until he rounded up thirty-eight from "the place" Casiphia (8:18–19). Perhaps there were few in Babylon to begin with, since the distinction between priests and Levites is not unambiguously attested for the period prior to the deportations, and seems to have resulted from internecine strife among the various branches of the priesthood, involving accusations of religious infidelity (Ezek. 44:10–14). It is not clear how many groups are listed here or what relationship existed between them. Ezra has three names: Jeshua, Kadmiel, Hodaviah (Neh. 7:43: Hodevah), while 1 Esd. 5:26 adds Bannas and Sudias and omits Hodaviah. Bannas corresponds to the well-known Levitical name Bani or Binnui (1 Chron. 16:31; Ezra 8:33; Neh. 3:17, etc.), suggesting that we should read Bani for *bᵉnê,* "sons of . . . ." This would give us four principal Levitical phratries, also named in the building of the temple

(3:9), the reading of the law (Neh. 8:7, Kadmiel missing), the great confession of sin (Neh. 9:4–5), the pledge (Neh. 10:10–11 [9–10]), and the alternative list of repatriated clergy (Neh. 12:8). The names are therefore: **Jeshua, Bani** (Binnui?), **Kadmiel, Hodiah** (Hodaviah, Hodevah, Judah?).

[41] The term *m^{e}šōrēr* covers the composition as well as the rendition of liturgical music, hence "musician" seems more appropriate than "singer." Since they are listed separately from Levites, it would be natural to conclude that they had not yet attained to Levitical status, as was certainly the case at the time of C (e.g., 1 Chron. 9:18, 26, 33–34; 16:4; 23:3–6; Ezra 3:10). The enhancement of status may be due to opening the Levitical ranks to other cult specialists at a later point in time in the Persian period (see, e.g., Rudolph 1949, 121). **Asaph,** a Kohathite Levite and contemporary of David according to C, was eponym of one of the three guilds of liturgical musicians in the Second Temple, the other two being Heman and Jeduthun (1 Chron. 16:4–5, 7, 37; 25; 2 Chron. 5:12, etc.). Psalms attributed to Asaph (50; 73–83) were presumably the work of this guild (see M. J. Buss, *JBL* 82, 1963, 382–391). Only Asaphites are mentioned here and at the laying of the foundations of the temple (Ezra 3:10–11). Other musicians returned with Ezra (7:7) and one, Eliashib, married a foreign woman (10:24). Others were appointed by Nehemiah (Neh. 7:1), some were signatories to the pledge (10:27), and the Asaphite Mattaniah seems to have played a prominent role in the liturgy during Nehemiah's mission (Neh. 11:17; 12:8–9).

[42] Gatekeepers are listed separately here and at Neh. 11:19. They appear to have achieved Levitical status later than the musicians. Both here and at Neh. 12:25 they are divided into six divisions, whereas the list in 1 Chron. 9 has four only. **Shallum,** a Korahite Levite, is the leading figure in 1 Chron. 9:17–19, though his group does not appear at the time of Nehemiah. The only two groups in all lists are those of **Talmon** and **Akkub.** More gatekeepers arrived with Ezra (7:7), some of whom agreed to divorce their foreign wives (10:24). Others were signatories to the pledge in Neh. 10 (vs. 29, 40). C assumes that they were founded by David as a distinct Levitical order closely associated with the temple musicians (1 Chron. 15:18; 16:38; 23:5; 26:1–19). One of their principal functions was to protect the ritual purity of the temple precincts (e.g., 2 Chron. 23:19), and some of them were in charge of the temple stores (1 Chron. 9:26–27).

[43–54] Thirty-five (thirty-two in Neh. 7) temple servants are listed in this first return, a further two hundred and twenty were recruited by Ezra from Casiphia (8:17–20), and at the time of Nehemiah some of them lived in Jerusalem (3:26, 31; 11:21) and took part in building the wall (3:26). The official explanation of the term *nātîn* (pl. *n*ᵉ*tînîm*) is that they were "given" (verbal stem *ntn*) to the Levites by David as servants (Ezra 8:20), but it is not attested for the preexilic period. They were not slaves, since some of them signed the pledge to observe the law (Neh. 10:29 [28]), but probably formed a distinct class or guild of temple personnel analogous to the *širkutu* of the Neo-Babylonian period, and possibly also to the *ytnm,* a list of whom occurs in a Ugaritic text (*spr ytnm,* text 301 I 1, *UM,* p. 169; cf. text 52:3, where *ytnm* occurs immediately after *šr*[*m*]). The repetition of the Gibeonite genealogy after laity, priests, Levites, gatekeepers, and musicians in C's list of repatriates (1 Chron. 9:35–44) confirms the connection between this originally Hivite group and the postexilic *n*ᵉ*tînîm,* a connection suggested by Josh. 9:23, 27 and taken for granted in later Jewish sources (e.g., *b. Yeb.* 71a; 78a–79b; *b. Hor.* 4b; *b. Makk.* 13a). Descendants of Gibeonites were not, however, the only non-Israelites whose employment in the temple is deplored in the temple law of Ezekiel (44:6–7).

Consistent with the non-Israelite origin of this class, several of the names listed here are of foreign origin. **Ziha,** perhaps identical with the overseer of the *n*ᵉ*tînîm* living on the Ophel (Neh. 11:21), is Egyptian-Aramaic (cf. *AP* 30:7), and the same may be the case with **Asnah. Rezin** is Syrian-Aramaic (cf. Isa. 7:1); **Bezai** is probably Babylonian; **Meunim** and **Nephisim** are Arabian, the former perhaps descended from prisoners taken in wars during the time of the monarchy (1 Chron. 4:41; 2 Chron. 20:1; 26:7; see J. R. Bartlett, *JTS* 20, 1969, 6), the latter related to the Ishmaelites (1 Chron. 5:19). **Barkos** is Edomite, meaning son of the Edomite deity Kos or Kaus (see T. C. Vriezen, *OTS* 14, 1965, 330–353; M. Rose, *JSOT* 4, 1977, 28–34; J. R. Bartlett, *JSOT* 5, 1977, 29–38). **Sisera** is certainly non-Semitic, perhaps Illyrian. Very few if any are formed with the theophoric element YHVH, though **Reaiah** is a possibility, and **Shalmai** (Neh. 7:48 for Shamlai), **Hanan,** and **Uzza** could be hypocoristics. **Hagabah, Hagab,** probably variants, correspond to a name in the Ugaritic *ytnm* list and on an ostracon from preexilic Lachish (see A. Lemaire, *Inscriptions Hébraïques* I, Paris, 1977, 182–183). Rather surprisingly, only one—**Hanan**—occurs in the Gibeonite lists (1 Chron. 8:38; 9:44). Very few are attested for the preexilic period, Hanan and Uzza being the exceptions. **Keros** has turned up on an ostracon from Arad from the late monarchy, which, however, does not prove a preexilic origin for the *n*ᵉ*tînîm* (*pace* Levine 1969). Several appear to have originated as nicknames, not unexpectedly in view of the low social status of this class. The following are more or less probable instances: **Hasupha** = Speedy, **Lebanah** = white (albino?), **Nekoda** = pockmarked, **Gazzam** = locust, **Paseah** = lame, **Bakbuk** = flask-shaped, **Hakupha** = crooked, **Harsha** = taciturn, **Neziah** = faithful, **Hatipha** = seized (as a prisoner of war?); the emendation of **Mehida** to Mehira (= hasty?) does not seem to be justified.

[55–58] The class known as descendants of Solomon's slaves, closely associated with the *n*ᵉ*tînîm,* traced its descent to those non-Israelites whom Solomon had made state slaves by subjecting them to forced labor (*mas-'ōbēd,* 1 Kings 9:20–21 = 2 Chron. 8:7–8), including service as galley slaves (2 Chron. 8:18; 9:10). Some of them were assigned to the newly built temple, a practice well attested in the ancient Near East. Their precise status in the Second Temple is uncertain. They were exempt from taxation (Ezra 7:24) but are not listed with the *n*ᵉ*tînîm* as signatories of the pledge (Neh. 10:29 [28]). Since they do not appear in C's list alongside the *n*ᵉ*tînîm* (1 Chron. 9), they may have merged with the latter by the time of writing.

The ten names listed (seventeen in 1 Esd. 5:33–34) are not particularly revealing. **Shephatiah** is the only well-attested Israelite name. **Hassophereth** (Sophereth at Neh. 7:57, Assaphioth at 1 Esd. 5:33) and **Pochereth-hazzebaim** denote occupations (cf. Qoheleth), meaning "scribe" and "gazelle hunter" respectively. **Peruda/Perida** (= solitary), **Darkon** (= stern?), **Hattil** (= talkative?) may have originated as nicknames. **Giddel** is also the name of a *nātîn* (2:47).

The total for both categories of servants, that is, three hundred and ninety-two (three hundred and seventy-two in 1 Esdras), results in very small families or phratries, an average of about 8.7 each, suggesting that their organization may have been different from that of the other classes listed.

[59–63] There follows the list of those of uncertain descent. The first two Babylonian place-names mentioned, taken with the Tel Abib of Ezek. 3:15, suggest that some of the deportees were settled on ancient sites no longer occupied (tel = a mound). **Tel Melah** (Salt Mound) may be the Thelma located in the salt flats near the Persian Gulf according to the geographer Ptolemy (5.20). **Tel Harsha** (= Mound of the Deaf-Mute?) is unidentified; it may be fanciful to suggest that it may have some connection with Ezekiel (Ezek. 3:24–27; 24:27; 33:21–22). The other three are also unidentified, though a Kfar Imra is mentioned in *j. Taan.* 4:69a. In 1 Esd. 5:36 they have been taken to be personal names. Those listed were unable to verify their ancestral house and descent (*zera'* is an unusual word for ancestors), and therefore their true Israelite stock. The list therefore demonstrates the importance of genealogy in establishing status in the golah community. It also illustrates the fierce determination of a segment of Babylonian Jewry to maintain its identity against the threat of assimilation.

The six hundred and fifty-two laity (six hundred and forty-two in Neh. 7:62) belong to three "houses." **Delaiah** is a good Israelite name attested both before and after the exile (e.g., Jer. 36:12, 25; 1 Chron. 3:24; Neh. 6:10; *AP* 30). **Tobiah** may be an ancestor of Nehemiah's opponent of the same name (see on Neh. 2:10) and of the Tobiads, rivals of the Oniads under the Diadochoi. **Nekoda** occurs elsewhere only in the *n^etînîm* list (2:48). The priests also belong to three families. **Habaiah** (Hobaiah at Neh. 7:63, Obdia at 1 Esd. 5:38) is otherwise unattested. **Hakkoz,** a priest during David's reign (1 Chron. 24:10), gave his name to a line which continued down into the Hasmonean period (1 Macc. 8:17), and which appears to have been reinstated (Neh. 3:4, 21; cf. Ezra 8:33). The last named claimed descent from the Barzillai of David's day on the distaff side (see 2 Sam. 17:27–29; 19:31–39; 1 Kings 2:7), a quite exceptional situation no doubt responsible for the dubious status of his descendants. According to 1 Esd. 5:38, this Barzillai's wife was called Augia.

The status of priests was more important because of the risk of contamination for the entire community from illegitimate office-bearers. The exclusion was not intended to be permanent, and it is significant that the civil authority (*tiršātā',* from the Old Persian *taršta,* revered) intervened in cultic matters, as did Nehemiah, who held the same office (Neh. 7:69 [70]; 8:9; 10:2; cf. 12:26), and Arsames, satrap of Egypt (*AP* 21). The governor is not named (1 Esd. 5:40 identifies him as Nehemiah and adds Attharias, an evident corruption of *hattiršātā';* cf. 1 Esd. 9:49) and his identity would depend on the date of the list which we have seen to be uncertain. His ruling, excluding them from the sacrificial food of the first degree of holiness, as opposed to ordinary priestly fare (see especially Lev. 7:1–10), was to remain in force until the issue could be decided by Urim and Thummim. This was an ancient oracular device which gave Yes-No answers to specific questions (1 Sam. 14:41–42; 28:6; Num. 27:21). It was manipulated by the priest (Deut. 33:8) and was later incorporated into the high priest's regalia (Ex. 28:30; Lev. 8:8). It is doubtful whether it was ever used in the postexilic period. According to *m. Soṭa* 9:12 (cf. *t. Soṭa* 13:2; *b. Yoma* 21b) it was one of the five things absent from the Second Temple, and according to *b. Soṭa* 48b it would be available again in the messianic age. 1 Esd. 5:40 defers the decision to a high priest *clothed* in Urim and Thummim *(dēlōsis kai alētheia),* which reflects a later situation; one of several indications of the secondary nature of this text. It would be very risky to posit an early date for the list as a whole, before the appointment of Jeshua as high priest, on the basis of this decision of the governor. The allusion would more naturally be to a priest who exhibited the prophetic gift which qualified him to decide this kind of issue (cf. 1 Macc. 4:46).

[64–67] The sum total of the *qāhāl* is given at the end, in the manner of C (cf. 1 Chron. 7:5, 11, 40, etc.). The figure of 42,360 does not correspond to the sum of the subtotals in the list, which would be 29,818 in Ezra, somewhat higher in Nehemiah and 1 Esdras. Various reasons for the discrepancy have been suggested, all of them speculative. The number of servants has been taken to imply a high level of prosperity, but a proportion of one to six is not so high, especially since the few members of the upper class would presumably have had a large retinue. The two hundred male and female singers (two hundred and forty-five at Neh. 7:67 and 1 Esd. 5:42) served for secular entertainment. There were no female singers in the Second Temple, and probably none in the First Temple either. (Even if we read *šārôt*, female singers, for *šîrôt*, songs, at Amos 8:3, the allusion is not to the Jerusalem temple, and perhaps not to a temple at all.)

It is quite a question why the list ends with an inventory of horses, mules, camels, and donkeys (the first two absent from Neh. 7:68 [69]). It seems unlikely that they were included to demonstrate that the newcomers had the wherewithal for rebuilding the temple, since horses and mules did not generally serve as pack animals. Perhaps they were added in view of the rescript of Cyrus (1:4, 6) and to fill in the picture of a single caravan which had made the long journey from Babylon. And, here too, there may be an echo of the exodus narrative (Ex. 12:38).

Final Stages of the Return and Resumption of Worship (Ezra 2:68–3:6)

In addition to bibliographies for the preceding and following sections see P. R. Ackroyd, *CHJ* I, 136–143; K. **Galling**, "Königliche und nichtkönigliche Stifter beim Tempel von Jerusalem," *ZDPV* 68, 1950, 134–142; E. **Janssen**, *Juda in der Exilzeit*, 94–104; D. R. **Jones**, "The Cessation of Sacrifice After the Destruction of the Temple in 586 B.C.," *JTS* 14, 1963, 12–31; H. G. M. **Williamson**, "The Composition of Ezra i–vi," *JTS* 33, 1983, 1–30.

2:68 When they came to the house of YHVH which is in Jerusalem, some of the heads of ancestral houses made votive offerings to the house of God to set it on its foundation. [69]According to their

means, they contributed to the treasury of the work sixty-one
thousand gold darics, five thousand silver minas, and a hundred
priestly vestments. [70]The priests, the Levites, and some of the
people settled in Jerusalem; [a] the musicians, gatekeepers, temple
servants, [b] and all Israel in their towns.

3:1 When the seventh month came around, and the Israelites
were in their towns, the people gathered together of one accord in
Jerusalem. [2]Jeshua son of Jozadak with his fellow priests, and
Zerubbabel son of Shealtiel with his kinsmen, set to work to build
the altar of the God of Israel in order to offer burnt sacrifices on
it, as prescribed in the law of Moses the man of God. [3]They set
the altar on its bases, for they lived in fear of the local inhabitants, [c]
and offered up burnt sacrifices to YHVH upon it, both the morning and the evening offerings. [4]They observed the feast of Booths
as prescribed, with the daily burnt sacrifices to the number prescribed for each day; [5]thereafter, the continual burnt offerings,
those for sabbaths, [d] new moons, for all the sacred feasts of
YHVH, and for those who had vowed a votive offering to YHVH.
[6]Beginning on the first day of the seventh month, they offered
burnt offerings to YHVH, though the foundations of the temple
of YHVH had not yet been laid.

a. "in Jerusalem" added with 1 Esd. 5:46.
b. MT adds "in their towns" by dittography; omitted with LXX[A] and 1 Esd.
   5:46.
c. MT reads "for in terror upon them from the peoples of the land," which is
   impossible. The conservative reading adopted here assumes '*ēmāh* for *b^e-*
   'ēmāh.
d. "sabbaths" inserted with 1 Esd. 5:51; for justification of this addition see
   commentary.

[2:68–69] The problem posed by the parallelism between this conclusion to the list and Neh. 7:69[70]–8:1 is discussed in the Introduction, sect. 4. C's narrative picks up from the point at which the list
was inserted, i.e., at 1:11. The theme is the endowment of the temple,
which, as noted, is out of place in the Nehemiah context. Endowment
by the heads of kinship groups raises the important issue of the status
of the Second Temple. Solomon's temple was a royal establishment;
like the Bethel temple it was "a royal sanctuary and temple of the
kingdom" (*miqdaš-melek ûbêt maml^ekāh*, Amos 7:13). David himself purchased the land on which it was built, the construction was
paid for out of royal funds, and the necessary endowments continued
to be provided by the monarchy (2 Kings 12:18). In his revised

account C insists that the heads of ancestral houses *(rā'šê hā'ābôt)* shared with David the responsibility for endowing the temple (1 Chron. 26:26), in keeping with the situation described here. His version of the restoration of worship during the reign of Joash, following on the dark days of the reign of the foreign queen Athaliah, is also instructive in this regard. The public collection solicited by Joash for the restoration was an innovation necessitated by the depletion of the royal treasury (2 Kings 12). C, however, changes this into a temple tax levied, according to Mosaic law, on the population as a whole (2 Chron. 24:6, 9–10), the same tax which the signatories of the covenant in Neh. 10 vowed to maintain (Neh. 10:33). According to this view, then, the temple was no longer a royal establishment but the responsibility of the community as a whole.

The discrepancy between the versions of Cyrus' decree may also be explained along these lines. According to the Aramaic version (Ezra 6:4–5), the expenses involved in the rebuilding are to be paid out of the royal treasury since the Persian king sees himself as the successor to the native dynasty and therefore acknowledges responsibility for the sanctuary. The Hebrew version, on the other hand, follows C's view that responsibility for the rebuilding lies with those returning from exile, the reconstituted Israel, even though the situation called for outside assistance. It is this theme which is taken up again in the present passage.

There is probably some textual corruption of the figures. The Nehemiah version has 41,000 gold darics in all as against 61,000 in Ezra. 1 Esd. 5:44 lists 1,000 gold minas, which is close to the Ezra figure since the mina was about sixty times the weight of the daric (about 525 grams). 1 Esdras also agrees with Ezra on the number of silver minas—5,000—as against a total of 4,200 in Nehemiah. Both 1 Esdras and Ezra list one hundred vestments as against a total of 597 in Nehemiah, or 97 if the text is emended following LXX. Whether these figures correspond in any way to historical reality is another matter. A community whose leaders could endow the temple in the amount of more than 1,132 pounds of gold and more than five times that amount of silver, and still presumably have something left over for themselves, must have been rich beyond dreams of avarice. One imagines, however, that the real situation was of a more modest and prosaic nature.

[70] The account of the settlement forms a kind of inclusion with 2:1. Those of the people who settled in Jerusalem would have included leaders and members of the upper class. At the time of Nehemiah the city was sparsely populated (Neh. 7:4), but this condition could be explained by events subsequent to the early settlements.

One can only imagine the difficulties, logistic and otherwise, involved in resettling about 50,000 people. C can at least ignore the severe problems created by relations with the native population since for him the land was already depopulated. This was therefore a new beginning. The typological character of his narrative is also apparent here. The exodus theme of gifts of gold, silver, and clothing (Ex. 3:21–22; 11:2; 12:35–36) reappears and the occupation concludes with the allotting of land (cf. Josh. 18–19). The diaspora group is "all-Israel" *(kol-yiśrā'ēl),* the authentic Israel of the early days. The stage is therefore set for the building of the temple in its proper place, that is, where it previously had stood, and for the community's access to it (cf. Ex. 15:17–18).

[3:1–6] The place of this incident in the narrative sequence is reasonably clear. The rescript of Cyrus resulted in an immediate return to the homeland and resettlement in it. The altar was at once set up to permit the resumption without delay of legitimate worship, essential for the community's well-being. In spite of the first intimations of opposition (3:3), the foundations of the rebuilt temple were laid and the service of dedication was held (3:7–13). After further opposition (4:1–23), work on the temple was resumed in the second year of Darius (4:24–5:2), who renewed the original authorization (5:3–6:12), thus permitting the work to be completed in the sixth year of his reign (6:13–15). The story ends with the service of dedication and the celebration of the great passover (6:16–22).

This is C's account of the first and decisive stage of restoration, and it goes without saying that it raises a number of historical problems which are not easily solved. A major sticking point is the author's presentation of the role of Zerubbabel. Taking the narrative at face value, Zerubbabel is presented as active in both stages of the rebuilding, first under Cyrus, then under Darius. While this is chronologically possible, and still has some defenders, it seems much more likely that the author has backdated Zerubbabel's activity into the first stage of the return in the interests of presenting a more unified story. It also allowed him to pass over internal problems and to describe the restoration as a triumph over opposition originating exclusively outside of the group. A very different picture emerges from a reading of Haggai and Zechariah 1–8.

[1] The seventh month (Tishri, in the autumn) belongs, in the logic of the narrative, to the first year of the return, followed by events in the second year "of their coming to the house of God" (v. 8). If 3:1–13, perhaps rounded out with 6:19–22, was originally an independent account of the rebuilding and dedicating of the temple under Darius (as suggested by Ackroyd), C has set it back into the

earliest period of the return, omitted any allusion to Darius, and made the service of dedication for the completed temple into a celebration of the laying, or re-laying, of the foundations (3:10–13; cf. 6:16–18). As it is, the narrative is designed to highlight the golah community's zeal in restoring the sacrificial system even before beginning the rebuilding. In so doing, they followed the example of David, who, according to 1 Chron. 21:28–22:1, averted disaster by building an altar and offering sacrifice before the temple was built.

The seventh month, in which the feast of Sukkoth fell, was the most important of the year and the most propitious for embarking on a new initiative (cf. 2 Chron. 5:3; 7:8–10; Neh. 7:72b [73b]; 8:2, 14–18). Emphasis is on the unanimous and enthusiastic participation of the entire community, as is generally the case in C; as, for example, when David brought up the ark to Jerusalem (1 Chron. 13:1–14). The author is not concerned with the problem how some 50,000 people could have returned en masse and settled in different parts of the country within the space of six months.

[2] Exceptionally, Jeshua is named before Zerubbabel, no doubt because of the nature of the task. He is not called high priest, as invariably in Haggai (1:1, 12, 14; 2:2, 4). Haggai, Zechariah, and Ezra 4:24–5:2 clearly attest to the activity of Zerubbabel and Jeshua under Darius. The most probable explanation is—as suggested—that the author, who was not concerned with precise historical reconstruction, chose to backdate Zerubbabel and ignore or downplay the role of Sheshbazzar. Zerubbabel was probably appointed governor of the province either at the time of Cambyses' Egyptian campaign in 525 or at the beginning of the reign of Darius (522–520). He seems to have disappeared from the scene, for reasons unknown, some time before 515. The altar may have survived the destruction of 586 and even continued in use during the subsequent decades (Jer. 41:5); but, if so, the author would not have found it acceptable. At this and other points in his narrative he stresses conformity with the Mosaic law. Allusions to this law in C's work can generally, but by no means invariably, be traced to Deuteronomy. Thus, the allusion here is probably to Deut. 27:6–7, which prescribes the building of an altar immediately on entering the land. It is also in Deuteronomy (33:1) that we find the designation "man of God" used of Moses (see R. Hallevy, *JNES* 17, 1958, 237–244).

[3] The language used here implies that the altar was built on the foundations (*mᵉkônôt;* cf. masc. form at 2:68 and Ps. 104:5 and the similar *matkōnet* at 2 Chron. 24:13) of the previous one, another indication of the author's interest in the vital theme of continuity (and therefore legitimacy). As at the time of David, the building of

an altar and offering sacrifice had the purpose of warding off danger
to the community. In this instance the source of the trouble is identified as "the peoples of the lands" *('ammê hā'ᵃrāṣôt),* referring either
to neighboring peoples, as, for example, the Edomites who had taken
over the Judean Negeb, or peoples of foreign extraction settled in the
northern and central regions (cf. 4:9–10). 1 Esd. 5:49 adds that some
of the other peoples of the land joined them, implying that they
assisted in setting up the altar, but then goes on to say that all the
peoples who were in the land (on the earth?) were hostile. The daily
morning and evening sacrifice—the Tamid—consisted in a lamb
with flour, oil, and wine (Ex. 29:38–42; Num. 28:3–8). The Tamid
was restored after the repair of the temple by king Joash (2 Chron.
24:14) and, after another period of neglect, by Hezekiah (2 Chron.
29:7, 27–29). How important it remained in the religious history of
Israel can be seen from Dan. 11:31 and 12:11 (cf. *m. Taan.* 4:6). It
signified by metonymy the sacrificial system as a whole.

[4–6] The celebration of Sukkoth was the appropriate way to
mark a new beginning, as at the dedication of the First Temple (2
Chron. 5:3) and during Ezra's mission (Neh. 8:13–18). The sacrifices
prescribed for the eight-day festival are listed only at Num. 29:12–38,
generally taken to be a P stratum. (For the legislation dealing with
this festival see de Vaux, *AI,* 495–506.) The rest of the prescribed
sacrifices follow according to the order which is routine in C (e.g.,
2 Chron. 2:3; 8:13). Sabbath and new moon usually go together, as
at Num. 28:9–15. They are both mentioned at 1 Esd. 5:51, leading
to the assumption that "sabbaths" has dropped out here. Votive
offerings were ad hoc, spontaneous, and private (cf. Deut. 12:17; Lev.
22:17–25; Num. 15:1–10) and correspond to a favorite topic of the
author (see on 1:4).

[6] This verse forms an inclusion with 3:1 by referring to the date
of the solemn inauguration of the liturgy and therefore of a new era.
It also leads into the next "moment" of the restoration by noting that
work on the temple still remained to be done. The precise meaning
of 6b, depending on the interpretation of the verb *yussād,* can be
conveniently deferred to the next section.

Laying of the Foundations and Dedication (Ezra 3:7–13)

P. R. Ackroyd, *CHJ* 136–143; F. I. **Andersen,** "Who Built the Second Temple?"
ABR 6, 1958, 1–35; N. H. **Baynes,** "Zerubbabel's Rebuilding of the Temple," *JTS*
25, 1924, 154–160; R. **Ellis,** *Foundation Deposits in Ancient Mesopotamia,* New
Haven, 1968; K. **Galling,** "Die Exilwende in der Sicht des Propheten Sacharja,"
Studien, 109–126; "Serubbabel und der Hohepriester beim Wiederaufbau des Tem-

pels in Jerusalem," ibid., 127–148; A. **Gelston,** "The Foundations of the Second Temple," *VT* 16, 1966, 232–235; J. **Goettsberger,** "Über das III Kapitel des Esrabuches," *JSOR* 10, 1926, 270–280; M. **Heltzer,** "A propos des banquets des rois achéménides et du retour d'exil sous Zerobabel," *RB* 86, 1979, 102–106; W. E. **Hogg,** "The Founding of the Second Temple," *PTR* 25, 1927, 457–461; W. Th. **In der Smitten,** *Esra,* 3–6; A. **Janssen,** *Juda in der Exilzeit,* 94–104; D. R. **Jones,** "The Cessation of Sacrifice After the Destruction of the Temple in 586 B.C.," *JTS* 14, 1963, 12–31; A. **Kapelrud,** "Temple Building: A Task for Gods and Kings," *Orientalia* 32, 1963, 56–62; M. W. **Leeseberg,** "Ezra and Nehemiah: A Review of the Return and Reform," *CTM* 33, 1962, 79–90; J. **Liver,** "The Return from Babylon, Its Time and Scope," *EI* 5, 1958, 114–116 (Heb.); D. L. **Petersen,** "Zerubbabel and Jerusalem Temple Reconstruction," *CBQ* 36, 1974, 366–372; A. **Petitjean,** "La mission de Zerobabel et la reconstruction du temple, Zech 3:8–10," *ETL* 42, 1966, 40–71; E. **Sellin,** "Noch einmal der Stein des Sacharja," *ZAW* n.F. 18, 1942/43, 59–77; L. A. **Snijders,** "Het 'Volk des lands' in Juda," *NTT* 12, 1958, 241–256; C. C. **Torrey,** *Ezra Studies,* 301–314; C. J. **Tuland,** " 'Uššayya' and 'Uššarna': A Clarification of Terms, Date and Text," *JNES* 17, 1958, 269–275.

3:7 They therefore gave silver to the masons and craftsmen, and food, drink, and oil to the Sidonians and Tyrians, to bring cedar logs by sea from the Lebanon to Joppa, in keeping with the authorization which Cyrus king of Persia had given them. [8]In the second year after they had come to the house of God in Jerusalem, in the second month, Zerubbabel son of Shealtiel and Jeshua son of Jozadak made a start, together with their fellow Israelites, the priests, Levites, and all who had come to Jerusalem from the captivity. They appointed Levites from the age of twenty upward to supervise work on the house of YHVH. [9]Jeshua with his sons and kinsmen, Kadmiel, Bani,[a] and the sons of Hodaviah[b] together undertook to supervise those who were doing the work[c] on the house of God. (Also the Henadad Levites, their sons and kinsmen.)[d] [10]When the builders laid the foundations of the temple of YHVH, the priests were standing clothed in their vestments with trumpets, and the Levites, sons of Asaph, with cymbals, praising YHVH as ordained by David, king of Israel. [11]They sang praises antiphonally and gave thanks to YHVH, "for he is good, his love for Israel endures for ever"; and all the people raised a great shout in praise of YHVH because the foundations of the temple had been laid.

[12]Many of the priests, Levites, and heads of ancestral houses, old men who had seen the First Temple when it yet stood—this was for them the real temple[e]—wept aloud, while others raised their voices in a shout of joy. [13]The people were unable to distinguish between the shouting for joy and the sound of weeping,[f] for the

people were raising a great cry, and the sound could be heard far off.

a. Bani (or Binnui) for *bnyv,* "his sons"; see on 2:40.
b. "Hodaviah" for MT "Judah"; see on 2:40.
c. Reading *'šy* (pl.) for *'šh* (sing.) with several MSS.
d. The phrase in parentheses is a gloss.
e. MT *zeh habbayit beʿênêhem,* lit., "this was the temple in their eyes," is best taken, in view of the syntax, as an explanatory gloss which understands the preceding *beyosdô* as referring to the Solomonic temple.
f. Omitting "of the people" with LXX.

[3:7] The author now turns to the laying of the foundations and their dedication. The description of the preparations recalls, and is intended to recall, those which preceded the building of Solomon's temple: the participation of masons, stonecutters, carpenters, Sidonians and Tyrians (1 Chron. 22:2, 4, 15), provisions supplied to the Phoenicians (2 Chron. 2:9, 15), and transport of timber by sea to Joppa (2 Chron. 2:16). The reference to the rescript is to be taken in general terms; it included no grant for timber, though 1 Esd. 4:48 alludes to such a grant from Darius to Zerubbabel, an allusion enlarged on by Josephus (*Ant.* 11.60). An anonymous seer of the early Persian period views the adornment of the temple with wood from Lebanon as divinely preordained (Isa. 60:8–14).

[8–9] According to the logic of the narrative up to this point, the second year would be during the reign of Cyrus (therefore 537/6). C makes no allusion to Sheshbazzar even though the Aramaic source attributes the laying of the foundations to him (5:16). Neither Haggai nor Zechariah alludes to him either, and they give no hint of any previous attempt to rebuild the temple, which at their time still lay in ruins (Hag. 1:4). Both prophets attribute the foundation-laying to Zerubbabel and place it in the reign of Darius not Cyrus (Hag. 2:18; Zech. 4:9). As suggested earlier, it seems that C has simply telescoped events in the early Persian period to fit in with his own theological perspective. This foreshortening involved limiting the role of Sheshbazzar to custody of the sacred vessels (1:8–11), and backdating the laying of the foundations to the reign of Cyrus to emphasize the exclusive role played by the golah group immediately after its return to the homeland. On this last point, it is noticeable that Haggai makes no allusion whatever to this group.

Work on the First Temple also began in the second month, that of Ziv, later Iyyar (I Kings 6:1, 37; 2 Chron. 3:2). While this spring month was in fact a good time to get started on a major project, after the winter rains and the sowing season had ended, the author's recapitulatory intent is quite clear, as it is in other details of his narrative. The work was done exclusively by the golah group under Levitical supervision. We can recover the four Levitical names of the census list (see 2:40) from the textually corrupt v. 9: Jeshua (not of course the high priest), Kadmiel, Bani or Binnui, Hodaviah or perhaps Hodiah. The Masoretic divider in the middle of the verse confirms the suspicion that the Henadad group was added subsequently, drawing on Neh. 10:10 [9] (see also 3:18, 24), perhaps because it was not originally diasporic. The minimum qualifying age is here and elsewhere (1 Chron. 23:24–27; 2 Chron. 31:17) set at twenty, but we also find twenty-five (Num. 8:24) and thirty (Num. 4:3, 23, 30; 1 Chron. 23:3). The age was probably lowered progressively as the range of functions associated with the Levitical office increased.

[10–11] While the verbal stem *ysd* does not invariably connote the laying of foundations (see Additional Note following), and while the parallel 1 Esd. 5:57 speaks only of building the temple, the solemnity with which the occasion was celebrated strongly indicates that this is what was happening. Following liturgical orthopraxy (cf. 1 Chron. 15:19; 16:5–6; 25:1, 6; 2 Chron. 5:12–13), priests blew trumpets, and Asaphite Levites (see 2 Chron. 29:25–26 and commentary on Ezra 2:41) clashed cymbals, no doubt to keep time and mark pauses in the antiphonal chant. The psalm fragment (cf. Ps. 106:1; 136:1) is a favorite of C, and he brings it in whenever he can (e.g., 1 Chron. 16:34; 2 Chron. 5:13; 7:3). The goodness and love *(ḥesed)* of YHVH recall to the worshiper the theme of covenant fidelity. The shout *(tᵉrû'āh),* also associated with warfare, was probably understood as acclaiming YHVH as king of Israel (cf. the psalms of divine kingship, Pss. 93; 95–99).

[12–13] The incident of the old men weeping seems to have been suggested by Hag. 2:3, with which v. 12 has significant parallels. If so, there may have been more to this weeping than nostalgia; a muted attitude of disparagement of the project in hand, understood as such by the scholiast who added the gloss "this was for them the (real) temple" (see Bewer 1922, 45–46). For his own good reasons C says nothing about *internal* opposition to the project, of the kind alluded to in Hag. 1:2–11 and perhaps also Isa. 66:1–2. He also suggests that the weeping of the "old guard" was drowned out by the triumphant acclamations of the majority. (There is, incidentally, no suggestion that this weeping was of the cultic sort.) Perhaps we should say that our author, while deeply conscious of the importance of continuity and tradition, was no reactionary.

Additional Note on the Laying of the Foundations
of the Second Temple

The Cyrus rescript mandated rather than permitted the building of
the temple (*bnh* is translated sometimes "build" and sometimes
"rebuild," reflecting the uncertainty as to what was involved). We
are later told that the gifts collected from the community were
contributions to the task of erecting it on its site (*l^{e}ha^{ca}mîdô 'al-
m^{e}kônô*, 2:68). The Aramaic version of the rescript also speaks of
it having to be built on its site (*'al 'atrēh*, 5:15; 6:7). The implication
is that it was to be built on the same site as the former temple, a
traditional practice in antiquity reflected at a much later time in the
building or rebuilding of synagogues. Logically, therefore, the
mākôn of Ezra 2:68 would be the base, foundation, or platform on
which the Solomonic temple was erected. We might compare Ps.
104:5, which speaks of God establishing the earth on its foundation
(*yāsad 'ereṣ 'al-m^{e}kônehā*), and 2 Chron. 24:13, in which we are told
that king Joash "raised the house of God on its foundation"
(*ya^{ca}mîdû 'et-bêt hā'^{e}lōhîm 'al-matkuntô*). The confessional prayer
of Ezra uses the same verbs favored by C, in speaking of the temple
ruins being "raised" (Ezra 9:9). This suggests a work of clearing
away debris and repairing rather than starting from scratch. And in
all probability this is what actually happened, since the fire set by the
Babylonians in 586 would not have destroyed the building entirely
and would certainly have left the foundations intact (see 2 Kings
25:9).

The first stage in the reestablishment of the cult was the setting up
of the altar on its foundations (*'al m^{e}kônōtāv*, Ezra 3:3), and this at
a time when the temple was not yet built (*hêkal* YHVH *lō' yussād*,
3:6). A crucial question arises here with the use of this verb *ysd*,
which has a range of meanings corresponding to "establish, found,
fix, appoint" (*BDB* ad loc.). The tendency in recent years has been
to assign it, in this context, the more general sense of repair, complete, or something of the sort (e.g., Ackroyd, Andersen, Clines
1984, Fensham 1982). C's account of work done on the temple under
king Joash, summarized as *y^{e}sôd bêt hā'^{e}lōhîm*, 2 Chron. 24:27, is
cited in support of this interpretation, since he had already informed
us that Joash was responsible for restoring and repairing the temple
fabric (using the verbs *ḥaddēš* and *ḥazzēq*, vs. 4–14). We therefore
have at least one instance where a cognate of *ysd* cannot refer to
laying foundations. This is so, but it remains to be seen what *yussād*
means in the present context (Ezra 3:6). The narrative goes on to
describe the preparations, comparable to those preceding the build-

ing of the First Temple, and then speaks of a solemn liturgical celebration accompanying the work of the builders (3:7–13). We are reminded of Job 38:4–7, which describes a heavenly liturgy, with the "sons of God" shouting for joy, when the earth was founded *(b^{e}yosdî hā'āreṣ)*. (The verb *vayyārî'û,* shouted, is cognate with *t^{e}rû'āh* at Ezra 3:11, 13.) That *ysd* can have this specific sense, the laying of foundations or of a foundation stone accompanied by appropriate solemnities, is also apparent in the tradition about the founding of Jericho by Hiel involving human sacrifice *(ba'^{a}bîrām b^{e}kōrô yis-s^{e}dāh,* 1 Kings 16:34; cf. Josh. 6:26). Analogy with the laying of the foundations of a temple is also implied in certain descriptions— especially in liturgical texts—of the creation of the earth (Pss. 24:2; 78:67; 89:12 [11]; 102:26 [25]; 104:5; Prov. 3:19; Amos 9:6; Isa. 48:13; 51:13, 16; Zech. 12:1). It therefore seems reasonable to conclude that where the term occurs in Ezra 3 it connotes, in the intention of the author if not in historical reality—a distinction often neglected—the solemn laying of the foundations or foundation stone of the new temple.

One of the most vexatious problems of interpretation in Ezra 1–6 stems from the report, in the Aramaic source, that Sheshbazzar, governor of the province, laid the foundations *(y^{e}hab 'uššayyā')* of the temple during the reign of Cyrus (5:16), an act which is attributed to Zerubbabel in Ezra 3 and at Zech. 4:9, with the clear implication that it took place later, under Darius. Here, too, the problem turns on the precise meaning of the terms used in describing what was done. *'uššayyā'* (*'uššāh* in sing.) occurs only in this section (4:12; 5:16; perhaps 6:3). The word can be traced back, through the Akkadian, to a Sumerian term *uš* meaning substructure, foundation. It may therefore be taken to correspond to the Hebrew *y^{e}sôd, mussad,* and possibly other related forms, which can certainly refer to the foundation(s) of a building (e.g., Micah 1:6; Ezek. 13:14). *y^{e}hab 'uššayyā'* would therefore be the equivalent of *yāsad,* and there is nothing in the context to rule out this meaning, certainly not considerations of historical plausibility. Other factors would have to be considered in deciding whether the report is a fabrication of the Judeans to strengthen their case at the Persian court, or of the author of the Aramaic source, or of C himself. There seems to be no compelling reason, therefore, to exclude the view that in both Hebrew and Aramaic texts we are being told that work on the Second Temple began with laying the foundations, celebrated with appropriate rituals, in keeping with an ancient thematic and ritual pattern.

More problems emerge when we take into account what Haggai and Zech. 1–8 have to say about the reestablishment of worship in the early Persian period. For both prophets the event took place early in the reign of Darius. Zerubbabel, representing the native dynasty, played the decisive role, and there is no hint of any previous attempt at rebuilding: the temple was lying in ruins (Hag. 1:4; cf. Zech. 1:16; Isa. 63:18; 64:11) and as yet no stone was placed upon a stone (Hag. 2:15). Then, as a result of prophetic urging, Zerubbabel took the decisive initial step, to describe which the same verb *ysd* is used: "the hands of Zerubbabel have founded this house *(yiss^edû habbayit haz-zeh);* his hands will complete it" (Zech. 4:9). Both also speak of the day when the temple was founded *(yussād;* cf. Ezra 3:6). Here too, however, recent commentary has inclined to the view that the verb has the more general sense of restoration or repair. Yet the distinct impression is given of a precise point in time—the *day* of foundation—marking the reversal from ill fortune and infertility to blessing and plenty (Hag. 2:15–19; Zech. 8:9–13). An act is therefore suggested which is distinct from the work of restoration and rebuilding (Zech. 4:9; 6:12–13; 7:9). Given the importance of this initial act and its ritual celebration in the ancient Near East, this is no more than what we would expect. And, in fact, in the present instance, there are indications of such a ceremony in which Zerubbabel, as a royal figure, played the leading role, in keeping with the well-attested theme of royal responsibility for temple-building (Kapelrud). Zech. 4:7–10 has been taken to allude to such a ritual of establishing a new temple on the site of the old, one in which a stone was taken from the foundations of the previous building and set in place to mark the beginning of the new. It was also customary then, as it still is, to deposit a tablet or tablets to mark the event, and this part of the ritual may be alluded to in the obscure reference to the *'eben habb^edîl* (= tin tablet?) at Zech. 4:10. The ceremony in question was known in ancient Mesopotamia as the kalu ritual *(kalû* = ritual singer), implying a liturgy of hymn-singing and inevitably recalling the situation as described in Ezra 3 and the metaphorical language of Job 38 (Petersen, Ellis; rather different interpretations in Sellin and Petit-jean).

Josephus also, following 1 Esdras (2:18; 5:57; 6:11, 20), distinguishes between the laying of the foundation and the work of rebuilding, the former under Cyrus and involving Sheshbazzar, whom he appears to identify with Zerubbabel (*Ant.* 11.19, 93). Then, after further work was stopped by Cambyses, who was evil by nature *(physei ponēros,* 11.26), it was allowed to continue under Darius, who was an old friend of Zerubbabel. The foundations had to be laid once again (11.79) and the work was then completed without further incident.

Opposition During the Reign of Cyrus (Ezra 4:1–5)

A. **Alt**, "Die Rolle Samarias bei der Entstehung des Judentums," *KS* 2:316–337; R. J. **Coggins**, "The Interpretation of Ezra iv.4," *JTS* n.s. 16, 1965, 124–127; *Samaritans and Jews*, 37–57; E. W. **Nicholson**, "The Meaning of the Expression *'am hā'āres* in the Old Testament," *JSS* 10, 1965, 59–66; J. W. **Rothstein**, *Juden und Samaritaner*, Leipzig, 1908; L. A. **Snijders**, "Het 'volk des lands' in Juda," *NTT* 12, 1958, 241–256; S. **Talmon**, "The Judean *'am ha'ares* in Historical Perspective," *Fourth World Congress of Jewish Studies* I, Jerusalem, 1967, 71–76; R. **de Vaux**, "Le sens de l'expression 'peuple du pays' dans l'Ancien Testament et le rôle politique du peuple en Israel," *RA* 58, 1964, 167–172; E. **Würthwein**, *Der 'Am Ha'arez im Alten Testament*, Stuttgart, 1936, 57–64.

4:1 When the adversaries of Judah and Benjamin heard that those who had returned from exile were building a temple to YHVH God of Israel, [2]they approached Zerubbabel, Jeshua[a] and the heads of ancestral houses and said to them, "Let us build with you, for we worship the same God as you, and we have been sacrificing to him[b] since the time of Esarhaddon, the king of Assyria who brought us here." [3]But Zerubbabel, Jeshua, and the other heads of ancestral houses said to them, "It is not right for both you and us to build a house for our God; rather we alone[c] must build for YHVH the God of Israel as His Majesty Cyrus king of Persia commanded us." [4]So the local population discouraged the people of Judah and made them too afraid to continue building. [5]They bribed officials to oppose them in order to frustrate their purpose; and this continued for the entire reign of Cyrus king of Persia down to the reign of Darius king of Persia.

a. Absent from MT; added with 1 Esd. 5:15.
b. Reading *lô* for *lō'* with Qere; the change may have been inspired by anti-Samaritan polemic.
c. A somewhat unusual meaning for *yaḥad* but demanded by the context. An alternative translation of *'aⁿaḥnû yaḥad* as "we a community," based on the meaning of *yaḥad* in the Qumran texts, has been proposed by Talmon (1953).

The purpose of this account of opposition from outside the golah community is to explain the delay in implementing the royal decree. C carefully avoids alluding to internal problems which, however, we know to have existed: indifference (Hag. 1:2–4), internal strife (Isa. 58:4; Zech. 8:10), unfavorable social and economic conditions (Hag. 1:5–6, 9–11; 2:16–19; Zech. 8:10), and perhaps also downright opposition to the rebuilding (Isa. 66:1–2). In the long section dealing with opposition which begins here it is particularly important to grasp the logic of the narrative. After the resumptive 4:24, 5:1–2 continues 4:1–5 and takes us down to the second year of Darius (520). The intervening passage 4:6–23, dealing with opposition under Ahasu-erus/Xerxes (486–465) and Artaxerxes (465–424), is obviously out of chronological order. This is not unusual in ancient historiography and neither calls for a theory of interpolation nor requires us to conclude that the author was ignorant about the correct order of the early Achaemenids. Having just dealt with opposition under Cyrus, he simply wished to carry this theme through the reigns of Darius (4:5), Xerxes (4:6), and Artaxerxes (4:7–23)—in the correct chrono-logical order—omitting Cambyses, for whose reign he probably had no comparable information. He then doubled back to continue the account of the rebuilding under Darius, including Tattenai's inter-vention, the imperial edict reaffirming the authorization and, finally, the completion and dedication of the temple in the sixth year of his reign.

The narrative sequence in 1 Esdras is very confused, beginning as it does with opposition under Artaxerxes (2:12–25) which continued until a more favorable situation was created as a result of Zerubba-bel's verbal skill at the court of Darius (2:26–4:63). The list of repatriates is then placed firmly in the context of that reign (5:1–45), followed by the first attempts at rebuilding (5:46–62), local opposi-tion which put a stop to the work—again—until the second year of that reign (5:63–71), resumption of the work (6:1–2), and so on as in Ezra down to the completion and dedication (6:3–7:15). Josephus follows 1 Esdras quite closely, but is clearly concerned to rectify the chronological confusion, which he does by substituting Cambyses (never mentioned in Ezra and 1 Esdras) for Artaxerxes and putting the mission of Ezra in the reign of Xerxes (*Ant.* 11. 21–30, 120). Neither 1 Esdras nor Josephus says anything about opposition dur-ing this reign as does Ezra 4:6. In making his major alteration, Josephus was probably influenced by the bad reputation which Cam-byses acquired, somewhat undeservedly, in the Greek historiograph-ical tradition (e.g., Herodotus 3.16, 25, 27–38; Diodorus Siculus 1.46; Strabo 17.27). As a general rule, it would be imprudent to rely on either 1 Esdras or Josephus where they diverge from Ezra 1–6.

[4:1–2] The connection with the preceding episode is brought out more clearly in 1 Esd. 5:63: "When the enemies of the tribe of Judah and Benjamin heard it, they came to find out what the sound of the trumpet meant." That those who offered their assistance are desig-nated adversaries from the outset implies that the author understood their offer to be interested and disingenuous. These adversaries identified themselves as descendants of foreigners forcibly resettled in the region of Samaria after the incorporation of the Northern Kingdom into the Assyrian empire in the late eighth century. According to the Deuteronomic historian these settlers combined the cult of YHVH with those of other deities (2 Kings 17:24–34), a situation which continued to the time of writing (17:34, 41; cf. 2 Chron. 13:9). That further deportations and relocations occurred under Esarhaddon (681–669), perhaps in connection with his campaign of 677/6 in Syria (*ANET,* 290; D. J. Wiseman, *Iraq* 14, 1952, 54–60), is entirely possible and may be alluded to in the obscure gloss at Isa. 7:8b. The Aramaic source (4:10) will refer to a different resettlement under Osnappar/Asshurbanipal (668–c. 627). As it stands, the statement of the adversaries—with the emendation suggested—does not reflect the author's animus against the Samaritans. It would be anachronistic to call these people Samaritans, as Josephus does (*Ant.* 11.84, etc.), since the Samaritans did not exist as a separate religious community in the early Persian period. There is no reason to doubt the claim of these inhabitants of the one-time Assyrian province of Samerina to be YHVH-worshipers. It will be recalled that a delegation from Samaria came south shortly after the destruction of Jerusalem to make offerings at the ruined site (Jer. 41:5).

[3] The rejection of the offer was justified on the technical point that those making it were not mentioned in the imperial firman. The real reason was, of course, quite different. The syncretic practice of the petitioners would have sufficed, in which respect a comparison is often made with Hag. 2:10–14, which declares the offerings of "this people" and "this nation" unclean. But the allusion here is almost certainly to the condition of the Judean community itself before the dedication of the new sanctuary (J. Blenkinsopp, *A History of Prophecy in Israel from the Settlement in the Land to the Hellenistic Period,* Philadelphia, 1983, 232; D. Petersen, *Haggai and Zechariah 1–8,* Philadelphia, 1984, 70–85). The fact that opposition to the resurgence of Judah continued to come predominantly from this region suggests a political motivation for both the offer and the rejection. The leaders in the province of Samaria may well have seen the emergence of a new, aggressive presence in Judah, and one which enjoyed the favor of the imperial government, as threatening, even though there is no clear evidence that Judah was under the administrative control of Samaria from the beginning of the Persian period. An offer to share the labor, and presumably also the expense, of rebuilding the sanctuary would have been taken to entail, and would in fact have entailed, a share in controlling the temple itself with all that that implied.

[4–5] The local population (literally, "the people of the land") who succeeded in holding up the work on the temple for so long may have included the adversaries of v. 1, but vs. 4–5 should probably be taken as a quite distinct piece of information. The term *('am hā'āreṣ)* has different connotations in different periods which need not be investigated here. In Ezra-Nehemiah the terms used are "the peoples of the land" (*'ammê hā'āreṣ,* Ezra 10:2, 11; Neh. 9:24; 10:31–32 [30–31]) and "the peoples of the lands" (*'ammê hā'ᵃrāṣôt,* Ezra 3:3; 9:1–2, 11; Neh. 9:30), which are used for all practical purposes interchangeably. They refer to the inhabitants of either Judah or neighboring provinces (Samaria, Idumea, etc.) who are outside the golah community and are therefore by definition religiously suspect. These outsiders, then, succeeded in discouraging the builders (lit., they "weakened their hands," a well-established idiom; cf. 2 Sam. 4:1; Isa. 13:7; Jer. 6:24; Lachish ostracon 6 [*ANET,* 322]), and they did so by suborning or bribing officials in the imperial bureaucracy (*yō'ᵉṣîm,* lit., "counselors") with a view to undermining the good standing of the Judeans with the imperial government. It was their machinations, rather than lack of will or of resources, which the author would have us believe were responsible for the unconscionable delay in implementing the royal decree.

Opposition During the Reigns of Xerxes and Artaxerxes (Ezra 4:6–24)

Y. **Aharoni,** *The Land of the Bible,* 358; P. S. **Alexander,** "Remarks on Aramaic Epistolography in the Persian Period," *JSS* 23, 1978, 155–170; G. G. **Cameron,** *Persepolis Treasury Tablets,* Chicago, 1945; W. **Eilers,** *Iranische Beamtennamen,* 5–43; J. A. **Fitzmyer,** "Some Notes on Aramaic Epistolography," *JBL* 93, 1974, 201–225; K. **Galling,** "Kronzeugen des Artaxerxes?" *ZAW* 63, 1951, 66–74; H. H. **Grosheide,** "Een geschrift van Tabeel?" *GTT* 50, 1950, 71–79; A. C. **Hervey,** "The Chronology of Ezra iv. 6–23," *The Expositor* 4/8, 1893, 50–63; A. **van Hoonacker,** "Néhémie et Esdras, une nouvelle hypothèse sur la chronologie de l'époque de la restauration," *Le Muséon* 9, 1890, 151–178; W. Th. **In der Smitten,** *Esra,* 105–148; R. G. **Kent,** "Old Persian Texts," *JNES* 4, 1945, 228; J. J. **Koopmans,** "Die eerste Aramese deel van het Boek Ezra 4:7–6:19," *GTT* 55, 1955, 142–160; C. **Kuhl,** "Die 'Wiederaufnahme'—ein literarkritisches Prinzip?" *ZAW* 66, 1952, 1–11; J. **Liver,** "The Problem of the Order of the Kings of Persia in the Books of Ezra and Nehemiah," *Studies,* 263–276 (Heb.); E. **Meyer,** *Die Entstehung des Judentums,* 12–41, 54–59; J. **Morgenstern,** "Jerusalem—485 B.C.," *HUCA* 27, 1956, 101–179; 28, 1957, 15–47; 31, 1960, 1–29; V. **Pavlovský,** "Die Chronologie der Tätigkeit Esdras. Versuch einer neuen Lösung," *Bib* 38, 1957, 428–456; A. F. **Rainey,** "The Satrapy 'Beyond the River,'" *AJBA* 1, 1969, 51–78; H. H. **Schaeder,** *Iranische Beiträge* I, 14–17, 212–225; *Esra der Schreiber,* 27–28; C. C. **Torrey,** *Ezra Studies,*

140–207; H. C. **Trumbull**, *The Covenant of Salt*, New York, 1899; G. E. **Wright**, *Shechem, The History of a Biblical City*, London, 1965, 167–169.

4:6 During the reign of Ahasuerus, at the beginning of his reign, they lodged a complaint in writing against the inhabitants of Judah and Jerusalem.

[7]In the days of Artaxerxes, Tabeel and his colleagues,[a] in accord with[b] Mithredath, wrote to Artaxerxes king of Persia. The letter was written in Aramaic and translated.[c] What follows is in Aramaic.[d]

[8]Rehum the chancellor and Shimshai the secretary wrote a letter concerning[e] Jerusalem to Artaxerxes the king as follows:

[9]From Rehum the chancellor and Shimshai the secretary, together with their colleagues the judges,[f] legates, officials, Persians,[g] men of Erech, Babylonians, men of Susa, that is, Elamites, [10]and the other peoples whom the great and esteemed Osnappar had deported and resettled in the city of Samaria and elsewhere in the Trans-Euphrates satrapy:[h]

[11]This is a copy of the letter which they sent to him:

"To King Artaxerxes: your servants, the men of the Trans-Euphrates satrapy, send greetings:[i]

[12]"Be it known to the king that the Jews who came up from you to us have arrived in Jerusalem and are rebuilding that wicked and rebellious city. They are completing the walls and reinforcing the foundations.[j]

[13]"Be it therefore known to the king that if this city is rebuilt and its walls completed, they will pay no tribute, tax, or duty,[k] with the result that the royal interests will certainly[l] suffer harm. [14]Now, since we have eaten of the salt of the palace, it is not seemly for us to be witness to the king's dishonor; therefore we have sent word to inform the king, [15]so that search may be made in the annals of your predecessors. You will discover in these annals and ascertain that this city is a rebellious city, harmful to kings and provinces, and that sedition has been going on in it[m] from ancient times; that is why this city was destroyed. [16]We therefore make known to the king that if this city is rebuilt and its walls completed, it will result in your having no possessions left to you in the Trans-Euphrates satrapy."

[17]The king replied with the following decree: "To Rehum the chancellor, Shimshai the secretary, and the rest of their colleagues who reside in Samaria and elsewhere in the Trans-Euphrates satrapy, greetings. [18]The letter which you sent to me has been read

clearly in my presence. [19]Pursuant to my orders, search has been made, and it has been found that from of old this city has been guilty of insurrection against kings, and that rebellion and sedition have been going on in it. [20]Moreover, powerful kings were over Jerusalem and controlled the entire region beyond the Euphrates, and tribute, tax, and duty were paid to them. [21]Therefore issue a decree that these men are to desist. The city is not to be rebuilt until a decree is issued by me. [22]Be careful not to neglect your duty in this matter, lest there be further damage to the royal interests."

[23]When a copy of the decree of King Artaxerxes was read in the presence of Rehum the chancellor,[n] Shimshai the secretary, and their colleagues, they went with all haste to the Jews in Jerusalem and forcibly compelled them to desist.

[24]Then work on the house of God ceased, and it remained suspended down to the second year of the reign of Darius king of Persia.

a. Lit., "the rest of his colleagues."
b. *bišlām*, from Aram. "peace," "accord," rather than a personal name. See commentary.
c. MT reads, "and he wrote the letter written in Aramaic," which is impossible. $k^e t\bar{a}b$, Aram., should be read as a gloss on the unfamiliar Old Persian loanword *ništ^{e}vān*.
d. An editorial note referring to 4:8–6:18; cf. Dan. 2:4.
e. Or "against" *('al)*.
f. Reading *dayyānayyā'* for *dînāyē'*.
g. MT has *'^{a}pārsāyē'* by dittography.
h. MT adds k^e'*enet*, "and now," the formula for beginning the substance of a letter after the salutation (see C. C. Torrey 1897, 166–168).
i. "Send greetings" supplied; *ûk^e'enet* belongs to the following verse.
j. MT has past tense, but vs. 13 and 16 require the imperfect, as translated here (cf. Vulg.).
k. "Tribute" is probably correct for *mindāh* (cf. Akk. *mandattu*), but the meaning assigned to $b^e l\hat{o}$ (cf. Akk. *biltu?*) and $h^a l\bar{a}k$ (cf. Akk. *ilku?*) is less certain.
l. *'app^{e}tôm* could also be translated "finally," "in the end," from Old Persian *apatam-am;* for a quite different derivation see W. F. Albright, *JBL* 40, 1921, 114–115. C. C. Torrey (1910, 175, and 1954, xiv) derives the word from the Gk. *epithēsis*, "impost," giving the meaning "and the royal impost will suffer damage."
m. Lit., "they have been doing sedition in it."
n. MT omits "the chancellor" *(b^e'ēl-ṭ^e'ēm).*

[4:6] Ezra 4:6–23 deals with opposition during the reigns of Xerxes (486–465) and Artaxerxes I (465–423). As already noted, there is no need to conclude that the author was confused about the order of the early Achaemenids. The successive mention of Cyrus and Darius at 4:5 suggested continuing the story of opposition into the next two reigns, even though it involved introducing another topic, that of the rebuilding of the city and wall, and necessitated a circuitous return to the restoration of the temple under Darius—beginning at 4:24 which is a "repetitive resumption" of 4:5. Ahasuerus *('ᵃḥašvērôš),* by some earlier scholars identified with Cambyses or Cyaxares, is certainly Xerxes *(Khšayāršæ).* His first regnal year would correspond to late 486 and early 485. This notice gives the impression of being a summary of a fuller account which would presumably have given us the names of the authors of the complaint and the reasons for it, information which C may have felt it advisable to suppress. In his first year Xerxes was occupied with Khabasha's revolt in Egypt, which was put down in 483. His early years were also taken up with revolts in Babylon led successively by Belsimanni and Shamash-eriba (484–482) which ended with the destruction of Babylon and the great esagila sanctuary. Henceforth Babylon existed as a satrapy distinct from Abar-nahara. This administrative reorganization may point to disturbances in the west also, including the province of Yehud, which may in turn have provided the occasion or pretext for accusations of complicity with or sympathy for the rebels. If, however, the chronological indication is to be taken literally, one would have to think rather of the Egyptian revolt which was already under way when Xerxes came to the throne. But the hypothesis of active involvement leading to widespread destruction in Judah and Jerusalem, proposed in its most extreme form by Morgenstern, is unfounded. The allusion to the restoration of the temple in Ezra's prayer (Ezra 9:9) is retrospective, and the archaeological evidence turns out, on closer inspection, to be either uncertain or nonexistent. The date of the destruction of the early postexilic settlement at Bethel is disputed, Gibeon provides no clear indication at all, and Shechem, where level V is said to have ended about 480, was not in Judah (see Wright; P. W. Lapp, *BA* 28, 1965, 6–10; L. A. Sinclair, *BA* 27, 1964, 60–62).

[7] 1 Esd. 2:12 lumps together the names in vs. 7 and 8 and, for good measure, adds Beelteemos, an obvious misunderstanding of the Aramaic *bᵉ'ēl-ṭᵉ'ēm,* meaning the one who issues decrees, i.e., the chancellor. The letter of Tabeel is, however, distinct from that of Rehum and associates. We know nothing about it but may assume, from the context, that it was unfavorable. If the proposed reading of *bišlām* is correct (see textual note b), it would appear that this Tabeel wrote to Artaxerxes *('Artaḥšaśtā')* with the approval of Mithredath,

clearly a different person from the treasurer of Ezra 1:8, and presumably a highly placed satrapal official with a common Persian name. The so-called "Tabeel hypothesis," proposed by Klostermann and argued at length by Schaeder (1930b, 14–27), holds that the entire Aramaic source (4:8–6:18) was composed as an apologia by the Jew Tabeel who, to make his point, quoted the letter of Rehum and the king's reply, concluding with a survey of earlier opposition down to the time of Xerxes. On this supposition, however, we would have to conclude that the tactic was remarkably inept since (1) the argument from the early history of Judah as endemically rebellious is not addressed; (2) the rebuilding and fortification of a city is an entirely different matter from the rebuilding of a temple; and (3) to quote the king's letter back to him would have been an unprecedented and probably suicidal act of folly. Besides, the resumptive verse 4:24 raises suspicions about the unity of the Aramaic section, a unity which at the very least cannot simply be assumed.

The name Tabeel (also at Isa. 7:6) means "God is good," or perhaps "God is my good," and is the Aramaic near-equivalent of Tobiah. While it is impossible to disprove the identity of the writer with the Ammonite opponent of Nehemiah (Neh. 2:10, 19; 3:35 [4:3], etc.; see B. Mazar 1957), it would be imprudent to assume it. The letter was written in Aramaic, the diplomatic lingua franca of the Persian empire, and translated into Persian (v. 8). The language of this verse suggests that it may have originally belonged to the Aramaic source *(bišlām, kᵉnôtāv* [Qere], *'al, kᵉtāb, ništᵉvān).*

[8–11] Here we have the problem of two, if not three, introductions to the letter accusing the Jews of seditious intent. While it is possible that vs. 9–10 have been interpolated (Torrey et al.), it is more likely that the duplication reflects the practice of writing the name of the sender and the recipient, sometimes accompanied by a brief résumé of the contents, on the outside of the papyrus scroll (for examples see the Arsham collection published by G. R. Driver in 1957). In its present context, however, v. 8 is a simple narrative statement, and vs. 9–10, which contain no verb, do not identify the recipient. We would therefore either have to supply a verb or take these verses to be a simple list of senders (as NEB and this translation). The first of these is Rehum, a satrapal official in the Samaria province. The Aramaic title *bᵉ'ēl-tᵉ'ēm* corresponds to Old Persian *framānakara (farmānkara),* one who gives orders or issues edicts (e.g., *AP* 26:4, 8), a high civilian rather than military official, hence "chancellor" rather than "governor" (RSV). As a highly placed official, the secretary or scribe *(sāpar),* was responsible for drafting official correspondence, translating into and from Aramaic, registering land for purposes of taxation, and so on. Such scribes were employed at satrapal courts (Herodotus 3.128) and provincial centers (*AP* 17:1, 6). Their activities are well attested at Elephantine (see Porten 1968, 55–57, 192–197). The letter offers no support for the *sāpar* as royal investigator, a sort of political commissar (*pace* R. A. Bowman 1954, 600). The other titles of officeholders are unclear. '*aparsatkāy* (Old Persian *fraštaka*) appears to mean legate or envoy (Eilers, 40; Porten 1968, 52 n. 93). *ṭarpᵉlāy* is unattested, but has been interpreted as a gentilic referring to Tripoli in Syria (K. Galling, *VT* 4, 1954, 418–422; other explanations in Eilers, 39–40, and H. Torczyner, *BJPES* 14, 1947/48, 1, 6). Interestingly, Persian officials are also frequently accompanied by "colleagues" in the Elephantine papyri (e.g., *AP* 6:6; 17:1), perhaps part of a system of checks and balances. The ethnic designations are explained with reference to a settlement of foreigners in the Samaria region by Osnappar, understood by some Greek versions as Shalmaneser but more probably Asshurbanipal (668–c. 627). While this particular deportation is unattested, it may have followed Asshurbanipal's suppression of a rebellion in Babylon in 648 or his defeat of a coalition of Elamites and Persians a few years later (see A. Malamat, *IEJ* 3, 1953, 28–29). The extension to the entire satrapy, here and in the superscription following, is transparently tendentious, with a view to strengthening the case against the Judeans.

[12–16] The wording of the opening sentence would more naturally refer to an aliyah during the reign of Artaxerxes I Long Hand (465–424) rather than to the return under Cyrus. In all probability, Ezra and his caravan arrived in Jerusalem in the seventh year of this reign (458) and Nehemiah thirteen years later (445). The allusion could not be to the latter, who received personal authorization from the king to rebuild the city. In his confessional prayer Ezra says that by the good grace of the Persian kings, they had been able to build the temple and had been given a *gādēr* in Judah and Jerusalem (Ezra 9:9). This has sometimes been taken to refer to the rebuilding of the city wall, but *gādēr*, more commonly translated "fence" or something of the sort, is an odd way of referring to a city wall, especially since it protected not just Jerusalem but the entire province. The allusion is therefore retrospective, and *gādēr* is used metaphorically of the protection afforded the province by the Persian government from the time of Cyrus (see on 9:9).

Another possibility is suggested by the report of Hanani to his brother Nehemiah in the twentieth year of the reign that the wall had been broken down and its gates burnt (Neh. 1:3). Since the natural assumption is that this had happened quite recently—it was news to

Nehemiah—the action of the authorities in Samaria may have taken place shortly before Nehemiah's mission (in 446, according to In der Smitten, 105, 147–149). In that case the correspondence could have been occasioned by the revolt of Megabyzus, satrap of Abar-nahara, some three years before Nehemiah's mission, which would also explain why the complaint was lodged by a provincial official without reference to the governor of the satrapy. That the king reversed his decision soon after at the request of Nehemiah does not rule out this possibility, especially since the revolt was of brief duration and Megabyzus won his way back into favor. Reversal is also contemplated in the king's reply (Ezra 4:21).

It is difficult to know precisely what was happening in Jerusalem. The verbs in v. 12 are in the past tense, but it transpires from what follows that the rebuilding of the wall was not yet complete. It is also unclear what they were alleged to be doing with the foundations *('uššayyā')*. The verbal form *yaḥîṭû* is found only here. Here too the syntax requires the past tense, and therefore the stem *yḥṭ* (Rosenthal, *Aramaic Grammar*, par. 178) rather than *ḥṭṭ* (dig) or *ḥyṭ* (inspect, survey, as G. R. Driver, *JTS* 32, 1931, 364, followed by NEB). But the meaning assigned in our translation is quite uncertain. Whatever it was they were doing, the anticipated consequences were that tribute and other taxes levied on the province would be withheld, an act tantamount to rebellion. The writers claim that they are obliged to act by virtue of their oath of allegiance as imperial officials. Eating the salt of the palace may, by analogy with Israelite practice (Lev. 2:13; Num. 18:19; 2 Chron. 13:5), indicate an oath ratified by partaking in common of a meal seasoned with salt (cf. *synalizomenos,* Acts 1:4). The annals to be consulted would be those of the Assyrian and Babylonian kings, for the Achaemenids claimed to be their legitimate successors. These annals contained accounts of rebellions in Judah and expeditions mounted against it, including the one which resulted in the capture of Jerusalem in 598/7 (*ANET,* 288, 563–564). The claim that the entire satrapy would be in jeopardy if the city were to be fortified as a prelude to rebellion (cf. Neh. 2:19) may appear at first sight a patent exaggeration. If, however, we bear in mind the critical situation which developed during the reign at that end of the empire, the claim would not have seemed incredible anytime between the outbreak of the Inaros rebellion in Egypt, backed by powerful Athenian land and sea forces, in 460, and the rebellion of the satrap Megabyzus about 448 B.C.E.

[17–22] Since it is unlikely that the firman was addressed to the entire satrapy, or even to the associates of Rehum residing throughout the satrapy, we may assume that "elsewhere in the Trans-Euphrates satrapy" (vs. 10, 17) is an editorial expansion. The same for the allusion to the Davidic-Solomonic empire in v. 20, which is irrelevant to the purpose of the decree and reflects a Judean perspective (cf. Ps. 72:8) rather than the result of research in the royal annals of Mesopotamia, which, to our knowledge, contain not even a passing allusion to the United Monarchy. The reading of the letter "clearly" *(m**pāraš)* in the king's presence implies translation into Persian by a royal scribe (cf. 4:7; Neh. 8:8), since we cannot assume that Artaxerxes knew Aramaic. Unlike "the laws of the Medes and the Persians, which cannot be revoked" (Dan. 6:8; cf. Esth. 1:19; 8:8), the decree allows for a future abrogation (v. 21b, absent from 1 Esdras). While this is historically quite credible, as we have seen, we cannot exclude the possibility of another editorial touch, anticipating the permission given Nehemiah to rebuild the city and its defenses (Neh. 2:8).

[23] The authorities wasted no time in implementing the firman by military intervention, a point made more explicit at 1 Esd. 2:30. It would be natural to suppose that the intervention resulted not only in stopping the work but also destroying what had been done, resulting in the situation as described by Hanani (Neh. 1:3).

[24] There is a verbal link with the preceding verse—"compelled them to desist" *(baṭṭēlû,* v. 23), "the work . . . ceased and remained suspended" *(b**ṭēlat, vah**vāt bāṭ**lā',* v. 24)—but the initial "then" *(bē'dayin)* cannot imply direct narrative sequence, for the subject is the entirely different one of the building of the temple. The verse, then, takes up again, with overlap, the narrative interrupted earlier (4:5). One disadvantage of this narrative technique, sometimes called "repetitive resumption," is that we learn nothing about the period from early in the reign of Cyrus, through the entire reign of Cambyses, to the second year of Darius. We also lack information on how the problem created by the opposition was resolved sufficiently to allow for a new start. This resumptive verse, or at least its second half (24b), must be from C, who could have taken the date from Hag. 1:1.

Resumption of Work During the Reign of Darius (Ezra 5:1–2)

P. R. Ackroyd, "Two Old Testament Historical Problems of the Early Persian Period," *JNES* 17, 1958, 13–27; W. A. M. Beuken, *Haggai-Sacharja 1–8,* Assen, 1967; K.-M. Beyse, *Serubbabel und die Königserwartungen der Propheten Haggai und Sacharja,* Stuttgart, 1972; R. A. Mason, "The Purpose of the 'Editorial Framework' of the Book of Haggai," *VT* 27, 1977, 413–421; A. **Petitjean,** *Les oracles du Proto-Zacharie. Un programme de restauration pour la communauté juive après l'exil,* Paris, 1969.

> 5:1 The prophets Haggai[a] and Zechariah son of Iddo prophesied against[b] the Jews in Judah and Jerusalem in the name of the God of Israel;[c] ²whereupon Zerubbabel son of Shealtiel and Jeshua son of Jozadak set to work and began to build the house of God which is in Jerusalem, and with them were the prophets of God supporting them.

a. MT adds $n^e\underline{b}\hat{\imath}yy\bar{a}'h,$ "the prophet," following Hag. 1:1, 12; 2:1, 10; absent from 1 Esd. 6:1.

b. *'al* could also mean "about," but see the following note.

c. MT adds $^a l\hat{e}h\hat{o}n,$ "against them," absent from 1 Esd. 6:1. It is unclear to which antecedent it refers, since it could also be translated "over them"; but absence of the relative pronoun suggests a gloss, the purpose of which was to clarify the sense of $'al\text{-}y^e\hat{h}\hat{u}\underline{d}\bar{a}y\bar{e}'.$

Reviewing once again the logic of C's narrative which incorporates the Aramaic material: the first stage of temple building occurred during the reign of Cyrus (3:1–13) when it was interrupted and remained in abeyance until the second year of Darius. At that time it was resumed with prophetic support, then delayed again by Tattenai's intervention, then resumed once more and completed in the sixth year of the reign (6:14–15). The resumptive verse 4:24 which links with 4:5, and 6:14 which links with 5:1–2, serve to maintain the narrative flow. The Aramaic material may have been excerpted from a more extensive history of the restoration and then incorporated, with editorial adjustments, into the work. With the exception of the finale, the service of dedication (6:16–18), there is, however, little of C's own characteristic language and idiom in it, and we would not be justified in concluding that the Hebrew narrative 3:1–4:6 was translated from this source. The section dealing with events under Darius has connections with Haggai and Zechariah 1–8, especially the editorial framework of these collections of sayings. Its theological character is much in evidence here: divine intervention, the role of the prophet, past infidelities, etc. Conspicuously absent, however, are messianic expectations associated with Zerubbabel, and the completion of their work is ascribed not to the latter but to the elders.

Zechariah is the son of Iddo here and his grandson at Zech. 1:1. If "son" is to be taken literally, the same persons may be named in the list of priests at Neh. 12:16. As a priestly name Iddo is elsewhere attested (e.g., Ezra 8:17). Both names—Haggai and Zechariah— occur several times in the Elephantine papyri (*ḥgy* at *AP* 12:5 and nine other times; *zkryh* at *AP* 5:5 and six other times). The implication that these prophets castigated their Judean contemporaries for delay in getting the temple built is confirmed by the prophecies themselves, in notable contrast to the Hebrew narrative 3:1–4:5. The designation "the God of Israel" is characteristic of the Aramaic material (6:14; 7:15; cf. 1 Chron. 5:26) but also occurs in the Hebrew narrative, usually in the form "YHVH the God of Israel" (1:3; 3:2; 4:1, 3). Zerubbabel and Jeshua are here responsible for undertaking the work, but at its completion their place is taken by the elders (6:14). Since it is unlikely that the omission of the names is accidental, they must have disappeared from the scene some time between 520 and 515. Whether they both died or were removed by the Persians for political reasons cannot be determined. The messianic expectations attested in Haggai (2:6–7, 20–23) may well have been the occasion for the removal of Zerubbabel. The "prophets of God" who lent their support were not necessarily restricted to Haggai and Zechariah (cf. Zech. 7:3; 8:9). The support was presumably moral, as Josephus states explicitly (*Ant.* 11.4–5), and may have had political implications of the kind just described.

As noted earlier, the Aramaic source does not explain what made it possible for the work of rebuilding to be resumed in Darius' second year. One factor may have been the arrival of new immigrants from Babylonia, perhaps as a result of the suppression of the two revolts in that region during the critical period of Darius' struggle for control (522–520). Zechariah, who may have been one of those immigrants (cf. Neh. 12:16), seems to appeal to Babylonian Jews to get out (Zech. 2:11 [6]). He also reports a ceremonial crowning of Zerubbabel, an event made possible by the financial backing of wealthy new arrivals from Babylon (6:9–14; in the present state of the text the high priest Joshua has replaced Zerubbabel).

Intervention of Tattenai and His Letter to Darius (Ezra 5:3–17)

P. S. Alexander, *JSS* 23, 1978, 155–170; F. I. Anderson, "Who Built the Second Temple?" *ABR* 6, 1958, 1–35; R. A. Bowman, *Aramaic Ritual Texts from Persepolis,* Chicago, 1970, 44–45, 73; and " '*eben g*ᵉ*lāl—aban galālu* (Ezra 5:8; 6:4)," in I. T. Naamani and D. Rudavsky (eds.), *Doron: Hebraic Studies,* New York, 1965, 64–74; P.-E. Dion, "Les types épistolaires hébréo-araméens jusqu'au temps de Bar-Kokhbah," *RB* 96, 1979, 544–579; M. Dunand, "Byblos, Sidon, Jérusalem. Monuments apparentés des temps achéménides," *VTSup.* 17, 1969, 64–70; J. A. Fitzmyer, *JBL*

93, 1974, 201–225; K. **Galling,** "Von Nabonid zu Darius," *ZDPV* 70, 1954, 4–32; *Studien,* 32–60; A. **Gelston,** "The Foundations of the Second Temple," *VT* 16, 1966, 232–235; P. **Joüon,** "Le Mot 'uššarnā' dans Esdras 5,3(9)," *Bib* 22, 1941, 38–40; J. J. **Koopmans,** "Die eerste Aramese deel van het Boek Ezra 4:7–6:19," *GTT* 55, 1955, 142–160; E. **Meyer,** *Entstehung des Judentums,* 41–46; S. **Mowinckel,** " 'uššarnā' Ezr. 5:3,9," *StTh* 19, 1965, 130–135; A. T. **Olmstead,** "Tattenai, Governor of 'Across the River,' " *JNES* 3, 1944, 46; A. F. **Rainey,** "The Satrapy Beyond the River," *AJBA* 1, 1969, 51–78; H. H. **Schaeder,** *Iranische Beiträge* I, 212–225; S. **Smith,** "Timber and Brick or Masonry Construction," *PEQ* 73, 1941, 5–6; E. **Stern,** *Material Culture,* 61–67; H. C. **Thompson,** "A Row of Cedar Beams," *PEQ* 92, 1960, 57–63; C. C. **Torrey,** "The Aramaic Portions of Ezra," *AJSL* 1907/08, 209–281; C. G. **Tuland,** " 'Uššayyā' and 'Uššarnâ'," *JNES* 17, 1958, 269–275; A. **Ungnad,** "Keilinschriftliche Beiträge zum Buch Esra und Ester," *ZAW* 58, 1940/ 41, 240–243.

5:3 At that time Tattenai, governor of the Trans-Euphrates satrapy, Shethar-bozenai, and their colleagues came to them and addressed them as follows: "Who gave you a decree of authorization to rebuild this house and finish its roofing?" [4]They then asked them:[a] "What are the names of the men engaged in building this edifice?" [5]However, their God looked kindly on the Jewish elders,[b] for they did not force them to suspend the work while the report was being sent to Darius and the letter with his reply was being returned.

[6]This is a copy of the letter which Tattenai, governor of the Trans-Euphrates region, and Shethar-bozenai and his colleagues, the inspectors of the Trans-Euphrates region, sent to King Darius. [7]They sent him a report in which was written as follows:

"To King Darius, all greetings!

[8]"Be it known to the king that we went to the province of Judah, to the house of the great God. We discovered that it was being rebuilt by the Jewish elders in the city of Jerusalem[c] with worked stones, and timber was being set in its walls. The work was being done with all diligence, and it was making good progress under their direction. [9]We then inquired of these elders, addressing them as follows: 'Who gave you a decree of authorization to rebuild this house and finish its roofing?' [10]For your information, we also asked them for their names, with a view to recording the names of the men who were the leaders.

[11]"Their reply was as follows: 'We are the servants of the God of heaven and earth, and we are rebuilding the house that was built a great many years ago; it was a great king of Israel who built and completed it. [12]But because our ancestors provoked the God of

heaven to anger, he delivered them over to Nebuchadnezzar the Chaldean, king of Babylon, who tore down this house and carried off the people into exile in Babylon. [13]However, in the first year that Cyrus ruled as king of Babylon, King Cyrus issued an edict that this house should be rebuilt. [14]As for the gold and silver vessels which Nebuchadnezzar had removed from the temple of Jerusalem and brought to the temple of Babylon, King Cyrus took them out of the temple of Babylon and consigned them to a man named Sheshbazzar, whom he had appointed governor. [15]He said to him, "Take these vessels and go, place them in the temple which is in Jerusalem. Let the house of God be rebuilt on its original site."[d] [16]This person Sheshbazzar then came and laid the foundations of the house of God which is in Jerusalem; and from then until now the work of building has continued but is not yet finished.'

[17]"Therefore, if it please the king, let search be made in the royal archives there in Babylon to ascertain whether King Cyrus issued an edict for the house of God in Jerusalem to be rebuilt, and may the king be pleased to send us his ruling in this matter."

a. Reading *'ᵃmarû* for MT *'ᵃmarnā'*, "we said," perhaps a slip occasioned by the use of first person in the letter (5:9).
b. Lit., "the eye of their God was on the Jewish elders."
c. "We discovered . . . Jerusalem" with 1 Esd. 6:8, necessitated by the context.
d. Lit., "in its place," *'al-'atrēh;* cf. *AP* 32:8: *lmbnyh b'trh kzy hyh lqdmn,* "to rebuild it in its place, as it was before."

The Aramaic account of events under Darius (5:1–6:18) had the purpose of legitimating the building in the eyes of the authorities: the Cyrus rescript is mentioned or quoted twice (5:15; 6:2–5), it is stated that the task was undertaken by royal appointees on command of the central government (5:14; 6:7), and prayers for the royal family were incorporated into the liturgy (6:10). Both the construction and the day-to-day operation of the temple were to be financed out of the royal treasury and satrapal funds (6:4, 8–9), and future hostile acts were prohibited under the most severe penalties (6:11–12). Unlike, C, this source is not concerned to explain the delay in completing the project; it states quite simply that the Cyrus rescript was acted on at once and that the work continued without interruption from then to the present (5:16)—a statement which the elders, if they made it, must have known to be untrue. Not surprisingly, Zerubbabel's role is not emphasized, if indeed it was even mentioned in the original form of the document. The reply of Darius refers only to a governor, unnamed, and the Jewish elders (6:7), and elsewhere in this source it is the latter who are the leaders and whose names were presumably enclosed with the letter (5:5, 8, 9; 6:8, 14).

The theological character of this account has already been noted. The work prospered because it was done under divine guidance (5:5, 8; 6:14) and with prophetic support (5:1–2; 6:14). The God for whom the temple was destined is the God of Israel who is the great God, God of heaven and earth. Especially noteworthy is the Deuteronomic designation "the God who has caused his name to dwell there" (6:12). The history is interpreted in traditional fashion, after the manner of the Deuteronomic historian: the destruction of Solomon's temple was due not to the weakness of Israel's God but to religious infidelity which provoked his anger. The great turning point, the moment of grace, was the accession of Cyrus and his edict commanding the restoration of the temple and its worship.

The Tattenai correspondence served to answer the charges contained in the Rehum letter, especially its interpretation of the history of Israel and the reason for the destruction of Jerusalem (4:15; 5:12). It also presents the Jews in their relations with the central government in a quite different light, a fact which may help to explain the present order of the material.

[5:3–5] The inspection would have taken place between the second and the sixth year of Darius and, since the work seems to have been well advanced, nearer to the end than to the beginning of that period. But the upheavals of the first two years of the reign were still close enough to warrant careful monitoring of new initiatives of this kind. (We may discount Josephus' point that the building looked more like a fortress than a temple, *Ant.* 11.89.) Tattenai, bearer of a Babylonian name *(ta-at-tan-ni,* perhaps from *nabu-tattanu-uṣur),* is known from a cuneiform text to have been governor of Abarnahara (Ebir-nari of the Assyrians) in 502, but this region did not form a satrapy distinct from Babylon until the reign of Xerxes. A contract tablet attests that in the early years of Darius the satrap of Babylon and Abar-nahara *(pihat babili u ebir nari)* was a certain Ushtanni, who was therefore Tattenai's immediate superior in the imperial administration. The former resided in Babylon, the latter probably in Damascus. The two are therefore not to be identified *(pace* B. Meissner, *ZAW* 17, 1897, 191–192, and Bertholet 1902, 20). Shethar-bozenai is a corruption of a Persian name, probably Satibarzana (cf. *AP* 5:16 and the Shethar of Esth. 1:14). His office of secretary or scribe corresponds to that of Shimshai in relation to Rehum (4:8). There is nothing to suggest hostile intent in this tour of inspection, for the work was allowed to continue while confirmation of the building permit was being sought.

The technical term *'uššarnā'* (also v. 9), here translated "roofing," was already a matter of speculation at the time of the Greek versions (LXX has *chorēgia,* supplies, apparatus, and 1 Esd. 6:4 has *stegē,* roof or ceiling). Its occurrence in the Elephantine papyri is not very helpful since in no case does the context place its meaning beyond doubt. It is used for something needed to repair a boat (*AP* 26:3, 5, 9, 21), for part of an altar (*AP* 27:18), for something combustible which was destroyed together with the doors and roof of the temple at Jeb (*AP* 30:11), for something, presumably made of wood, which could be put on or into a house *(BMAP 3:23: wkl 'šrn zy yhkn 'l byt' zk).* The translation given here is therefore only one of several possibilities.

The list of names was presumably forwarded with the letter. Since it contained only those of the elders, it has no connection with the list of Ezra 2.

[6–10] The account of the inspection breaks off rather abruptly, probably because the author realized that the information would be repeated in the letter. Following normal epistolary style, the letter opens with a salutation, gives a brief account of action taken, with a verbatim report of the elders' reply, and finally requests a ruling. The salutation "every greeting" (*šᵉlāmā' kollā';* lit., "all peace") is probably an abbreviation of a more elaborate form as, for example, in *AP* 30:1–3: "the health *(šᵉlām)* of your lordship may the God of heaven seek after exceedingly at all times" (cf. also *AP* 41:1). Missing are the date and the names of the senders, generally written on the outside of the despatch. The colleagues are here identified more specifically as investigators or inspectors (*'ᵃparsᵉkāy,* from Old Persian *frasaka/patifrāsa;* see W. Eilers 1940, 5–43, and Porten 1968, 53–54), which should not be emended to "Persians."

It is interesting to observe that the writer of the letter expresses no opinion; he simply states the facts. The only additional information provided is that the temple was being built of worked stones and timber was being set in the walls. The term used for the type of stone, *'eben gᵉlāl,* has often been interpreted from the familiar stem as referring to stones which, on account of their weight, had to be rolled. More probably, however, they were ashlars (cf. Akk. *aban galāla* [*CAD* 5:11]; R. A. Bowman 1954, 610, has another explanation). The function of the wooden beams is less clear. We may have an anticipation of the injunction that the walls be built with three courses of ashlars and one of timber, a technique used in building Solomon's temple, probably aimed at countering the effects of earthquake (6:4; cf. 1 Kings 6:36; 7:12). But it could also refer to the crossbeams or rafters over which the roof would eventually be built.

[11–16] The reply of the elders is a carefully and subtly phrased piece of religious propaganda, quite apart from the question of its historical character. The essential component of the appeal to history in support of a petition has an interesting parallel in the letter written in 408 B.C.E. by the priests of Jeb to the governor of Judah after their temple had been destroyed. It too refers to the time when the temple was built and makes appropriate allusion to the beneficial effects of the Persian conquest (*AP* 30:13–14). The crux of the matter was the Cyrus edict which is paraphrased except for the command to return the temple vessels, which is quoted verbatim (vs. 13–15). The sequel is not, as at 1:10, the return of the vessels to their proper place, but the implementation of the permission to build, beginning with the laying of the foundations by Sheshbazzar (v. 16). If we read synoptically this Aramaic paraphrase, the version reportedly found at Ecbatana, also in Aramaic (6:2–5), and the Hebrew version with its connective narrative (1:1–11), we note that they have in common: the date, the rebuilding of the temple, and return of the sacred vessels. That all three are based on a historical text is entirely possible, though in no case is it reproduced verbatim and *in extenso*. It is also unlikely that the Hebrew version depends on the Aramaic or vice versa. Each of the three has its variations and amplifications. The Hebrew version adds permission to return and the command addressed to the local population to provide monetary assistance, additions probably suggested by the narrative context in which the quotation occurs. The list of vessels has the appearance of a genuine archival item (cf. *AP* 61 and 63), either preserved independently or attached to the edict. The Aramaic version adds the dimensions of the sanctuary and details of its construction, together with the important point that the operation is to be financed out of the royal treasury. It says nothing about Sheshbazzar. Peculiar to the Aramaic paraphrase is the addressing of the command to Sheshbazzar, governor *(peḥāh)* of Judah, who at once complied by laying the foundations. This, too, is in keeping with the apologetic intent of the elders' deposition. We cannot avoid the suspicion that the manner of alluding to Sheshbazzar—"one whose name was Sheshbazzar," "this (person) Sheshbazzar," was not meant to be complimentary. It has been observed (Clines 1984, 87–88) that both expressions are used of slaves in the papyri (e.g., *AP* 28:4, 11; *BMAP* 5:2; 8:7–8), which may imply that, for reasons about which we can only speculate, Sheshbazzar had become *persona non grata* to the Persian authorities. If this is so, it would help to explain the silence of Haggai and Zechariah on his contribution to the work of restoration.

The command addressed to Sheshbazzar to deposit the vessels retrieved from the great esagila sanctuary in Babylon (Herodotus 1.181–183) in the Jerusalem temple sounds contradictory, for the temple still remained to be built. The contradiction (made much of by Batten 1913, 137–138) does not, however, call for textual emendation. The way it is put may be confused, but the idea is clear enough: put the vessels in the temple once it has been built. On the role of Sheshbazzar, and related issues pertaining to the history of the province before Darius, we are at several removes from the *nuda facta historica*. We must take into account not only the obvious apologetic intent of the elders, but also the *Tendenz* of the author or editor of this part of the Aramaic section and of C himself. Of the real course of events we can have only few and uncertain glimpses.

The Cyrus Rescript Rediscovered (Ezra 6:1–5)

K. Galling, "Kyrusedikt und Tempelbau," *OLZ* 40, 1937, 473–478; A. H. J. Gunneweg, "Die aramäische und die hebräische Erzählung über die nachexilische Restauration—ein Vergleich," *ZAW* 94, 1982, 299–302; R. T. Hallock, "A New Look at the Persepolis Treasury Tablets," *JNES* 19, 1960, 90–100; E. Otto, *Die biographischen Inschriften der ägyptischen Spätzeit,* Leiden, 1954, 169–173; see also bibliography to 1:1–4.

6:1 Then King Darius issued a decree, and they searched in the archives where the treasures were stored[a] there in Babylon. [2]However, a scroll was found in Ecbatana, in the citadel, which is in the province of Media, on which was written the following: "A memorandum: [3]In his first year King Cyrus issued a decree: With respect to the house of God in Jerusalem, let that house be rebuilt, the place where sacrifices are offered and to which burnt offerings are brought.[b] Its height is to be sixty cubits and its breadth sixty cubits, [4]with three courses of worked stone and one course of wood.[c] The expenses are to be paid out of the royal treasury.[d] [5]Item: the gold and silver vessels of the house of God which Nebuchadnezzar removed from the temple which is in Jerusalem and brought to Babylon are to be restored and brought back to the temple which is in Jerusalem, each to its proper place. They are to be deposited[e] in the house of God."

a. Retaining MT *bêt siprayyā' dî ginzayyā'* on the assumption that the text alludes to documents with fiscal implications. Reversing the order of nouns brings it more into line with *bēt ginzayyā' dî malkā'* of 5:17 but is not otherwise an improvement.

b. Reading *'ešōhî* for *'uššôhî* with 1 Esd. 6:24, which sits better with the syntax of the sentence.

c. Reading *had,* one, for MT *hadat,* new; putting fresh (unseasoned) timber in the walls of a building would not be a particularly good idea. 1 Esd. 6:24, typically, keeps both *(kainou henos).*

d. Lit., "the royal palace" *(bêt malkā').*

e. Reading *yānḥat* for *taḥēt;* the change to the second person is unexpected (but see E. Bickerman 1946, 251).

The text of Darius' decree begins at v. 6 but it assumes that the Cyrus rescript has just been quoted, no doubt prefaced by the conventional prescript and salutation, with perhaps a word about its recovery. It was natural to assume that the rescript was filed in Babylon, capital of the satrapy to which Judah belonged—the fifth of the twenty into which Darius reorganized the empire (Herodotus 3.91). It was written on a rolled-up piece of leather or papyrus. (For its probable appearance see Kraeling, 1953, illustration XXI, or Porten 1968, plate 14a.) In general, however, the records of the early Achaemenids were written on clay tablets. Ecbatana (Aram. *'Aḥmᵉtā'*) is Hamadan, the Hagmatana of the Greeks, the Median capital captured by Cyrus in 550 which became the summer residence of the Persian kings on account of its high altitude and temperate climate (see Xenophon, *Anabasis* 3.5.15; *Cyropaedia* 8.6.22). The citadel of Ecbatana *(bîrtā';* Akk. *bîrtu)* is referred to by Herodotus (1.98).

The reply of Bigvai governor of Judah and Delaiah governor of Samaria to the request to rebuild the Elephantine temple destroyed by the Egyptians in 408 provides an interesting parallel: "Memorandum *(zkrn)* from Bigvai and Delaiah: Let it be an instruction to you in Egypt to say to Arsames about the house of the altar of the God of heaven which was built a long time ago, before Cambyses, in the fortress of Jeb, and which Waidrang, that reprobate, destroyed in the fourteenth year of king Darius (II): that it be rebuilt on its (original) site as it was before, in order that cereal offering and incense be offered on this altar, as was done previously" (*AP* 30; Cowley 1923, 123).

As noted earlier, the decree has in common with the Hebrew version the date, permission to rebuild, and return of the vessels. It differs from it in that there is no reference to a return from Babylon, and the expenses are to be defrayed from government funds rather than from the private sector. It also adds measurements and some details of construction. It is unnecessary to suppose that Cyrus issued two edicts with regard to Judah. Restoration of the sacred vessels implied that someone had to return, if only Sheshbazzar and an escort. It is in fact entirely possible that this is about all that happened in the period immediately following the imposition of the *pax Persica* in the west.

It was only natural that if the central government was footing the bill, it would have something to say about the dimensions of the building, if only to avoid a cost overrun. But the dimensions given here and in 1 Esdras are odd, to say the least. If we supply sixty cubits for the missing length, as for the First Temple (1 Kings 6:2), we have a perfect cube. This could then only be seen as a symbolic reference, as with the immense cube (one hundred and twenty cubits in length, breadth, and height) in which Utnapishtim survived the deluge (*Gilgamesh* 11.28–30, 57–59; A. Heidel, *The Gilgamesh Epic and Old Testament Parallels,* Chicago, 1946, 82 n. 173). The alternative would be to align it with 1 Kings 6:2—sixty cubits long, thirty high and twenty broad—but this necessitates rather drastic textual surgery. For the other details of construction see notes on 5:10. We saw earlier that the financing of local cults was a feature of Persian policy as, for example, in the Udjahorresnet inscription, lines 24–30, 43–45 (Otto; other examples in de Vaux 1937, 30–43). All the more remarkable, then, that nothing was done for almost two decades. On the sacred vessels see on 1:7–11 and 5:14–15.

Darius Replies (Ezra 6:6–12)

G. G. **Cameron**, *Persepolis Treasury Tablets,* Chicago, 1948, 12–13; "Persepolis Treasury Tablets Old and New," *JNES* 17, 1958, 161–176; E. **Meyer**, *Entstehung des Judentums,* 46–54; D. M. **Lewis**, *A Selection of Greek Historical Inscriptions to the End of the Fifth Century B.C.,* Oxford, 1969, 20–22; F. **Parente**, "Ezra 6.11. La pena comminata a chi altera l'editto di Dario," *Henoch* 1, 1979, 189–200; F. **Rundgren**, "Über einen juristischen Terminus bei Esra 6,6," *ZAW* 70, 1958, 209–215; J. **Teixidor**, "The Aramaic Text in the Trilingual Stele from Xanthus," *JNES* 37, 1978, 181–185; R. **de Vaux**, *AI,* 415–422.

6:6 "Now, Tattenai, governor of the Trans-Euphrates region, Shethar-bozenai and your colleagues,[a] the inspectors of the Trans-Euphrates region, keep away from them. 7Leave the governor of the Jews and the Jewish elders alone to continue their work[b] rebuilding that house of God on its original site. 8I also decree regarding what you are to do for these Jewish elders with respect to the rebuilding of that house of God: the expenses are to be paid in full to these men from the royal revenue deriving from the tribute of the Trans-Euphrates region, so that the work may not be brought to a standstill.[c] [9]Whatever is needed, whether steers, rams, or lambs for burnt offerings to the God of heaven, whether wheat, salt, wine, or oil, as the priests who are in Jerusalem dictate, let it be given them on a daily basis without delay, [10]that they may offer pleasing sacrifices to the God of heaven and pray for the well-being[d] of the king and his sons. [11]Item: I decree that if any person alters this edict, a beam shall be pulled from his house, he shall be impaled upright upon it,[e] and his house shall be turned into a midden.[f] [12]May the God who has caused his name to dwell there overthrow any king or people who may venture to alter this edict or destroy that house which is in Jerusalem. I, Darius, have so decreed. Let it be done with all diligence."

a. MT has "their colleagues," $k^e n\bar{a}v\bar{a}t^e h\hat{o}n$.
b. MT adds $b\hat{e}t$-$'^e l\bar{a}h\bar{a}' d\bar{e}k$ after $la'^a b\hat{i}dat$ by dittography, as is clear from the resulting syntactic disarray. 1 Esd. 6:27 does not repeat the phrase.
c. $d\hat{i}$-$l\bar{a}' l^e batt\bar{a}l\bar{a}'$, "so as not to make (it) cease," the verb referring to the work, not the payments; cf. LXX and Syr.
d. Lit., "life."
e. The meaning of $z^e q\hat{i}p yitm^e h\bar{e}' '^a l\bar{o}h\hat{i}$ is uncertain. Assuming the stem mh' = strike (cf. Dan. 2:34–35; 5:19 in Peal), we might translate "upright he shall be struck upon it," i.e., the offending party would be tied to a stake taken from his house and flogged. The context, however, favors the harsher alternative.
f. $n^e v\bar{a}l\hat{u}$, also Dan. 2:5 and 3:29 ($n^e v\bar{a}l\hat{i}$), of uncertain meaning, differently translated at 1 Esd. 6:32. The meaning given here is also found in Mishnaic Hebrew.

Such detailed stipulations regarding the cult of a local deity in a remote province are not in themselves historically implausible; witness the Gadatas inscription concerning the cult of Apollo in Magnesia (Lewis), the trilingual Xanthos inscription (Teixidor), and the so-called Passover Papyrus from Elephantine (*AP* 32). The incorporation of prayers for the royal family into the liturgy is also consistent with Persian practice (cf. the Cyrus cylinder [*ANET,* 316] and *AP* 30:25–26); the allusion would be to prayers accompanying the daily sacrifice, which may explain why the reply does not promise support of the festal liturgy. It is also possible that certain features may be explained by the employment of a Jewish scribe in the redaction of the letter, someone to whom could be attributed the Deuteronomic allusion to the residence of the divine name, the mention of sacrificial materials, perhaps also "this house of God" (four times). But the tone of the letter, with its enthusiastic and unconditional endorsement, cannot fail to arouse suspicion. Darius may conceivably have required that the day-to-day operation of the temple be financed out of satrapal revenues, but it is highly unlikely that the subsidy would be practically on demand. It is also worth noting that the sacrificial materials are listed in the order favored by C (cf. 1 Chron. 29:21; 2 Chron. 29:21, 32; cf. Ezra 6:17; 7:22; 8:35) and that the phrase "on a daily basis" *(yôm bᵉyôm)* is also characteristic of C (1 Chron. 12:22; 16:23; 2 Chron. 8:13; 24:11; 30:21). We must also ask whether Darius would have absolved a subject people in advance and in perpetuity of any wrongdoing, making use of sanctions to protect them from the consequences of possible future rebellion.

It would therefore not be hypercritical to conclude that the royal reply, with the preceding account of the successful archival search, is a free composition elaborated on the historical basis of a confirmation of the Cyrus rescript issued during the reign of Darius.

The injunction on Tattenai and his colleagues to "be distant from there" *(raḥîqîn hᵃvô min-tammāh)* is more peremptory than we would expect, especially in view of the objective and uncontentious nature of the inquiry. Moreover, it was clearly Tattenai's responsibility to monitor what was going on anywhere within his jurisdiction, and the central government would be highly unlikely to exempt any part of it from supervision. Use of the verb "be distant" *(rḥq)* has suggested a technical legal injunction, in the sense of the dismissal of a charge, by analogy with the deed of renunciation *(spr mrḥq)*, attested in the Elephantine papyri *(AP* 6:22; 8:25; cf. 13:7; 35:4; Rundgren). But the analogy does not fit the context, since Tattenai was neither making an accusation nor staking a claim; he was simply seeking confirmation of a building permit. Since there is no allusion to a governor in Tattenai's inquiry, the phrase "the governor of the Jews" in the reply may have been added; characteristically, 1 Esd. 6:27 goes on to identify this governor with "Zerubbabel, the servant of the Lord." The provision of animals and commodities for the daily sacrifice (for details see de Vaux) was, perhaps, entailed in the mandated prayers for the royal family. The summarizing phrase "pleasing sacrifices" *(nîḥôḥîn)*, corresponding to the Hebrew *rêaḥ nîḥôaḥ* (literally, "smell of appeasement"), is certainly of Jewish origin. The affixing of penalties or curses to be incurred by anyone tampering with an official document (decree, law, treaty) was routine in the ancient Near East; a similar example occurs in the Behistun inscription (par. 67) in the name of Darius' own deity, Ahura Mazda. Impaling was a Persian practice (e.g., Behistun, par. 32; Herodotus 3.159) inherited from the Assyrians (see, for example, the Lachish

reliefs [*ANEP,* 131; H. Shanks, *BAR* 10.2, 1984, 62]), generally
reserved for the most serious crimes, especially sedition and the
violation of treaty oaths. The treatment of the offender's house is
reminiscent of what happened to the temple of Baal in Samaria
during Jehu's reign (2 Kings 10:27). The decree ends with what is
in effect the king's signature, no doubt validated by the royal seal.

The Temple Finished and Dedicated (Ezra 6:13–18)

J. **Gray,** *I & II Kings,* London and Philadelphia, 1963, 215–219; F. X. **Kugler,** *Von
Moses bis Paulus,* Münster, 1922, 215; J. M. **Myers,** *II Chronicles,* Garden City,
1965, 31–41; H. G. M. **Williamson,** *Israel in the Book of Chronicles,* Cambridge,
1975, 87–130; *1 and 2 Chronicles,* Grand Rapids, 1982, 213–224.

6:13 Then Tattenai, governor of the Trans-Euphrates region, Shethar-bozenai, and their colleagues carried out with all diligence the
instructions which King Darius had sent them. [14]So the elders of
the Jews continued successfully with the building, aided by the
prophesying of Haggai[a] and Zechariah son of Iddo. They finished
building by command of the God of Israel and by command of
Cyrus,[b] Darius, and Artaxerxes king of Persia. [15]By the twenty-
third[c] of the month of Adar, in the sixth year of the reign of King
Darius, this house was completed. [16]Then the Israelites, priests,
Levites, and the rest of the exiles celebrated with joy the dedication
of this house of God. [17]At its dedication they sacrificed a hundred
steers, two hundred rams, four hundred lambs, together with
twelve he-goats as a sin offering on behalf of all Israel, corresponding to the number of the tribes of Israel. [18]They established the
priests in their divisions and the Levites in their sections for the
service of the house[d] of the God who is in Jerusalem, as prescribed
in the book of Moses.

a. Omitting "the prophet"; see 5:1.
b. In their own way the Masoretes have avoided the impression of parity between
   the two commands by different vocalization: *ta'am* for God's command, *t^e'ēm*
   for that of Cyrus.
c. With 1 Esd. 7:5 followed by Josephus, *Ant.* 11.4–7; MT has "third"; see
   further the commentary.
d. "of the house" added, following some OG readings and Syr.

[6:13–15] The prompt compliance of Tattenai and associates with
the decree confirms the impression that their intervention was not

inspired by hostile intent, in contrast to that of Rehum under Artaxerxes. The allusion to the two prophets who sustained the work forms an inclusion with 5:1, and the same stylistic feature may help to explain the unexpected reference to Artaxerxes (cf. 4:7–8 at the beginning of the Aramaic section). It seems to be suggested that prophetic support continued up to the time of completion, i.e., to the sixth year of Darius (515 B.C.E.). Since, however, the latest dated saying of Haggai is from November–December 520 (Hag. 2:10, 18), and that of Zechariah is from November–December 518 (Zech. 7:1), the allusion is more probably retrospective, in the sense that they provided the initial impetus. The rebuilding of the temple was therefore mandated by divine authority mediated through both prophecy and the secular arm. The author, then, accepts the possibility of a genuine religious life under foreign rule. We note again (cf. 5:5, 9) the absence of any allusion to Zerubbabel at this vital stage. In light of the author's, or his source's, political views, it is understandable if the hopes for emancipation focusing on Zerubbabel, which were thought to be contingent on the rebuilding of the temple (Hag. 2:6, 20–23; cf. Zech. 4:9–10; 6:9–14), were passed over in silence. At any rate, we are ignorant as to what happened to Zerubbabel between the beginning of the work in 520 and its completion about five years later.

The inclusion of Artaxerxes, the first of that name, serves to round out the Aramaic narrative. Here too it is unnecessary to suppose that the author was unfamiliar with the correct chronological order of these rulers. It also permitted a preview of that king's measures in favor of the Jerusalem temple and its cult (7:15–24; cf. 9:9), which were also in keeping with the divine command (7:23).

The date of completion is carefully noted. Adar (Akk. *adaru*) is the twelfth month of the Babylonian calendar, corresponding to February–March, and the sixth year of Darius is 515 B.C.E. MT has the third day of the month, and it has been widely accepted that this date would correspond to March 12, 515. According to a more adventurous calculation (Kugler), the third of Adar/March 12 of that year fell on a sabbath, which it is claimed would rule it out for the completion of the work. But even if the calculation is correct, analogy with the creation of the world in seven days concluding with Sabbath would raise a query. There are also too many problems with this kind of calculation to inspire confidence; in any case, an easier explanation is at hand. The date given in 1 Esdras and Josephus, the twenty-third, is to be preferred on textual grounds since it is easier to explain the loss of a digit in MT than the addition of one in 1 Esdras. It should also be noted that in his description of the dedication of Solomon's temple, C diverges from 1 Kings in one small but significant detail: the solemn assembly convened for the occasion is prolonged beyond the eight days of the festival to the twenty-third day of the month (2 Chron. 7:9–10; cf. 1 Kings 8:66). The later date also has the advantage of narrowing the gap between the completion of the work and the new year, in the first month of which Passover was celebrated. If the dedication service lasted a week, as did that of the First Temple (1 Kings 8:64–66), the gap would in fact be eliminated. We may observe, finally, that the Second Temple was completed about seventy years from the destruction of the First in 586. Here, too, we note a significant structuring element in Ezra 1–6, leading us back to the prophecy with which it all started. This history which begins with prophecy therefore ends with it.

[16–18] The description of the dedication ceremony has much in common with the liturgy at the beginning of the work (3:8–13): participation of priests, Levites, golah community; the temple as "the house of God"; the joy of the participants. In addition, everything is done according to the law of Moses (3:2, 4). Up to this point the Aramaic source has referred to the people as Jews (*yᵉhûdāyē*, 4:12, 23; 5:1, 5; 6:7–8, 14), the people of Judah (4:4), or the inhabitants of Judah and Jerusalem (4:6). Here, by contrast, the term *bᵉnê-yiśrā'ēl* is used, consisting in priests, Levites and the rest of the golah community (see on 1:4–5). This language is characteristic of C, for whom the returned exiles embodied the true Israel in continuity with the past. This paragraph, therefore, which is somewhat out of character with the rest of the Aramaic material, should be assigned to C, who was quite capable of writing in Aramaic. Its purpose is to round out the sequence of events in his source material. For him the founding of the temple and the reconstitution of the community belong together.

The number of animals sacrificed at the dedication is scanty compared with the veritable hecatomb at the dedication of Solomon's temple (1 Kings 8:63; 2 Chron. 7:5). The offering of twelve goats in expiation for the sins of all Israel, repeated after the arrival of Ezra (8:35), is based on priestly ritual (Lev. 4:22–26; 9:3; Ezek. 43:18–27), and specifically on the sin offering of tribal leaders as described in Num. 7, a later strand of the Priestly source. The twelve-tribe theme, first expressed in the genealogies (1 Chron. 2–8), appears often in Ezra (2:2; 8:24, 35). It is one way of saying that the historical Israel is now located in this particular group which has rediscovered its identity and links with the past after a long period of alienation. If the expiatory offering is read as a preparation for Passover, it would signify the cancellation of a long period of infidelity from the time of Josiah when the last great Passover was celebrated.

The setting up of the sacerdotal and Levitical orders is done according to the law of Moses. What the author means by "the law of Moses," "the book of Moses," and similar expressions is not easy to determine, but it at least included some of the priestly and ritual legislation, in this case such passages as Ex. 29 and Lev. 8. It comes as something of a surprise that no allusion is made to the activity of David as founder of the cult and its personnel (1 Chron. 23–26). The reason may be that the reorganization was in preparation for a Passover which, like that of Josiah, had to be carried out in conformity with Mosaic law (2 Chron. 35:6). It is hardly coincidence that the terms used here for the clerical divisions *(p*e*luggāh, maḥl*e*qāh)* occur together in C's account of Josiah's Passover (2 Chron. 35:4–5), and that both accounts speak of these dispositions as in function of "the service of the house of God" (cf. 2 Chron. 35:2).

The Great Passover (Ezra 6:19–22)

M. **Noth**, *US,* 145; B. **Porten**, *Archives from Elephantine,* 122–124, 128–132, 280–282, 311–314; J. B. **Segal**, *The Hebrew Passover from the Earliest Times to A.D. 70,* London, 1963; R. **de Vaux**, *AI,* 484–493.

6:19 On the fourteenth day of the first month the exiles kept the Passover, [20]for the Levites[a] had, without exception, purified themselves; they were all in a state of ritual purity. So they slaughtered the Passover animal for all the exiles, for their fellow priests, and for themselves. [21]Those who partook were the Israelites who had returned from exile and all those who had joined them, separating themselves from the impurity of the nations of the land to seek YHVH the God of Israel. [22]They also kept the feast of Unleavened Bread for seven days with rejoicing; for YHVH had given them cause for joy in making the king of Assyria well disposed toward them, so that he assisted them in the work on the house of God, the God of Israel.

a. Following 1 Esd. 7:11; MT has "for the priests and Levites," but v. 20b shows that only Levites were intended.

[6:19–20] C rounds off his Aramaic source with this paragraph in Hebrew, though we have just seen that the final section in Aramaic also appears to be his. The recapitulatory intent is clear: Ezra 1–6 begins and ends with the house of the God of Israel (cf. 1:3) being rebuilt with the help of the secular ruler acting as agent of the same God. The dedication of the temple and the subsequent celebration of the Passover mark, for the writer, one of the great turning points in the history of Israel. These events brought to an end the long dark period stretching back to the end of Josiah's reign. The exodus from exile in Babylon ended, appropriately, with the festival of freedom and access to the temple, in fulfillment of an ancient aspiration:

> You will bring them in and plant them on your holy mountain,
> The place, O YHVH, that you have made for your dwelling,
> The sanctuary, O YHVH, which your hands have established.
> YHVH will reign for ever and ever!
>
> (Ex. 15:17–18, RSV)

In the context of C's history as a whole, which must always be borne in mind, this is the third new beginning marked by the celebration of this festival with the participation of all the people. The first was during Hezekiah's reign following the apostate Ahaz (2 Chron. 30), the second that of Josiah after the dark days of Manasseh and Amon (2 Chron. 35:1–19). In both instances the festival marked the climax of religious renewal including the restoration of temple worship. The close verbal and thematic parallels between the three Passover narratives leave us in no doubt that we have here a structural fact of the greatest importance for understanding C's intentions in Ezra 1–6 and the history as a whole.

The date, the fourteenth of Nisan (cf. 2 Chron. 30:2–3, 15; 35:1), follows the Priestly calendar (Ex. 12:1–6; Lev. 23:5–6; Num. 9:3, 5; Ezek. 45:21). Hezekiah's Passover was celebrated on the fourteenth of the second month to allow all participants to purify themselves, following a later provision of Priestly law (Num. 9:9–14). The need for this ritual purification is stressed on all three occasions (2 Chron. 30:2–3, 15; 35:6), though Hezekiah allowed for exceptions in his anxiety to include well-disposed participants from the northern tribes (30:18–19). The role of the Levites is emphasized, and it is they who slaughter the sacrificial animals (2 Chron. 30:17; 35:11). In all three cases the organization of the clergy in their several divisions (cf. 2 Chron. 31:2; 35:2, 4–5) follows on the repair and restoration of the temple as an essential prerequisite for the celebration (2 Chron. 29:3; 34:8, 10). Impurity *(ṭum'āh),* meaning in the first place false worship, must be set aside; and the achieving of this end was, of course, the reason for the reforms in the first place (cf. Ezra 6:21).

[21] Despite its quasi-sectarian character, the golah community

was joined in the celebration of the festival by those of the local population, including no doubt some from the region of Samaria, who were willing to accept the cult of YHVH alone, for which the phrase used here is to *seek YHVH,* a key expression of C, also used of the northerners who accepted Hezekiah's invitation (2 Chron. 30:18–19 and cf. Ezra 4:2). While these "seekers" are not called proselytes *(gērîm),* their inclusion illustrates the openness of the postexilic Jewish community to outsiders who wished to become insiders. While there were, very naturally, differences of opinion on qualifications for membership (on which the remainder of Ezra-Nehemiah will have much to say), a similar attitude is attested in roughly contemporary prophetic texts (especially Isa. 56:1–8) and is enshrined in the later strata of Pentateuchal law. Thus, the Priestly legislation on Passover allowed for the inclusion of *gērîm* on condition of circumcision (Ex. 12:43–49), a requirement which, perhaps significantly, is here passed over in silence. Any judgment on the attitude of the postexilic community to outsiders which leaves this matter of the *gērîm* out of account will certainly be inadequate.

[22] The feast of Unleavened Bread (*ḥag-maṣṣôt,* Ex. 12:15–20; Lev. 23:6–8; Num. 28:17) was also part of the ritual during Hezekiah's and Josiah's reign (2 Chron. 30:13; 35:17). The joy of the festival is accentuated here, as it is in the account of Hezekiah's festival, and in practically identical language (2 Chron. 30:21). C ends this chapter of the history by giving the reason for the rejoicing: the God of Israel, working through the secular ruler, had brought his purpose to fruition with the completion of the temple and restoration of worship. Thus the story which began with the "stirring up" of the spirit of Cyrus by YHVH ends with the "turning of the heart" of his descendant. Much has been written on the unexpected allusion to "the king of Assyria" in this last verse. Inevitably, it has been taken to be a scribal error, but the versions provide no support for this view. Or again, the Persian kings were, in a certain sense, successors of the Assyrians; or perhaps "Assyria" could simply stand for Mesopotamia; or could even reflect later usage, with reference to the Seleucid empire, as may be the case in some late additions to prophetic books (e.g., Isa. 19:23–25). To these we may add yet another possibility. In view of the close parallels between this paragraph and the account of Hezekiah's Passover, the allusion in the latter to the remnant which has escaped from the hand of the king of Assyria (2 Chron. 30:6) may well have been in the writer's mind as he brought his story of the return and restoration to a close.

II

Ezra 7–10

Ezra's Mission to Jerusalem (Ezra 7:1–10)

P. R. **Ackroyd**, "The Chronicler as Exegete," *JSOT* 2, 1977, 2–32; M. **Ararat**, "Ezra and His Activity in the Biblical and Post-Biblical Sources," *BM* 17, 1972, 451–492 (Heb.); J.R. **Bartlett**, "Zadok and His Successors at Jerusalem," *JTS* n.s. 19, 1968, 1–18; J. **Begrich**, "Sofer und Mazkir," *ZAW* 58, 1940, 1–29; H. L. **Ellison**, "The Importance of Ezra," *EvQ* 53, 1981, 48–53; H. H. **Grosheide**, "Ezra de Schrift-geleerde," *GTT* 56, 1956, 84–88; A. H. J. **Gunneweg**, "Zur Interpretation der Bücher Esra-Nehemia," *VTSup.* 32, 1981, 146–161; W. Th. **In der Smitten**, *Esra, 7–11*; H. J. **Katzenstein**, "Some Remarks on the Lists of the Chief Priests of the Temple of Solomon," *JBL* 81, 1962, 377–384; K. **Koch**, "Ezra and the Origins of Judaism," *JSS* 19, 1974, 173–197; F. X. **Kugler**, *Von Moses bis Paulus. Forschungen zur Geschichte Israels,* Münster, 1922, 218–219; S. **Mowinckel**, *Studien* III, 18–20; M. **Noth**, *US,* 145–148; H. H. **Schaeder**, *Esra der Schreiber,* 39–59.

7:1 Following on these events, in the reign of Artaxerxes king of Persia, there went up from Babylon Ezra son of Seraiah, son of Azariah, son of Hilkiah, [2]son of Shallum, son of Zadok, son of Ahitub, [3]son of Amariah, son of Azariah, son of Meraioth, [4]son of Zerahiah, son of Uzzi, son of Bukki, [5]son of Abishua, son of Phinehas, son of Eleazar, son of Aaron the chief priest. [6]This man Ezra was a scribe skilled in the law of Moses which YHVH God of Israel had given. Since he enjoyed the favor of YHVH his God,[a] the king granted his every request.

[7]Some of the laity,[b] priests, Levites, musicians, gatekeepers, and temple servants also went up to Jerusalem in the seventh year of King Artaxerxes. [8]He arrived[c] in Jerusalem in the fifth month— that is, in the seventh year of the king— [9]for on the first day of the first month he fixed the date[d] of departure from Babylon,

arriving in Jerusalem on the first day of the fifth month, since he enjoyed the good favor of his God. [10]For Ezra had set his mind on studying and observing the law of YHVH, and on teaching both statute and ordinance in Israel.

a. Lit., "since the hand of YHVH his God was on him."
b. Lit., "Israelites."
c. MT *vayyābô'* should not be emended to *vayyābô'û* (pl.); v. 9 continues in the sing.
d. Reading *yāsad* or *yissad* for MT *yᵉsud,* a substantive which could mean "beginning," "establishing." No consonantal change is required.

Ezra 7:1–10 is C's introduction to the Ezra narrative based on Ezra's own autobiographical memoir. Not surprisingly, therefore, its theological character is at once observable. Assuming that Ezra's journey took place in the seventh year of Artaxerxes I nicknamed Long Hand (465–424; see Additional Note following), there would be a gap of some fifty-seven years (515–458) between the events just recorded and this new phase of activity. While it is not unlikely that C had some knowledge of events during this interval (see on 4:6ff. for problems arising under Xerxes), there may have been nothing that he cared to record. Malachi and at least part of Isa. 56–66 were in all probability written during this interval, and the situation which they describe suggests that C would have viewed it as a time of failure. It therefore fits into the pattern of a new beginning after a dark period, a conclusion strengthened by the close parallelism between the description of the mission and that of the first return and restoration in chapters 1–6. Ezra's journey from Babylon is also subtly presented as a replication of the first exodus. It may easily be overlooked that the departure from the river Ahava is dated two days before the festival of Passover (8:31), which therefore the caravan, in imitation of the first Israelites, must have celebrated as the end of their sojourn in "the house of bondage." Thus the second episode in the history recorded in this book begins as the first one ends, with the celebration of the festival of freedom.

[7:1–5] It would be natural to assume that the Artaxerxes mentioned here is the same as the ruler introduced in the first section (4:7–23; 6:14), and that therefore the year is 458 B.C.E. Josephus (*Ant.* 11.120) has substituted Xerxes for Artaxerxes in a misguided attempt to correct the chronology of his source. The Aramaic form Ezra corresponds to the common Hebrew name Azariah ("YHVH has helped"), attested in preexilic biblical texts, seal impressions, jar handles from Gibeon, postexilic lists (Neh. 10:3; 12:1, 13, 33), and the Elephantine papyri (*AP* 1; 20; 62; 63). The author has provided Ezra with an Aaronite genealogy, placing him in the sixteenth generation after the putative eponym of the priesthood. Since sixteen generations cover four centuries at the outside, the list must be either defective or selective, most probably both. The author has drawn on the priestly genealogy in 1 Chron. 5:27–41 [6:1–15], itself incomplete, in the process omitting by haplography Azariah (a third priest of that name), Amariah, Ahitub, and Zadok. It is also apparent that Ezra cannot be literally the son of Seraiah, the high priest executed by the Babylonians after the fall of Jerusalem (2 Kings 25:18–21). It is possible that the name of Ezra's father was Seraiah—a fairly common postexilic name (Ezra 2:2; Neh. 7:7; 10:3 [2]; 11:1, 11; 12:1, 7, 12)—and that this coincidence with the name of the last preexilic high priest suggested providing Ezra with a priestly pedigree, perhaps by a later hand. The basic idea, at any rate, seems to have been to establish a line of continuity with the past analogous to the temple vessels. Ezra was not, of course, high priest. He appears in none of the lists (Neh. 12:10–11, 22) and is nowhere described as such (see also on Ezra 8:33). If the genealogy is to be considered at all historical, he must have stood in the collateral line of descent. But it is much more likely that the genealogy is a fiction designed to convey the message that Ezra's function with respect to the law and the cult continued that of the preexilic priesthood.

[6] C provides little biographical information on Ezra apart from what pertains to his mission. He was a resident of the Babylonian diaspora and may have been attached in some capacity to the satrapal court in Babylon, as Nehemiah was to the imperial court in Susa. In the rescript he is addressed as "scribe of the law of the God of heaven" (7:12, 21), which, since Schaeder, has been widely understood to correspond to an official function at the imperial court. As a high-level functionary, the scribe (*šāpiru* in Akkadian, *sāprā'* in Aramaic) is attested from the earliest times in the ancient Near East, inclusive of Israel (2 Sam. 8:17; 20:25; 1 Kings 4:3; 2 Kings 12:11; 18:18, 37; 19:2; 22:3–12). The duties attached to the office were not confined to redaction of official documents, since we hear of them overseeing the temple treasure (2 Kings 12:11; cf. Neh. 13:13), being sent on important missions (2 Kings 19:2–7; 22:14–20), and engaging in negotiations involving a knowledge of foreign languages (2 Kings 18:18–27). Throughout the Persian period scribes of this kind were employed in the central government and at satrapal and provincial courts (Herodotus 3.128; *AP* 17; cf. Ezra 4:8–24). The seven counselors of the Persian king (Ezra 7:14–15; cf. Esth. 1:13–14) no doubt

belonged to the same class. Their role was not unlike that of the half-legendary and ubiquitous Ahiqar, court scholar *(ummānū)* of the Assyrian king Esarhaddon, described as "a wise and skillful scribe" *(spr ḥkym wmhyr; AP, Ahiqar* 1.1).

Starting from Ezra 7:12, 21, Schaeder argued that Ezra occupied an official position at the imperial court, a kind of High Commissioner for Jewish Affairs, or at least was endowed with that office for the duration of his mission. As is clear from the wording of the decree, his principal responsibility was the implementation and administration of Jewish law, a charge entirely consonant with what we know of the scribal function in general. Taking his cue from the decree, which is part of the Ezra memoir, C gave the office a peculiarly Jewish connotation, that of expertise and instruction in Torah (7:6, 11), further exemplified in the public reading and explanation of the law at which Ezra presided. Schaeder believed that, in this capacity as described by C, Ezra marked the beginning of the process leading to Judaism as we know it, characterized above all by the study, observance, and teaching of Torah.

While Schaeder's view is ingenious and plausible, and has been widely accepted, it relies heavily on the detailed authenticity of the decree, or at least of its description of Ezra as "the priest, the scribe of the law of the God of heaven" (7:12, 21). While it is generally acknowledged that the decree was redacted by a Jewish functionary at the court, it is also possible that it has been subsequently touched up in the course of its transmission and incorporation into the book. The combination of priest and scribe must especially arouse suspicion, since this is how Ezra is described at other points in the narrative (Neh. 8:9; 12:26). It is therefore equally possible that C's perception of Ezra's role vis-à-vis the law has influenced the formulation in the decree on which Schaeder's hypothesis rests. Other indications of editing in Artaxerxes' letter serve to strengthen this interpretation, which stands Schaeder's hypothesis on its head.

C, then, describes Ezra as a "skilled scribe" *(sōpēr māhîr);* as with Ahiqar (and cf. Ps. 45:2 [1]), the adjective denotes scribal competence including fast and accurate scrivening. The exercise of this skill, further defined at v. 10, includes knowledge of the law of Moses, its interpretation and application to specific cases, a procedure later known as *midrash halakah.* While C nowhere else associates the scribal function with the law, it is unlikely that Ezra represents, in this respect, an absolute beginning. The existence of a written law necessarily involves a professional class of legal specialists. According to Deuteronomy, the law book was the responsibility of the priesthood (Deut. 17:18; 31:9–13, 24–26), which was also charged with its public reading (31:10–11). Deuteronomy itself does not speak of scribes, but an authentic saying of Jeremiah condemns "handlers of the law" *(tōš^epê hattôrāh)* in a context which associates them with priests (2:8). We have no direct clue to the identity of these scribes who handled—that is, were skilled in—the law, but since both Deuteronomy and Jeremiah (18:18; cf. Ezek. 7:26) acknowledge that law is the province of the priesthood, it seems reasonable to conclude that in the postexilic period we are dealing with a specialization of the priestly function created by the need to interpret legal texts and hand down decisions in keeping with these interpretations.

Here again we note how the author emphasizes the benevolence of the Persian ruler while attributing it to the providence of YHVH for his people (cf. 1:1; 6:22). The laying on of the hand of YHVH, a recurring motif in the book (Ezra 7:9, 28; 8:18, 22, 31; Neh. 2:8, 18), signifies the bestowal of blessing (cf. Gen. 48:14). Whether the mission originated in a request of Ezra addressed to the king, as with Nehemiah (Neh. 2:4–8), is uncertain; the sentence could be understood in a more general sense.

[7] Some commentators have bracketed this verse as intrusive, since it neither mentions Ezra nor even connects this aliyah with him. Others have suggested that we read "he brought up" *(vaya'al,* Rudolph 1949, 67) for the plural "went up" *(vayya^alû).* The context, however, suggests fairly clearly that they accompanied Ezra. The caravan consisted of laity (Israelites), priests, Levites, musicians, gatekeepers, and temple servants, listed in the same order as in Ezra 2. The lesser temple functionaries are not represented in the list of phratries in Ezra's memoir (8:1–14), nor are they alluded to in the rescript itself. C, however, who describes this repatriation in terms parallel to the first under Cyrus, would simply have assumed their presence. One of the principal objects of the mission, after all, was the restoration of temple worship.

[8–9] The dates of departure and arrival are carefully noted. The departure date was fixed for the first of the first month (Nisan) in the seventh year of the reign. Later (8:31) we will be told that the caravan actually set out on the twelfth of Nisan. The arrival date was the first of the fifth month (Ab) of the same year. Since it was midsummer, they would have taken the northern route, following the Euphrates into northern Syria, down to Damascus, and then to Jerusalem, probably along the coastal route rather than down the Jordan valley. Since this involved a trek of around eight hundred miles, the rate of progress was no more than about ten miles a day, a reasonable rate in view of the season, the children who accompanied them, and the baggage. That Ezra *fixed* the date of departure alerts us to the religious significance of these chronological indications. Like the exodus from Egypt, the departure is to be in the first month (cf. Ex. 12:2; Num. 33:3). The actual date of departure is two days before Passover, which means that they also imitated the ancient Israelites by celebrating the festival at the beginning of their journey to the promised land. This circumstance, which was certainly not lost on the author, allowed him to begin this new episode at the same point in the liturgical calendar at which he had concluded the three preceding chapters of his history (see on 6:19–22). After their arrival in Jerusalem on the first of Ab, there was an interval of three days after which the endowments for the temple were handed over (8:32). This too may have a special calendric significance, since Solomon's temple was destroyed on the seventh of Ab (2 Kings 25:8). Some have made the further suggestion that 458 B.C.E. may have been a sabbatical year, counting back from the one which came up in 164 B.C.E. according to 1 Macc. 6:49, 53 (Koch). The first day of the fifth month may also have fallen on a sabbath in 398 (see Kugler and, in reply, van Hoonacker 1923). This may or may not be so, but if it is, it would not rule out that year for Ezra's mission since the actual date of departure was the twelfth not the first. What is at least clear is that the mission represented for C, and possibly for Ezra also, a new beginning, a replica of the first exodus to be followed, then as now, by the giving of the law.

[10] The causal connection between this verse and the two verses preceding should not be overlooked. Ezra arranged the time of departure and arrival because of his assiduous study of the law and his determination to observe and teach it. These three activities—study, observance, instruction—fill out the description of Ezra as scribe (cf. Sir. 38:24–39:11) and lay the basis, first adumbrated in Deuteronomy, of the kind of religion Judaism was to remain thereafter. The law which Ezra taught is further explicated in the twinned terms statute *(ḥōq)* and ordinance *(mišpāṭ)*, the former referring to the basic provisions or stipulations of the law, the latter to their application in judicial cases (cf. Deut. 4:1, 5, 8, 14; 5:1; 11:32; 12:1; 26:16).

Additional Note on the Chronology of Ezra and Nehemiah

In addition to the commentaries see W. F. **Albright**, *JBL* 40, 1921, 104–124; *The Biblical Period*, 93, 112–113; J. **Bright**, "The Date of Ezra's Mission to Jerusalem," in M. Haran (ed.), *Yehezkel Kaufmann Jubilee Volume*, Jerusalem, 1960, 70–87; *A History of Israel*, Philadelphia, 1981 (3rd ed.), 391–402; H. **Cazelles**, "La mission d'Esdras," *VT* 4, 1954, 113–140; F. M. **Cross**, "A Reconstruction of the Judean

Restoration," *JBL* 94, 1975, 4–18; J. A. **Emerton**, "Did Ezra Go to Jerusalem in 428 B.C.?" *JTS* 17, 1966, 1–19; K. **Galling**, *Studien*, 149–184; A. **van Hoonacker**, "Néhémie et Esdras, une nouvelle hypothèse sur la chronologie de l'époque de la restauration," *Le Muséon* 9, 1890, 151–184, 317–351, 389–401; "La succession chronologique Néhémie-Esdras," *RB* 32, 1923, 481–494; 33, 1924, 33–64; W. Th. **In der Smitten**, *Esra*, 91–105; A. **Jepsen**, "Nehemia 10," *ZAW* 66, 1954, 87–106; U. **Kellermann**, "Erwägungen zum Problem der Esradatierung," *ZAW* 80, 1968, 55–87; A. **Lefèvre**, "Néhémie et Esdras," *DBSup*. 6:393–424; S. **Mowinckel**, *Studien* III, 99–109; V. **Pavlovský**, "Die Chronologie der Tätigkeit Esras: Versuch einer neuen Lösung," *Bib* 38, 1957, 428–456; H. H. **Rowley**, "The Chronological Order of Ezra and Nehemiah," in S. Löwinger and J. Somogyi (eds.), *Ignace Goldziher Memorial Volume* I, Budapest, 1948, 117–149 (= Rowley, *The Servant of the Lord and Other Essays on the Old Testament*, London, 1965, 137–168); R. J. **Saley**, "The Date of Nehemiah Reconsidered," in G. A. Tuttle (ed.), *Biblical and Near Eastern Studies* (La Sor Festschrift), 1978, 151–165; W. M. F. **Scott**, "Nehemiah-Ezra?" *ExpT* 58, 1946/47, 263–267; M. **Smith**, *Parties and Politics That Shaped the Old Testament*, 120–123; N. H. **Snaith**, "The Date of Ezra's Arrival in Jerusalem," *ZAW* 63, 1951, 53–66; S. **Talmon**, "Ezra and Nehemiah," *IDBSup*. 317–328; C. G. **Tuland**, "Ezra-Nehemiah or Nehemiah-Ezra?" *AUSS* 12, 1974, 47–62; R. **de Vaux**, "Israël (Histoire de)," *DBSup*. 4:764–769; G. **Widengren**, "The Chronological Order of Ezra and Nehemiah," in J. H. Hayes and J. M. Miller (eds.), *Israelite and Judaean History*, 503–509; J. S. **Wright**, *The Date of Ezra's Coming to Jerusalem*, London, 1958; E. M. **Yamauchi**, "The Reverse Order of Ezra/ Nehemiah Reconsidered," *Themelios* 5, 1980, 7–13.

According to the present order of the book, Ezra arrived in Jerusalem in the seventh year of Artaxerxes (Ezra 7:8) and Nehemiah in the twentieth year of a king of the same name (Neh. 2:1; the slight difference in spelling cannot serve to distinguish different rulers of the same name). Thereafter, both were present and active simultaneously in the city (Neh. 8:9; 12:36). Josephus (*Ant.* 11.135, 168) puts Ezra's arrival in the seventh year of Xerxes and Nehemiah's in the twenty-fifth year of the same reign, a praiseworthy but misguided attempt to correct the chronology of his source, since Xerxes reigned for only twenty-one years; however, it at least confirms the impression gained from the biblical narrative that both men arrived during the same reign. The date of Nehemiah's arrival, in the twentieth year of Artaxerxes I Long Hand (465–424), i.e., 445/444, is beyond reasonable doubt, and his administration lasted until some short time after the same king's thirty-second year, i.e., 432/431. The alternative dating in the reign of Artaxerxes II nicknamed Memory Man (404–359), i.e., 384/383–372/371, was espoused occasionally in the last century and has been recently defended by Saley, but is generally abandoned and for excellent reasons. The biblical narrative does not fit the historical context of the early fourth century, and this dating ignores the Elephantine letter from 408 B.C.E. (*AP* 30) which gives the name of the high priest as Johanan (cf. Neh. 12:22–23) and mentions Sanballat as the father of the chief official in Samaria. Artaxerxes III (359–338) is ruled out *a fortiori,* and in any case he did not reign for thirty-two years.

In its present form, then, the book invites the conclusion that Ezra and Nehemiah arrived in Jerusalem during the same reign, the former about thirteen years before the latter. The identification of the ruler as Artaxerxes I is also a natural conclusion from the earlier allusions to an Artaxerxes who succeeded Xerxes (Ezra 4:6–7). The date of Ezra's arrival would then be 458/457, a conclusion which was taken for granted until the late nineteenth century, when it was challenged first by Vernes (1889), then by the Belgian scholar van Hoonacker in a string of publications spread over thirty-four years. While van Hoonacker's arguments, often restated, occasionally refined, but never substantially augmented, won considerable support (e.g., Rowley, Snaith, Cazelles, Galling, Mowinckel, Widengren), they have not proved decisive enough to create a new consensus. The result has therefore been a stalemate and it is by now clear that, in the absence of new information, certainty is unattainable. Given this situation, it seems reasonable to take the position that, if none of the arguments advanced against the sequence Ezra-Nehemiah of the biblical text proves decisive, that sequence should be adopted as the one in possession, at least as a working hypothesis.

Alternative views, resting on arbitrary emendation of Ezra 7:7–8 in order to date Ezra's mission in the twenty-seventh (Wellhausen, Procksch, Bright), thirty-second (Kosters, Rudolph 1949), or thirty-seventh year (Albright, Pavlovský, Lefèvre) should be considered only if no other solution is feasible. Since this is not the case, and since all these variations labor under other difficulties (see in detail Emerton against the thirty-seventh year, 328 B.C.E.), they need be pursued no further.

One of the principal arguments advanced against the priority of Ezra is that the condition in the province and in Jerusalem at the time of Ezra's arrival is intelligible only if Nehemiah had already been active there. The city wall was already in place (Ezra 9:9), Jerusalem was populated with clerical and civic leaders (Ezra 8:29; 10:5) as also with the common people (10:1, 7), and Ezra handed over the temple endowments and vessels to a panel of four established by Nehemiah and entrusted with responsibility for the temple treasure (Ezra 8:33; cf. Neh. 13:13). On closer inspection, however, this argument carries little weight. If Ezra 9:9 does indeed refer to the city wall, it may well have been broken down again as a result of the intervention described at Ezra 4:23. But it must be observed that the allusion comes in a prayer which may or may not be contemporary with Ezra; the word used, *gādēr*, usually refers to a fence or hedge rather than a city wall (Micah 7:11 may be an exception, but the word occurs there in the plural, not necessarily with reference to city walls); and the "wall" is for the entire province, not just for Jerusalem. The allusion is therefore allegorical rather than literal. The depopulation of Jerusalem leading to Nehemiah's *synoikismos* may also have been caused by disturbances subsequent to Ezra's mission (as Neh. 1:3 would suggest) and, in any case, the city was underpopulated rather than depopulated. Several allusions in the Nehemiah history, especially in the list of wall builders, testify clearly to houses and people in Jerusalem before the transfer of population. There is, finally, no suggestion that the management of the temple treasury was an innovation of Nehemiah's. It is just as likely that he restored it, as he did other aspects of temple administration. In any case, Nehemiah's panel was different in both function and composition from the one to which Ezra consigned the gifts from Babylon.

Along rather similar lines, it is pointed out that, assuming the secondary nature of Neh. 8:9 and 12:36 where the two men are associated, Nehemiah never mentions Ezra, and his measures designed to protect the religious and ethnic purity of the community make better sense as a follow-up to the more comprehensive measures pushed through by Ezra. But the argument would have to assume that Ezra's measures met with complete success, which is doubtful, to say the least. Quite apart from the distinct possibility that they failed, and that therefore Nehemiah would have good reason not to allude to them, there would be nothing surprising if abuses had crept in again here and there after the passage of about a quarter of a century.

That Nehemiah is named before Ezra (Neh. 8:9; 12:26) throws no light on their relative chronology. Apart from the fact that Nehemiah's name is not original in the account of Ezra's law assembly (see on Neh. 8:9), it would be natural for the governor's name to come first. The linking of Zerubbabel with Nehemiah in a later retrospective summary (12:47) is also a matter of civil administration. Failure to mention Ezra is therefore unremarkable and has no bearing on the chronological issue.

Proponents of the early fourth century date for Ezra's arrival in Jerusalem have also argued that the political situation in the early years of the reign of Artaxerxes I, with Egypt in revolt backed by a powerful Athenian fleet, was not the most propitious time for such a mission. Artaxerxes would have been too busy to bother about Judah and the journey of some eight hundred miles from Babylon far too dangerous to contemplate. By 398, on the other hand, Egypt had already won its independence and the rebellion of Cyrus the Younger had been crushed. It could as easily be argued, however, that precisely on account of the unstable situation in the west in 458 Artaxerxes would have taken measures to assure support in the strategically crucial region of the Palestinian corridor. The matter has now been under discussion for at least a century with the result that one thing at least is clear, namely, that the earlier date for Ezra's mission cannot be excluded on these grounds.

The strongest and clearest argument for reversing the order in the biblical narrative, the trump card, has always been the high priestly succession as presented in the book. Eliashib was the high priest contemporary with Nehemiah (Neh. 3:1, 21; 13:28). According to one listing his grandson was Jonathan (Neh. 12:10), but elsewhere a certain Johanan (Jehohanan) appears as either his son (Neh. 12:23) or grandson (v. 22), though Joiada (Jehoiada) is also listed as his immediate successor (12:10, 22; 13:28). From one of the more interesting of the Elephantine letters (*AP* 30) we know that a Johanan was high priest around 410 B.C.E. During the foreign marriage crisis Ezra withdrew into the room of a certain Jehohanan son of Eliashib in the temple precincts (Ezra 10:6). If this Eliashib is identical with the high priest during Nehemiah's administration, it would be difficult to avoid the conclusion that Ezra's reforms took place a generation or so later. Eliashib is, however, a fairly common name (three are listed in one document, Ezra 10:24, 27, 36), and this person is not called high priest, which we would expect if he were such. There is also a question whether Ezra would be consorting with the high priestly family which, on the assumption of Nehemiah's priority, had already seriously compromised itself and "defiled the priesthood" (Neh. 13:28–29).

Arguments based on names, especially those of frequent occurrence, require careful handling. It is often urged in support of Nehemiah's priority, for example, that at the time of the wall-building Meremoth was young and active enough to not only take part but do double duty (Neh. 3:4, 21), whereas when Ezra arrived he was a priest in a senior position in the temple bureaucracy (Ezra 8:33). This is, of course, possible in spite of the elapsed time of almost half a century. But if the reverse order is assumed, the lapse of time would be only thirteen years (458 to 445), which would create even less of a problem, especially since the priests who assumed responsibility for sections of the wall need not themselves have done the physical work.

Other arguments of a similar kind, which do not call for extensive treatment, will be dealt with at the appropriate points in the commentary.

Our conclusion is, then, that the case for reversing the chronological order of the two men has not been sustained, and that therefore we may assume that Ezra arrived in the seventh year (458) and Nehemiah in the twentieth year (445) of Artaxerxes I Long Hand. This is not to say that positive arguments advanced in support of this order are necessarily any stronger. The argument from the so-called "Passover papyrus" from Elephantine (*AP* 21), dated 419 B.C.E., is one of these. Though damaged, it appears to prescribe the correct procedure for celebrating Passover–Unleavened Bread. The contention is that such detailed prescriptions of ritual law on the frontiers of empire in southern Egypt could not have been enforced before Ezra promulgated his law in Jerusalem. We must recall, however, that Ezra's law, whatever it was, was deemed to be familiar to Jews in the region, and the injunction of the Egyptian satrap may have consisted simply in the reaffirmation of the right to celebrate a festival unpopular with the local population whose gods included Khnum in the guise of a ram (so B. Porten, *BA* 42, 1979, 74–104). If, however, we take a broader view of the editorial tendency of the book, we will agree that C had good reasons for putting Ezra after Nehemiah, on the grounds that his office as priest and his mission as lawgiver were of paramount importance. If he did not do so, the reason may be that the facts were too well known and that, in consequence, he had to be content with contemporaneity. And if, finally, he knew that Ezra's mission was (to say the least) somewhat less than a total success, we can understand why he chose to rearrange his material in order to present Ezra's activity as part of a more comprehensive operation which was brought to a successful conclusion.

The Rescript of Artaxerxes (Ezra 7:11–26)

P. R. Ackroyd, "The Temple Vessels—A Continuity Theme," *VTSup.* 23, 1972, 166–181; F. Ahlemann, "Zur Esra-Quelle," *ZAW* 59, 1942/43, 77–98; Y. Bin-Nun, "g^{e}mîr," *BM* 65, 1976, 296–302 (Heb.); H. Cazelles, "La Mission d'Esdras," *VT* 4, 1954, 113–140; Z. W. Falk, "Ezra vii 26," *VT* 9, 1959, 88–89; K. Galling, *Studien,* 165–178; G. Garbini, "Aramaic g^{e}mîr (Esdras 7,12)," *Studi in Onore di Edda Bresciani,* Pisa, 1985, 227–229; W. Th. In der Smitten, *Esra,* 11–17; "Eine aramäische Inschrift in Pakistan aus dem 3. Jhdt. v. Chr.," *BeO* 28, 1971, 309–311; A. S. Kapelrud, *The Question of Authorship in the Ezra-Narrative: A Lexical Investigation,* Oslo, 1944, 40–42; U. Kellermann, "Erwägungen zum Problem der Esradatierung,"

ZAW 80, 1968, 55–87; R. **Meiggs** and D. M. Lewis, *A Selection of Greek Historical Inscriptions to the End of the Fifth Century B.C.*, Oxford, 1969, 20–22; P. **Nober,** " *'adrazdā'* (Esdras 7,23)," *BZ* n.F. 2, 1958, 134–138; "Lexicalia iranico-biblica," *VD* 36, 1958, 103–104; R. H. **Pfeiffer,** *Introduction to the Old Testament,* New York, 1948 (2nd ed.), 826–828; F. **Rundgren,** "Zur Bedeutung von ŠRŠW—Esra vii 26," *VT* 7, 1957, 400–404; C. C. **Torrey,** *Ezra Studies,* 157–158; A. C. **Welch,** *Post-exilic Judaism,* Edinburgh and London, 1935, 245–279.

7:11 This is a copy of the memorandum which King Artaxerxes gave to Ezra the priest, the scribe, versed in matters concerning the commandments of YHVH and his ordinances to Israel.

[12]"Artaxerxes, king of kings, to Ezra the priest, scribe of the law of the God of heaven, greetings.[a] [13]I hereby decree that anyone in my kingdom of the people of Israel, their priests and Levites, who volunteers to go to Jerusalem may go with you. [14]For you are sent by the king and his seven counselors to inquire about Judah and Jerusalem with respect to the law of your God with which you are entrusted.[b] [15]You are also to convey the silver and gold which the king and his counselors have given as a votive offering to the God of Israel, whose dwelling is in Jerusalem, [16]together with whatever gold and silver you may collect[c] throughout the entire province of Babylon, and the votive offerings of the people and priests which they freely give for the house of their God in Jerusalem. [17]With this money, then, you will without delay purchase steers, rams, and lambs, with their cereal and drink offerings, and you will offer them in sacrifice on the altar of the house of your God in Jerusalem. [18]With the rest of the silver and gold you may do whatever you and your brethren consider appropriate, according to the will of your God. [19]As for the vessels which have been given to you for the service of the house of your God, you shall hand them over to the God of Jerusalem; [20]and if anything else is needed for the house of your God, which it is your responsibility to provide, you may requisition it from the royal treasury.

[21]"I, Artaxerxes the king, hereby issue a decree to all the treasurers in the Trans-Euphrates satrapy: whatever Ezra the priest, the scribe of the law of the God of heaven, requests of you, be it done with all haste, [22]up to a hundred talents of silver, a hundred cors of wheat, a hundred baths of wine, a hundred baths of oil, and an unspecified amount of salt. [23]Whatever is decreed by the God of heaven, let it be assiduously carried out on behalf of the house of the God of heaven, lest his wrath descend on the kingdom, the king, and his sons. [24]We also notify you that it is not permitted to impose tribute, tax, or duty on any of the priests, Levites, musi-

cians, gatekeepers, temple servants, or other cult personnel of this house of God.

[25]"As for you, Ezra, in keeping with the wisdom of your God which is yours, [b] appoint magistrates and judges who will judge all the people in the Trans-Euphrates satrapy, all who are familiar with the laws of your God; and those who are not familiar with them you shall instruct. [26]Whoever will not obey the law of your God and the law of the king, let judgment be swiftly executed upon him, whether sentence of death, corporal punishment, confiscation of property, or imprisonment."

a. The puzzling *g^{e}mîr,* "complete," "perfect," is taken to be an abbreviated form of greeting; cf. 5:7 and see commentary.
b. *dî bîdāk,* lit., "which is in your hand."
c. Lit., "find."

After the introductory v. 11 the decree itself, like those of Cyrus (6:3–5) and Darius (6:6–12) is in Aramaic. It consists in the following: (1) permission for Ezra and those wishing to accompany him to emigrate from Babylon to Judah; (2) the sending of Ezra on a fact-finding mission with respect to the observance of the Jewish law, with instructions to set up and enforce judicial procedures and teach the law where necessary; (3) instructions to convey to Jerusalem votive offerings from the court and private individuals, monies collected in Babylon, and cultic vessels or utensils donated by the king; (4) instructions on how the Jerusalem cult is to be funded by the imperial and satrapal authorities, and how these funds are to be used; (5) an order to the local authorities freeing the Jerusalem cultic establishment from taxation. The decree is addressed to Ezra, though it slips into the plural here and there (17, 25), with the exception of a paragraph addressed to the local authorities (21–24). The latter may have been copied from a separate decree forwarded directly to the satrapy or it may have been left to Ezra to deliver it (as Nehemiah did later, Neh. 2:9). If the decree was really issued, C may have come upon it in the Ezra memoir, which may also have contained an account of how it came to be written, somewhat after the manner of Neh. 2:1–8. There is a hint of this in Ezra 7:27–28 and in the introduction to the decree at 1 Esd. 8:8.

The authenticity of this Aramaic text has long been in dispute. At one end of the spectrum, it has been thought to be a pure invention of C (Torrey, Pfeiffer). Others (Mowinckel 1964–65, Ahlemann, Kapelrud) have been somewhat less categorical though still basically negative. Others again have accepted some parts and rejected others. Batten, for example (1913, 307–308), rejected everything except the permission to return and the injunction about the law, while In der Smitten (19) ruled out the rescript addressed to the satrapal authorities. While there has been a tendency to accept that the major provisions of the decree are consonant with Persian imperial policy vis-à-vis local cults (e.g., Cazelles), the problem has been the equally clear indications of Jewish coloring. Beginning with Eduard Meyer (1896), this problem seemed to have been solved by the hypothesis of redaction by a Jewish functionary in the imperial service, perhaps by Ezra himself; and this hypothesis seemed to be strengthened by Schaeder's argument (1930a) that Ezra the scribe was acting in an official capacity as commissioner for Jewish affairs in the satrapy. The question, however, remains: are the indications of Jewish authorship so extensive as to collapse the hypothesis of Meyer and Schaeder? Do not also some of these indications point unmistakably to the authorial or editorial role of C himself?

The view adopted here can be briefly stated as follows, leaving detailed argument for the commentary. The mission of Ezra, like that of Udjahorresnet in Egypt under Darius I, is certainly historical. The purpose of the mission, as mandated in an imperial firman, was to restore the Jerusalem cultus and put the administration of the Jewish law on a firm basis, and this in the interests of peace and stability in the province and perhaps elsewhere in the satrapy. With or without editorial retouching, the decree was incorporated into Ezra's personal account of his tour of duty, from which it was subsequently excerpted by C who, as elsewhere in the history, did not scruple to engage in extensive rewriting.

[7:11] C's introduction to the document, in Hebrew, borrows the technical terms from Old Persian for "copy" *(paršegen)* and "memorandum" *(ništ^{e}vān);* cf. 4:11, 23. For the description of Ezra as priest and scribe see the commentary on the preceding section.

[12–13] As is customary, the superscription gives the names of the writer and the recipient of the letter. The title "king of kings" is commonly used in Persian official documents, e.g., the Behistun inscription. It was taken over from old Mesopotamian protocol (Akk. *šar šarrāni;* cf. Ezek. 26:7 and Dan. 2:37). The description of Ezra here and later as "priest and scribe of the law of the God of heaven" is taken from C's introduction rather than the reverse *(pace* Schaeder 1930a, 39–59, and Rudolph 1949, 73). The specifically Israelite term for "priest" *(kāh^{a}nā', Heb. kōhēn)* is used rather than the more general *kumrā',* and the twofold office has the advantage of corresponding to the two principal aspects of the mission—the restoration of the cult and the reform of the judicial system. For the designation "the God of heaven" see on 1:2. The words $g^e m\hat{\imath}r\ \hat{u}k^e$-*'enet,* which defy translation as they stand (RSV prudently omits them), conclude the superscription; k^e*'enet* is used to introduce the substance of a letter and therefore belongs to the following verse; $g^e m\hat{\imath}r$, from a verbal stem meaning "end," "complete," or something of the sort, has had various interpretations, none of them secure. It has been interpreted as the title of an official document (cf. Akk. *dinu gamru;* G. Rinaldi, *BeO* 3, 1961, 85); as meaning "the matter has been completely dealt with," therefore a bureaucratic note put in the margin (but then why here rather than at the end?); as a formula of abbreviation, either with the meaning "etc." (as in modern Hebrew $v^e g\hat{o}mar$) or as a conventional contraction for the usual greeting formula. The last option, which is supported by *chairein* at 1 Esd. 8:9 and in Syr., is taken here. The letter, then, opens by granting permission to return to the homeland. While there is no reason to doubt that those listed in 8:1–20 did in fact return with Ezra, allusion to "the people of Israel" as laity alongside clergy, and especially to volunteering (from *hitnaddēb;* see on 1:4), betrays C's hand. In addition, we find here the first of several conscious parallels with the first return, e.g., the sacred vessels and the generous subventions from public and private sources.

[14] The first object of the mission was to ascertain to what extent the laws were being observed. While we are not told that this aspect of the mission was instigated by reports from the province, similar to those received by Nehemiah (1:1–3), the possibility is suggested by the sad state of affairs described in Malachi (2:7–9, 17; 3:8, 13–15) and here and there in Isa. 56–66. The extent of Ezra's jurisdiction is here limited to Judah and Jerusalem, a familiar combination in C's history (about twenty-five times), but it is later extended to the entire satrapy. The phrase "with which you are entrusted," literally "which is in your hand," does not imply that Ezra actually brought the law with him, and it later becomes clear that it is, or should be, known in the province (v. 25). The mission emanated directly from the king and his cabinet of seven princes (cf. Herodotus 3.31, 71, 83–84; Xenophon, *Anabasis* 1.6.4–5; Esth. 1:14).

[15–16] The royal endowment of local cults, primarily for political reasons, was a feature of the imperial policy of the early Achaemenids; cf. Cyrus in respect to the cult of Marduk in Babylon, and Cambyses (in spite of his bad reputation) in respect to the great sanctuary of Neith in Sais. Private offerings of the faithful were, of course, common (cf. *AP* 21). C would no doubt have us recall the immense amounts donated for the First Temple under David (1

Chron. 29:6–9) and the votive offerings for Zerubbabel's temple (Ezra 1:4; 2:68–69). Ezra was also authorized to collect funds in Babylonia, presumably from fellow Jews and sympathizers, in much the same way that wealthy Jews in the diaspora support the State of Israel today.

[17–20] The decree goes on to stipulate how the funds are to be disbursed. The note of urgency, expressed in the adverbial phrase "without delay" (*'āsparnā';* see also 5:8; 6:12–13; 7:21), is frequently heard in these decrees. As noted earlier (see on 6:9), the sacrificial animals are listed in the order which is standard for C, but here there are joined to them the offerings of flour mixed with oil and of wine as prescribed in the P legislation (Num. 15:1–16); hence *their* cereal and drink offerings. There could be no clearer indication of a Jewish hand at work in the redaction of the document. Whatever is left over is to go into a discretionary fund, presumably to be used for religious purposes ("according to the will of your God"). The theme of the sacred vessels (or utensils) replicates the generous gesture of Cyrus at the first return (1:7–11; 5:14–15; 6:5). Here, too, they are listed, and mention is made of those to whom they are entrusted and what is to be done with them on arrival in Jerusalem (8:26–27, 33–34). In C's history as a whole, this theme forms another link of continuity with the past, the remote past of the First Temple and the proximate past of the first return. In spite of the evident expectation that the public and private subventions will more than suffice for Ezra's needs (v. 18), he is promised additional support from the royal treasury (literally, "the house of the king's treasures," corresponding to Old Persian *ganzataka*), and that according to need. In this respect also Artaxerxes is represented as following the lead of Cyrus (6:4), in the best tradition of Persian generosity toward the Jewish population in the empire.

[21–24] This section forms, in effect, a separate decree addressed not to Ezra but to the satrapal authorities in Abar-nahara. It runs parallel to the decree of Darius (6:9–10) in requiring them to provide the wherewithal for the sacrificial system in Jerusalem, with the exception that it sets limits to what can be demanded in money and kind. Like the sums donated to the sanctuary after the first return (2:69), the amounts are impossibly high, over three and a quarter tons of silver; the more so, of course, if the contributions were to be made on an annual basis. According to Herodotus (3.91), the income from the entire satrapy in the early Achaemenid period amounted to only three and a half times that amount. Ezra could, in addition, require delivery of some 650 bushels of wheat, 600 gallons of wine, the same quantity of oil (*mᵉšaḥ,* literally, "anointing"; cf. *AP* 30:20;

31:20) and an unlimited amount of salt. All of these commodities were for use in the temple liturgy (cf. Num. 15:1–16 and, for wine libations, Ex. 29:40 and Hos. 9:4). The authenticity of this part of the document is clearly not above suspicion. After the generous, almost limitless subventions already promised, it is surprising that more would be thought necessary, especially since Ezra had already been commanded to purchase these commodities out of funds provided from the royal treasury and private donations (v. 17). The motive for the generosity—to appease the anger of a powerful deity—is, however, by no means implausible, and is paralleled in the Darius rescript (6:10). The word for wrath—*q*ᵉ*ṣap, qeṣep* in Hebrew—is a term which carries a special theological connotation since it is used exclusively of the divine anger (e.g., Num. 1:53; 18:5; Josh. 9:20; 2 Kings 3:27). In one passage, to be considered shortly, C represents King Jehoshaphat enjoining the priests and Levites to instruct the people in the law "that his wrath *(qeṣep)* may not come upon you and your brethren" (2 Chron. 19:10). It may therefore be the case that, while the formulation is C's, the historical situation presupposed is quite plausible. At the time of Ezra's mission Egypt was in revolt under the Lybian Inaros backed by a large Athenian fleet, the Persian army sent to quell the revolt had been defeated, the satrap of Egypt had been killed, and it seemed entirely possible that Egypt and the Syro-Palestinian area might be lost to the empire. It was therefore a time when the cooperation of the local deities was especially necessary. One way to secure that cooperation, illustrated by the Gadatas inscription from Magnesia in Asia Minor (see Meiggs and Lewis), was to exempt the cultic personnel of the sanctuary in question from taxation. (For the terms used see textual note on 4:13.) The list of these personnel is C's, following the order in the census of Ezra 2. The only difference is the substitution of the generic "cult personnel" *(pālᵉḥîn)* for the specific "descendants of Solomon's servants" (1 Esd. 8:24 has "scribes of the temple," in keeping with later usage illustrated in Josephus).

[25–26] The decree now returns to Ezra and the matter of the law broached earlier. The order is somewhat confused, but perhaps it was thought appropriate to end with the threat of punishment, as does the Darius rescript (6:11–12). Ezra is commanded to appoint magistrates and judges, and it is now assumed that his jurisdiction is not limited to Judah and Jerusalem. The terms for these officials —*šāp*ᵉ*ṭîn, dayyānîn*—are in fact synonymous, the former borrowed from the Hebrew *šōp*ᵉ*ṭîm,* judges. The injunction inevitably recalls the Deuteronomic provisions for establishing a comprehensive judiciary system (Deut. 1:16–17; 16:18; 17:8–13) in which the officials in question are judges and officers (*šōpᵉṭîm, šōṭᵉrîm,* 16:18). The Deuteronomic connection is strengthened by the injunction to teach, a dominant theme in Deuteronomy and related writings. "The wisdom of your God which is in your hand" is also parallel to "the law of your God which is in your hand" (v. 14); a phrase which is totally out of place in an official document of this kind but entirely intelligible when we recall the Deuteronomic equation of the law with wisdom (Deut. 4:6; cf. Ps. 37:30–31; 119:98). An instructive parallel in C's history, also of Deuteronomic inspiration, is the establishment of a comprehensive judicial machinery by the Judean king Jehoshaphat (2 Chron. 19:4–11). He appointed judges throughout the land with the purpose of bringing the people back to the traditional observances. He then set up a central judiciary in Jerusalem composed of priests, Levites, and laity, enjoining them to instruct the people in order to ward off the divine wrath *(qeṣep).* Interesting also is the distinction between "the matter of YHVH" and "the matter of the king" (*dᵉbar* YHVH, *dᵉbar hammelek,* 2 Chron. 19:11), the former under clerical, the latter under secular jurisdiction. This sounds very similar to the distinction in the decree between the law of your God and the law of the king (cf. also 1 Chron. 26:32). The construction of this sentence, with *dātā'* repeated, strongly suggests that these are not to be identified, in the sense that the king endows the Jewish law with his own authority (*pace* Rudolph 1949, 75; R. A. Bowman 1954, 630, et al.). Unlike the situation at the time of Jehoshaphat, however, Ezra could assume responsibility for both in view of his double office of priest and scribe.

Ezra's jurisdiction now covers the entire satrapy. It is tempting to read this as an example of C's utopianism, a vision of the Greater Israel of the United Monarchy restored (cf. 4:20; see Ackroyd 1973, 246). But it seems tolerably clear that only those "familiar with the law of your God" are intended, that is, Jews and proselytes *(gērîm),* insofar as the latter came under the law. The command to instruct is not therefore a license to proselytize. It is also unlikely that it has children in mind; they would be taken for granted. It envisages rather those who had lost sight of traditional observance, a process accelerated by living in a Gentile environment and intermarrying with the local population. We must suppose that by now many Jewish communities had been established throughout the satrapy outside of Judah, some indications of which appear in the census of Ezra 2 (vs. 20–35) and in the Nehemiah material (Neh. 13:4–9, 23–27).

Penalties for violation of the law in both the religious and the secular sphere are listed in descending order of severity. The death sentence is levied in Pentateuchal law on a wide range of transgressions. The second penalty is often translated "banishment" (e.g., by RSV), but this appears to be mistaken since the Persian word from which it derives means something different. (1 Esd. 8:24, which has *timōria*, physical punishment, points in the right direction.) Corporal punishment (*šᵉrōšî*, from Old Persian *sraušyā*), especially flogging, is characteristic of Persian rather than Israelite penal practice. Confiscation of property is actually the only one of these penalties threatened during Ezra's mission (10:8). With the exception of prisoners of war and political prisoners (e.g., Jer. 37:15–38:13), imprisonment was not part of Israelite penal law either, to judge by the extant legislation. While the list of penalties is hardly complete, it seems that the Persian penal code was invoked even for infractions of traditional Jewish law.

Additional Note on Ezra's Law

J. **Blenkinsopp**, "The Mission of Udjahorresnet and Those of Ezra and Nehemiah," *JBL* 106, 1987, 409–421; G. C. **Cameron**, "Darius, Egypt, and the 'Lands Beyond the Sea,' " *JNES* 2, 1943, 307–313; H. **Cazelles**, "La Mission d'Esdras," *VT* 4, 1954, 113–140; M. **Fishbane**, *Biblical Exegesis in Ancient Israel,* Oxford, 1985; P. **Grelot**, "Le Papyrus Pascal d'Eléphantine et le Problème du Pentateuque," *VT* 5, 1955, 250–265; "La dernière étape de la rédaction sacerdotale," *VT* 6, 1956, 174–189; C. **Houtman**, "Ezra and the Law," *OTS* 21, 1981, 91–115; W. Th. **In der Smitten**, *Esra,* 123–130; U. **Kellermann**, "Erwägungen zum Esragesetz," *ZAW* 80, 1968, 373–385; R. G. **Kent**, "The Restoration of Order by Darius," *JAOS* 58, 1938, 112–121; R. W. **Klein**, "Ezra and Nehemiah in Recent Studies," in F. M. Cross et al. (eds.), *Magnalia Dei,* 361–376; K. **Koch**, "Ezra and the Origins of Judaism," *JSS* 19, 1974, 173–197; H.-J. **Kraus**, "Zum Gesetzesverständnis des nachprophetischen Zeit," *Biblisch-theologische Aufsätze,* Neukirchen-Vluyn, 1972, 179–194; S. **Mowinckel**, *Studien III: Die Esrageschichte und das Gesetz Moses;* N. **Reich**, "The Codification of the Egyptian Laws by Darius and the Origin of the 'Demotic Chronicle,' " *Mizraim* 1, 1933, 178–185; R. **Rendtorff**, "Esra und das Gesetz," *ZAW* 96, 1984, 165–184; H. H. **Schaeder**, *Esra der Schreiber,* 39–77; Morton **Smith**, *Parties and Politics That Shaped the Old Testament,* 122–125; W. **Spiegelberg**, *Die sogenannte demotische Chronik des Pap. 215 der Bibliotèque Nationale zu Paris,* Leipzig, 1915, especially 30–32; G. **Widengren**, "The Persian Period," in J. H. Hayes and J. M. Miller (eds.), *Israelite and Judaean History,* 514–515.

One of the major issues in the interpretation of Ezra-Nehemiah is the identity of the law which Ezra was commissioned to teach and administer. It was not a new law, since it was presumed to be familiar in principle to Jews in the province (Ezra 7:25), and it is unnecessary to conclude that he brought it with him (see on 7:14). The law of which the commission speaks is presumed to be identical with the

law of Moses or of YHVH mentioned in C's introduction to the
rescript (7:6, 10–11) and, by implication, throughout his history. The
traditional view in Judaism identifies this law with the Pentateuch
(Torah), or at least its legal portions, and there have been many
scholars since Wellhausen willing to accept the identification. The
alternative is to opt for some specific collection of Pentateuchal law,
Deuteronomic, Priestly, or Holiness Code (Lev. 17–26), or some
combination of them. Others again, much less plausibly, deny any
connection with Pentateuchal law (e.g., Houtman). Surprisingly,
however, the option is rarely argued on the basis of the allusions to
law, direct or indirect, in Ezra-Nehemiah or in C's history as a
whole.

Numerous allusions to an authoritative law occur in Ezra-Nehemiah, some in the Ezra material (especially, of course, the public
reading of the law, Neh. 8), others in the Nehemiah memoir, others
again in the editorial additions and connective editorial narrative.
The variations are legion: the law (Neh. 8:2, 7; 9:13–14, 26, 29, 34;
12:44), the book of the law (Neh. 8:3), the book *tout court* (Neh. 8:5,
8), the law of Moses (Ezra 3:2; 7:6), the book of the law of Moses
(Neh. 8:1), the book of Moses (Ezra 6:18; Neh. 13:1), the law of
God/YHVH (Ezra 7:10, 14, 26; Neh. 8:8, 18; 9:3), the law of the God
of heaven (Ezra 7:12, 21, in the rescript itself), the words (Ezra 9:4;
Neh. 8:9, 12–13), the ordinance (Ezra 3:4; Neh. 8:18—unless *mišpāṭ*
is to be translated "custom"), commandments, statutes, and ordinances (Ezra 7:11; 9:11; Neh. 1:5, 7; 9:16, 29, 34; 10:30 [29]), the law
commanded/given by Moses (Neh. 8:14; 10:30 [29]). In addition,
there are the allusions to practices and observances carried out in
keeping with legal stipulations, some accompanied by a standard
formula, e.g., "as it is written" (*kakkātûb,* Ezra 3:2, 4; 6:18; Neh.
8:15), but for the most part simply recorded as having been done in
a certain way. It might be worth asking what relation, if any, exists
between these instances and legal stipulations in the Pentateuch.

The most obvious places are those in which Pentateuchal law is
either directly quoted or paraphrased. Ezra's confessional prayer
refers to the law forbidding intermarriage with the natives, in keeping with the Deuteronomic character of the prayer as a whole. The
same verse (Deut. 7:3) is quoted by Nehemiah (13:25) and is the basis
for the first article of the covenant sworn to by the golah community
(Neh. 10:31 [30]). It is also Deuteronomic law to which Nehemiah
appeals in excluding Ammonites and Moabites from the temple
community (Neh. 13:1–2; cf. Deut. 23:4–5 [3–4]). Nehemiah's prayer
on hearing the bad news from Judah, also Deuteronomic in character, paraphrases Deut. 30:1–5 in a way suggesting that by the time

of composition (perhaps later than Nehemiah) the entire book rather than the legal corpus alone (12–26) was understood as Mosaic law (see on Neh. 1:8–9). Add that the only direct quote from the book of Moses in 1–2 Chron. is also from Deuteronomy (2 Chron. 25:4 following 2 Kings 14:6; Deut. 24:16).

While Deuteronomic law was therefore basic to the reforms of Ezra and Nehemiah, there are also instances where Priestly legislation (P) and the Holiness Code (H) have to be taken into account. Sukkoth, following on the reading of the law, is celebrated on the basis of provisions found only in this material; specifically, the injunction to dwell in booths (Neh. 8:14–15; cf. Lev. 23:42–43 H), the solemn assembly on the eighth day (Lev. 23:36, 39), and the sacrifices mandated for the festival (Ezra 3:4; cf. Num. 29:12–28, a later provision of Priestly law). The same for the celebration of Passover and Unleavened Bread in Ezra 6:19–22 (and cf. *AP* 21), the importance of which for C's history as a whole was noted in the commentary. The date (fourteenth of the first month) is specified in Ex. 12:6 (P) but not in Deut. 16:1–8, which also does not legislate on the important issue of qualifications for participating in the festival (Ezra 6:21; cf. Ex. 12:19, 45). For those convinced of the essential unity of Chronicles-Ezra-Nehemiah, it will come as no surprise to see that the Passovers of Hezekiah and Josiah are celebrated on the basis of the same law. The former avails itself of a provision of Priestly law allowing for a month's postponement for those not ritually pure (2 Chron. 30:2, 15; cf. Num. 9:6–14). The latter follows "the book of Moses" with respect to the distribution of the burnt offerings (2 Chron. 35:12). The Passover sacrifice is to be roasted following Priestly law (2 Chron. 35:13; cf. Ex. 12:8–9), not boiled as stipulated at Deut. 16:7. Likewise, the daily burnt offering *(tāmîd)* is reinstituted after the return following Priestly law (Ezra 3:3, 5; cf. Ex. 29:38–42; Num. 28:3–8). Sabbath was obviously of great importance for Nehemiah (13:15–22). While the manner of observance is assumed rather than stated, Nehemiah speaks of profaning the sabbath, following Priestly usage (e.g., Ex. 31:14; Ezek. 20:16). On the subject of tithing, finally, the covenant stipulation in Neh. 10 corresponds to Priestly law rather than to anything in Deuteronomy in obliging the community to "the tithe of tithes," i.e., the tenth part of the Levitical tithe destined for the priests (Neh. 10:38b–40 [37b–39]; cf. Num. 18:25–32).

In other instances observance could be on the basis of either Deuteronomy or Priestly law—for example, the prohibition of lending at interest to a fellow Israelite (Neh. 5:7–13; cf. Deut. 23:19–20; Lev. 25:36–37) and the law of firstlings and firstfruits (Neh. 10:36–

38a; cf. Deut. 15:19–20; 26:1–4; Lev. 23:14; Num. 18:15–16). In one case at least we find a combination of both: the stipulation in the sworn covenant concerning the sabbatical year (Neh. 10:32b [31b]) which combines the forgiveness of debts (Deut. 15:1–3) with the requirement that the land be left fallow (Lev. 25:1–7, 18–24).

Our survey would therefore suggest the conclusion that "the law" in Ezra-Nehemiah, and therefore Ezra's law *as understood by the redactor,* refers basically to Deuteronomic law supplemented by ritual legislation in the Pentateuchal corpora conventionally designated P and H. This conclusion is, however, complicated by another factor: those indications in Ezra-Nehemiah of practice in accord with neither Deuteronomic nor Priestly law. The clearest example is the observance of a day of repentance and fasting on the twenty-fourth rather than the tenth of Tishri, the latter being the date fixed for Yom Kippur in the Priestly laws (Neh. 9:1; cf. Lev. 16:29; 23:27–32; Num. 29:7–11). The most natural explanation would be that at that point in time Yom Kippur was either unknown or at least not firmly established. Somewhat less clear is the fixing of the temple tax at a third of a shekel (Neh. 10:33–34 [32–33]) rather than a half as in P (Ex. 30:11–16; cf. 38:25). Since taxation generally tends to increase rather than decrease, we would be inclined to conclude that the Pentateuchal stipulation is later in date, and it remained at that amount into the Roman period (Matt. 17:24; Josephus, *War* 7.6.6). The wood offering for the sanctuary (Neh. 10:35 [34]; 13:31), though implicit in sacrificial procedures, is absent from the Pentateuch, becoming the subject of explicit concern only in the rabbinical period (*b. Taan.* 28a). The minimum age for Levites, fixed at twenty in Ezra 3:8 (also 1 Chron. 23:24–27; 2 Chron. 31:17), twenty-five in Num. 8:24 (P) and thirty in 1 Chron. 23:3 (cf. Num. 4:3, 23, 30), might suggest a progressive lowering of the age in keeping with the increasing range of duties assigned to the office. But it is also possible that the minimum age was changed both ways in response to circumstances unknown to us; in which case conclusions about relative dating of sources would be invalid.

These results are corroborated by a survey of Chronicles which uses much the same language, predominantly Deuteronomic, in speaking of the law (e.g., 1 Chron. 6:49; 22:13; 28:7–8; 29:19; 2 Chron. 25:4; 30:16; 33:8; 34:31–33). It is assumed that the law was known and available in writing from the beginning of the monarchy (1 Chron. 16:40; 22:12–13; 28:7, 19; 2 Chron. 5:10). There were times, however, when it was lost, or at least lost sight of, and had to be rediscovered. When the prophet Azariah ben Oded told king Asa that "for a long time Israel was without the true God, without a teaching priest *(kōhēn môreh),* and without law" (2 Chron. 15:3), he was presumably referring to the days of the Judges. Right from the beginning, therefore, the law required a priest-teacher (like Ezra) for its implementation. Saul neglected this law and died as a result, his specific transgressions being consultation of mediums, forbidden by the Deuteronomic law (1 Chron. 10:13; Deut. 18:11). During David's reign the Levites carried the ark "as Moses had commanded according to the word of YHVH" (1 Chron. 15:15; cf. Deut. 10:8; 31:9, 25). The command to teach the law, much emphasized in Deuteronomy, was fulfilled in exemplary fashion by Jehoshaphat during whose reign a team of five princes, nine Levites, and two priests toured the cities of Judah teaching the people out of a law-book which they had with them (2 Chron. 17:7–9)—an operation parallel to that of Ezra and perhaps reflecting practice at the time of writing. Jehoshaphat also appointed judges in all the cities (2 Chron. 19:5–7; cf. Deut. 1:16–17; 16:18) and set up a central judiciary in Jerusalem composed of clergy and laity (19:8–11; cf. Deut. 17:8–13). As noted in the commentary on Ezra 7:26, the distinction made at this point between "the matter of YHVH" and "the matter of the king" is reflected in the language of the Artaxerxes decree.

Where law is referred to in C's history of the Judean monarchy, the wording is more often than not Deuteronomic and there are frequent allusions to the laws in Deut. 12–26. But as in Ezra-Nehemiah, the Deuteronomic law is supplemented by cultic legislation of the P variety; e.g., the *tāmîd* and the celebration of Passover by Hezekiah and Josiah. In reading through this material, we may also observe how Ezra's mission was seen to fit into the history taken as a whole. A basic pattern is that of failure to observe the law leading to disaster and followed by a movement of renewal and restoration. Saul disregarded the law (1 Chron. 10:13); David was a model of observance. After the lawlessness of Ahaz, Hezekiah did everything in accord with the law, renewed the covenant (2 Chron. 29:10) and crowned it with Passover. The same for Josiah following Manasseh and Amon. The same pattern obtains in Ezra 1–6, and the author is at pains to tell us that everything was done according to the law. Since Ezra's task was to restore the law, we may assume that his mission, together with that of Nehemiah, was seen as a distinct, similar phase, following on a half century of failure (from the sixth year of Darius to the seventh of Artaxerxes) which he passes over in silence.

In the context of C's history, then, Ezra's law was no innovation. It was the law available from the beginning in writing, which had to be reaffirmed, retaught, and even rediscovered from time to time after periods of infidelity. The author of the Ezra Apocalypse follows the same line in presenting his hero as reproducing, under divine inspiration, the entire law after it had perished with the fall of Jerusalem (2 Esd. 14). This law cannot simply be identified with the Pentateuch, not even with the legal sections of the Pentateuch. Its basic content appears to have been Deut. 12–26, in what precise form we cannot say, supplemented with cultic legislation conventionally attributed to P and H. It is tempting to think of the Deuteronomic core as the law which obtained uninterruptedly in Judah from preexilic times and the cultic legislation as the product of priestly-scribal activity in the Babylonian diaspora. This conclusion would, however, be oversimplified. Much of the cultic legislation may have achieved its mature formulation at that time and later, and all of the laws were undergoing exegetical development as exemplified in the matter of foreign marriages in Ezra-Nehemiah (see especially Fishbane). What can perhaps be safely said is that Pentateuchal law had not reached its final form by the mid-fifth century but was well on its way to doing so.

The Artaxerxes rescript also raises the issue of Persian policy vis-à-vis the legal practices and traditions of subject peoples and the Jews in particular. Darius I was long remembered as one of the great legislators (Plato, *Ep.* 7.332b; Xenophon, *Oecon.* 14.6; Diodorus Siculus 1.95). He refers often to his law *(dāta)* in the Behistun inscription, and he seems to have drawn on the ancient Mesopotamian legal tradition in ruling his Babylonian subjects. He also appointed a commission to codify traditional Egyptian law, the final draft of which was written up in Aramaic and demotic Egyptian (Spiegelberg, Reich). The mission of the Egyptian notable Udjahorresnet, sent back to Egypt by Darius to reorganize the hieratic scribal schools or "houses of life," was probably connected with this work of codification and redaction, its purpose being to consolidate the *pax Persica* in that generally troubled part of the empire (Cameron, Blenkinsopp). The laws in question certainly included the regulation of cult, which, needless to say, had important political and economic implications. We have no direct evidence of similar activity in the province of Yehud during that reign, but it would be reasonable to surmise—given its strategic importance and proximity to Egypt—that Persian imperial policy also influenced the codification of Jewish law and therefore the formation of the laws in the Pentateuch. The mission of Ezra mandated by Artaxerxes, who was also faced with the need for extensive reform and reorganization (Diodorus Siculus 2.69, 71), could then be seen as a second phase in the consolidation of Israel's legal heritage.

Response to the Rescript (Ezra 7:27–8:14)

F. Ahlemann, "Zur Esra-Quelle," *ZAW* 59, 1942/1943, 77–98; G. Fohrer, *Introduction to the Old Testament*, Nashville, 1968, 243–244; G. Hölscher, *Esra und Nehemia* II, 519–520; W. Th. In der Smitten, *Esra*, 19–21; A. Kapelrud, *The Question of Authorship in the Ezra-Narrative*, 45–46; H. G. Kippenberg, *Religion und Klassenbildung im antiken Judäa*, Göttingen, 1978, 23–41; K. Koch, "Ezra and the Origins of Judaism," *JSS* 19, 1974, 173–197; R. du Mesnil du Buisson, *Nouvelles études sur les dieux et sur les mythes de Canaan*, Leiden, 1973, 232–233; S. Mowinckel, *Studien* I, 116–123; " 'Ich' und 'Er' in der Esrageschichte," *Verbannung und Heimkehr. Wilhelm Rudolph zum 70. Geburtstage*, Tübingen, 1961, 211–234; R. H. Pfeiffer, *Introduction to the Old Testament*, 830–831; O. Plöger, "Reden und Gebete im deuteronomistischen und chronistischen Geschichtswerk," in W. Schneemelcher (ed.), *Festschrift für Günther Dehn*, Neukirchen-Vluyn, 1957, 35–49; H. C. M. Vogt, *Studie zur nachexilischen Gemeinde in Esra-Nehemia*, Werl, 1966, 118–141.

7:27 Blessed be YHVH, God of our fathers, who has so disposed the mind of the king to beautify the house of YHVH which is in Jerusalem, [28]and has made the king, his counselors, and all his powerful officials well disposed toward me. Since, therefore, I enjoyed the favor of YHVH my God,[a] I strengthened my resolve and assembled leading men out of Israel to go up with me.

8:1 These are the heads of their ancestral houses and the list of those who went up with me from Babylon in the reign of King Artaxerxes:

[2]Of the descendants of Phinehas: Gershom;

Of the descendants of Ithamar: Daniel;

Of the descendants of David: Hattush son of Shecaniah;[b]

[3]Of the descendants of Parosh: Zechariah, with whom were listed 150 males;

[4]Of the descendants of Pahath-moab: Eliehoenai son of Zechariah, accompanied by 200 males;

[5]Of the descendants of Zattu:[c] Shecaniah son of Jahaziel, accompanied by 300 males;

[6]and of the descendants of Adin: Ebed son of Jonathan, accompanied by 50 males;

[7]and of the descendants of Elam: Jeshaiah son of Athaliah, accompanied by 70 males;

[8]and of the descendants of Shephatiah: Zebadiah son of Michael, accompanied by 80 males;

[9]of the descendants of Joab: Obadiah son of Jehiel, accompanied by 218 males;

¹⁰and of the descendants of Bani:ᵈ Shelomothᵉ son of Josiphiah, accompanied by 160 males;

¹¹and of the descendants of Bebai: Zechariah son of Bebai, accompanied by 28 males;

¹²and of the descendants of Azgad: Johanan son of Hakkatan, accompanied by 110 males;

¹³and of the descendants of Adonikam: these are the names of the last of the family:ᶠ Eliphelet, Jeiel, Shemaiah, accompanied by 60 males;

¹⁴and of the descendants of Bigvai: Uthai son of Zabbud,ᵍ accompanied by 70 males.

a. Lit., "as the hand of YHVH my God was on me"; cf. 7:6.
b. With LXXᴬ and 1 Esd. 8:29 instead of MT: "of the descendants of David: Hattush; of the descendants of Shecaniah . . ."; see commentary.
c. Zattu, missing in MT, is supplied from 1 Esd. 8:32 and LXX (Zathoes); cf. Ezra 2:8.
d. Bani, missing in MT, supplied from 1 Esd. 8:36 and LXX (Boani); cf. Ezra 2:10.
e. MT Shelomith is a female name (e.g., 1 Chron. 3:19); for Shelomoth see 1 Chron. 23:9; 24:22, etc. (M. Noth 1928, 165 n. 6).
f. MT has simply "the last (*'aḥᵃrōnîm),* and these are the names . . ."; for the present translation see commentary.
g. With 1 Esd. 8:40, in keeping with the singular *'immô;* MT has "Uthai and Zabbud (Qere: Zakkur) accompanied by 70 males."

At this point begins a fairly long first-person narrative attributed to Ezra (7:27–9:15), which the corresponding section in 1 Esdras introduces, unnecessarily, with the words "then Ezra the scribe said" (8:25). Assuming that this Ezra memorandum is not a pure invention of C, it included the rescript (presupposed by 7:27–28), and perhaps also some account of how the mission came about, analogous to the opening of Nehemiah's memoir (2:1–8). It would then remain to be determined whether the third-person Ezra material (7:1–11; 10; Neh. 8) derives from an independent source available to C (as, e.g., Ahlemann) or consists in C's selective paraphrase of the first-person narrative (as, e.g., Rudolph 1949, 165).

[7:27–28] The short prayer or doxology which follows the rescript is, with the exception of the long penitential prayers in Ezra 9:6–15 and Neh. 9:6–37 (the latter attributed to Ezra in LXX), the only one in the Ezra narrative. By contrast, the Nehemiah narrative is punctuated by short prayers which, however, are of a quite different kind (see commentary ad loc.). Ezra's prayer, beginning with the blessing form (*bārûk* YHVH), is more in line with the sort of prayers which C, occasionally but not always following his source, puts into the mouths of his characters throughout the history (e.g., David, 1 Chron. 29:10–19; Huram of Tyre, 2 Chron. 2:11; Solomon, 2 Chron. 6:4–11; the Queen of Sheba, 2 Chron. 9:8; see also the prayer of Jehoshaphat addressed to "the God of the fathers," 2 Chron. 20:5–12). The phrase "who has so disposed the mind of the king," literally, "who has put (something) like this into the heart of the king," is also found at Neh. 2:12 and 7:5. C is evidently using his own language to express Ezra's sentiments and restate a theme dominant throughout the book.

It is worth noting that no allusion is made here to the law; the main concern is with the temple, its equipment and adornment. We find the same emphasis in Ezra's preparations for the journey to Jerusalem (8:15–20, 24–30). The confessional prayer also speaks of YHVH working through the kings of Persia with a view to reestablishing the temple and its cult (9:9). Since both Jewish tradition and modern scholarship tend to stress almost exclusively Ezra's role vis-à-vis the law, it will be well to bear this in mind in evaluating his mission. It may also, incidentally, help to explain the puzzling allusion to Artaxerxes at Ezra 6:14. One of several clues that Ezra's mission is presented as the fulfillment of prophecy (see especially Koch) is the verb rendered "beautify" *(pā'ēr),* which occurs frequently in Isa. 40–66, in two instances with reference to the new sanctuary (Isa. 60:7, 13). Together with the frequent bringing in of the number twelve (2:2; 6:17; 8:3–14, 24, 35) and the hints of a new exodus from Babylon, it might suggest an interpretation of Ezra's work significantly different from the one which has prevailed in modern scholarship.

We note once again the theme of the benevolence of the Persian kings. It is arguable that Ezra represents a political stance more characteristic of the Babylonian diaspora than the homeland, one which allowed for a full religious life even without political autonomy. With this in mind, then, Ezra proceeded to the first and most difficult stage, that of persuading civic and religious leaders in the diaspora—many of them now fifth- or sixth-generation Babylonians—to follow the example of Abraham and set out for a strange land.

[8:1] The list of participants in Ezra's caravan amounts to 1,513 males (1,690 in 1 Esd. 8), suggesting a total inclusive of women and children of around 5,000; hence about a sixth of the number in the

Ezra 2 repatriation list. The groups are listed according to a set formula: name of eponym, name of the living head or patriarch of the group, number of males in the phratry or extended family. There are some divergencies from this pattern. The numbers accompanying the two priestly groups and one Davidic group with which the list opens are not given. The second-last of the twelve lay phratries, that of Adonikam, lists three names, adding that they are the last— meaning that none of that family remained in Babylon (see below on 3–14). It will come as no surprise to learn that the authenticity of the list has often been questioned (e.g., by Hölscher, Kapelrud, Fohrer). It has been argued that the list interrupts the sequence of the narrative between 7:28 and 8:15, dealing with the assembling of the caravan. This may be so, but the fact that the list has been spliced into the story does not impugn its authenticity. And, in any case, it could as well be argued that 8:15 is a resumptive verse, of a kind which we have seen to occur frequently in the book. The list also follows on quite naturally from 7:28. The occurrence of all twelve names of the lay eponyms (excluding David) in the Ezra 2 list has also aroused suspicion. But again, it could be countered that Ezra would naturally seek recruits among families some of whose members had already made aliyah, in some cases in the not so distant past. We have every reason to believe that close ties existed between the Babylonian diaspora and the homeland, especially between members of the same extended family. As for the number twelve, reminiscent of the twelve leaders of the first return (2:2), and sometimes taken as evidence of an artificial and fictive schematizing: if it necessitated some editorial arrangement of the data (as with the twelve "minor" prophets in the canon), this would not impugn the essential authenticity of the list.

[2] The list opens with priests and the representative of the Davidic line, as with the Ezra 2 list but in reverse order. Phinehas, son of Eleazar, and Ithamar represented the two surviving branches of the Aaronite priesthood after the elimination of Nadab and Abihu by a precisely engineered earthquake (Lev. 10). This arrangement, which contrasts with the priestly courses in Ezra 2:36–39, points to the increasing ascendancy of the Aaronites, an ascendancy now enshrined in the Pentateuch (Ex. 6:23–25; 28:1; Num. 3:2–4; 25:6–13; cf. 1 Chron. 24:1–2). The need for new blood is also indicated by the fierce denunciation of the Jerusalem priesthood in Malachi (1:6–2:9; 3:3) which ends with the promise, or threat, of a purge to be carried out by an emissary of YHVH—by some identified with Ezra himself, but perhaps more likely Nehemiah. Ezra himself belonged to the

Phinehas line, represented in the list by Gershom, an old priestly name (1 Chron. 6:1, etc.). The cadet branch of Ithamar was represented in the caravan by a certain Daniel, whose name also appears among the signatories to the sworn covenant (Neh. 10:7 [6]). That these were not the only priests to make the journey is clear from the subsequent narrative (8:24).

Following the text as amended, the Davidic house was represented by Hattush, son of Shecaniah in the list and his grandson in C's Davidic genealogy (1 Chron. 3:21–22). If the latter is correct, Hattush would be a fourth-generation Davidide after Zerubbabel (born around 570), which makes a possible fit with a mission in 458 but practically eliminates the rival date sixty years later in the reign of Artaxerxes II. No other Davidic participants are mentioned, perhaps because there were none. That Hattush is listed separately from the others, and yet is passed over without comment, is consonant with C's political views, which may well have been no different from those of Ezra, at least at the outset of his mission.

[3–14] All of the twelve phratries mentioned here occur also in the first part of the laity roster for the first return (Ezra 2:3–15), but none of the names in the second half of the Ezra 2 list (16–20) occurs here. The only name in the first half of this list which is absent from the Ezra 2 list is Zaccai. Of the twelve names in our list the first, the fifth, and the last five are in the same order as the list of the first return. The question of priority cannot easily be decided. In any case, it is possible that both draw on a census of families known to be of Babylonian origin (the *beně haggôlāh* of C). Members of seven of the twelve pledged themselves to divorce their foreign wives (Ezra 10), and all—with the sole exception of Shephatiah—are represented among the signatories to the sworn covenant (Neh. 10; assuming that Adonijah is identical with Adonikam and that Joab is included under Pahath-Moab). Several also took part in the wall-building under Nehemiah. Most of the names are fairly well attested for the period. Ebed (v. 6) is probably hypocoristic, from Obadiah (cf. 1 Esd. 8:32 and LXX Obeth); Jeshaiah, an alternative transliteration of Isaiah, appears to have been common in the Persian period (e.g., Ezra 8:19; Neh. 11:7); Joab represents the cadet branch of the Pahath-moab phratry (cf. 2:6); Hakkatan (the Small) is a nickname to distinguish its bearer from an older or larger member of the family (cf. James the Less). The Adonikam phratry diverges from the pattern in naming three leaders who are "the last" or "the latest." This has been understood as the last in the list (e.g., NEB), the last to arrive (presumably meaning that they set out later than the others), or the youngest members of the family. Most likely, however, we are being told that with these three the entire family group had made aliyah, leaving none behind in Babylon. For further comment on the names of the families see on 2:3–15.

Recruiting for the Mission (Ezra 8:15–20)

E. **Auerbach**, "Das Aharon-Problem," *VTSup.* 17, 1968, 37–63; A. **Bentzen**, "Priesterschaft und Laien in der jüdischen Gemeinde des fünften Jahrhunderts," *AfO* 6, 1930/31, 280–286; L. E. **Browne**, "A Jewish Sanctuary in Babylonia," *JTS* 17, 1916, 400–401; A. **Causse**, *Les dispersés d'Israël*, Paris, 1929, 76–77; A. **Cody**, *A History of Old Testament Priesthood*, Rome, 1969, 168–170; A. **Falkenstein**, "Die babylonische Schule," *Saeculum* 4, 1953, 125–137; A. H. J. **Gunneweg**, *Leviten und Priester*, Göttingen, 1965, 204–215; W. Th. **In der Smitten**, *Esra*, 21–22; S. **Klein**, "Die Schreiberfamilien: I Chron. 2:55," *Monatschrift für Geschichte und Wissenschaft des Judentums* 70, 1926, 410–416; I. **Mendelsohn**, "Guilds in Babylonia and Assyria," *JAOS* 60, 1940, 68–72; A. **Menes**, "Tempel und Synagoge," *ZAW* 50, 1932, 268–276; E. **Meyer**, *Die Entstehung des Judentums*, 176–177; K. **Möhlenbrink**, "Die levitischen Überlieferungen des Alten Testaments," *ZAW* 52, 1934, 209; R. **de Vaux**, *AI*, 388–390; J. **Vink**, "The Date and Origin of the Priestly Code in the Old Testament," *OTS* 15, 1969, 73–77; D. E. **Weisberg**, *Guild Structure and Political Allegiance in Early Achaemenid Mesopotamia*, Baltimore, 1967; H. **Winckler**, "Kasiphja-Ctesiphon," *Altorientalische Forschungen*, Reihe 2, Band III, Leipzig, 1901, 509–530.

8:15 These I assembled by the canal which flows to Ahava, where we set up camp for three days. When I reviewed the people and the priests, I found no Levites there. [16]So I sent[a] Eliezer, Ariel, Shemaiah, Elnathan,[b] Jarib, Elnathan, Nathan, Zechariah, and Meshullam, leading men, together with Joiarib and Elnathan, instructors.[c] [17]I ordered them[d] to go to Iddo, the leading man in the place Casiphia, with instructions as to what they were to say[e] to Iddo, his kinsmen,[f] and the temple servants[g] in the place Casiphia: they were to send us ministers for the house of our God. [18]Since we enjoyed the favor of our God,[h] they sent us Sherebiah,[i] a skilled man of the descendants of Mahli, son of Levi, son of Israel, with eighteen of his sons and kinsmen; [19]also Hashabiah together with Jeshaiah of the descendants of Merari and twenty of his kinsmen and their sons. [20]Of the temple servants, whom David had assigned as ministers[j] for the service of the Levites, there were two hundred and twenty, all of them designated by name.

a. Each of the following names is preceded by *lamed;* since, however, they cannot be the ones to whom the message was sent, we must either translate "sent for" or, better, take *lamed* as the sign of the accusative.

b. Some MSS have "Jonathan."

c. 1 Esd. 8:43 omits the last two men, thus applying the designations *rā'šîm* and *mᵉbînîm (hēgoumenous kai epistēmonas)* to all ten individuals named; probably a result of overlooking the meaning "teacher" for *mēbîn*.

d. With Qere *vā'ᵃsavveh* rather than Ketib *vā'ôṣî'āh*, lit., "I sent them out."

e. Lit., "I put in their mouths words to say."

f. Reading *vᵉehāv* for MT *'āhîv*, "his brother," following LXX. Torrey's emendation *'āhî*, "my brother" (i.e., Ezra's), is interesting but speculative (1910, 265).

g. Reading *vᵉhannᵉtînîm;* Ketib has *hannᵉtûnîm*.

h. Cf. 7:7, 28.

i. MT has "and Sherebiah," thus distinguishing him from the "skillful man." This, however, would leave Sherebiah without a pedigree and would raise the question why the *'îš śekel* is not named.

j. Reading *mᵉšārᵉtîm* for MT *vᵉhaśśārîm*, "and his princes." The verb is singular, and C makes David alone the founder of the clerical orders; see also the commentary.

[8:15] The first-person narrative takes up from 7:28 with the repetition of the verb "assembled" *(vā'eqbᵉṣāh . . . vā'eqbᵉṣēm)*, another example of the resumptive technique by means of which C maintains narrative continuity. The recruitment of Levites is a logical consequence of their absence from the preceding list and the terms in which the permission was granted (7:13); and for C as editor the mission of Ezra would have been inconceivable without them. It would nevertheless be unwise to impugn the essential historicity of this incident, especially in view of the plausible topographical and onomastic detail. The location of the assembly point is unknown. Ahava is here a place-name, whereas later it is a river or, more probably, a canal (vs. 21, 31). Identification with Scenae (= tents), a caravanserai near Babylon (Strabo, *Geog.* 6.1, 27) is speculative, but it could not have been far from the city. The choice of a site by water was dictated by practical and possibly also ritual requirements (cf. Ps. 137:1; Ezek. 1:1, 3; 3:15). The three-day pause is repeated after the arrival in Jerusalem by both Ezra (8:32) and Nehemiah (Neh. 2:11). A frequent feature in traditional narrative, it stands for a brief period of time. As a result of his efforts, Ezra recruited thirty-eight Levites, about half the number given in the census of the first return. For possible reasons for the low numbers see commentary on 2:40. Other reasons, some rather fanciful, are proposed by several rabbis (e.g., *t. B.K.* 7:3; *b. Pes.* 87b).

[16–17] Following MT, the eleven deputies are divided into two groups: nine "heads," short for "heads of ancestral houses" (see on 1:5), and two instructors. 1 Esd. 8:43–44 has only ten names, omits the last two, and describes them all without distinction as leaders and men of discernment (see textual note c). But here and elsewhere in C's history the term mēbîn (active participle of the verb hēbîn; stem byn) can also designate a person with a special skill and, more specifically, one who teaches that skill to others. In C's history almost all occurrences refer to Levites. The liturgical precentor Chenaniah has this title (1 Chron. 15:22), as also Levitical musicians in general (1 Chron. 25:7–8; 2 Chron. 34:12), the distinction between teacher and pupil (mēbîn 'im-talmîd) being made explicitly at 1 Chron. 25:8. The teaching function of the Levites is also indicated by the same verbal form in C's account of Josiah's reform (2 Chron. 35:3) and in connection with Ezra's reading of the law (Neh. 8:8–9). It seems, then, that the distinction in MT should be retained, which means that Joiarib and Elnathan were singled out as having a special function, that of instruction, even though they were not themselves Levites.

Some confusion has probably occurred in the transmission of the eleven names: there are too many Elnathans, and Jarib is a variant of Joiarib. Only two of them—Shemaiah and Zechariah—occur in the preceding list, a circumstance sometimes misguidedly used as an argument against the authenticity of the list, which, needless to say, gives only a few of the names of the repatriates. Five of the eleven names here occur in the list of those who married outside the community (Ezra 10), and a Meshullam is one of the few who are named as opposing Ezra's measures (10:15). Two—Zechariah and Meshullam again—are noted as participants in the public reading and explanation of the law (Neh. 8:40), though the names are quite common and the individuals may therefore not be the same.

The delegates were required to consult with a certain Iddo, described as the leading person in a place called Casiphia, literally "Casiphia the place." This place-name is otherwise unattested. It might suggest something to do with silver (kaspā' in Aramaic), perhaps named after a guild or guilds of silversmiths who had settled there (cf. ksp' in AP 13:18, 19; BMAP 3; 12). In Babylonia, as in Israel, artisans working at the same trade tended to group together. Others, however, have connected the name with "Caspian" (Herodotus 7.67) or with the idea of a treasury, following 1 Esd. 8:45, while Winckler identified it with the Ctesiphon of the Greeks. Whatever the explanation, it was clearly a place of some importance for the Babylonian diaspora. It must have been the site of a cultic establishment of some kind, and the peculiar construction "Casiphia the place," repeated twice in the same verse, recalls the Deuteronomic use of "place" (māqôm) for temple (e.g., Deut. 12:5; 1 Kings 8:29;

Jer. 7:3, 6, 7; cf. Ezra 9:8). This in its turn has raised the question whether the Babylonian exiles, like their coreligionists in Elephantine, worshiped in their own temple. The possibility cannot be dismissed out of hand on account of the Deuteronomic centralization of the cult. The measure was designed to put rival sanctuaries in Israel out of business, and even if it was interpreted as applying outside the land of Israel, we have no guarantee that the prohibition was successful. About half a century after Ezra's mission the Jewish leaders in Elephantine requested and obtained the support of the governor of Judah for the rebuilding of their temple destroyed in a pogrom (*AP* 30–32). It is true that the high priest and his colleagues in Jerusalem had not replied to a previous letter dealing with the same matter (*AP* 30:18), but their silence is adequately explained by disapproval of the syncretic type of worship practiced in the settlement; and the governor's reply betrays no hint of disapproval. The same situation may have obtained in Babylon, and some have found confirmation in Zechariah's vision of the woman called Wickedness (the goddess Anath?), for whom a temple was to be built in the land of Shinar (Zech. 5:5–11). This, however, was only a proposal, and it comes from a rather later time. At the least, there must have existed at Casiphia a school, comparable to the Egyptian "house of life," for the training of temple personnel. Whatever conclusion is reached about the origins and location of the P source in the Pentateuch, the study of law, including ritual law, which was going on in the diaspora must have had some such institutional basis. Iddo may not have been Ezra's brother, as Torrey supposed, but it is reasonable to suppose that they both shared the same kind of background.

[18–20] Iddo was able to provide thirty-eight Levites and two hundred and twenty temple servants for Ezra's caravan, as against seventy-four and three hundred and ninety-two (the latter inclusive of descendants of Solomon's servants) in the census of the first return. No musicians or gatekeepers are mentioned, though some may have been included among the Levites. Three leaders are mentioned by name: Sherebiah, Hashabiah, Jeshaiah. All three belonged to the Merari division (Gen. 46:11; Ex. 6:16; Num. 3:17, etc.), which had special responsibility for carrying the tabernacle and other holy objects in the wilderness (Num. 4:29–33). Sherebiah and Hashabiah, together with ten other Levites, will form half of the team charged with the conveyance of the vessels and offerings (8:24). The former played a prominent role in subsequent events—the public reading of the law (Neh. 8:7) and the service of repentance (Neh. 9:4–5)—and was a signatory of the covenant (Neh. 10:13 [12]). The term *šekel,* skill, occurs elsewhere in C's history where he treats of Levites and their associates (1 Chron. 26:14; 2 Chron. 30:22).

It is tolerably clear that C has added the clause in v. 20 purporting to explain the origin of the temple servants and the etymology of their name (*n^{e}tînîm,* from the verbal stem *ntn,* give). The phrase "for the service of the house of God" is typical of C (e.g., 1 Chron. 25:6), but the late form of the relative pronoun *(š^e* for *'^{a}šer)* is not. (It occurs only at 1 Chron. 5:20 and 27:27, the latter probably added.) The list of two hundred and twenty names may well have been available to the editor, but its inclusion would have interfered with the narrative flow.

Preparations for Departure (Ezra 8:21–30)

A. **Cody,** *A History of Old Testament Priesthood,* 190–192; A. **Kapelrud,** *The Question of Authorship in the Ezra-Narrative,* 52–53; B. **Pelzl,** "Philologisches zu Esra 8:27," *ZAW* 87, 1975, 221–224; D. J. **Wiseman,** "A Late Babylonian Tribute List?" *BSOAS* 30, 1967, 499.

8:21 I proclaimed a fast there by the Ahava canal, so that we might humble ourselves before our God and ask of him a safe journey for ourselves, our children, and all our possessions. [22]I was ashamed to ask the king for an armed escort with cavalry to assist us against enemies along the way, for we had told the king that the favor of our God works for the good of all those who seek him,[a] but his fierce anger[b] is on all those who forsake him. [23]So we fasted and entreated our God about this, and he answered our prayers.

[24]Then I set aside twelve of the leading priests and Sherebiah and[c] Hashabiah together with ten of their kinsmen, [25]and I weighed out to them the silver, gold, and vessels, the offerings for the house of our God which the king, his counselors and lords, and all Israel present there, had contributed. [26]I weighed out into their keeping six hundred and fifty talents of silver, a hundred silver vessels weighing two talents,[d] and a hundred talents of gold; [27]also twenty gold bowls worth one thousand darics and two vessels of fine burnished copper, as precious as gold. [28]I said to them, "You are consecrated to YHVH, and the vessels also are consecrated; and the silver and gold are a votive offering to YHVH God of our fathers.[e] [29]Guard them carefully[f] until you weigh them out in the presence of the leading priests, the Levites, and the leaders of ancestral houses of Israel in Jerusalem, in the rooms of the house

of YHVH." [30]So the priests and Levites took delivery of the full weight of silver, gold, and sacred vessels, to convey them to Jerusalem, to the house of our God.

a. Lit., "the hand of our God is on (over) all who entreat him, to (their) good."
b. Lit., "his strength and anger"; hendiadys.
c. For MT *l^ešērēbyāh* read *v^ešērēbyāh* with 1 Esd. 8:34.
d. MT has "a hundred silver vessels worth talents." Either the number of talents has fallen out (as Myers 1965, Batten 1913, R. A. Bowman 1954, et al.) or we are to read the dual *l^ekikkārāym* for the plural *l^ekikkārîm*. This translation favors the dual.
e. Reading *'^abōtēnû* for MT *'^abōtēkem*, second person pl., with LXX, Vulg., and other ancient versions.
f. MT has "watch over and guard" *(šiqdû v^ešimrû)*, another example of hendiadys.

[8:21–23] As we would expect, preparation for the arduous journey was both practical and spiritual. In the preexilic period fasting, often accompanied by sacrificial ritual, was practiced as an accompaniment to mourning the dead (1 Sam. 31:13; 2 Sam. 1:12; 12:16, 21–23) or in a situation of national or individual emergency (Judg. 20:26; Jer. 14:12; 36:6, 9; Pss. 35:13; 69:11 [10]; 109:24). After the massive disasters of the late sixth century it became more common (e.g., Jer. 41:4–5 at Mizpah; cf. 1 Sam. 7:6), with liturgical fasting commemorating the fall of Jerusalem and destruction of the temple (Zech. 7:2–7; 8–19; cf. Isa. 58:3–9). As in the present passage, it often acts as a reinforcement of prayer, not infrequently involving confession of sin (cf. Neh. 9:1; Dan. 9:3; 2 Chron. 20:3). The very ancient idea of fasting as a form of mortification, in the etymological sense of bringing oneself to the point of death in order to bring into play the saving power of God, is also present here in connection with self-abasement (see also 1 Kings 21:27–29; Isa. 58:3–9; Lev. 16:29–34). Thus the fast at the Ahava canal points to the grave dangers anticipated—with reason—during the arduous journey to Judah. The prayer for a safe journey, literally, a straight or level way *(derek y^ešārāh)*, is almost certainly intended to recall the exilic Isaiah's call to straighten or level the way for the homecoming of the exiles (Isa. 40:3); another indication that Ezra's mission is seen as the fulfillment of prophecy.

This aspect of the mission may also help to explain why Ezra's caravan made the journey without a military escort, unlike the earlier journey of Udjahorresnet from Susa to Egypt and the later one of Nehemiah, also originating in Susa (Neh. 2:9). While this circumstance need not point to dependence of the Ezra account on the Nehemiah memoir (as suggested by Kapelrud, In der Smitten 1973a, et al.), it is extraordinary that the Persian officials did not insist on an armed escort, especially since a good part of the treasure being conveyed came from them. The reason for Ezra's refusal of help is given in a psalm-like couplet, identified as such by the parallelism between "all who seek him" and "all who forsake him" (cf. 1 Chron. 28:9; 2 Chron. 15:2; Isa. 58:2; 65:1, 11). The problems which Ezra may well have anticipated would have originated not (as is often suggested) from apostate Jews but from the unsettled political situation in the west at that time.

[24–27] Assuming that the Sherebiah and Hashabiah here mentioned are identical with the Levites so named in vs. 18–19, the group charged with conveying the votive offerings for the temple would have consisted in twelve priests and twelve Levites, consistent with the duties assigned to the clergy elsewhere in C's history. This further example of interest in the number twelve (cf. 2:2; 6:17; 8:35; also 1 Chron. 25:9–21, the divisions of Levitical musicians) is noteworthy in spite of the fact that the clergy by itself is not representative of Israel. Somewhat parallel to the votive offerings for the First Temple (1 Chron. 26:26), the gifts come from the king, his attendants, and Babylonian Jews. They indicate, once again, both the munificence of the Persian ruler and the acknowledged legitimacy of the Jerusalem shrine. As elsewhere in C's history (1 Chron. 21:25; cf. 2 Sam. 24:24; 2 Chron. 7:5), the amounts are greatly exaggerated: 650 talents of silver, calculating the talent at about 75 pounds, amounts to more than 21 tons (cf. 2:69). If the reading proposed is correct (see textual note d), the vessels would average about one and a half pounds each. A hundred talents of gold would be well in excess of three tons weight, and the twenty gold bowls would add up to about twenty-one pounds. The two copper vessels must have been manufactured from a special and rare type of ore, perhaps the rich, reddish kind known as orichalc, but unfortunately the term used to describe it (*muṣhāb*, perhaps related to *ṣāhōb*, red or yellow, Lev. 13:30) occurs only here. The combination of the plausible and the implausible in this inventory suggests that C was working with real data which he has elaborated, in his accustomed way, *ad maiorem templi gloriam* and to convey more vividly Ezra's trust in divine providence.

[28–30] Ezra reminds the bearers that both they and the vessels with which they are charged are consecrated (*qōdeš*, usually translated "holy"), that is, removed from the profane sphere and set aside for divine service. The idea was not only to emphasize the sacred nature of their task but to discourage theft. The silver and gold were not in the same category, since they were to be used to purchase the necessities for worship (cf. 7:17–18). Here again, the motif of votive or freewill offering (*n*^{e}*dābāh;* see on 1:4) reappears. Those to whom the treasure was to be consigned included laymen, but since laymen are not mentioned in the account of the delivery (v. 33), their inclusion here has been taken to be an editorial addition (Rudolph 1949, 82). Perhaps so, but absolute consistency is not to be looked for in this kind of narrative. The temple rooms in which the treasure is to be deposited are no doubt storerooms of the kind which surrounded the main hall and inner sanctuary of the First Temple (1 Kings 6:5–10).

The Journey Successfully Completed (Ezra 8:31–36)

F. M. **Abel**, *La géographie de la Palestine* II, Paris, 1933, 108–120; N. **Avigad**, "A New Class of Yehud Stamps," *IEJ* 7, 1957, 146–150; A. **Bentzen**, "Priesterschaft und Laien in der jüdischen Gemeinde des fünften Jahrhunderts," *AfO* 6, 1930/31, 260–286; P. C. **Hammond**, "A Note on Two Seal Impressions from Tell es-Sultan," *PEQ* 89, 1957, 68–69; A. **Jaubert**, "Le Calendrier des Jubilés et de la Secte de Qumrân: Ses Origines Bibliques," *VT* 3, 1953, 261; O. **Leuze**, *Die Satrapieneinteilung in Syrien und Zweistromlande von 520 bis 320,* Halle, 1935, 19–23; J. **Milgrom**, *Studies in Cultic Theology and Terminology,* Leiden, 1983, 47–66, 67–74; N. H. **Snaith**, "A Note on Ezra viii.35," *JTS* n.s. 22, 1971, 150–152.

8:31 We set out on the journey to Jerusalem from the Ahava canal on the twelfth day of the first month; [32]and since we enjoyed the favor of our God,[a] he kept us safe from enemies and ambush along the way. [32]So we arrived in Jerusalem and rested[b] there for three days. [33]On the fourth day we weighed out the silver and gold and the vessels in the house of our God into the keeping of Meremoth son of Uriah the priest, with whom were Eleazar son of Phinehas together with the Levites Jozabad son of Jeshua and Noadiah son of Binnui. [34]Everything was in order with respect to number and weight, and the weight of the entire consignment was recorded there and then.

[35]Then the exiles who had returned from the captivity offered in sacrifice to the God of Israel twelve steers for all Israel, ninety-six rams, seventy-two[c] lambs, and twelve he-goats as a sin offering: all a burnt offering to YHVH. [36]They delivered the king's instructions to the royal satrapal authorities and the governors of the Trans-Euphrates satrapy, who then provided support for the people and the house of God.

a. Lit., "the hand of our God was upon us"; cf. 7:6, 9, 28; 8:18, 22.
b. *vanneseb;* "rested" rather than "stayed" since they did not leave after three days.
c. With 1 Esd. 8:65 and Josephus, *Ant.* 11.137; MT has "seventy-three."

The narrative continues in the first person (vs. 31–34) but the conclusion (vs. 35–36) is third person, the language and ideas betraying the hand of C. The first-person narrative, which justifies the refusal of an armed escort and emphasizes the safe delivery of the entire consignment, suggests a report to the Persian authorities. The sequel in the third person is of a quite different nature, though the statement that the king's orders had been passed on to the satrapal authorities (cf. 7:21–24) may have been taken from Ezra's memorandum.

[8:31–34] For the chronological indications in 7:7–8, C could have drawn on the Ezra memorandum. The actual departure from the Ahava was on the twelfth of Nisan, which, as noted earlier, implies that Passover was celebrated ten days after the caravan had left base. The journey lasted over a hundred days and was apparently uneventful, remarkably so in view of the politically disturbed situation in the early years of Artaxerxes I, the treasure being transported, and the lack of a military escort. Use of the verb *hissil* (rescue, save; stem *nsl*) does not necessarily imply that they came under attack but survived. The date of arrival was the first of Ab, the month in which the destruction of the First Temple was commemorated (2 Kings 25:8; Zech. 7:3; 8:19). It has also been calculated that, according to the calendar of the Book of Jubilees and the Qumran community, they would have arrived on a Friday, corresponding to the day of the week on which Joshua entered Canaan (Jaubert). This would neatly explain one of the three days' rest, but unfortunately we do not know that the golah community followed this calendar in the fifth century B.C.E. Three days is a conventional designation for a short period of time (cf. 8:15; 10:8; Neh. 2:11) and cannot be used to demonstrate dependence on the Nehemiah narrative. It may, however, have been meant to recall the three days' pause of Joshua after crossing the Jordan (Josh. 3:1) in keeping with the exodus-occupation typology of the narrative as a whole. Practically, of course, three days would be an absolute minimum for finding at least provisional shelter for some five thousand immigrants.

On the fourth day, which would be the fourth or fifth of Ab, the offerings and sacred vessels were turned over to the clerical authorities designated to take delivery of them. These consisted in two priests and two Levites under the leadership of Meremoth. During Nehemiah's tenure of office the temple treasury was also administered by a board of four: a priest, a scribe, a Levite, and a temple musician (Neh. 12:44; 13:13). Since the relevant passages do not imply that this arrangement was first set up at that time, they cannot be used to demonstrate the chronological priority of Nehemiah. The name Meremoth has been another red herring in this respect. He belonged to the Hakkoz family (Neh. 3:4, 21), which, according to the census in Ezra 2, had been unable to document its priestly credentials and was therefore debarred from office. The argument runs that Meremoth was not functioning as a priest at the time of the wall-building, but by the time Ezra arrived he had not only been reinstated but was occupying an important office (Rudolph 1949, 17, 69; Myers 1965, 72; et al.). Bentzen (1930/31) would even have us believe that he was reinstated for doing double duty on the wall. Further, if the priest Meremoth who signed the covenant is the same person (Neh. 10:6 [5]), the rehabilitation must have occurred while Nehemiah was still in office. All of this is, however, quite speculative. If Ezra preceded Nehemiah, it could as well be argued that the unfrocking of the Hakkoz priests took place after Ezra's arrival, and that the Meremoth of Neh. 10:6 [5] is a different person—the name is by no means uncommon. No less fragile is the supposition of Koch (1974, 190–191) that Meremoth was high priest and that he was deposed by Ezra, who took his place—hence the descent from Seraiah in his genealogy. The designation "the priest" *(hakkōhēn)* does not necessarily mean "high priest" with reference to either Meremoth or Ezra, and neither occurs in the lists of postexilic high priests (Neh. 12:10–11, 22). At any rate, this Meremoth ben Uriah was in charge of the temple treasury assisted by the priest Eleazar ben Phinehas and the Levites Jozabad ben Jeshua (see also Ezra 2:40; Neh. 11:16) and Noadiah ben Binnui (see also Neh. 12:8). The greatest care was taken to check the treasure and make a detailed inventory. While such measures are entirely plausible, they happen to match quite closely the concerns and style of C as, for example, in David's detailed dispositions for the building of the First Temple (1 Chron. 28:14–19).

[35–36] As was noted a moment ago, this last section is third-person narrative and may be taken to lead directly into the account of the public reading of the law (beginning at Neh. 7:72 [73]). There can be little doubt that this is the work of C. "The exiles" *(bᵉnê-haggôlāh)* is his preferred designation for the restored community (see on 1:5). He is at pains to point out that the royal command to sacrifice was carried out. The sacrificial animals correspond to those offered at the dedication of the temple (see 6:17) and, further back, at the rededication of the First Temple by Hezekiah (2 Chron. 29:20–24; note also the similarity in dating, 29:17). The difference here is the obvious concern to bring into play once again the number symbolic of the old Israel: twelve and its multiples (96 and 72). The repetition of the sin offering (*ḥaṭṭā't;* cf. 6:17) acknowledges that the period preceding the return was one of infidelity. The author also notes that the instructions addressed to the satrapal authorities in the edict were carried out. Like Nehemiah after him (Neh. 2:9), Ezra delivered them himself. The Persian title *'aḥašdarpan* (Old Persian *khshathrapāvan*)—on which the immediately following *peḥāh* (pl. *paḥ avôt*), "governors," may be an explanatory gloss—would normally refer to the satrap, but since the word is in the plural it must allude to local officials. It would therefore be consistent with the treasurers *(gizzabrayyā')* addressed by Artaxerxes in the edict (7:21), and it may indicate that, due to political disturbances, the satrapal office was then vacant, as it must have been some years later during the short-lived rebellion of Megabyzus. The final statement, obviously retrospective, assures the reader that these local officials faithfully carried out the king's commands.

The Foreign Marriage Crisis (Ezra 9:1–5)

M. **Avi-Yonah,** *The Holy Land from the Persian to the Arab Conquest (536 B.C.–A.D. 640),* Grand Rapids, 1977 (2nd ed.), 19–23; P. R. **Ackroyd,** "The Jewish Community in Palestine in the Persian Period," in *CHJ* 143–147; J. **Blenkinsopp,** "The 'Servants of the Lord' in Third Isaiah," *Proceedings of the Irish Biblical Association* 7, 1983, 1–23; D. **Bossman,** "Ezra's Marriage Reform: Israel Redefined," *BTB* 9, 1979, 32–38; R. L. **Braun,** "Chronicles, Ezra and Nehemiah: Theology and Literary History," *VTSup.* 30, 1979, 52–64; J. **Bright,** *A History of Israel,* 387–390; W. **Eilers,** "Kleinasiatisches," *ZDMG* 94, 1940, 225–227; L. M. **Epstein,** *Marriage Laws in the Bible and Talmud,* Cambridge, Mass., 1942; S. **Herrmann,** *A History of Israel in Old Testament Times,* Philadelphia, 1975, 307–310; P. **Humbert,** "Le Substantif to'ēbā et le verbe t'b dans l'Ancien Testament," *ZAW* 72, 1960, 217–237; W. Th. **In der Smitten,** *Esra,* 24–25, 130–149; M. **Jastrow,** "The Tearing of Garments as a Symbol of Mourning," *JAOS* 21, 1900, 23–29; "Baring of the Arm and Shoulder as a Sign of Mourning," *ZAW* 22, 1902, 117–120; A. **Kapelrud,** *The Question of Authorship in the Ezra Narrative,* 59–63; N. **Lohfink,** "Enthielten die im Alten Testament bezeugten Klageriten eine Phase des Schweigens?" *VT* 12, 1962, 260–277; M. **Smith,** *Parties and Politics That Shaped the Old Testament,* 123–125; "Jewish Religious Life in the Persian Period," *CHJ* 244–245, 269–270; C. C. **Torrey,** *Ezra Studies,* 255–260; *Composition,* 14–21.

9:1 When these matters had been settled, the leaders approached me and said, "The people of Israel, and the priests and Levites, have not kept themselves apart from the local populations and the abominations of the Canaanites, Hittites, Perizzites, Jebusites, Ammonites, Moabites, Egyptians, and Edomites.[a] ²For they have taken wives from among their womenfolk for themselves and their sons, so that the holy race has mingled with the local populations; moreover, the leaders and officials have been to the fore in this unfaithful conduct." ³When I heard this report I tore my tunic and mantle, plucked hair from my head and beard, and remained seated in a stupor. ⁴Then there gathered round me all those who trembled at the word[b] of the God of Israel on account of the infidelity of the exiles who had returned, while I remained seated in a stupor until the evening sacrifice. ⁵I rose from my fasting, with my tunic and mantle torn; I knelt down and spread out my hands in prayer to YHVH my God.

a. "Edomites" with 1 Esd. 8:69 in preference to MT "Amorites"; cf. Deut. 23:4–7 [3–6]; 1 Kings 11:1. In the stereotypical list Amorites are generally third or higher in order.
b. With 1 Esd. 8:72 and LXX; cf. Ezra 10:3. MT has "words."

[9:1] The opening phrase *(ûkᵉkallôt 'ēlleh)* is one of the more common connective links in C's history (2 Chron. 7:1; 20:23; 24:10, 14; 29:29; 31:1). It could be functioning here to paper over a gap in the memoir (Batten 1913, 331), but more probably it was necessitated by the relocation of the public reading of the law which, like Ezra 8:35–36, is in the third person. We have already seen that an original location of Neh. 8 at this point makes for a more satisfactory chronological sequence, filling the gap between the fifth and the ninth months. Decisive action of the kind described here would also more naturally follow the promulgation and explanation of the law, and the problem of the four-month delay in Ezra's discovery of this abuse is mitigated though not entirely removed. (Against Rudolph 1949, 85–87, there is no indication that previous attempts of Ezra at solving the problem had failed.)

The ones who brought the news were leading laymen *(śārîm)*, obviously not the ones who are reported to have been among the ringleaders (v. 2). In postexilic usage the term includes the chief administrators of the six districts into which the province was divided (Avi-Yonah 1966). The complaint dealt with intermarriage with inhabitants of the province and surrounding regions (the *'ammê hā'ᵃrāṣôt* of 3:3 and 4:4) who were outside of the community referred to as the *gôlāh* and the holy race *(zera' haqqōdeš)*. This community is described as a well-defined entity: it had its own assembly *(qāhāl, 10:8–12)*, its leaders exercised judicial and punitive power, including excommunication and confiscation of property (10:8, 14), and it was united in support for and participation in the temple cult. In describing such a community as existing in the mid-fifth century C is, however, involved in something of a contradiction. On the one hand, he would have us believe that the *bᵉnê haggôlāh* entered into possession of a depopulated province while, on the other, he sees them threatened by assimilation to the native population. The actual situation was, of course, somewhat different. By no means all of the population of Judah lost their lives or went into exile with the fall of Jerusalem, and at the time of Ezra there were many who had no connection with the Babylonian diaspora. Prophetic texts from the early Persian period attest to tension, often acrimonious, between the more anti-assimilationist elements (Morton Smith's "Yahweh alone party"; 1971) and their syncretic co-religionists, with the former more likely to be found among those who returned at different times from the diaspora. They also confirm the impression conveyed by Ezra-Nehemiah that control of the temple was a crucial issue. But it is doubtful that the "congregation of the returned exiles" (10:8) was as sectarian in ethos and organization as the editor makes it out to be.

To describe those outside the community whose womenfolk constituted a mortal danger, the author falls back on the standard list (generally but not invariably seven) of native peoples (e.g., Gen. 15:19–20; Ex. 3:8, 17; 33:2; 34:11; Deut. 7:1; 20:17; Judg. 3:5; cf. Neh. 9:8). The present version of the list exhibits an interesting exegetical blend of Deut. 7:1–5, prohibiting intermarriage with the standard seven nations, and Deut. 23:4–8 [3–7], which excludes Ammonites and Moabites absolutely and Edomites and Egyptians to the third generation from membership in the community. We note the same combination in the historian's censure of Solomon's foreign marriages, which actually quotes from Deut. 7:1–5 (1 Kings 11:1–2); one wonders, in fact, whether it reflects the situation at the time of Ezra and Nehemiah (cf. Neh. 13:26). In itself, the list fills out the exodus-occupation pattern which we have noted at several points, while the inclusion of Ammonites, Moabites, Egyptians, and Edomites gives it contemporary relevance. The Deuteronomic law of the *qāhāl*—the same term is used for Ezra's community (10:8)—excludes Ammonites and Moabites *in perpetuum*. This stipulation of the law was of obvious relevance during the administration of Nehemiah, and remained so, controversially, long after (see, for example, Ruth and Judith 14:10). Egyptians and Edomites, on the contrary, qualified for membership in the third generation, suggesting a situation like that of the Jewish colony in Elephantine where intermarriage with Egyptians (e.g., *AP* 14) and Arameans (e.g., *AP* 25; 28) must have been fairly common. This did not mean that relations with Edomites (Idumeans) and Egyptians created no problems. The short haggadic passage in the so-called Holiness Code dealing with the offspring of an Egypto-Israelite marriage (Lev. 24:10–23), and the generally hostile allusions to Edomites in exilic and early postexilic writings (Lam. 4:21–22; Ps. 137:7–9; Isa. 63:1–6; Mal. 1:2–5), would be a better guide to the real situation.

[2] The way in which the situation is described points unmistakably to the editorial hand of C. Marriage outside the community is described as *ma'al*—infidelity, unfaithful conduct—a key term characteristic of C (1 Chron. 2:7; 5:27; 9:1; 10:13; 2 Chron. 12:2; 26:1, 6, 18; 28:19, 22; 29:6, 19; 30:7; 33:19; 36:14; cf. Ezra 10:2, 5, 10; Neh. 1:8; 13:27). The result of seduction by the alien "abominations" (*tô'ēbôt,* a Deuteronomic term for false gods and their cults) is the corruption of the "holy race," literally, "holy seed" (cf. Neh. 9:2; Mal. 2:15; and the late gloss at Isa. 6:13). It is this kind of language which has given rise to the conception of early Judaism as racially exclusive. The factor of biological descent was certainly important and continues to be so, as is clear from the juridical definition of Jewish identity in the State of Israel today. What this means is that, unlike Christianity, Judaism has continued to think of itself in terms of peoplehood. But it will be clear from the passage under discussion that the primary concern is with the *religious* identity of the community, a concern which continued to be paramount throughout the Second Temple period. What characterized Second Temple Judaism was neither particularism nor universalism but rather a tension or dialectic which allowed it to open itself to adherents without losing its identity. Thus the severe measures proposed by Ezra have to be balanced by the remarkable openness of early Judaism to proselytes. We should, in addition, bear in mind the important social and economic factors involved. Since according to Priestly law (Num. 27:1–11) daughters could in certain circumstances inherit, exogamous marriage could lead to alienation of family property, a concern also reflected in the stories in Gen. 12–50 about the ancestors. The situation obtaining at the time of Nehemiah, when the priesthood was involved in intermarriage with non-Judean families (Neh. 13:4, 28), reminds us also that control of the temple, an obviously crucial

issue, could have played a part in discouraging such marriages in the ranks of the clerical and lay aristocracy.

It would be necessary to add that the measures taken by Ezra against intermarriage were not successful. With all its dangers, the practice continued to be one of the principal sources of recruitment, without which it is impossible to explain the immense demographic expansion of Judaism between the Persian and Roman periods. The concern of both Ezra and Nehemiah to exclude marriage with foreign *women* is also subject to misunderstanding, but here the situation is much less clear since we do not know when and under what circumstances the emphasis on matrilinear descent originated. The Deuteronomic prohibition (7:3) includes both sexes and Lev. 24:10–23 presents the case of an Israelite woman married to an Egyptian man. On the assumption that the mother has the greater influence on the child's religion, emphasis on excluding foreign women as marriage partners is readily understandable. On the other hand, the assumption would have probably been made, as it appears to have been among the Jews of Upper Egypt (e.g., *AP* 14), that a Jewish woman who married a foreign man also adopted his cult and therefore no longer belonged to the Jewish community.

[3–5] Ezra's reaction on hearing the report appears almost absurdly intemperate, especially since four months had passed since his arrival. The tearing of the clothes and disheveling of the hair were, of course, conventional expressions of mourning (cf. 2 Sam. 13:19; 2 Kings 22:11), the former a modified form of ritual nakedness, the latter of ritual shaving of the hair, a practice forbidden on account of its pagan connotations (Lev. 19:27; 21:5; Deut. 14:1). More to the point, there is here what we would today call the P.R. angle for, as Josephus notes (*Ant.* 11.142), these demonstrative acts had the advantage of drawing public attention to his protest. The demonstration continued throughout the day as Ezra sat on the ground in the temple precincts (10:1) in a catatonic state, reminiscent of Ezekiel by the Chebar canal (Ezek. 3:15; the same term, *mᵉšōmēm* [MT *mašmîm*], is used). This continued until the evening sacrifice (see on 3:3), a conventional designation of time, that is, the ninth hour or 3 P.M., and one of the appointed times for prayer (cf. 1 Kings 8:29, 36; 2 Kings 16:15; Dan. 9:21; *m. Ber.* 4:1; Matt. 27:46; Acts 3:1). Ezra prayed on his knees, an exceptional position since one usually prayed standing or sitting, and one which, with its penitential connotations, became common only from the time of the exile (cf. 1 Kings 8:22, an exilic passage). The spreading out of the hands (cf. Ex. 9:29; 1 Kings 8:22; Isa. 1:15; Ps. 28:2), familiar from ancient Near Eastern iconography and the *orantes* of the Roman catacombs, was the gesture appropriate for petitionary or intercessory prayer. That the prayer is preceded by fasting (the word *ta'⁴nît*—cf. 1 Esd. 8:73, *nēsteia*—occurs only here in HB) points forward to the kind of milieu in which the book of Daniel circulated (e.g., Dan. 9:3–4). It is worthy of note that Ezra, like Moses interceding for the apostates at Sinai (Ex. 32:30–34), identifies himself with the sinful people and prays as one of them.

Ezra's public demonstration of grief attracted the sympathetic attention of "all those who trembled at the word of the God of Israel," a category which appears to have formed the nucleus of his support group (cf. also 10:3). The verbal noun *ḥārēd, ḥᵃrēdîm,* with reference to the manifestation of religious emotion (cf. Quakers, Shakers), occurs in the Hebrew Bible, with one exception (1 Sam. 4:13), only in Third Isaiah (66:2, 5), which is also from the early Persian period. The prophetic saying at Isa. 66:5 is spoken by an anonymous seer to a group, those who tremble at God's word, who have been "excommunicated" by their brethren, i.e., fellow Jews, on account of their association with the speaker ("for my name's sake"). Their words, quoted derisively by their opponents, point unmistakably to their eschatological beliefs. Since excommunication implies exclusion from the temple community and from participation in the cult, their opponents must have included some at least of the temple authorities. And in fact, in a saying immediately preceding, commitment to the temple is contrasted with the religious attitude of these devout "quakers" (Isa. 66:1–2). We are therefore dealing with a prophetic-eschatological group whose members have a well-defined identity over against their fellow Jews, a group which is at the center of religious conflict. The impression will be strengthened when we go on to note that the "quakers" of chapter 66 are identical with the "servants of YHVH" of the preceding chapter (65:8–16); in fact, the eschatological vindication of "the servants" in 65:13–14 may be read as their answer to the taunts of the opposition in 66:5: they mourn in the present age but will rejoice in the age to come. A similar situation, with its quasi-sectarian undertones, appears also in Mal. 3:13–21, where the God-fearers who mourn in this age are assured of ultimate well-being.

Assuming that Isa. 66:1–5 dates from the early Persian period, it would be natural to ask whether any connection exists between these "quakers" and the pietists of similar designation who formed Ezra's principal support group (Ezra 9:4; 10:3). The former are described as prophetic-eschatological, the latter have a special concern for the law. There is, of course, no contradiction here. The group addressed in Isa. 66, forerunner of the pietist sects of the Hasmonean period, would be expected to espouse a rigorist interpretation of the law. That a connection exists is already suggested by the designation *ḥᵃrēdîm,* which occurs only in these two contexts. Also, the opponents of the *ḥᵃrēdîm* in Third Isaiah are denounced as syncretists (65:3–5, 7, 11), and the danger of syncretism is the basic issue in the matter of foreign marriages (cf. also Mal. 2:10–12, where the connection is explicit). The emphasis in both contexts on mourning and, by implication, fasting, points in the same direction. The designation "mourners" *(ᵃbēlîm, mit'abbᵉlîm)* is used throughout Third Isaiah for the devout minority (Isa. 57:18; 61:2–3; 66:10), while Ezra keeps night vigil—no doubt in the company of his supporters—fasting and mourning over the faithlessness of the golah community (9:4; 10:6). In view of the common evaluation of Ezra and his work the conclusion suggested is surprising, even disconcerting: he appears to have found his principal support among a prophetic-eschatological group which espoused a rigorist interpretation of the law and which was out of favor with the religious leadership in the province.

Other supporters named or implied—the *śārîm* who brought the matter to his attention (9:1), Shecaniah of the Elam phratry (10:2; cf. 2:7; 10:26)—are laymen. The commission appointed to oversee the matter was also composed of laymen—at least priests are not mentioned (10:16). At the time of Nehemiah, not many years later, the high priestly family was involved in foreign marriages (Neh. 13:4, 28), and the situation was probably no different when Ezra arrived. The narrator wishes to leave us with the impression that the matter was settled amicably, almost unanimously, but the real situation was probably rather different. Since exogamous marriage involved community leaders lay and clerical, both they and the equally distinguished families of the women threatened with divorce must have been offended. Moreover such action, which was not required by any law known to us, exceeded Ezra's mandate. The likelihood of stirring up a hornet's nest would not have been welcomed by the Persian authorities who sent Ezra out precisely as an instrument of the *pax Persica* at a difficult moment and to a sensitive part of the empire. This may explain why the story breaks off suddenly rather than, as we might have expected, on an upbeat note. We do not know the outcome, but it would be a reasonable guess that Ezra was recalled after a stay of no more than a year.

A Public Confession of Sin (Ezra 9:6–15)

P. R. **Ackroyd,** *Exile and Restoration,* Philadelphia, 1968, 73–78; R. S. **Ellis,** *Foundation Deposits in Ancient Mesopotamia,* New Haven, 1968, 46–93; A. **Fer-**

nández, "La Voz GDR en Esr. 9,9," *Bib* 16, 1935, 82–84; "Esdr. 9,9 y un Texto de Josefo," *Bib* 18, 1937, 207–208; G. F. **Hasel**, *The Remnant,* Berrien Springs, Mich., 1980; B. **Hornig**, "Das Prosagebet in der nachexilischen Literatur," Diss., Leipzig, 1957 (summary in *TLZ* 83, 1958, 644–646); W. Th. **In der Smitten**, *Esra,* 25–28; "Die Gründe für die Aufnahme der Nehemiaschrift in das chronistische Geschichtswerk," *BZ* n.F. 16, 1972, 216–221; H. **Kaupel**, "Die Bedeutung von Gādēr in Esr. 9:9," *BZ* 22, 1934, 89–92; "Zu *gādēr* in Esr. 9,9," *Bib* 16, 1935, 213–214; O. **Plöger**, "Reden und Gebete im deuteronomistischen und chronisti-schen Geschichtswerk," in W. Schneemelcher (ed.), *Festschrift für Günther Dehn,* Neukirchen-Vluyn, 1957, 35–49; J. B. **Pritchard**, *Hebrew Inscriptions and Stamps from Gibeon,* Philadelphia, 1959, 9–10; G. **von Rad**, "Die levitische Predigt in den Büchern der Chronik," *Festschrift für Otto Procksch,* 1934, 113–124 (= "The Levitical Sermon in I and II Chronicles," Von Rad, *The Problem of the Hexateuch and Other Essays,* New York, 1966, 267–280); C. C. **Torrey**, *The Composition and Historical Value of Ezra-Nehemiah,* 19–20.

9:6 I said, "O my God, I am too ashamed and confused to lift up my face to you, O my God, for our iniquities have piled up over our heads[a] and our guilt is so great it reaches to heaven. [7]From the time of our ancestors even to this day we have incurred great guilt,[b] and on account of our iniquities we, our kings, and our priests have been delivered to the sword, to captivity, plunder, and humiliation at the hands of foreign kings,[c] as is the case today.

[8]"But now YHVH our God has suddenly[d] shown us mercy, leaving us some survivors[e] and giving us a firm hold[f] on his holy place. Our God has cheered us[g] and accorded us in some measure a new lease of life in our bondage. [9]Bondsmen we surely are, yet our God has not forsaken us in our bondage, but has made the kings of Persia so well disposed toward us[h] that they have given us a new lease of life, allowing us to rebuild the house of our God and repair its ruins, and have provided us with a protective wall in Judah and Jerusalem.

[10]"And now, O my God, what can we say after all this, seeing that we have forsaken your commandments [11]which you gave through your servants the prophets when you said, 'The land which you are about to enter to take possession of it is a land rendered unclean by the pollutions of the local inhabitants, and their abominable practices have filled it from one end to the other with their impurity. [12]Now, therefore, do not give your daughters to their sons in marriage, nor take their daughters as wives for your sons; do not ever seek their welfare and well-being, that you may grow strong and eat the good things of the land, leaving it as an inheritance for your children for ever.'

¹³"After all that has happened to us on account of our evil deeds and our great guilt—though you, our God, have inflicted less punishment on us than our iniquities have merited, and have allowed us to survive, as we do—¹⁴shall we once again transgress your commandments, intermarrying with the peoples who practice these abominations? Would you not be angry with us to the point where there would be no surviving remnant at all? ¹⁵O YHVH, God of Israel, you are righteous, for we the survivors are still here today. We are here in your presence, guilty as we are, for none can stand in your presence because of this guilt."

a. Lit., "have become many over a head." MT should probably read *lᵉma'lāh mē'al hārō'š*, assuming haplography; cf. 2 Chron. 34:4.
b. Lit., "we are in (a state of) great guilt."
c. *malkê hā'ᵃrāṣôt*, "kings of the lands."
d. *kim'at rega'*, lit., "almost a moment" or "for a little while," is more often than not understood as the interval elapsed since the first return. But if this were so, one would have expected a phrase which indicated the past without the implication that the time of grace will not last long. For the present rendering see Galling 1964, 61–62.
e. *pᵉlêṭāh* (also vs. 13, 14), a collective feminine referring to people who have escaped some disaster or have been rescued; cf. 1 Chron. 4:43; 2 Chron. 12:7; 20:24; 30:6.
f. *yāṭēd*, a stake or tent peg, should not be emended to *yeter*, remnant, a reading attested only in cod. 1 Kennicott. For the metaphorical sense of *yāṭēd* see commentary.
g. Lit., "brightened our eyes"; cf. 1 Sam. 14:29; Ps. 13:4 [3].
h. Lit., "he extended to us favor before the kings of Persia"; see on 7:28.

Formally, Ezra 9:6–15 is a prayer addressed to YHVH which passes almost immediately from the first person singular to the first person plural, and therefore could be classified as a communal confession of sin, comparable to certain psalms so designated. The genre is, however, adapted to the context, being aimed rhetorically at persuading those present to get rid of their foreign wives. Hence the reference to YHVH in the third person (v. 8) and the rhetorical questions (vs. 10, 14); hence also the historical survey which passes rapidly over the entire preexilic period as one of infidelity (6–7), then takes in the new beginning made possible by the Persians (8–9), then presents the golah community with the demand for decision (10–15, beginning "and now," *vᵉ'attāh*).

Communal confession of sin, whether in the form of prayer or of sermon, is a prominent form of religious expression in the Second

Temple period. We find it in the homiletic framework to Zech. 1–8 (1:7–8; 7–8) which speaks of the sins of the ancestors (1:2, 4, 6; 7:11–12; 8:14), the prophet as preacher of law whose message is spurned (1:4, 6; 7:12), exile and dispersion as the outcome of religious infidelity (7:14), and its effect on the land (7:14). Many of the same themes appear in the prayer at Neh. 9:6–37, attributed to Ezra in LXX, and in the confession of sin in Dan. 9:4–19, here too coinciding with the evening sacrifice (Dan. 9:21). Psalms classified as national or communal confessions of sin (78; 106) also follow the same pattern, which continues into the Roman period (e.g., 1QS I 4–II 1; 4QDibHam[a]; see M. Baillet, *RB* 68, 1961, 195–250).

On the much-debated issue of authorship there is no consensus. If the narrative immediately preceding is attributed to the Ezra memoir, it would be difficult not to attach the prayer to it also. But, on the other hand, the narrative proceeds in the third person (10:1), and we have seen more than one indication in 9:1–5 of C's style and vocabulary. The practice of putting prayers, speeches, and exhortations into the mouths of characters was common in ancient historiography in general, and C is no exception (see, e.g., 1 Chron. 29:10–19; 2 Chron. 12:4–8; 20:6–12, 20; 30:6–9). A close reading of these passages, which are free compositions of the author, will bring to light several parallels with Ezra's prayer. The prayer is also consonant with the theological ideas, of Deuteronomic inspiration, which inform C's history. God, who is righteous (cf. 2 Chron. 12:6), is not responsible for the disasters which have befallen Israel since he not only gave the law as a guide but sent "his servants the prophets" to warn of the consequences of nonobservance. The history of the monarchy ended in exile because Israel neglected these prophetic warnings. One interesting corollary is that Ezra represents himself as heir to the prophets and to Moses as prophet *kat' exochēn*. Adaptation to the historical context—e.g., in the allusion to the kings of Persia— would not exclude the hypothesis of composition or redaction by C, any more than would the reference to Ammon, Moab, and Edom in the prayer of Jehoshaphat, which no one doubts is a free composition of the author (2 Chron. 20:10). All we can say about the authorship of the prayer, then, is that if Ezra did pray publicly on this occasion, and if he recorded his prayer for posterity, it has been thoroughly edited by C, using his own characteristic style and vocabulary.

[9:6] The invocation begins in the first person singular but passes at once to the plural as Ezra identifies himself with the sinful community past and present. The prayer begins and ends with the sense of guilt and shame, the inability to stand in the presence of God. The fact that much of the language is conventional, borrowed from cultic and prophetic *loci communes* (e.g., shame and confusion, Ps. 6:11 [10]; Jer. 6:15), does not take away from its evocative possibilities. The theme of communal guilt (*'ašmāh,* 1 Chron. 21:3; 2 Chron. 24:18; 28:10, 13; 33:23), its causes, effects, and the possibility of its removal, plays a major role in C's history. In the larger context of that history Ezra emerges here as intercessor, in direct line of descent from Moses and later prophetic servants of YHVH.

[7] The prayer goes on to summarize the religious history of Israel from the ancestors to the present as a history of infidelity. The perspective is more radical than that of Hosea, who traces Israel's fall from grace to the occupation of the land; or of Ezekiel, who goes further back to Egypt (Ezek. 20). This one verse recapitulates C's history, pressing the point that Israel's subjection to foreign rule— Assyrian, Babylonian, and now Persian (cf. 2 Chron. 30:6–9; Neh. 9:32)—is the result of religious infidelity. We will have noted that exactly the same point is made in the reply of the elders to Tattenai (Ezra 5:12). The final phrase—"as is the case today" *(kᵉhayyôm hazzeh)*—may seem out of place and contrary to the otherwise benign view of Persian rule in the book; it would certainly be inappropriate in a document destined for Persian consumption. But it would be a mistake to make too much of this prudential attitude, as if Ezra and his contemporaries were not aware of the basic unacceptability of political subjection, a point made much more clearly in the similar confessional prayer in Neh. 9.

[8–9] The contrast between Israel's condition before and after the moment of grace represented by the decree of Cyrus is now emphasized. The difficult phrase *kim'aṭ rega'* (see textual note d) refers to the lapse of time since the first return. This would still be true if we follow those who translate it "suddenly," which would add the idea of the unexpected and unanticipated in the gracious act of God on behalf of his people. Taking up the old prophetic idea of the remnant, the prayer represents the golah people as the survivors, those who had come through the judgment of exile with their faith intact (cf. 1 Chron. 4:43; 2 Chron. 12:7; 20:24; 30:6; Neh. 1:2). Here, too, the benevolence of the Persians is acknowledged, manifested especially in permission to rebuild the temple (cf. 6:14; 7:28). Israel is still in servitude to a foreign power, no less than in the days of the Assyrians and Babylonians, but this is a new and different dispensation. The metaphor of a peg or stake *(yātēd)* in the temple—here translated "firm hold"—has been explained with reference to the practice of putting an object of this kind in the foundations of a temple in ancient Mesopotamia as a symbol of the union between royal builder and the deity to whom the building is dedicated (Ellis). More probably, however, the allusion is to the nomadic practice of "staking" a claim to a plot of land on which to pitch tents for the family or clan. There is also the association with the tent-sanctuary in the wilderness, prototype of the temple, which was secured with bronze pegs (Ex. 27:19; 35:18; Num. 3:37), and the prophetic metaphor of Zion as a tent immovably anchored in the same way (Isa. 33:20; cf. 54:2). Thus, the visible sign that they have not been abandoned by God— another characteristic theme of C (1 Chron. 28:9; 2 Chron. 12:5; 15:2; 24:20)—is the fact that the temple has indeed been rebuilt.

The other allusion to a "protective wall" is still occasionally taken literally to refer to Nehemiah's rebuilt wall, thereby serving as an argument for the priority of Nehemiah's mission. But apart from the fact that Nehemiah's wall did not surround the entire province, the word *gādēr* nowhere refers to a city wall, with the possible but by no means certain exception of Micah 7:11. It connotes for the most part a fence or low stone wall protecting a vineyard (Num. 22:24; Isa. 5:5; Ps. 80:13 [12]; Prov. 24:31). Depending on how one translates the same word on jar handles discovered at el-Jîb, it may also, by metonymy, stand for the vineyard itself as an enclosed space (Pritchard). Its metaphorical use was facilitated by the prophetic image of Israel as God's vineyard (Hos. 2:8; Isa. 5:5; Ezek. 13:5). The allusion, therefore, is to measures taken by the Persian authorities to protect the province from its enemies, thus allowing work on the temple to be completed.

[10–12] After this brief historical review, the matter in hand, marriage outside the community, is addressed. The commandment forbidding this practice is quoted at length. That it is communicated through "his servants the prophets" does not mean that we are to look for it in the prophetic books, which—with the exception of Mal. 2:11–12—nowhere contain this prohibition. The term "his servants the prophets" is the standard Deuteronomic designation for the prophetic succession beginning with Moses, the fountainhead of prophecy (Deut. 18:15–18; 34:10; 2 Kings 17:13, 23; 21:10; Jer. 7:25–26; etc.). It corresponds to the Deuteronomic representation of the prophet as mediator and continuator of the legal tradition (see especially 2 Kings 17:13), a view which would come to classic expression in the opening verse of *m. Abot* (The Sayings of the Fathers). The basic text, reinterpreted to apply to the contemporary situation in Ezra-Nehemiah, is the Deuteronomic law forbidding marriage with the native populations (Deut. 7:1–5). But the quotation given here is put together from a wide range of sources, suggesting a somewhat eclectic approach to scripture on the part of C or his source. The principal passages used in this collage are as follows:

"the land which you are about to enter to take possession of it" (Deut. 7:1);

"a land rendered unclean by the pollutions of the local inhabitants" (the term *niddāh* occurs in ritual law dealing with the woman's menses in Leviticus and Numbers and, by extension, to any source of ritual contamination, e.g., Lev. 20:21; Ezek. 7:19–20; the term is not used in Deuteronomic law; the closest parallel, though using the more common term *ṭāmēʾ*, is Lev. 18:24–30);

"their abominable practices" (*tôʿēbôt*, abominations, is typically Deuteronomic, e.g., Deut. 18:9; 2 Kings 16:3; 21:2);

"which have filled it from one end to the other" (2 Kings 10:21; 21:16);

"do not give your daughters, etc." (Deut. 7:3);

"do not ever seek their welfare or well-being" (Deut. 23:7 [6]);

"that you may . . . eat the good things of the land" (Deut. 6:11);

"as an inheritance for your children for ever" (Deut. 1:38–39).

We see, once again, the decisive bearing of Deuteronomy on legal practice and the theological understanding of the law at the time of Ezra and Nehemiah.

[13–15] The conclusion is now stated: given the historical experience of religious infidelity and its consequences, and faced with the clear demands of the law, further violations put the community at risk of total disappearance. Israel exists only by divine favor, by the grace of God. The new lease of life, the breathing space, afforded through the goodwill of the Persians is a last chance. Israel, whose only surviving legitimate representative is the golah people, is responsible for its own destiny. By his dealings with his people throughout its history YHVH has demonstrated his righteousness (cf. 2 Chron. 12:16). Indeed, he has not punished Israel according to the strict measure of justice; if he had, the exile would have been the end of the story. Marriage with outsiders and contamination by their cults is therefore terminally dangerous. As extreme as the measures to be proposed seemed, and indeed were, the basic question was whether they were prepared to do whatever it took for Israel to preserve its identity and continue its saga. The author would no doubt have agreed with Rilke: "Who speaks of winning? Surviving is everything."

The Decision to Take Action (Ezra 10:1–8)

F. Ahlemann, "Zur Esra-Quelle," *ZAW* 59, 1942/43, 97–98; K. Baltzer, *The Covenant Formulary,* Philadelphia, 1971, 47–48, 51–52; G. J. **Blidstein**, "Atimia: A Greek Parallel to Ezra x.8 and to Post-Biblical Exclusion from the Community,"

VT 24, 1974, 357–360; J. C. L. **Gibson**, *Textbooks of Syrian Semitic Inscriptions* I, Oxford, 1971, 51–54; F. **Horst**, "Der Eid im Alten Testament," *EvTh* 17, 1957, 366–384; W. Th. **In der Smitten**, *Esra*, 28–30; "Die Gründe für die Aufnahme der Nehemiaschrift in das chronistische Geschichtswerk," *BZ* n.F. 16, 1972, 216–221; A. **Kapelrud**, *The Question of Authorship in the Ezra Narrative*, 71–75; M. R. **Lehmann**, "Biblical Oaths," *ZAW* 81, 1969, 74–92; A. **Malamat**, "The Ban in Mari and in the Bible," *Biblical Essays*, 1966, 40–49; E. **Meyer**, *Die Entstehung des Judentums*, 91; S. **Mowinckel**, *Studien* I, 124–135, 158–162; "'Ich' und 'Er' in der Esrageschichte," in A. Kuschke (ed.), *Verbannung und Heimkehr*, 211–233; M. **Noth**, *US*, 146–147; M. **Pope**, "Devoted," *IDB* 1:838–839; "Oaths," *IDB* 3:575–577; J. R. **Porter**, "Son or Grandson (Ezra x.6)?" *JTS* 17, 1966, 55–67.

10:1 As Ezra was praying and making confession of sin, prostrate in tears before the house of God, there gathered to him a great assembly of Israelites, men, women, and children, for the people with Ezra were weeping bitterly.[a] ²Then Shecaniah son of Jehiel of the descendants of Elam spoke up and said to Ezra, "We have acted faithlessly toward our God and have married foreign women from the local populations, but there is yet hope for Israel in this matter. ³Let us therefore pledge in covenant to our God to send away all our women[b] and their offspring, in accordance with the decision of my lord[c] and of those who tremble at the commandment of our God; and let it be done according to the law. ⁴Arise, for it is your responsibility; you have our support. Act with decision!"[d] ⁵So Ezra arose and made the leaders of the priests, the Levites, and all Israel swear to act accordingly; and they took the oath.

⁶Then Ezra left his place in front of the house of God and went to the room of Jehohanan son of Eliashib. He spent the night[e] there, eating no food and drinking no water, for he was in mourning over the faithlessness of the returned exiles. ⁷Then a proclamation was issued throughout Judah and Jerusalem to all the returned exiles to assemble in Jerusalem. ⁸In keeping with the decision of the leaders and elders, all the property of anyone not arriving within three days was to be confiscated, and he himself was to be banned from the congregation of the returned exiles.

a. MT has "for the people were weeping with a great weeping." Since the weeping was clearly not the cause of the assembling, some emend *ky bkv* to *vybkv* with Vulg. ("and the people wept bitterly"). The alternative possibility, followed here, is that the people already with Ezra were doing the weeping.
b. MT has "all women" *(kol-nāšîm);* 1 Esd. 8:90: "all our wives who are of alien race"; cf. LXX.

c. MT *'ᵃdōnāy*, referring to YHVH; emended to *'ᵃdōnî*, "my lord," with reference to Ezra, following 1 Esdras and some Heb. MSS.

d. Lit., "be strong and do" *(hᵃzaq vaʿᵃśēh)*; hendiadys.

e. Emending MT *vayyēlek* to *vayyālen*, with 1 Esd. 9:2.

Read in its narrative context, this passage is not without its problems. The most obvious of these is the change from first to third person. While this does not necessarily rule out the possibility that both 9:1–5 and 10:1–8 are drawn from the Ezra memoir—the same change occurs, for example, in the Cyrus cylinder—it is also possible that the editor either paraphrased his source (Noth, 146–147; Rudolph 1949, 93) or had at his disposal an alternative account. The close parallelism between the two passages certainly suggests the latter alternative: both speak of the infidelity *(ma'al)* of the golah people, the community consists of Israelites, priests and Levites, marriage is with "the peoples of the land(s)," Ezra is supported by the "tremblers," and his fasting is noted. The first- and third-person narratives have been edited into a consecutive account with the help of connective prose, a procedure similar to that employed in the first part of Hosea (1–3). Juxtaposition of source is also suggested by a closer reading of the narrative sequence. In 10:1–5 the fasting, prayer, weeping, etc., leads to the successful outcome of the imposition of an oath on the plenary assembly, which is surprising if, as is suggested, it took place spontaneously there and then in front of the temple. Even more surprising is the sequel in which Ezra keeps vigil, fasts, and mourns for the community's infidelity *after* the issue appears to have been resolved (6–8). Here, too, it seems that C has incorporated parallel versions into his history. While these editorial procedures complicate the task of historical reconstruction, the main outline of events is fairly clear. Another problem has been perceived to arise out of comparison with Nehemiah's measures faced with the same issue (Neh. 13:23–29). Similarities do exist—violent emotional reaction (Ezra at least confined himself to pulling out his own hair), the taking of an oath, allusion to infidelity *(ma'al,* Neh. 13:27)—but they are not so close as to require the dependence of the one on the other.

[10:1] The third-person narrative opens with a temporal clause, a stylistic feature of C. The verb *hitvaddōt* ("to confess sin"; stem *ydh*) belongs to the stock of cultic terminology (Lev. 5:5; 16:21; 26:40; Num. 5:7) and occurs elsewhere with the verb *hitpallēl*, "pray" or, more precisely, "intercede" (Neh. 1:6; Dan. 9:4, 20). Those who were drawn by Ezra's demonstrative grief are called a *qāhāl*, meaning a

crowd, not a liturgical assembly (cf. 10:8). The sense seems to be that
it was the weeping and wailing of those already in Ezra's company
which attracted the crowd, somewhat like the effects of the shouting
and weeping accompanying the laying of the foundations of the
temple (3:13–4:1). In that case, the allusion would include the
$ḥ^arēdîm$ or "quakers" (cf. 9:4), and their behavior would be the more
understandable if, as suggested, they are identical with the sectarians
alluded to in Isa. 66.

[2–4] The one fact known about Shecaniah is that he was a layman, belonging to the Elam phratry, a large number of whose members made aliyah at the beginning (2:7) and rather fewer with Ezra
(8:7). Six "Elamites" had in the meantime married foreign wives
(10:26). One of these was a certain Jeiel, who is sometimes identified
as Shecaniah's father. If this were correct, it would lend a certain
urgency to Shecaniah's intervention. The names, however, are quite
common, and since the wrongdoers were about to pledge themselves
to put away their foreign wives *with the children,* either Jeiel's status
had been rectified in the meantime or, more likely, they were not
related. Shecaniah, at any rate, followed Ezra in identifying himself
with the sinful community, acknowledged the wrongdoing, but held
out the possibility of hope, perhaps inspired by Ezra's prayer. His
proposal was to make (literally "cut") a covenant to dismiss foreign
wives and their offspring, and to do so "according to the law." As
the term "covenant" *(b^erît)* is used in the period of the Second
Temple, the emphasis is on a collective commitment to certain stipulations of law confirmed by an oath. The closest parallel is the
covenant in Neh. 10 which, however, is not called a $b^erît$ but a pledge
(*'^amānāh,* Neh. 10:1 [9:38]) or, in other words, a firm commitment
confirmed by an oath and a self-imposed curse (*š^ebû'āh, 'ālāh,* Neh.
10:30 [29]). It consists, in other words, in swearing an oath to observe
certain specific stipulations, the names of the signatories being recorded. Something of the same may be implied in Mal. 3:16 where
we hear of the "God-fearers" conferring together and learn that their
names are recorded in God's book. C records a $b^erît$ of King Asa
involving an assembly, an oath to put aside idolatry, and the death
penalty for those who refuse to participate (2 Chron. 15:8–15). A
similar covenant was initiated by Hezekiah (2 Chron. 29:10), also in
a free composition of C, and even in his account of Josiah's covenant,
where he follows his source, the element of obligation receives special
emphasis (2 Chron. 34:30–33; cf. 2 Kings 23:1–3). This is not the
place to trace the development of this idea throughout the history.
In view of later developments, especially the Qumranic and early
Christian use of the term, it will be enough to signal the quasi-

sectarian character of covenant as presented throughout C's history. Shecaniah's speech suggests that the decision about such a covenant had already been made by Ezra in collaboration with the *ḥᵃrēdîm*. While we obviously do not know what the specific contribution of the latter was in this instance, their radical commitment to the law, indicated both here and in Isa. 66, will explain their enthusiastic promotion of this rigorist solution to the problem.

The requirement that this be done "according to the law" is puzzling at first sight, since Pentateuchal law nowhere requires an Israelite to divorce his foreign wife. We must conclude that what is implied here is a particular interpretation of law, and specifically a rigorist interpretation of the Deuteronomic law forbidding marriage with the native population, such an interpretation as the *ḥᵃrēdîm* would be likely to espouse. This, then, would be one of several indications in the book of the crucial importance of biblical interpretation as a factor in the struggle to determine the identity and character of the community. The kind of institutional act by which the interpretation is implemented and imposed also takes us back to Deuteronomy. Deut. 29:9–14 [10–15] speaks of "cutting" a covenant which involves women and children and in which the curse *('ālāh)* is the operative element. The concluding exhortation to act decisively ("be strong and act," *ḥᵃzaq va'ᵃśēh*) provides one more example of C's editorial activity (1 Chron. 28:10, 20; 2 Chron. 19:11; see also the slightly different form at 1 Chron. 22:13 and 2 Chron. 32:7).

[5] Following on Shecaniah's speech, Ezra proceeded at once to administer the oath to the leaders of the priests, Levites, and laity. Since it does not seem necessay to emend the Hebrew text, we may note that only the leaders of the priesthood, presumably including the high priest, are singled out for special mention. During Nehemiah's administration a grandson of the high priest had married the daughter of Sanballat (Neh. 13:28). The general implication seems to be that Ezra drew his support in the main from the laity, and especially those elements alienated from the temple and its clerical bureaucracy (see also 9:3–5). The action of Ezra as here described seems, however, to anticipate the plenary assembly which followed a few days later. The administration of the oath could hardly have taken place spontaneously even if a quorum of priests, Levites, and laity just happened to be present. It would also leave us wondering why Ezra continued to fast and mourn *after* the successful outcome of his appeal. As suggested earlier, the solution is to be found in the editorial activity of C in combining the sources at his disposal.

[6–8] The vigil, fasting, and mourning in the temple precincts suggest preparation for a solemn religious occasion. The strongly penitential note also suggests the participation of Ezra's support group, something of whose ethos can be divined, as suggested earlier, from Isa. 66 and perhaps also Mal. 3:13–21. The identity of the permanent occupant of the room in which Ezra spent the night continues to be the subject of much speculation. If the Eliashib mentioned here is identical with the high priest of the same name during Nehemiah's mission (Neh. 3:1), it would be difficult to avoid the conclusion that Ezra followed Nehemiah. But there are sound reasons for rejecting the identification, not the least of which is the improbability of Ezra consorting with a family which, on the hypothesis of Nehemiah's chronological priority, had "defiled the priesthood" (Neh. 13:28–29; see the Additional Note on the Chronology of Ezra and Nehemiah).

Significantly, preparations for the plenary assembly were in the hands of lay authorities rather than the temple personnel. According to C's terminology, the "leaders" *(śārîm)* were tribal heads (e.g., 1 Chron. 23:2; 27:22; 28:1, 21; 29:6), though the term could also be used, by extension, of Levitical (1 Chron. 15; 2 Chron. 35:9) and priestly groups (1 Chron. 24:5; 2 Chron. 36:14). It also served to designate district and city governors (Neh. 3:9–19) and therefore represented a higher administrative level than the elders. These "leaders," then, were to play a primary role and the elders and judges a subordinate role in implementing the decision, and the commission appointed to adjudicate individual cases was also composed of laity (Ezra 10:16). In all of these arrangements, the temple clergy is conspicuous by its absence. If nothing is said of Ezra himself, the reason will be that he chose to work through agents who had their own reasons for supporting him. And if, as suggested, the outcome was less than successful, the reason may lie with the temple authorities, who no doubt had their own contacts with the imperial administration in the satrapy.

The issuance of the proclamation was probably by courier, and allowed three days (cf. 8:15, 32) for assembly, adequate in view of the size of the province, no more than about thirty-five miles north to south and twenty-five east to west. The punishment threatened for nonparticipation, though less severe than on a similar occasion during Asa's reign (2 Chron. 15:13), could hardly be disregarded. The verb used for the confiscation of property *(ḥrm)* originally connoted dedication to the deity and therefore destruction (e.g., Deut. 20:16; Josh. 6:21). In this instance, it was destined to become property of the temple, as is explicitly noted at 1 Esd. 9:4 and by Josephus *(Ant.* 11.148). The other punishment, excommunication from the golah community, is closely related since the province constituted, in effect, a temple community in which title to real estate was contingent on participation in and, of course, support of the cult (cf. Ezek. 11:14–15). The formula itself may be compared with the one frequently recurring in the Priestly laws and narrative (e.g., Gen. 17:14; Ex. 12:15, 19). It appears from Isa. 66:5 (where the verb *niddāh*, expel, is used) that it was invoked in the case of the *hᵃrēdîm*. But to what extent it was implemented, and how it fitted in with the ordinary administration of law in the province, cannot be determined.

The Assembly Is Convened (Ezra 10:9–17)

D. Bossmann, "Ezra's Marriage Reform: Israel Redefined," *BTB* 9, 1979, 32–38; J. Bright, "The Reforms of Nehemiah and Ezra," in *Kaufman Jubilee Volume*, 1960, 70–87; H. Grimme, "Die Begriffe von hebräischen *hwdh* und *twdh*," *ZAW* 58, 1940/41, 234–240; W. Th. In der Smitten, *Esra*, 30–33; P. Joüon, "Notes philologiques sur le Texte Hébreu d'Esdras et de Néhémie," *Bib* 12, 1931, 85; C. U. Wolf, "Traces of Primitive Democracy in Ancient Israel," *JNES* 6, 1947, 98–108.

10:9 All the men of Judah and Benjamin assembled in Jerusalem within the three days. It was the ninth month, the twentieth day of the month, and all the people were sitting in the open space in front of the house of God, trembling because of this matter and shivering[a] on account of the rain. [10]Ezra the priest rose to his feet and addressed them: "You have acted faithlessly in marrying foreign women, and in so doing you have added to Israel's guilt. [11]Give praise now to YHVH, God of your fathers, and do his will by separating yourselves from the local inhabitants and from the foreign women."

[12]The entire assembly gave a loud reply: "Yes, indeed, it is up to us to do as you say; [13]but there are many people here and it is the rainy season; we cannot stay out here in the open. Besides, the task cannot be completed in a day or two, for we have transgressed in great measure in this matter. [14]Let our leaders represent the assembly as a whole; then let all those in our cities who have married foreign women present themselves at set times, each one accompanied by the elders of his city and its magistrates, until the fierce anger of our God, brought on by this matter, has been averted from us." [15]Only Jonathan son of Asahel and Jahzeiah son of Tikvah opposed this proposal,[b] with Meshullam and Shabbethai the Levite supporting them.

[16]So the returned exiles acted accordingly. Ezra the priest set aside for himself men who were heads of ancestral houses,[c] one

for each ancestral house, all of them designated by name. They held sessions to inquire^d into the issue beginning on the first of the tenth month; ^{17}and by the first of the first month they had finished dealing with all the men who had married foreign women.

a. "trembling" and "shivering" to mitigate the zeugma in MT, which has only one verb *(marʿîdîm)*.

b. MT *ʿāmdû ʿal-zōʾt* is ambiguous. It could also be translated "insisted on this," but account must be taken of the adversative *ʾak* with which the sentence opens. LXX has "were with me on this (issue)" *(metʾ emou peri toutou)*, which presupposes *ʿimmādî* for *ʿāmdû*. 1 Esd. 9:14 has the expansive reading," took charge on these terms, and Meshullam, Levi, and Shabbethai served with them as judges."

c. MT has "Ezra the priest, men, heads of ancestral houses were set aside"; cf. LXX. 1 Esd. 9:16, *kai epelexato heautō Esdras,* suggests a reading *vayyabdēl lô* for MT *vayyibbādᵉlû.*

d. Reading *ldrvš* for MT *ldryvš,* "of Darius."

The narrative continues with the account of the plenary assembly (cf. the Greek *ekklēsia* convening in the *agora*) in the forecourt of the temple. As in the previous section, there are hints here and there of a conflation of two versions or a reworking of source material in the interests of a certain editorial point of view. These can be identified especially at those points where the textual tradition is unclear. The most interesting occurs with the intervention of named individuals (v. 15). LXX suggests that these people constituted Ezra's sole support, and it is even possible to understand MT in this sense, though the subsequent course of the narrative is meant to give a quite different impression. The 1 Esdras version (9:14), on the other hand, which has the first two named implementing the decision assisted by Meshullam, Levi, and Shabbethai acting as magistrates, looks like an alternative account of the commission of inquiry described in vs. 16–17. LXX also puts Ezra on the same level as the family heads in the setting up of the commission, and in this instance MT, unemended, gives the same sense as against 1 Esd. 9:16. There are therefore grounds for assuming that there existed a version in which the role of Ezra was not so prominent and support for his measures was far from unanimous. This version would then have been rewritten by C to highlight Ezra's role and the wholehearted acceptance of his program.

[10:9] C's hand is apparent from the outset in the description of the assembled as the men of Judah and Benjamin (cf. 1 Chron. 9:3; 2 Chron. 11:1, 12, 23; 15:2, 8, 9; 25:3; 31:1; 34:9; Neh. 11:36; 12:34;

see also on Ezra 1:5). The location is the same as for Ezra's public prayer and probably also for the reading of the law (Neh. 8). The twentieth of Kislev corresponds to a day in the third week in December, a time when Jerusalem can be miserably cold and rainy, as anyone who has lived in the city during the winter months will testify. While it is a common feature of ancient historiography to exaggerate the emotive reactions of individuals and groups (cf. 3:13; 9:3; 10:1; Neh. 13:25), the prospect of forcible separation from wives and children for some of those present, and of trouble for all, combined with the downpour, would explain more than adequately the general misery. This is one of the more realistic scenes in the book which could hardly have been invented.

[10–11] Ezra addresses the assembly in the same vein as in the prayer; witness the key terms *māʿal* ("act faithlessly"; see 9:2) and *'ašmāh* ("guilt"; see 9:6–7, 13, 15), both of frequent occurrence throughout C's history. The prayer described the guilt incurred by Israel throughout its history; given the present situation, they were now in danger of adding another chapter to that history of guilt (cf. 9:13–14). They are therefore admonished to acknowledge God in praise and thanksgiving, in the same terms in which Joshua addressed Achan, who had compromised the successful outcome of the occupation (Josh. 7:19). The practical expression of this acknowledgment was to do God's will, an essential aspect of which according to the Priestly law in the Pentateuch (e.g., Lev. 20:22–26) is separation from the nations. It is for this reason that Ezra is here designated not as scribe but as priest.

[12–14] The political purpose of the plenary gathering was to isolate the assimilationists in the community by a kind of plebiscite. The situation is only superficially analogous to the Athenian assembly of freemen, and therefore it is inappropriate to speak of a democratic element in the political setup in the province (*pace* Wolf). A degree of popular support was, nevertheless, necessary in order to carry through a measure opposition to which, especially in the higher social echelons, was assured in advance. We have seen some reasons to suspect that support was not so overwhelming as C would have us believe; and even taking the narrative as it is, we cannot avoid the suspicion of reluctance to implement the proposal. After all, the classical way of shelving a proposal is to send it to committee. The assembly, therefore, presumably through its spokesmen, proposed a delay. The reasons were, in themselves, entirely reasonable: the great number of people present, the inclement weather, the large number of cases which would have to be considered on their individual merits or demerits. The counterproposal was, therefore, to delegate author-

ity to act to the lay leadership (*śārîm,* see textual note on 9:1), who
would form a commission to examine the individuals concerned.
This commission would take each district, and within each district
each town or village in turn, and summon those suspected of exogamous marriage to make a deposition and accept the commission's
verdict. The suspect parties were to be accompanied by the local
elders and magistrates, both to give evidence based on information
locally available and to protect the rights of the innocent. The administrative pattern operative here is based on the system which, according to C, was set up by Jehoshaphat in the ninth century (2 Chron.
19:8–11; cf. Deut. 17:8–13). It will be noted that the purpose of this
disposition, still according to C, was to avoid incurring guilt and the
divine anger (2 Chron. 19:10). To sound a realistic note, we can easily
imagine the problems involved in implementing this plan: Were
wives of different ethnic background all on the same footing? How
many generations did it take to establish the legitimacy of this or that
marriage? Such problems, and the widespread disruption which the
measure necessarily brought with it, must have considerably reduced
its chances of success from the outset.

[15] As this verse is generally understood (e.g., RSV, NEB,
NAB), it refers to a small minority of four in opposition to the
proposal; in other words, it functions to emphasize the overwhelming
support which it enjoyed. This may well be the way C intended it to
be understood, in keeping with a tendency in his history to record
opposition to various proposals (e.g., 1 Chron. 21:6; 2 Chron. 28:12;
30:10–11, 18). It is also possible, however, that the objection was
directed at the recommendation to postpone action rather than settling the matter there and then, an alternative suggested by 1 Esd.
9:14 (see textual note b). In other words, the four in question (five
in 1 Esdras) would represent a rigorist minority. Some support may
be found for this view in the names. A Meshullam was among the
prominent associates of Ezra before the return (8:16), and a Shabbethai is listed among leading Levites resident later on in Jerusalem
(Neh. 11:16). Another Shabbethai, or perhaps the same one, played
an active role in the public reading of the law (Neh. 8:7). This is
possible, but the frequency with which these names occur in that
period suggests caution.

[16–17] All that remained now was to follow through with the
implementation of the decision. Here too there is some uncertainty
(see textual note c). If, as seems likely, we are being told that the
selection was made by Ezra himself, the committee was composed
of the lay leaders of phratries (see on 1:5) and not, as we might have

expected, of clerical and lay members (cf. 2 Chron. 19:11). We are told that their names were all a matter of record, but the list, if known to C, was passed over. The commission began its work after a delay of only ten days, continuing from the first of the tenth month (Tebeth) to the first of Nisan in the following year. On our reckoning, this would be from about December 29, 458, to about March 27, 457 B.C.E. It is tempting to calculate the rate of progress on the basis of the number of working days—about seventy-five—and the number of cases in the list which follows, namely, one hundred and nineteen. This would probably be a waste of time, however, since we do not know how many cases were examined and cleared, nor can we be sure that the commission sat every working day. It would have been of interest to know what procedures were followed; whether, for example, the disqualifications listed in Deut. 23 played any part in reaching decisions. For what was at issue here was a matter of the greatest importance for the future: the definition and identity of the Jewish people in its relation to the Gentile world.

The List of Offenders (Ezra 10:18–44)

A. T. Clay, *Business Documents of Murashu Sons of Nippur Dated in the Reign of Darius II (424–404 B.C.)*, Philadelphia, 1904, 148; M. Cogan, "The Men of Nebo—Repatriated Reubenites," *IEJ* 29, 1979, 37–39; S. Mowinckel, *Studien* I, 124–135; H. G. M. Williamson, "The Origins of the Twenty-four Priestly Courses: A Study of Chronicles xxiii–xxvii," *VTSup.* 30, 1979, 251–268.

10:18 Of the members of priestly families who had married foreign women there were discovered to be the following:

Of the descendants of Jeshua son of Jozadak and his kinsmen: Maaseiah, Eliezer, Jarib, Gedaliah. [19]They pledged themselves[a] to dismiss their wives; their guilt offering was a ram of the flock for their guilt.[b]

[20]Of the descendants of Immer: Hanani, Zebadiah;

[21]Of the descendants of Harim: Maaseiah, Elijah, Shemaiah, Jehiel, Uzziah;

[22]Of the descendants of Pashhur: Elioenai, Maaseiah, Ishmael, Nethanel, Jozabad, Elasah;

[23]Of the Levites: Jozabad, Shimei, Kelaiah (that is, Kelita), Pethahiah, Judah, Eliezer;

[24]Of the musicians: Eliashib;

Of the gatekeepers: Shallum, Telem, Uri;

²⁵Of Israel:

Descendants of Parosh: Ramiah, Izziah, Malchijah, Mijamin,ᶜ Eleazar, Malchijah,ᵈ Benaiah;

²⁶Descendants of Elam: Mattaniah, Zechariah, Jehiel, Abdi, Jeremoth, Elijah;

²⁷Descendants of Zattu: Elioenai, Eliashib, Mattaniah, Jeremoth, Zabad, Aziza;

²⁸Descendants of Bebai: Jehohanan, Hananiah, Zabbai, Athlai;

²⁹Descendants of Bani: Meshullam, Malluch, Adaiah, Jashub, Sheal,ᵉ Jeremoth;ᶠ

³⁰Descendants of Pahath-moab: Adna, Chelal, Benaiah, Maaseiah, Mattaniah, Bezalel, Binnui, Manasseh;

³¹Descendants of Harim: Eliezer, Isshijah, Malchijah, Shemaiah, Shimeon,ᵍ ³²Benjamin, Malluch, Shemariah;

³³Descendants of Hashum: Mattenai, Mattattah, Zabad, Eliphelet, Jeremai, Manasseh, Shimei;

³⁴Descendants of Bani:ʰ Maadai, Amram, Joel,ⁱ ³⁵Benaiah, Bedeiah, Cheluhi,ʲ ³⁶Vaniah, Meremoth, Eliashib, ³⁷Mattaniah, Mattenai, Jaasu;

³⁸Descendants of Binnui:ᵏ Shimei, ³⁹Shelemiah, Nathan, Adaiah, ⁴⁰Machnadebai,ˡ Shashai, Sharai, ⁴¹Azarel, Shelemiah, Shemariah, ⁴²Shallum, Amariah, Joseph;

⁴³Descendants of Nebo: Jeiel, Mattithiah, Zabad, Zebina, Jaddai, Joel, Benaiah.

⁴⁴All of these had married foreign women; so they sent them away, women and children alike.ᵐ

a. Lit., "they gave their hand."
b. MT "and guilty, a ram of the flock for their guilt" does not make sense. For *'ªšēmîm* read *'ªšāmām*, "their guilt-offering."
c. *miyyāmin* is identical with Minjamin (Neh. 12:17, 41); Syr. has "Benjamin" which, however, is a different name (see commentary).
d. Perhaps an error for Hashibiah (cf. 1 Esd. 9:26, *Asibias*).
e. An unlikely formation; read either "Yishal" with some Oriental MSS (cf. 1 Esd. 9:30, *Asaēlos*) or Shaul (Saul) with Syr.
f. MT: Jeramoth.
g. 1 Esd. 9:32 has Simon Chosamaios; it is not clear whether this corresponds to two names in Heb., one of which has fallen out in MT.
h. Suspect on account of the earlier Bani (v. 29); perhaps Bigvai (cf. 2:14; 8:14).
i. MT "Uel" is implausible; L and Syr. have "Joel"; cf. 1 Esd. 9:34 *Iouēl* and Neh. 11:9.
j. Qere: Chelulu; LXX: Chelia.
k. MT has "and Bani and Binnui"; for *vbny* read *vmbny;* cf. LXX ᴮᴬ.

    l. MT *mkndby* is implausible; LXX has "Machad Nabou" (cf. Nebo, v. 43), which is no better. Perhaps we should read *mbny* ("of the descendants of . . .") as the beginning of a new phratry; cf. 1 Esd. 9:34 "and of the sons of Ezora (= Azzur)." See Mowinckel, 124.

    m. MT 44b has: *vyš mhm nšym vyšymv bnym* ("and some of them are women, and they put sons") which is corrupt beyond repair. The translation given follows 1 Esd. 9:36: *kai apelysan autas syn teknois.* LXX *(kai egennēsan ex autōn huious)* presupposes a *Vorlage* close to MT (cf. also Syr. and Vulg.). Among emendations of a more or less extensive nature we may mention the following: *vyš mhm gršym nšym vbnym* ("there were some of them who expelled wives and children"), Bertheau 1882, 126; *vyšymv mhm nšym vyš bnym* ("they put their wives [from them] even if there were children"), Schneider 1959, 160; *vyš mhm bnym vyšybv bnym* ("and some of them [i.e., the men] had children, and they restored the children [to their mothers]"), Batten 1913, 350–351.

Unlike the lists in Ezra 2:1–67 and 8:1–14, this one has no title. Also, C's account of proceedings following on the assembly continues naturally after the listing of the first family of priests; in other words, v. 19 appears to be the natural continuation of v. 17. Confirmation of this conclusion is at hand in the language of v. 19 which echoes the dispositions for guilt offerings in Lev. 5:14–19; for these dispositions refer to anyone guilty of a breach of faith or act of disobedience, not just to priests. We conclude, then, that the account of the assembly and its sequel (10:9–17) continued with v. 19 and concluded with the now garbled v. 44b. When the list was inserted into this account, either by C or a later editor, the members of the high priestly family were given special prominence by being isolated from the other transgressors and alone subjected to the guilt-offering obligation.

The list includes 17 priests, 6 Levites, 4 other temple functionaries and 84 laity, the last figure dependent on an emended v. 38 (see textual note k). These figures are extremely low, about 1 in 270 of the male population listed in the census of the province (Ezra 2). A possible solution, certainly not ruled out by C's reference to "all the men (of Judah and Benjamin)" (10:9, 17), is that the list is confined to the upper strata of Judean society (Galling 1954, 215; Rudolph 1949, 97–98). This appears to be the case with temple personnel, since the *n^etînîm* are conspicuous by their absence, and none of the inhabitants of the provincial towns listed in the census (2:20–35) is included. A great deal depends on whether the list is confined to transgressors who actually went through with the divorce. The narrative leading up to the list (v. 17) suggests that it was intended to include all those whom the commission of inquiry found to be out of order, while the pledging and the guilt offerings (v. 19), and probably also the concluding sentence (v. 44), indicate that it was restricted to those who sent their wives back to their families. In that case we would be inclined to suspect that by no means all found in violation took the extremely hard and sacrificial option of separation from wife and children. And, in fact, if the "reform" had been as successful as C would have us believe, we would have expected a conclusion rather different from the somber and uncertain note on which the present narrative ends.

[10:18–22] The priests are listed according to houses or families as in the census (2:36–39), but in a somewhat different order. Unlike the priest list in Ezra's caravan (8:2), it does not follow the Aaronite genealogy, which may not have been firmly established by that time. The ancestor of the high priest Jeshua's house was Jedaiah, eponym of the second of the twenty-four courses established, according to C, by David (1 Chron. 24:7; cf. 1 Chron. 9:10; Neh. 11:10). As high priest at the time of the rebuilding of the temple, Jeshua was the most illustrious member of the phratry, and one of the courses, the ninth, was eventually to be named for him (1 Chron. 24:11). He appears to have compromised himself in the eyes of the anti-assimilationist party prior to the reestablishment of the cult (Zech. 3:1–5). At the time of Nehemiah, the high priestly family was involved in foreign marriage alliances (Neh. 13:28–29), and certain indications in Isa. 56–66 and Malachi suggest that this liberal attitude had been characteristic of the ruling priestly class for some time.

Of this, however, we have no hint in the list. At the time of the census there were 973 members of the Jeshua house; only four are mentioned here. The names are common, especially Maaseiah ("YHVH's doing"), which occurs four times in the list. The Immer house, later the sixteenth course (1 Chron. 24:14), numbered 1,052 in the census; it shows only two out of line. The houses of Harim and Pashhur have the most. The former constituted the third course (1 Chron. 24:8), the latter is not in the course list. Pashhur is the largest of the houses in the census (1,247) and also has the largest number of delinquents, which may help to explain why it did not maintain its place in the ranks of the priesthood.

[23–24] The absence of the temple servants from the list of lesser clerics has already been noted. This cannot be because they did not fall under the law as interpreted by Ezra, for which there is no evidence, and it is unlikely that none of their number had fallen foul of the committee of inquiry (see the commentary on their names in

2:43–57). Six Levites are listed as against seventy-four in the census (2:40). The first named, Jozabad, is probably identical with the Levite who held an important administrative position in the temple both before Ezra's arrival (Ezra 8:33) and during Nehemiah's tenure of office (Neh. 11:16) and who also took part in the reading of the law (Neh. 8:7). Kelaiah is identified in a gloss unknown to 1 Esdras with the Kelita (= cripple or dwarf) who helped out on the same occasion (Neh. 8:7; see also Neh. 10:11 [10]). Remarkably, the musicians, who number 128 in the census, have only one black sheep. He shares the name Eliashib with the high priest of Nehemiah's time and two others in the list. The gatekeepers, 139 in the census (2:42), have three delinquents. Two of the three names are identical with those of gatekeepers listed in the census (Shallum and Telem = Talmon). Here, too, it is clear that temple musicians and gatekeepers have not yet graduated to Levitical status.

[25–43] The laity are listed under the title "Israel," as elsewhere in the book (7:7; 9:1; Neh. 11:3; etc.). As the Hebrew text stands, they are divided into ten phratries, but the ninth, named for a second Bani, should be broken down into two, possibly three. The number may therefore have originally stood at twelve, like the number of lay families which returned with Ezra (Ezra 8:3–14). If Bigvai is read for the second Bani (v. 34; see textual note h), all the names in this list appear in the census with the exception of the textually uncertain Binnui (see textual note k). Likewise, seven of the names feature in the list of Ezra's caravan. Again, we can only speculate that the remaining five (Adin, Shephatiah, Joab, Azgad, Adonikam) had either been cleared by the commission or simply ignored the injunction to divorce their wives.

A study of the eighty-four names (eighty-six in the unemended text) suggests that the list is not an invention of C (*pace* Hölscher 1923 and Mowinckel). An interesting feature is the use of traditional patriarchal nomenclature (Judah, Manasseh, Shimeon, Benjamin, Joseph; see also Amram and Elijah). This practice, which is not attested earlier, may bear on the disputed issue of the date at which the narrative traditions about the ancestors were redacted. Many of the names are frequently attested in the postexilic period, several of them also in nonbiblical texts; e.g., Benjamin in the Murashu tablets (Clay, nos. 104, 205), Shashai in the Elephantine papyri (*AP* 49:1). Some are repeated several times in the list itself (Maaseiah, Mattaniah, Eliezer, Shimei, Eliashib, Malchijah, Jeremoth). Over thirty of them are formed with the theophoric element Ya or Yahu, from the Tetragrammaton, not counting the hypocoristics or caritatives: Abdi (Abdiah), Zabad (Zebediah), Zabbai—a remarkable contrast with

the family eponyms, none of which is of this type. This may well
reflect religious development between the first return and the time of
Ezra. Correspondingly, very few of the names are of foreign origin,
a conspicuous exception being the Persian Vaniah (Old Persian
vānya; see also *AP* 22:40).

[44] The first part of the verse takes up the narrative thread from
the conclusion of the inquest ("all the men who had married foreign
women," v. 17), leading us to expect a further and final statement
about the success of the operation. Unfortunately, however, the brief
sentence with which this chapter of the history concludes is unintelligible, and none of the many attempts to extract meaning from it has
been fully successful. The more important ancient versions (LXX,
Syr., Vulg.) construed it to mean that some of these women had
borne children, but this would be so obvious as not to be worth
mentioning, and it is hardly the note on which the story of a successful reform would be likely to conclude. Also, the verb in MT
(vayyāśîmû) cannot mean to bear children. Most attempts at recon-
structive surgery involve arbitrary emendation and shuffling the
order of the five words in the Hebrew text. 1 Esd. 9:36, "they sent
them away with their children," makes good sense and can, with a
little goodwill, be derived from a reconstructed Hebrew text (*vyšlḥvm*
instead of *vyšlh[v]m; nšym vbnym* with *vyśym* inserted by dittography). The adoption of this text must, however, be regarded as a *faute
de mieux,* since it is also possible that the Greek translator of 1
Esdras imposed his own meaning on a text which was as unintelligible to him as it is to us. On any reading, the conclusion to an
important episode in the religious history of the community is, for
C, uncharacteristically abrupt. We might have expected some remarks on the beneficial effects of the reform on the community and
something further about Ezra himself. As suggested earlier, the most
likely explanation is that this measure of Ezra's was not successful.
The practice of marrying outside the community was still widespread
during Nehemiah's administration, and it would be impossible to
explain the remarkable demographic expansion of Judaism in the
following centuries if this measure had taken hold. We conclude,
then, that the strict anti-assimilationism of Ezra, supported by a
rigorist minority (the *ḥᵃrēdîm*) and opposed by the more liberal
among the Judean nobility and the temple clergy, not only failed to
obtain adequate support but stirred up enough trouble to necessitate
Ezra's recall, or at least the termination of his mandate. Hence the
failure of the historian to conclude this part of his narrative in his
accustomed way (cf. 2 Chron. 15:15; 29:36; 30:26–27; 34:33).

It would be natural for us today to deplore the ethical insensitivity revealed in this measure, the single-minded concentration on a certain interpretation of the law, the disregard for the toll exacted on the parties concerned, not least on the women. It is this, more than anything else, which has given Ezra the reputation of the rigorous anti-assimilationist, in the process contributing to the generally pejorative assessment of early Judaism in modern biblical scholarship. At the least, however, we should acknowledge the problem which the marriage program was designed to confront: how to maintain the characteristic way of life, the religious traditions, even the language (cf. Neh. 13:23) of a community, against the threat of assimilation. In the event, Ezra's solution proved too drastic to win support. The problem remained, and the descendants of those Jews who shivered in the rain in the temple courtyard continued to plot a hazardous course between exclusiveness and assimilation under Persian, Macedonian, and Roman rule.

III

Nehemiah 1:1–7:5a

Hanani Brings Bad News (Neh. 1:1–4)

N. **Ararat,** "Nehemiah's Sole Arrival in the Twenty-fifth Year of Ezra's Arrival," *BM* 65, 1976, 293–295 (Heb.); W. R. **Arnold,** "The Passover Papyrus from Elephantine," *JBL* 31, 1912, 30–31; J. A. **Bewer,** "Josephus' Accounts of Nehemiah," *JBL* 43, 1924, 226–227; E. J. **Bickerman,** "En marge de l'Ecriture, I. Le comput des années de règne des Achéménides (Neh. i,2; ii,1 et Thuc. viii,58)," *RB* 88, 1981, 19–23; R. A. **Bowman,** *Aramaic Ritual Texts from Persepolis,* Chicago, 1970; D. J. A. **Clines,** "The Evidence for an Autumnal New Year in Pre-exilic Israel Reconsidered," *JBL* 93, 1974, 22–40; F. M. **Cross,** "The Discovery of the Samaritan Papyri," *BA* 26, 1963, 110–121; G. **de Deliceto,** "Epoca della Partenza di Hanani per Gerusalemme e Anno della Petizione di Neemia ad Artaserse: Neem. 1,1 e Neem. 2,1," *Laurentianum* 4, 1963, 431–468; W. Th. **In der Smitten,** "Erwägungen zu Nehemias Davidizität," *JSJ* 5, 1974, 41–48; U. **Kellermann,** *Nehemia,* 8–11, 154–159; J. **Morgenstern,** "Jerusalem—485 B.C.," *HUCA* 27, 1956, 101–179; 28, 1957, 15–47; 31, 1960, 1–29; S. **Mowinckel,** *Studien* II, 7–17; R. J. **Saley,** "The Date of Nehemiah Reconsidered," in G. A. Tuttle (ed.), *Biblical and Near Eastern Studies: Essays in Honor of William Sanford LaSor,* Grand Rapids, 1978, 151–165; J. **Schaumberger,** "Die neue Seleukiden-Liste BM 35603 und die makkabäische Chronologie," *Bib* 36, 1955, 423–455; C. J. **Tuland,** "Hanani-Hananiah," *JBL* 77, 1968, 157–161.

1:1 The chronicle of Nehemiah son of Hacaliah.

In the month of Chislev, in the twentieth year, while I was in the citadel of Susa, ²Hanani, one of my brothers, arrived accompanied by men from Judah. I inquired of him about the Judeans, those still remaining who had survived the captivity, and about Jerusalem. ³They said to me, "Those still remaining over there in the province who have survived the captivity are in great distress and disgrace. The wall of Jerusalem has been broken down and its gates gutted by fire." ⁴When I heard the report I sat down and wept. I mourned for several days and continued in fasting and in prayer to the God of heaven.

The title, added by C or a later editor, could be translated "words of Nehemiah" *(dibrê n^eḥemyāh),* which might then suggest analogy with the superscriptions of some prophetic books (Jer. 1:1; Amos 1:1). But what follows is not a collection of sayings, and there is no reason to think that Nehemiah is presented as a prophetic figure *(pace* Ackroyd 1973, Coggins 1976). C's history of the monarchy is punctuated by allusions to sources entitled "chronicles" *(d^ebārîm)* in which the deeds (also *d^ebārîm*) of the various kings are recounted (1 Chron. 29:29; 2 Chron. 9:29; 12:15; 13:22; 16:11; 20:34; etc.). The title of the Nehemiah source probably follows this usage, with Nehemiah understood as the subject rather than the author of the narrative. The Nehemiah material, therefore, takes its place as one of the many sources used in the "secondary history." There seems to be no compelling reason to regard it (with the possible exception of the last section, 13:4–31) as a much later appendage to the history (see further on "The Composition of Ezra-Nehemiah" in the Introduction, sect. 4).

It has already been noted that Ezra-Nehemiah forms one book in MT and LXX (cf. also Josephus, *C. Apion* 1.40), an arrangement which is readily understandable in view of the twinning of the two protagonists at an early stage of development (cf. Neh. 8:9; 12:26, 36). Yet the transition from Ezra to Nehemiah is far from smooth. Ezra ends abruptly and, leaving aside the title, the beginning of Nehemiah is equally abrupt. No attempt is made to link the two parts either chronologically *(pace* Ararat, who changes the date to the twenty-fifth year after Ezra's arrival) or thematically. One might speculate that some connective narrative has been omitted, leaving the edges jagged at both ends of the excision. In that case, a possible candidate would be Ezra 4:7–23, recording the hostile intervention of the Samarian authorities under Artaxerxes. If an editor could displace the public reading of the law (Neh. 8), as is generally acknowledged, he could also have moved this episode to its present position with a view to treating various phases of opposition together. Less felicitously, 1 Esdras relocates it after Cyrus and before Darius (2:16–30), misled by the apparent chronological sequence in the *Vorlage.* The hypothesis has, at any rate, the advantage of solving the problem of the truncated date at Neh. 1:1, since it would then be evident that the twentieth year referred to the reign of the Artaxerxes whose letter authorized the forcible termination of the rebuilding of the walls. It would also lead naturally into the next phase of the history, in which the king reversed his decree, a possibility explicitly left open in the decree itself (Ezra 4:21).

At the historical level, the implication would be that the bad news brought by Hanani concerned events in the recent past rather than under Babylonian rule (Ackroyd 1973) or at the beginning of Xerxes' reign (Morgenstern). Rehum's complaint was instigated by an influx of Jews from the east during Artaxerxes' reign and their allegedly seditious activities in Judah after their arrival (Ezra 4:12). This could hardly have happened before Ezra's arrival in the seventh year of the reign (458 B.C.E.), since the Ezra narrative makes no allusion to the kind of situation which prompted Nehemiah's emotional reaction to the bad news. We might then entertain the possibility that Rehum's complaint was occasioned by Ezra's arrival and subsequent activities. In view of what has been said about Ezra's support group, prophetic-eschatological aspirations of national restoration may have led to political action contributing to the failure of Ezra's mission and the termination of his mandate; and one might find support for this hypothesis in the allusion to the Davidic monarchy in Artaxerxes' reply (Ezra 4:20). In that case, however, we still have a gap of some twelve years, after which the situation in Judah would hardly have been news to a court official in Susa. A connection with the short-lived revolt of the satrap Megabyzus about 448 B.C.E. would shorten the gap considerably, but the information available (from the unreliable Ctesias) is too scanty to go beyond a guess. The suggestion of Morton Smith (1971, 127–128) that the situation may have been caused by an Arab raid is also a possibility, but no more than that. The allusion in 1 Esdras (4:45, 50) refers to events under Neo-Babylonian rule, the Hasmonean tradition attributing the rebuilding of the temple to Nehemiah (2 Macc. 1:18) is unsupported, and Ezra 6:14, suggesting that the temple was completed under Artaxerxes, is susceptible of a quite different explanation (see commentary ad loc.). All we can say, then, is that some serious disturbance had taken place shortly before 445 B.C.E. the cause of which remains obscure.

[1:1] The name of the protagonist (= Yahu/YHVH has comforted) is of a type frequently attested in the preexilic period and during the Second Commonwealth (Neh. 3:16; see also F. M. Cross for the Daliyeh texts and B. Porten, 1968, for Elephantine; for the name at Ezra 2:2 = Neh. 7:7, see on Ezra 2:2). The name of his father, here and at 10:2 [1], has not been successfully explained. The absence of a royal lineage, and of either name in C's Davidic genealogy (1 Chron. 3), seriously weakens the hypothesis that Nehemiah belonged to the Judean royal house (Kellermann et al.; on which see especially J. A. Emerton, *JTS* n.s. 23, 1972, 177–179).

As noted above, the opening of the first-person narrative is very abrupt. If this were the beginning of the Nehemiah Memoir (hereafter NM) we would expect the author to introduce himself, but for this we have to wait until the end of the chapter (1:11b). The date is also incomplete, since we are not told to what the twentieth year refers. Here too we have to wait for an explanation (2:1; cf. 5:14). We then have the problem that if Hanani's visit occurred in Chislev, i.e., the ninth month (November-December), the conversation with Artaxerxes could not have taken place in the first month (Nisan) of the same year (2:1). It is possible that Nehemiah, as a high official at the Persian court, reckoned according to the regnal year. *If* he did, and *if* Artaxerxes' reign began any time between the second and the eighth month inclusively, Nisan would follow Chislev in that year. Unfortunately, however, we do not know in which month Artaxerxes I began to reign (*pace* Bickerman), and it would have been less misleading for Nehemiah to have referred to the months by number rather than by name. An alternative suggestion is that at this point the dating follows the older calendar according to which the year begins in the autumn (Myers 1965, 92; Fensham 1982, 150), or that a later glossator has "corrected" the text following the Seleucid calendar with its similar reckoning (Schneider 1959, 163; Kellermann 1967, 75; Clines 1974, 36). A simpler and more plausible explanation, however, is that "twentieth" is a mistake, and that we should read "in the nineteenth year" (Rudolph 1949, 102–103), which would confirm the impression that the original opening of NM has been curtailed and modified in the course of transmission.

In spite of occasional demurrals and challenges (most recently by Saley), the broad consensus is that Nehemiah was active during the reign of Artaxerxes I (465–424). The well-known letter from the Elephantine priests to Bigvai, governor of Judah, names the family of Sanballat as governing Samaria and Johanan as high priest in Jerusalem (*AP* 30). That the same individuals (Sanballat and Johanan) were contemporaries of Nehemiah excludes the possibility that the latter was active under the second or, *a fortiori*, the third king of that name. Evidence for another Sanballat, also governor of Samaria, from the as yet unpublished Daliyeh papyri, adds a complicating factor but does not affect the fifth-century date for Johanan the high priest and Geshem/Gashmu the Arab (see on Neh. 2:19). It is therefore beyond reasonable doubt that Nehemiah arrived in Jerusalem in the twentieth year of Artaxerxes I, therefore in 445 B.C.E.

In spite of putting Nehemiah's mission in the twenty-fifth year of

Xerxes, which is impossible since Xerxes reigned for only twenty-one
years (486–465), Josephus offers a more satisfactory and certainly
more entertaining introduction which diverges considerably from
the biblical text:

> Now one of the Jewish captives, named Nehemiah, who was cup-
> bearer of king Xerxes, was walking about before the walls of Susa, the
> metropolis of Persia, when he overheard some strangers, who were
> entering the city after a long journey, speaking Hebrew to one another,
> and so he went up to them and inquired where they had come from.
> When they replied that they had come from Judaea, he began to
> inquire further how the people and the metropolis Jerusalem were
> getting on. They said that these were in a bad way, for the walls had
> been torn down to the ground, and the surrounding nations were
> inflicting many injuries on the Jews, overrunning the country and
> plundering it by day and doing mischief by night, so that many had
> been carried off as captives from the country and from Jerusalem itself,
> and every day the roads were found full of corpses. Then Nehemiah
> burst into tears out of pity for the misfortunes of his countrymen, and
> looking up to heaven said, "How long, O Lord, wilt thou look away
> while our nation suffers these things, having thus become the prey and
> spoil of all?" And as he lingered near the gate, lamenting these things,
> someone came up to him and informed him that the king was now
> about to recline at table. Thereupon, just as he was, and without
> bathing, he at once hastened to perform the service of bringing the
> king his drink. (*Ant.* 11.159–163)

While it is possible that Josephus had before him an alternative
version of the prologue to the mission (which would be consistent
with the hypothesis of an Arab raid), it appears more likely that he
is embellishing in his own way, and in tune with the novelistic style
then in vogue, the more succinct version which he had before him.
It would therefore be risky to reconstruct the "original" introduction
to either the narrative or the wording of the prayer on this basis (*pace*
Mowinckel, *Studien* II, 7–13, 16–19).

This opening scene takes place in Susa, the winter residence of the
Achaemenids (Xenophon, *Cyropaedia* 8:6, 22), in southwest Iran.
The qualification *bîrāh*—which accompanies the name of the town
here and throughout Esther—is translated "citadel" rather than
"capital" (RSV), following usage in the Aramaic ritual texts from
Persepolis (R. A. Bowman 1970, 20 and *passim*).

[2] According to Josephus, as we have just seen, the news came
to Nehemiah by way of a chance encounter, but in the biblical text
the situation is not so clear. It is tempting to think that the Judeans
comprised a delegation to the imperial court with a petition for

redress, and that the strategy was to route it through a highly placed Jew who had access to the king. This is by no means impossible, even though Nehemiah is the first to speak. His brother Hanani, later to be governor of Jerusalem (7:2), may have simply introduced the group to Nehemiah. It is not entirely clear that he came with them, even though his family had roots in Jerusalem (2:5). Identification of this person with the Hananiah who went on an important mission to the Jewish settlement in Elephantine (*AP* 21:2, 11; 38:7–8) is chronologically just possible but speculative, especially since the name is common—there are seven or eight with this name in Ezra-Nehemiah and two more at Elephantine. The way in which Nehemiah refers to the inhabitants of the province is also problematic. Use of the term *pᵉlēṭāh*, "escaped remnant," often used by C (1 Chron. 4:43; 2 Chron. 12:7; 20:24; 30:6; Ezra 9:8, 13–15), has a distinctly theological connotation inherited from prophetic preaching. But the sense as a whole would more naturally point to those who had never left the land, resulting in a perspective quite different from that of C. In general, Nehemiah, unlike Ezra, is not at all concerned with return from exile, and the heavily charged language used here occurs nowhere else in the Nehemiah material. This does not, however, justify the conclusion that there was no return before Nehemiah (*pace* Kosters, 44–45) or, less drastically, that Nehemiah preceded Ezra (Rudolph 1949, 105).

[3–4] We have already seen that Nehemiah's reaction precludes the possibility that events in the distant past were the cause. The description of that reaction follows the conventions of postexilic piety (see on Ezra 9:3–5), including sitting on the ground while in mourning (cf. Job 2:8, 13). This continued for several days. We are not told how long; assuming that the news was brought in the nineteenth year of Artaxerxes, he was still in mourning when he resumed service at the royal table at least three months later (2:1–3).

Nehemiah's Prayer (Neh. 1:5–11a)

B. **Hornig**, "Das Prosagebet in der nachexilischen Literatur," Diss., Leipzig, 1957 (see *TLZ* 83, 1958, 644–646); U. **Kellermann**, *Nehemia*, 8–11; S. **Mowinckel**, *Studien* II, 17–19; O. **Plöger**, "Reden und Gebete im deuteronomistischen und chronistischen Geschichtswerk," in W. Schneemelcher (ed.), *Festschrift für Günther Dehn*, Neukirchen-Vluyn, 1957, 35–49.

1:5 I said, "I beseech you, YHVH God of heaven, the great and fearful God, who observes covenant fidelity[a] with those who love him and keep his commandments; [6]may your ears[b] be attentive and your eyes open, to hear the prayer of your servant which I now address to you, day and night, on behalf of your servants, the people of Israel. I confess the sins which we, the people of Israel, have committed against you; both I and my ancestral house have sinned. [7]We have greatly wronged you in not observing the commandments, statutes, and ordinances which you commanded your servant Moses. [8]Remember the admonition[c] which you addressed to your servant Moses when you said, 'If you are unfaithful, I will scatter you among the nations, [9]but if you return to me, observing the commandments and fulfilling them, even if your dispersed ones be at the far end of the heavens, I will gather them in from there and bring them back to the place which I have chosen to make my name dwell there.' [10]They are your servants, your own people, whom you have redeemed with your great power and strong hand. [11a]I beseech you, Lord, let your ear be attentive to my humble prayer[d] and that of your servants who delight in revering your name. Give your servant success at this time[e] and extend your mercy to him in his dealings with this man."[f]

a. Lit., "covenant and fidelity" (*habbᵉrît vāhesed* [or *vᵉhāhesed*]; asyndeton.
b. With LXX[BL], Syr., and Vulg.; cf. 2 Chron. 6:40; 7:15; MT has the sing.
c. Lit., today *(hayyôm)*.
d. Lit., "the prayer of your servant."
e. Lit., today *(hayyôm)*.
f. Mercy *(raḥᵃmîm)* is to be shown by God, not by "this man."

There has been much discussion on the authenticity of the prayer (see Kellermann, 9 n. 16, for principal references). In effect, the question is whether the prayer was part of the NM or was inserted into it by an editor, C or another. The allusion to "this man" (i.e., Artaxerxes) at the end, the only exception to the generalizing tone of the prayer, is the clearest indication that it is not indigenous to its present context, with which, in fact, it does not make a good fit. "YHVH" and "the children of Israel" *(bᵉnê yiśrā'ēl)* are also uncharacteristic of NM, being attested only at 5:13. It is also quite unlike the other brief prayers with which the memoir is interspersed. If it was added, the addition may have been suggested by the rapid prayer of Nehemiah before making his request at the royal table (2:4)—the last sentence would, at any rate, fit that context very well. The Deuteronomic language and style in which the prayer is couched would not, of course, prove that C composed it, but certain expressions and turns of phrase (see especially vs. 6, 8, 10) suggest that C, or someone from the same ambient, has edited and expanded a brief prayer which originally stood either here or at 2:4.

Confession of sin, in which the individual and the people blend together, is characteristic of Second Temple piety (cf. Ezra 9:6–15; Neh. 9:6–37; Dan. 9:4–19; 1QS I 24–II 1; Bar. 1:15–3:8). Form-critically, this type of prayer may be viewed as a development from the preexilic psalms of public lamentation. The prayer begins and ends with invocation and appeal for a hearing; these encapsulate the confession of sin, involving a review of the nation's history which may be brief and generalizing, as here, or quite lengthy and specific, as in some of the examples cited. The prayer may be taken as illustrating one of the most characteristic features of Second Temple religion: a deep sense of sin and a profound conviction of the need to remove it.

[1:5] While more characteristic of official documents (see on Ezra 1:2), the title "God of heaven" is not out of place in this kind of prayer; we may compare C's version of the prayer of Jehoshaphat in which God in heaven is invoked (2 Chron. 20:6). The language throughout is Deuteronomic in character: "the great and fearful God" (also Neh. 4:8 [14]; 9:32; cf. Deut. 7:21; 10:17), "who observes covenant fidelity with those who love him and keep his commandments" (cf. Deut. 7:9; 1 Kings 8:23). It will be observed that the opening invocation of Daniel's prayer is practically identical (Dan. 9:4).

[6] The wording of the appeal to God to hear and see occurs also in C's version of Solomon's prayer (2 Chron. 6:40; cf. 7:15), which at this point diverges from its source in 1 Kings 8:52 (cf. 8:29). The allusion to Nehemiah himself and his house is not so unusual, and certainly provides no basis for Nehemiah's Davidic status (as Kellermann et al.).

[7] Here too the language is typically Deuteronomic: "commandments, statutes, and ordinances" (cf. Deut. 5:31); "your servant Moses" (cf. Deut. 34:5; Josh. 1:2; 9:24).

[8–9] These verses are a paraphrase of Deut. 30:1–5 (cf. 4:25–31), but it is noteworthy that the verb *mā'al* (act unfaithfully) occurs, characteristic of C and not at all of Deuteronomy (see on Ezra 9:2). The idea of the ingathering, the annulment of the curse of exile, is also a dominant theme of the exilic Deuteronomist. The far end of the heavens (Deut. 30:4; cf. 4:32) signifies the point where the earth and sky merge, that is, the furthest horizon, from which the dispersed of Israel will be brought back to the place where YHVH has elected to be worshiped (Deut. 12:11, 14; 1 Kings 11:13; etc.). This is an idea which dominates much of the prophetic and sermonic writing of the exilic age.

[10] Redemption by the strong hand of God is also a Deuteronomic theme (Deut. 3:24; 4:34; 5:15; 7:8; 9:26; 13:5; etc.). The verb *pādāh*, which occurs at this point in the prayer and frequently in Deuteronomy, points once again to the exodus, a major theme in Second Isaiah and in Ezra-Nehemiah, which would be further developed typologically in early Christianity and throughout Jewish history. The phrase "your own people whom you have redeemed" occurs also in C's version of David's prayer (1 Chron. 17:21), being one of the few points at which this version departs from its source in 2 Sam. 7.

[11a] Reverence for the divine name, leading eventually to the substitution of other expressions (the Name, the Place) and circumlocutions, was another mark of Second Temple piety (e.g., Mal. 3:16). The appeal to win the king's favor (for a similar expression see *AP* 30:1–2) suddenly brings the prayer to bear on a particular situation, but one for which the narrative to this point has not prepared us. "This man" *(hā'îš hazzeh)* contrasts sharply with allusions to Persian kings in the official correspondence in Ezra and dramatizes the distinction between official, public attitudes and private convictions. If the prayer in its present context belonged to the NM, which we have seen to be very doubtful, it was certainly not meant to be read by the political authorities.

Nehemiah Is Granted a Leave of Absence
(Neh. 1:11b–2:10)

W. F. **Albright**, "Dedan," in *Geschichte und Altes Testament [Festschrift Albrecht Alt]*, Tübingen, 1953, 1–12; A. **Alt**, "Judas Nachbarn zur Zeit Nehemias," *KS* 2:338–345; J. A. **Bewer**, "Josephus' Accounts of Nehemiah," *JBL* 43, 1924, 225–227; P. A. H. **de Boer**, "Vive le Roi!" *VT* 5, 1955, 225–231; F. M. **Cross**, "Aspects of Samaritan and Jewish History in Late Persian and Hellenistic Times," *HTR* 59, 1966, 201–211; "Papyri from the Fourth Century B.C. from Dâliyeh," in D. N. Freedman and J. C. Greenfield (eds.), *New Directions in Biblical Archaeology*, Garden City, 1969, 41–62; "The Historical Importance of the Samaria Papyri," *BAR* 4, 1978, 25–27; S. **Feigin**, "Etymological Notes," *AJSL* 43, 1926/27, 58; R. T. **Hallock**, *Persepolis Fortification Tablets*, Chicago, 1969, 40–44; W. Th. **In der Smitten**, "Nehemias Parteigänger," *BO* 29, 1972, 155–157; "Erwägungen zu Nehemias Davidizität," *JSS* 5, 1974, 41–48; B. S. J. **Isserlin**, "Ancient Forests in Palestine: Some Archaeological Indications," *PEQ* 86, 1955, 87–88; A. **Jepsen**, "Pardes," *ZDPV* 74, 1958, 65–68; U. **Kellermann**, *Nehemia*, 11–13, 154–159, 166–

170; P. W. **Lapp,** "The Second and Third Campaigns at 'Arâq el-Emîr," *BASOR* 171, 1963, 8–39; P. W. and N. **Lapp,** "Discoveries in the Wâdi ed-Dâliyeh," *AASOR* 41, 1974, 17–24; B. **Mazar,** "The Tobiads," *IEJ* 7, 1957, 137–145, 229–238; C. C. **McCown,** "The 'Araq el-Emir and the Tobiads," *BA* 20, 1957, 63–76; J. **Naveh,** "The Development of the Aramaic Script," *The Israel Academy of Sciences and Humanities,* Jerusalem, 1970, 62–64; H. H. **Rowley,** "Nehemiah's Mission and Its Background," *Men of God,* London and Edinburgh, 1963, 211–245 (= *BJRL* 37, 1954/55, 528–556); "Sanballat and the Samaritan Temple," *Men of God,* 246–276 (= *BJRL* 38, 1955/56, 166–198); C. C. **Torrey,** "Sanballat the Horonite," *JBL* 47, 1928, 380–389; M. E. **Will,** "Iraq el Amir. Histoire d'une famille: les Tobiades," *Le Monde de la Bible,* 22, 1982, 12–13; E. M. **Yamauchi,** "Was Nehemiah the Cupbearer a Eunuch?" *ZAW* 92, 1980, 132–142; H. **Zimmern,** "Über Bäcker und Mundschenk im Altsemitischen," *ZDMG* 53, 1899, 115–119.

1:11b I was wine steward to the king. 2:1 In the month of Nisan, in the twentieth year of King Artaxerxes, when I had charge of the wine, [a] I took the wine and gave it to the king. Since I had never been sad in his presence, [b] [2]the king said to me, "Why are you looking sad when you are not sick? You must be in a bad mood." [c] I was very much afraid [3]and said to the king, "O king, may you live for ever! How can I not look sad when the city where my ancestors are buried lies in ruins with its gates burnt down?" [4]The king then said to me, "What is it you are asking?" I offered a prayer to the God of heaven [5]and replied to the king, "If it please the king, and if you are well disposed toward your servant, I request [d] that you send me to Judah, to the city where my ancestors are buried, that I may rebuild it." [6]The king, with the royal consort sitting beside him, then said to me, "How long will you be gone and when will you return?" So the king agreed to send me, and I told him how long it would take. [e]

[7]Then I said to the king, "If it please the king, let them give me letters for the governors of the Trans-Euphrates satrapy which will grant me passage until I arrive in Judah; [8]also, a letter to Asaph, keeper of the royal reserve, with instructions to supply me with timber to make beams for the gates of the temple fortress, for the city wall, and the house which I am to occupy." Since I enjoyed the good favor of my God, [f] the king granted my request.

[9]So I came to the governors of the Trans-Euphrates satrapy and handed over to them the royal letters. The king had sent with me an escort of army officers and horsemen. [10]When Sanballat the Horonite and Tobiah the "servant," the Ammonite, heard of it, they were very displeased that someone had come to take care of the interests of the people of Israel.

a. Reading *l^epānāy* with LXX (cf. Syr.) for MT *l^epānāv*, as many of the commentators (e.g., Bertholet 1902, 49; Rudolph 1949, 106; R. A. Bowman 1954, 671; Batten 1913, 190). While MT is not impossible, the more natural sense is that it was Nehemiah's turn to serve wine.

b. MT *v^elō'-hāyîtî ra' l^epānāv*, lit., "and I had not been bad (unhappy) before him," the verb having the pluperfect sense. LXX *ouk ēn heteros enōpion autou* ("there was no one else in his presence") presupposes *v^elō'-hāyāh rēa' l^epānāv* and carries the added implication that the royal consort appeared at a later stage and presumably influenced the royal decision. Some emend *lō'* to the asseverative particle *lû* (cf. NEB "as I stood before him, I was feeling very unhappy"), but this usage is infrequent in postexilic texts.

c. Lit., "this is nothing but sadness (badness) of heart." The phrase *rōa' lēb* can mean "evil disposition" (cf. 1 Sam. 17:28), but the context, and especially the subsequent action of the king, suggests sadness rather than badness.

d. "I request" added for the sense.

e. Lit., "I gave him a (fixed) time." There is no need to emend with Syr. to "he gave me a (fixed) time."

f. Lit., "as the good hand of God was on (over) me"; cf. Ezra 7:6.

As suggested earlier, Nehemiah's prayer may have been spliced into the narrative, a procedure well attested in the Hebrew Bible. If so, the lack of narrative continuity between 1:4 and 1:11b permits the further suggestion that the prayer may have been elaborated on the basis of a briefer invocation (perhaps 1:11a) which originally stood at 2:4, when Nehemiah was about to make his petition. We may compare the brief prayer of Judith as she prepared to decapitate Holophernes (Judith 13:4–5, 7). At both points in Nehemiah prayer is addressed to the God of heaven. Josephus puts into Nehemiah's mouth a brief prayer after he heard the bad news. He also alludes to, but does not quote, the prayer at the king's table, putting it at a somewhat earlier point than in Nehemiah (*Ant.* 11.162, 165). There is no reason to believe that he had access to a source significantly different from our Hebrew text.

[**1:11b**] The essential piece of information, that Nehemiah was a royal wine steward (Heb. *mašqeh,* lit., "one who gives to drink"), is given first. For the wine steward (or cupbearer or butler) had an important and influential office and could therefore serve ideally as a means of access to the king. Classical authors (e.g., Herodotus 3.34; Xenophon, *Cyropaedia* 1:3, 8–9, 11) attest to the high status attaching to this office. The sage Ahiqar, also a cupbearer, is described as second in rank to Esarhaddon at the Assyrian court (Tobit 1:22). Nehemiah, therefore, was one of those Jews who, like the patriarch Joseph, rose to high estate in the service of a foreign king. His subsequent conduct also shows that he discharged his duties without compromising his Jewish identity. The position was one of great trust since, *inter alia,* the cupbearer had to taste the wine to forestall any attempt at poisoning, a favorite means of disposing of the opposition at the Persian court.

The conclusion has been drawn from Nehemiah's position at the court that he must have been a eunuch. On closer inspection, however, none of the arguments advanced is very persuasive. Some royal wine stewards were eunuchs but others were not. The presence of the royal consort is far from decisive since the case is exceptional, women usually not being present at Persian royal banquets (cf. the case of Haman in Esth. 7:8, certainly no eunuch). If Nehemiah had been a eunuch, one or another of his many enemies would surely have brought it up against him, especially in view of the fact that the sexually mutilated were excluded from the cult community (Deut. 23:2 [1]). Contrary to what used to be argued (e.g., by E. Meyer 1896, 194), the term *tiršātā',* translated "governor" at Ezra 2:63, cannot have this meaning. Bertholet's interpretation of Ps. 127, which speaks of building and the blessing of children, as a covert attack on Nehemiah, is ingenious but unconvincing; and, finally, there is no need to interpret Nehemiah's many appeals to be remembered as the eunuch's longing for a "monument and a name" (*yād vāšēm,* Isa. 56:5).

[2:1–2] The fateful approach to the king was made in Nisan, the first month in the Babylonian calendar, corresponding to March–April, and therefore rather more than three months after Hanani brought the news with its implicit appeal for Nehemiah's cooperation. The delay may be explained by the king's absence in Babylon during the winter months, or there may have been several royal butlers serving on a rota system. Herodotus (9.110–111) speaks of a special banquet called *tukta* during which it was considered *de rigueur* for the king to grant any request addressed to him. Parties thrown by the Achaemenids were famous for their opulence and extravagance (e.g., Esth. 1:1–12; Dan. 5:1–4; 1 Esd. 3:1–3). Nehemiah, who was not lacking in shrewdness, probably waited for such an occasion—the royal birthday, or a spring festival, or an occasion when (exceptionally) one of the king's favorite harem women would be present. The allusion to his previous deportment may be of a quite general nature, with the purpose of emphasizing the unusual circumstances which caught the king's attention, or it may imply that, since hearing the bad news, he had kept up appearances and was now deliberately seeking an occasion to win the royal sympathy. If so, the strategy was not without risk. Court etiquette required a cheerful and pleasant demeanor (cf. Dan. 1). Any hint of moroseness could arouse suspicion of intrigue. Nehemiah was therefore naturally apprehensive as he approached the decisive moment for which he had patiently waited.

[3–6] After the customary salutation (cf. 1 Kings 1:31; Dan. 2:4), Nehemiah explained the reason for his dejection. His answer, no doubt well rehearsed in advance, is worded with great care. There is no mention of Jerusalem, the "rebellious and wicked city" of the royal firman issued just a few years earlier (Ezra 4:17–22). The issue is couched in personal rather than political terms with the mention of his ancestral tombs, a subject likely to arouse the sympathy and interest of the king. While Nehemiah does not exactly dissimulate his intent to rebuild the city, he manages to convey the impression that his main purpose is to restore the sepulchers of his ancestors. Those who hold that Nehemiah was of the blood royal have found an argument here, on the grounds that only royal tombs would be *in* the city. It is also argued that the phrase *bêt-qibrôt,* literally "house of tombs," bears the same construction and is meant to recall those royal Achaemenid tombs built in the shape of a palace (Stronach 1978). But all of this is highly speculative. Nehemiah's answer need not imply that the tombs were inside the city and—whatever the construction in Persian, the language in which the conversation was presumably conducted—the Hebrew term *bêt-qibrôt* is in apposition to *hāʿîr,* the city.

The king understood at once the point of Nehemiah's complaint and invited him to make his request. The silent invocation may illustrate the practice of private prayer, characteristic of Second Temple piety but rare in the preexilic period; it will be recalled how Hannah's silent praying at Shiloh was misconstrued by Eli (1 Sam. 1:13). Later on, Nehemiah dated his tenure of office as governor from this time (Neh. 5:14), but the request did not have this implication, and it is clear that the king did not contemplate a twelve-year leave of absence. The task of rebuilding the city nevertheless implied considerable authority, and we must assume that Nehemiah was appointed governor shortly after his arrival, thus arousing the animosity of the authorities in Samaria whom he had circumvented. Perhaps this was the plan from the outset. It may seem surprising that Artaxerxes did not even bother to inquire further about the supposed hotbed of rebellion, the subject of his response to Rehum's letter of complaint (Ezra 4:19–20). The most likely explanation is that Artaxerxes was not "taken in," but decided that this was the opportune moment for reversing the decree (cf. Ezra 4:21), for shrewdly calculated political reasons. In view of the disturbances in the west during the first two decades of the reign, he may well have considered the fortification of Jerusalem, carried out by a Jewish subject of unimpeachable loyalty, as a significant strengthening of his position in Abar-nahara, especially in view of its proximity to Egypt where revolt was endemic.

Mention at this point of the "royal consort" has intrigued the commentators from early times. The woman in question was almost certainly not Artaxerxes' queen, whose name, according to Ctesias (*Persika* 15:44), was Damaspia. The term used is not *hammalkāh*, the queen, but the relatively rare *haššēgal* (LXX *pallakē*), harem woman (cf. Judg. 5:30; Ps. 45:10 [9]; Dan. 5:2–3, 23). Her introduction at this point of the narrative, as the king was about to reply favorably to Nehemiah, is clearly intended to be significant, and the most natural assumption would be that her presence was beneficial. Ctesias (14:39), not the most reliable of historians, reports that Artaxerxes was susceptible to feminine charms, and it is possible that this perhaps temporary favorite of the king had agreed to cooperate in the furtherance of Nehemiah's plan the details of which, as the course of subsequent events reveals, had been carefully worked out in advance.

[7–8] Having achieved his main point, Nehemiah went on at once to make two further requests: documents which would guarantee him safe passage, and a requisition order for timber. An official passport for journeys of this kind was probably quite routine. One of the Elephantine papyri records such a document issued in the name of the satrap of Egypt which also allowed for provisioning along the route (G. R. Driver 1957, 27–28). The situation in the Abar-nahara satrapy, now separate from Babylon, may still have been unsettled after the recent revolt of Megabyzus, and Nehemiah may have anticipated trouble from the Samarian authorities. Timber was requested for the gates of the temple fortress, the city wall, and his own house. The location of the temple fortress *(habbîrāh 'ašer labbayit)* is unknown. It may have included the Tower of Hananel and the Tower of the Hundred (Neh. 3:1). Topographical constraints suggest that it occupied more or less the same site, north of the temple, as the Hasmonean citadel (1 Macc. 13:52) and Herod's Antonia fortress (*Ant.* 15.403; 18.91). The use of timber in wall-building has already been noted (see on Ezra 5:8). Nehemiah's family dwelling may have been still standing but in need of repair. Though "house" *(bayit)* can also mean "palace" or, in other words, the governor's mansion, Nehemiah states his personal needs last and in appropriately modest terms. Judging by his name—Asaph—the custodian of the royal reserve appears to have been Jewish, though Asaph (Addaios in Josephus, *Ant.* 11.167) could be the Hebrew form of a Persian or, at any rate, non-Jewish name. The location of this "paradise" (*pardēs,* from Old Persian *pairidaeza,* LXX *paradeisos;* cf. Qoh. 2:5; Cant. 4:13) is unknown. It would be natural to think of the Lebanon, a principal source of timber (Ezra 3:7). There were other sources nearer to hand, however, as Hag. 1:8 suggests; perhaps in the foothills to the west of Jerusalem (the Shephelah, 1 Chron. 27:28) or southeast in the region of Tekoa (cf. the place-name Jebel Ferdēs near the Herodium). These additional requests were also granted, the total success of the operation being attributed to the divine intervention and guidance (the "hand of God"; cf. Ezra 7:6, 9, 28).

[9–10] Provision of an armed escort, together with guides and travel rations, was standard procedure, as can be seen from the Persepolis Fortification Tablets (Hallock). The absence of such an escort for Ezra's caravan (Ezra 8:22) was meant to emphasize his faith in divine providence, but it is gratuitous to interpret it as setting up a contrast unfavorable to Nehemiah's acceptance of the offer. (Whether Ezra, in the circumstances, would have been permitted to make the journey unescorted is another matter.) Nehemiah's itinerary is not given. It would probably have taken him first to Babylon, then up the Euphrates, across to Damascus, seat of the satrapal government, and finally to Samaria and Jerusalem. Since there is no mention of Rehum, Samarian commander *(bᵉ'ēl ṭᵉ'ēm)* earlier in the reign, he may have been recently succeeded by Sanballat. Though the latter is not designated governor, he is named immediately after the notice that Nehemiah came to the governors of Abar-nahara, and the description of his activities is consistent with holding that office.

This Sanballat has a Babylonian name (*sin-uballit,* "the god Sin has given life"), possibly as a descendant of a family settled in the north by the Assyrians in the eighth century (2 Kings 17:24). At several points he is described as "the Horonite" (2:10, 19; 13:28). This designation has been variously explained. His origin has been traced to Haran in northern Mesopotamia, center of the worship of the moon god Sin (Klostermann, Galling 1954, Feigin), or to the one-time Assyrian province of the Hauran in the northern Transjordan region (Kraeling 1953, 107–108), or to Horonaim in Moab (Kellermann, following Kittel and Hölscher; cf. Isa. 15:5 and Jer. 48:3). The more likely candidate, however, is one of the Beth-horons settled by Ephraimites in the Shephelah northwest of Jerusalem; in which case, there is no reason to suppose that the designation itself was meant to be uncomplimentary. It may be worth noting that it was to this region, the plain of Ono, that Sanballat attempted to lure Nehemiah (6:2; cf. Ezra 2:33 = Neh. 7:37; 11:34). That Sanballat was a YHVH worshiper may be deduced from the names of his sons known from an Elephantine letter (Delaiah and Shemaiah). His determination to compromise Nehemiah and abort his mission was dictated by political rather than religious concerns, since the intervention of the Samarian authorities in Jerusalem (Ezra 4:23–24) must have given them temporary control of the province of Judah. Influential contacts in Jerusalem (6:10–14) and the marriage of his daughter into the Jerusalemite high priestly family (13:28) would have helped significantly to consolidate his position.

The Elephantine letter just referred to (*AP* 30:29 = 31:28) informs us that in 408 B.C.E. two of his sons were actively involved in public affairs, but it is neither stated nor implied that he himself was still alive at that time. By 433 at the latest he had a married daughter (Neh. 13:28), which would mean that in 408, if alive, he must have been in his late sixties if not older. The same letter makes it clear that at that time Samaria and Judah were separate provinces, each with its own governor. That the successor of Nehemiah as governor of Judah bore a Persian name—Bigvai or Bagohi—*may* suggest that the quarrel between Nehemiah and Sanballat necessitated the intervention of the central government, though a Persian name does not necessarily imply that its owner was Persian. Another letter (*AP* 32), in which the answer to the one just mentioned is recorded, informs us that Delaiah was the acting governor—or, if Sanballat was no longer alive, the actual governor—of Samaria. That he replied jointly with the governor of Judah further suggests that by that time conflict between the two provinces had by some means been settled.

Two of the papyri discovered in the Wadi ed-Dâliyeh name a Sanballat governor of Samaria in the last decades of Persian rule (Cross, Lapp and Lapp). This Sanballat is very probably identical with the Sanballat active during the reign of Darius III (336–330) according to Josephus (*Ant.* 11.302–325). Josephus has it that his daughter married Manasseh, brother of the high priest Jaddua, and that Manasseh subsequently became the first high priest of the temple built by Sanballat on Mount Gerizim. On the historicity of this incident something will be said later, but it appears that the Sanballat family maintained its control over Samaria for at least a century, during which time its connections with the high priestly family in Jerusalem remained close.

Closely associated with Sanballat in his opposition to Nehemiah, here and throughout the narrative (2:10, 19; 3:35 [4:3]; 4:1 [4:7]; 6:1, 12, 14), was Tobiah, described curiously as "the servant, the Ammonite." On one occasion at least he was actually in Samaria with Sanballat (3:35 [4:3]). He had close ties with the Judean nobility and the Jerusalem priesthood (6:17–19; 13:4), and even managed to obtain accommodation in the temple precincts—probably in connection with a commercial venture—during Nehemiah's temporary absence (13:4–9). "The servant, the Ammonite" has given rise to a great deal of discussion. "Servant" *('ebed)* is an honorific title borne by high officials, but since it also means "slave," the title has been widely understood as a double entendre with obviously uncomplimentary implications. But however Nehemiah may have chosen to understand it, it is also possible that the title was traditional in the family, perhaps as an abbreviated form of "servant of the king of Persia" or something of the sort. By interesting coincidence, if it is that, one of the Lachish ostraca from the last days of the monarchy refers to a Tobiah "servant of the king" (3:19–21), and the most imposing feature of the Tobiad settlement at 'Araq el-Emir east of the Jordan bears the name Qaṣr el-'Abd. The alternative suggestion (Albright, 4), that the verse originally referred to three opponents, one of them a certain Abd known from the proto-Arabian inscription of Nûrân as governor of Dedan in the Arabian peninsula, is intriguing, especially since he is there associated with a chieftain named Gashmu (cf. Geshem, Neh. 2:19). But the proposed emendation is unsupported, and has the further disadvantage of breaking the connection between Tobiah and Ammon. For it seems likely that Tobiah was in fact governor of the Ammonite region, whatever its precise status under the Persians, as Sanballat was of Samaria and Geshem (Gashmu) of the Kedarite region. His close association with Sanballat, and his occasional presence in Samaria, do not oblige us to conclude that he served under Sanballat in that city, any more than we are justified in concluding that Geshem was stationed there. It would also be risky to base an argument on the identification of this Tobiah with the Tabeel of Ezra 4:7 (as Mazar, 236–237, and Kellermann, 167–170), which is possible but speculative. On the assumption that Nehemiah's three principal opponents had distinct territorial jurisdictions, it will also be easier to understand the plan to invade Judah involving Samarians, Ammonites, and Arabs (4:1 [7]).

About two centuries later the aristocratic Tobiad family, which was closely related to the Jerusalem priesthood, established itself as a quasi-autonomous power in the Ammonite region, where they presumably already had connections among the Jewish settlers there (cf. Jer. 40:11, 14; 41:10, 15; 49:2). Something of the history of this family can be reconstructed from Josephus (*Ant.* 12.160–236), the Zeno papyri from the mid-third century, and the excavations at 'Araq el-Emir (cf. also 1 Macc. 5:10–13; 2 Macc. 12:17). It would be quite natural to conclude that the Ammonite foe of Nehemiah was the ancestor of these Tobiads, of whom we may also find traces here and there in texts from the Persian period (Zech. 6:9–15; Ezra 2:60 = Neh. 7:61). We conclude, then, that Tobiah belonged to a distinguished Jerusalemite family with close ties to the high priesthood and the aristocracy, and that at the time of Nehemiah's mission he was the Persian-appointed governor of the Ammonite region. It is also possible, but no more than possible, that following on the events recorded in Ezra 4:8–23, he was assigned some form of temporary jurisdiction over affairs in Judah, either in coordination with or under the supervision of the authorities in Samaria.

The contrast between "Ammonite" and "Israelites" *(bᵉnê yiśrā'ēl)*—rather than "men of Judah"—is certainly deliberate. Ammonites were excluded *in perpetuum* from the congregation of Israel (Neh. 13:1). It may also be reinforced by a play on the name Tobiah in the allusion to a man who has now arrived to "seek the good" *(lᵉbaqqēš ṭôbāh)* of Israel.

Nehemiah's Night Ride (Neh. 2:11–20)

W. F. **Albright**, "Dedan," in G. Ebeling (ed.), *Geschichte und Altes Testament. Beiträge zur historischen Theologie* (Alt Festschrift), Tübingen, 1953, 1–12; A. **Alt**, "Das Taltor von Jerusalem," *PJB* 24, 1928, 74–98 = *KS* 3:326–347; J. **Braslavi**, "En Tannin," *EI* 10, 1971, 90–93 (Heb.); M. **Burrows**, "Nehemiah's Tour of Inspection," *BASOR* 64, 1936, 11–21; F. M. **Cross**, "Geshem, the Arabian, Enemy of Nehemiah," *BA* 18, 1955, 46–47; W. J. **Dumbrell**, "The Tell el-Maskhuṭa Bowls and the 'Kingdom' of Qedar in the Persian Period," *BASOR* 203, 1971, 33–44; P. **Haupt**, "Nehemiah's Night Ride," *JAOS* 39, 1919, 143; J. **Heller**, "Die abgeschlagene Mauer," *CV* 11, 1968, 175–178; W. Th. **In der Smitten**, "Nehemias Parteigänger," *BO* 29, 1972, 155–157; H. **Kaupel**, "Der Sinn von *'ośēh hammᵉlā'kāh* in Neh 2,16," *Bib* 21, 1940, 40–44; U. **Kellermann**, *Nehemia*, 13; W. S. **LaSor**, "Jerusalem," in G. W. Bromiley et al. (eds.), *The International Standard Bible Encyclopedia* II, Grand Rapids, 1982, 998–1032; I. **Rabinowitz**, "Aramaic Inscriptions of the Fifth Century B.C.E. from a North-Arab Shrine in Egypt," *JNES* 15, 1956, 1–9; J. **Wilkinson**, "The Pool of Siloam," *Levant* 10, 1978, 116–125; H. G. M. **Williamson**, "Nehemiah's Wall Revisited," *PEQ* 116, 1984, 81–88; T. F. **Wright**, "Nehemiah's Night Ride," *PEF Quarterly Statement*, April 1896, 172–173.

2:11 When I arrived in Jerusalem, and had been there three days, [12] I set out by night together with a few men, but I did not tell anyone what my God had prompted me[a] to do on behalf of Jerusalem. No beast of burden accompanied me except the one on which I was riding. [13] I left at night by the Valley Gate, facing the

Dragon Spring, going in the direction of the Dung Gate, inspect-ing[b] the walls[c] of Jerusalem which were broken down[d] and their gates gutted by fire. [14]I continued to the Fountain Gate and to the King's Pool, where there was no room for the animal on which I rode to pass. [e] [15]I proceeded through the night, going up the wadi, inspecting the wall; then I returned, entering by the Valley Gate. [16]The officials did not know where I had gone or what I was doing; up to this point I had not told the Jews, the priests, the nobles, the officials, and the rest of the people who were to do the work.

[17]Then I said to them, "You see the sorry state in which we are, with Jerusalem in ruins and its gates destroyed by fire. Come, let us rebuild the wall of Jerusalem that we may no longer be an object of disgrace." [18]I went on to tell them how God had shown his gracious favor to me, [f] and also what the king had said to me. They replied, "Let us make a start with the rebuilding," whereupon they went to work with a will. [g]

[19]When they heard about it, Sanballat the Horonite, Tobiah the "servant," the Ammonite, and Geshem the Arab derided us and held us in contempt. They asked, "What is this thing that you are doing? Are you rebelling against the king?" [20]I sent them a reply, saying, "The God of heaven will grant us success. We his servants are making a start with the rebuilding. But as for you, you have no share or claim or traditional right in Jerusalem."

a. Reading *nātan* for MT *nōtēn;* cf. Syr. and Vulg.
b. *šōbēr* (Qal) occurs only here; otherwise in Piel with the sense of "hope," "wait"; cf. LXX *katanoōn* and Vulg. *considerabam.* LXX[BAS] have *kai ēmēn syntribōn,* reading *šōbēr,* which makes no sense (*pace* Heller).
c. The consonantal text *(bhvmt)* could be sing. or pl.; LXX[BAS] and Vulg. have sing.; LXX[L] has pl. The verb is in pl.
d. Reading, with Qere, *hēm pᵉrûsîm,* Qal participle passive, meaning strictly "breached" (cf. 1:3, *mᵉpōrāṣet*), but not in agreement with *hômôt* (fem.).
e. Lit., "there was no room for the animal to pass under me."
f. Lit., "I told them (about) the hand of God which was good on me"; cf. Ezra 7:6; Neh. 2:8.
g. Lit., "they strengthened their hands for the good," the more natural implica-tion being that they actually made a start, a conclusion also suggested by the following verse.

The Nehemiah Memoir continues with Nehemiah's arrival in Je-rusalem and tour of inspection of the wall. Josephus (*Ant.* 11.168–171) omits the nocturnal inspection, proceeding at once to Nehemiah's address to the people and command to the officers to measure the walls and assign the work gangs their sections. The conclusion to this bit of additional information is that "the Jews prepared for the work" (cf. Neh. 2:16), which suggested to Mowinckel (*Studien* II, 22–23) that Josephus had before him a somewhat fuller version of the Nehemiah story. It would be more prudent to conclude, however, that here and in similar instances Josephus is rewriting his source, with both omissions and expansions, to produce a smoother narrative line and a more interesting story for his public. He concluded, no doubt correctly, that the topography of Jerusalem was a subject of limited appeal to his Gentile audience.

[2:11–12] Like Ezra (8:32), Nehemiah waited only three days before getting down to work. As noted at Ezra 8:32, the similarity is not significant, since "three days" is simply a conventional way of designating a brief passage of time. The need for haste was no doubt prompted by awareness that his enemies already knew about his mandate (v. 10) and might move against him at any time. Nehemiah was also doubtless aware that these enemies had allies in the province who would be watching him closely (6:17–19; 13:4–9, 28); hence also the need for secrecy. The plan, obviously not free of risk, was to present them with a *fait accompli*. We are not told who the "few men" were. Nehemiah would presumably have needed guides, and he would have been in touch with sympathizers in the city since hearing the news back in Susa. His insistence that he was the only one of the party mounted is rather curious. The explanation usually offered, that he wished to avoid the impression of a show of force, is hardly satisfactory since the whole point of a night operation was to avoid detection completely. Use of the generic term *bᵉhēmāh* (animal, beast of burden) also helped allay any suspicion of messianic pretensions (of the kind with which he was actually charged, 6:6–7) which the use of a horse, or even a mule (cf. 1 Kings 1:38–40), might have encouraged. We have to keep in mind that this is Nehemiah's *apologia pro vita sua*, and that it was written as much for posterity as for his contemporaries.

[13–15] The exact determination of the route followed by Nehemiah in his night ride has long been a matter of debate. The location of the six topographical features mentioned depends on a prior decision about the dimensions of Jerusalem in the fifth century B.C.E. (see Additional Note on Nehemiah's Jerusalem). The tour began and ended at the Valley Gate, situated at a distance of some thousand cubits (about five hundred meters) from the Dung Gate (Neh. 3:13), which stood near the southern extremity of the eastern hill (the Ophel). According to C (2 Chron. 26:9), the Valley Gate was fortified by King Uzziah in the eighth century B.C.E. The valley to which this

gate led must be the Tyropeon or Cheesemakers Valley between the
eastern and western ridges—the Ophel and Mount Zion respectively.
Nehemiah, therefore, left the city on the western side, turned left,
and proceeded south. He then passed opposite or facing a feature
otherwise unattested called Dragon Spring or possibly Dragon's Eye
(LaSor). (The rendering "Jackal's Well" in RSV is based on an
unsupported emendation of *hattannîn* to *hattannîm;* LXX^B has "toward the mouth of the Fig Spring," reading *hatt^e'ēnîm.*) This feature
is often identified with En Rogel, close to a local landmark known
as Serpent Stone (*'eben hazzōḥelet,* 1 Kings 1:9). But En Rogel, now
Bir 'Ayyub (Job's Well), lies more than two hundred meters south
of the Ophel, and therefore the party could hardly be said to have
passed opposite or facing it. Identification with the Pool of Siloam
(Braslavi) is topographically more feasible, but it is safer to assume
an allusion to a source of water in the Tyropeon now dried up. The
Dung Gate *(ša'ar hā'ašpōt),* more correctly the Rubbish Gate (cf. 1
Sam. 2:8 = Ps. 113:7; Lam. 4:5), was at the extreme south leading
directly to the city dump in Hinnom. It is almost certainly identical
with the more elegantly named Potsherd Gate mentioned by Jeremiah (19:2), broken pottery forming the bulk of the city refuse at that
time (cf. the Testaccio of ancient Rome).

After passing the Dung Gate, the party continued outside the
walls until they arrived opposite the Fountain Gate, probably near
the southeast corner leading to En Rogel (Fuller's Spring?) in the
Kidron Valley (Josh. 15:7; 18:15; 2 Sam. 17:17; 1 Kings 1:9). This
gate is also mentioned in the account of the rebuilding (3:15) and the
solemn dedication of the wall (12:37). The King's Pool is not mentioned elsewhere, but we will hear of a certain Shallum working on
the wall of the Pool of Shelah of the King's Garden, in close proximity to the Fountain Gate and the stairs leading down from the City
of David (3:15). The King's Pool may therefore be identical with the
Pool of Shelah or Shiloah (cf. Isa. 8:6; the consonants are identical),
a basin fed by a canal or aqueduct from the Gihon Spring, also
known as the Lower Pool (Isa. 22:9) and probably to be identified
with the modern Birket el Hamra. At this point, as he headed north
along the narrow ridge overlooking the Kidron Valley, Nehemiah
was forced to dismount and proceed on foot. Very probably debris
from the collapsed wall and ruined terraces forced him and his
companions to the bottom of the eastern slope where the Jericho
road now passes. They continued up the valley northward, then
retraced their steps and reentered the city through the same gate by
which they had left it. The repetition of the verb (*'āšûb,* returned,
turned round) leaves little doubt that they did not follow the wall

further north and around the city. Perhaps they saw as much as they needed to see, though from the lower route which they were obliged to take this could hardly have been more than a general impression, and Nehemiah would have had an idea of the state of the northern peimeter on his first entrance into the city. At any rate, the tour of inspection seems to have been limited to the southwest and southeast part of the city wall.

[16] The element of secrecy is emphasized once again after the completion of the tour. It seems to have been especially important to keep the "officials" in the dark. As used in the book, this term *(sāgān;* cf. Akk. *saknu)* applies to administrators, including district governors (see on Neh. 4:13). It does not refer to the hereditary nobility *(ḥôrîm)* or to Persian officials in the province, for the *s^egā-nîm* took part in the dedication of the wall (12:40) and shared responsibility for tithing and the upkeep of the temple (13:11). At Elephantine the *s^egan* generally, but not invariably, had a judicial function (e.g., *AP* 8:13; 10:13, 18–19; 26:9, 21–22). The same was probably the case in Judah, though the term "magistrate" would be too restrictive. Nehemiah was probably aware that his enemies had allies among these local officials, and therefore did not at the outset invite them to share in his plans.

The delay in announcing his intentions would also have allowed time to rally support and test the strength of the opposition. The listing of the people who were not told has some interesting features which call for discussion. The first category, "Jews" *(y^ehûdîm),* applies in the first instance to the inhabitants of the province of Judah *(Y^ehûd).* As Josephus put it: "This name *(Ioudaioi),* by which they have been called from the time when they went up from Babylon, is derived from the tribe of Judah; as this tribe was the first to come to those parts, both the people themselves and the country have taken their name from it" *(Ant.* 11.173). The territorial connotation is, however, attested before the exile in both biblical texts and Assyrian inscriptions. In these instances (e.g., 2 Kings 16:6; 25:25; Jer. 32:12) "Judean" would be a more appropriate translation-word than "Jew." The same usage continues after the return (e.g., Ezra 6:7; Neh. 1:2; 13:23), together with the practically synonymous "Judah," "house of Judah," "children of Judah" (Neh. 4:4, 10 [10, 16]; 13:12, 16). Although Sanballat was a devotee of YHVH, he refers to Nehemiah and his associates as *y^ehûdîm* while at the same time dissociating himself from them (3:33–34 [4:1–2]; 6:6). But we also detect a shift from the purely territorial to the ethnic sense with religious overtones, especially with reference to people of Judean origin living outside the province (Neh. 4:6 [12]; 5:8). And even members of the

Elephantine colony, not descended from Judeans, refer to themselves as *y*ᵉ*hûdîn* (*AP* 6:3–10; 8:2; 10:3; etc.). By the time of the composition of Esther (see Esth. 2:5 and *passim*) the term is used in much the same sense as it is today.

To return to the list of people in v. 16. It consists in three categories: Jews, community leaders civic and religious, the common people. It is tempting to reduce these to two by interpreting "the people who were to do the work" *('ōśê hammᵉlā'kāh)* as referring to other administrative officials ("beamtete Leute," Kaupel). In that case "the Jews" would be the common people as opposed to the community leaders (cf. 5:17, "Jews and officials"). But against this reading is the practice common in the NM of referring to the community as "nobles, officials, and the rest of the people" (4:8, 13 [14, 19]; 7:5). In addition, the designation *'ōśê hammᵉlā'kāh* occurs elsewhere in the book only with reference to cultic personnel (11:12; 13:10), which is certainly not the case here. We are therefore led to suspect that in this instance *y*ᵉ*hûdîm* means something other than the common people as distinct from the leadership. The same distinction between "Jews" and common people appears at a later point, when we hear of complaints of the people and their wives against their Jewish brethren (5:1). The context provides little help in identifying these latter, but Nehemiah's allusion to Jewish brethren who had been sold to the nations and have now been repatriated (5:6) suggests the possibility that diaspora Jews formed a privileged segment of the population of the province. It is perhaps these golah Jews whom Nehemiah names first among those who are destined to share his vision and labors.

[17–18] At this point the narrative is very compressed. Nothing is said of the circumstances leading to the public announcement, or of when and where it took place. As was to be expected, Josephus (*Ant.* 11.168–172) remedied this situation by locating the public address in the temple precincts immediately after Nehemiah's arrival in the city. Here, Nehemiah speaks of the condition of Jerusalem and its defenses in words practically identical with the description given him back in Susa (1:3). The work of restoration was necessary in order to regain respect after the humiliations suffered by the city in recent years and thus silence the taunting *(ḥerpāh)* of their enemies (cf. 3:36 [4:4]; 5:9). Since trouble was clearly anticipated, it was also necessary for him to inform his supporters of the royal authorization to rebuild, a remarkable coup which he could with justice present as a sign of the divine favor (cf. 2:8). The unanimously favorable response would have come as no surprise since Nehemiah must have carefully screened his supporters in advance. But it will become apparent as the story proceeds that not all the opposition was to come from outside the province.

[19–20] The theme of opposition confronted and overcome is a major structural feature of the first part of the NM (1–6). Nehemiah arrives from Susa, Sanballat et al. hear of it and are displeased (2:10); the decision to rebuild the wall is taken, they hear of it and accuse the Nehemiah faction of sedition, and Nehemiah counters with trust in YHVH (2:19–20); the work on the wall begins, Sanballet et al. react angrily, and Nehemiah counters with a prayer directed against them (3:33–37 [4:1–5]); the project is well under way, the enemies hear of it and plot military action, which again evokes a prayer (4:1–3 [7–9]); the work on the wall is finished, the enemies hear of it and plot to assassinate Nehemiah, and once again their action is countered with prayer (6:1–9). And, finally, as the last day of the operation dawns, the enemies hear of it, they are obliged to acknowledge the hand of God, and the reproach *(ḥerpāh)* comes back to rest on their heads, thus fulfilling the prayer of Nehemiah (6:15–16; cf. 3:36 [4:4]). This pattern is close to that of the lamentation psalms: hostile accusation or action against an innocent party who counters with trustful prayer to God and thus overcomes (e.g., Pss. 7; 9; 54; 56; 59). The comparison may help to explain some features of the genre in which the NM is cast, and should be borne in mind in evaluating the historical character of his *apologia.*

In addition to Sanballat and Tobiah (see on 2:10), we now hear of a third enemy, a certain Geshem (2:19; 6:1–2) or Gashmu (6:16) the Arab, who joins in the accusation of sedition and in concerted action against Nehemiah. The name occurs on a dedicatory bowl from the Persian period discovered in 1947 at Tell el-Maskhuṭa near Ismailia in Lower Egypt. The donor's name, inscribed on the bowl, is "Cain son of Gashmu king of Kedar" *(qynv br gšm mlk qdr).* The North Arabian Kedarites, mentioned frequently in the Old Testament (Gen. 25:13; Isa. 21:16–17; 42:11; 60:7; Jer. 2:10; 49:28–33; Ezek. 27:21; 1 Chron. 1:29), are also known from Assyrian records as *Qidri.* They were subdued by the Babylonians (Jer. 49:28) and supported the Persians, assisting Cambyses during his invasion of Egypt (Herodotus 3.4, 88). The same name (Gashmu bin Shahru) also occurs in a roughly contemporary Lihyanite inscription together with a certain 'Abdu governor of Dedan, and it is probable that both inscriptions refer to the enemy of Nehemiah. It seems that by the fifth century B.C.E. the Kedarites had settled a broad area from the Transjordanian plateau to the Nile delta. It results that Judah was surrounded on all sides by hostile forces: Samaria to the north, Ammon to the east, the Kedarites to the east and south, the city of Ashdod to the west. At a certain point all of these planned concerted military action against Judah, a repeat of the intervention of Samaria earlier in the reign, but on a more ambitious scale (Ezra 4:23). The basic issue was the separate autonomy of Judah, which must have fallen under Samarian control after the intervention of Rehum, a situation which Nehemiah aimed to reverse.

Within the province itself Nehemiah clearly did not have the undivided support of the population. The nucleus of the opposition consisted in those of the hereditary nobility, public officials, and priests who were allied with Sanballat and Tobiah either by marriage or by common interest (6:17–19; 13:4–9, 28). Several of these were not enthusiastic about his social and religious reforms, which threatened their position (5:6–13; 13:10–11, 17). There is also a suggestion of lack of support in the southern part of the province (3:5, the nobles of Tekoa), probably on account of links with Geshem and the Kedarite Arabs. He must have drawn his support principally from the faction represented by the delegation to Susa (1:2–3), probably identical with the *yᵉhûdîm* or golah Jews mentioned in 2:16 and 5:1, whose influence must have greatly increased during Nehemiah's administration. He also advanced his own kinsmen (5:14; 7:2), and he alludes several times to his "servants" (4:10, 17 [16, 23]; 5:10, 16), a corps of loyal supporters not further identified. His social measures were designed to win popular support, which they probably did. Since a similar social stratification existed among temple personnel, it was natural for him to seek support among the Levites, especially in view of the family connections and economic interests of the priestly aristocracy. The memoir also speaks of both support and opposition from prophetic circles (6:7, 10–14), but the polemical tone of the narrative at this point makes it difficult to determine what the real situation was.

Instead of answering directly the charge of sedition, Nehemiah simply affirmed his confidence in the successful outcome of the operation based on the certainty of divine assistance. In language reminiscent of Zerubbabel's rejection of outside help in building the temple (Ezra 4:1–5), he rejected outside intervention in any shape or form. The terms used are drawn from customary law. The denial of a "share" *(ḥēleq)* corresponds to a traditional formula denoting political dissociation (cf. 2 Sam. 20:1; 1 Kings 12:16), while "claim" *(ṣᵉdāqāh)* stands for the legal right to exercise jurisdiction. The third term, translated "traditional right," literally, "memorial, remembrance" *(zikkārôn),* is less clear but probably alludes to the right to participate in the Jerusalem cult (cf. Josh. 4:7; Zech. 6:14). How important this right was will be appreciated if we recall that membership in the cult community also conferred civic status. So this statement is, in effect, a declaration of independence on behalf of the province. It reveals what must have been the ultimate aim of Nehemiah's mission from the outset.

Work on the Wall (Neh. 3:1–32)

Y. **Aharoni**, "Beth-haccherem," in D. Winton Thomas (ed.), *Archaeology and Old Testament Study,* Oxford, 1967, 171–184; N. **Avigad**, *Discovering Jerusalem,* Nashville, 1980, 1–62; N. **Avi-Yonah**, "The Walls of Nehemiah—A Minimalist View," *IEJ* 4, 1954, 239–248; "The Newly-Found Wall of Jerusalem and Its Topographical Significance," *IEJ* 21, 1971, 168–169; M. **Broshi**, "The Expansion of Jerusalem in the Reigns of Hezekiah and Manasseh," *IEJ* 24, 1974, 21–26; M. **Burrows**, "Nehemiah 3:1–32 as a Source for the Topography of Ancient Jerusalem," *AASOR* 14, 1933/34, 115–140; A. **Demsky**, "*Pelekh* in Nehemiah 3," *IEJ* 33, 1983, 242–244; H. **Geva**, "The Western Boundary of Jerusalem at the End of the Monarchy," *IEJ* 29, 1979, 84–91; R. **Grafman**, "Nehemiah's 'Broad Wall,' " *IEJ* 24, 1974, 50–51; U. **Kellermann**, *Nehemia,* 14–17; K. **Kenyon**, *Digging Up Jerusalem,* London and Tonbridge, 1974; *EAEHL* II, 1976, 591–597; J. **Kirchner**, *Inscriptiones Atticae* II, Berlin, 1927; B. **Mazar**, *The Mountain of the Lord,* New York, 1975; "Jerusalem in the Biblical Period," *EAEHL* II, 1976, 580–591; I. **Mendelsohn**, "Guilds in Ancient Palestine," *BASOR* 80, 1940, 17–21; "Guilds in Babylonia and Assyria," *JAOS* 60, 1940, 68–72; S. **Mowinckel**, *Studien* I, 109–116; J. **Simons**, *Jerusalem in the Old Testament,* Leiden, 1952, 226–281; C. G. **Tuland**, " '*ZB* in Nehemiah 3:8. A Reconsideration of Maximalist and Minimalist Views," *AUSS* 5, 1967, 158–180; A. D. **Tushingham**, "The Western Hill Under the Monarchy," *ZDPV* 95, 1979, 39–55; R. P. **Vincent**, "Les murs de Jérusalem d'après Néhémie," *RB* 13, 1904, 56–74; D. F. **Weisberg**, *Guild Structure and Political Allegiance in Early Achaemenid Mesopotamia,* Baltimore, 1967; see also bibliography to Neh. 2:11–20.

3:1 Eliashib the high priest and his priestly colleagues[a] set to work and rebuilt the Sheep Gate. They consecrated it,[b] hung its doors, and consecrated the section[c] as far as the Tower of the Hundred (as far as the Tower of Hananel).[d] [2]Next to him[e] the men of Jericho did the rebuilding, and next to them[f] Zaccur son of Imri. [3]The people of Hassenaah rebuilt the Fish Gate; they fixed its beams[g] and hung its doors with their bolts and bars. [4]Next to them Meremoth son of Uriah son of Hakkoz worked at the repairs; and next to him[h] Meshullam son of Berechiah son of Meshezabel repaired; and next to him[h] Zadok son of Baana. [5]Next to them the people of Tekoa repaired, but their nobles would not demean themselves[i] to work for their lord.[j]

[6]Joiada son of Paseah and Meshullam son of Besodeiah repaired

the Mishneh Gate;[k] they fixed its beams and hung its doors with
their bolts and bars. [7]Next to them Melatiah the Gibeonite and
Jadon the Meronothite did the repairing, together with[l] the people
of Gibeon and Mizpah. The latter was under the jurisdiction of the
governor of the Trans-Euphrates satrapy.[m] [8]Next to them[f] Uzziel
son of Harhaiah, a member of the goldsmiths' guild,[n] did the
repairing; and next to him Hananiah, a member of the perfumers'
guild. They restored[o] Jerusalem as far as the Broad Wall.

[9]Next to them Rephaiah son of Hur, ruler of one half of the
Jerusalem district, did the repairing. [10]Next to him[h] Jedaiah son
of Harumaph repaired opposite[p] his own house; and next to him
Hattush son of Hashabneiah. [11]Malchijah son of Harim and Hasshub son of Pahath-moab repaired a second section and[q] the
Tower of the Ovens; [12]and next to him Shallum son of Hallohesh,
ruler of one half of the Jerusalem district, did the repairs together
with his daughters.[r]

[13]Hanun and the inhabitants of Zanoah repaired the Valley
Gate; they rebuilt it and hung its doors with their bolts and bars.
They also repaired a thousand cubits of the wall as far as the Dung
Gate.[s]

[14]Malchijah son of Rechab, ruler of the Beth-haccherem district,
repaired the Dung Gate. He rebuilt it and hung its doors with their
bolts and bars. [15]Shallum[t] son of Col-hozeh, ruler of the Mizpah
district, repaired the Fountain Gate. He rebuilt it, roofed it, and
hung[u] its doors with their bolts and bars. He also repaired the
retaining wall of the Pool of Shelah, which was part of the King's
Garden, and as far as the steps which go down from the City of
David.

[16]After him Nehemiah son of Azbuk, ruler of one half of the
Beth-zur district, repaired up to a point opposite the David
tombs,[v] and as far as the Artificial Pool and the House of the
Heroes.[w] [17]After him the Levites repaired: Rehum son of Bani,
and next to him Hashabiah, ruler of one half of the Keilah district,
repaired on behalf of his district. [18]After him their brethren repaired: Binnui[x] son of Henadad, ruler of one half of the Keilah
district. [19]Next to him Ezer son of Jeshua, ruler of Mizpah, repaired a second section from a point opposite the Ascent of the
Armory and the Angle.[y] [20]After him[z] Baruch son of Zabbai[aa]
repaired a second section from the Angle to the door of the house
of Eliashib, the high priest. [21]After him Meremoth son of Uriah
son of Hakkoz repaired a second section from the door of Eliashib's house to the end of his house.

[22]After him the priests from the Jordan valley[bb] did the repairs.

[23]After them[f] Benjamin and Hasshub repaired opposite their houses; and after them[f] Azariah son of Maaseiah son of Ananiah repaired beside his own house. [24]After him Binnui son of Henadad repaired a second section from the house of Azariah to the Angle and the Corner. [25]After him Palal son of Uzai did the repairs from opposite the Angle and the tower projecting from the upper royal palace which was part of the courtyard of the guard; and after him Pedaiah son of Parosh did the repairing [26](the temple servants were living on the Ophel[cc]) to a point opposite the Water Gate to the east and the projecting tower. [27]After him the people of Tekoa repaired a second section from opposite the great projecting tower to the Ophel wall.

[28]From the Horse Gate the priests did the repairs, each opposite his own house. [29]After them[n] Zadok son of Immer repaired opposite his house; and after him Shemaiah son of Shecaniah, the custodian of the East Gate, did the repairs. [30]After him[dd] Hananiah son of Shelemiah and Hanun sixth son of Zalaph repaired a second section. After him Meshullam son of Berechiah did the repairs opposite his room. [31]After him[dd] Malchijah, a member of the goldsmiths' guild,[ee] repaired as far as the house of the temple servants and the merchants, opposite the Parade Gate and as far as the upper room of the Corner. [32]Between the upper room of the Corner and the Sheep Gate the goldsmiths and the merchants did the repairs.

a. Lit., "his brethren the priests."
b. *qidd^{e}šûhû* is often emended to *gēršûhû* (following A. B. Ehrlich 1914, 188), which, however, is unattested, or *gērûhû* (cf. vs. 3, 6 and 2:8). But this emendation is unsupported by the ancient versions and is based on a misapprehension of the role of the priesthood in the work (see commentary).
c. "the section" supplied; the masc. pronominal suffix of the verb cannot refer either to the gate or to the wall (= *hômāh,* fem.).
d. Lack of the conjunction suggests that the phrase in parentheses was added in the interests of topographical clarity (cf. 12:39).
e. Referring back to Eliashib.
f. MT has sing.
g. *qērûhû,* denominative verb from *qôrāh,* beam; exact meaning uncertain.
h. MT has pl.
i. Lit., "would not bring their necks into the work," i.e., they refused to participate out of pride or resentment.
j. MT has pl. *'^{a}dōnêhem,* sometimes taken to mean that they refused to work under their overseers; but in that case the pl. would still be a problem and we would expect a different term; perhaps a pl. of majesty referring to God or (the option taken here) Nehemiah.

k. Emending the consonantal text from *hyšnh* to *hmišnh;* see commentary.

l. Supplying the conjunction with Syr.

m. An attempt to make sense of the difficult *l*ᵉ*kisse' pahat 'ēber hannāhār,* lit., "belonging to the throne of the governor of Across the River"; see commentary.

n. Reading *ben-harh*ᵃ*yāh ben-hassōrpîm* for *ben-harh*ᵃ*yāh sōrpîm* (haplography); closer to the expression in vs. 8b and 31 and less drastic than *ben-heber hassōrpîm.*

o. MT *vayya'*ᵃ*zbû* has become one of the principal bones of contention in this chapter over the last few years. The usual meaning "they abandoned" must itself be abandoned in spite of desperate efforts to retain it: (1) the stem *'zb* cannot mean "leave out," "omit" (*pace* Williamson 1986, 194); it means to abandon a person or place—which makes no sense whether the subject is the two artisans named here or the work force as a whole; (2) the only exception to the basic meaning occurs at Neh. 3:34 [4:2], where the context requires the meaning "restore" or something of the sort, and this alternative meaning is supported by Ugaritic and Sabaean *'db.* Since the meaning "abandon" does not fit the context, and this alternative is available, the reading proposed seems the best in the circumstances.

p. Omitting "and" *(v*ᵉ*neged)* with LXXᴸ and Vulg.

q. LXX *kai heōs* presupposes *v*ᵉ*'ad,* which fits with the formulaic language of the list. Alternatively, the conjunction could be omitted and *'ēt* translated "with," giving a smoother reading. MT is, however, defensible and has been retained.

r. *ûb*ᵉ*nôtāv* should not be emended to *ûbānāv,* "and his sons," or to *ûbônāv,* "and his builders"; see commentary.

s. Reading *ša'ar hā'ašpôt* (cf. v. 14) for *ša'ar hāš*ᵉ*pôt.* While the meaning "curds," "cheese" for *š*ᵉ*pôt* (2 Sam. 17:29) recalls the Tyropeon or Cheesemakers Valley of Josephus (*War* 5.140), it is clear from the following verse that the Dung Gate is intended. Thus MT is the result of a scribal error rather than a "verschönernde Korrektur" (Rudolph 1949, 117), which would not explain why the scribe was not equally fastidious in copying v. 14.

t. MT has Shallun, an alternative form or simple scribal error.

u. Sing. with Qere for Ketib *v*ᵉ*ya'*ᵃ*mîdû.*

v. MT *qibrê dāvîd,* LXX, Syr., and Vulg. have sing., understandably since David would need only one tomb, but misguided nevertheless; see commentary.

w. A literal translation of *bêt haggibbōrîm,* which might also mean "barracks" or, somewhat less likely, a burial place or shrine for the heroes of David's day (cf. 2 Sam. 23:8–39).

x. MT has *bvy,* Bavvai, but cf. v. 24.

y. This entire phrase is obscure. "Ascent" takes *'lt* to be singular *('*ᵃ*lat)* rather than plural *('*ᵃ*lōt);* "armory" for *nešeq* is possible, but LXX *synaptousē* suggests the juncture between the Ascent and the Angle; though generally translated "corner," *miqsōa'* has a meaning distinct from *pinnāh,* see, for example, 2 Chron. 26:9, where the Corner Gate *(ša'ar happinnāh)* is distinguished from the *miqsōa'.* See further the commentary.

z. MT adds *hhrh,* which could have infiltrated by dittography with *'hryv,* "after him," or mean "up the hill"; cf. LXX *eis to oros autou* and Vulg. *in monte;* perhaps a gloss introduced into the text at the wrong point.

aa. "Zakkai," Qere, several MSS, Syr., and Vulg. We have kept MT (cf. Ezra 10:28).

bb. Lit., "men of the plain/valley" *('anšê hakkikkār);* see commentary.

cc. A gloss (cf. 11:21) inserted here since the survey has reached the Ophel, the northern and higher part of the eastern ridge.

dd. Emending MT *'ah^arāy,* "after me," with Qere and major versions.

ee. Reading *ben-hassōrpîm* for MT *ben-hassōrpî.*

The list of builders and their assignments is not an original and integral part of the NM. It interrupts the first-person narrative, refers to him in the third person (v. 5), and betrays inconsistency with the timetable for completion of the work given elsewhere in the memoir (6:1; 7:1). It provides the first of several indications that more than one account of Nehemiah's activity may have been available. The same conclusion is suggested by the overall structure of the memoir from this point: decision to undertake the work—opposition (2:17–20); work begun—opposition (3:33–37 [4:1–5]); work half finished—opposition (3:38–4:3 [4:6–9]); work completed—opposition (4:9[15]–6:14). Very likely, then, the list derives from an independent source which supplements and greatly expands the allusions to the wall-building in NM.

The list is clearly not an invention of C, as argued by Torrey (1895, 37–38; 1910, 225, 249). It may have been preserved in the temple archives, but in any case it reflects the careful plans laid by Nehemiah and his associates. Topographically, it covers the entire perimeter of the fifth-century B.C.E. city, beginning and ending at the Sheep Gate to the north of the temple area and moving anticlockwise. Some think it to be incomplete, but the few omissions of second sections—possibly only one (v. 20)—can be explained by simple scribal error. The absence of work gangs from certain localities—e.g., Bethel and Bethlehem—may simply mean that Nehemiah did not succeed in persuading everyone to take part, which would hardly be surprising (cf. 3:5 and the complaints recorded in 4:4–6 [10–12]). There has been some support for the view that two originally separate records have gone into the making of the list: 3:1–15 dealing with the north and west sections, and 3:16–32 dealing with the eastern section beginning at the southern extremity. In the former X builds or repairs *next to* Y, while in the latter X works *after* Y. Correspondingly, the former lists topographical features along the wall, while the latter locates the groups with reference to features within the city, including houses. Finally, all of the six gates repaired are in the first section, none in the second (see especially Burrows). There is certainly a significant change after v. 15, but the main part of it can be explained by the different situation encountered along the eastern perimeter, where it was no longer possible to follow the line of the old wall down the western slope of the Kidron Valley. (It would have been especially here that the complaint about there being "much rubbish" would have been justified.) The change in formula, of no particular significance, may indicate a different scribe at work; it does not require us to postulate a different source. And, finally, most of those who did double duty are mentioned in both of the allegedly distinct sections.

The participants, divided into forty-one work details, represent different social and professional classes: priests, Levites, gatekeepers, artisans and tradesmen, private individuals. The governors of five of the administrative districts (*peˡākîm*) into which the province was divided also assumed responsibility for manning one section or, more commonly, two. The list is therefore an important source for the political and social life of Yehud in the fifth century B.C.E. Its importance for the topography of Jerusalem in the Persian period is obvious, but unfortunately none of the nine gates or eighteen other features mentioned can be identified with absolute certainty. While some progress has been made, especially by eliminating some earlier hypotheses, and as a result of excavation over the last two decades, it is unlikely that the debate on the extent of Nehemiah's Jerusalem can be settled in the present state of our knowledge (see Additional Note on Nehemiah's Jerusalem).

An interesting parallel to the situation in Jerusalem is that of Athens following on the Persian defeat at Plataea in 479 B.C.E. The Athenians no sooner began to rebuild the city wall destroyed by the Persians than they were ordered to desist by Spartan emissaries. As a result of a clever plan by Themistocles, however, they were able to continue. Everyone took part—including women, children, metics, and slaves—and the work was completed in record time (Thucydides 1.89–93; Diodorus Siculus 11.39–40; Plutarch, *Themistocles* 19). Eighty-six years later a system rather similar to that of Nehemiah was used in the rebuilding of the long wall of the Piraeus after Conon's defeat of the Spartan fleet off Cnidus. An inscription records how one section was completed: "In the archonship of Euboulides: starting at the boundary marker, as far as the facade of the gates by the Aphrodision, moving to the right 790 (units); Demosthenes the Boiotian paid for this and for the transportation of the stones" (Kirchner, 290, no. 1657; M. Smith 1971, 129–130). This last may serve to remind us that those Judeans who assumed responsibility for sections of the wall did not necessarily themselves do the physical work involved.

The circuit of the walls can be divided for convenience as follows: the northern section with eight work details (1–5); the west with ten (6–13); the southern extremity with two (14–15); the eastern side with twenty-one (16–32). The sections on the east were clearly much shorter than the others, since on this side the original line of the wall had to be abandoned and a new wall built on the ridge overlooking the Kidron Valley.

To the *north* (1–5) the work began and ended at the Sheep Gate, northeast of the temple area (the site now occupied by the White Fathers' monastery and church of St. Anne; cf. John 5:2). It was perhaps the usual entrance for sheep destined for sacrifice and the site of a sheep market. The northern perimeter sustained the brunt of the Babylonian attack in 587, which explains the need for eight work details along a fairly short section. The condition of the wall may also be gauged by the fact that between the Sheep Gate and the Fish Gate the workers built *(bnh)* rather than reinforced *(hhzyq)*. The priest contingent worked as far as the Tower of the Hundred (see 12:39), perhaps the headquarters of a centurion (cf. the phrase *rb m't', AP* 2:11), and the Tower of Hananel (Jer. 31:38; Zech. 14:10; see also on 2:7–8). The high priest Eliashib (3:20–21; 12:10, 22; 13:28) had close contacts with the families of both Sanballat and Tobiah and fell foul of Nehemiah later in his administration. If there was already bad blood between them, Nehemiah may have either persuaded him to take part notwithstanding or felt obliged to co-opt him for the initial ceremony of consecration. And, for his part, the high priest may have felt that he could not afford to be conspicuously absent from the enterprise. Significantly, however, he is not named in the account of the dedication of the wall (12:27–43). It was to be expected that so important an enterprise would begin with a solemn act of consecration and end with an equally solemn dedication (*ḥᵃnukkāh*, 12:27).

The length of the sections assigned between the Sheep Gate and the Fish Gate are not given. The latter was east of the Tower of Hananel (12:39), probably near the northwest corner where the wall turned south (2 Chron. 33:14). Zeph. 1:10 suggests that the Mishneh, the second quarter of the city, lay beyond the Fish Gate. The name probably is connected with a fish market at the gate. Jericho and Hassenaah (Senaah) are also listed together in the census (see Ezra 2:35). They were probably the principal centers of an administrative district, the Jordan Valley area or *kikkār* (Avi-Yonah 1966, 20, 22).

No significant information can be extracted from the builders' names. Zakkur is a common postexilic name, belonging to a member of Ezra's caravan (Ezra 8:14). Imri is hypocoristic for Amaryahu or Amariah (Neh. 11:4). Their position on the wall suggests association with the Jordan Valley people. After the Fish Gate the work details no longer build but reinforce or repair. The choice of verbs suggests that the northern part of the wall was completely demolished. Meremoth was one of those who did double duty (v. 21). Probably identical with the Meremoth who took delivery of the bullion and sacred vessels from Ezra (Ezra 8:33), he belonged to a priestly family of dubious lineage, that of Hakkoz (Ezra 2:61 = Neh. 7:63). We do not know whether he was functioning as a priest at the time of the rebuilding (see on Ezra 8:33). Meshullam was probably a person of high rank since his daughter married Tobiah's son (Neh. 6:18). Another Zadok is mentioned later in the list (v. 29).

Tekoa, about twelve miles south of Jerusalem in the Judean wilderness, may have been the secondary capital of the district of Bethzur (Avi-Yonah 1966, 22). Its people took on a second section of wall further south (v. 27). As noted earlier, the refusal of the Tekoan nobles to accept Nehemiah's leadership may, given the location of Tekoa, be explained by proximity to Geshem the Kedarite whose sphere of influence extended to those parts. The notice serves as a reminder that support for the project was by no means unanimous.

On the *west* (6–13), the first to be mentioned are Joiada ben Paseah ("son of the cripple," Ezra 2:49) and Meshullam, repairers of the Mishneh Gate. They are mentioned only here. In MT this gate is called *ša'ar hayᵉšānāh,* often translated "Old Gate" which, however, is incorrect since, first, we then have a feminine adjective modifying a masculine noun (*ša'ar* is, exceptionally, feminine only at Isa. 14:31 and Ezek. 40:19) and, second, *ša'ar* would also have to carry the article. An alternative explanation, that it is an abbreviated form of "the gate of the old city" *(ša'ar hā'îr hayᵉšānāh),* is unlikely, if only on account of the gate's location. The most probable, though by no means certain, solution is therefore to emend to *mšnh,* reading "the Mishneh Gate," that is, the gate associated with the second quarter of the city (2 Kings 22:14 = 2 Chron. 34:22; Zeph. 1:10). Since the name of a gate would more naturally indicate a destination outside the city (e.g., the Damascus and Jaffa gates of the Old City today), the wall of which this gate formed a part did not enclose the Mishneh, though the latter appears to have been surrounded by the eighth-century B.C.E. wall, a section of which was discovered in 1969–1970.

The names of the two individuals from the Gibeon region are not attested elsewhere. Meronoth (see also 1 Chron. 27:30) was presumably a village near Gibeon, northwest of Jerusalem. Mizpah, probably Tell en-Nasbeh eight miles north of Jerusalem, was the administrative center of the province after the destruction of Jerusalem (2 Kings 25:23, 25; Jer. 40–41). It would therefore not be surprising if it served as the residence of the Persian governor during his visits to the province and, in consequence, enjoyed a special status vis-à-vis the local administration. The alternative explanation, that this work detail repaired the wall as far as the "throne" of the satrapal governor, would require a different preposition (*'ad* rather than *l^e*). Moving to the next detail (8), it seems that some guilds, goldsmiths, apothecaries, and merchants, provided their own work forces, perhaps for segments of the wall corresponding to their quarters. Guilds tended to cluster, for obvious reasons of professional convenience. The guilds mentioned were perhaps among the more affluent whose work allowed for a more lengthy absence. Their work extended as far as the Broad Wall. From the only other mention of this feature, in the account of the dedication service (12:38), it seems to have been located between the Ephraim Gate and the Tower of the Ovens, neither of which however can be clearly identified. The wording suggests that it was not itself in need of repair. The proposal that it is to be identified with the wall seven meters wide recently discovered in the Jewish Quarter (Avigad, 62) is, in the present state of our knowledge, no more than a guess. More of the wall would have to be discovered to give it plausibility.

The five sections between the Broad Wall and the Valley Gate (9–12) cover the western perimeter of the Ophel going down to the City of David (the eastern ridge), a distance of some five hundred yards. Clearly, the sections were not all of equal length (especially Jedaiah's), the length of each depending on the state of disrepair, the size of the work group, and possibly other factors. The only topographical feature mentioned, apart from Jedaiah's house, is the Tower of the Ovens (see also 12:38), used either for baking or for firing pottery. Two of the sections are manned by administrators of the two districts into which Jerusalem was divided. It appears from the list that the province was divided into five districts (*p^{e}lākîm;* cf. Akk. *pilku):* Jerusalem (9, 12), Beth-haccherem (14), Mizpah (15), Beth-zur (16), Keilah (17–18), but to these we should probably add Jericho and the Jordan Valley area, though its governor is not mentioned. At least three of these (Jerusalem, Beth-zur, Keilah) were divided into two subdistricts, each with its own administrator. It appears likely, however, that the province was divided into six districts and twelve subdistricts each with its principal and secondary administrative center: Jerusalem (Netophah), Beth-zur (Tekoa), Keilah (Adullam), Beth-haccherem (Zanoah), Mizpah (Gibeon), and Jericho (Senaah). Of these all but two (Netophah and Adullam) provided manpower, and in one instance womanpower, for work on the wall.

Rephasiah ben Hur came of an old Judean family (cf. 1 Chron. 2:19–20; 4:1), perhaps originally of Hurrian stock. Harumaph (= mutilated nose) presumably originated as a nickname. Malchijah is a very common postexilic name; two others occur in the list (14, 31). He appears to be identical with the Malchijah who agreed to divorce his foreign wife (Ezra 10:31). A Hasshub is mentioned later (23) who may be identical with the son of Pahath-moab (cf. Ezra 2:6) who did double duty; repetition here and elsewhere in the list may explain the absence of patronymic (8, 13, 23, 31). Shallum's daughters should not be disposed of by textual surgery. Either he had no sons or his daughters distinguished themselves by volunteering. In any case, their presence in the work detail was considered noteworthy.

Zanoah in the southern Shephelah (cf. Josh. 15:34) was reoccupied after the return (Neh. 11:30). It may be the missing half of Beth-haccherem (14), in which case Hanun would be the opposite number of Malchijah ben Rechab. For the location of the two gates, separated by about five hundred meters, see commentary on 2:13. We must suppose either that the Zanoah group was especially numerous or that this length of wall required only minor repair.

On the *south* (3:14–15), responsibility for repairing the Dung Gate fell to the governor of the Beth-haccherem district, perhaps of the Rechab phratry (1 Chron. 2:55). The location of Beth-haccherem is uncertain. The traditional identification with Ain Karem about eight kilometers west of Jerusalem has been challenged by Aharoni (1962), who locates it at Ramat Rahel between Jerusalem and Bethlehem, a site which he himself excavated. His arguments are not, however, persuasive. The excavation produced nothing to support the identification. Since Jer. 6:1 speaks of an attack from the north not the south, the allusion to Beth-haccherem together with Jerusalem and Tekoa does not settle the issue. The Karim of Josh. 15:59 (LXX) may or may not be identical with Beth-haccherem; the towns with which it is listed indicate a location south of Jerusalem, but that is all. And if Beth-haccherem is the administrative center of a separate district with its own governor, it would hardly be so close to Jerusalem. Perhaps all we can say is that the Beth-haccherem district was west of Jerusalem between Mizpah to the north and Keilah to the south. The next section, which included the Fountain Gate (see on 2:14), was the responsibility of the governor of the Mizpah district (see 3:7), to be distinguished from the city governor (v. 19). The curious name Col-hozeh, also at 11:5, seems to indicate a mantic or seer ("the all-seeing one"), though such derivations can be deceptive. The retaining wall of the Pool of Shelah (see 2:14) within the King's Garden (cf. 2 Kings 25:4) was part of the city defenses. The steps probably led down from the summit of the eastern ridge, through the Fountain Gate, to En Rogel in the Kidron Valley.

On the *east* side (16–32), the sections are identified with reference to features for the most part, if not entirely, within the city. This was about the point where Nehemiah had to dismount in order to continue his nocturnal tour of inspection. The assumption is that the preexilic eastern wall enclosed terraced buildings some way down the slope, that these had collapsed together with the wall, and that Nehemiah therefore was obliged to build higher up on the ridge where traces of his work have been discovered (Kenyon, 183–184). Beth-zur (Khirbet et-Tubeiqah about six kilometers north of Hebron), governed by Nehemiah's namesake, was the center of an administrative district, the secondary "capital" being Tekoa (Avi-Yonah 1966, 22). None of the three features which mark the limit of the governor's assignment can be identified. The sepulchers were no doubt those of the royal Judean house located in the City of David (1 Kings 2:10; 11:43; 14:31; etc.), though not necessarily identifiable with the tombs (cisterns?) discovered by R. Weill in 1913–1914 (on which see Kenyon, 31–32). The Artificial Pool, named to distinguish it from the Pool of Shelah, was further north, as was the House of the Heroes, the meaning of which is quite uncertain.

Something may have been lost or scrambled in transmission at this point (vs. 17–18), with the result that it is not clear how far the list of Levites extends. Bani is a good Levitical name (cf. 8:7; 9:5; 11:22). Both governors of the Keilah district bear Levitical names, but it is surprising to find Levites serving in this capacity. Keilah itself (Khirbet Qila, twelve kilometers northwest of Hebron) was the principal administrative center, with either Adullam or Azekah as the seat of the other administrator. The topographical details in the next section (19–20) are obscure. The location of the steps, or ascent, of the Armory is unknown. It was probably close to an architectural feature within the city (see also 24–25 and 2 Chron. 26:9), perhaps a right angle turn or abutment projecting from a wall.

Several of the remaining sections on the east are identified with reference to private houses (20–24, 28–29, 30–31), and generally the work is assigned to the owner of the house. The exception is Meremoth (see 3:4 and Ezra 8:33), who was given the important additional assignment of building up the wall opposite the length of the high priest's house. The priests who worked next to him are called "men of the plain," and thus distinguished from other worker-priests. When used topographically, as a proper name, *kikkār* (22) always stands for the Jordan Valley around Jericho (e.g., Gen. 13:10–12; 19:28; Deut. 34:3; 2 Sam. 18:23; 1 Kings 7:46). Neh. 12:28, which speaks of musicians coming together from the *kikkār* around Jerusalem, does not invalidate this translation since the context suggests the more general meaning of "region." After the stretch opposite the houses of Benjamin, Hasshub (also v. 11), and Azariah, Binnui the Levite was responsible for another section as far as the Angle and the Corner, the names indicating a point where the wall took a sharp turn from north-northeast to north-northwest.

Palal ben-Uzai's section began at the point where the wall turned, probably not far from the southeast corner of the Turkish wall. The other point of reference here (25) is a projecting tower or turret, clearly a prominent and well-known feature. The rest is obscure. The syntax suggests that "from the upper royal palace" *(mibbêt hammelek hā'elyôn)* has been added as a further attempt at clarification, and that the tower was part of the courtyard of the guard (cf. Jer. 32:2). The only problem is that we are not yet past the Gihon spring and would expect the palace to lie further north. The note about the *n*ᵉ*tînîm* (see on Ezra 2:43) is a gloss taken from 11:21 and placed here since the survey has now reached the Ophel, the northern and higher part of the eastern ridge. The Water Gate was presumably the entrance in the old city wall down the ravine which led to Gihon. The Ophel wall must have been the northern defensive perimeter of the Jebusite and Davidic city repaired by Jotham in the eighth century (2 Chron. 27:3). Nehemiah's wall may therefore have either crossed it at right angles or incorporated part of it running south–north. In what way, if at all, it related to Manasseh's outer wall which surrounded the Ophel we cannot say (cf. 2 Chron. 33:14).

Assuming that a section has not been omitted, the Horse Gate (28) must have been close to the Ophel wall. It could be a city gate overlooking the Kidron Valley (Jer. 31:40) or an entrance for cavalry into the palace courtyard (2 Kings 11:16; 2 Chron. 23:15). Zadok ben-Immer was a priest (cf. Ezra 2:37; Neh. 10:22 [21]). His northern neighbor on the wall belonged to the order of gatekeepers, who had not attained Levitical status in Nehemiah's day (cf. 10:29 [28]; 11:19), though the name Shemaiah is of frequent occurrence among Levites. He is to be distinguished from another Shemaiah, roughly contemporary, who was of Davidic lineage (1 Chron. 3:21–22). The East Gate (29), not elsewhere attested, may be identical with the eastern entrance to the temple mentioned by Ezekiel, though a different name is used (Ezek. 10:19; 11:1). The next three workers were all doing double duty. Hananiah may be identical with the apothecary of v. 8 and Hanun with the Zanoahite of v. 13. Meshullam's room was probably in the temple precincts; the term *niškāh* occurs elsewhere only in connection with the temple (Neh. 12:44; 13:7). This Meshullam was related by marriage to Tobiah, who was to be ejected from his *niškāh* in the temple by Nehemiah (Neh. 6:18; 13:4–9). Next along the line was Malchijah, the third of that name in the survey. The house of the temple servants, which they shared with merchants, must have been part of the temple complex. Trading was, of course, a necessary concomitant of the sacrificial system, which must have given rise to numerous problems (cf. Neh. 13:15–22 and, much later, Mark 11:15–17). The temple servants were responsible for the provision of fuel and water, and probably much else besides (cf. Josh. 9:27); hence their connections with traders who were lucky or well connected enough to obtain a franchise for temple provisions. The last features mentioned in the survey are the Parade Gate *(ša'ar hammipqād)* and the Corner. The precise meaning of the former is disputed. A plausible suggestion would be that it was a designated point for assembly and review, perhaps for the temple or palace guard (cf. 2 Chron. 32:6). The latter was not a unique feature (see also 24). In this instance it probably stands for the point where the wall turned to the west. The upper room may have served as a lookout point, providing an open view to the north and south. That the goldsmiths and merchants repaired this last section may indicate the presence of a commercial quarter in the northeast corner of the temple mound.

Additional Note on Nehemiah's Jerusalem

The debate on the extent of Jerusalem in the fifth century B.C.E. has been going on for more than a century. The possibility of a solution hangs on the interpretation of the data in Nehemiah (2:13–15; ch. 3; 12:31–40) interpreted in the light of relevant archaeological data. Unfortunately, the features alluded to in Nehemiah are hardly ever identifiable with certainty, while the interpretation of the archaeological data, long a matter of dispute, is always under threat of subversion by the discovery of new evidence. *If* we could be certain of the extent of the preexilic city, and *if* Nehemiah's wall followed the line of the wall destroyed by the Babylonians in 587 B.C.E., a solution would be at hand. Since, however, neither point can be established with certainty, the best we can hope for is a reasonable but provisional hypothesis.

The Jebusite city conquered by David (2 Sam. 5:6–9) was confined to the eastern ridge enclosed by the Central Valley or Tyropeon to the west, the Hinnom to the south, and the Kidron Valley to the east. The Jebusite-Davidic wall, partially excavated by Dame Kathleen Kenyon, enclosed an area of about fifteen acres at the southern end of the eastern ridge. To the east the wall followed a line some way down the terraced slope, providing an occupation area known as the Millo which was built up under David and Solomon (2 Sam. 5:9; cf. 1 Chron. 11:8; 1 Kings 9:24; 11:27) and repaired by Hezekiah (2 Chron. 32:5). Solomon enlarged the city to the north, taking in the temple mound and thus doubling the enclosed area. This necessitated continuing the wall to the north and enclosing the northern end of the ridge, known as the Ophel, a distance of some 230 meters between the northern extremity of the City of David and the temple mound (1 Kings 3:1; 11:27).

During the two centuries following, all that was needed was occasional repairs, perhaps as a result of Pharaoh Shishak's campaign (1 Kings 14:25–28; 2 Chron. 12:1–12), certainly as a result of the partial demolition of the wall (some 180 meters) during a brief occupation by troops from the Kingdom of Samaria in the early eighth century (2 Kings 14:13; 2 Chron. 25:23). It was no doubt to remedy this situation that extensive repairs were carried out at crucial points along the wall during the reigns of Uzziah and Jotham immediately following the invasion (2 Chron. 26:9; 27:3). The walls may have been damaged once again during the Syro-Ephraimite war in 734 B.C.E. when the forces of the Israel-Damascus axis laid siege to the city (2 Kings 16:5; Isa. 7:1). The reign of Hezekiah (c. 715–687) marked a decisive turning point in the fortunes of Jerusalem. In addition to securing the water supply by means of the famous tunnel, 533 meters in length from the Gihon spring to the pool of Siloam (2 Kings 20:20; 2 Chron. 32:30; cf. 32:4; Isa. 22:9–11), he patched up the existing wall and built another wall outside of the old one (2 Chron. 32:5). Rather surprisingly, C also speaks of Hezekiah's successor Manasseh building an outer wall *(ḥômāh ḥiṣônāh)* for the City of David, a wall which passed west of Gihon, surrounded the Ophel, incorporated the Fish Gate, and reached a great height (2 Chron. 33:14). Since it is difficult to accept that Manasseh built an entirely new wall so soon after Hezekiah built his, the author may be speaking of the repair, reinforcement, or completion of Hezekiah's "other wall."

The more inclusive late eighth/early seventh century wall, which

C credits to both Hezekiah and Manasseh, was necessitated by a significant increase in the city's population following on the Assyrian conquest of Samaria (722 B.C.E.) and the consequent influx of refugees from the north. The territorial encroachments of Sennacherib during his campaign in Judah in 701 (*ANET,* 288) may also have played a part. The wall must have enclosed at least part of the western ridge, including the residential district known as the Mishneh (2 Kings 22:14 = 2 Chron. 34:22; Zeph. 1:10–11; Neh. 11:9), though the exact extent of this district is unknown. Sections of a wall dated to this same period were discovered by Kenyon on the eastern slope of the Ophel and by Avigad in the Jewish Quarter of the Old City. Though the line followed by this wall along the northern, western, and southern sides remains a matter of conjecture, it is a reasonable surmise that the sections uncovered formed part of the same defensive system. It would also be reasonable to suppose that Hezekiah's outer wall enclosed the Siloam reservoir, a conclusion suggested by Isa. 22:9–11 and perhaps also by Josephus' description of the first city wall (*War* 5.142–145), though Kathleen Kenyon ruled out preexilic settlement at the southern end of the western ridge and argued that Siloam must have been an underground reservoir outside the city wall. This eighth–seventh century wall was the one breached by the Babylonians during the siege (2 Kings 25:4), certainly on its northern line, and then systematically demolished after the capture of the city (2 Kings 25:9–10).

Coming now to Nehemiah's wall, we at least know that he left the line of the preexilic wall on the eastern side, building along the top of the steep slope of the Kidron Valley rather than some way down the side; hence the need for points of reference within the city rather than on the wall. The situation is not so clear with the rest of the circuit. Since it is entirely possible that the repopulation of the city was contemplated from the outset, Nehemiah may well have enclosed a greater space than was warranted by the existing population. After the completion of the wall he observes, in fact, that "the city was wide and large, but the people within it were few" (7:4). The objection that the much longer line of the Hezekian wall would have exceeded the capacity of his workers cannot be pressed, since we know neither the condition of the wall in the fifth century nor the size of the work details. It seems more probable, however, given the limited resources available and the need for speedy completion, that to the west and south he kept to the line of the old pre-Hezekiah wall. It may still have been in reasonably good condition, which would explain the ability of just one group to cover the five hundred meters from the Valley Gate to the Dung Gate. This conclusion is also suggested by the names of the gates in this sector. Zeph. 1:10, which speaks of the Fish Gate, the Mishneh, and the hills, presumably in topographical order viewed from inside the city, assumes that this gate led out into the Mishneh or Second Quarter at the time of writing (late Judean monarchy). That one of the gates in Nehemiah's wall was called the Mishneh Gate (3:6) suggests the same conclusion. The Valley Gate to the west (3:13) also belonged to the pre-Hezekian wall since it was fortified by King Uzziah a half century or so before Hezekiah (2 Chron. 26:9). While the debate will no doubt continue, and further relevant archaeological data emerge, this would seem to be the most likely explanation in the present state of our knowledge.

Renewed Opposition (Nehemiah 3:33–38 [4:1–6])

J. B. Bauer, "Der 'Fuchs' Neh 3,35: ein Belagerungsturm?" *BZ* n.F. 19, 1975, 97–98; J. Blenkinsopp, "The Mission of Udjahorresnet and Those of Ezra and Nehemiah," *JBL* 106, 1987, 409–421; M. Burrows, "The Origins of Neh. 3:33–37," *AJSL* 52, 1936, 235–244; C. C. Torrey, *Ezra Studies,* 225–226; G. von Rad, "Die Nehemia-Denkschrift," *ZAW* 76, 1964, 176–187.

3:33 [4:1] When Sanballat heard that we were building the wall, he became angry and greatly incensed. He derided the Jews [34[2]]and said in the presence of his associates and the Samaria militia, "What do these wretched Jews think they are doing?[a] Are they going to leave it all to God?[b] Will they offer sacrifice?[c] Will they finish it in a day?[d] Will they retrieve[e] the stones out of the heaps of rubble, even though they are burnt?" [35[3]]Tobiah the Ammonite, who was beside him, added, "Yes, and whatever they manage to build, if a fox climbs on it, it will break down the wall made with these stones of theirs."

3:36 [4:4] "Hear, O our God, for we have become an object of contempt. Turn their taunt back on their own heads, and deliver them up to be plundered[f] in the land of their[g] captivity. [37[5]]Do not cover up their iniquity and let not their sin be blotted out from your sight, for they have provoked you[h] to anger in the presence of the builders."

3:38 [4:6] So we built the wall, and all of it was joined together up to half of its height.[i] The people were determined to get on with the work.[j]

a. Supplying "these" *(hā'ēlleh)* with LXX[L].
b. MT *h^aya'azbû lāhem,* the first of a notoriously difficult series of four rhetorical questions, has been variously explained. Those who find here and at 3:8

(see textual note ad loc.) a second meaning of the verb *'zb*, i.e., restore (cf. *UM* 303, no. 1374, *'db;* also Ex. 23:5 and 1 Chron. 16:37) translate "will they restore for themselves?" which is not very satisfactory. The other possibility is to retain the more common meaning of the verb (= abandon) and emend *lāhem* to *lēlōhîm*, "God," on the assumption that *lāhem* is a reverential *tiqqun* (cf. 1 Sam. 3:13). But "will they abandon God?" hardly seems to call for theological correction, even if spoken by a reprobate (*pace* Williamson 1986, 214). More acceptable, therefore, is the meaning "Will they leave it (all) to God?" (cf. the use of *'zb* in Ps. 10:14).

c. MT *hᵃyizbāhû* is textually uncertain, but since it makes some sense in the context none of the proposed emendations is followed.

d. MT *hayᵉkallû bayyôm;* here too emendations have been suggested. LXX has "will they sacrifice or eat in their place (of worship)?," based on *hᵃyō'klû* for *hayᵉkallû,* which, however, is not an improvement over MT.

e. MT *hayᵉhayyû,* meaning "restore," "bring alive," "resurrect"; cf. the verb *hvy* in the inscription of Yehimilk of Byblos (line 2) and Karatepe 1.5; also the probable meaning "restore" or "rebuild" at 1 Chron. 11:8.

f. *bizzāh* from *bzz,* "plunder"; cf. 2 Chron. 14:13 [14]; 25:13; 28:14; playing on assonance with *bûzāh,* "object of contempt," from *bûz.*

g. Supplied; cf. Syr.

h. MT has "they have provoked to anger in the presence *(lᵉneged)* of the builders." Use of this preposition rules out the builders as direct object of the verb. Since *hik'îs* is (except at 1 Sam. 1:7 and Ezek. 32:9) used with God/ YHVH as object, we assume ellipsis of the pronoun; cf. ellipsis of the divine name at Hos. 12:15 and Ps. 106:29.

i. MT has *'ad-hesyāh,* "to its half(way mark)"; see commentary.

j. Lit., "the people had a heart to do (it)."

The opposition theme is prominent in the first part of the NM, punctuating the progress of the story from the arrival in Jerusalem (2:10) to the completion of the work (6:16). With only minor variations it begins "when Sanballat et al. heard . . ." followed by hostile action and Nehemiah's counteraction, generally through prayer. This structural element confirms the impression that the list of builders, whatever its origin, was inserted into the autobiographical narrative. Less certain is the suggestion that the present passage is a textually more obscure variant of the mocking reaction of Sanballat and Tobiah in 2:19–20, the repetition of which was occasioned by the insertion of the list (*pace* Batten, Burrows). More likely, the two passages represent distinct phases of the opposition which reaches its climax in chapter 6. The similarity is more readily explained by the formulaic presentation of the opposition theme throughout this part of the work.

[3:33–35 (4:1–3)] As will be apparent from the textual notes, the point of Sanballat's remarks is no longer clear. If it were possible to interpret his questions as real rather than rhetorical, they could be taken to reflect genuine concern at the prospect of the refortification of Jerusalem. Then, perhaps, Sanballat was arguing for a second intervention (cf. Ezra 4:23–24), while Tobiah was trying to assure him that it would not be necessary. On balance, however, it is more likely that he is saying, in effect, that it would take a miracle for them to achieve their purpose. This would be the point of the second question, "Are they going to leave it all to God?" The next question, about sacrifice, is even more problematic. If MT is allowed to stand, it could imply that the sacrificial cult has been suspended, for reasons unknown, or, more plausibly, the allusion could be to the sacrifice of dedication to follow completion of the wall. Or, again, the implication might be that offering sacrifice would somehow result in the miraculous completion of the work by divine intervention. The mocking allusion to a miracle is perhaps confirmed by asking whether they intended to finish it in a day (cf. "Destroy this temple, and in three days I will raise it up," John 2:19). The last question, about the stones, could also be of the same kind. Perhaps Sanballat is asking sarcastically whether they are planning to bring the stones to life (the literal meaning of the verb used) so that they will emerge from the rubble on their own and take their place in the wall. This is all quite speculative, admittedly, but it is the best we can do with the text as it is.

Tobiah's lame witticism is of a kind, suggested by Sanballat's allusion to the damaged stones. The agile animal in question is a fox *(šû'āl)* not a jackal *(tan)*. The suggestion that it is a technical term for a siege engine of some kind (Bauer) is possible but speculative and unnecessary. Foxes tend to gather in ruins (cf. Ps. 63:11 [10]; Lam. 5:18) so that the point, absurd as it is, is easily understandable.

[3:36–37 (4:4–5)] Nehemiah's prayer is of the private psalm of lamentation type (e.g., Pss. 44; 74; 79) which dwells on the wrongs inflicted on the speaker and often concludes with imprecations designed to bring down a variety of unpleasant consequences on the head of the offending party (e.g., Pss. 35; 58:7–10 [6–9]; 69:23–29 [22–28]; 109:6–19). It is also related to what von Rad has called the remembrance motif *(Gedächtnismotiv)* in Nehemiah, that is, the appeal to God to remember the suppliant and his good works, a feature also found in late Egyptian votive inscriptions (von Rad, Blenkinsopp). Of these short supplications which punctuate, irregularly, the first-person narrative (3:36–37 [4:4–5]; 5:19; 6:14; 13:14, 22, 29, 31) three (3:36–37 [4:4–5]; 6:14; 13:29) are directed against enemies and consist in an appeal to God to remember their evil deeds

and treat them accordingly. Since this kind of appeal is not represented in the late Egyptian votive inscriptions (e.g., that of Udjahorresnet from the time of Darius), it probably results from a
contamination of that form with the kind of imprecation psalm
alluded to. That the enemy is represented as opposing God's will will
probably not suffice to reconcile most Christians and Jews to it today.
It is, admittedly, an unpleasant kind of prayer and one best avoided.
Understood in the context of the opposition theme referred to, however, it has a role to play in the unfolding story of the triumph of
a project willed by God over obstacles which, at the time, appeared
almost insurmountable.

The conclusion of the prayer is rather abrupt and not entirely clear
(see textual note h). It seems to suggest that the disparaging remarks
of Sanballat and Tobiah were meant to be heard by the builders,
rather like those of the Assyrian *rab shaqu* in the days of Hezekiah
(2 Kings 18). If so, the incident must have occurred just outside
Jerusalem rather than in Samaria, a circumstance which would
heighten the element of danger and explain the allusion to the military escort.

[3:38 (4:6)] Completion of the work required sealing the joints
between adjacent sections of the wall where this was necessary, a
conclusion confirmed by the following verse. The halfway mark
referred to the height of the wall, consonant with Tobiah's remark,
since it was already complete in length and presumably also in
breadth. The enthusiasm of the builders is emphasized, though we
have seen one indication (3:5) that the opposition was not entirely
without effect, and we will have occasion to note others in due
course.

The Opposition Intensifies (Neh. 4:1–8 [7–14])

A. **Alt,** "Judas Nachbarn zur Zeit Nehemias," *KS* 2:338–345; M. **Held,** "The Root
zbl/sbl in Akkadian, Ugaritic and Biblical Hebrew," *JAOS* 88, 1968, 90–96; U.
Kellermann, *Nehemia,* 17–18.

4:1[7] When Sanballat, Tobiah, the Arabs, Ammonites, and Ash-
dodites[a] heard that the repair of the walls[b] was progressing, since
the gaps were beginning to be closed up, they became very angry.
²[8]They all plotted together to come and fight against Jerusalem
and create havoc.[c] ³[9]But we prayed to our God and posted a
guard day and night over the walls[d] because of them.

⁴[10]Then the people of Judah[e] said, "The strength of the load

carriers has failed, and there is too much rubble; we cannot go on building the wall." [5[11]]Meanwhile our adversaries were saying, "Before they are aware of it or notice it, we will be among them, killing them and putting a stop to the work."

[6[12]]When the Jews who were living near them came to us from all sides,[f] they said to us time and time again,[g] "You must return to us."[h] [7[13]]Then I stationed[i] the people on the lowest parts of the area behind the wall, in the open spaces,[j] according to families with their swords, spears, and bows.

[8[14]]After seeing to this,[k] I at once addressed the nobles, leaders, and the rest of the people: "Do not be afraid of them. Remember the Lord God[l] great and terrible, and fight for your brothers, your sons and daughters, your wives and your homes."

a. Absent from LXX, probably through homoiarkton.

b. Generally sing. in Nehemiah. Syr., Vulg., and some Gk. minuscules also have the sing. MT, however, has pl., and there is no compelling reason to change it.

c. Translating *tôʿāh*, only here and Isa. 32:6, from *tʿh*, to stray, get lost. MT adds *lô*, "for it (him)," which cannot refer to Jerusalem (fem.); hence the proposed emendation to either *lî*, "for me," or *lānû*, "for us."

d. MT *ʿalêhem*, which could mean "against them," but *mippᵉnêhem* would then be redundant. One would expect the fem. *ʿalêhen*, agreeing with *hômôt*, but the distinction is often overlooked in later Biblical Hebrew (e.g., Ruth *passim*).

e. MT has "Judah."

f. V. 6[12] suffered serious damage at an early stage, as is clear from the versions, and is barely intelligible as it stands: lit., "when the Jews who were living near them came to us, they said to us ten times, 'from all the places which you will return to (against) us.'" Many attempts at emendation are on record: *kl-hmzmvt ʾšr hšbv ʿlynv*, "all the schemes which they have devised against us," for MT *mkl-hmqmvt ʾšr tšvbv* (Ehrlich 1914, 192; Rudolph 1949, 124); the addition of *yaʿᵃlû* before *ʿālênû* (with LXX), reading, "wherever you turn, they will attack us"; reading *yšbv* for *tšvbv*, "from all the places where they dwell they will attack us" (Bertholet 1902, 59). The translation offered assumes that *mikkol-hammᵉqōmôt* is out of place.

g. Lit., "ten times"; cf. Gen. 31:7, 41; Lev. 26:26; Num. 14:22; 1 Sam. 1:8; Job 19:3.

h. MT *ʾašer tāšûbû ʿālênû; ʾašer* introduces direct speech, and the preposition *ʾel* is occasionally used interchangeably with *ʿal* in late Biblical Hebrew.

i. *vāʾaʿᵃmîd* occurs twice in the verse, the first time without object, leaving open the possibility that the intervening five words were added to the original narrative which then resumed with the repetition of the verb.

j. Reading *sᵉḥîḥîm* with Qere, of uncertain meaning, perhaps from a stem *šhh* (bright, shining, white); cf. *sᵉḥîaḥ*, Ezek. 24:7–8; 26:4, 14; *sᵉḥîḥāh*, Ps. 68:7

[6]. "Open spaces" is admittedly speculative, as indeed is the translation of the entire phrase.

k. Lit., "I saw, I arose, and I said . . . ." It is unnecessary to insert *kî yār^e'û*, "that they were afraid," after *vā'ēre',* "I saw" (Rudolph 1949, 126; Bertholet 1902, 59).

l. MT "the Lord."

The opposition-response pattern continues in this section. The unfolding conflict falls into the traditional holy war pattern: enemies conspire together, the people call to God for help, their human resources are limited, they form battle lines according to the ancient tribal levy, they are urged not to fear since God will fight for them, and finally the enemy's plans are frustrated. The pattern is particularly clear in Deuteronomy, but follows somewhat different lines in C (e.g., 2 Chron. 13:2–20; 14:10–16; 20:1–30; 25:5–13; 32:1–23). The narrative continues in the first person—singular and plural—though there are signs of disturbance, due to the imperfect integration of the theme of internal opposition, hardly more than hinted at so far. These hints of internal problems (vs. 4, 6 [10, 12]) may derive from a source distinct from the NM, though this hypothesis is hardly necessary since the memoir goes on to discuss other problems internal to the community quite openly (chapter 5). There is therefore no need to question substantial Nehemian authorship at this point (*pace* Mowinckel, *Studien* II, 24–26).

[4:1–3 (7–9)] The city and province are now surrounded on all four sides by enemies. On Sanballat to the north see commentary at 2:10, 19; his people, the inhabitants of Samaria, are not mentioned. On Tobiah, here exceptionally without gentilic, and the Ammonites to the east see commentary on 2:10. The political status of Ammon under the Persians is not clear; it may have been a separate province in the Abar-nahara satrapy. The Arabs, no doubt including the Edomites of the province of Idumea (Diodorus Siculus 19.95.2; 98.1), were to the south and southeast; their leader Geshem (see 2:19) is not mentioned at this point. Arabia was not part of the satrapy. It enjoyed special privileges under the early Achaemenids due to assistance rendered to Cambyses during his conquest of Egypt (Herodotus 3.88, 91, 97). Ashdod to the west (see also 13:23–24), one of the cities of the Philistine pentapolis, gave its name to the Assyrian province of Asdūdu carved out of the southern coastal plain and the Shephelah after Sennacherib's campaign of 711. It included the Philistine area with the exception of Gaza, an independent city, and Ashkelon, which belonged to Tyre (Herodotus 2.157).

Renewed opposition was occasioned by unexpectedly rapid progress on the wall. The word translated "repair" (*'arûkāh*) is used literally of the healing of a wound (Isa. 58:8; Jer. 8:22; 30:17; 33:6). Only here and at 2 Chron. 24:13 is this substantive, with the verb *'lh* ("proceed," literally "go up") used as an architectural metaphor. It may be observed, in passing, that C seems to have had a special interest in the building activities of the kings of Judah. At numerous points he provides details not given in his principal source (1 Chron. 11:8; 22:3; 2 Chron. 2:1, 17; 3:3; 14:6; 15:8; 24:4–14; 26:9–10; 27:3–4; 29:3; 32:2–5, 30; 33:14–16). There are also several instances of architectural terminology which occur only in 1-2 Chron. and Ezra-Nehemiah. In addition to *'arûkāh,* just mentioned, there are the verb *hāyāh* (Piel) for restoration work (1 Chron. 11:8; Neh. 3:34 [4:2]); *sabbāl,* load carrier, porter (2 Chron. 2:1 [2]; 2:17; 34:13; Neh. 4:4 [10]; cf. *nōśēʿ sabbāl* at 1 Kings 5:29); *'āmad* (Hiphil), set up, erect (2 Chron. 24:13; Ezra 2:68; 9:9; Neh. 3:1, etc.); *kûn* (Hiphil), set up (e.g., an altar; 2 Chron. 33:16; Ezra 3:3). The closing of the gaps probably alludes to the bonding of adjacent sections after the work details had built to half the projected height. The concerted effort on the part of neighboring provinces to frustrate the work being done with imperial authorization in Jerusalem gives us a glimpse into the problems faced by the central government in the more distant satrapies. The conflict is, naturally, cast in religious terms in the NM, but the motivation must have been predominantly political and perhaps also commercial. Probably all the allies had something to lose with the creation of an independent province in Judah under its own governor. Nehemiah, who was already acting in that capacity whatever his official status, reacted to the threat with a Cromwellian combination of prayer and military vigilance.

[4–5 (10–11)] At this point we have a rather sudden transition to a quite different problem, that of the morale of the builders, after which we are brought back with equal suddenness to the external enemies. The problems begin with what appears to be a short snatch of verse in the *qinah* or lament form (3 + 2) recited by the Judeans, literally, "Judah," a collective term favored by C (e.g., 2 Chron. 14:6 [7]; 16:6; 20:24; cf. Neh. 12:44):

> *kāšál kóah hassabbál*
> *vᵉheʿāpár harbéh,*
> *vaʾanáhnû lóʾ nûkál*
> *libnót bahômáh*

This quatrain is generally explained as one of those occupational ditties—somewhat along the lines of "Ol' Man River"—sung by the weary builders as they tried to keep going. But a moment's reflection will suffice to show that this is quite unlikely. The passage is certainly in verse and even has the unusual feature of internal rhyme, but the words are altogether too prosaic for the proposed *Sitz im Leben*. An alternative suggestion is that it was a kind of slogan chanted by builders who had put down their tools and gone on strike. If so, we can only regret that they could not have come up with something less pedestrian. It remains something of a mystery, therefore, why the editor would have preserved or introduced this fragment of verse in a narrative otherwise spare to the point of terseness. It may be noted that the preceding sentence (3b [9b]) can also be written as verse, forming a rhymed couplet:

> vanna'ʻᵃmíd mišmᾱ́r 'ᵃlêhém
> yômᾱ́m vālᾱ́ylāh mippᵉnêhém

Moreover, it has the advantage of a phrase *(yômām vālaylāh,* "day and night") which occurs often in poetry or, as elsewhere in Nehemiah (1:6; 9:12, 19), in the context of prayer. It would be tempting to conclude that these are fragments of a verse account of the wall-building epic, a hypothesis which would have the advantage of explaining the exceptionally disturbed state of the text in this section. Whatever the explanation, the failure of nerve or morale among the builders constituted a major crisis for Nehemiah and his supporters.

[6–8 (12–14)] It will be obvious from the textual notes that the proposed translation is but one of several options for making sense of a badly damaged text. LXX understood the Jewish neighbors of Nehemiah's enemies as coming to warn against imminent attack ("they will come up from every side against us"). This makes eminently good sense, but it may have been obtained in spite of an intractable Hebrew text as unclear then as it is now. Josephus (*Ant.* 11.175) paraphrases, representing the report of an imminent attack as a rumor spread by the enemy to discourage the builders, a ploy which in fact almost succeeded. If, however, we opt to stay closer to MT, we may conclude that these other Jews were repeatedly urging the builders to leave the city. The appeal may have been inspired by fear for the safety of the workers, especially those from the towns and villages listed earlier. Prolonged absence must have caused much inconvenience and hardship, and would have had a significant impact on the economy of the province. Nehemiah reacted to the threat by assembling the entire corps of builders in a military or paramilitary parade ending with a stirring address, of which the memoir provides no more than the gist. The purpose was less to deter the threatened attack than to boost the morale of the workers, which had reached a dangerously low point. The assembly was arranged according to kinship groupings, reminiscent of the ancient tribal levy, in order to reinforce the motivation provided by the harangue.

Nehemiah Holds Firm (Neh. 4:9–17 [15–23])

N. **Avigad**, "New Light on the Na'ar Seals," in F. M. **Cross** et al. (eds.), *Magnalia Dei,* 294–300; J. **Macdonald**, "The Status and Role of the Na'ar in Israelite Society," *JNES* 35, 1976, 147–170; H.-P. **Stähli**, *Knabe—Jüngling—Knecht: Untersuchungen zum Begriff N'R im Alten Testament,* Frankfurt am Main, 1978, 162–167; H. J. **Warner**, "A Simple Solution of Nehemiah iv.23 (Heb. verse 17)," *ExpT* 63, 1951/ 52, 322.

4:9[15] When our enemies heard that we had been informed,[a] and that God had frustrated their plan, we all returned to our several tasks at the wall. [10][16]From that day on, half of my servants were engaged in the work, while the other half[b] held the shields,[c] spears, bows, and coats of mail[d] behind all the house of Judah [11][17]engaged in building the wall.[e] The load carriers did their work[f] supporting[g] the burden with one hand, and with the other holding their weapon. [12][18]As for the builders, each had his sword fastened at his belt[h] as he built, while the trumpeter stayed at my side.

[13][19]Then I said to the nobles, the officers, and the rest of the people, "The work is widely spread out[i] and we are some distance apart from each other along the wall. [14][20]You must rally to us wherever you hear the sound of the trumpet. Our God will fight for us." [15][21]So we continued with the work[j] from dawn of day until the stars came out. [16][22]I also told the people at that time, "Let every man and his servant spend the night in Jerusalem so that he can do guard duty for us at night and work during the daytime." [17][23]Neither I nor my kinsmen nor my servants nor my bodyguard[k] took off our clothes; each kept his weapon in his right hand.[l]

a. Lit., "it was known to us."
b. Lit., "half of them."
c. MT has "held and the spears and the shields and the bows." The conjunction before *hār^emāhîm* could be simply omitted, giving good sense, but it seems marginally better to reverse the order of *hār^emāhîm* and *hammāginnîm,* resulting in a more conventional sequence; cf. 2 Chron. 26:14.
d. Omitting *v^ehaśśārîm* ("and the leaders") as dittography with the relatively rare *v^ehaśśiryōnîm (vhśrym/vhśrynym).* There is also no verb governing *haśśārîm.*

e. *habbônîm bahômāh* belongs with v. 10.

f. MT has sing., *'ōśeh,* but the distributive sense would require *'îš* before *'ōśeh.*

g. Lit., "carrying" *('ōmśîm);* LXX has *en hoplois* (for *enoploi,* "armed," presupposing *hᵃmušîm).*

h. Lit., "at his loins."

i. MT has "the work is much and wide," hendiadys.

j. "Half of them held their spears" *(vᵉhesyām mahᵃzîqîm bārᵉmāhîm),* intruded here by dittography with the similar phrase in v. 10, also following *'ōśîm bammᵉlā'kāh.*

k. MT adds "who were after me" *('ᵃšer 'ahᵃray).*

l. MT *'îš šilhô hammāyim,* "each his weapon the water," is unintelligible. Perhaps some words fell out at an early stage. Thus, L has "every one who was sent to the water (went) each with his weapon to the water." LXX simply omits. Vulgate *unusquisque tantum nudabatur ad baptismum* tries to make sense of it by assuming that they took their clothes off only to get washed, but this would require a rather different Hebrew *Vorlage.* The present translation follows the safer route of emending *hmym* to *hymynv,* from the verbal stem *ymn* (Hiphil); *-m* and *-nv* are not infrequently confused. (See R. Weiss, *JBL* 82, 1963, 188–194.)

[4:9 (15)] The same pattern can be detected here as in the previous section. It begins with information coming to the opposition and refers to the anticipated assistance of YHVH, warrior-god. It is possible that a clause has dropped out of the opening sentence stating what it was that had come to the attention of Nehemiah's people. It may have been news of impending attack brought by those other Jews (v. 6 [12]), which enabled Nehemiah to take timely countermeasures. We get the impression that the allies were engaged in psychological warfare to demoralize the builders without having to take the very serious step—in view of the imperial authorization—of large-scale military intervention. As usual, Nehemiah credits YHVH with negating these hostile plans (cf. 2 Sam. 15:34; Ezra 4:5).

[10–12 (16–18)] Nehemiah's countermeasures consisted in: (1) withdrawing half of his personal retinue *(nᵉ'ārîm)* from construction work to form an armed force stationed within the perimeter and just behind the work squads—a move which had the additional advantage of discouraging unrest among the builders; (2) arming the work force, both the gangs carting away the rubble and hauling stones, probably with the help of donkeys, and the actual builders; the disparity between their arms and those of Nehemiah's professionals would lessen the likelihood of trouble from the workers; (3) having a trumpeter stationed at his side to call the builders to rally at the point of imminent attack (for the role of trumpeter in warfare cf. Judg. 3:27; 6:34; 7:18; 1 Sam. 13:3); (4) ordering the workers to spend the night in the city, still more or less depopulated (cf. 7:4), doubtless in close proximity to the work area, to guard against surprise attack and, perhaps even more so, to discourage defections and absenteeism among those commuting from neighboring villages. These measures testify to the vigorous faith and self-confidence of the new governor. While we can hardly speak of an imminent mutiny among the wall builders (as argued by Hölscher 1923 and Mowinckel, *Studien*), there was disaffection, as we have seen, and the Sanballat-Tobiah axis had sympathetic contacts within Judean society. We see how crucial was the role of the trained "servants" *(nᵉ'ārîm)*. They are distinguished from his kinsmen and probably formed a special militia seconded to him in his capacity as governor of the province (cf. 5:15–16). They therefore formed a kind of national guard whose function was to police the province and maintain law and order. While their arms as described here correspond to Persian equipment (cf. Herodotus' description of Xerxes' army, 7.61), they were probably recruited locally. Nehemiah's tactics were never put to the test, perhaps fortunately for him. The point of attack—probably a surprise attack—would have to be identified and the news brought to Nehemiah, his trumpeter would have to make his way there before sounding the alarm (loud enough to be heard round the entire perimeter of the city?), and the people would have to put down their tools to repel the incursion. It may be for this reason that Josephus, rather more experienced in military matters, has trumpeters stationed at intervals of five hundred feet (*Ant.* 11.177).

[13–15 (19–21)] Nobles *(ḥôrîm)* and officers *(sᵉgānîm)* are often mentioned together in the book (Neh. 2:16; 4:8, 13 [14, 19]; 5:7; 7:5). The former were the hereditary Judean nobility (e.g., Jer. 27:20; 39:6; Isa. 34:12; see H. C. M. Vogt 1966, 107–111). The function of the latter never emerges clearly. In prophetic texts from the sixth century they are almost invariably linked with provincial governors, which would suggest regional administration (cf. Jer. 51:23, 28, 57; Ezek. 23:6, 12, 23). Both classes come in for considerable censure in Ezra-Nehemiah. The *sᵉgānîm* were among the worst offenders in the matter of foreign marriages (Ezra 9:2). Both were charged by Nehemiah with economic exploitation (5:7). Several of the nobles maintained close contacts with his enemies (6:17). Neither class seemed particularly zealous in the specifics of religious observance (13:7, 11).

[16–17 (22–23)] The fact that round-the-clock sentry duty had already been set up (4:3 [9]) further emphasizes Nehemiah's aim of avoiding defections by obliging the workers to stay overnight in Jerusalem. The final reference to Nehemiah's own outstanding example is understandable in itself and a requirement of the genre. By naming together his kinsmen—including presumably his brother Hanani—and his "servants" and bodyguard, the narrative once again emphasizes the distinction between Nehemiah's own support group and the rest of the province, a point of great importance to be borne in mind throughout the book.

Social and Economic Problems (Neh. 5:1–13)

A. **Barrois**, "Debt, Debtor," *IDB* 1:809–810; M. **Dandamaev**, *Politische und wirtschaftliche Geschichte*, Historia Einzelschriften 18, Wiesbaden, 1972, 33–45; H. **Gamoran**, "The Biblical Law Against Loans on Interest," *JNES* 30, 1971/72, 127–134; U. **Kellermann**, *Nehemia*, 19–21, 154–166, 178–179; H. G. **Kippenberg**, *Religion und Klassenbildung im antiken Judäa*, Göttingen, 1978, 42–77; H. **Kreissig**, *Die sozialökonomische Situation in Juda zur Achämenidenzeit*, Berlin, 1973; N. P. **Lemche**, "The Hebrew Slave," *VT* 25, 1975, 128–144; R. P. **Maloney**, "Usury and Restrictions on Interest-Taking in the Ancient Near East," *CBQ* 36, 1974, 1–20; E. **Neufeld**, "The Rate of Interest and the Text of Nehemiah 5.11," *JQR* 44, 1953/54, 194–204; "The Prohibitions Against Loans at Interest in Ancient Hebrew Laws," *HUCA* 26, 1955, 355–412; R. **North**, *Sociology of the Biblical Jubilee*, Rome, 1954, 37–38, 205–206; J. P. M. **van der Ploeg**, "Slavery in the Old Testament," *VTSup.* 22, 1972, 72–87; H. C. M. **Vogt**, *Studie zur nachexilischen Gemeinde in Esra-Nehemia*, 72–75, 106–117; J. **de Zwaan**, "Shaking Out the Lap," *The Expositor* 7:5, 1908, 249–252.

5:1 There arose a great outcry of the common people and their wives against their fellow Jews.[a] [2]Some were saying, "We are putting up our sons and daughters as surety[b] to buy grain in order to stay alive," [3]while others were saying, "We are mortgaging our fields, vineyards, and houses in order to get grain during the famine." [4]Others again were saying, "We have borrowed money against[c] our fields and vineyards to pay the king's tax. [5]Our bodies are no different from the bodies of our fellows,[d] and our children are no different from theirs; yet here we are, at the point of forcing our sons and daughters to become slaves. Indeed, some of our daughters have already been forced into that condition,[e] but there is nothing we can do,[f] since our fields and vineyards belong to others."[g]

[6]I was very angry when I heard their complaint and what they had to say. [7]I controlled myself,[h] however, and took their nobles and officials to task, saying to them, "You are distraining the persons and property of your own kinsfolk."[i] I convoked a great assembly against them[j] [8]and said to them, "To the best of our ability, we have bought back our fellow Jews who have been sold

into slavery to the Gentiles, while you are selling your own kinsfolk so that they will have to be bought back by us!"[k] They
remained silent and found nothing to reply. [9]So I continued, "This
business which you are engaged in is not good. Should we not walk
in the fear of our God to turn back the taunts of our Gentile
enemies? [10]I myself and my kinsfolk and servants are advancing
them money and grain; so let us leave off this seizing in pledge for
debts. [11]Give back to them at once their fields, vineyards, olive
orchards, and houses, together with the percentage of interest[l] in
money and grain, new wine and fine oil, which you have taken
from them." [12]They replied, "We will make restitution, and we will
exact nothing more from them. We will do as you say." I therefore
summoned the priests, and put them on oath to act in this manner.
[13]I also shook out the fold of my robe with the words, "Thus may
God shake out from his home and his property any one who does
not keep this promise; thus may he be shaken out and left empty!"
All the assembly said "Amen" and praised YHVH, and the people
did as they had promised.[m]

a. In MT the complaint is addressed to *('el)* not against *('al)* their fellow Jews;
   cf. LXX *pros* and similar cases with *'el* in MT (Gen. 18:21; Ex. 3:9; 1 Sam.
   9:16). But since *'el* and *'al* are easily confused (e.g., Job 34:28 where we would
   expect *'ēlāv* rather than *'ālāv*), the translation will depend on the identity of
   the fellow Jews, on which see the commentary.
b. MT reads "our sons and daughters we are many," which will not do; and it
   is clear from what follows that the problem was not large families. We therefore read *'rbym* for *rbym*, an emendation which goes back to the eighteenth
   century. This may suggest that v. 2 originated as a variant of v. 3 with *bntynv*
   (our daughters) for *btynv* (our houses).
c. Reading *'al;* the preposition is omitted in MT.
d. Lit., "Like the flesh of our fellows is our flesh."
e. The same verb occurs here as earlier in the sentence *(kbš).* Since, however,
   the daughters are singled out, one might also translate "ravage" as at Esth.
   7:8.
f. Lit., "it is not within the power of our hands," taking *'el* = power; the idiom
   occurs quite frequently (Gen. 31:29; Deut. 28:32; Micah 2:1; Prov. 3:27). F.
   M. Cross (*TDOT* 1:260–261) and W. G. E. Watson (*Bib* 58, 1977, 213–215)
   find here an occurrence of the stem *l'y,* to be strong, attested in Ugaritic,
   Phoenician, and Akkadian but not elsewhere in MT. The redivided phrase
   would then be *'yn l' lydnv,* "there is no strength to our hands"; cf. M. Dahood's
   discovery of a derivate of the same stem in Ps. 7:13 [12] (*Psalms* I, Garden
   City, 1965, 46). While the redivision of the words is plausible and ingenious,
   lack of attestation in Hebrew suggests caution. The sense is not, in any case,
   materially affected.

g. LXX reads *tois entimois*, presupposing *lḥrym* for *l'ḥrym*, but MT need not be changed.

h. The choice here is between taking *mlk* with the meaning "take counsel with oneself," as in Aramaic, and an otherwise unattested Niphal of *mlk*, "exercise control." The latter option is followed here since the former is unattested in Biblical Hebrew. On the basis of an Arab cognate L. Kopf (*VT* 9, 1959, 261–262) reads "I was beside myself."

i. The verb *nš'* and the substantive *mš' (maššā')* do not mean simply "lend" and "loan," respectively. Nor is it simply a matter of lending at interest, as is clear from other texts where the terms occur (see commentary). The proposal of Rudolph (1949, 130) to read *maššā'* and *noš'îm* ("eine Last legt ihr einer wie der andere auf seinen Brüder") is syntactically more awkward and less in keeping with the context.

j. *qᵉhillāh*, an alternative form of *qāhāl* (Deut. 33:4; Sir. 7:7; 42:11) is rare but attested (cf. LXX *ekklēsian megalēn* and Vulg. *contionem magnam*). NEB "I rebuked them severely" relates *qhlh* to an Arabic cognate (see F. Zimmermann, *JBL* 50, 1931, 311–312), which seems less likely, apart from the fact that v. 13 refers to the *qāhāl* during which the decision was taken.

k. MT has *vᵉnimkᵉrû-lānû*, "that they may be sold to us." If this reading is maintained, it would suggest that the nobles and officials were attempting to make a profit out of the redemption of those enslaved by their creditors. While this is possible, the more natural sense is the one given, reading *vᵉnikrû-lānû* (with Rudolph 1949, 130).

l. Lit., "hundredth part of" *(mᵉ'at hakkesep . . .)*, generally understood as 1 percent per month or 12 percent annually. Since this is very low for that time, we take *mē'āh* in the more general sense of interest (more commonly *nešek*, literally "bite") or profit accruing from the transaction. *m't* need not be emended to *mš't*, pledge (cf. Deut. 24:10), a suggestion that goes back to Abraham Geiger.

m. Lit., "according to this word."

The narrative continues in the first person with an incident that interrupts the wall building and the pattern of opposition/countermeasure described earlier. Severe social and economic problems were encountered and, as often in Ezra-Nehemiah, a solution was reached through a plenary assembly (Ezra 10:5, 7–8; Neh. 2:17–18; 8–10; 13:1–3). It is of course possible that the incident is in correct historical sequence. Social unrest may have been aggravated by the prolonged absence of the rural population from their homesteads and farms, which would also explain the explicit mention of the womenfolk. On the other hand, Ezra-Nehemiah has undergone several displacements, and it would not be surprising if this were a case in point. The forcible repopulation of Jerusalem, involving a (literal) decimation of the rural population (11:1–2), must have caused con-

siderable disruption and unrest, and the conduct of creditors is one
of the matters regulated in the covenant of chapter 10 (v. 32 [31]).
We are also told that the wall was finished on the twenty-fifth of Elul,
the sixth month, after only fifty-two days' work (6:15). This means
that it was going on from about the middle of July to early September
or, in other words, *before* the olive and grape harvest which was so
important for the economy of the Judean highlands (*pace* Neufeld).
This would be the obvious time for calling in debts in money and
kind. And finally, the narrative itself tells us that a famine precipitated the unrest (v. 3).

[5:1] The subject is introduced with typical abruptness, and we
are given little help in understanding precisely what form the disturbance took. The term corresponding to "outcry" *(ṣeʿāqāh)* can be
used in a legal sense (cf. Gen. 18:20–21; Ex. 12:30; Job 34:28), and
the trouble seems to have been occasioned by the disparity between
the condition of the common people and their wives on the one hand
and others known simply as "Jews" *(yehûdîm)*. We had occasion
earlier to note the ambiguity in the use of this term in the book (see
on Neh. 2:16). While it is often used of the inhabitants of the province
in general (e.g., Ezra 5:5; 6:7, 14; Neh. 3:33–34 [4:1–2]; 13:23), it can
also refer to those outside the province (e.g., Jer. 40:11–12; 44:1; Ezra
4:12; Neh. 4:6 [12]; 5:8), even such as did not originate there (e.g.,
the "Jews" of Elephantine). Thus the word carries a religious as well
as a strictly territorial connotation, the antonym of "Gentile" as in
Esther and later texts. In addition, it can designate a category distinct from the common people of the province, as well as from the
priests, nobles, and officials (2:16; 5:17). On the assumption that the
protest was directed *against* these other "Jews" (see textual note a),
we take the term to stand for a privileged stratum of the population,
most probably the more affluent of those who had returned from the
Babylonian diaspora with their leaders (for indications of their af-
fluence see Ezra 1:4–6; 2:68–69; 7:16; Zech. 6:9–14). This was, of
course, the stratum to which Nehemiah himself belonged and on
which he drew for support; a circumstance which may explain why
he concentrated his attack on the nobles and officials (v. 7), even
though these *yehûdîm* had occasioned the unrest in the first place.

[2–4] While at an earlier stage the text may have mentioned only
two aspects of the problem—pledging property and children to buy
grain and borrowing money to pay taxes (see textual note b), in its
present form it differentiates between pledging the labor of family
members and the use and usufruct of property. While the three
instances are not necessarily in order of severity (Kippenberg, 56–
57), it may well have seemed a less desperate expedient to pledge the

labor of (grown) children than to risk forfeiting the family parcel of land on which survival depended. The law prescribed a maximum of seven years of indentured labor or slavery for debt (Ex. 21:2–11; Deut. 15:12–18; cf. three years in the Hammurabi code, no. 117) after which the debt-slave went free. Thus, debt-slavery was practiced and permitted throughout the history of Israel (e.g., 2 Kings 4:1–2). It was also not unusual in this kind of transaction for the family member's service to begin at once and continue until the debt was amortized.

The second complaint was that family holdings, the only source of income in the subsistence economy of the Judean farmer, were being mortgaged in order to stay alive during the famine. Here, too, the normal procedure was that produce from these holdings would be computed toward the amortization of the loan. If practice in the Jewish colony in Upper Egypt is at all comparable, loans of grain carried extraordinarily heavy interest rates and stiff penalties for nonpayment (*BMAP* 56, 259–265; Porten 1968, 78–79). The third and last complaint arose out of the need to borrow money in order to pay the imperial tax (see on Ezra 4:13, 20). The central government levied a fixed amount of bullion on each satrapy. Herodotus (3.91) gives the figure of three hundred and fifty talents for the fifth satrapy, to which Judah belonged. From the time of Darius at least, the principal imposition was a land tax (the *ilku* of the Babylonians) computed according to the estimated produce of the holding. The burden seems to have increased appreciably from the reign of Xerxes, in good part on account of his campaigns in Asia Minor and Europe. Since it was the governor's task (and therefore Nehemiah's) to collect at the provincial level and then, after deductions for expenses and collector's fee, pass on the takings to the satrapal court, we can understand Nehemiah's concern to distance himself from the nobles and officials and to stress his own fairness and liberality over against previous incumbents (5:6–10, 15). The rate of interest on such loans at Elephantine, in some instances practically contemporary with Nehemiah, could be as high as 60 percent or even 75 percent with severe penalties, including distraint of property, for default. The only way in which the Judean farmer, who practiced a subsistence economy, could possibly meet his tax obligation was by producing and marketing a surplus. His situation drove him inevitably, therefore, into the hands of the middleman or wealthy landowner, and the frequent cases of default and expropriation contributed to the great estates and absentee landlords of the late Persian and Hellenistic periods.

Important factors in the political unrest were, therefore, Persian fiscal policy and economic disparity between the long-term residents of the province and the more wealthy Babylonian *olim*. To these we must add the requirement of supporting the sacrificial cult of the temple and an untaxed corps of clergy which appears to have constituted about 10 percent of the total population. Given this situation, there was no buffer against the occasional bad harvest, apparently of rather frequent occurrence in the sixth and fifth centuries B.C.E. (Hag. 1:5–6, 10–11; 2:15–16, 19; Mal. 3:9–12; Joel 1–2). While, therefore, the outcry of the common people described in this section may reflect a specific occurrence, it may also serve to illustrate a situation which tended to recur, which is borne out by other allusions in the writings from the period (e.g., Zech. 8:10; Isa. 58:3–4), and which should be borne in mind when discussing the emergence of parties and sects, generally identified exclusively on the basis of their religious beliefs.

[5] This is not a new gravamen, but a peroration with poignant emphasis on the fate of the children, sons and daughters. The appeal is to equality and unity: we are the same flesh and blood, we are one people, yet you allow this to happen. Neither the common people nor Nehemiah himself alleges that the law has been violated—with the exception of selling fellow Jews into slavery to Gentiles (v. 8). Debt-slavery, mitigated by the septennial release, is contemplated in the laws (Ex. 21:1–11; Deut. 15:12–18). It was also widely practiced. We hear a prophet's widow lamenting that the creditor is on his way to seize her two children for defaulting on debts (2 Kings 4:1–2). But the appeal to solidarity as "brethren" *('aḥîm),* members of the same community, introduces considerations which were part of the broad intent of the law from the beginning. In both the so-called Covenant Code and Deuteronomic law procedures permissible in themselves are excluded in the case of the poor, and one of these is forcible seizure of pledges against defaulting (Ex. 22:24 [25]; Deut. 24:10–11). The same solicitude for the poor fellow Israelite is expressed in the Holiness Code, which requires support of the poor, as an obligation not as charity, and states explicitly that the insolvent "brother" who sells himself must not be treated as a slave (Lev. 25:35–39). A similar requirement is expressed in C, for we hear of a prophet during the reign of Ahaz forbidding the victorious Northerners to force male and female Judeans into slavery (2 Chron. 28:10–11, using the same language as here). It was this traditional ethos, which comes to only partial expression in the laws, to which the common people and their wives are appealing.

The daughters are singled out for mention because of the immediate risk of the girl being taken as wife for her new master or his son, a situation which could well be irreversible (cf. Ex. 21:7–11). Since their holdings were already mortgaged, the landlords did not in any case have the means to redeem the children whose services had already been entailed.

[6–11] Characteristically, the complaint provoked an immediate and emotional reaction from Nehemiah. It is interesting that he assigned responsibility to the nobles and officials rather than "the Jews." His accusation is not that they had loaned at interest (as RSV), but that they were acting the part of the *nōšeh,* the seizer of persons and property pledged against nonpayment of debt. This, as we have just seen, was forbidden in the case of the poor (Ex. 22:24 [25]). The strategy was the same as that pursued by Ezra in the matter of foreign marriages: convoke a plenary assembly in order to win popular support, isolate the opposition and "put them on the spot," and thus force them to take immediate action. His diatribe rested on the contrast between the efforts of himself and his party to buy back Jews enslaved in the diaspora and the current practice of reducing to slavery for defaulting on debts. It seems that the accused were not only seizing the persons of fellow Judeans but selling them to foreigners, thus swelling the numbers of those who would have to be bought back and, at the same time, provoking the derision of Gentile neighbors (v. 9). The accusation is in itself quite credible. Phoenicians, Greeks, and Arabs, all of whom had commercial interests in the province, were involved in the lucrative slave trade (cf. Ezek. 27:13; Joel 4[3]:3, 4–8; Amos 1:9), and it would be unremarkable if the assimilationist Judean aristocracy also had a hand in it.

Nehemiah's proposal was to stop the practice of seizing the persons and property of insolvent fellow Jews, to return pledged property which had already been seized, together with money and produce taken to liquidate the interest on the loan. We would assume that they would also be obliged, *a fortiori,* to release those indentured for defaulting. The strategy, therefore, seems to have been to use the occasion of economic crisis to proclaim an emergency jubilee, somewhat comparable to the manumission of slaves by Zedekiah during the siege of Jerusalem (Jer. 34:8–22). Some interesting parallels with the stipulations for the jubilee year in the Holiness Code (Lev. 25) may be noted: the fear of God as the motivating force (v. 9; cf. Lev. 25:17, 36, 43); restitution of ancestral property (Lev. 25:27–28, 41); prohibition of reducing fellow Israelites to slavery (Lev. 25:39, 46) and of charging interest on loans to the poor (25:36).

Nehemiah adds that he and the members of his family and party also loaned money and goods. He is not confessing guilt in order to make it easier for them to do so. On the contrary, he is saying that it is possible and necessary to do so without the abuses which they had come together to abolish. They are to return not only the property seized as surety but also the money and the percentage of the produce from the mortgaged property applied against the loan and interest—a solution *in radice* which gives a fair idea of the gravity of the situation which threatened the peace and stability of the province.

[12–13] The outcome was successful: the guilty parties agreed to the proposal without reservation. In all likelihood, they had no choice, since Nehemiah as governor had the military resources to force compliance, and would no doubt have done so if necessary. The priests were summoned to administer the oath, not primarily and certainly not exclusively on themselves, which was then confirmed by a symbolic gesture of a type used frequently by the prophets. The occasion was therefore a covenant, analogous to the one recorded in greater detail later (Neh. 10). The shaking out the fold of the robe, which served as a kind of pocket, is functionally parallel to the threat of banning or excommunication in Ezra's assembly to deal with foreign marriages (Ezra 10:8). The liturgical conclusion looks very much like an editorial addition in the manner of C, practically identical with the conclusion to the setting up of the ark in Jerusalem during David's reign (1 Chron. 16:36).

Nehemiah's Record (Neh. 5:14–19)

A. Alt, "Die Rolle Samarias bei der Entstehung des Judentums," *KS* 2:328–337; N. Avigad, *Bullae and Seals from a Post-exilic Judean Archive,* Jerusalem, 1976; K. Galling, "Bagoas und Esra," *Studien zur Geschichte Israels im Persischen Zeitalter,* 149–184; "Serubbabel und der Wiederaufbau des Tempels in Jerusalem," in A. Kuschke (ed.), *Verbannung und Heimkehr,* 96; Y. M. Grintz, "Jehoezer—Unknown High Priest?" *JQR* 50, 1960, 338–345; U. Kellermann, *Nehemia,* 154–166; I. M. Linforth, *Solon the Athenian,* Berkeley, 1919; S. E. McEvenue, "The Political Structure in Judah from Cyrus to Nehemiah," *CBQ* 43, 1981, 353–364; R. North, "Civil Authority in Ezra," *Studi in Onore di Eduardo Volterra,* vol. 6, Milan, 1971, 377–404; G. von Rad, "Die Nehemia-Denkschrift," *ZAW* 76, 1964, 176–187; W. Schottroff, *"Gedenken" im Alten Orient und im Alten Testament,* Neukirchen-Vluyn, 1967, 218–219, 222; M. Smith, *Parties and Politics That Shaped the Old Testament,* 193–201; E. Stern, *Material Culture,* 200–214; G. Widengren, "The Persian Period," in J. H. Hayes and J. M. Miller (eds.), *Israelite and Judaean History,* 509–511; E. M. Yamauchi, "Two Reformers Compared: Solon of Athens and Nehemiah of Jerusalem," in G. Rendsburg et al. (eds.), *The Bible World: Essays in Honor of Cyrus H. Gordon,* New York, 1980, 269–292.

5:14 Moreover, from the day when I was appointed[a] governor[b] in the land of Judah—from the twentieth to the thirty-second year of King Artaxerxes, twelve years in all—neither I nor my kinsfolk partook of the governor's food allowance. [15]The former governors, my predecessors, imposed a heavy burden[c] on the people and exacted from them for their daily food allowance[d] forty shekels of silver. Their retainers also lorded it over the people. Moved by the fear of God, however, I did not behave in this way. [16]Rather, I put my best effort into the work on this wall, I purchased[e] no land, and all my retainers were gathered there on the job. [17]A hundred and fifty people enjoyed my hospitality,[f] Jews[g] and officials, together with those who came to us from the surrounding nations. [18]This is what was prepared for each day: one ox and six choice sheep; fowl[h] was also prepared for me and, at ten-day intervals, every kind of wine[i] in abundance. In spite of this I did not claim the governor's food allowance because the service weighed heavily on the people. [19]Remember for my good, O my God, all that I have done for this people.

a. MT has "from the day when . . . appointed me"; we must therefore either supply a subject, transposing *hammelek* from its later position in the verse (it is absent in LXX[BA]; Vulg. has it in both places), or read *suvvē'tî* for *ṣivvāh 'ōtî* (Rudolph 1949, 132). The latter alternative is followed here.

b. Reading *peḥāh* for MT *peḥām* (*paḥᵃtām*, "their governor"); cf. LXX *eis archonta autōn.*

c. In MT the verb *hikbîdû* is without object. *'ōl*, yoke, may have been lost through haplography before the preposition *'al* (cf. the combination of the same verb and substantive in 1 Kings 12:10, 14; Isa. 47:6; also L *kloion*, collar, yoke) or, equally probable, *'ōl* may have been read as the preposition *'al.*

d. MT reads *bᵉlehem vāyayin 'aḥar*, "in bread and wine afterwards," from which neither the ancient (LXX) nor the modern translator has been able to extract meaning. Vulg. introduces *quotidie*, "daily," suggesting *bᵉlehem lᵉyôm 'eḥād*, lit., "for their food for one day."

e. MT "we purchased" *(qānînû).*

f. Lit., "(were) at my table."

g. *yᵉhûdîm* should not be emended to *hôrîm*, nobles.

h. *sippᵒrîm*, birds; cf. LXX[BA], Syr., Eth., which read *ṣᵉpîrîm*, he-goats; see A. Cohen, *BM* 12, 1966/67, 139–140.

i. MT *bᵉkol-yayin lᵉharbēh* has been variously emended. 2 MSS read *nēbel yayin*, a skin of wine, but *lᵉharbēh* requires the pl., therefore perhaps *niblê kol-yayin*, skins of every kind of wine, or *kᵉlê kol-yayin*, vessels of every kind of wine. The simplest expedient is to omit the preposition, as in the present translation.

The account of the assembly in which the social problem was confronted and apparently solved is rounded off by a more general defense of Nehemiah's conduct as governor contrasted with that of his predecessors. Here especially the language of the NM is reminiscent of the late Egyptian votive inscriptions referred to earlier and, in particular, that of Udjahorresnet from the early years of Darius I:

> I was a good man in my city, rescuing my people from the very great turmoil which happened throughout the entire land, the like of which had never happened in this land. I protected the weak against the powerful; I rescued the timid person when it was his turn to suffer; I did for them whatever was to their advantage when the time came to act on their behalf. . . . O great gods who are in Sais! Remember all the useful things accomplished by the chief physician Udjahorresnet! May you do for him whatever is useful and make his name endure in this land forever! (lines 33–36, 47)

A parallel of a rather different kind is the verse account of Solon's good works on behalf of the Athenians as preserved in Aristotle's *Constitution of Athens.* Appointed archon in or about 594 B.C.E., he carried out social reforms similar to those of Nehemiah: abolition of loans secured with the person of the debtor *(epi tois sōmasin),* general cancellation of debts and manumission of debt-slaves, curtailing the forced purchase of holdings, buying back of the indigent who had been sold into slavery—all accompanied by denunciation of the unjust accumulation of wealth, expressions of piety toward the gods, and the hope of a good repute in the memory of generations to come.

[5:14] Nehemiah was appointed governor in the twentieth year of Artaxerxes I, therefore in 445/444 (see on 1:1), and returned to Susa for an unknown period of time in 433/432 (13:6). The present section at least could therefore not have been written before this last date. It is, of course, possible that the chronological note was added by a glossator drawing on 1:1 and 13:6 (as Hölscher 1923, 535; Mowinckel, *Studien* II, 27; Rudolph 1949, 131–132), but it seems to be integral to the passage as a whole and the point being made. If the request for a leave of absence is historical, it does not seem that he was appointed governor before his departure from Susa, though he must have been shortly after his arrival in Jerusalem. He tells us that during all of the twelve years that followed, he and his family did not avail themselves of the governor's per diem allowance, ordinarily a substantial drain on the resources of the province.

[15] Allusion to earlier governors, whose performance is compared unfavorably with that of Nehemiah himself, raises the question

of the identity of these officials, and in turn that of the political status of Judah prior to Nehemiah's arrival. Nehemiah is clearly not contrasting his conduct with that of officials in Samaria, whom he would not be likely to speak of as his predecessors. Judah is called a province (*yᵉhûd mᵉdîntā'*, Ezra 5:8; cf. Ezra 2:1 = Neh. 7:6; Neh. 1:3; 11:3), in other words, an administrative subdivision of a satrapy (cf. Esth. 1:1, 3, 16, etc.). It was not just a tax district, since taxes were collected through the satrapal and provincial system (*pace* McEvenue, 359–360). Provinces were administered by a governor (*peḥāh*, cf. Akk. *paḥātu*). We are, unfortunately, in no position to reconstruct the political history of the province in the century between the ascendancy of Cyrus and the arrival of Nehemiah on the scene. In their reply to Tattenai, the elders referred to Sheshbazzar as the governor appointed by Cyrus at the time of the first return (Ezra 5:14), and Zerubbabel is also said to have filled that office for some time in the early part of the reign of Darius (Hag. 1:1, 14; 2:2, 21). An unnamed governor is mentioned in Malachi (1:8), which was written in all probability shortly before Nehemiah's administration. The allusions to the *tiršātā'* (the Persian equivalent of *peḥāh*) in Ezra 2:63 and Neh. 7:65, 69 [70] are less certainly relevant since they cannot be dated with any assurance.

Archaeological data which may bear on the issue can be used only with caution on account of uncertainty of dating. Seal impressions from Ramat Rahel, south of Jerusalem, bear the names of Yeho'ezer and Ahzai, governors of Judah, and the archive of bullae and seals published by Avigad includes some with the name Elnatan, also governor (*yhd 'lntn pḥv'*). If Avigad is correct in dating these to the late sixth or early fifth century, we could fill in one or other of the "former governors" criticized by Nehemiah and begin to fill in the gap between Zerubbabel and Nehemiah. Avigad's dating is, however, disputed, so the matter must remain *sub judice* for the time being. The name of another governor, Yehezqiyah, occurs on coins from the late Persian period discovered at Beth-zur and Tell Jemneh, and this person has been identified with the priest Ezekias mentioned by Josephus (*C. Apion* 1.187–189). The prevalence of Yehud stamps and indigenous mints in the later Persian period would be consistent with a distinct provincial administration, but would not prove that its separate status was the result of Nehemiah's efforts. His administration must, nevertheless, have marked a decisive moment in the political history of the province.

The view that Judah became a distinct province independent of Samaria only at the time of Nehemiah was argued by Albrecht Alt in an important paper first published in 1934 and has been champi-

oned sporadically since then (Galling 1961, Rudolph 1949, Kellermann, McEvenue, North, et al.). Alt argued that the Assyrian province of Samaria (Samerina), formed in the eighth century B.C.E.,
maintained its identity through the Neo-Babylonian period whereas
Judah, on account of its size and the circumstances of its incorporation into the Babylonian empire, never became a distinct province.
This hypothesis, he claimed, best explains the course of events in the
Persian period down to the arrival of Nehemiah in Jerusalem, especially the silence of the sources on a governor in Judah with whom
Rehum, Tattenai, and Ezra himself had to deal. Nehemiah's achievement was to free Jerusalem from Samarian control and get himself
appointed the first governor of the province.

The problem with Alt's hypothesis is that it fails to take account
of the clear allusions in the sources to governors in Judah prior to
Nehemiah and the designation *medînāh (medîntā'),* a term used in
the Persian chancellories for a province or administrative subdivision
of a satrapy. The failure of both Tattenai and Ezra to mention the
provincial governor may be due to political unrest which resulted in
a temporary vacancy in the office. The more probable view, therefore, is that Judah was indeed an administrative unit distinct from
Samaria from the beginning of Persian rule, that as a result of the
events recorded in Ezra 4:7–23 it was placed provisionally under
Samarian control, and that Nehemiah was responsible for regaining
provincial autonomy. This would also explain more adequately the
politically inspired opposition of Sanballat and associates who had
much to lose by the unexpected turn of events in Jerusalem after
Nehemiah's arrival.

The contrast between his own conduct and that of his predecessors
is a regular feature of the apologetic genre to which the memoir
belongs. Nehemiah was himself quite capable of using forceful per-
suasion when the occasion warranted (e.g., 13:8, 25). The one specific
point is the exaction of a tax for victualing the governor's mansion
amounting to forty shekels of silver (about one pound in weight) per
diem. Nehemiah no doubt had private means which allowed him to
discontinue this exaction, though we have no reason to question the
religious motive which he adduces.

[16–18] Also in keeping with the requirements of the genre, Nehemiah lists his contributions to the common good: the rebuilding of
the city wall—allusion to "this wall" suggests that the memoir was
written in Jerusalem rather than at the imperial court; abstention
from the purchase of land, presumably the forced purchase of land
from insolvent debtors (cf. 5:3, 5, 11); keeping under control the
military detachment assigned to the governor, and even using it for

public works; in spite of entertaining lavishly, he did not draw the governor's entertainment allowance but paid all expenses out of his own pocket. The total number thus supported included the provincial bureaucracy, native and Persian (this may be the sense of "Jews and officials"), delegations and visitors from other parts of the empire, family members, acquaintances, and assorted freeloaders. The provisions listed suggest a number well in excess of one hundred and fifty (Batten 1913, 246–247, estimates six to eight hundred), unless the governor and his guests had gargantuan appetites. In any case, the amount pales in comparison with Solomon's daily provisioning, which included ten oxen, twenty cattle, and a hundred sheep (1 Kings 5:2–3 [4:22–23]). It is unclear why a special mention is made of fowl (if the reading is correct). Wild fowl of various kinds were certainly caught and eaten (e.g., Amos 3:5; Ps. 124:7; Prov. 6:5; Eccl. 9:12), but the Hebrew Bible is quite unspecific on the subject, and there is no allusion to domestic poultry (turkey, goose, duck, hen), though representations of a cock—perhaps a fighting cock—have turned up on a cooking pot at Gibeon (el-Jîb) and a seal from Tell en-Nasbeh (see *IDB* 1:656 and W. F. Badè, *ZAW* 51, 1933, 150–156).

[19] Leaving aside the short formulaic prayer directed against enemies (3:36–37 [4:4–5]; 6:14; 13:29), all other appeals to God to remember occur in the last chapter of the book (13:14, 22, 31). This may provide a further indication that the present summary of Nehemiah's career as governor belongs logically, and perhaps belonged originally, at the end of the memoir, and was transferred to this point to serve as a contrast to the behavior castigated in the previous section (5:1–13). It was perhaps inevitable that Nehemiah's anxiety that God acknowledge and reward his good works should be viewed as symptomatic of a venal and legalistic religious attitude characteristic of *Spätjudentum* (see, for example, the remark of Rudolph 1949, 133). This kind of appeal is, however, characteristic of the genre, as can be verified from ancient Near Eastern royal inscriptions (see, e.g., *ANET*, 307, 316, 317) and the Egyptian votive texts referred to earlier. And if Nehemiah's desire to be acknowledged by God is venal and self-serving, the same must be said of many of the psalms and indeed of much of Christian prayer from the beginnings down to the present.

A Campaign of Intimidation (Neh. 6:1–14)

K. Baltzer, "Das Ende des Staates Juda und die Messias-Frage," *Studien zur Theologie der alttestamentlichen Überlieferungen,* 1961, 33–43; A. Bentzen,

"Quelques remarques sur le mouvement messianique parmi les Juifs aux environs de l'an 520 avant Jésus-Christ," *RHPR* 10, 1930, 493–503; L. **Delekat**, *Asylie und Schutzorakel am Zionheiligtum,* 1967, 320–325; A. L. **Ivry**, "Nehemiah 6,10: Politics and the Temple," *JSJ* 3, 1972, 35–45; U. **Kellermann**, *Nehemia,* 21–23, 154–159; E. **Kutsch**, "Die Wurzel 'SR im Hebräischen," *VT* 2, 1952, 57–69; D. **Pardee** et al., *Handbook of Ancient Hebrew Letters,* Chico, 1982; R. **Schiemann**, "Covenanting with the Princes: Neh. vi.2," *VT* 17, 1967, 367–369.

6:1 When it came to the hearing of Sanballat, Tobiah,[a] Geshem the Arab, and the rest of our enemies that I had rebuilt the wall so that no gap remained in it—though up to that time I had not hung the doors in their gates—[2]Sanballat and Geshem sent me the following message: "Come, let us meet in Chephirim[b] in the Vale of Ono." They were planning to do me harm, [3]so I sent messengers to tell them, "I am engaged in a great task; I cannot come down. Why should the work be suspended while I leave it to come down to you?" [4]They sent me the same message four times, and I gave them the same answer. [5]On the fifth occasion Sanballat sent his servant to me in the same way, but this time bearing an unsealed letter. [6]Its contents were as follows: "It is reported among the nations, and Gashmu also is saying it,[c] that you and the Jews are planning to rebel, and it is for this reason that you are rebuilding the wall. To judge by these reports, you are to be their king, [7]and you have even set up prophets to proclaim in Jerusalem that there is a king in Judah[d]—this with reference to yourself. Word of what is going on will come to the hearing of the king. Come, therefore, let us confer together." [8]I sent him a reply saying, "None of the things of which you speak has happened; you are inventing them out of your own imagination." [9]They were all trying to intimidate us, thinking, "They will be discouraged from continuing with the work so that it will not be finished." But I strengthened my resolve the more.[e]

[10]When I entered the house of Shemaiah son of Delaiah, son of Mehetabel, as he was in seclusion,[f] he said:

"Let us meet at the house of God, inside the sanctuary,
  Let us shut the doors of the sanctuary, since they are coming to kill you,
  They are coming to kill you at night!"

[11]I answered, "Should one in my position[g] run away? Who in my position would enter the sanctuary in order to stay alive?[h] I will not go." [12]Then I realized that it was not God who had sent him; he had uttered the prophecy against me because Tobiah and Sanballat[i] had hired him. [13]It was for this purpose that he was

suborned,[j] that I should act in this way out of fear and thus commit sin, providing them with the occasion to give me a bad name[k] and thus discredit me. [14]Bear in mind, O my God, Tobiah and Sanballat on account of these their[l] deeds, as also Noadiah the prophetess and the rest of the prophets who were intent on intimidating me!

a. Often omitted as a gloss since it is the only name of the three without the preposition, and the following verse names only Sanballat and Geshem. But the preposition *(l^e)* is attested in twenty-three Hebrew MSS, Syr., and L, and v. 1 may be intended to introduce the machinations of all three.

b. The name (= Lions) is unusual but not impossible; cf. Chephirah (Tell Kefireh) further east and the Amarna letter (Knudtzon 1907–15, no. 273) written by a certain "lady of the lions" *(belit neše)* from a place near Aijalon. LXX *(en tais kōmais)* and Vulg. *(in viculis)* read *bkprym* for MT *bkpyrym*, but we would then expect "in one of the villages."

c. The omission of *gšmv* by dittography with *nšm'* finds some support in LXX, but it is safer to retain MT.

d. Or, reading *mālak* for *melek*, "He reigns in Judah!"

e. MT *v^e'attāh ḥazzēq 'et-yādāy*, "and now strengthen my hands," which suggests another short ejaculatory prayer addressed to God. On the other hand, the verb is never used with God as subject, and the other prayers of this kind in the book always invoke God explicitly. In spite of the unusual *v^e'attāh*, therefore, the verb should be read as infinitive absolute or emended to *ḥizzaqtî*, following LXX, Syr., and Vulg.

f. The obscurity of *'āsûr* does not oblige us to emend to *śākûr* (Kellermann, 180 n. 25), for which there is no support.

g. Lit., "a man like me."

h. Lit., "and live" *(vāḥāy);* see commentary.

i. The naming of Sanballat after Tobiah and the sing. verb do not necessitate the excision of Sanballat, which is unsupported by the versions.

j. MT *l^ema'an śākûr hû' l^ema'an-'îrā'* is grammatically and syntactically impossible. The most plausible suggestion is that *śākûr hû' l^ema'an 'îrā'*, "he was hired in order that I should fear," originated as an alternative reading for *śāk^erû(hû) l^ema'an 'îrā'*, "they hired him in order that I should fear."

k. Lit., "so that it would be for them a bad name."

l. MT "his deeds" *(ma^{'a}śāv)*, which does not necessitate the omission of Sanballat as a gloss; cf. v. 12.

The narrative returns to the wall-building, with another incident which threatens to delay the completion of the work. The patterning of this part of the memoir is clear. Three incidents conclude with an allusion to attempted intimidation (1–9, 10–14, 15–19), and the completion of the work is mentioned at the beginning, in the middle, and at the end (6:1, 15; 7:1). The first two (1–9, 10–14) are, however, more closely related, and are preceded and followed by a call to God to remember—the *Gedächtnismotiv* (5:19; 6:14). There is no reason to doubt their substantial authenticity as belonging to the NM.

[6:1–4] The first ruse involves Sanballat and Geshem (Gashmu) acting in concert. The opening formula (cf. 2:10, 19; 3:33 [4:1]; 4:1, 9 [7, 15]) uses an unusual passive construction which may reflect a Persian idiom (E. V. Kutscher, *Hebrew and Aramaic Studies,* Jerusalem, 1977, 70–89). For the dramatis personae see 2:10, 19; the other enemies presumably include some of those referred to earlier (4:1 [7]). The closing up of the gaps has already been mentioned (4:1 [7]), as also the final stage of hanging the wooden doors (3:1, 3, etc.), since the list of builders presupposes that the entire job had been finished. Whatever the intentions of Sanballat and Geshem, Nehemiah prudently suspected mischief, no doubt due to the proposed venue of the conference, not to mention their previous record. A site in the Vale of Ono (for the location see on Ezra 2:33 and cf. Neh. 11:35, where it is called *gēy haḥᵃrāšîm,* "the valley of craftsmen"; also see 1 Chron. 8:12, which mentions Ono and Lod with their "daughters," i.e., villages) may have been chosen for any one of several reasons. If Sanballat's family was from one of the two Beth-horons (see on 2:10), it would have been near his home territory. It may have been in a neutral zone between Ashdod and Samaria (so Alt, *KS* 2:343 n. 4) or on the border between them. We should assume that *at that time* it lay outside the territory of Judah, in spite of the presence of people from Ono in the list of repatriates, the date of which is uncertain (so M. Avi-Yonah 1966, 17–18, and Y. Aharoni 1979, 416; against E. Stern 1982, 245–249). Why they persisted in their attempt so long it is difficult to say. There is perhaps a touch of conscious humor in Nehemiah's giving work on the wall as an excuse when he knew perfectly well that their whole point was to put a stop to it (Clines 1984, 173).

[5–9] In the next stage the offensive moved into high gear with an attempt on Nehemiah's life. Sanballat's messenger brought an open letter, that is, one written on papyrus to which no seal had been affixed and which could therefore be read and its contents divulged in transit. Since it is by no means certain that the letter is quoted verbatim, nothing much is gained by comparison with the form and style of other letters which have survived from the Second Temple period. The two copies of a document, one open for immediate delivery, the other sealed for future reference, in the account of Jeremiah's purchase of real estate (Jer. 32:11–14) are also of doubtful relevance since the text in question is a contract not a letter. The report emanates from Sanballat alone but is supported by Geshem, here in the more original form of Gashm(u). It conveys to Nehemiah the news that: the rebuilding of the city wall had been widely reported among the neighboring nations; it was being interpreted as preparation for a messianic uprising focusing on the person of Nehemiah himself; this insurrection had prophetic support, and the nationalistic prophets were about to proclaim him king, if they had not done so already. It looks as if Sanballat is merely repeating the charges of Rehum and the Samarian authorities of a few years earlier in the reign, precipitated by the same kind of activity and supported by the same kind of interpretation (Ezra 4:8–16). While there was no explicit reference to the restoration of the native dynasty on that occasion, the allusion in the royal reply to the United Monarchy (v. 20) would at least indicate a connection in the mind of the redactor, if not of Artaxerxes himself. While we do not hear of prophetic endorsement on that occasion either, prophets, including Haggai and Zechariah, supported the rebuilding of the temple as a prelude to the messianic rule of the Davidide Zerubbabel (Hag. 2:6–9, 20–23; Zech. 6:9–14). According to the Masoretic reading, the prophetic proclamation runs "there is a king in Judah!" But a slightly different vocalization brings it into line with other acclamations from an earlier period: "Absalom reigns in Hebron!" (*mālak 'abšālôm bᵉḥebrôn*, 2 Sam. 15:10), "Jehu reigns!" (*mālak yēhû'*, 2 Kings 9:13)— both were usurpers, incidentally.

Not unexpectedly, Nehemiah dismissed these charges as pure fabrication. The allegations may well have been made since it is unlikely that Nehemiah would otherwise have recorded them. They would also have had a certain plausibility in view of the recent history of unrest in the province. To what extent, if at all, they were justified is quite another matter. We have no reason to believe that Nehemiah was of Davidic descent. Neither the confession of the sins of his father's house (1:6) nor the allusion to Jerusalem as the place of his ancestral sepulchers (2:3) warrants this conclusion (*pace* Kellermann). Granted, the credibility of the accusation did not necessarily depend on Nehemiah's Davidic descent since non-Davidides had risen to the throne earlier, as they would later in the days of the Hasmoneans. It seems unlikely, however, that Nehemiah would have even mentioned the accusation if there had been any truth in it. It is possible, of course, that nationalistic prophets had, on their own initiative and prompted by the rebuilding of the city's defenses, endorsed Nehemiah as king, as others had Zerubbabel during the reign of Darius. Prophetic endorsement of royal candidates, legitimate or otherwise, was a regular feature of the history of Israel from the early days of the monarchy (e.g., 1 Sam. 9–10; 1 Kings 1:32–40;

2 Kings 9:1–13), and the interval of seventy years between the completion of the temple and the fortification of the city may have been noted as significant (cf. Ezra 1:1; Hag. 1:2; Zech. 1:12). True or not, the allegation could have caused Nehemiah embarrassment or worse if it reached the central government, especially in view of the intervention of Artaxerxes in the not so distant past. If the NM was intended to serve, *inter alia,* as a report to the king, we can understand Nehemiah's anxiety to prove that the allegation was unfounded.

[**10–13**] The transition to this next episode is very abrupt. No reason is given for Nehemiah's visit to Shemaiah's house. Presumably, Shemaiah summoned him on the pretext of having a prophetic message to deliver. As stated here, the proposal does not make good sense. As governor, Nehemiah had an armed retinue at his disposal and had no need to take refuge in the temple in order to save his skin. Up to this point we have been given no indication that the situation was desperate enough for him to seek sanctuary, and in any case sanctuary did not involve entering the actual building, which was off-limits to laymen (Ex. 21:14; Num. 18:7; 1 Kings 1:50). Perhaps the incident has not been fully recorded, for whatever reason, or has been altered in the process of transmission. Its rather cryptic character has therefore encouraged a great deal of speculation: that Shemaiah was planning to designate Nehemiah as king in the sanctuary (Kellermann) or preparing to endorse a military takeover of the temple area (Ivry). Taking the episode as it stands, it is at least clear that Shemaiah wanted to get Nehemiah into the temple. Since the plot originated with Tobiah, we would be led to recall his close contacts with temple personnel (13:4–9), suggesting that Nehemiah was not expected to leave the temple alive.

Shemaiah's lineage is given, but his position and office are not clearly stated. The name itself is common and frequently attested in Levitical (e.g., 1 Chron. 9:14; 15:8; Neh. 11:15) and prophetic circles (1 Kings 12:22; Jer. 26:20; 29:4–7). There is also a Davidic descendant of that name who would have been a contemporary of Nehemiah (1 Chron. 3:22). It is possible that his family was one of those repatriated from Babylon (Ezra 2:60). The passive participle *'āṣûr,* translated "in seclusion," has provoked interminable and inconclusive discussion. It has been taken to mean that he was in a state of ritual impurity and therefore debarred from leaving his house (Bertholet 1902)—which is odd, since he proposed to do so that same day; or that his confinement was intended to symbolize Nehemiah's being shut up in the temple (Keil 1870); or that Nehemiah came upon him in an ecstatic seizure (Hölscher 1923, Mowinckel, *Studien*) or in a state of depression (Kutsch); or, finally, that it was mentioned only to explain why the governor visited him rather than the reverse (Rudolph 1949; but again, why?). The verb has the meaning to restrain, hold back, imprison, or something of the sort. Perhaps the closest parallel is the condition of the Edomite or Aramean Doeg (1 Sam. 21:8 [7]), who was "detained before YHVH" (*ne'ṣār lipnê* YHVH), presumably for some religious reason, e.g., the fulfillment of a vow or employment in a cultic function. Shemaiah is presented as a prophet. His message is described as a prophecy *(n*ᵉ*bû'āh)* and, appropriately, is set in verse or doggerel in what may well be intended as a parody of prophetic speech. In that capacity he was probably on the temple staff and therefore his house may have been in the temple precincts. This type of prophecy continued throughout the Second Temple period (Zech. 7:2–7; 8:9) but did not enjoy the best of reputations (e.g., Isa. 56:10–12; Zech. 10:2; 13:2–6). Shemaiah and other temple prophets and prophetesses (or wives of prophets), including Noadiah mentioned only here, appear then to have been part of a plot hatched in the temple precincts at the instigation or with the backing of Tobiah with the purpose of eliminating Nehemiah and thus aborting his mission.

Nehemiah's answer shows that he understood Shemaiah's message as an attempt to expose him to the charge of cowardice. But since he assumes that taking refuge in the temple would be not only cowardly but sinful, there was also inducement to sacrilege, since laypeople were forbidden under pain of death to enter the temple (Num. 18:7). While this aspect may have been added to the story by C or an editor from his circle (cf. the account of Uzziah's sin in entering the sanctuary, 2 Chron. 26:16–20; 27:2), since Nehemiah did not scruple later on to enter the temple (13:8), it fits in well enough with the episode. The Tobiah temple connection seems to have suddenly dawned on Nehemiah, leading him to the conclusion that Shemaiah was no true prophet (cf. Jer. 23:21; 28:15). The episode ends with the prayer or imprecation of the remembrance type (cf. 13:29), in which the prophetess Noadiah comes in for special mention for reasons unknown.

The Wall Completed in Spite of Opposition (Neh. 6:15–19)

J. A. Bewer, "Josephus' Account of Nehemiah," *JBL* 43, 1924, 226–227; I. Löw, "Miscellen: No. 3, TÔBŌTĀV Neh 6:19," *ZAW* 33, 1913, 154–155; R. A. Parker and W. H. Dubberstein, *Babylonian Chronology 626 B.C.–A.D. 75*, Providence, 1956; S. M. Paul, "Nehemiah 6:19—Counter Espionage," *Hebrew Annual Review* 1, 1977, 177–179.

6:15 So the wall was finished on the twenty-fifth of Elul, in the space of fifty-two days. ¹⁶When our enemies heard of it, and all the nations which surrounded us saw it,ᵃ it seemed to them a truly astonishing achievement,ᵇ and they realized that this work was our God's doing.

¹⁷At that time, moreover, many of the princes of Judah were sending letters to Tobiah,ᶜ and Tobiah's replies were coming back to them. ¹⁸For there were many in Judah who were his sworn associates, for he was the son-in-law of Shecaniah son of Arah, while Johanan his son had married the daughter of Meshullam son of Berechiah. ¹⁹They kept on singing his praises in my presence,ᵈ and reporting what I said back to him. Tobiah also sent letters with the purpose of intimidating me.

a. MT *vyr'v,* by the Masoretes understood to derive from the stem *yr',* fear, rather than *r'h,* see; a reading supported by the plene spelling in some Hebrew MSS and by LXX *(ephobēthēsan)* and other ancient versions. It also fits the common theme of the fear, wonder, bewilderment, etc., of a discomfited enemy (e.g., 1 Chron. 14:17). But on the other hand, the idea of all the nations fearing when all our enemies heard of it is forced, and the sense is considerably improved by reading "and all the nations . . . saw (it)" as a continuation of the subordinate clause, parallel with "when all our enemies heard (of it)."

b. MT reads *vayyippᵉlû mᵉʿōd bᵉʿênêhem,* lit., "and they fell very much in their eyes/sight," an idiom elsewhere unattested. A slight emendation, first proposed by Klostermann in 1896, gives *vayyippālēʾ,* it was/appeared wonderful (accepted by Siegfried 1901, 96–97; Rudolph 1949, 137; et al.); cf. the similar *mēʾēt* YHVH *hāyᵉtāh zōʾt hîʾ niplāʾt bᵉʿênēnû,* "this is YHVH's doing; it is wonderful in our sight" (Ps. 118:23).

c. The Hebrew construction is extremely awkward; lit., "the princes of Judah were increasing their letters going to Tobiah." Following LXX and Vulg. we read *rabbîm mᵉhōrê yᵉhûdāh* for *marbîm hōrê yᵉhûdāh.* The initial *m-* of *marbîm* resulted from dittography with the final *-m* of the preceding *hāhēm,* and the initial *m-* of *mᵉhōrê* lost as a result of haplography with final *-m* of *rabbîm.*

d. Lit., "also his good deeds/qualities they were saying in my presence." The suggestion, first proposed by Abraham Geiger in 1857, to emend *tôbōtāv,* and his good deeds, to *tibbōtāv,* his rumors, evil reports (from *tibbāʾ,* Aramaic equivalent of Hebrew *dibbāh*) does not improve the sense; for why should Tobiah inform Nehemiah of evil reports he was spreading about him, thus enabling him to take countermeasures? *tôbōtāv* also allows another pun (see on 2:10) on the name Tobiah.

[6:15–16] The work of rebuilding the walls was completed in the astonishingly short time of fifty-two days and in the hottest season of the year. Since Elul (only here and 1 Macc. 14:27) is the sixth month, corresponding to August-September, the work must have begun in the first week of the previous month, Ab, corresponding to late July, and continued into mid-September. More precise reckoning is speculative, and the often quoted date of October 2 for the completion, based on the Parker and Dubberstein chronology, is certainly too late. Josephus (*Ant.* 11.179) gives the much longer period of two years and four months. While the discrepancy could be due to a copyist's error in the text which he was following (Bewer), it was more probably Josephus' own doing, especially if he was thinking of the length of the city wall in his own day. It will also be recalled that he placed Nehemiah's mission in the reign of Xerxes, and his chronology of events is not even internally consistent (e.g., 11.168). There is, at any rate, nothing impossible about the fifty-two-day period. Much of the wall, especially to the south and west, only needed repairing, and there was no shortage of labor. We may compare the rather similar circumstances under which the Athenians made short work of rebuilding the city wall destroyed by the Persians (Thucydides 1.89–93; Diodorus Siculus 11.39–40; Plutarch, *Themistocles* 19).

At this point too Nehemiah records the reaction of the opposition, individuals and nations, to the progress of his mission. Perhaps unconsciously, the writer draws on the theme, familiar from hymns and prophetic sermons, of the nations being forced to acknowledge the hand of God in the fortunes of Israel (e.g., Pss. 118:23; 126:2).

[17–19] The vague temporal phrase—literally, "in those days"—which introduces the next paragraph leaves the chronology indeterminate. The exchange of correspondence and accompanying psychological warfare waged by Tobiah need not be contemporary with the rebuilding of the wall. It links up with the Shemaiah incident orchestrated by Tobiah (6:10–14) and seems to suggest a weaving together and alternating of the wall-building and opposition themes. There is no reason to exclude any of this from the NM, which certainly continued beyond 6:15 (*pace* Torrey 1910, 226–227). It was argued earlier that Tobiah's base of operations was Ammon and not Samaria, and that he may have had special responsibilities in Judah following on the earlier unsuccessful attempt to fortify Jerusalem (see on 2:10). He had close connections with leading families in Jerusalem, including that of the high priest (see on 13:4). We can reconstruct only a small part of this Tobiah network:

```
Arah (Ezra 2:5; Neh. 7:10)                    Meshezabel (Neh. 3:4)
  |                                              |
Shecaniah                                      Berechiah
  |                                              |
  ┌──────────────────────┐                       |
Shemaiah (Neh. 3:29?)  daughter  =  Tobiah     Meshullam (Neh. 3:4)
                         |                       |
                       Johanan    =            daughter
```

The presence of sworn associates—literally, "masters of the oath" *(ba‘ᵃlê šᵉbû‘āh;* cf. Akk. *bēl adē)*—in Jerusalem points to a Tobiad party with its own covenant or compact. The forming of such associations seems to have been a characteristic of the period. The bond is not simply that of blood or marriage, though he could have drawn on a considerable number of relatives among the Jerusalemite lay and priestly aristocracy for support. It might appear at first sight that they spoke well of Tobiah in the governor's presence in order to bring about a rapprochement, one which would favor Tobiah's commercial interests in the capital. While such efforts may well have been made, the reporting back and forth is interpreted as a sustained effort to undermine Nehemiah's morale and hinder his program of restoration in the province.

Jerusalem Secured (Neh. 7:1–5a)

J. Barr, "Hebrew *'ad,* especially at Job i. 18 and Neh. vii. 3," *JSS* 27, 1982, 177–188; G. R. Driver, "Forgotten Hebrew Idioms," *ZAW* 78, 1966, 4–6; P. Haupt, "Batim lo benuyim," *Johns Hopkins University Circulars* 13, 1894, 108; C. G. Tuland, "Hanani-Hananiah," *JBL* 77, 1958, 157–161.

7:1 When the wall had been rebuilt and I had hung the doors, the gatekeepers[a] were appointed. [2]I put Hanani my brother,[b] commander of the citadel, in charge of Jerusalem, for he was a more dependable and God-fearing man than most. [3]He said[c] to them, "The gates of Jerusalem are not to be left open during the hottest time of the day,[d] but while they are still on guard duty[e] they are to shut and bar[f] the gates; and dispose the inhabitants of Jerusalem in watches,[g] some at their guard posts, others opposite their houses."

[4]Now the city was wide and spacious but the people in it were few, and no houses had yet been rebuilt. [5]Then my God prompted me to convene the nobles, officers, and common people to be enrolled.

a. MT adds "and the musicians and the Levites," a scribal addition due to the fact that these classes are generally listed together, if not in this order. See commentary.

b. MT adds v^e'*et-h*^{a}*nanyāh,* an explanatory gloss, as is clear from the rest of the sentence; see Mowinckel, *Studien* II, 29; Rudolph 1949, 138; R. A. Bowman 1954, 724).

c. There is no need to emend to "I said" with Qere and some ancient versions. Hanani, the person responsible for the security of the city, is now addressing the gatekeepers.

d. Lit., "to the heat of the sun" *('ad-hōm haššemeš)*. This could mean that the gates were to remain shut until about midmorning when, depending on the season (cf. 6:15, midsummer), the sun does get hot. But this and similar phrases refer rather to the afternoon, the siesta hour (cf. Gen. 18:1 k^e*hōm hayyôm;* 1 Sam. 11:9, cf. v. 11; 2 Sam. 4:5). Since it makes no sense to open the gates only at or from that time of day, we should probably give *'ad* the alternative meaning "during" *(BDB 'ad* I 2b, II 2).

e. v^e'*ad hēm 'ōmdîm,* lit., "and until they (are) standing," often emended to v^e'*ōd hû' 'ōmēd* or v^e'*ōd hahōm 'ōmēd,* "while it (i.e., the heat) lasts," which is possible but fails to account for the pl. form of the participle, which would most naturally apply to the gatekeepers (cf. LXX and Vulg. *cumque adhuc assisterent*). If this second *'ad* is assigned the same meaning as the first, the sense could be that the gates are to be closed and secured before the guards go off duty for the siesta hour. The entire sentence remains very obscure, however, and one can only hope that the gatekeepers understood their instructions better than the modern commentators. "Standing at ease" or "standing about inactive" (cf. NEB following Driver, 5) seems somewhat farfetched and is not well supported by the parallels adduced (2 Chron. 20:17; Job 32:16).

f. For this meaning of *'ḥz,* cf. Aram. *'ḥd (BMAP* 9:13), though the meaning of the verb here and elsewhere in the papyri is not entirely clear.

g. In MT "the inhabitants of Jerusalem" is in apposition to "watches" *(mišm^e-rôt).*

[7:1–3] The NM continues in the first person. Now at last, work on the wall was really completed (cf. 6:1, 15) with the setting up of the gates. The next step was the installation of a guard or security system, accomplished by the appointment of gatekeepers. The addition of "musicians and Levites" (textual note a) is understandable since elsewhere in C, including Ezra-Nehemiah, the gatekeeper *(šô'ēr)* has a cultic function associated with the temple not the city. In the repatriation list (Ezra 2:70; cf. Neh. 7:72 [73]; Ezra 10:24; Neh. 10:29, 40 [28, 39]), gatekeepers are distinct from musicians and Levites. According to the census in Neh. 11 musicians are included among Levites but gatekeepers are not (vs. 15–21), while in the last two chapters of the book their function is clearly liturgical, they receive tithes, and are numbered among the Levites (Neh. 12:25, 45,

47; 13:55). Their Levitical status is also assumed throughout 1-2 Chronicles (e.g., 1 Chron. 9:2, 17–32; 15:18, 23–24; 16:38; 23:5; 26:1–19; 2 Chron. 23:4; 31:14; 34:13). Their duties include guarding the entrances to the temple, preserving its ritual purity, and looking after furniture and supplies. The change in their status might therefore provide a useful clue to the dating of the sources. The gatekeepers mentioned here are, of course, different. Their role is to guard the city gates, no doubt working in tandem with lookouts posted on the towers set into the walls (cf. 2 Sam. 18:26 and the metaphoric use of the term at Isa. 62:6).

The appointment of his brother Hanani (see on 1:2) was understandable but required justification in view of anticipated charges of nepotism. Surrounded as he was by people of uncertain allegiance, not to mention downright enemies, Nehemiah had to rely heavily on family members (4:17 [23]; 5:10, 14) and his *n^e'ārîm,* the armed detachment assigned to him. The translation offered here assumes that Hanani was already commander of the fortress or citadel *(bîrāh),* perhaps the temple fortress *(habbîrāh '^{a}šer labbayit)* for the rebuilding of which Nehemiah had requisitioned timber (2:8), and therefore the probable precursor of the Akra in the Hellenistic period (e.g., 1 Macc. 11:20) and Herod's Antonia fortress. This appointment represented another important step toward putting the province on a firm political footing after the disturbances which had led to Nehemiah's mission. It appears from the list of builders (the date of which is, however, uncertain) that the district administration was already in place with two civil governors for the Jerusalem region (3:9, 12). Hanani probably functioned as military governor with special responsibility for the security of the city, a situation which may also have obtained in Mizpah (3:15, 19).

Given the state of the text, we can only speculate on Hanani's instructions to his newly appointed gatekeepers. On the reading offered here, they dealt not with the regular times of opening and closing the gates, but with the couple of hours following the midday meal when vigilance would be at a low ebb. Driver appositely recalls the storming of Rome's *porta Salariana* by Alaric in 410 C.E. at midday when the guards were dozing. A further security measure consisted in drafting the few people living in the city for guard duty. Some of these were assigned to guard posts along the wall (cf. 3:1, 11, 25–27), others whose houses abutted the wall (e.g., 3:10, 20–21, 23–24, 28–31) were asked to take responsibility for the section opposite their residence. These emergency measures show that the danger of direct attack from Sanballat and his allies had not yet passed.

[4–5a] The narrative moves on to the next logical step of political consolidation, one no doubt intended from the outset: the repopulation of the city. Jerusalem had never completely recovered from the devastation at the hands of the Babylonians a century and a half earlier, and many of the common people must have fled into the countryside after the disturbances reported to Nehemiah while he was still in Susa. The result was that the space enclosed by the rebuilt wall was "wide of hands" (cf. Gen. 34:41; Ps. 104:25; 1 Chron. 4:40; etc.) but relatively empty. (See the Additional Note on Nehemiah's Jerusalem.) The statement that no houses had been (re)built cannot be taken literally, since it is contradicted by the previous verse and by other indications in Nehemiah (3:20, 29; cf. Hag. 1:4). This does not, however, oblige us to understand it metaphorically, in the sense of families or households (as Haupt, Batten 1913, Rudolph 1949, et al.). It may simply be taken to mean that only after the completion of the wall was an extensive building operation undertaken (cf. Sir. 49:13; Josephus, *Ant.* 11.181). It certainly provides no ammunition for the proponents of the chronological priority of Nehemiah.

The assembly for the purpose of taking a census provided a natural point for the insertion of the repatriation list. Nehemiah's insistence that the decision was taken under divine inspiration is perhaps intended to recall David's census represented by C as an exercise in pride inspired by Satan (1 Chron. 21:1). This first half of the verse (5a) is certainly from the NM, as is clear from the series "nobles, officers, people" (cf. 2:16; 4:8, 13 [14, 19]; 5:7), the characteristic expression "my God" (2:8, 12, 18; 5:19; 6:14), and the idea of divine prompting (2:12). The proposed census was clearly intended to serve as a basis for Nehemiah's *synoikismos,* which would lead us to expect not a list of earlier immigrants but something more like the list in Neh. 11. For the resumption of the theme introduced here and at once broken off we have to wait until Neh. 11:1.

IV

Nehemiah 7:5b–10:40 [39]

A Census of the Temple Community (Neh. 7:5b–72a [73a])

For bibliography see Ezra 2:1–67 and 2:68–3:6.

7:5b I found the genealogical record of those who had returned in the early days,[a] in which I found written the following:

[6]These are the inhabitants of the province who came up from captivity in the diaspora, whom Nebuchadnezzar king of Babylon had taken into exile.[b] They returned to Jerusalem and Judah, each to his own town.

[7]They came[c] with Zerubbabel, Jeshua, Nehemiah, Azariah,[d] Raamiah,[e] Nahamani, Mordecai, Bilshan, Mispereth,[f] Bigvai, Nehum,[g] Baanah.

The sum total of the men of the people of Israel:

[8]Descendants of Parosh, 2,172

[9]Descendants of Shephatiah, 372

[10]Descendants of Arah, 652

[11]Descendants of Pahath-moab, of the descendants of Jeshua and Joab, 2,818

[12]Descendants of Elam, 1,254

[13]Descendants of Zattu, 845

[14]Descendants of Zaccai, 760

[15]Descendants of Binnui,[h] 648

[16]Descendants of Bebai, 628

[17]Descendants of Azgad, 2,322

[18]Descendants of Adonikam, 667

[19]Descendants of Bigvai, 2,067

[20]Descendants of Adin, 655

[21]Descendants of Ater, of Hezekiah, 98

[22]Descendants of Hashum, 328[i]
[23]Descendants of Bezai, 324
[24]Descendants of Hariph,[j] 112
[25]Descendants of Gibeon, 95
[26]Men of Bethlehem and Netophah, 188[k]
[27]Men of Anathoth, 128
[28]Men of Beth-azmaveth, 42[l]
[29]Men of Kiriath-jearim, Chephirah, and Beeroth, 743
[30]Men of Ramah and Geba, 621
[31]Men of Michmas, 122
[32]Men of Bethel and Ai, 123
[33]Men of the other Nebo, 52[m]
[34]Descendants of the other Elam, 1,254
[35]Descendants of Harim, 320
[36]Descendants of Jericho, 345
[37]Descendants of Lod, Hadid, and Ono, 721
[38]Descendants of Senaah, 3,930.
[39]Priests: descendants of Jedaiah, of Jeshua's house, 973
[40]Descendants of Immer, 1,052
[41]Descendants of Pashhur, 1,247
[42]Descendants of Harim, 1,017.
[43]Levites: descendants of Jeshua, of Kadmiel, of the descendants of Hodevah,[n] 74.
[44]Musicians: descendants of Asaph, 148.
[45]Gatekeepers: descendants of Shallum, Ater, Talmon, Akkub, Hatita, Shobai, 138.
[46]Temple servants: descendants of Ziha, Hasupha, Tabbaoth,
[47]Keros, Sia,[o] Padon,
[48]Lebanah, Hagabah, Shalmai,[p]
[49]Hanan, Giddel, Gahar,
[50]Reaiah, Rezin, Nekoda,
[51]Gazzam, Uzza, Paseah,[q]
[52]Besai, Meunim, Nephushesim,[r]
[53]Bakbuk, Hakupha, Harhur,
[54]Bazlith,[s] Mehida, Harsha,
[55]Barkos, Sisera, Temah,
[56]Neziah, Hatipha.
[57]Descendants of Solomon's slaves:
Descendants of Sotai, Sophereth, Perida,[t]
[58]Jaala, Darkon, Giddel,
[59]Shephatiah, Hattil, Pochereth-hazzebaim, Amon.[u]
[60]All the temple servants and the descendants of Solomon's slaves, 392.

⁶¹These are the ones who came up from Tel Melah, Tel Harsha, Cherub, Addon,ᵛ and Immer, but were unable to declare their ancestral house and descent, as to whether they belonged to Israel: ⁶²Descendants of Delaiah, Tobiah, Nekoda, 642.

⁶³Of the priests: descendants of Hobaiah, Hakkoz, Barzillai (he had taken one of the daughters of Barzillai the Gileadite as his wife and was therefore named after them).

⁶⁴These looked up their registration in the official list but did not find it, and were therefore excluded from the priesthood. ⁶⁵His Excellency the governorʷ ordered them not to partake of the consecrated food until there should be a priest to consult Urim and Thummim.

⁶⁶The sum total of the congregation: 42,360, ⁶⁷not counting their male and female slaves, who came to 7,337. They also had 245 male and female singers,ˣ ⁶⁸⁽⁶⁹⁾435 camels, and 6,720 donkeys.

⁶⁹⁽⁷⁰⁾Now some of the heads of ancestral houses contributed to the work. His Excellency the governor contributed to the treasury a thousand gold darics, fifty bowls, and five hundred and thirty priestly vestments.ʸ ⁷⁰⁽⁷¹⁾Some of the heads of ancestral houses contributed to the treasury of the work 20,000 gold darics and 2,200 silver minas. ⁷¹⁽⁷²⁾What the rest of the people contributed amounted to 20,000 gold darics, 2,000 silver minas, and sixty-seven priestly vestments. ⁷²ᵃ⁽⁷³ᵃ⁾The priests, Levites, gatekeepers, musicians, some of the people, the temple servants, and all Israel settled in their towns.ᶻ

a. *hā'ōlîm bāri'šōnāh* cannot belong with the preceding *hayyahaś* in a construct chain; one or the other must be omitted, or possibly read *hityahaś* for *hayyahaś.*

b. Some MSS add "to Babylon" with Ezra 2:1.

c. *habbā'îm;* cf. Ezra 2:2, *'ašer bā'û.*

d. Ezra 2:2 Seraiah (Zaraios). In these notes the 1 Esdras variant is given, where relevant, in parentheses.

e. Ezra 2:2 Reelaiah (Rēsaios).

f. Ezra 2:2 Mispar (Aspharos).

g. Ezra 2:2 Rehum (Roïmos).

h. Ezra 2:10 Bani (Bani).

i. The order in Ezra 2:17–19 is different; 1 Esdras adds five names.

j. Ezra 2:18 Jorah (Ariphos).

k. Ezra 2:21–22 lists them separately with combined total of 179; 1 Esd. 5:17–18 has a total of 178.

l. Ezra 2:24 Azmaveth (Baitasmōn).

m. Ezra 2:29–32 has a different order.

n. Ezra 2:40 Hodaviah.

o. Ezra 2:44 Siaha (Sua).

p. Ezra 2:46 Shamlai; the order is different.

q. The order in Ezra 2:46–49 is different.

r. Ezra 2:50 Nephisim (Naphisi).

s. Ezra 2:52 Bazluth (Basalōth).

t. Ezra 2:55 Hassophereth (Assaphiōth), Peruda (Pharida).

u. Ezra 2:57 Ami (Amon).

v. Ezra 2:59 Addan.

w. MT *hattiršātā'*, as at Ezra 2:63.

x. Ezra 2:66 also lists 736 horses and 245 mules. The inclusion of this extra verse in RSV accounts for the difference in numbering.

y. LXX omits "five hundred." Since the hundreds usually come before the tens the emendation "thirty priestly vestments and five hundred silver minas" (supplying *kesep mānîm* before *(va)h^a mēš mē'ôt*) is often made; possible, but requiring more extensive alteration in the text than seems warranted.

z. Usually corrected following Ezra 2:70 and 1 Esd. 5:46, but see commentary.

As noted in the previous section, the next stage in the implementation of Nehemiah's policy, the repopulation of Jerusalem, is introduced at 7:4–5a and not resumed until 11:1. Thus, the large block of material 7:5b–10:40 [39], none of which is from the NM, has been inserted at this point, modifying significantly the course of the narrative in the interests of a particular editorial point of view. The *ostensible* reason for the editorial splicing in of the list at this point is to provide a demographic basis for the relocation of population to Jerusalem. In the context of the narrative strategy as a whole, however, it gives concrete expression to the *qāhāl,* the entire golah people gathered together "as a church" to hear the law and commit themselves to its observance. (See further Introduction, sect. 4.) This arrangement was suggested by the assembly in the seventh month, also introduced by the golah list, in Ezra 3. The connection is apparent in the way Ezra 3:1 has been taken over and adapted to the new context. "When the seventh month came around, and the Israelites were in their towns, all the people gathered together of one accord. . . ."

The theological significance of the list could easily be overlooked. The first part of Nehemiah (1:1–7:5a) records a time of trials and eventual triumph over opposition with the securing of the city and the reform of social ills. Only then is the entire community in its divinely ordained divisions, clerical and lay, presented as a community which obediently attends to the law and observes the festivals. This community on behalf of which God has made up his mind is constituted by repatriated Jews and those who choose to join them.

It is a community which claims legitimacy on the basis of links with the past, and one to which one can adhere, or from which one can be excluded, on the basis of a profession of faith and a level of moral performance consonant with it. Only when the existence of this "great company" (Jer. 31:8) is assured does the NM proceed with the event, of central importance in C's history, of the reconstitution of Jerusalem as an inhabited city.

It is only fairly recently in the history of Christian Old Testament scholarship that the negative estimate of the work of Ezra and Nehemiah has been set aside sufficiently to allow for other perspectives— the influence of prophecy and the restorative intent and effect of their missions as fulfilling prophecy. The twelvefold leadership of the restored community has already been noted (see on Ezra 2:1–2), and it may be in some related way significant that the total, 42,360, is divisible by twelve. Whether this points to an eschatological perspective which informed the production of the list (cf. the 144,000 of Rev. 7:1–8), even some form of "realized eschatology" (as maintained by Gunneweg 1981), in the sense that this is the saved community whose names are written in God's book (cf. Mal. 3:16), is less certain. What is certain is the intent, in all of this, to identify and embody the true "Israel of God," to give it a form and substance which would enable it to survive.

Liturgical Reading and Explanation of the Law
(Neh. 7:72b[73b]–8:12)

F. **Ahlemann,** "Zur Esra-Quelle," *ZAW* 59, 1942/43, 77–98; G. R. **Driver,** "Studies in the Vocabulary of the Old Testament, II," *JTS* 32, 1931, 251–253; M. **Fishbane,** *Biblical Interpretation in Ancient Israel,* 107–109; K. **Galling,** "Erwägungen zur antiken Synagoge," *ZDPV* 72, 1956, 163–178; M. **Gertner,** "Terms of Scriptural Interpretation: A Study in Hebrew Semantics," *BSOAS* 25, 1962, 1–17; I. **Heinemann,** "The Development of Technical Terms for the Interpretation of Scripture," *Leshonenu* 15, 1947, 108–115 (Heb.); W. Th. **In der Smitten,** *Esra,* 35–47; U. **Kellermann,** *Nehemia,* 26–28, 90–92; S. **Mowinckel,** *Studien* I, 50–59; III, 7–11, 44–61; K.-F. **Pohlmann,** *Studien zum dritten Esra,* 127–148, 151–154; H. J. **Polotsky,** "Aramäisch *pr̆s* und das Huzvaresch," *Le Muséon* 45, 1932, 273–282; H. H. **Schaeder,** *Iranische Beiträge* I, 199–202; C. C. **Torrey,** *Ezra Studies,* 252–284.

7:72b[73b] When the seventh month came around, and the Israelites had settled in their towns,[a]   8:1 all the people gathered together of one accord to the open space in front of the Water Gate. They asked Ezra the scribe to bring the book of the law of Moses which YHVH had prescribed for Israel. [2]On the first day of the seventh month, therefore, Ezra the priest brought the law before the congregation—men, women, and all those capable of understanding it[b]—[3]and read aloud from it in the open space in front of the Water Gate from dawn to midday in the presence of the men, women, and those capable of understanding. All the people listened attentively to the book of the law.[c] [4]Ezra the scribe stood on a wooden platform which had been made for the purpose,[d] and there stood by him, to his right, Mattithiah, Shema, Anaiah, Uriah, Hilkiah, and Maaseiah; and, to his left, Pedaiah, Mishael, Malchijah, Hashum, Hashbaddanah, Zechariah, and Meshullam.[e]

[5]Ezra opened the book in the sight of all the people, for he was higher than them all, and when he opened it they all rose to their feet. [6]Ezra then pronounced a blessing on YHVH the great God, and all the people responded "Amen, Amen" while raising their hands, bowing their heads, and prostrating themselves before YHVH with their faces to the ground. [7]The Levites[f] Jeshua, Bani, Sherebiah, Jamin, Akkub, Shabbethai, Hodiah, Maaseiah, Kelita, Azariah, Jozabad, Hanan, and Pelaiah instructed the people in the law while the people stayed in their place. [8]They read[g] from the book, the law of God, distinctly, rendering the meaning and expounding the recited text.[h]

[9](Nehemiah the governor[i]), Ezra the priest and scribe, and the Levites who instructed the people said to all the people, "This day is consecrated to YHVH your God; do not mourn or weep"; for they were all weeping while they listened to the words of the law. [10]Then he said to them, "Go, eat choice foods and drink sweet wine[j] and send portions to those who have nothing prepared for them, for this day is consecrated to our Lord. Do not be sad, for joy in YHVH is your strength." [11]The Levites stilled the people with the words, "Be quiet, for this day is holy. Do not be sad." [12]So all the people went off to eat, drink, and send portions, and to make a great and joyous feast, for they had understood the meaning of the things[k] which had been announced to them.

a. The verse is not in order, and the phrase *ûbᵉnê yiśrā'ēl bᵉ'ārêhem* is suspect because of the possibility of dittography with the preceding *vᵉkol-yiśrā'ēl bᵉ'ārêhem*.

b. *vᵉkōl mēbîn lišmōa'* here and *hammᵉbînîm* in the following verse are sometimes referred to Levitical instructors, but the context is speaking of those competent to participate, therefore more naturally minors and/or *gērîm;* cf. Neh. 10:29 [28]; Deut. 31:10–13; Josh. 8:5; 2 Chron. 20:13.

c. Lit., "the ears of all the people (were) to the book of the law."

d. Or "which they had made for the sermon" *(dābār);* the entire phrase is absent from LXX.

e. Meshullam, which lacks the conjunction, is missing from 1 Esd. 9:44, which has seven on the right and six on the left. Meshullam may have been added, perhaps a corrupt form of *mśmylv,* "to the left."

f. In MT "and the Levites" follows the names, but 1 Esd. 9:48 is without the conjunction, and most of the names are characteristically Levitical.

g. The pl. need not be emended to the sing., referring to Ezra (Schaeder 1930a, 52–53; Rudolph 1949, 147; Pohlmann, 133).

h. For justification of this translation of *m e pōrāš* and *śôm śekel* see commentary.

i. "Nehemiah" has been added; the verbs in this and the following verse are in the sing. The text originally read simply *hattiršātā',* later identified with Nehemiah. See commentary.

j. Lit., "sweet drinks," *mamtaqqîm,* only here and Cant. 5:16; cf. Vulg. *mulsum,* i.e., wine mixed with honey, a kind of mead.

k. Or "they had understood the words" *(hadd e bārîm).*

We saw that the issue of the repopulation of Jerusalem, introduced at Neh. 7:4–5a, is only taken up again at 11:1. This last, which refers to the leaders of the people (and they alone, understood) dwelling in Jerusalem served as a resumptive link with 7:72 [73], which, in the Nehemiah context, both concludes the list and links up with what follows. We also noted that 7:5a provided a point of entry for inserting the repatriation list, narrative continuity being maintained by the theme of assembling, taken up again after the list (8:1). The list itself was inserted, somewhat awkwardly, as an introduction to the reading of the law. The bulk of the long insertion (7:5b–10:40 [39]), therefore, consists in the reading of the law, celebration of Sukkoth, a service of repentance, and a covenant. Though these may be read as a unit with its own internal logic, only the reading of the law (ch. 8) was originally part of the Ezra material. It deals with Ezra alone, since the mention of Nehemiah at 8:9 is an addition from the time when the work of the two had been synchronized (cf. 12:26, 36). Conversely, Ezra is not mentioned in chapters 9–10. Stylistically too, Neh. 8 has little in common with the NM.

On the original location of Neh. 8 see Introduction, sect. 4. Since it is in the third person, it cannot be a verbatim extract from the Ezra memoir. This is hardly surprising, since much of the Ezra material has come to us in the third person, including the final paragraph of Ezra 8 (vs. 35–36), which at an earlier stage may have stood directly before the reading of the law. Thus Neh. 8 is either a paraphrase of a first-person account or a narrative complementary to it, not unlike Ezra 7:1–26 or 8:35–36. It would not be hypercritical to suspect a conflation of two versions or perhaps an expansion by an editor for whom the role of Ezra vis-à-vis the Levites was less important: there are distinct lists of assistants (thirteen in each list in the present state of MT), both Ezra and the Levites are said to read the law (vs. 3, 8), and both exhort the congregation to put aside sadness (vs. 9, 11). These indications will be discussed more fully in the commentary.

A question much less often asked than that of the original location of the passage is the reason for its relocation to this point in the Nehemiah story. One possibility is that the text originally referred to the presence of an unnamed governor (*tiršātā',* 8:9; cf. 7:65, 69 [70]), who was later mistakenly identified with Nehemiah, since the term is also used of him (10:2 [1]). This error then necessitated the removal of the passage to a point in time after Nehemiah's arrival on the scene. 1 Esd. 9:49, in which the people are addressed by a certain Attharates, certainly a corruption of *hattiršātā',* would seem to support this supposition. More probably, however, the identification with Nehemiah was made *after* the incident had been relocated, part of the process of linking the work of the two leaders and thus (as we have argued) discreetly covering over the failure of Ezra's marriage policy. The later expansion of the role of Levites in the ceremony may have been dictated by the same considerations.

The public reading and explanation of the law is represented as a one-time event which took place on a specific date—the first of Tishri, and at a specific location—the open space in front of the Water Gate. Not unexpectedly, however, doubts have been raised about the historical reality behind the description. One difficulty, already alluded to, is the simultaneous presence of Ezra and Nehemiah. Commentators have also detected in it elements of a religious service: the assembling of the congregation, procession with the Torah scroll, the people standing when the book is opened, recital of a blessing *(berākāh),* the repeated Amen of the congregation with the raising of hands and prostration in prayer, *lectio divina* and explanation (sermon), and finally the dismissal. That it reflects an early form of synagogue worship has often been suggested (e.g., Galling, In der Smitten, Kellermann), but unfortunately we know nothing of the conduct of synagogue worship before the Roman period, and some essential elements seem to be missing. More generally, it embodies some of the characteristics of worship as described by C, e.g., the need to rejoice and the teaching role of Levites. The overall sequence in Neh. 8–10 is quite similar to the ceremony described as taking place during the reign of Josiah following on the discovery of the law book: a plenary gathering in Jerusalem, public reading of the law, and sealing of commitment to observance by a

covenant (2 Chron. 34:29–32). The connection with Booths (Sukkoth) could have been suggested by the stipulation that the law be
read publicly during that festival every seventh year (Deut. 31:9–13).
We may therefore conclude that Neh. 8:1–12 is a free composition
of an editor, either C or one from the same milieu, which reflects
different facets of liturgical praxis during the Second Commonwealth.

[7:72b–8:1] On this opening phrase see the commentary on Ezra
3:1. The first day of Tishri (September-October), corresponding to
New Year's Day *(rō'š haššānāh),* is designated in Priestly legislation
as "the day of the trumpet blast" *(yôm t^erû'āh)* and "a holy convocation" *(miqrā'-qōdeš)* (Lev. 23:23–25; Num. 29:1–6). It was therefore
a day well chosen for a new beginning. The year is not given. In its
present context it would be the seventh month of Nehemiah's first
year in office (445), following on the sixth month toward the end of
which the rebuilding of the wall was completed (6:15). In its original
context, however, it would have followed the fifth month during
which Ezra arrived in Jerusalem (Ezra 7:8) and preceded the ninth
month during which the assembly convoked to dissolve foreign marriages took place (Ezra 10:9). It is extremely unlikely, as we have
seen, that Ezra would have waited more than twelve years to promul-
gate and explain the law. It is even less probable that he withdrew
to Babylon and then returned with Nehemiah in 445 B.C.E.

The assembly took place in the plaza connected with Jerusalem's
Water Gate, on the east side of the city opposite the temple area (see
3:26). It is perhaps significant that it took place here rather than in
the temple area (where 1 Esd. 9:38 locates it). Though the editor has
given it a strongly religious and liturgical coloring, the public promulgation and explanation of traditional law is entirely in keeping
with Persian policy, expressed in the firman of Artaxerxes. It is also
not the only instance in the Ezra narrative where the initiative comes
not from Ezra himself but from the laity. On the identity of the law
read and explained by Ezra and his associates see the Additional
Note on Ezra's Law.

[8:2–4] In this first part of the account we hear only of the leadership role of Ezra accompanied by thirteen assistants, presumably
laymen since they are not otherwise identified. Only later do the
Levites have a role to play. We may therefore suspect a combination
of two narrative layers. In the first and presumably earlier one Ezra
reads the law (3), he is assisted by thirteen laymen (4), and it is he
who admonishes the people not to be sad (9). In the second and later
strand the Levites both read and explain the law (8), there are
thirteen of them (7), and it is they who issue the final admonition

(11). In view of the importance which C attaches to the teaching and liturgical roles of Levites (for the former see especially 2 Chron. 17:7–9; 35:3), one would be tempted to assign this expanded version either to C himself or a later editor sharing the same enthusiasm for the Levitical office.

It is interesting to note that women and children, at least those children old enough to understand what was going on, are included in the congregation (cf. Deut. 31:10–13; 2 Chron. 20:13; Neh. 10:28–29 [27–28]). Nothing certain can be concluded as to the identity of the law scroll from the duration of the reading, presumably five or six hours, since Ezra read *from* it. The wooden platform (lit., "tower") does not correspond to the *bemah* of the synagogue since it had to accommodate at least fourteen people. It would have been closer in size to the bronze platform, more than four feet high and seven feet square, occupied by Solomon during the dedication of the temple according to C (2 Chron. 6:13). Not much is to be gained from a study of the names of the assistants. The temptation to reduce them to twelve should probably be resisted since (1) it is without textual support, (2) there are also thirteen Levites, and (3) one of them may have been the leader, thus obtaining a twelvefold group either way. It is perhaps worth noting that only one of these names of laymen occurs in the golah list (Hashum, Neh. 7:22), and only four are among the signatories to the covenant of Neh. 10 (Anaiah, Maaseiah, Hashum, Meshullam). We are reminded once again that the impetus for the reforms of Ezra and Nehemiah seems to have come primarily from the laity, a fact to some extent obscured by later editing.

[5–8] Out of respect for the law, the congregation stood during the reading. The blessing was probably of the kind found in C (e.g., 1 Chron. 16:36; 2 Chron. 6:4), beginning "Blessed art thou, YHVH God of Israel . . ." and giving the reason for the blessing in a relative clause following. This and similar liturgical forms must have achieved a degree of fixity during the years of exile and the period of restoration. The raising of the hands during prayer (cf. Ps. 28:2; Ezra 9:5), the prostration or *proskynēsis* (Ezra 9:5; 10:1), the invocation of "the great God" (Deut. 10:17; Jer. 32:18; Neh. 1:5; 9:32; *AP* 72:15) all reflect aspects of liturgical practice. Of the greatest importance historically is the veneration accorded to the law in the context of an act of worship, a factor which must be taken into account in any discussion of canonicity.

As already noted, at this point we begin to get a rather different picture of the proceedings. In vs. 1–4 Ezra reads the scroll surrounded by a group of laymen on a raised dais. There is nothing liturgical about the event which takes place in a secular location. From now on, however, the description is of an explicitly liturgical event. Ezra opens the book (from which he had already read), there is the blessing, the Amen, and the Levites take over the reading and interpretation of the law. The list of thirteen Levites has every appearance of having been put together out of other easily available lists: nine (including repetitions) of the sixteen Levitical signatories to the covenant (Neh. 10), and eight of the sixteen at the service of repentance (9:4–5), are represented here. They perform the task of instruction familiar from C, for whom it is also important that the people stay in their liturgical station (cf. 2 Chron. 30:16; 34:31; 35:10). What exactly the Levites did at this point depends on the meaning assigned to the Hebrew word *mᵉpōrāš,* from a verbal stem *prš* meaning divide, separate, specify (passive participle agreeing with *hassēper,* the book). Later Jewish tradition found here the biblical origin of the scriptural targum. According to *b. Meg.* 3a, "they read in the book, in the law of God" refers to the Hebrew text; *mᵉpōrāš,* "with an interpretation," indicates the targum; "they gave the sense" refers to the verse stops; and "they caused them to understand the reading" refers to the accentuation or the Masoretic notes which had been forgotten and were now reestablished. Leaving aside the backdating of the Masoretes, some modern exegetes have endorsed this interpretation, relating it to early Iranian chancellory praxis (Schaeder, Polotsky). Another option is that the Levites read the text section by section, thus anticipating the Masoretic *perashot* (Bertholet 1902, 69). While there is probably some truth in both of these interpretations, it seems safer to take it in the more general sense indicated by the adverb "distinctly," i.e., implying "care for the exact pronunciation, intonation, and phrasing, so as to make the units of the piece and its traditional sense readily comprehensible" (Fishbane, 109). The following phrase "rendered the meaning" *(śôm śekel)* would therefore serve to make this somewhat more explicit, while the final *vayyābînû bammiqrā'* would indicate the quite distinct procedure of interpreting the passage just read. Whatever conclusion is reached on the historicity of the narrative, we have here invaluable information on the study, interpretation, and teaching of Torah in the centuries preceding the emergence of Pharisaic scribalism.

[9–12] As the sing. verb in vs. 9 and 10 suggests, the admonition was delivered by Ezra alone in the earlier form of the narrative. Nehemiah the governor and the Levites were added at a later stage. The day, the first of the seventh month, is a day of "holy convocation" to which any manifestation of grief is foreign. It is remarkable how often Ezra-Nehemiah, generally thought to be gloomy and jejune, reports demonstrations of anger, grief, and joy. The reason for the weeping and mourning in this instance is the sense of inadequacy and failure vis-à-vis the law and the threat posed by the curses appended to it. We may compare the reaction of King Josiah when the newly discovered law was read to him (2 Kings 22:11). The admonition is to put aside sadness and enjoy the good fare and fellowship associated with the festal sacrifices (cf. Num. 29:2–6). The theme of rejoicing, closely associated with worship in Deuteronomic-Chronistic preaching (e.g., Deut. 12:12; 14:26; 2 Chron. 29:36; 30:25), is rounded off with a psalmlike asseveration: joy in YHVH is your strength. The word for "joy" *(ḥedvāh)* occurs only here and in a psalm cited by C (1 Chron. 16:27)—a different word is used in the variant Ps. 96:6:

> Honor and majesty are before him,
> Strength and joy are in his place.

The passage ends, therefore, on a note which calls into question the indictment—so often repeated in the modern period—of early Judaism as fearful and joyless.

Celebration of the Feast of Booths (Neh. 8:13–18)

M. **Fishbane**, *Biblical Interpretation in Ancient Israel,* 109–113; A. S. **Kapelrud**, *The Question of Authorship in the Ezra-Narrative,* 80–94; F. **Mezzacasa**, "Esdras, Nehemias y el Año Sabatico," *RevBibl* 23, 1961, 1–8, 82–96; J. **Morgenstern**, "Studies in Calendars," *HUCA* 10, 1935, 70; A. **Pavlovský**, "Die Chronologie der Tätigkeit Esdras. Versuch einer neuer Lösung," *Bib* 38, 1957, 273–305, 428–456; H. H. **Schaeder**, *Esra der Schreiber,* 7–15, 20–26; A. C. **Welch**, *Post-exilic Judaism,* Edinburgh and London, 1935, 262–275.

8:13 When, on the second day, the heads of ancestral houses of all the people, with the priests and the Levites, came together to Ezra to study the stipulations of the law, [14]they found it written in the law which YHVH had prescribed through Moses[a] that the Israelites should dwell in booths during the festival of the seventh month. [15]They were also to make[b] the following announcement and proclamation throughout all their towns and in Jerusalem: "Go out into the hills and fetch branches of olive, pine,[c] myrtle, palm, and other trees in leaf to make booths, as it is written." [16]So the people went out, fetched them, and made booths for themselves, each on his own roof, in their courtyards, in the courts of the house of God, in the square of the Water Gate and the

Ephraim Gate. [17]All the assembly of those who had returned from captivity made booths and dwelt in them. The Israelites had not done so from the days of Joshua[d] to that time; so there was very great rejoicing. [18]Each day, from the first day to the last, the book of the law of God was read.[e] They kept the feast for seven days, and on the eighth day there took place a closing ceremony according to the ordinance.

a. Taking *'ašer sivvāh* YHVH *b^eyad-mōšeh* as a subordinate adjectival clause rather than a noun clause; cf. the parallel at 8:1.
b. There is no reason to excise *'ašer,* reading "and they made the following announcement. . . ." See commentary.
c. Lit., "oil tree" *('ēs šemen),* hence often translated "wild olive."
d. MT has *yēšûa',* "Jeshua."
e. Reading *vayyiqārē'* for MT *vayyiqrā',* "he read." The antecedent, Ezra, is too far distant from the verb.

This account of the celebration of Sukkoth continues and concludes C's Ezra narrative. As noted earlier (Introduction, sect. 4), such liturgical occasions are structurally important in the history as a whole:

1. Dedication of the First Temple—Booths (2 Chron. 5–7)
2. Completion of Hezekiah's reforms—Passover (2 Chron. 30)
3. Completion of Josiah's reforms—Passover (2 Chron. 35:1–19)
4. Conclusion of the first return—Booths (Ezra 3:1–4)
5. Completion of the Second Temple—Passover (Ezra 6:19–22)
6. Completion of Ezra's reforms—Booths (Neh. 8:13–18)

The parallelism between the first Passover after the return and those of Hezekiah and Josiah (see on Ezra 6:19–22) is matched by the parallelism between Solomon's celebration of Booths (especially 2 Chron. 7:8–10) and the present passage: the entire *qāhāl* participates, there is a closing ceremony *('^aseret)* on the eighth day, and the entire festival is marked by general rejoicing. It was also noted that, in describing the festivals of Hezekiah, Josiah, and Ezra, the author refers back to earlier occasions: Hezekiah back to Solomon (2 Chron. 30:26), Josiah back to Samuel (2 Chron. 35:18), and now Ezra back to Joshua (8:17). The implied analogy between Joshua and Ezra as leader of a new occupation guaranteed by observance of the law newly promulgated fits the typological pattern which we have noted at several points in the narrative to date.

[8:13] The date is the second of Tishri, following the first day of that month on which the law was read (8:2). The reading and study of the law on these two days does not correspond to any extant stipulation of law. The gap of twelve days between the discovery of the law about Sukkoth and the beginning of the festival itself on the fifteenth of the month (Lev. 23:33; Num. 29:12) highlights the omission of the Day of Expiation (Yom Kippur) which Pentateuchal legislation prescribes for the tenth of the month (Lev. 16:29–34; 23:26–32; Num. 29:7–11). Some have suggested that Ezra may have celebrated Sukkoth from the third to the tenth or shifted Yom Kippur from the tenth to the twenty-fourth (9:1). But it will be obvious that there is not enough time for an eight-day festival from the third to the tenth (in reality, the ninth), and time must also be allowed for the collection of the flora stipulated by the law. There is also no obvious reason why the observance should have been postponed. The most likely explanation, therefore, is that Yom Kippur had not yet attained a firm place in the liturgical calendar, though the practice of a fast some time in the seventh month, attested for the early Persian period (Zech. 7:5; 8:19), may be seen as a step in that direction. This inconsistency between the historical narrative in Ezra-Nehemiah and Pentateuchal law is one of several indications that the latter had not yet attained its final form.

The public reading of the law is followed by a study session or seminar limited to the lay and clerical leadership. Mention in this connection of the heads of ancestral houses (see on Ezra 1:5) provides another indication that the clerical monopoly of legal expertise, obviously an important aspect of social control, was already being breached by the laity. Their educational role, already emphasized in Deuteronomy (e.g., 6:7), may be seen as a remote preparation for the Pharisees, and indeed for the essentially lay character of Judaism as it took shape throughout the Second Temple period.

[14–15] The opening expression, "they found it written in the law," already appears to function as a formulaic introduction to a biblical quotation (Fishbane, 109–110). Of the Pentateuchal laws concerning Sukkoth (Ex. 23:16; 34:22; Lev. 23:33–43; Num. 29:1–38; cf. Ezek. 45:25) the only one which prescribes dwelling in booths is found in the Holiness Code (Lev. 23:42). Either some part or all of this collection was, therefore, in some form, considered part of Mosaic law at that time. The same law prescribes that on the first day of the festival the people shall take "the fruit of splendid (myrtle?) trees, branches of palms, boughs of trees in leaf, and willows of the stream" (Lev. 23:40). It does not say what is to be done with them, but later attestations confirm that the four species (palm, myrtle, willow, citrus fruit) were carried in procession (2 Macc. 10:7; Jose-

phus, *Ant.* 3.245; 13.372; *m. Sukk.* 4:1–7). Since, however, the law
goes on to prescribe dwelling in booths (Lev. 23:42), the Ezra seminar inferred that the branches were to be used to cover *(skk)* the
lean-to or shanty serving to commemorate the wandering in the
wilderness. We can therefore observe the process by which a new
law, prescribing the making of booths out of these materials, is
generated by inference from an old law and endowed with the same
authority ("as it is written," v. 15).

The law in Lev. 23:40 does not speak of a public proclamation (cf.
Ezra 1:1; 10:7) and has only two of the species mentioned at Neh.
8:15 (palm, tree in leaf). The "oil tree" (see textual note c) is probably
a member of the pine or cypress family (M. Zohary, *IDB* 2:293–294).

[16–17] We are not told whether the execution of the command
followed at once. It would not have to, since there was an interval
of twelve days before the beginning of the festival. The location
suggests an occasion which was both domestic and civil. The erection
of some of the booths in the temple precincts is sometimes taken to
imply a conscious allusion to the Deuteronomic law of centralized
observance (Deut. 16:15), but the Holiness Code (Lev. 23:40) also
speaks of festal rejoicing "before YHVH your God," namely, at the
sanctuary. The choice of the Water Gate (see 3:26) and the Ephraim
Gate may also point in the same direction, since the former was along
the eastern wall opposite the temple area, while the latter, situated
about two hundred yards from the Corner Gate (2 Kings 14:13), was
in the northern wall, also in close proximity to the temple.

Characteristic of C is the participation of the totality of Israel, and
for him the Israel of that time is embodied in "all the assembly
(qāhāl) of those who had returned from captivity" (cf. Ezra 2:1; 3:8;
6:21; 8:35) or, more succinctly, "the exile assembly" (*qᵉhal haggôlāh*,
Ezra 10:8, 12, 14). The statement that it had not been done *in this
manner* since the time of Joshua must be taken programmatically
rather than literally, as in the other instances where this kind of
formula is used in C (2 Chron. 30:26; 35:18). It implies a correspondence between Ezra's aliyah and the exodus from Egypt, and between return to the homeland of the deportees and Joshua's
occupation of the land. The reader is therefore invited to think of
Joshua's assembly at Shechem in the course of which statutes and
ordinances were made and written and the people rededicated itself
to the service of YHVH (Josh. 24). If, therefore, we are to look for
any historical innovation, it is not in the celebration of the festival
itself, which was already well established (e.g., Judg. 21:19; 1 Sam.
1:3; Hos. 12:9; Zech. 14:16), or even in the dwelling in booths,
implied in the very name of the festival (Deut. 16:13, 16), but in the

use of the species to construct and cover the *sukkāh*. The festive joy which marked the occasion (cf. Deut. 16:13–15; Lev. 23:40), and the pilgrim feasts in general (e.g., Ezra 6:22), is another reminder of the character of religious life at that time which can so easily be overlooked.

[18] According to the later calendric ordinances (Lev. 23:33–36; Num. 29:35), Sukkoth lasted from the fifteenth to the twenty-second of Tishri, the last day being reserved for the closing ceremony *(ᵃṣeret)*. C follows the same dispositions for the festival in the course of which the First Temple was dedicated (2 Chron. 7:8–10; the parallel 1 Kings 8:64–66 does not speak of a closing ceremony), and it is worth noting that the phrase "each day" *(yôm bᵉyôm)* occurs only in C and the Ezra narrative (1 Chron. 12:22; 2 Chron. 8:13; 24:11; 30:21; Ezra 3:4; 6:9). The reading and study of Torah throughout the festal week recalls Deut. 31:10–13, which, however, prescribes the reading only in the seventh year. If we could be sure that 458 B.C.E. coincided with the year of release or *šᵉmiṭṭāh* (Morgenstern, Pavlovský, Mezzacasa), the matter would be neatly solved, but such calculations do not inspire confidence. It is still possible that with respect to the reading of the law the account reflects a well-established practice in the liturgical life of Israel. Whatever the actual situation may have been, the connection between law and worship, mirrored in psalms and prayers expressive of early Jewish piety, is a datum of central importance for understanding the age of Ezra and Nehemiah and of the Second Commonwealth in general.

A Penitential Service (Neh. 9:1–5)

F. Ahlemann, "Zur Esra-Quelle," *ZAW* 59, 1942/43, 77–98; E. Sellin, *Geschichte des israelitisch-jüdischen Volkes* II, Leipzig, 1932, 140, 160.

9:1 On the twenty-fourth day of the same month,[a] the Israelites convened for a fast, wearing sackcloth and with earth on their heads.[b] [2]Those of Israelite stock[c] separated themselves from all foreigners. They stood and confessed their sins and the iniquities of their ancestors. [3]Standing in their place, they read from the book of the law of YHVH their God for a quarter of the day, and for another quarter they confessed their sins and worshiped YHVH their God. [4]On the raised podium of the Levites there were standing[d] Jeshua, Bani, Kadmiel, Shebaniah, Bunni, Sherebiah, Bani,[e] and Chenani. These cried out aloud to YHVH their God. [5]The Levites Jeshua, Kadmiel, Bani, Hashabneiah, Sherebiah, Hodiah,

Shebaniah, and Pethahiah said, "Arise and bless YHVH your God":

From age to age
May they bless your glorious name[f]
Exalted beyond every blessing and praise!

a. Lit., "this month."
b. Lit., "on them" (*ᵃlêhem).*
c. Lit., "the seed of Israel" *(zera' yiśrā'ēl).*
d. The verb *(vāyyāqom)* is in the sing.
e. Or, perhaps, Binnui; the names are easily confused and the redactor, who was probably not working under strict historical constraints, would not have repeated a name. LXX[A] has "sons of . . ." (*bᵉnê* . . .) for both occurrences.
f. *vîbārᵉkû* also permits the translation "may your glorious name be blessed" (impersonal pl. for passive), but need not be emended to either passive participle *(bārûk)* or third-person imperfect Pual *(vayᵉbōrak).* For the arrangement of this verse see commentary.

The much-discussed question of the historical and chronological situation of this episode naturally depends on the results of literary analysis—on which, as so often in Ezra-Nehemiah, the adage *tot capita quot sententiae* applies. Much has been made of the change from rejoicing to mourning and fasting, a change which, following the overt chronology of Neh. 8–9, took place in the course of a single day, since Sukkoth ended on the twenty-second and the penitential service began on the twenty-fourth of the month (see, for example, Torrey 1895, 31–33). A complicating factor is the unexpected severance from foreigners, which has persuaded some commentators that Neh. 9 is the natural sequel to Ezra 9–10 (e.g., Rudolph 1949, 154), and others that it is the natural preface to Neh. 13:1–3 (Sellin). The variation on the former of these alternatives, according to which Neh. 9 is to be spliced in between Ezra 10:15 and 10:16, is vitiated by the quite arbitrary emendation of *'al-zō't* to *'al-ṣôm,* conveniently crediting the two individuals mentioned at Ezra 10:15 with the request for a fast (Ahlemann).

A close reading of this passage reveals a striking parallelism with the public reading of the law in the previous chapter (8:1–12). There is the assembly of the congregation *(vayyē'ās̄ᵉpû,* 8:1; *ne'espû,* 9:1), the public reading of the law, the ceremony in both cases occupying the same space of time (8:3; 9:3), the Levites operating from a raised platform during the ceremony (8:4; 9:4), the people on their feet (8:5; 9:3) and in their place (8:7; 9:3), and the pronouncement of a blessing. This extensive overlap suggests that 9:1–5a incorporates a parallel version of 8:1–12, one in which Ezra is conspicuous by his absence. It will be recalled that the analysis of 8:1–12 suggested a conflation of two strands, one featuring Ezra and lay assistants, the other emphasizing the role of Levites. The present passage appears to be related to the latter, and the penitential service may have been suggested by the allusions to mourning and weeping in the account of the public reading of the law (8:9, 11).

[9:1] Sukkoth was celebrated from the fifteenth to the twenty-second of Tishri. The interval of one day between the conclusion of the festival and the penitential service, rather than existing liturgical praxis, may adequately explain the date assigned to the latter. A fast in the seventh month is attested from the early Persian period (Zech. 7:5; 8:19), one of several commemorating the destruction of Jerusalem, the burning of the temple, and subsequent disasters (2 Kings 25:8–9, 25; Jer. 41:1). Whether there is any connection between this observance and Yom Kippur we do not know, but it is possible that the date of the latter was originally indeterminate and only later fixed on the tenth of the month (Lev. 16:29; 23:27). It remains, at any rate, historically implausible that the joyful celebration of Sukkoth—a climactic event, as we have seen—should be followed within a few hours by fasting and mourning. In the preexilic period fasting was occasional, accompanying either public disaster (e.g., Jer. 14:1–12) or private misfortune (e.g., 2 Sam. 12:15–23). Only after the fall of Jerusalem did it begin to find a regular place in the liturgical calendar. In keeping with the symbolism of diminution and death, the wearing of sackcloth (e.g., Job 1:21; Joel 1:8, 13; Jonah 3:5, 8) represented the shroud in which the corpse was wrapped, and the sprinkling of earth on the head (e.g., Josh. 7:6; 1 Sam. 4:12; 2 Sam. 1:2; Job 2:12) stood for burial in the earth. The danger of routine and insincerity associated with these practices, alluded to in the New Testament (Matt. 6:16–18), was in evidence much earlier, as can be seen in the sermon on true fasting in Isa. 58:3–9. The present allusion, therefore, as brief as it is, probably reflects contemporary practice, as elsewhere in C's opus (e.g., the fast proclaimed by Jehoshaphat, also followed by a prayer of petition, 2 Chron. 20:3–12).

[2] The separation from foreigners has proved to be the most recalcitrant aspect of a passage bristling with problems. It inevitably recalls Ezra 9–10, which uses the same verb for separation *(bdl)*, speaks of the community as a "holy seed," and features fasting accompanied by a confessional prayer. There is, however, one important difference, often overlooked—namely, that the present passage speaks of foreigners in general rather than foreign women, in which

respect it anticipates Neh. 13:1–3 rather than repeating Ezra 9–10. Perhaps the simplest explanation is that those of foreign descent who, according to Deut. 16:14, participated in Sukkoth (though according to Lev. 23:42 they did not dwell in booths), could not be expected to identify with the collective and cumulative sin of Israel confessed in the prayer which follows. In the same way the dwelling in booths was restricted to the native-born *('ezrāḥîm)* since only they shared in this particular aspect of the tradition.

[3] The third element in the narrative, besides penitential ritual and exclusion of foreigners, is the reading of the law, which, as noted earlier, parallels Neh. 8:1–12. Here, as in 8:3, the time is probably from early morning to midday, with the difference that it is now divided between the reading and confession of sin, perhaps a more liturgically precise restatement of the mourning and weeping which accompanied the reading in the earlier passage. The suggested elision of this verse as an editorial attempt to align the incident with the preceding one (Rudolph 1949, 156) misses the point that the passage in its entirety is a recapitulation of themes in the Ezra narrative.

[4–5] In the preceding account of the reading of the law the podium or dais was occupied by Ezra and his thirteen assistants (8:4) balanced, in the final form of the narrative, by a group of thirteen Levites. In the present incident eight Levites occupy the raised position and intone the liturgy. But there immediately follows another list of eight Levites (only two in LXX) who issue the invitation to prayer and presumably go on to lead it. Since five of these, including the three leaders Jeshua, Bani, and Kadmiel (cf. 10:9; 12:8), are also in the preceding list, it seems reasonable to conclude that the lists were originally identical (as, for example, Torrey 1910, 279–280), and that the differences have arisen in the course of transmission. Even on the improbable assumption of historicity, it seems unlikely that the names of participants would have been recorded, and even less likely (as the ancient versions attest) that they would have been transmitted without error. The main point is that the Levites took the lead in calling to the liturgy of repentance and, as the text now stands, in intoning the psalm. It should be noted, however, that the three psalm verses which follow are of a type which belongs not to the beginning but to the end of a liturgical psalm (see especially Pss. 41:14 [13]; 106:48; also Pss. 45:18 [17]; 72:19; 89:53 [52]; 115:18). It would therefore be reasonable to conclude that they are quite distinct from the long confessional prayer which begins at v. 6. Since the only example of a similar formulation at the beginning of a psalm or prayer occurs in

C's history (1 Chron. 29:10: "Blessed are you, YHVH, God of Israel our father, from age to age"), it may also be suggested that the present arrangement of the text is the work of C.

A Confessional Prayer (Neh. 9:6–37)

P. R. **Ackroyd,** "God and People in the Chronicler's Presentation of Ezra," in J. Coppens (ed.), *La notion biblique de Dieu,* Leuven, 1976, 149–162; M. **Baillet,** "Un recueil liturgique de Qumran, Grotte 4: Les Paroles des Luminaires," *RB* 68, 1961, 195–250; F. C. **Fensham,** "Neh. 9 and Pss. 105, 106 and 136: Post-exilic Historical Traditions in Poetic Form," *JNSL* 9, 1981, 35–51; M. **Gilbert,** "La place de la loi dans la Prière de Néhémie 9," in J. Doré et al. (eds.), *De la Tôrah au Messie. Melanges Henri Cazelles,* Paris, 1981, 307–316; W. Th. **In der Smitten,** *Esra,* 47–51; U. **Kellermann,** *Nehemia,* 32–37; L. J. **Liebreich,** "The Impact of Nehemiah 9:5–37 on the Liturgy of the Synagogue," *HUCA* 32, 1961, 227–237; S. **Mowinckel,** *Studien* I, 50–59; O. **Plöger,** "Reden und Gebete im deuteronomistischen und chronistischen Geschichtswerk," *Aus der Spätzeit des Alten Testaments,* Göttingen, 1971, 50–66; G. **von Rad,** "The Levitical Sermon in I and II Chronicles," *The Problem of the Hexateuch and Other Essays,* New York, 1966, 267–280; M. **Rehm,** "Nehemia 9," *BZ* n.F. 1, 1957, 59–69; E. **Sellin,** *Geschichte des israelitisch-jüdischen Volkes* II, Leipzig, 1932; G. Vermes, *The Dead Sea Scrolls in English,* Harmondsworth, 1962, 202–205; A. C. **Welch,** "The Source of Nehemiah ix," *ZAW* 47, 1929, 130–137; *Post-exilic Judaism,* Edinburgh, 1935, 26–46.

9:6 You, O YHVH, are the only God, [a, b]
You made the heavens, the uttermost heavens, and all their host,
The earth, and all that is on it,
The seas, and all that is in them.
You preserve them all, and the host of heaven worships you.

[7]You are YHVH, the God who chose Abram,
Who brought him out from Ur of the Chaldeans
And assigned him the name Abraham.
[8]When you found his heart to be faithful to you
You made a covenant with him
To give to his descendants the land of the Canaanites,
Hittites, and Amorites,
The Perizzites, Jebusites, and Girgashites;
And you kept your promise, because you are just.

[9]You saw the misery of our ancestors in Egypt
And heard their cry at the Red Sea. [c]
[10]You wrought signs and wonders against Pharaoh,

Against his servants, and all the people of his land,
For you knew how insolently they had treated them,
So you made a name for yourself, which lasts to this day.
¹¹You split the sea before them,
They passed through the sea as on dry land,
But their pursuers you cast into the depths
Like a stone in mighty waters.

¹²With a column of cloud you led them by day,
With a column of fire by night,
To light for them the way in which they should journey.
¹³On Mount Sinai you came down and spoke with them from
heaven,
You gave them just ordinances, true laws, good statutes and
commandments.
¹⁴You made known to them your holy sabbath,
You prescribed for them commandments, statutes, and a law
through Moses your servant.
¹⁵You gave them food from heaven to appease their hunger,
You drew water from the rock to appease their thirst,
You told them to come and take possession of the land which you
had sworn ᵈ to give them.

¹⁶But they, our ancestors, ᵉ acted insolently, they were obdurate ᶠ
And would not obey your commandments.
¹⁷They refused to obey, unmindful of the wonders which you
performed among them;
They were obdurate, ᶠ appointing a leader ᵍ in order to return to
their bondage in Egypt. ʰ
But you are a forgiving God, gracious and merciful, long-suffer-
ing and abounding in faithful love;
So you did not abandon them.
¹⁸Even when they made for themselves a molten calf
And said, "This is your god who brought you up from Egypt,"
Holding you in great contempt,
¹⁹You, in your mercy, did not abandon them in the wilderness,
The column of cloud did not cease to guide them on their journey
by day,
Nor the column of fire by night, lighting them on the way they
should go.
²⁰You gave your good Spirit to instruct them,
You did not withhold your manna from their mouth,
And you gave them water to appease their thirst.

[21]For forty years you sustained them in the wilderness where they
  lacked for nothing;
Their clothes did not wear out and their feet did not swell.

[22]You gave them kingdoms and peoples, allotting them as a boundary;[i]
They took possession of the land of Sihon[j] king of Heshbon and
  the land of Og king of Bashan.
[23]You made their descendants numerous like the stars of heaven,
  You brought them into the land which you had told their ancestors to enter and possess.
[24]The descendants entered and possessed the land,
  You subdued before them the Canaanites, its inhabitants,
  Delivering into their power their kings and the peoples of the
  land
  To do with them as they pleased.
[25]They occupied fortified cities and rich, arable land,
  They took over houses full of good things, hewn cisterns, vine-
  yards, olive orchards, fruit trees in abundance—
  They ate, were filled, and grew sleek, reveling in your great
  goodness.
[26]Yet they were defiant and rebelled against you,
  They cast your law behind them,[k]
  They killed your prophets who gave them warning,
  To bring them back to you;
  They held you in great contempt.[l]
[27]So you delivered them into the power of their enemies who
  oppressed them,
  In the time of their distress they cried out to you
  And you heard them from heaven.
  In your abundant mercy you gave them saviors
  Who saved them from the power of their adversaries,
[28]Yet once they obtained relief they again did evil in your sight,
  So you abandoned them to their enemies who subdued them, so
  that once again they cried out to you,
  And you heard them from heaven and delivered them many
  times in your mercy.
[29]You gave them warning, to bring them back to your law,
  But they acted insolently, and would not obey your commandments.
  They sinned against your ordinances, by doing which one may
  live,

Stubbornly turning their backs,[m] obdurately refusing to obey.[n]
[30]For many years you were patient with them,
Warning them through your Spirit, by means of your prophets,
But they would not heed, so you delivered them
Into the power of the peoples of the lands.
[31]Yet in your great mercy you did not make an end of them,
You did not abandon them, for you are a gracious and merciful
    God.

[32]Now therefore, O our God, the great God, the mighty and awe-
    some One,
Who faithfully keeps covenant,
Do not make little of the hardship which has come upon us,
Our kings and princes, our priests and prophets, our forebears,[o]
    and all our people
From the time of the kings of Assyria to this day.
[33]You have been just with respect to all that has happened to us,
For you acted faithfully, whereas we have done wrong.
[34]For our kings and princes, our priests and our forebears[o] have
    not observed your law,
Nor did they heed your commandments and the warnings which
    you gave them.
[35]They neither served you nor turned away from their evil deeds,
Though in their own kingdom, and surrounded by the great
    goodness which you bestowed on them
In the broad and fertile land which you gave them.

[36]And so now we are slaves,
Slaves in the land which you gave to our ancestors,
To eat of its fruit and partake of its goodness.
[37]Its produce profits the kings whom you have placed over us on
    account of our sins,
They have power over our bodies and dispose of our beasts as
    they please,
And we are in great distress.

a. LXX adds "and Ezra said" at the beginning of the verse.
b. *'attāh-hû' YHVH l*^{e}*baddekā* can hardly be translated "you alone are YHVH."
    What is expressed is the incomparability and uniqueness of YHVH, as in Isa.
    44:6, 8; 45:6, 21–22; 46:9; etc.
c. Or "the Reed Sea."
d. Lit., "raised your hand" (to pronounce an oath).
e. *va'*^{a}*bōtênû* with explicative *vav*: they, that is, our ancestors.
f. Lit., "they hardened their necks."

g. *vayyittᵉnû-rōʾš;* Num. 14:4, on which this phrase is based, rules out the meaning "they proposed," "they determined" (*pace* Fensham, 231, et al.).

h. Reading *bᵉmiṣrayim* for MT *bᵉmiryām,* "in their rebellion."

i. *pēʾāh* (cf. Ug. *pat*), usually "corner," "side"; see Jer. 48:45 (cf. Num. 24:17) parallel with *qodqod,* "head," presumably therefore the side or crown of the head and, by a somewhat obscure semantic extension, "boundary" (cf. Akk. *pāṭu*). NEB "spoils of war" relies on a somewhat less secure Arabic cognate.

j. MT "the land of Sihon, the land of the king of Heshbon" is syntactically possible, assuming *vav* explicative, but stylistically improbable; *vᵉʾet-ʾereṣ* due to dittography.

k. Lit., "behind their backs."

l. Not to be removed as a gloss (cf. v. 18).

m. Lit., "they gave (presented) a stubborn shoulder."

n. Lit., "they hardened their backs and did not listen."

o. *ʾᵃbōtênû,* our ancestors, but here with a rather different connotation from vs. 9, 16, 23 since the context deals with the less distant past.

In the present context, the long prayer which follows is part of the penitential liturgy of the twenty-fourth of Tishri. But if, as suggested, 9:5b forms the conclusion to a liturgical psalm, 9:6–37 must have been added subsequently. It also seems unlikely that it belonged to either the Ezra or the Nehemiah material. With the sole exception of sabbath, references to the law and its nonobservance are quite unspecific; they do not justify the conclusion that the prayer formed the conclusion to the reading of the law and celebration of Sukkoth (*pace* Sellin, 139). And if it had originated as part of the Ezra material—as the Old Greek translator assumed (see textual note a)—we might have expected some allusion to foreign marriages as a prominent example of infidelity. In addition, the outright claim to independent possession of the land, which is one of the dominant themes of the prayer, and allusion to the oppressive and arbitrary nature of foreign rule, create further difficulties for this hypothesis. For while Ezra-Nehemiah never loses sight of the basic unacceptability of foreign domination, allusions to it are carefully nuanced (Ezra 9:8; Neh. 1:11) and are outweighed, if only for prudential reasons, by emphasis on the benevolent and providential aspects of Persian rule (see further Rudolph 1949, 156–157, and R. A. Bowman 1954, 746).

The prayer consists in a historical recital (6–31) leading up to petition to be free of a present situation of distress (32–37), the latter introduced by the phrase "now therefore" (*vᵉʾattāh*), which frequently marks such a passage in similar compositions (e.g., Ps. 39:8 [7]). The historical review begins with creation (6), then the ancestors

(7–8), exodus (9–11), wilderness including the giving of the law at Sinai (12–21), occupation of the land on both sides of the Jordan (22–25), the period of the Judges and the monarchy (26–31). The purpose of the review is not, as often in the psalms (e.g., Pss. 105; 135; 136), praise and thanksgiving of God, though these are implied, but the communal confession of a sinful history leading up to the "great distress" in which the people now finds itself. Other examples of this genre are often adduced from the canonical psalms, but the only one which is close is Ps. 106, which narrates the history in the same sequence, though beginning only with the exodus, and from the same perspective. It goes on to emphasize the refusal to enter the land (vs. 24–27; cf. Neh. 9:17), and it tells the history of judges and kings in terms of alternating chastisements and salvific interventions. It concludes with a petition for the ingathering of dispersed Israel and a blessing formula similar to Neh. 9:5 (vs. 47–48). Similar reservations are in order with respect to prophetic influence. In spite of Gunkel's derivation of the genre from prophetic preaching, possibly the only passage in the prophetic books which is reasonably close is the communal lament in Isa. 63:7–64:12 in which, however, the element of historical recital is much reduced. The prayer in Dan. 9, certainly comparable, also lacks the sustained historical recital, though exhibiting similarities in theme and phrasing (especially vs. 6, 8, 10, 12, 14, 15). Much closer is the liturgical text from the fourth Qumran cave (4QDibHam[a]), the so-called "Words of the Heavenly Luminaries," dated to the early second century B.C.E. (Baillet, 246–247; Vermes, 202–205); this text also surveys the history from the exodus and speaks of political vassalage as the result of sin. Other later texts which fit the genre would include Baruch 1:15–3:8 and the Prayer of Manasseh (structurally similar, though individual rather than communal). Both of these mark the transition from recital to petition in the same way as here (*v^e'attāh;* Bar. 2:11; Pr. Man. v.11).

I have been content to designate the passage a prayer, since it is at least certain that it is addressed to YHVH in the name of the people. Though it has been arranged psalm-like in strophes and verses, evidence of metric regularity is sporadic, so that it might be more properly described as a sermon in rhythmic liturgical prose (Ackroyd 1973, 301) than a psalm. In this respect it is somewhat similar to the homiletic framework of Zech. 1–8 (1:1–6; 7:8–14). Neither the form nor the content provides firm clues to its origin. It has little in common with the Chronicler's characteristic style. Allusion to political servitude beginning with the Assyrians suggests a date in the Persian period at the earliest—against Welch, who places its composition in the period of Assyrian hegemony—but a date between Alexander and the Maccabees would not be ruled out. It was presumably composed for liturgical use, perhaps by a Levitical author (see especially von Rad), and played a significant part in the development of early Jewish liturgical prayer (Liebreich).

More will be said about the structure, themes, and purpose of the composition in the commentary which follows. No attempt will be made to trace all the biblical references and allusions (for a convenient though incomplete list see Myers 1965, 167–169). It is, in a sense, a pastiche of biblical phrases, but it is much more than that. A detailed study of these references would perhaps contribute to determining the extent to which the historical tradition was already in place and assimilated to liturgical usage at the time of composition.

[9:6] *Creation.* The prayer begins with an invocation to the God of Israel as creator. The God who chose Abraham and promised possession of the land is the God who made the heavens, the earth, and the seas, and who is worshiped in the heavenly liturgy of which worship in temple and synagogue is the earthly counterpart (cf. Isa. 6:1–5; Job 38:4–7). Though praise of YHVH as creator is common in the psalms (e.g., Pss. 104; 148:1–4), only one of the "historical" psalms begins with creation (136:4–9). Reference to the heavens and all their host presupposes the Priestly creation recital (Gen. 2:1), the first of several allusions to this source. Though rooted in ancient Near Eastern theology, the theme of God as creator, and the related theme of the incomparability of YHVH, achieved prominence only from the time of the Babylonian exile (Gen. 1:1–2:4; Isa. 40–48; Amos 4:13; 5:8–9; 9:5–6).

[7–8] *Ancestors.* The prayer moves on at once to the founding of the people with the election of Abraham. Three themes are emphasized: the divine call to go on a journey, the change of name, the promissory covenant guaranteeing land and peoplehood. Abraham is called out of Ur of the Chaldeans, that is, Mesopotamia, to go on a journey of faith, the same journey on which the exiles in Babylon were summoned to venture. The representation of Abraham as journeyer—in later tradition even as the first proselyte—will help to explain why the figure of Abraham became prominent, outside of Genesis, only in exilic and postexilic writings (e.g., Isa. 51:2; 63:16). The change of name, dependent on a Priestly tradition (Gen. 17:5), carries the same implication of a new role and destiny. But the decisive point is the Abrahamic covenant, the only one referred to in the prayer. By this means the indefectible promise of the land is emphasized; for God is just *(ṣaddîq)* and does not go back on his promises, all appearances to the contrary notwithstanding. The author of the prayer seems to have been familiar with both versions of the Abrahamic covenant (Gen. 15 and 17). The faithfulness of Abraham is stressed in the former (Gen. 15:6), which also gives prominence to the land. The list of nations given here is, however, significantly different from those named in Gen. 15:19–21, which may suggest that a rather different form of the tradition is reproduced at this point. The election of the ancestors is a prominent theme in Deuteronomy (e.g., 4:37; 10:15), and it is clear throughout that the prayer is much indebted to Deuteronomic ideas and formulations.

[9–11] *Exodus.* The recital of the exodus story follows fairly closely the hymnic memorializing of the event (Pss. 78:12–14; 105: 23–38; 106:6–12; 135:8–9; 136:10–16), echoing also the homiletic formulations of Deuteronomy (e.g., the "signs and wonders," Deut. 4:34; 6:22; 34:11) and utilizing key phrases from the basic narrative in Exodus (e.g., 3:7; 7:3; 14:10, 21; 15:5). The exodus as passage from servitude to freedom as a paradigm of divine action is taken up in Second Isaiah and at several points in the Ezra narrative. This is how YHVH "made a name for himself" (cf. Ex. 9:16; Ps. 106:8; Isa. 63:12, 14; Dan. 9:15), and the power displayed then is still available in the present to those who invoke that name.

[12–21] *Wilderness.* The principal theme in this part of the prayer is the contrast between divine providence and the rebellion of Israel culminating in refusal to enter the land. By acting insolently the ancestors imitated the conduct of the Egyptians faced with the divine command (v. 10, the same verb). Unfaithful conduct results from forgetting the tradition, for it is the collective memory of tradition, actualized in the liturgy, which preserves the community in existence. The chronological order of the biblical narrative is abandoned in favor of a thematic sequence: divine providence (12–15), rebellion (16–18), renewed evidence of divine benevolence (19–21). The familiar motifs of divine guidance and provision of sustenance bracket the giving of the law at Sinai, which is therefore exhibited as the supreme example of divine providence. The only legal prescription to be named is observance of the "holy sabbath" (a Priestly term; cf. Ex. 16:23), of major concern in the postexilic period (e.g., Neh. 10:31 [30]; 13:15–22; Isa. 56:2, 4, 6). The Sinai event is not described as a covenant. The only covenant alluded to is the one made with Abraham, permitting a total concentration on the promise of land and nationhood. The command to possess the land is given special prominence (v. 15).

The theme of the land as a place of freedom is further emphasized by the people's refusal to take the risks essential for being free; they appointed a leader to take them back to the familiar bondage in Egypt (the diaspora?), where at least their bodily needs were satisfied (cf. Ex. 16:2–3; Num. 14:4). The political implication is the impossibility of acquiescing in foreign rule if they are to inherit the promises.

Divine guidance was not withdrawn even after the apostasy of the golden calf—a bull calf of metal cast in a mold and plated with gold, anticipating the bull cult practiced among the Canaanites and widespread in the Northern Kingdom (1 Kings 12:28; Hos. 8:5). The reference to the good Spirit of YHVH which continued to instruct them (cf. Pss. 51:13 [11]; 143:10; Isa. 63:10) restates the tradition about the seventy elders endowed by charismatic succession with the spirit of Moses (Num. 11:16–17, 24–30). The connection between the Spirit and prophecy, frequently attested during the time of the Second Temple (e.g., 2 Chron. 36:15–16), will recur later in the prayer (v. 30).

[22–25] *Conquest.* The prayer moves from the promise of land to providential guidance in their journey to it and now, finally, to the actual occupation of the land. The exact sense of the statement in v. 22 is obscure (see textual note i). I take it to refer to the Transjordanian kingdoms which bordered Israelite territory west of the Jordan. The religious status of territory occupied on the east bank caused problems at different times. Conquest of the kingdoms of Sihon and Og (Num. 21:21–35; 32:33; Deut. 1:4; 2:16–3:11)—a typical example of "twinning" in these ancient traditions—was already firmly established in the hymnic celebration of the conquest (Pss. 135:10–12; 136:17–22). The seventy descendants of Jacob in Egypt (Ex. 1:5) expanded into a people numerous as the stars of heaven (Gen. 15:5; 22:17; 26:4; etc.) in fulfillment of the promise to Abraham and in obedience to the divine command at creation (Gen. 12:2; 1:28). We may take this to reflect the demographic expansion of the Judean community after the exile. The subjection of the Canaanites could likewise correspond to rejection of "the peoples of the land(s)" who opposed the work of restoration during the missions of Ezra and Nehemiah. The riches of every kind which fell to their lot in the land are described in terms drawn from Deuteronomy: fortified cities (Deut. 3:5; 6:10), houses, cisterns, vineyards, and the like (6:11), the fertile earth giving of its abundance (8:7–10; 32:13–14). This part of the prayer ends with an intimation of spiritual failure which often accompanies material prosperity. The wording is borrowed from the Song of Moses (Deut. 32:15) and leads directly into the history of infidelity which follows.

This interpretation of the conquest, like so much else in the prayer, is basically Deuteronomic, but it could easily be overlooked that there is no mention of Joshua. The omission is probably deliberate, serving to emphasize the idea of the land as a divine gift rather than the outcome of human effort. This perspective is more consonant with that of the Priestly source, which passes over the actual conquest in silence, focusing exclusively on the setting up of the wilderness sanctuary in the land and the allotment of territory to the tribes (Josh. 18:1; 19:51).

[26–31] *Rebellion.* This section reproduces the cyclical pattern of apostasy, disaster, prayer for deliverance, divine reaction, relief, renewed relapse, and so on. The cycle is repeated three times, ending with the contemporary situation with only a remnant left (cf. the conclusion to the historical survey in Ezra's prayer, Ezra 9:13–15). The source for this part of the prayer is the Deuteronomic historian's summary of the period of the Judges (Judg. 2:11–23), filled out with themes from prophetic preaching, especially Ezek. 20. Here, however, the record of human failure is more firmly linked with reliance on the mercy of God (vs. 27, 28, 31). The language of rejection in v. 26 draws on the same Deuteronomic source (1 Kings 14:9; cf. Ezek. 23:35). The prophetic role of testifying against neglect of the law is also a Deuteronomic theme (e.g., 2 Kings 17:13; cf. 2 Chron. 24:19). As Clines observes (1984, 197), the accusation of murdering prophets, which was to become an important strand of early Christian anti-Jewish polemic (e.g., Luke 11:47–51; Acts 7:52), is based on rather slim evidence (Jer. 26:20–23; 2 Chron. 24:20–22; in 1 Kings 18:4 the perpetrator is Jezebel). The entire history of rejection is then summed up in the phrase "great contempt"—not restricted to blasphemy, as in RSV and other modern versions. The first of the three cycles refers to the Judges sent as "saviors" *(môšî'îm)* in a time of distress (Judg. 2:16, 18; 3:9, 15; etc.), the first of many acts of mercy abounding (2 Sam. 24:14 = 1 Chron. 21:13; Ps. 119:156).

The same pattern continues in the theological reflection on the history of the kingdoms which follows. The Deuteronomic theme of the unheeded warning of the prophet is given great prominence (cf. especially 2 Kings 17:7–20). With the giving of the law Israel was offered the choice of life or death, another Deuteronomic-sapiential theme (Deut. 30:15–20), though the actual wording ("by doing which one may live") betrays affinity with the Holiness Code and Ezekiel (Lev. 18:5; Ezek. 20:11). The summation of the history concludes in the same terms. Inspired by the Spirit of God (cf. Zech. 7:12), prophets warned continually but to no avail. With enslavement to the "peoples of the lands," a significant variation on "enemies" or "adversaries," the perspective is that of subjection within the vast Persian empire.

[32–37] *Final petition.* The historical survey leads up to the present situation of hardship which is dated from the beginning of Assyrian hegemony in the eighth century B.C.E. The invocation reflects the language of Nehemiah's prayer (1:4–5). The balance between transcendence (great, mighty, awesome) and intimacy ("our God," a common form of address in Nehemiah) is characteristic of Second Temple discourse about God. A basic postulate of faith is that God is faithful to his covenant commitment (cf. Neh. 1:5), and that therefore the disasters of history must be due to human failure not divine indifference. This again is a dominant theme of the Deuteronomic history, to which the prayer closely hews throughout (cf. Deut. 7:9; 1 Kings 8:23). This last phase of the history is one of hardship. *t^{e}lā'āh*, a word chosen to bring to mind the hardships undergone by Israel in Egypt and in the wilderness (Ex. 18:8; Num. 20:14). Though "Assyria" appears to stand for Persia in Ezra 6:22, and served later still as a code name for the Seleucids (Isa. 19:23–25), it should in the present context be taken literally, dating the present situation of political subjection either from the reign of Ahaz or from the fall of the Northern Kingdom in 722 B.C.E. It is implied, though of course not stated explicitly, that there was not much to choose between the Assyrians and their imperial successors, the Babylonians and Persians.

Both at the beginning and the end of the prayer (8, 33) it is affirmed that God is just *(ṣaddîq),* that is, free of blame for what had happened. He has kept his side of the bargain, he has not gone back on his promises but has warned continually through prophetic intermediaries, and the warnings have not been heeded. This too is a major (Deuteronomic) theme of the prayer. The ironic outcome is that those who would not serve (i.e., worship) him during their independent existence are now compelled to serve (also *'bd*) a hard taskmaster. In spite of the pro-Persian sentiments in Isa. 40–48 and favorable allusions to the Persians' providential role in Ezra-Nehemiah, there is no reason to believe that their rule was significantly more benign than that of their Semitic predecessors. The allusion to military conscription, forced labor, and the requisitioning of livestock recall references elsewhere to the heavy burden of taxation during the early Persian period (Ezra 4:13; 7:24; Neh. 5:4). One of the worst aspects of imperial policy under the Achaemenids was the draining away of local resources from the provinces to finance the imperial court, the building of magnificent palaces, and the interminable succession of campaigns of pacification or conquest, especially after the accession of Xerxes in 486 B.C.E. For these reasons, then, the situation is one of great distress. The prayer is therefore, by implication, an aspiration toward political emancipation as a necessary precondition for the fulfillment of the promises.

The Sworn Covenant (Neh. 10:1–40 [9:38–10:39])

H. C. **Brichto,** *The Problem of "Curse" in the Hebrew Bible,* Philadelphia, 1963, 22–76; G. **Brin,** "The Firstling of Unclean Animals," *JQR* 68, 1978, 1–15; D. J. A. **Clines,** "Nehemiah 10 as an Example of Early Jewish Biblical Exegesis," *JSOT* 21, 1981, 111–117; O. **Eissfeldt,** *Erstlinge und Zehnten im Alten Testament,* Leipzig, 1917; M. **Fishbane,** *Biblical Interpretation in Ancient Israel,* 123–134, 165–166, 213–216; A. **Ibañez Arana,** "Sobre la colocación original de Neh. 10," *EstBib* 10, 1951, 379–402; H. **Jagersma,** "The Tithes in the Old Testament," *OTS* 21, 1981, 116–128; A. **Jepsen,** "Nehemia 10," *ZAW* 66, 1954, 87–106; U. **Kellermann,** *Nehemia,* 37–41, 100–103; H. G. **Kippenberg,** *Religion und Klassenbildung im antiken Judäa,* 69–77; M. R. **Lehmann,** "Biblical Oaths," *ZAW* 81, 1969, 74–92; J. **Liver,** "The Half-Shekel Offering in Biblical and Post-Biblical Literature," *HTR* 56, 1963, 173–198; S. **Moscati,** "I sigilli nell'Antico Testamento: Studio esegetico-filologico," *Bib* 30, 1949, 314–338; S. **Mowinckel,** *Studien* I, 135–145; III, 142–155; R. **Negah,** "Why Is Ezra's Name Absent from the List of Signatories of the Covenant?" *BM* 80, 1979, 79–80 (Heb.); B. **Porten,** *Archives from Elephantine,* 122–133; M. **Smith,** *Parties and Politics That Shaped the Old Testament,* 136–144, 173–174; "The Dead Sea Sect in Relation to Ancient Judaism," *NTS* 7, 1961, 347–360; A. C. **Welch,** "The Share of N. Israel in the Restoration of the Temple Worship," *ZAW* 48, 1930, 179–187; *Post-exilic Judaism,* 69–86.

10:1 [9:38] In spite of all this,[a] we make a firm commitment in writing,[b] and on the sealed document are the names of our leaders, our Levites, and our priests.

10:2 [10:1] Those who sealed it with their signatures[c] were: Nehemiah the governor,[d] son of Hacaliah, and Zedekiah; [3[2]]Seraiah, Azariah, Jeremiah, [4[3]]Pashhur, Amariah, Malchijah, [5[4]]Hattush, Shebaniah,[e] Malluch, [6[5]]Harim, Meremoth, Obadiah, [7[6]]Daniel, Ginnethon, Baruch, [8[7]]Meshullam, Abijah, Mijamin, [9[8]]Maaziah, Bilgai, Shemaiah. These are the priests.

[10[9]]The Levites: Jeshua[f] son of Azaniah, Binnui of the descendants of Henadad, Kadmiel, [11[10]]with their fellow Levites Shebaniah,[g] Hodiah,[h] Kelita, Pelaiah, Hanan, [12[11]]Mica, Rehob, Hashabiah, [13[12]]Zaccur, Sherebiah, Shebaniah,[i] [14[13]]Hodiah, Bani, Beninu.[j]

[15[14]]The leaders of the people: Parosh, Pahath-moab, Elam, Zattu, Bani, [16[15]]Bunni, Azgad, Bebai, [17[16]]Adonijah, Bigvai, Adin, [18[17]]Ater, Hezekiah, Azzur, [19[18]]Hodiah, Hashum, Bezai, [20[19]]Hariph, Anathoth, Nebai,[k] [21[20]]Magpiash, Meshullam, Hezir, [22[21]]Meshezabel, Zadok, Jaddua, [23[22]]Pelatiah, Hanan, Anaiah,

[24][23]Hoshea, Hananiah, Hasshub, [25][24]Hallohesh, Pilha, Shobek, [26][25]Rehum, Hashabnah, Maaseiah, [27][26]Ahiah, Hanan, Anan, [28][27]Malluch, Harim, Baanah.

[29][28]The rest of the people—priests, Levites, gatekeepers, musicians, temple servants, and all those who had separated themselves from the local population[1] out of regard for the law of God, together with their wives, sons, and daughters, all such as had sufficient knowledge and understanding[m]—[30][29]associate themselves with their noble kinsmen[n] in taking upon themselves[o] a curse and an oath to act in accord with the law of God which was given through Moses the servant of God, to observe and fulfill all the commandments of YHVH our Lord, together with his ordinances and statutes;

[31][30]To wit: we will not give our daughters in marriage to the local population or take their daughters as wives for our sons;

[32][31]Item: if the local people bring merchandise or any kind of grain to sell on the sabbath we will not buy from them on the sabbath or on a holy day;

Item: we will forgo the harvest of the seventh year and return anything held in pledge;

[33][32]Item: we take on ourselves the obligation to contribute[p] the third of a shekel annually for the service of the house of our God, [34][33]for the showbread, the daily cereal and burnt offering, for sabbaths, new moons, established festivals, the holy offerings and sin offerings to make atonement for Israel, and for any work to be done on the house of our God;[q]

[35][34]Item: we—priests, Levites, and people—have cast lots for the wood offering, to bring it to the house of our God at the set times annually, according to our ancestral houses, to burn upon the altar of YHVH our God, as prescribed in the law;

[36][35]Item: we undertake to bring in the firstfruits of our land and the first yield of every fruit tree annually to the house of YHVH; [37][36]also the firstborn of our sons and of our livestock as prescribed in the law; we will bring to the house of our God, to the priests on duty in the house of our God, the firstborn of our cattle and sheep; [38][37]also the best of our dough, our contributions,[r] the fruit of every tree, of new wine and fine oil we will bring to the priests, to the storehouses of the house of our God. The tithe of our land we will bring in for the Levites, for it is the Levites who collect the tithe in all the country towns.[s] [39][38]An Aaronite priest shall be with the Levites when they collect the tithe; and the Levites shall bring up the tenth part of the tithe to the house of our God, to the rooms in the storehouse. [40][39]For Israelites and Levites shall bring

the contribution of grain, new wine, and fine oil to the storerooms, where the vessels of the sanctuary are kept, and where the priests on duty, the gatekeepers, and the musicians reside. We will not neglect the house of our God.

a. The phrase *b*ᵉ*kol-zō't* has this meaning at Isa. 5:25; 9:11; Ps. 78:32 (see *BDB* at *b*ᵉ, p. 90, III 7), which would be consonant with the confession of sin immediately preceding; but "on account of all this" (*BDB* III 5) would also be possible.

b. Lit., "to make (cut) a firm commitment and write (it)."

c. MT has *v*ᵉ*'al hah*ᵃ*tûmîm,* "and on the sealed documents." If emended to the sing. it would read "and on the sealed document were (the names of) . . . ," but the ancient versions (LXX, Syr., Vulg.) favor emending to *v*ᵉ*hahōt*ᵉ*mîm,* "those who sealed it."

d. Though *hattirSātā'* stands between the name and the patronym, it should not be struck since this construction is attested (see Myers, 173).

e. Some MSS have "Shecaniah"; cf. 12:3.

f. MT has *v*ᵉ*yēSûa',* but the conjunction is out of place.

g. Some Heb. MSS, Syr., and L read "Shecaniah"; cf. v. 5 and the same name at v. 13.

h. Cf. Hodaviah at Ezra 2:40 (see commentary ad loc.).

i. Again, some Heb. MSS and Syr. read "Shecaniah," but it probably should be deleted. The repetition of the name may have been occasioned by Hodiah, which follows here and at v. 11.

j. A suspicious formulation otherwise unattested. Some substitute Chenani (cf. 9:4), but in the absence of confirmation MT should probably stand.

k. Or, with Ketib, LXX, and L, "Nobai."

l. Lit., "the peoples of the lands."

m. Reading with LXX *yôdēa' ûmēbîn;* cf. Neh. 8:2.

n. MT has "their kinsmen, their nobles"; hendiadys.

o. Lit., "entering into."

p. Omit MT *'ālênû,* "upon ourselves."

q. Lit., "for every work *(kōl m*ᵉ*lā'kāh)* of the house of our God."

r. *ût*ᵉ*rûmōtênû,* "and our contributions," is not in LXX. It may have entered through association with Num. 15:20–21 and Ezek. 44:30.

s. Lit., "the towns of our labor" *('ārê* ᵃ*bōdātēnû).*

There follows a solemn, public commitment to the law, and to certain specifics of the law, which is put in writing and signed by the clerical and lay leadership. Read as the conclusion to this section of the work (Neh. 8–9), it makes good sense. The public reading and explanation of the law on the first of Tishri is followed by the celebration of Sukkoth from the fifteenth to the twenty-second. On the twenty-fourth of the same month there takes place a penitential service with a communal confession of sin past and present, leading to a solemn rededication of the people to the law. Though this last is not dated, the natural assumption would be that it concludes the penitential service on the twenty-fourth of the month. Thus the sequence which begins with the law ends with it. Though less clearly detectable, the presence of the two great leaders also seems to be implied. There is no doubt about Nehemiah (8:9; 10:2 [1]), and the absence of Ezra from the list of signatories, though disconcerting, could conceivably be explained by the fact that, as author of the document, he did not have to sign it (Torrey 1910, 284; Negah). There is also the curious fact that in the lists of priests, which closely correspond to those who signed the document (Neh. 12:1–7, 12–21), Ezra occurs in place of Azariah, the two being alternative forms of the same name.

In its present arrangement, therefore, Neh. 8–10 has a logic and unity of its own. It is, nevertheless, an editorial construct put together out of disparate elements. We therefore conclude that the opening phrase of the present passage—"in spite of all this" (or possibly "because of all this")—serves as a connective link with the prayer immediately preceding, though at an earlier editorial stage it may have connected with an introduction to the ceremony which is no longer extant. The binding agreement would fit the context well enough if restricted to law observance in general, that is, without the stipulations in vs. 31–40 [30–39]. But the narrative up to this point has not prepared us for these specifics, which would be more readily intelligible *after* Nehemiah's measures described later in the book (ch. 13). The list of names also appears to have been inserted at a later point in time. They are arranged in a different order from the categories listed in the introduction (10:1 [9:38]), and we would expect the names of signatories to follow rather than precede the stipulations of the contract. The manner of their insertion will be seen more clearly if (following Rudolph 1949, 172–173) we observe that the direct speech beginning at 9:5 is continued at 10:1 [9:38] and, following the insertion, at 10:29–30 [28–29], though the syntax has been disturbed by adjustments necessitated by the insertion. The same conclusion is suggested by the awkward passage from 10:1 to 10:2 [9:38 to 10:1], repetition in the latter verse pointing to a new beginning.

While the results of this kind of literary analysis are rarely definitive, we may suggest the following stages in the formation of this section: (1) a continuation of the penitential service with renewal of commitment to the law in general on the part of the entire community; (2) insertion of the lists of priests, Levites, and laity drawn from sources available elsewhere in Ezra-Nehemiah; (3) addition of the stipulations which presuppose and therefore are later than Nehemiah's reforms. How much later we have no means of determining, but this final version anticipates in some respects the sectarian covenanting of the Hasmonean period and later (e.g., Qumran).

[10:1–9 (9:38–10:8)] The opening phrase connects the pledge with the fast and prayer immediately preceding. Assuming this connection, the voice speaking in the name of the group carries over from the public confession of sin. In that case the affirmation is made by the Levites (9:5), and it is interesting to note that at Qumran the Levites recited the communal confession of sin and pronounced the curses which were part of the covenant ceremony (1QS i–ii; cf. Deut. 27:14). As the text now stands, this is what happens here where a communal confession of sin is followed by a solemn commitment sealed by an oath.

Only the civic and religious leaders sign the covenant; the rest take an oath involving a self-imposed curse. As happens occasionally in C (2 Chron. 19:8; 30:21), Levites are named before priests. Though the old language of covenant-making survives in the use of the expression "cutting a covenant" (stem *krt*), the traditional term *bᵉrît* for covenant is not used. Its substitute *'ᵃmānāh*, which occurs only here and at Neh. 11:23, connotes firmness of resolve (stem *'mn*), and was perhaps chosen to distinguish this kind of covenant from the historical covenant in which YHVH is directly involved as commanding or promising. The writing of the stipulations gave them additional authority, and the signing of the names (not the affixing of personal seals; there were far too many involved for that) gave it the force of a valid contract (cf. the form of contracts at Elephantine, e.g., *AP* 20:2; 28:2).

The list of signatories begins with Nehemiah and Zedekiah, then twenty-one priests, seventeen Levites, and forty-four laymen. Torrey (1910, 284) observed that the total, eighty-four, is a multiple of twelve and saw this as a significant hallmark of C (cf. Ezra 2:2; 6:17; 8:24). The suggestion is interesting and plausible, but the possibility of scribal error, especially in the Levitical list, leaves it open to question. The priest list begins with Seraiah. No priest called Zedekiah is known from that time, and Seraiah stands at the head of other priest lists. Since it was customary to put the scribe's name next to that of the principal in correspondence (cf. Ezra 4:8–9), this Zedekiah may be identical with the scribe Zadok mentioned later (13:13).

For the names of the twenty-one priests the redactor drew on lists referring back to an earlier period, that of the high priests Jeshua and Joiakim (Neh. 12:1–7, 12–21). The first three—Seraiah; Azariah = Ezra; Jeremiah—are identical in all three lists. The last five in our list are identical with and in the same order as the last five in the other two lists, allowing for slight textual variations (Maaziah = Maadiah = Moadiah). However, the last six of the lists in Neh. 12 are missing from our list, requiring the insertion of six other names at different points in the list. For none of these names (Pashhur, Malchijah, Obadiah, Daniel, Baruch, Meshullam) would the redactor have had far to seek. There is some overlap with names in C's list of the twenty-four courses (1 Chron. 24), which may mean that we are dealing with an earlier stage in the formation of the priestly courses or *maḥlᵉqôt*. The conclusion seems inevitable that the list is not an actual record of signatories, especially since the names represent patronyms rather than individuals. Jepsen's hypothesis that the names of individuals, written in the left-hand column of the scroll, were accidentally lost, leaving only the patronyms in the right-hand column, is ingenious but speculative. It seems that the editor who inserted the names simply drew on the most complete list of priestly families available in order to convey the impression of wholehearted support for the reforms of Nehemiah.

[10:10–14 (9–13)] The list of Levites ostensibly contains seventeen names, but if the second occurrence of Shebaniah and Hodiah is due to scribal error, as is likely, there would be three leaders plus twelve, thus salvaging something of Torrey's hypothesis. The first three, generally found together (Neh. 9:4–5; 12:8; cf. Ezra 2:40 = Neh. 7:43; Ezra 3:9), are patronymics but the others appear to be personal names. There is considerable overlap with Levitical names elsewhere in Neh. 8–10. Seven of the thirteen assistants at the reading of the law (8:7) and seven or eight out of the sixteen who took part in the penitential rite (9:4–5) occur here. It is worthy of note that the percentage of Levites to priests is much higher here than in the earlier narrative strata in the book.

[15–28 (14–27)] The names of the forty-four lay leaders are also drawn from sources readily available. In the first part (Parosh to Magpiash inclusive) all of the names except three (Bunni, Azzur, Hodiah) are taken from the census of Ezra 2 = Neh. 7, generally in the same order. These, therefore, are family or phratry names. Anathoth and Nebai (= Nebo), place names in the census (Ezra 2:23, 29), serve here as personal names. Of the remaining twenty-three (21–28), three, possibly four (assuming Malluch = Malchijah) occur in the list of Ezra's lay assistants (Neh. 8:4). More significantly, thirteen occur, with some slight variations, in the list of wall builders and, with one exception, in the same order. It would be difficult to find a clearer indication of the artificial nature of the list. Whoever inserted it may have wished to acknowledge the demographic expansion which had occurred since the first return and chose this way to do it.

[29–30 (28–29)] These verses form the continuation of 10:1 [9:38], which connects with the penitential service, but the insertion of the list has led to certain adjustments, including the change from first to third person. The text may have referred originally only to the rest of the people. The other categories, especially the allusion to children old enough to understand what was going on, were added in order to recall the assembly with which Neh. 8–10 begins (7:72 [73]; 8:2–3). Those who had severed their relations with the local population constitute a separate category of people who qualified for participation by eschewing idolatry and accepting the demands of the law. A similar situation occurs in C's description of the Passover following on the dedication of the rebuilt temple (Ezra 6:21) and, further back, in the covenant ceremony of Deut. 29:9–15 [10–16], a passage which has certainly influenced the description of this covenant. This, then, would be one of several allusions to proselytism in the early Second Temple period.

The pledge by means of which the community commits itself to the observance of the law is, like so much else in Ezra-Nehemiah, of Deuteronomic inspiration. The phrase "the curse and the oath" (*'ālāh, š^ebû'āh*) expresses by hendiadys the idea of a pact confirmed by an oath which, like all oaths, is reinforced by a curse. We are therefore very close to the "sworn covenant" (literally, "covenant and oath") of Deut. 29:11 [12]. Neh. 10 may also be better understood in the light of covenants which punctuate C's history of the monarchy. After a period of infidelity, Asa entered with his people into a *b^erît* confirmed by an oath (2 Chron. 15:12–15). The priest Jehoiada, guardian of the young king Joash, made a covenant with the entire *qāhāl* in the temple (2 Chron. 23:3, 16). Hezekiah's covenant (2 Chron. 29:10) is particularly interesting since it follows a communal confession of sin ending with a reference to a present situation of distress caused by the Assyrians ("as you see with your own eyes," 29:8; cf. Neh. 9:32–37). Josiah's covenant is preceded by a public reading of the law and stipulates that the people "walk" according to the law and observe it (*lāleket . . . lišmôr*, 2 Chron. 34:31; cf. Neh. 10:30 [29]). Of these four covenants only the last reproduces a passage in C's principal source. The Deuteronomic history does refer to Jehoiada's covenant (2 Kings 11:4), but C transforms it into an explicitly religious occasion. We can therefore trace a development in the understanding of covenant from Deuteronomy to the author of 1-2 Chronicles, and from there to Neh. 10

and, eventually, the sectarian covenant-making of the Greco-Roman period.

[31 (30)] We pass now from the generalized commitment to observe all the commandments to the specific covenant stipulations. To repeat, the latter are not in their original context since logically they must follow rather than precede the reform measures described in chapter 13. The first article anticipates the oath imposed on those Jews who had married foreign women (13:25). It is based on Deut. 7:3–4, which, unlike the earlier prohibition of Ex. 34:11–16, applies to both men and women. The present stipulation contemporizes the Deuteronomic law by substituting "the peoples of the land" for the traditional list of seven nations. As we see from Neh. 13:23, this in effect broadens the scope of the prohibition, resulting in a more rigorous formulation. While the pledge also corresponds to an important element in Ezra's program, it is noteworthy that there is no requirement to dissolve existing marriages.

[32a (31a)] This second article is closely related to Nehemiah's measures occasioned by the operation of an obviously profitable sabbath market in Jerusalem, involving in addition to buying and selling the associated activities of traveling, setting up booths, hauling goods, etc. (13:15–22). While the sabbath law may originally have applied only to agricultural labor (Ex. 23:12; 34:21), it eventually came to cover the activities of everyone in the household (Ex. 20:8–11; Deut. 5:12–15), and to include such things as lighting a fire (Ex. 35:3), gathering firewood (Num. 15:32–36), preparing food, and traveling (Ex. 16:22–30—all three passages assigned to the Priestly source). While selling, as the active element in doing business, was prohibited from early times (Amos 8:5), buying apparently was not. The present stipulation, then, extends the scope of the sabbath law in two respects. It prohibits not only selling but buying, and it applies to festival days as well as sabbaths. The pledge therefore represents a move in the direction of the comprehensive Mishnaic sabbath law involving thirty-nine categories of forbidden activities (*m. Shabb.* 7:2). In general, the exilic and early postexilic periods seem to have been particularly important in the evolution of sabbath observance, to judge by the Priestly creation recital (Gen. 1:1–2:4) and allusions in prophetic writings (Ezek. 20:12, 16, 20, 24; Isa. 56:1–8; 58:13–14). For sabbath in the Jewish colony at Elephantine and the name Shabbetai, see Porten 1968, 124–128.

[32b (31b)] This briefly worded stipulation, the only one which has no counterpart in Neh. 13, but which corresponds to his program of social reform already described (5:1–13), illustrates the process by which a more comprehensive law evolves out of existing legislation. The law of the seventh fallow year (Ex. 23:10–11; Lev. 25:1–7 P) is combined with the quite distinct law requiring the release in the seventh year of debt-slaves and the restitution of persons and property taken in pledge (Deut. 15:1–18; cf. Ex. 21:2–6). It is therefore made clear that both laws are binding simultaneously, to the exclusion of other possible interpretations. Whether this stipulation was ever put into effect, or indeed whether the law of the sabbatical year was ever practiced on a regular basis, is an open question. Apart from the emergency measure of the manumission of slaves during the siege of Jerusalem, which in any case was quickly reversed (Jer. 34:8–16), the only instances known to us are from several centuries later (1 Macc. 6:49, 53; Josephus, *Ant.* 13.8.1).

[33–34 (32–33)] The next three articles deal with support of the temple—the principal agenda of reform in C's history of both the preexilic and postexilic periods. Pentateuchal law (Ex. 30:11–16; 38:25–26 P) stipulated the payment of a half shekel for support of the sanctuary, levied on the basis of a census and incumbent on all, rich and poor alike (Ex. 30:15). While it is possible to read this as a one-time payment, it also reflects a regular feature of temple administration at the time of redaction, and so it was understood by C where he describes the funds raised by King Joash for repair of the temple as the Mosaic sanctuary tax (*maś'at mōšeh,* 2 Chron. 24:4–14; cf. 2 Kings 12:4–16). If the denomination is the same, and if we may assume that taxation tends inexorably to increase, this Priestly law reflected in Chronicles would be later than the lower rate pledged here. The half-shekel temple tax continued down into the Roman period (Matt. 17:24–27), when it was the equivalent of two Tyrian drachmas (Josephus, *War* 7.216–218; *Ant.* 18.312).

Since the temple was a royal establishment financed out of the exchequer in the preexilic period, the fixed temple tax is probably of postexilic origin. Whether it was levied before the time of the pledge we do not know. As successors to the native dynasty, and in keeping with their policy throughout the empire, the Achaemenids subsidized the establishment and operation of local cults (Ezra 6:9–10; 7:21–24) and encouraged private donations (Ezra 1:4, 6; 2:69). It is therefore possible that the assumption of the burden of support by the province reflects another aspect of the goal of provincial autonomy pursued by Nehemiah.

The itemization of different aspects of temple worship requiring support uses much of the cultic terminology of C, and may have been added at a later stage (as Rudolph 1949, 179). The showbread or Bread of the Presence (Ex. 25:23–30; Lev. 24:5–9; cf. 1 Chron. 9:32;

32:39; 2 Chron. 13:11) was a permanent thanksgiving offering representing the twelve tribes. The perpetual daily offering *(tāmîd)* consisted in cereal and a lamb offered morning and evening (Ex. 29:38–42; Num. 28:1–8), and many more animals were required for the sacrifices prescribed for sabbaths, new moons, and the festal calendar in general (Num. 28–29). The "holy things" *(qodāšîm)* probably allude to public offerings on special occasions (e.g., 2 Chron. 29:33; 35:13). Sin offerings *(ḥaṭṭā'ôt)*, as the name suggests, were those made on extraordinary penitential occasions (2 Chron. 29:21; Ezra 6:17; 8:35; cf. Lev. 4:1–5:13; Num. 15:22–29). Some such provision for support by members of temple communities must have been fairly common in the Persian empire. Unfortunately, however, the only analogous case known to us is the list of contributors and contributions from the Elephantine settlement in Upper Egypt (*AP* 22; see Porten, 160–164, 320–327).

[35 (34)] The pledge to provide wood for sacrifice, a not inconsiderable burden given the scarcity of this commodity in the province, affords another example of the development of the legal tradition in early Judaism. For while this stipulation is not "prescribed [lit., written] in the law," it is implicit in the requirement that the priests keep the fire for the morning and evening sacrifice burning continuously, for which of course fuel was required (Lev. 6:2, 5–6 [9, 12–13]; cf. 1:17). The later development and formalization of the requirement is attested in Josephus (*War* 2.425) and in *m. Taan.* 4:5 (cf. *b. Taan.* 28a), which gives a list of families contributing and the times at which the contribution was to be made. How this fitted with the role of the *n^etînîm,* descendants of the Gibeonites condemned to be "hewers of wood and drawers of water" for the sanctuary (Josh. 9:27; see on Ezra 2:43), we do not know. Perhaps the task of the latter was restricted to preparing and stacking the wood. Several commentators (e.g., Rudolph 1949, 180; Ackroyd 1973, 307) have suspected that this pledge is out of place and should come at the end, as it does in Neh. 13:31. Given the uneven syntax this may be so, but the meaning would not be affected.

[36–40 (35–39)] The final article deals with offerings in support of the temple and its personnel; specifically: firstfruits, firstborn, prime produce, and the tithe. Here too, the resolution reflects the situation which obtained toward the end of Nehemiah's administration and the measures taken to rectify it (Neh. 13:10–11, 31). The offering of the fruitfruits of the earth *(bikkûrîm)* was an ancient practice associated with the wheat harvest festival or Shavuoth (Ex. 23:19; 34:26; Deut. 26:1–11; Num. 28:26). By giving over to the deity the first sheaf, the crop was deconsecrated and made available for pro-

fane use. The inclusion of fruit trees, not specified in Pentateuchal
ritual law, provides another example of halakic development from
the implicit to the explicit. Offering of the firstborn *(bᵉkôrôt)*, equally
ancient (Ex. 13:2; 22:30 [29]; 34:19–20; Deut. 15:19–20; Num. 18:
15), does not include a rider about the need to redeem children and
unclean animals (cf. Ex. 13:12–13; 34:20; Deut. 12:6; Num. 18:17).
It is noticeable, however, that the qualification "as prescribed in the
law" refers only to sons and livestock generically, distinguishing
these from the cattle and sheep which are destined for sacrifice. It
may therefore be taken as an implicit allusion to redemption, and
therefore the rest of the verse should not be excised as an editorial
expansion (*pace* Rudolph 1949, 178). The tribute of the first and best
(rēˀšît) of produce appears to combine two supplementary items of
Priestly legislation: Num. 15:20–21 dealing with the offering of a
batch of dough, and Num. 18:12 listing wine, oil, and grain but not
the produce of fruit trees.

Provision of support for Levites by means of the tithe was particularly significant in view of their support for Nehemiah's program and
indications of priest-Levite tension. It is therefore not surprising that
the editorial expansion in vs. 38b–40a [37b–39a], which cannot be
attributed to the pro-Levitical Chronicler, modifies the tithe stipulation in several important respects. First, the earlier method of collection by the laity (e.g., Amos 4:4) is discontinued in favor of collection
by Levites at designated provincial centers. The tithe is therefore
now thought of as a kind of tax and the Levite as tax collector as well
as beneficiary. Second, the collection is to be supervised by an Aaronite priest, a step toward the complete control of the process by the
priesthood which was achieved by the Roman period and possibly
earlier (Josephus, *Ant.* 20.8.8; 20.9.2). Third, Levites are required to
surrender a tithe of their tithe to the priests, a requirement which
came to be enshrined in the supplementary Priestly legislation in the
Pentateuch (Num. 18:25–32). Fourth and finally, the obligation to
tithe is imposed on Levites and laity, and its purpose is support of
the temple and its personnel as a whole, not exclusively of the Levitical order. In later tradition this priestly takeover was justified by the
reluctance of Levites to make aliyah with Ezra (*b. Keth.* 26a; *b. Yeb.*
86a, b; *b. Ḥull.* 131b). Historically, it was one phase of a struggle
which had been going on from the early days of the return and
perhaps even earlier (see especially Ezek. 44:10–14).

The final statement relates to the neglect of the temple (the same
verb) of which Nehemiah complained after his return from Susa
(13:11). It recapitulates the last three articles of the pledge.

The relation between these stipulations and Pentateuchal legislation can therefore be observed at several points and in some detail. While the existence of an authoritative corpus of laws is assumed—note the formulaic "as it is written in the law" (35, 37 [34, 36])—it does not necessarily follow that the redactor had the Pentateuch in front of him in the form in which we know it. In general, the articles are more rigorist than corresponding legislation in the Pentateuch; witness the prohibition of intermarriage, the extension of the sabbath commandment, and the more comprehensive law of the seventh year. It is tempting to think of the pledge as a sectarian document, a forerunner of the halakah of Pharisee and Essene which went beyond the demands of the Mosaic law while acknowledging its ultimate authority. While it is certainly later than Nehemiah—how much later we cannot say—it deals with issues of concern during his administration and purports to show how his program was brought to a successful conclusion.

V

Nehemiah 11–13

The Repopulation of Jerusalem (Neh. 11:1–24)

J. R. **Bartlett**, "Zadok and His Successors at Jerusalem," *JTS* n.s. 19, 1968, 1–18; H. **Gese**, "Zur Geschichte der Kultsänger am zweiten Tempel," *Vom Sinai zum Zion*, Munich, 1974, 147–158; M. D. **Johnson**, *The Purpose of the Biblical Genealogies*, Cambridge, 1969, 37–76; U. **Kellermann**, *Nehemiah*, 41–44, 103–105; F. X. **Kugler**, *Von Moses bis Paulus*, Münster, 1922, 289–290; E. **Meyer**, *Entstehung des Judentums*, 94–102, 184–190; S. **Mowinckel**, *Studien* I, 48–49, 145–151; W. **Richter**, "Die nāgīd-Formel," *BZ* n.F. 9, 1965, 71–84.

11:1 The leaders of the people were living in Jerusalem, and the rest of the people cast lots to bring one in ten to settle in Jerusalem, the holy city, while the remaining nine stayed in the other towns. [a] ²The people blessed all those who volunteered to settle in Jerusalem.

³These are the chiefs of the province who were living in Jerusalem, while Israelites, priests, Levites, temple servants, and the descendants of Solomon's slaves settled in the towns of Judah, each on his own property in their towns. ⁴Some Judeans and Benjaminites settled in Jerusalem. Among the Judeans were: Athaiah son of Uzziah, son of Zechariah, son of Amariah, son of Shephatiah, son of Mahalalel, of the descendants of Perez; ⁵and Maaseiah son of Baruch, son of Col-hozeh, son of Hazaiah, son of Adaiah, son of Joiarib, son of Zechariah the Shelanite. [b] ⁶All the descendants of Perez who settled in Jerusalem came to 468, men capable of bearing arms. [c]

⁷These were the Benjaminites: Sallu son of Meshullam, son of Joed, son of Pedaiah, son of Kolaiah, son of Maaseiah, son of

Ithiel, son of Jeshaiah; [8]with his kinsmen[d] Gabbai, Sallai, 928 in all. [9]Joel son of Zichri was their overseer, and Judah son of Hassenuah was second in command of the city.

[10]Among the priests: Jedaiah, Joiarib, Jachin;[e] [11]Seraiah son of Hilkiah, son of Meshullam, son of Zadok, son of Meraioth, son of Ahitub, ruler of the house of God; [12]with their colleagues who carried out the work on the temple: 822 in all. Adaiah son of Jeroham, son of Pelaliah, son of Amzi, son of Zechariah, son of Pashhur, son of Malchijah; [13]with their kinsmen, heads of ancestral houses: 242 in all. Amasai[f] son of Azarel, son of Ahzai, son of Meshillemoth, son of Immer; [14]with his kinsmen, men capable of bearing arms:[c] 128 in all. Their supervisor was Zabdiel son of Haggedolim.[g]

[15]Among the Levites: Shemaiah son of Hasshub, son of Azrikam, son of Hashabiah, son of Bunni. [16]Shabbethai and Jozabad were the Levitical leaders in charge of the external work of the house of God. [17]Mattaniah son of Micah, son of Zabdi, son of Asaph, leader of psalm-singing in thanksgiving and petition;[h] Bakbukiah, second in command among his kinsmen, and Abda son of Shammua, son of Galal, son of Jeduthun. [18]The Levites in the holy city were 284 in all.

[19]The gatekeepers Akkub, Talmon, and their colleagues who stood guard at the gates were 172 in all.

[20]The rest of Israel[i] were in all the towns of Judah, each on his own ancestral plot. [21]The temple servants were living on the Ophel; Ziha and Gishpa were in charge of the temple servants. [22]The official in charge of the Levites in Jerusalem was Uzzi son of Bani, son of Hashabiah, son of Mattaniah, son of Mica, of the descendants of Asaph, musicians. They were responsible for the work of the house of God, [23]for there was a royal decree concerning the musicians which imposed obligations on them, as each day required. [24]Pethahiah son of Meshezabel, of the descendants of Zerah son of Judah, was the king's adviser[j] in all matters concerning the people.

---

a. Lit., "and ten parts (*yādôt,* hands) in the towns."

b. MT has "Shilonite" but Shiloh is not in Judah, and the allusion is clearly to Shelah son of Judah (Gen. 38:5; Num. 26:20; 1 Chron. 3:2; 9:5). The consonants are identical.

c. *'anšê-ḥāyil* could be translated "men of substance" (as NEB; it is noticeable, however, that at Prov. 31:10 NEB translates *'ēšet-ḥayil* as "a capable wife" not "a woman of substance"). However, the occurrence of *gibbôrê ḥayil* at v.

14, clearly with the same sense, suggests a military connotation. "Valiant
men" is archaic and "warriors" inappropriate in the context; hence "capable
of bearing arms."

d. Emending MT *v'hryv,* "and after him," to *v'hyv* with L.

e. MT reads "Jedaiah son of Joiarib, Jachin . . ." The last name, standing by
itself, is suspicious since it departs from the genealogical pattern in this section. The suggested emendation of *ykn* to *bn,* resulting in "Jedaiah son of
Joiarib son of Seraiah . . . ," disposes of this problem but is arbitrary. I have
followed 1 Chron. 9:10–11, which lists Jedaiah, Jehoiarib, Jachin, and then
begins a linear genealogy with Azariah (Seraiah).

f. MT has *ᵃmaśśay,* which is an impossible conflation of *ᵃmaśay* and *ᵃmāśay.*
The corresponding form in 1 Chron. 9:12, *maᶜśay,* results from metathesis.

g. *haggᵉdôlîm,* "the great ones," is an improbable personal name. If we read
haggādôl, sing., assuming dittography with the following word, it becomes no
less improbable without an accompanying proper name, though it might stand
for the high priest, as suggested by Rudolph (1949). Other possibilities are
Giddel (cf. Ezra 2:47) or Gedaliah (cf. Ezra 10:18).

h. Reading *hattᵉhillāh,* the psalm, for *hattᵉhillāh,* the beginning, with L and
Vulg.; though it is just possible that *rōʾš hattᵉhillāh,* lit., "leader of the
beginning," was a technical term for precentor, the one who intones and takes
the lead in liturgical music.

i. MT has *hakkōhᵃnîm halᵉviyyîm,* "the Levitical priests," which is intrusive.

j. Lit., "at the king's hand" *(lᵉyad hammelek).*

After a brief notice about the repopulation of Jerusalem (1–2), we
have lists of laity, priests, Levites, and other cult personnel living in
Jerusalem (3–19). The list of provincial towns and villages is quite
distinct. The general heading at v. 3 may have been amplified when
the topographical list was added; v. 20 may also have served as a
heading, though it is now separated from the place-names by a series
of notes added subsequently (21–24). Thus the chapter reached its
present form in several stages and, as we shall see, subsequent to the
administration of Nehemiah, who is not even mentioned in it.

[11:1–2] This account of the transfer of population or synoecism
appears to follow logically on 7:4–5a, where the NM speaks of the
underpopulated city and what Nehemiah proposed to do about it.
But the wording is very close to the conclusion of the census (7:71–
72a [72–73a]), which also speaks of people settling in their towns,
which suggests that the list in Neh. 7, intended as an introduction
to chapters 8–10, was already in place when the present chapter was
added. The brief statement on the repopulation of Jerusalem is not
from the NM. Unlike 7:4–5a, it is in the third person, uses terminology foreign to the memoir (e.g., *śārîm* rather than *ḥōrîm, sᵉgānîm*
for leaders, the holy city, etc.), and attributes the decision not to

Nehemiah but to the people. We assume that Nehemiah did have an account of this event, surely one of the more important of his administration, but that for some reason it has been replaced by another which serves merely to introduce the lists of clerical and lay families living in Jerusalem. That the transfer of population was accomplished by casting lots, probably Urim and Thummim manipulated by the priesthood (cf. Neh. 7:65), suggests that the material in this chapter, including this brief introduction, was redacted by clerical scribes and deposited in the temple archives.

We are told that only the clerical and lay leaders had settled in Jerusalem. The houses of several of these are mentioned in the list of workers on the wall, and some were resident there when Ezra arrived (Ezra 8:29, 33). So the city was underpopulated rather than depopulated, and therefore some means had to be found to bring a substantial number of the common people, including artisans, into it. In spite of what is said about people volunteering—a familiar theme in C—this need could hardly have been adequately satisfied on a purely voluntary basis. On the contrary, recourse to a system of "decimation" suggests rather a forcible transfer of population which must have created significant social and economic problems (for parallels see R. A. Bowman 1954, 770). There may also be a theological undertone here, an echo of the bringing of the tithe or tenth of produce to Jerusalem alluded to in the passage immediately preceding. We may also perhaps detect allusion to the prophetic motif of the tenth part as the remnant (Amos 5:3; 6:9; Isa. 6:13). Another nuance is that the verb *hitnaddēb* ("to volunteer") also has military connotations, preparing us for the description of the settlers, lay and clerical, as capable of bearing arms (vs. 6, 14). Once the wall had been built, the provision of a military or paramilitary reserve, supplementing the governor's militia, would have furthered the process of turning the city into a fortress, a process which was certainly consistent with Persian policy in the region as long as the city remained under the control of pro-Persian elements.

[3] The heading to the list of lay leaders in Jerusalem in the first part of the verse is quite clear, but the remainder, which is syntactically very awkward, is almost certainly an addition. At this point it is important to note that the lists in 11:4–19 parallel at many points the list of first settlers in 1 Chron. 9:2–17, and that the parallelism extends to the respective headings. This similarity makes it somewhat less likely that both lists have drawn on a common archival source, though the question of priority cannot easily be settled. It is, at any rate, quite possible that the heading at Neh. 11:3 has been expanded secondarily with borrowings from 1 Chron. 9:2–3. The

latter reads: "The first to settle *on their own property, in their towns, were: Israelites, priests, Levites, and temple servants; and some Judeans, Benjaminites,* Ephraimites, and Manassehites *settled in Jerusalem*" (identical words italicized). The principal difference would therefore be that our version omits the people of Ephraim and Manasseh; naturally, since it is now a question of the southern tribes alone. It also adds the descendants of Solomon's slaves, for what reason we do not know. These considerations do not, needless to say, suffice to decide the issue of priority with regard to the lists themselves. That here (1 Chron. 9:26) and elsewhere C describes both temple musicians and gatekeepers as Levites, whereas Neh. 11 puts only musicians into this category, would however support the priority of the Nehemiah list (as argued by Mowinckel, *Studien* I, 146–147, and Rudolph 1949, 183–184, *inter alios*). This is, however, no more than a plausible hypothesis.

[4–9] Unlike 1 Chron. 9, the Nehemiah list restricts lay leaders to Judeans and Benjaminites. If Ephraimites and Manassehites have been added to C's list, it would confirm what we already know, that this author never loses sight of the pan-Israelite ideal. In contrast to the repatriation list in Neh. 7, listing here is according to large tribal subdivisions. The three subdivisions or "sons" of Judah are Shelah, Perez, and Zerah (cf. Gen. 46:12; Num. 26:19–20). While all three appear in 1 Chron. 9, our list has only Shelah and Perez represented by Maaseiah and Athaiah respectively, each with a linear genealogy of six or seven generations. Numbers are given only for the Perezites, and these are restricted to men who could be drafted into the militia. While the list obviously has something in common with 1 Chron. 9, none of the names is actually identical, though there are alternative forms (Athaiah/Uthai, Amariah/Imri, Maaseiah/Asaiah). Some of the differences may be explained by the different historical and demographic situations to which the lists correspond, though it is clear that considerable corruption has occurred in transmission (cf. the much shorter list in LXX). Only one Benjaminite paterfamilias is given, a certain Sallu with a genealogy of seven generations—as against four in 1 Chron. 9. These Benjaminite names cannot fail to arouse suspicion since not one of them occurs in Benjaminite lists elsewhere (Gen. 36; Num. 26:38–41; 1 Chron. 7:6–12; 8:1–40). Only the first two names in Sallu's genealogy are identical in the two lists, though two other names in 1 Chron. 9 (Hodaviah/Judah, Hassenuah) correspond to names of commanders at Neh. 11:9. The former, from an important and numerous family (Ezra 2:35), was second in command of the city, while another Benjaminite, Joel ben Zichri (cf. 1 Chron. 8:19, 23, 27), was military commander, perhaps successor to Nehemiah's brother Hanani (Neh. 7:2). The relative prominence of Benjaminites, reflected in these offices and in the large number of settlers, can be explained by the dense population of the Benjaminite region noted in our discussion of the census, not to mention the fact that Jerusalem itself was within Benjaminite tribal territory.

The occurrence of Zaccur son of Imri in the list of wall builders (Neh. 3:2), probably identical with Zechariah son of Amariah (= Imri, 1 Chron. 9:4) in our list, and of Col-hozeh who also participated in the wall-building (3:15), may point to the date of the present list since both are two generations earlier than their descendants named here as settlers in Jerusalem.

[10–14] According to our reading six houses of priests are represented, including three of the four occurring in Ezra 2:36–39 (see commentary ad loc.). Jedaiah and Joiarib (or Jehoiarib) occur elsewhere together (Neh. 12:6, 19). The former, of the house of Jeshua (Ezra 2:36 = Neh. 7:39; see W. F. Albright, *JPOS* 6, 1926, 96–100), is listed among the first repatriates (Neh. 12:6) and gives his name to the second of the twenty-four priestly courses (1 Chron. 24:7). The latter is the patronymic for the first of the courses (1 Chron. 24:7). He is also the ancestor of the Maccabees (1 Macc. 2:1), and it has been suggested that the name was inserted in the list at that late date. Jachin is less prominent but should not be eliminated. He has given his name to the twenty-first course (1 Chron. 24:17). The six-member linear genealogy of Seraiah, last preexilic high priest (2 Kings 25:18; Jer. 52:24), is defective since Azariah not Hilkiah was Seraiah's father (1 Chron. 6:14; Ezra 7:1). Rather curiously, 1 Chron. 9:11 omits Seraiah, beginning the genealogy with Azariah. Both abbreviated versions should be compared with the much fuller genealogies in 1 Chron. 5:29–41 [6:3–15] and Ezra 7:1–5. The designation "ruler *(nāgîd)* of the house of God," which could be used of more than one temple official (cf. 2 Chron. 35:8), came to be restricted to the high priest (1 Chron. 9:20; 2 Chron. 31:13), which is clearly its meaning here. It may be taken to indicate that the jurisdiction of the high priest, while exercised primarily in the religious sphere, also had important political and social implications. An interesting parallel (suggested by R. A. Bowman 1954, 775) would be the Islamic imām whose influence, as recent history has amply demonstrated, is not restricted to the religious sphere. There follows the seven-member linear genealogy of Adaiah. The first two and the last two names are identical in 1 Chron. 9, the middle three are absent, but the genealogy there continues for six more generations. The four-generation line of Amasai (= Amasiah), of the Immer branch of the postexilic priesthood (cf. Ezra 2:37), completes the list of priests. The total of 1,192 priests—considerably higher in C's list—is probably quite realistic for the period in question.

[15–18] The total number of Levites is 284, less than a quarter that of priests. Six are mentioned by name. Shemaiah, whose descent is traced through four generations, is identified in 1 Chron. 9:14 as belonging to the Merari group, Merari being the third son of Levi according to Priestly genealogical tradition (Ex. 6:16; etc.). The name Merari may have fallen out of the list in the course of transmission. Shabbethai and Jozabad are assigned responsibility for outside work relating to the temple, probably involving such things as collecting tithes and revenues. Levites with the same names took part in the public reading of the law and are elsewhere named as contemporaries of Ezra and Nehemiah (Ezra 8:33; Neh. 8:7; 10:15). Since this conflicts with the later date which we have assigned to the list, the names, which are absent from C's list, may have been added to fill out the picture. Mattaniah, an Asaphite Levitical musician, has a four-member genealogy in both lists. Abda (Obadiah at 1 Chron. 9:16), whose descent is traced back through three generations, represents the Jeduthun guild of musicians (cf. 1 Chron. 25:1). Bakbukiah, finally, appears to have been an assistant to Mattaniah the precentor. He may be identical with the Bakbakkar of 1 Chron. 9:15 and the liturgical singer Bukkiah mentioned at 1 Chron. 25:13. As suggested earlier, the list fits into a stage intermediate between the early postexilic period when musicians and gatekeepers were distinct from Levites and the time of C when both functions had been absorbed into the Levitical office.

[19] The temple gatekeepers are listed next. In the census (Ezra 2:42 = Neh. 7:45) and at Neh. 12:25 there are six names of gatekeepers, in 1 Chron. 9 there are four, and of these four only two, Akkub and Talmon, occur here. These two occur in all lists and always together. No information on this class of temple employees is provided except the laconic statement that they stood guard at the gates, which, while hardly unexpected, does not merit deletion as a gloss (R. Zadok, *ZAW* 94, 1982, 298). The 1 Chron. 9 list provides much more information: they were Levites, they guarded the King's Gate to the east, they were established by Samuel and David and functioned on a rota system, they had responsibility for the temple's security and for its furniture and utensils, and they lodged in the temple precincts. For the names see on Ezra 2:42.

[20–24] The register of settlers in Jerusalem is followed by a list of provincial settlements (25–36). This list should follow directly after v. 20 which introduces it. The connection has, however, been broken by three notes or appendices to the register dealing with temple servants, Levites, and a layman who served as a royal official (21–24). The appendices are therefore in inverse order to that of the list. In the heading to the settlement list (20), "priests and Levites"— or, as MT now stands, "levitical priests"—is probably an addition suggested by Neh. 7:72a. The statement that all of the repatriated Israelites reoccupied their ancestral holdings is probably idealistic.

The first note (21) deals with the temple servants (n^e *tînîm;* see on Ezra 2:43) since this class was not included in the list. Their overseers were Ziha (see Ezra 2:43) and Gishpa, otherwise unknown and hardly a scribal error for Hasupha who follows Ziha in the census. Their location would have been known from the list of wall builders (3:26, 31). Mention of overseers suggested a second note about a certain Uzzi—a familiar Levitical name—an Asaphite who was supervisor of temple liturgy or chief sacristan at the time of writing. Since he was great-grandson of the Mattaniah named as precentor in the list immediately preceding (v. 17), the note must have been added at least half a century after the list. The royal decree echoes the language of C (1 Chron. 25) with reference to David's dispositions for the temple liturgy. Neh. 12:24 also alludes to a command of David *(miṣvat dāvîd)* which specifies liturgical tasks to be discharged at regular intervals (cf. 1 Chron. 25:9–31). The author of the last note (24) may have understood this, quite naturally, as referring to the Persian king, since he goes on to name a royal counselor from the Zerah phratry of Judah. This person, Pethahiah, is sometimes thought to have been resident at the court in Susa, which might then explain the absence of the Zerah phratry from the register. Since, however, the phrase "at the king's hand" (see textual note j) need not be interpreted literally, he may have been a local official reporting to the central government via the satrapal and provincial authorities and representing the interests of the local population.

The rebuilding of the wall and the peopling of the "holy city" (11:1), brought to completion amid great hardships, ensured that this community, an insignificant component of a vast empire, would survive to face other challenges even after that empire had passed from the scene. It was to Nehemiah, with his remarkable combination of idealism and political realism, that early Judaism owed its ability to survive these challenges.

A Catalog of Settlements (Neh. 11:25–36)

Y. Aharoni, *The Land of the Bible: A Historical Geography,* Philadelphia, 1979 (2nd ed.), 347–356, 409–411; "The Negeb of Judah," *IEJ* 8, 1958, 26–38; W. F. Albright,

The Biblical Period, 52–53; "The Topography of Simeon," *JPOS* 4, 1924, 149–161; A. **Alt,** "Judas Gaue unter Josia," *KS* 2:276–288; "Bemerkungen zu einigen judäischen Ortslisten des Alten Testaments," *KS* 2:289–305; "Festungen und Levitenorte im Lande Juda," *KS* 2:306–315; F. M. **Cross** and G. E. Wright, "The Boundary and Province Lists of the Kingdom of Judah," *JBL* 75, 1956, 202–226; M. **Har-El,** "The Valley of the Craftsmen (Ge' Haharašim)," *PEQ* 109, 1977, 75–86; F. J. **Helfmeyer,** *"hānâ; mahᵃneh,"* *TDOT* 5:4–19; U. **Kellermann,** "Die Liste in Nehemia 11, eine Dokumentation aus den letzten Jahren des Reiches Juda," *ZDPV* 82, 1966, 209–227; B. **Mazar,** "The Cities of the Priests and Levites," *VTSup.* 7, 1959, 193–205; K. **Möhlenbrink,** "Die levitischen Überlieferungen des Alten Testaments," *ZAW* n.F. 11, 1934, 184–231; G. **von Rad,** *Das Geschichtsbild des chronistischen Werkes,* Stuttgart, 1930, 21–25.

11:25 These are[a] the settlements with their fields:

Some Judeans settled in Kiriath-arba and its dependencies,[b] Dibon and its dependencies, Jekabzeel and its dependencies. [26]Also in Jeshua, Moladah, Beth-pelet; [27]in Hazar-shual, Beersheba and its dependencies; [28]in Ziklag and Meconah and its dependencies; [29]in En-rimmon, Zorah, Jarmuth, [30]Zanoah, Adullam and its settlements, Lachish and its fields, Azekah and its dependencies. They encamped from Beersheba to the Valley of Hinnom.

[31]Some Benjaminites settled in Geba,[c] Michmas, Aijah, and Bethel and its dependencies; [32]Anathoth, Nob, Ananiah, [33]Hazor, Ramah, and Gittaim, [34]Hadid, Zeboim, Neballat, [35]Lod, Ono, and the Valley of the Craftsmen.[d] [36]Among the Levites some Judean divisions were attached to Benjamin.[e]

a. Reading *vᵉ'ēlleh* for MT *'el,* assuming loss of the final consonant to the following word.
b. Lit., "daughters."
c. Reading *bᵉgeba'* for MT *miggeba'.*
d. Or "of the Woods" *(hᵒrāšîm).*
e. Uncertain; lit., "belonging to Benjamin."

The catalog of Judean and Benjaminite settlements which follows is rather tenuously related to the preceding list of settlers in Jerusalem. As noted earlier, 11:20 may have been the heading for this section, though it speaks of cities or towns *('ārê yᵉhûdāh)* whereas here it is a question of small settlements *(hᵃṣērîm,* literally, "enclosures") with their attached farms and fields. The catalog lists seventeen locations in Judah and fifteen in Benjamin. There are some odd features of this list which have given rise to a lot of discussion. The first is the high percentage of place-names, especially Judean place-names, which occur nowhere else in Ezra-Nehemiah. Only one of the Judean locations mentioned here—Zanoah—occurs among the twenty-six in the census (Ezra 2 = Nehemiah 7). On the other hand, ten of the fifteen Benjaminite locations in the catalog are mentioned in the census. In contrast to this situation, eight of the Judean locations occur, some with slight variations, among the thirty-six in the Judean town list of Josh. 15:20–33, and generally in the same order. Another problem is the location within the province of those settlements which can be identified. The list begins with Kiriath-arba, the archaic name for Hebron, and the ten settlements following are all in the Negeb, within a radius of about twenty miles from Beersheba. This, however, is a region which we know to have been under Edomite-Arab control at the time of Nehemiah. The remaining six—Zorah to Azekah—are situated in the Shepelah, the lowlands going down to the coastal plain. If we compare the Benjaminite place-names (31–35) with the much longer list in Josh. 18:11–28 (cf. 1 Chron. 8), we see that towns on the southern border of Benjamin are completely absent from the catalog. How are we to explain these anomalies?

One conclusion which can be drawn at once is that it is not a list of places where diaspora Jews settled at different times during the Persian period. While some must have settled outside of the province of Yehud (see, for example, Ezra 7:25; Neh. 4:6 [12]; 13:24–25), eleven of the Judean settlements are in territory which came under Edomite-Arab control after the fall of Jerusalem and remained outside of the Jewish sphere until Maccabean times (1 Macc. 5:65; 11:34). It is also unlikely, in spite of the concluding note (36), that it consists in a list of Levitical settlements (*pace* Alt, *KS* 2:289–305), since no more than four of the names (assuming Dibon = Debir and En-rimmon = Ain) occur in the list of Levitical cities (Josh. 21:9–19). Attempts to backdate it to preexilic times or the period shortly after the return (e.g., Aharoni, Kellermann) fail to explain why it has been located at this point in the Nehemiah story, and the hypothesis of a Maccabean insertion, while not impossible, is unsupported.

We may fare somewhat better if we return to the boundary lists and town lists following the narrative of the conquest in the book of Joshua. The first Judean city to be assigned—to Caleb—was Hebron, Kiriath-arba (Josh. 14:6–15; 15:13–14), and Kiriath-arba is named first in the catalog. The territorial lists then describe the boundaries of Judah (Josh. 15:1–12), and in the catalog (25–30) the places listed mark the southern and western boundaries of Judah. Description of the northern boundary was unnecessary since Judah and Benjamin are taken to be one entity. There follows in Joshua a list of towns in the Negeb with their dependent settlements (Josh. 15:20–32). The catalog follows suit: all of the Negeb settlements which it names—with the sole exception of Meconah—are taken from the Joshua list and reproduced in the same order. The six settlements in the Shephelah are all likewise taken from the Joshua list. The towns in the hill country and the Wilderness of Judah (Josh. 15:48–62) are omitted, since the purpose of the catalog is to mark out the ideal boundaries of the province. The list of Benjaminite settlements, which omits the southern boundary points contiguous with Judah, completes the circuit in the north.

Our list, then, fits very well with the exodus-settlement pattern which we have observed at several points in our reading of Ezra-Nehemiah. It illustrates an important facet of the C narrative as a whole, namely, that history must always conform to ancient patterns. The statement which summarizes and concludes the Judean section of the catalog—that they encamped from Beersheba in the south to Ge-hinnom on the northern boundary of Judah (cf. Josh. 15:8; 18:16)—makes the same point. The idea of the land as an encampment around the sanctuary, a reproduction of the arrangement during the wilderness journeying, is based on ancient tradition. The idea is expressed in Deuteronomy (23:10–15 [9–14]) but is more fully developed in the Priestly source. The tent-sanctuary was set up at Shiloh, where the distribution of land took place under civil and religious leadership (Josh. 18:1; 19:51). Levites and people were to encamp around the sanctuary (Num. 1:53; 2:2; etc). The military allusion, noted also in the previous section (11:6, 14), finds its explanation here (cf. Num. 1:3). Also the requirement of ritual purity, a prominent aspect of postexilic thought, perhaps reflected in what Deuteronomy has to say about the purity of the camp (Deut. 23:10–15 [9–14]). The metaphor retained its vigor in C's history (1 Chron. 9:18–19; 2 Chron. 31:2) and indeed down into the Roman period, conspicuously in the Qumran community (see especially 1QM and CD).

[25–30] It remains to add a brief note on the place-names in the list. The Judean settlements begin with **Kiriath-arba,** the old name for Hebron (Judg. 1:10), about nineteen miles south of Jerusalem. Then **Dibon,** perhaps identical with Debir, immediately following Kiriath-arba in the settlement list in Joshua (15:15–19); less probably identified with Dimona in the Negeb (Josh. 15:22) = el-Qebâb about twenty-two miles east of Beersheba. **Jekabzeel** or Kabzeel (Syr., L, Vulg.) in the Joshua list (15:21) is either Kh. Ḥōra (Tel Ira) or Kh. al-Gharra, twelve and fifteen miles respectively east of Beersheba. Most of these identifications are hypothetical, but they all point to the same general area. **Jeshua,** probably Shema (Josh. 15:26), has also been identified with Tell es-Sa'aweh (Tel Jeshua) fifteen miles east of Beersheba. **Moladah** (Josh. 15:26) has been located at Khereibet el-Waten (Ḥorvat Yittan), Kh. Quṣeifeh and Tell el-Milḥ, all in the same area. **Beth-pelet** (Josh. 15:27) may be either Tell es-Saqati (Tel Shoquet) or Kh. el-Meshash, though Tell el-Milḥ has also been suggested. **Hazar-shual** (= Jackal enclosure, Josh. 15:28) was located by Abel at Kh. Waṭan and by Albright at Kh. el-Meshash. **Beersheba** (Josh. 15:28), the ancient site of which is situated at Tell es-Saba' (Tel Beer-sheba) about two miles east of the well-known modern city, is the focal point in this part of the catalog. **Ziklag** (Josh. 15:31) may be either Tell esh-Shari'ah (Tel Sera') about thirteen miles northwest of Beersheba or Tell el-Khuweilfeh (Alt, *KS* 3:429–435). The only site absent from the Joshua list is **Meconah,** emended unnecessarily to Meronah by Albright (*JPOS* 4, 1924, 152), and perhaps identical with Madmannah (Kh. Umm ed-Deimneh) about ten miles northeast of Beersheba. **En-rimmon** (= Pomegranate Spring, Josh. 15:32; 19:7) may be located at Kh. Umm er-Ramāmîm, about nine miles northeast of Beersheba.

As noted, the last six of the Judean place-names are in the Shephelah. **Zorah,** attributed to Dan in Josh. 19:41 and associated with Samson in Judg. 13:2, is generally identified with Ṣar'ah, about twenty miles west of Jerusalem. In the same region is **Jarmuth** (Josh. 15:35), identified with Kh. Yarmuk. Close by is **Zanoah** (Josh. 15:34), perhaps Zānûḥ, and **Adullam** (Josh. 15:35), either Tell esh-Sheik or Kh. Idelmā. **Lachish** (Josh. 15:39), Tell ed-Duweir, about twenty miles southwest of Jerusalem, was the center of an agricultural region (cf. "and its fields"). **Azekah** (Josh. 15:35), mentioned in the Lachish letters, is often identified with Tell ez-Zakarîyeh about six miles southeast of Lachish.

[31–36] For the names of Benjaminite settlements which also occur in the repatriation list see Ezra 2:26–33. The first four, within a range of about ten miles north of Jerusalem, mark the northern limits of the tribal boundary. **Aijah** (Kh. Ḥaiyān near Kh. et-Tell) is identical with Ai (Ezra 2:28). The next three are within a range of some three miles north of Jerusalem. **Nob** is identical with Nebo of Ezra 2:29, where the Elide priesthood settled after the destruction of Shiloh by the Philistines (1 Sam. 21–22). **Ananiah** is generally identified with el-'Azariah or Bethany—the name perpetuates the memory of Lazarus. **Hazor,** not to be confused with the great city of the Northern Kingdom, is identified with either Kh. Ḥazzûr five miles northwest of Jerusalem or Tel Aṣur = Baal-nazor (2 Sam. 13:23) ten miles further north. The site of **Gittaim** (= the two Gaths) has been much discussed (see especially A. Alt, *PJB* 35, 1939, 100–104, and B. Mazar, *IEJ* 4, 1954, 227–235); it may be identical with Tell Râs Abū Ḥamîd near Ramleh. On the western extreme of the province are **Zeboim,** perhaps Kh. Sabieh near Lod, **Neballat,** perhaps Beit Nabala (Ḥorvat Nevallat) northeast of Lod, **Lod, Ono** and the **Valley of the Craftsmen** (if this is the correct translation; see textual note d). The final statement, the meaning of which is obscure, perhaps intends to say that Levitical settlements were not confined to the tribal territory of Judah.

Lists of Temple Personnel (Neh. 12:1–26)

F. M. **Cross,** "A Reconstruction of the Judean Restoration," *JBL* 94, 1975, 4–18; U. **Kellermann,** *Nehemia,* 105–110; E. **Meyer,** *Die Entstehung des Judentums,* 102–104, 168–183; S. **Mowinckel,** *Studien* I, 151–162; G. **Widengren,** "The Persian Period," in J. H. Hayes and J. M. Miller (eds.), *Israelite and Judaean History,* 506–509; H. G. M. **Williamson,** "The Historical Value of Josephus' *Jewish Antiquities* xi.297–301," *JTS* n.s. 28, 1977, 49–66.

12:1 These are the priests and the Levites who came up with Zerubbabel son of Shealtiel and Jeshua: Seraiah, Jeremiah, Ezra, [2]Amariah, Malluch, Hattush, [3]Shecaniah, Rehum, Meremoth, [4]Iddo, Ginnethon,[a] Abijah, [5]Mijamin, Maadiah, Bilgah, [6]Shemaiah. Also Joiarib, Jedaiah, [7]Sallu, Amok, Hilkiah, Jedaiah. These were the chiefs of the priests and of their colleagues in the days of Jeshua.

[8]The Levites: Jeshua, Binnui, Kadmiel, Sherebiah, Judah, and Mattaniah who, with his kinsmen, was responsible for thanksgiving hymns.[b] [9]Bakbukiah, Unni,[c] and[d] their colleagues were opposite them when their turn came to serve.

[10]Jeshua was the father of Joiakim, Joiakim was the father of Eliashib, Eliashib of Joiada, [11]Joiada was the father of Jonathan, Jonathan was the father of Jaddua.

[12]In the days of Joiakim the following were priests, heads of ancestral houses: of Seraiah, Meraiah; of Jeremiah, Hananiah; [13]of Ezra, Meshullam; of Amariah, Jehohanan; [14]of Malluchi,[e] Jonathan; of Shebaniah, Joseph; [15]of Harim, Adna; of Meraioth,[f] Helkai; [16]of Iddo,[g] Zechariah; of Ginnethon, Meshullam; [17]of Abijah, Zichri; of Miniamin, . . .;[h] of Moadiah, Piltai; [18]of Bilgah, Shammua; of Shemaiah, Jehonathan. [19]Also, of Joiarib, Mattenai; of Jedaiah, Uzzi; [20]of Sallai, Kallai; of Amok, Eber;[i] [21]of Hilkiah, Hashabiah; of Jedaiah, Nethanel.

[22]In the days of Eliashib,[j] Joiada, of Johanan and Jaddua, the heads of ancestral houses of the priests[k] were recorded down to[l] the reign of Darius the Persian. [23]The Levites, heads of ancestral houses, were recorded in the Book of Chronicles down to the time of Johanan son of Eliashib.

[24]The chiefs of the Levites were: Hashabiah, Sherebiah, Jeshua, Binnui,[m] Kadmiel, with their colleagues opposite them, engaged in praise and thanksgiving, following the decree of David the man of God, turn by turn, namely: [25]Mattaniah, Bakbukiah, Obadiah, Meshullam, Talmon, and Akkub, gatekeepers, mounted guard over the storerooms at the gates.

[26]These served[n] in the days of Joiakim son of Jeshua son of Jozadak, and in the days of Nehemiah the governor and Ezra the priest and scribe.

a. With several Heb. MSS and Vulg. (cf. 10:7 [6]) for MT "Ginnethoi."
b. Reading *hôdôt* for MT *huyyᵉdôt*.
c. MT Ketib has "Unno," Qere "Unni"; cf. 1 Chron. 15:18, 20. Unno is hypocoristic for Aniah (cf. Neh. 8:4) or Ananiah (cf. Neh. 3:23).
d. The conjunction is absent from MT but attested in several ancient versions and demanded by the context.
e. Rather than Qere "Melichu"; cf. Malluch (LXX, L), Malchijah (Syr.).
f. Or possibly Meremoth, with L and Syr.; cf. 10:5 [4]; 12:3.
g. With Qere; cf. Adaiah (L, Vulg.).
h. The name has dropped out.
i. It is unnecessary to emend to Ebed following LXX and Syr.
j. Omitting *halᵉviyyim*, "the Levites," the first word of the sentence, mistakenly inserted here but originally a marginal heading for v. 23 (or vs. 24–25) or a gloss on *bᵉnê lēvî*, "sons of Levi," an expression rare in Ezra-Nehemiah, used only here and at Ezra 8:15. In addition, this type of heading usually begins "in the days of . . ."; cf. v. 12. See Meyer 1896, 103, and Rudolph 1949, 194.
k. MT has "the heads of ancestral houses and the priests."
l. Reading *'ad* for MT *'al*. The latter cannot mean "in" or "during" in spite of LXX *(en basileia)* and Vulg. *(in regno)*. An alternative possibility, suggested by Rudolph (1949, 194) is that *sēper dibrê hayyāmîm* has been lost between *'al* and *malkût dārᵉyāveš happārsî* by haplography. If so, the preposition *'ad* must still be supplied. Less probably Albright *(JBL* 40, 1921, 112–113) emended to *mᵉ'al*, "from," the allusion then being to Darius I.
m. With LXX and Syr. against MT *bēn*, "son of"; cf. v. 8. This list does not provide patronymics and the relationship is otherwise unattested.
n. The verb is supplied.

The lists of names and the notes which follow fall into the following parts: priests, Levites, and gatekeepers in office under the high priest Joiakim (12–21, 24–26a); priests and Levites under Joiakim's predecessor Jeshua (1–9); brief notes on sources for both of these lists (22–23); the high-priestly succession from Jeshua to Jaddua, drawn up on the basis of the lists just named, with the possible exception of Jonathan (10–11). The concluding phrase (26b) has either been added to link these lists with the Ezra-Nehemiah story or it has been detached from the account of the dedication ceremony immediately following.

All of this heterogeneous material, which has nothing to do with the NM, was placed here as a supplement to the lists in 11:10–24, with which it has certain features in common: brief notes on the functions of temple personnel (12:8—cf. 11:17; 12:25—cf. 11:19), and allusion to the Davidic origin of the liturgical musicians (12:24—cf. 11:23).

Determining the time of composition is complicated by the clear indications of updating (vs. 6, 19, 22, 23), the uncertain chronology of the high priests, especially the last named Jaddua, and the compiler's failure to specify which Darius of the three is alluded to (v. 22). In its final form it cannot be earlier than the late fourth century, and probably postdates the conquests of Alexander. If Joiarib, ancestor of the Maccabeans (1 Macc. 2:1), was added or substituted for another name in the Hasmonean period (Hölscher 1923, 553; Rudolph 1949, 191), the last touches would have been put to the lists almost two centuries later still. While there are indications of schematizing and creative filling in, we may assume that the compiler was drawing on material available in the temple archives.

[12:1–7] The compiler first lists priests at the time of Jeshua. The twenty-two names purport to be those of priests who were part of the original immigration during the reign of Darius I. (See chart on page 337.) This list is parallel to the twenty-one patronyms in the list of priests serving at the time of Joiakim, who was high priest between Jeshua and Eliashib the contemporary of Nehemiah, and whose *floruit* must therefore have been the first half of the fifth century. Hattush is missing from 12:12–21 and there are some minor variants (Malluch/Malluchi, Shecaniah/Shebaniah, Rehum/Harim, Meremoth/Meraioth). In the Joiakim list the priests' names are attached to patronymics, but in the Jeshua list these are presented as the actual names of individuals who immigrated from Babylon. It will be obvious, however, that this list has little in common with the fourfold division of priests in the repatriation list (Ezra 2:36–39). It therefore seems proper to conclude that the Jeshua list (1–7) depends on the Joiakim list (12–21), the patronymics in the latter serving as personal names in the former.

There are also parallels between these two lists and the roster of priests who signed the solemn pledge in Neh. 10 (vs. 3–9 [2–8]). With the exception of Iddo, all of the first sixteen names in the two lists under discussion (12:1–7, 12–21) occur in the list of signatories, some in slightly different form. The absence of the last six (17 to 22 in the accompanying chart) from the pledge list, taken with the conjunction before the first of the six (Joiarib), makes it practically certain that these names were added at a later stage. The conclusion seems to be unavoidable that the list of signatories has drawn on the same archival source as the two lists here, at least for the priests, which strongly suggests that it is an artificial compilation. It is also rather curious that the covenant list has six additional names (italicized in the chart) which bring it up to the number of the Joiakim list. Comparison with 1 Chron. 24:7–18 permits the further suggestion that the master list (12:12–21) with its two derivates (12:1–7 and 10:3–9) marks a certain stage in the development of the priestly courses. This is true also of the master list before it was expanded (*pace* Williamson 1986, 360–361). A development from sixteen to twenty-four presents no problems since the number would tend to increase, probably in multiples of two or four, and seven of the names in the Joiakim list occur in the courses list. It will be noted that the first two of the six added names correspond to the first two courses.

[8–9] With the much shorter Levitical lists (8–9, 24–25) we have a quite different situation. Eight are listed from the time of the high priest Jeshua (8–9) and eight from the time of Joiakim (24–25). In this first section the names are patronymics but serve as personal names. To the four of the Zerubbabel caravan (Jeshua, Kadmiel, Binnui, Hodaviah = Judah) are added Sherebiah, the precentor Mattaniah and two others, probably also specialists in liturgical music. The later list (24–25) has six names in common with this one. It omits Judah, adds Hashabiah and substitutes Obadiah for Unni. What we are to make of this is difficult to say. If the first two names of the later list, Hashabiah and Sherebiah, refer to individuals who returned with Ezra (Ezra 8:18–19) and took part in the penitential liturgy (Neh. 9:5, with Hashabneiah for Hashabiah), the compiler must have backdated them to the time of the high priest Joiakim who certainly antedated Ezra. There are also parallels with the Levitical signatories of the pledge (Neh. 10:10–11 [9–10]), of whose names six appear in the two lists of Levites in this chapter. In all probability, both drew on the same temple archive.

It may be deduced from these lists that liturgical musicians, and perhaps also gatekeepers (25b), had Levitical status. In the repatriation list (Ezra 2:40–42 = Neh. 7:43–45) both musicians and gatekeepers are listed separately from Levites, whereas by the time the Chronicler composed his work they had been assimilated to the Levitical ranks. During Nehemiah's administration liturgical musicians were regarded as Levites (Neh. 11:15–18, 22–23), though the fact that they can still be listed separately (e.g., Neh. 13:5, 10) suggests caution in drawing conclusions about dating on this basis alone.

[10–11] This extremely brief section lists the high-priestly succession from Jeshua to Jaddua. The first, Jeshua, is a familiar figure whose time frame is certain. Son of Jehozadak (Ezra 3:2, 8; 5:2; 10:18; Hag. 1:1; Zech. 6:11; etc.), he was born in the diaspora and served as high priest under Darius I (522–485). The chronology of the last of the six, Jaddua, is unfortunately less certain. Josephus tells us that he succeeded Johanan in the high priesthood during the reign of Darius III (336–331), that he was greeted deferentially by Alexander on the latter's visit to Jerusalem, and that he died some time before the death of Alexander (*Ant.* 11.302, 325–339, 346–347). Since Alexander's visit to Jerusalem is certainly legendary, the only question remaining is whether the contemporaneity of Jaddua with Darius III and Alexander is based on independent information or simply deduced from the biblical text (Neh. 12:22). Since there are some aspects of Josephus' account of the period which have the semblance of historicity, and since he is likely to be informed about the high priesthood if about anything, we should perhaps incline to accept his testimony at this point. And if so, the six-member linear genealogy of the postexilic high priesthood would cover about two centuries; barely possible, but not at all probable.

An ingenious solution to this problem, proposed by F. M. Cross, is to expand the list from six to ten on the assumption that, first, papponymy (the naming of a child after the grandparent) was practiced in the high priestly family and, second, the resulting duplicates were subsequently eliminated through haplography. He thus inserts a second Eliashib and a second Johanan between the second and third names in the list and adds a third Johanan and a third Jaddua (assuming Jaddua and Joiada are the same) at the end. This, he believes, brings the average tenure of office of each incumbent down to a reasonable figure. The most obvious problem with this hypothesis, however, is that the actual list contains no alternation of names and therefore no point of departure for assuming papponymy. There is also no papponymy in the preexilic priestly genealogies. Moreover, Eliashib was the son of Joiakim (Neh. 12:10; *Ant.* 11.158), not his brother as Cross supposes. It is also by no means certain that the Eliashib whose son Jehohanan provided hospitality for Ezra in the

LISTS OF PRIESTS

Neh. 12:1–7 *(under Jeshua)*	Neh. 12:12–21 *(under Joiakim)*	Neh. 10:3–9 [2–8] *(signatories)*	1 Chron. 24 *(courses)*
1. Seraiah	Seraiah/Meraiah	Seraiah	
2. Jeremiah	Jeremiah/Hananiah	Azariah	
3. Ezra	Ezra/Meshullam	Jeremiah	
		Pashhur	
4. Amariah	Amariah/Jehohanan	Amariah	
5. Malluch	Malluchi/Jonathan	Malchijah	Malchijah (5)
6. Hattush		Hattush	
7. Shecaniah	Shebaniah/Joseph	Shebaniah	Shecaniah (10)
		Malluch	
8. Rehum	Harim/Adna	Harim	Harim (3)
9. Meremoth	Meraioth/Helkai	Meremoth	
		Obadiah	
		Daniel	
10. Iddo	Iddo/Zechariah		
11. Ginnethon	Ginnethon/Meshullam	Ginnethon	
		Baruch	
		Meshullam	
12. Abijah	Abijah/Zichri	Abijah	Abijah (8)
13. Mijamin	Miniamin/———	Mijamin	Mijamin (6)
14. Maadiah	Moadiah/Piltai	Maaziah	Maaziah (24)
15. Bilgah	Bilgah/Shammua	Bilgai	Bilgai (15)
16. Shemaiah	Shemaiah/Jehonathan	Shemaiah	

17. Joiarib	Joiarib/Mattenai		Jehoiarib (1)
18. Jedaiah	Jedaiah/Uzzi		Jedaiah (2)
19. Sallu	Sallai/Kallai		
20. Amok	Amok/Eber		
21. Hilkiah	Hilkiah/Hashabiah		
22. Jedaiah	Jedaiah/Nethanel		

temple was high priest (Ezra 10:6). He is not called high priest, and
it is unlikely that in the circumstances Ezra would have consorted
with the high priestly family (see commentary on the passage). It is
even less likely that the Eliashib described at Neh. 13:4 as "placed
in charge of the rooms of the house of God" was the high priest of
our list. This would be an odd way of referring to the high priest,
and would more likely suggest that this individual, charged with
rather more humble responsibilities, is being distinguished from his
namesake the high priest. These considerations considerably reduce
the attraction, and eliminate the necessity, of creating a second Eliashib holder of the high priestly office. Similar considerations discourage the creation of additional Jadduas, the first of whom in any case
bears the quite different name Joiada. The situation is not improved
by assuming the practice of papponymy in the Sanballat family. This
may be so, but the fact remains that the Sanballat intermediate
between the contemporary of Nehemiah and the governor of Samaria
in the Daliyeh papyri exists only by courtesy of the hypothesis.

A simpler solution is that the list is incomplete, and that the
compiler has arranged the names known to him in the usual form
of a linear genealogy. There may also have been times of political
crisis, not infrequent in the Persian period, when the office was
vacant.

It remains to comment briefly on the remaining names in the list.
The next in line after Jeshua, Joiakim, is the son of Jeshua according
to the compiler followed by Josephus (*Ant.* 11.121). He fills the gap
between Jeshua, contemporary of Zerubbabel, and Eliashib, contemporary of Nehemiah (Neh. 3:1, 20–21; 13:28). A name may have
fallen out, or there may have been some discontinuity in this period
of about seventy years during which more than one political crisis
occurred. According to Josephus (*Ant.* 11.121), Joiakim was high
priest *(archiereus)* at the same time that Ezra was serving as first
priest *(prōtos hiereus)* in the Babylonian diaspora. Since the author
of 1 Esdras (9:39–40) describes Ezra as high priest during his mission
in Judah, he may be reflecting an early tradition, which survived for
centuries, that Ezra replaced or deposed Joiakim. The only part of
all this which has serious plausibility, and which fits the chronological order of Ezra and Nehemiah defended in this commentary, is that
Joiakim held the office at the time of Ezra's arrival.

The listing of Joiada, son and successor of Eliashib, is the only one
which diverges from the formula by omitting the verb *(hôlîd)*. At a
later point we hear of a certain Jehoiada son of Eliashib one of whose
sons married Sanballat's daughter (13:28). While it is uncertain
whether the designation "high priest" refers to him or his father, the

compiler may have taken his cue either from this text or from the
other list of high priests at 12:22. The next in succession is Jonathan
son of Joiada and grandson of Eliashib. The temptation to emend to
Johanan on the basis of Neh. 12:22 and Ezra 10:6 (assuming that
"son" here means "grandson") should be resisted. It has no textual
support, the names are quite different, and we are told explicitly that
Johanan was the son, not the grandson, of Eliashib (12:23). This
Johanan was the high priest in office about 410 B.C.E. when he was
the recipient of a letter from the Elephantine community which
remained unanswered (*AP* 30:18). Josephus' story about the sacrile-
gious murder of Jeshua in the temple by his brother Johanan the high
priest, an event which is recorded as having taken place under either
Artaxerxes II (404–359) or Artaxerxes III (358–338), appears to
involve the same person. But since, as is generally recognized, Josephus' chronology of the later Persian period is seriously defective, it
would be unwise to put too much weight on this information.

[12–21] The list of priests at the time of Joiakim in the early fifth
century shows no signs of artificiality. Its connection with the list in
vs. 1–7, the covenant signatories (10:3–9 [2–8]), and the priestly
courses (1 Chron. 24) was discussed earlier. A brief note on some of
the names may be helpful. Ezra is an alternative form of Azariah (see
on Ezra 7:1 and cf. Neh. 10:3 [2]). The name of Hattush, sixth in the
list of priests at the time of Jeshua (12:2), has been lost in transmission. Joseph is another example of the use of patriarchal names at
this time (cf. Ezra 10:42—a layman). The name corresponding to
Harim in the Jeshua list is Rehum, which is probably the result of
metathesis *(ḥrm—rḥm);* Harim is undoubtedly original. Adna,
Helkai (Hilkiah), Iddo (Adaiah) all occur elsewhere as the names of
laymen (Ezra 10:30; Neh. 8:4; Ezra 10:29). It is commonly assumed
that Zechariah, descendant of the Iddo listed here, is the canonical
prophet. Iddo is his father at Ezra 5:1 and his grandfather in the
superscription to the book which bears his name (Zech. 1:1)—which,
however, was probably influenced by the quite distinct Zechariah son
of Jeberechiah of Isa. 8:2. Both names are common, however, and
the prophet Zechariah was a contemporary of Jeshua not Joiakim.
The name of the descendant of Miniamin has been lost. Piltai,
hypocoristic of Paltiel, occurs in the Elephantine papyri (*AP* 40:1,
5), and Shammai is elsewhere (Neh. 11:17) the name of a Levite.

As noted earlier, the last six names, missing from the list of covenant signatories, were added at a later stage. Joiarib and Jedaiah
represent the first two courses (1 Chron. 24:7). Mattenai belongs
elsewhere to a layman (Ezra 10:33, 37) and Uzzi (cf. Ezra 7:4) is a
typical Levitical name. Kallai occurs only here. Since there are sev-

eral examples of these rhyming names (e.g., Gabbai, Sallai; Neh. 11:8), it may have been invented to fill a small gap in the record. Amok (= the Deep One?) sounds like a nickname. Eber is another example of patriarchal nomenclature (Gen. 10:21; 1 Chron. 5:13; 8:12, 22). It would be unwise to eliminate the second Jedaiah purely on the grounds of repetition. Nethanel (cf. Ezra 10:22) belonged to the Pashhur phratry; the patronymic occurs in the list of covenant signatories but is absent from both priest lists in this chapter. Whether this is due to the hazards of textual transmission or the vicissitudes of this group's history we do not know. Nor do we know when or why the Joiakim list was expanded to include these six names.

[22–23] Wishing to assure the reader of the reliability of his information, the compiler added a brief note about his sources. First, he claims to be relying on written information for the names of the heads of priest families, and the records are available from the time of Eliashib (and therefore Nehemiah) to "Darius the Persian." This title does not in itself presuppose the perspective of the Hellenistic period, for Herodotus (2.110, 158) speaks of Darius I in this way. If Jaddua, last of the four high priests named, was a contemporary of Alexander, as Josephus says, then Darius III Codomannus (336–331) is the king referred to. In that case, some names of high priests during this period of about a century and a half must have been omitted. The alternative is Darius II Nothus (423–404), which reduces the time span considerably but leaves unsolved the problem of Jaddua. The problem for the modern reader is probably due to the foreshortening of the Persian period which is already in evidence in Josephus, caused especially by confusing or conflating the second and third Artaxerxes and the second and third Darius. Second, for the Levitical lists he refers the reader to a written source, a Book of Chronicles, not the canonical book but a compilation of names and genealogies preserved, we may suppose, in the temple archives. For some reason Levitical records available to the compiler ended a generation after Nehemiah, in the late fifth or early fourth century.

[24–26] This list of Levites and gatekeepers at the time of the high priest Joiakim gives only family names. For the names of Mattaniah the precentor and his stand-in Bakbukiah the compiler probably drew on the notice in the previous chapter (11:17). Dependence on the lists to which this notice belongs is also apparent in the allusion to David's arrangements for liturgical music (cf. 11:22–23). The description of David as "man of God," that is, prophet, follows C's usage (1 Chron. 25:2; 2 Chron. 8:14). It was no doubt among the Levitical guilds of musicians, heirs of the cultic prophets of the First Temple, that the tradition of David as prophet developed. It continued into the Roman period, determining the way in which the Psalms, attributed to David, were used in both the Qumran community (1QPs[a]) and early Christianity (e.g., Acts 1:16; 2:25–31, 34).

The last three in the list are identified as temple gatekeepers. Their names—Meshullam (Shallum), Talmon (Telem), and Akkub—appear in other lists (1 Chron. 9:17; Ezra 10:24; Neh. 11:19). The task of guarding the temple storerooms *(ʾasuppîm)*—less probably the thresholds *(sippîm;* cf. 1 Chron. 9:19; 26:15)—is attested in 1 Chron. 26:15, 17. It is not clear whether they were considered Levitical by the compiler; C, in any case, provides them with an unimpeachable Levitical pedigree (1 Chron. 9:17–19, 26).

The addition of a phrase at the end of the lists synchronizing the high priesthood of Joiakim with Nehemiah and Ezra allows the compiler to conclude with a recall of the great personalities of that decisive epoch of reform and consolidation. The synchronism is correct for Ezra but not for Nehemiah, contemporary of the high priest Eliashib. By the compiler's time, however, the two names were already firmly linked, both were present simultaneously in Jerusalem, and their respective activities had been amalgamated into one continuous work of salvage and restoration. The order in which their names appear does not, therefore, have any bearing on the issue of chronological priority. As at 8:9, the governor has precedence over anyone else in the province and so is named first.

The Dedication of the Wall (Neh. 12:27–43)

M. Burrows, "The Topography of Nehemiah 12:31–43," *JBL* 54, 1935, 29–39; K. Fullerton, "The Procession of Nehemiah," *JBL* 38, 1919, 171–179; B. Mazar, "The Cities of the Priests and Levites," *VTSup.* 7, 1960, 193–205; J. Simons, *Jerusalem in the Old Testament,* Leiden, 1952, 446–450; N. H. Snaith, "Nehemiah xii. 36," *VT* 17, 1967, 243; R. de Vaux, *Ancient Israel,* 460–461.

12:27 For the dedication of the wall of Jerusalem they sought out Levites from all sides, to bring them to Jerusalem to carry out the dedication with joyful thanksgiving[a] and singing accompanied by cymbals, lutes, and zithers. [28]The musicians[b] also assembled from both the region surrounding Jerusalem and the Netophathite settlements; [29]also from Beth-gilgal and the countryside[c] of Geba and Azmaveth; for the musicians had built themselves settlements around Jerusalem.

³⁰The priests and Levites purified themselves; then they purified the people, the gates, and the wall.

³¹I led the leaders of Judah up onto the wall and appointed two large choirs to offer thanksgiving.[d] One proceeded[e] to the right on top of the wall in the direction of the Dung Gate. ³²Following them were Hoshaiah and half of the princes of Judah, ³³together with Azariah, Ezra,[f] and Meshullam, ³⁴Judah, Mijamin,[g] Shemaiah, and Jeremiah, ³⁵of the priestly ranks[h] with trumpets. Zechariah son of Jonathan, son of Shemaiah, son of Mattaniah, son of Micaiah, son of Zaccur, son of Asaph, ³⁶together with his colleagues Shemaiah, Azarel, Milalai, Gilalai, Maai, Nethanel, Judah, and Hanani,[i] with the musical instruments of David the man of God; and Ezra the scribe went ahead of them.

³⁷They passed by the Fountain Gate and went up directly by the stairs of the City of David, by the ascent to the wall, past the House of David, and so to the Water Gate on the east.

³⁸The second choir[d] went[j] to the left,[k] and I followed it with one half of the people on top of the wall, past the Tower of the Ovens to the Broad Wall; ³⁹then past the Ephraim Gate to the Mishneh Gate,[l] the Fish Gate, the Tower of Hananel and the Tower of the Hundred, and so to the Sheep Gate. They halted at the Gate of the Guard. ⁴⁰So both choirs[d] took up their stations in the house of God. I too, and the half of the officials who were with me, ⁴¹with the priests Eliakim, Maaseiah, Miniamin, Micaiah, Elioenai, Zechariah, and Hananiah with trumpets. ⁴²Also Maaseiah, Shemaiah, Eleazar, Uzzi, Jehohanan, Malchijah, Elam, and Ezer. The musicians then made loud music[m] under the leadership of Izrahiah. ⁴³On that day they offered great sacrifices, for God had given them cause for joy in abundance. The women and children also rejoiced, and the rejoicing of Jerusalem could be heard from afar.

a. MT has "the dedication and the joy," which could be read as hendiadys, giving *śimḥāh* the concrete sense of a joyful occasion (cf. 8:12; 2 Chron. 30:23). In view of similar expressions in 1 Chron. 15:25; 2 Chron. 30:21; and especially 2 Chron. 23:18 *(bᵉśimḥāh ûbᵉšîr),* it would nevertheless seem preferable to read *bᵉśimḥāh* with L.

b. Lit., "sons of the musicians," that is, members of guilds versed in liturgical music.

c. Lit., "fields"; cf. 13:10.

d. Heb. *tôdōt* ("thanksgivings," "thanksgiving choirs"), used with this meaning only in the present passage (vs. 31, 38, 40).

e. MT $v^e tah^a luk\bar{o}t$, a hapax, generally taken to mean "processions" or as an adj. "processing" (stem *hlk*, walk); but the parallel with v. 38 suggests the reading $v^e h\bar{a}$'*ahat hôleket*.

f. Since Ezra is the hypocoristic form of Azariah (cf. Neh. 10:3 [2]; 12:1, 13), it is often assumed either that one of the two is a gloss or that an editor erroneously identified Azariah with *the* Ezra (cf. 12:36). The absence of the conjunction before Ezra also points to a gloss. On the other hand, both are needed to balance with the seven priests in the northbound group (41), and we already know of another priest called Ezra (12:1, 13).

g. MT has Benjamin, probably misled by Judah immediately preceding.

h. MT has *ûmibb^e nê hakkōh^a nîm*, "and of the sons of the priests," but the conjunction appears to have been inserted as the result of a wrong division of the sentence. The phrase must refer to the persons named in the preceding verse since, first, Zechariah is a descendant of Asaph, therefore a Levite, and, second, trumpeting was a priestly prerogative (Num. 10:8; 31:6; 1 Chron. 15:24; 16:6; 2 Chron. 29:26; Ezra 3:10).

i. MT has "and Judah, Hanani."

j. Reading *hôleket* for *hahôleket*, "the one which went."

k. Reading *liśmō'l* for *l^e mô'l*.

l. See Neh. 3:6.

m. Lit., "made themselves heard" *(yašmî'û)*; cf. the same verb (*šm'*, Hiphil) frequently in C (1 Chron. 15:16, 19, 28; 16:5, 42; 2 Chron. 5:13). The usual translation "sang out loud" neglects the musical instruments.

At this point we return finally to the NM after the long insertion 7:5b–12:26. The remainder of the book draws on the NM with much editorial paraphrase, expansion, and no doubt omissions. The dedication of the wall is the expected finale to the completion of the city's defenses, including the synoicism. It brings Nehemiah's work to an appropriately solemn and satisfactory conclusion, even though several problems still awaited solution. The event is not dated. It would be natural to assume that it took place soon after the completion of the wall and the repopulation of the city, therefore within the first year of his administration (cf. 1:1; 2:1; 6:15). If so, it has been moved to make way for the Ezra material. What still remains to be narrated is connected only very loosely with this event ("on that day," "in those days," 12:44; 13:1, 15, 23).

Since there is no reason to assume that the dedication ceremony is an invention of C or someone from his circle (as Torrey 1895, 43–44; 1910, 248–249), we have the task of distinguishing between direct excerpt from the NM, paraphrase, and free editorializing. The assembling of Levitical musicians (27–29), the lists of cultic personnel (33–36, 41–42), and the concluding comment about the joy of the occasion are reminiscent of the Chronicler and were probably added by him or someone from his circle. This does not imply that the editing has transformed a secular event (e.g., a tour of inspection of the wall) into one which is explicitly religious. The outline of a religious ceremony is clear: assembly of community representatives lay and clerical, a rite of purification, circumambulation of the wall, and concluding sacrifices and sacrificial meal.

[12:27–29] Participation of Levitical musicians and allusion to thanksgiving and joyful liturgical music are characteristic of C (2 Chron. 23:18; 29:30; 30:23; Ezra 3:11–13). Musical instruments—cymbals and zithers played with the fingers or a pick—also figure routinely in liturgical celebrations described by C (1 Chron. 13:8; 15:16, 28; 16:5; 25:1, 6; 2 Chron. 5:12; 29:25). The information about the places where Levites resided is sometimes taken to indicate a situation which obtained after Nehemiah's administration (13:10) but before the solemn pledge of chapter 10 (v. 37 [36]), though it is unlikely that all Levites lived in Jerusalem at any time then or later. The places named are all within a radius of a few miles from Jerusalem: Netophah about six miles to the south, Geba and Azmaveth five to six miles north (see Ezra 2:22, 24, 26). If Beth-haggilgal is the site associated with the conquest traditions (Josh. 4:19; 15:7), it would be the most distant but still within easy reach. All the places named except Netophah are in Benjaminite territory (cf. 11:36).

Dedication—in Hebrew *ḥᵃnukkāh,* also the name of the Maccabean winter festival (1 Macc. 4:52–59)—is the giving over of a person or object to God symbolized by a complex of ritual acts. The idea of divine ownership and disposal is especially evident with those persons (e.g., Nazirites) or buildings (e.g., the temple) intended for the exclusive use of the deity, though it was also customary to dedicate private houses (Deut. 20:5). During the Persian period the dedication of the altar (Ezra 3:12–13), the rebuilt temple (Ezra 6:22), and the city symbolized by its wall mark progressive steps in the reconstitution of a people which thinks of itself in essentially religious terms.

[30] Purification rituals are carried out before not after a religious ceremony (e.g., Ex. 19:10, 14–15; Ezra 6:20). Purification of the participants is well attested. It could involve sexual abstinence, putting on clean clothes, and the offering of sacrifices. We are not told what it involved in this instance; perhaps the sprinkling of water over the walls and gates (cf. Num. 19:18; Ezek. 36:25). While such rituals were performed throughout the history of Israel, the need for freedom from contamination seems to have been a particular concern of the postexilic community (see also Ezra 6:20; Neh. 13:9, 22, 30).

[31–37] At this point we return to the first-person Nehemiah narrative after a long interval. Use of the first person does not provide an infallible guide to source division. One could argue, for example, that the division of the participants into two choirs was dictated by the antiphonal character of liturgical music (cf. 12:9, 24). Certainty is unattainable, and all we can say is that use of the first person creates a presumption in favor of direct excerpt from the NM. The most natural sense of the wording in the opening verse is that the procession took place on the wall, which, to judge by the section excavated by Kenyon, would allow for two or three to walk abreast. As governor, Nehemiah led the civil officials (*śārîm;* cf. 3:9, 7:2) to their starting point and marshaled the clergy. The point of departure was almost certainly the Valley Gate on the west side (2:13), from which the first group proceeded south and the second north, the eventual point of convergence being in the temple.

The parallel arrangement of the groups can be shown as follows:

I. *Southbound Group*	II. *Northbound Group*
first choir (31)	second choir (38)
seven priests (33–35a)	seven priests (41)
Zechariah, precentor (35b)	Izrahiah, precentor (42)
eight musicians (36)	eight musicians (42)
Hoshaiah (32)	Nehemiah (38)
half of the leaders (32)	half of the officials (40)

The liturgical character of the event is highlighted, especially in the term "choir" (lit., "thanksgiving") for each of the groups. True to form, the Chronistic editor also gives the names and, in one case, the genealogy of the clerical participants. As the text now stands (see textual notes f and g), the priests in the southbound group number seven, as when David brought the ark to Jerusalem (1 Chron. 15:24). All of the names, with the exception of Judah elsewhere belonging to a Levite (12:8), are attested for the period. They occur either among the covenant signatories (10:3, 8–9 [2, 7–8]) or in the list of residents in Jerusalem (12:1, 5–6, 12–13, 16–18), or in both. In keeping with liturgical orthopraxy (according to C) the priests blow trumpets. The eight Levitical musicians are under the baton of the Asaphite precentor Zechariah. Comparison of his genealogy with that of the musical director Mattaniah mentioned at 11:17 (reading Zichri for Zabdi with 1 Chron. 9:15 and L) suggests that he was Mattaniah's great-grandson, and therefore active some seventy-five or more years later; a conclusion which makes no sense in terms of actual chronology but may point to the time when the present narrative was composed or edited. Most of the eight Levitical names are attested elsewhere. Shemaiah, the name of a priest at Ezra 10:21, may be the equivalent of Shammua, a Levitical name at Neh. 11:17. Azarel is unattested, but the LXX variant Uzziel is of a well-known Levitical type (e.g., 1 Chron. 25:4). Milalai is also unattested and may be the rhyming twin of Gilalai (= Galal, Neh. 11:17). Maai, probably hypocoristic, is unattested, and Nethanel belongs to a preexilic Levite (2 Chron. 35:9). Judah, with its variants (Hodah, Hodaviah, etc.) is well attested, and Hanani is the name of one of C's Davidic musicians (1 Chron. 25:4, 25). For the description of David as man of God see on 12:24.

There can be little doubt that the inclusion of Ezra the scribe at the head of the southbound group, corresponding to Nehemiah in the other, is an editorial addition from the time when the activity of the two men had been amalgamated into one movement of reform. His inclusion disturbs the symmetry, and Nehemiah's counterpart, a certain Hoshaiah otherwise unknown, has already been mentioned.

[38–40] The essential part of the ceremony was the circumambulation of the wall, a ritual which was a common feature of the dedication of cities and buildings in antiquity and is still in use in the consecration of churches in some denominations. A good part of its rich significance is often lost on the modern reader as a result of anachronistic and misleading distinctions between "magic" and "religion." As M. Eliade has pointed out (*Patterns in Comparative Religion,* London, 1958, 371), its purpose is to affirm or reaffirm the idea of enclosure around a sacred center within which the threatening forces of chaos and disorder are brought under control. Some hints of the idea, and possibly also the ceremonial, can be detected in certain psalms (48:13–15 [12–14]; 68:25–28 [24–27]). One would therefore be led to think of a complete circuit of the wall. It appears, however, that the section between the Water Gate and the Sheep Gate, that is, a good part of the east side, was omitted, no doubt for practical reasons. The point of departure was almost certainly the Valley Gate on the west (2:13, 15; 3:13). The southbound group passed by the Dung Gate (2:13; 3:13) to the Fountain Gate near the southeast corner (2:14; 3:15), thence to the stone steps leading up the steep incline to the Ophel (3:15). The course of this part of the itinerary is uncertain. The procession may have had to leave the wall on account of the steep gradient, returning to it at a point further along. The House of David may indicate the site of David's palace, long destroyed but still remembered, or it may be connected with the Tombs of David mentioned in the list of builders (3:16). It seems that this group stayed with the wall only as far as the Water Gate opposite Gihon (3:26; 8:1), at that point turning west into the temple area.

Alternatively, the description may be defective at this point, in which case the two groups would have met at the Sheep Gate northeast of the temple area.

The northbound group to which Nehemiah belonged proceeded past the Tower of Ovens (3:11) and the Broad Wall (3:8) to the Ephraim Gate. This gate was part of the preexilic city wall, situated some two hundred yards from the Corner Gate (2 Kings 14:13). The name was probably retained for the corresponding gate in Nehemiah's wall. It had a spacious plaza where the people built booths during the celebration of Sukkoth (8:16). Passing the Mishneh and Fish Gates (3:3, 6), and the twin towers at the northwest corner (3:1), the procession arrived at the Sheep Gate where the work of rebuilding had been consecrated and initiated (3:1). At that point it left the wall to assemble with the southbound group at the Gate of the Guard. This place of assembly is often associated with the Court of the Guard (3:25), but this seems unlikely since the feature in question was part of the royal palace and therefore south of the temple (Jer. 32:2). It is more probably to be identified with the Parade Gate (3:31; perhaps also 2 Chron. 32:6) which was closer at hand and which, as the name suggests, was designed for such occasions. From there the entire company proceeded to the temple (40).

[41–42] The second group also contained seven priests and eight Levitical musicians with their leader. With the exception of Micaiah, all the names of priests occur either among those who had married foreign women (Ezra 10:18, 21–22, 28) or in the supplementary lists (Neh. 12:5, 12, 16–17), or in both. The eight Levitical names are less characteristically Levitical than we might expect; six of them occur elsewhere as priests' names (Ezra 7:5; 8:33; Neh. 12:2, 6, 13–14, 18–19). The only other Elam known to us is a layman (Ezra 2:7). Ezer, administrator of Mizpah, appears to be grouped with Levites (Neh. 3:19), though this is not entirely clear. Izrahiah (Jezrahiah), otherwise unattested, is the precentor corresponding to Zechariah in the southbound choir.

[43] The great (that is, many) sacrifices recall the dedication of the altar (Ezra 3:3–5) and of the rebuilt temple (Ezra 6:17). Now, as at the beginning, the sound of rejoicing was heard from afar (Ezra 3:13); now, as then, God gave them all, men, women, and children (cf. 8:2–3), cause for joy. There are so many indications of the rounding out of an epoch here, forming a kind of inclusion with the dedication of the temple, that we may suspect that C's edition of the history may have originally ended here. And it is worth noting once again how this part of the history begins and ends on a note of joy. Throughout the work of this author, so often disparaged as the

purveyor of interminable lists and genealogies, the joyful worship of God runs like a silver thread, from the ark procession of David (1 Chron. 15:16, 25) to the procession around Nehemiah's wall. The joy which finds expression in worship is, for this author, of the essence of religion:

> Glory in his holy name;
> Let the hearts of those who seek YHVH rejoice!
>   (1 Chron. 16:10)

Various Dispositions (Neh. 12:44–13:3)

M. **Fishbane**, *Biblical Interpretation in Ancient Israel*, 126–129; K. **Galling**, "Das Gemeindegesetz im Deuteronomium 23," in W. Baumgartner et al., *Festschrift A. Bertholet zum 80. Geburtstag*, Tübingen, 1950, 176–191; U. **Kellermann**, *Nehemia*, 47–48, 55–56; S. **Mowinckel**, *Studien* II, 34–35; W. A. **van der Weiden**, "Radix hebraica 'rb," *VD* 44, 1966, 97–104.

12:44 At that time men were appointed to take charge of the storerooms for contributions, firstlings, and tithes, and to gather into them the portions prescribed by the law for the priests and Levites according to the holdings of the towns; for Judah delighted in the priests and Levites then in office. [45]They performed the service of their God and the service of purification, with the musicians and gatekeepers, in keeping with the decree of David and of Solomon his son. [46]For at the time of David and Asaph, long ago,[a] there were chiefs[b] of musicians and leaders[c] of praise and thanksgiving to God. [47]At the time of Zerubbabel and that of Nehemiah[d] all Israel contributed the portions of the musicians and gatekeepers, as each day required. They set aside what belonged to the Levites, and the Levites set aside what belonged to the Aaronite priests.

13:1 On that day, as the book of Moses was being read to the people, it was found written in it that no Ammonite or Moabite should ever enter the assembly of God, [2]because they did not come to meet the Israelites with food and water, but rather hired Balaam against them to curse them, though our God turned the curse into a blessing. [3]When they heard the law, they separated from Israel all those of mixed descent.

a. *miqqedem* is sometimes emended, e.g., to *mupqādîm*, appointed (Bertholet 1902, 89), but unnecessarily; the form is well attested (Isa. 45:21; 46:10; Micah

5:1; Hab. 1:12; Pss. 74:12; 77:6, 12 [5, 11]; 143:5) and makes good sense in the context.

b. With Qere, several MSS, and Vulg. Other versions have sing. with Ketib.

c. MT has "leader(s) of the musicians and gatekeepers and song *(šîr)* of praise and thanksgiving," which does not make sense. Assuming a simple metathesis we read *śry (śārê)* for *šyr (šîr)*, which is consonant with *rāʾšê*, "chiefs"; see A. B. Ehrlich 1914, 210.

d. Sometimes omitted with LXX but unnecessarily.

The section now to be considered consists in two brief supplements to the dedication ceremony. They deal with support of the clergy, clerical responsibilities with special reference to liturgical music, and exclusion of certain categories from the worshiping community. They are tied in loosely with the narrative context by the phrase "on that day" (12:44; 13:1), and the theme of rejoicing forms an additional link (12:43–44). The chronological linkage is quite artificial, however, since the passage itself testifies that the epoch of Nehemiah is past history (12:47). Functionally, they bridge the gap between the achievements of Nehemiah at the beginning of his administration and events toward its end (13:6; cf. 5:14–18). The passage is often attributed to C, but the characteristic style and terminology of C are not much in evidence (*pace* Kellermann, 47–48). C would not have passed over Jeshua and Ezra in favor of Zerubbabel and Nehemiah (12:47), and the more obvious connections are with the stipulations of the covenant in Neh. 10, which is unrelated to C. All of these stipulations are referred to here with the exception of firstfruits and the wood offering, the omission of which is rectified in the concluding statements in the book (Neh. 13:30–31). This conclusion also summarizes the content of the present passage, referring as it does to purification, clerical service (*mišmeret*, 12:45), and the exclusion of everything foreign (*kol-nēkār*, 13:30; cf. *kol-ʿēreb*, 13:3). We conclude, then, that the covenant stipulations, the interstitial passage 12:44–13:3, and the last excerpt from the NM (13:4–31) are closely related in the literary formation of the book. The intent of the first two is to show that, in spite of problems, the outcome of Nehemiah's activity was a community united in observance of the law.

[12:44] The first concern is with support of the clergy. The appointment of officials in charge of the temple treasury (*ʾôṣār*) perhaps reflects Nehemiah's setting up a panel of four supervisors representing different constituencies (13:13). At the time of the Chronicler this function was performed by four gatekeepers, a situation backdated to David's reign (1 Chron. 9:26; cf. Neh. 12:25). It bears repetition that during the Persian period temples were often wealthy institutions with considerable capital and land holdings, which also served a function roughly comparable to banks in the modern period. It was natural, therefore, that C should show much more interest in the temple treasury than his principal source (1 Chron. 26:20–27; 27:25–31; 28:12; 29:8; 2 Chron. 5:1; 12:9; 16:2; 36:18). For the different contributions specified here see Neh. 10:33–34, 36–40 [32–33, 35–39]. The holdings (literally, fields) of the towns implies the assessment of contributions on a property-holding basis. The delight of the people in the temple clergy may have been real enough, but it must have been tempered by the heavy economic burden of supporting a tax-free institution with numerous employees. The editor inserted this remark to explain why the clergy were so well supported (though cf. 13:10–11), but also to link with the theme of rejoicing at the end of the previous passage.

[45–47] The correct performance of liturgical duties, which left the people so satisfied, is based on the dispositions of David referred to in the supplementary lists (11:23; 12:24). It also reflects a view of the origins of the temple liturgy, including purification rituals, which was probably standard at the time of writing (see 1 Chron. 23–26). According to this same view, these dispositions were faithfully implemented by Solomon (2 Chron. 8:14). The functions of liturgical musicians, organized in guilds under master liturgists of whom the most prominent was Asaph (see Ezra 2:4), are traced back to the same ideal epoch. The term *śar,* leader, in the text as emended perhaps reflects the title assigned to Chenaniah in David's reign (1 Chron. 15:22, 27); according to S. Mowinckel (*The Psalms in Israel's Worship,* Nashville, 1967, II, 56), *śar hammaśśā'* could be translated "master of the oracle." That the writer goes on at once to speak of the days of Zerubbabel and the days of Nehemiah implies the perspective of a considerably later time. While the writer probably did not think of the two men as contemporaries (witness the repetition of the phrase "in the days of . . ."), the linking of their names helps explain the backdating of Nehemiah to the time of the first return in 2 Macc. 1:18–36 and in rabbinic tradition. More generally, the passage illustrates the tendency to foreshorten or telescope events in the Persian period, a tendency which resulted in rabbinic chronology assigning no more than some thirty years to Persian rule (*Seder Olam Rab.* 30).

[13:1–3] The retrospective allusion in 12:47 to the laymen Zerubbabel and Nehemiah, with the implication that they played the leading roles in the refounding of the community, betrays a rather different perspective from that of C and may have influenced the linking of these two men, to the exclusion of Ezra, in the Wisdom of Jesus son of Sirach (49:11–13). The episode which now follows, represented as an extension of the dedication liturgy ("on that day," v. 1), takes the same line in attributing the public reading of the law and action resulting from it to Nehemiah, even though he is not explicitly mentioned. The reading is from "the book of Moses" (cf. 2 Chron. 25:4; 35:12; Neh. 8:1) and the text is the community law in Deut. 23:4–7 [3–6]. The text is not quoted *ad litteram*. Only the part dealing with Ammonites and Moabites is cited. The preceding stipulation excluding the sexually mutilated and the "bastards" *(mamzērîm)*, and the following section admitting third-generation Edomites and Egyptians, are omitted. The quotation is also recast in the third person, not the *oratio recta* of Deut. 23. Omission of the stipulation concerning eunuchs would be understandable if Nehemiah himself were such, but we have seen that this is very doubtful (1:11b). More probably, the issue being addressed had to do exclusively with "ritualized ethnicity" (Fishbane, 114). It would also be hazardous to conclude that the law concerning Edomites and Egyptians was too liberal for Nehemiah, especially in view of Edomite-Arab encroachments on Judean territory and the opposition of Geshem. We cannot be sure, in the first place, that this has any historical connection with Nehemiah himself or that it is reporting a specific occasion when this law was read and these results ensued. It is equally possible that it represents an editorial construct, reflecting the liturgical practice of reading scripture in temple and synagogue, and with the purpose of providing scriptural warranty for Nehemiah's action against Ammonites and Moabites which the narrative goes on to describe (13:4–9, 23). Whether 13:1–2 is an abridged version of the law as we know it, or an earlier draft which was later expanded, we have no way of knowing.

The reason for the exclusion of Ammonites and Moabites in the Deuteronomic law fits very well the situation during Nehemiah's career on account of the opposition of Sanballat, Tobiah, and their associates who also hired (the same verb *śkr*) a prophet against him (6:10–14), a stratagem which was likewise defeated with divine help. Balaam, a non-Israelite prophet now known also from the Deir 'Alla inscriptions, became in the course of time a sinister figure who led Israel into sin and deserved to die at their hands (Num. 31:8, 16; Josh. 13:22; 2 Peter 2:15; Jude 11; Rev. 2:14).

The result of the reading was the separation (stem *bdl* as in Ezra 9:1; 10:11; Neh. 10:29 [28]) from Israel of those of mixed descent. The term used here *('ēreb)* cannot refer to Arabs or Bedouin as in Ezek. 30:5 (*pace* Meyer 1896, 130); rather, it refers to those within the community of foreign or mixed descent (cf. Ex. 12:38; Jer. 25:20; 50:37), the equivalent of those who had "mingled" (*hit'ārᵉbû,* Ezra 9:2) with the local and neighboring non-Jewish population. This action seems to duplicate that of Ezra described at much greater length in Ezra 9–10. It may even have been intended to duplicate it, part of the strategy of presenting the reforms of the two men *ad modum unius.* There is, however, the significant difference that the requirement of divorcing foreign wives is passed over both here and in the covenant stipulations. The incidents related in the final extract of the NM confirm that this omission was not by oversight. For even though the bad effects of exogamous marriage are stressed (13:23–27), this remedy is not adopted, and the member of the high priestly family who married a Sanballat woman was himself expelled from the community. We would be justified in finding here another confirmation of the predictable failure of this measure of Ezra's.

Abuses Remedied (Neh. 13:4–14)

U. **Kellermann,** *Nehemia,* 48–51; S. **Mowinckel,** *Studien* II, 35–37; K. D. **Sakenfeld,** *The Meaning of Hesed in the Hebrew Bible,* Missoula, 1978; S. J. **Spiro,** "Who Was the Ḥaber? A New Approach to an Ancient Institution," *JSJ* 11, 1980, 186–216.

13:4 Now before this, Eliashib the priest who was placed in charge of the storerooms of the house of God, a relative of Tobiah, ⁵had provided a large room for him where previously there had been deposited the cereal offering, the frankincense, the vessels, and the tithe of grain, new wine, and fine oil prescribed by law for the Levites, musicians, and gatekeepers, together with the contributions[a] for the priests. ⁶While all this was happening I was not in Jerusalem, for in the thirty-second year of Artaxerxes king of Babylon I went to the king, and after some time I requested his permission[b] ⁷and returned to Jerusalem. Then I discovered the wicked thing that Eliashib had done on behalf of Tobiah, providing a room for him in the courts of the house of God. ⁸I was very upset and threw all Tobiah's household goods out of the room. ⁹I commanded them to purify the room[c] and then brought back into it the vessels of the house of God, the cereal offering and the frankincense.
  ¹⁰I also learned that the Levites had not been given their portions, and that both they and the musicians who had specific tasks to perform[d] had departed,[e] each to his own holding. ¹¹I therefore

remonstrated with the officials. "Why," I asked, "is the house of God being neglected?" So I brought them back together and reinstated them in their positions. [12]Then all Judah brought the tithe of grain, new wine, and fine oil into the storerooms. [13]I appointed[f] over them Shelemiah the priest, Zadok the scribe, and Pedaiah from the ranks of the Levites, with Hanan son of Zaccur son of Mattaniah to assist them, for they were considered trustworthy. Their task was to distribute shares to their colleagues.

[14]Remember me, O my God, on account of this, and do not wipe out these good deeds of mine which I have done for the house of God and its services.

a. MT *t^erûmat hakkōh^anîm,* collective sing.
b. *niš'altî min-hammelek;* for the idiom cf. 1 Sam. 20:6, 28.
c. MT has *l^ešākôt,* pl., but the context suggests sing., as L.
d. MT *'ōśê hamm^elā'kāh,* lit., "who did the work."
e. Lit., "fled."
f. Reading *vā'^asavveh* (cf. 7:2) with LXX, Syr., and L for MT *vā'ôṣrāh,* a Hiphil form otherwise unattested ("appoint as treasurer"?).

The structure and literary history of this last part of the book are difficult to determine, due to a complicated and not very satisfactory editorial arrangement of the material. If C's history ended with the dedication ceremony, 12:44–47 and 13:1–3 could be read as supplements, both introduced by the same phrase, "on that day" *(bayyôm hahû'),* which often marks additions to prophetic collections in the postexilic period (e.g., Zech. 12–14). But there still remained to be fitted in a rather longer extract from the NM dealing with various problems encountered toward the end of his administration and how he solved them. This last excerpt has been arranged in three sections (13:4–14, 15–22, 23–31), each of which is introduced by a rather vague temporal phrase and rounded off with the brief prayer to be remembered. We cannot help noticing throughout the sense of an epoch which at the time of writing belonged to the past (e.g., "in those days," 13:15, 23).

[13:4–5] The first of the three sections (13:4–14) deals with three issues: the expulsion of Tobiah from the temple precincts, the reorganization of the temple storerooms, and reform of the tithing system. They are connected by virtue of the fact that there was no longer any tithe to be stored after the expulsion of Tobiah. As noted earlier, the Eliashib who accommodated Tobiah in the temple is not the contemporary high priest of that name (3:1, 20–21; 12:10, 22; 13:28); his function is mentioned precisely to distinguish him from his namesake

mentioned shortly afterward. This function was similar to that of
Meremoth, to whom Ezra consigned the sacred vessels and donations on his arrival from Babylon (Ezra 8:33). The broad range of
Tobiah's contacts in Jerusalem have already been mentioned (2:10;
6:17–19). It appears that both he and Sanballat had established close
links with the Jerusalem priesthood through marriage alliances
which served to promote their political and economic interests, the
kind of situation which continued throughout the Persian period and
beyond (e.g., Josephus, *Ant.* 11.302–303). Provision of space in the
temple was no doubt connected with commercial concessions. The
word translated "room" *(liškāh)* connotes both residence and storeroom, but the latter is more common in Second Temple texts (1
Chron. 9:26; 2 Chron. 31:11; Ezra 8:29; Neh. 10:38–40 [37–39]).
Commercial interest, either as supplier or as middleman, was therefore the prime reason for wanting a *pied-à-terre* in the temple. Eliashib was obviously profiting by Nehemiah's absence to promote the
interests of the party opposed to the governor's policies, which no
doubt coincided with his own interests, and it is difficult to see how
he could have done so without the at least tacit approval of his
namesake the high priest.

[6] The memoir goes on to explain how such a situation could
have arisen. The explanation could imply a fairly brief absence, for
example, to report to the king on the state of the province. While he
would presumably have made much better time than Ezra and his
caravan, the round trip would have taken at least two months and
a stay of less than several weeks at the court is hardly conceivable.
In a somewhat similar situation in Egypt under Darius II, the governor Arsames was absent at the court for some three years, during
which time opponents of the Jewish community at Jeb profited by
his absence to destroy their temple (*AP* 27; 30; 32). It appears,
notwithstanding, that something more than a brief absence is implied. Neh. 5:14 speaks of a twelve-year tenure of office (445–433),
and his actions upon his return suggest that he was vested with the
same authority as before. Eliashib and Tobiah do not seem to have
expected him to return, at least not in the foreseeable future. It is
possible that he was recalled to explain allegations or complaints
made by one or other of his opponents, which he was evidently able
to do to the king's satisfaction, and thus secure his confirmation in
office. The last possible date for his return would be the year of the
death of Artaxerxes I Long Hand, that is, 423 B.C.E., but it was
almost certainly much earlier. There is no compelling need to demote
the verse to a gloss inserted later to explain how such a situation
could have arisen (as Mowinckel, *Studien* II, 35–37; Kellermann,

49–51). However the unusual title "king of Babylon" is explained—either by analogy with the same title used of Cyrus (*ANET,* 316), or by analogy with the title "king of Assyria" at Ezra 6:22, or because Babylon was the royal residence at that time—it need not imply the perspective of a much later time.

[7–9] We have seen that Nehemiah's absence at the court and return to Jerusalem may be seen as a chapter in the political history of the province and the struggle between the governor and the Sanballat-Tobiah-Geshem axis, with the former holding off the encroachments of the latter. In this struggle, which also divided loyalties within the province, the basic political issue seems to have been the establishment of the province's autonomy over against its neighbors. In pursuing this goal Nehemiah must have been walking a political tightrope since several of his actions could be, and in fact were, interpreted as seditious by opponents who must have had their own contacts in the satrapal and central government. Whether his return was occasioned by disturbing news which reached him from Jerusalem, as happened at his initial appointment, we do not know. The way in which he summarily rectified the situation points unmistakably to gubernatorial jurisdiction over the temple and its operations. Tobiah was expelled, the contaminated area purified, and the room restored to its original use. Most of the commodities stored there were those pledged in the covenant to support the cult (10:34, 38–40 [33, 37–39]). Use of the term "frankincense" permits a distinction between $l^e b\hat{o}n\bar{a}h,$ which was offered together with other things (Lev. 2:1–2), and $q^e t\bar{o}ret,$ which was offered by itself (cf. Ex. 30:1–10; for details see G. W. Van Beek, *BA* 23, 1960, 70–94). The significant omission from the list of commodities kept in the storeroom, compared with those which were returned to it, is the Levitical tithe. This omission provides the transition to another and equally serious problem which had to be dealt with.

[10] That Levites and liturgical musicians are here named separately does not necessarily imply that at the time of writing the latter had not yet been co-opted into the Levitical ranks. The collection of the tithe by the Levites themselves (10:38 [37]) may have come about as a result of this phase of neglect (cf. also Mal. 3:8–9). Theoretically the Levites did not own land, but we have encountered them more than once settled in various locations outside Jerusalem (7:72 [73]; 11:20; 12:27), which locations have nothing to do with the Levitical cities—if, indeed, these were anything more than an ideal projection (see M. Haran 1961b, 45–54, 156–165). Since the Levites provided important support for Nehemiah's policies, especially where these came into conflict with the interests of the higher clergy, we can

understand his anxiety to have them settled in Jerusalem rather than scattered around the province.

[11–13] Though Nehemiah held the civil officials (s*egānîm;* see on 2:16) responsible and remonstrated with them—not for the first time—one wonders whether the higher clergy were also involved. The accusation of neglecting the house of God has an exact counterpart in the final stipulation of the covenant (10:40 [39]). At this and similar junctures Nehemiah may convey the impression of being a highly contentious individual. He probably was, and if he had not been he probably would not have survived. At all events, the Levites and musicians were brought back without delay and, to avoid a recurrence of the crisis, Nehemiah put into effect an arrangement to ensure equitable distribution of resources (cf. 12:44). This consisted in a panel of four to supervise distribution of the tithe, the panelists representing the parties with a direct interest in the administration of resources: priests, Levites, musicians, and the governor himself. Shelemiah the priest bears a name unattested elsewhere in Ezra-Nehemiah but found at Elephantine (*AP* 30:29; 31:28). Zadok the scribe, whose task was no doubt to keep accurate inventory of resources and disbursements, may be identical with the Zedekiah of 10:2 [1]. He would have represented the interests of the governor. Pedaiah has a name otherwise unattested for Levites (but cf. Neh. 3:25 and *AP* 43:12). The musician Hanan (Hananiah) appears to have been grandson of the precentor Mattaniah (11:17; 12:35), which would strengthen the suspicion that the list of Levitical participants in the dedication ceremony is several decades later than the events described.

The argument for the chronological priority of Nehemiah, according to which this arrangement was in place when Ezra arrived in Jerusalem (Ezra 8:33), was briefly criticized in the commentary on that verse and should now be laid to rest. There is no suggestion that this was an innovation at the time of Nehemiah, and both the composition and the function of the officials mentioned at the two points of the narrative are different.

[14] The short prayer for remembrance which concludes this section, of a type which punctuates the last part of the NM (13:14, 22, 29, 31), has already been discussed (see 3:36–37 [4:4–5]; 5:19; 6:14). The metaphor of a record or ledger on which God records the good and bad deeds of humanity (cf. Isa. 65:6; Dan. 7:10), analogous to the book in which the names of the elect are registered (Mal. 3:16), will naturally be looked at askance when viewed through the prism of the Christian doctrine of grace and works. One can only say that

this is not the only option for understanding the implications of Nehemiah's prayer. The word *ḥesed,* used here, connotes both a fundamental attitude of fidelity and commitment and its expression in the conduct of one's life. There may be higher levels of religious sensitivity, but to look for assurance that one's life and work are of some worth in the sight of God is hardly an attitude to be despised.

Sabbath Observance (Neh. 13:15–22)

N. E. A. Andreasen, *The Old Testament Sabbath,* Missoula, 1972; M. **Fishbane,** *Biblical Interpretation in Ancient Israel,* 129–134; M. **Greenberg,** "The Sabbath Pericope in Jeremiah," *Iyyunim beSefer Yirmeyahu,* Jerusalem, 1971, 23–51 (Heb.); D. **Harden,** *The Phoenicians,* London, 1963 (2nd ed.), 157–179; A. **Kapelrud,** "Tyre," *IDB* 4:721–723; B. Z. **Luria,** "The Tyrians Also Who Lived in the City Brought in Fish and All Sorts of Wares, Nehemiah 13:16," *BM* 15, 1970, 363–367 (Heb.); R. **de Vaux,** *AI,* 475–483.

13:15 In those days I saw people treading winepresses in Judah on the sabbath, bringing in heaps of produce[a] and loading donkeys. They were also bringing into Jerusalem wine, grapes, figs, and all sorts of loads on the sabbath day. So I warned them against selling food.[b] [16]The Tyrians[c] who lived in the city[d] were also bringing in fish and all sorts of merchandise and selling them on the sabbath to Judeans in Jerusalem. [17]I remonstrated with the nobles of Judah saying, "What is this wicked thing you are doing, profaning the sabbath day? [18]Did not our ancestors do likewise, bringing on us and on this city all of these evils?[e] In profaning the sabbath you are bringing yet more wrath down on Israel." [19]When quiet had returned to the gates of Jerusalem,[f] just before the sabbath,[g] I commanded that the entrances[h] be closed and that they should not be opened again[i] until after the sabbath.[g] I also stationed some of my men at the gates so that[j] no load should enter on the sabbath day.

[20]On one or two occasions, however, the merchants and vendors of all kinds of wares spent the night outside Jerusalem. [21]I therefore warned them, saying, "Why are you camping out in front of the wall? If you do it again I will lay hands on you." So from then on they came no more on the sabbath. [22]I told the Levites to purify themselves and come and guard the gates[k] to preserve the sanctity of the sabbath day.

Remember this also to my credit, O my God, and spare me in your abundant mercy.

a. MT has simply "heaps" *(ʿᵃrēmôt,* LXX *dragmata),* not restricted to grain, as RSV and other modern versions.

b. MT "I warned them on the day of their selling food" *(vāʾāʿîd bᵉyôm mikrām ṣāyid)* is unsatisfactory since the verb has no object. I therefore read *bāhēm* for *bᵉyôm,* with Syr., and *mimmᵉkōr* for *mikrām* with Ehrlich 1914, 211, and Rudolph 1949, 206. Since *mimmᵉkōr* can be explained by haplography with the last letter of the preceding word, it is preferable to *kᵉmokrām,* "when they were selling" (Bertholet 1902, 92; et al.). Vulg., "I warned them that they should sell on a day when it was permitted to sell," makes good sense but is paraphrastic. *ṣāyid* means "food" as well as "game," *pace* Mowinckel, *Studien* II, 40–41.

c. Though missing from LXX^BA and Syr., *haṣṣōrîm* should neither be excised nor emended to *sayyᵉdîm,* "hunters" (Mowinckel, *Studien* II, 41).

d. MT has *bāh,* "in it"; the antecedent could be either Judah or Jerusalem.

e. Sing. in MT.

f. The difficulty here is caused by the verb *sālᵉlû.* The meaning "darken," "become shaded," is poorly attested and does not make good sense. L *hēsychasan* and Vulg. *quievissent* suggest a different approach, supported by Akk. and Syr. cognates, i.e., become quiet, inactive; cf. "when the entrances to Jerusalem had been cleared" (NEB based on G. R. Driver, *VTSup.* 16, 1967, 62–63), and "when the gates of Jerusalem had begun to empty" (Clines 1984, 244).

g. Rather than "the day before sabbath" and "the day after sabbath" respectively, since there is no evidence that this technical meaning applied in the Persian period (*pace* J. H. Tigay, *VT* 28, 1978, 362–365).

h. Lit., "doors" *(dᵉlātôt).*

i. "again" supplied.

j. *ʾᵃšer* supplied before *lōʾ yābôʾ,* following the more important ancient versions and the requirements of syntax.

k. More literally, "come as guardians of the gates"; asyndeton.

The two remaining passages from the NM (13:15–22, 23–29) are structurally parallel. They open in the same formulaic manner ("in those days I saw . . ."); they describe a problematic situation which provokes a response from Nehemiah, and the response takes the form of remonstrance with appeal to history. The final paragraph serves to round off the entire excerpt by returning to and recapitulating 12:44–13:3.

[13:15] The opening temporal phrase "in those days" is less determinate than "on that day" (12:44; 13:1) and does not help in placing the incidents in their historical context. They need not have taken place toward the end of Nehemiah's tenure of office. His observations of what was happening in the province do not necessarily imply a tour of inspection which must have taken place on the sabbath. We do not know whether at that time travel on sabbath was regulated by law, as it certainly was in the Roman period—based on an interpretation of

Ex. 16:29—when the maximum distance (the *'erub*) was two thousand cubits (Jub. 50:8, 12; CD 13:20–21; Josephus, *Ant.* 12.8.4; Acts 1:12; *m. Shabb.* 1:1; 5–6; *m. Erub.* 4–5; *Lev. Rab.* 34:16). Since the grapes were being pressed, the time of year must have been Tishri (September-October). The winepress generally consisted in a smoothed rock surface with a shallow channel along which the grape juice flowed into a lower rock basin in preparation for fermentation. Several have come to light in Israel, e.g., at Gibeon (el-Jîb), where this feature remained virtually unchanged for centuries.

If the people observed doing these things in Judah were Gentiles, the complaint addressed to the Jewish leadership would have been limited to buying on sabbath, which is precisely the issue in the covenant stipulation of Neh. 10:32a [31a]. The obvious tactic, in that case, would be to prevent Gentile trading on sabbath by closing the sabbath market at least in "the holy city" (11:1). This interpretation would also be consistent with one reading of the obscure verse 15b, "So I warned them [i.e., Gentiles] against selling food." Since it had long been understood that the Israelite was forbidden to sell on sabbath (Amos 8:5), the only doubtful issue would then be the legality of buying from Gentiles, and it would be this issue which was decided by Nehemiah and the covenant signatories, who stood by his decision. The difficulty is that the incident as reported here is closely related to the sabbath pericope in Jer. 17:19–27, acknowledged by most commentators to reflect a situation no earlier than the Babylonian exile. Only in these two passages is there a prohibition of transporting merchandise through the gates of Jerusalem, couched in the same language, and the parallelism is strengthened by the statement that sabbath violation was responsible for the destruction of the city and the evils which flowed from that disaster. The most probable solution, then, is that Nehemiah enforced what to many would have seemed a rigorist interpretation of the sabbath law in the decalogue (Ex. 20:8–11; Deut. 5:12–15). The decalogic prohibition of any kind of work *(kol-m^elā'kāh)* is interpreted to cover not only treading grapes, loading animals, porterage of goods and selling, none of which would have seemed exceptional, but also buying from Gentiles and thus encouraging trade on the sabbath. That the covenant stipulation alludes only to this last point does not imply a mitigation of Nehemiah's demands since the other exclusions were taken for granted.

[16] The Phoenicians (Sidonians and Tyrians), the most famous navigators and traders of the ancient world, as the Hebrew Bible also attests (Isa. 23:2–3, 8, 18; Ezek. 27:12–25; 28:5; Amos 1:9–10; Joel 4:6 [3:6]; Ezra 3:7), were well established during the Persian period

along the entire coastal region from Dor to Ashkelon (E. Stern 1982, 241–244). Further inland they set up trading stations, for example, the Sidonian settlement at Marissa (Tell Sandakhanna about eighteen miles southeast of Ashkelon), which almost certainly dates back into the Persian period. Not surprisingly, one of these was in Jerusalem, with a flourishing market perhaps located at the Fish Gate (see 3:3). The sabbath was obviously considered an ideal day for the market, and the Jewish inhabitants of the city must have flocked there in much the same way that the present-day inhabitants patronize the Arab markets in the Old City and Bethlehem on sabbath. The full implementation of the sabbath law as interpreted by Nehemiah, not to mention fair-trade practice, therefore seemed to call for the abolition of the sabbath market.

[17–18] The responsibility of the civic leadership for law observance is once again illustrated as Nehemiah takes to task not the priests but the nobles of Judah (on the *ḥôrîm* see commentary on 4:13). The language of sanctification (cf. Ex. 20:8, 11; Deut. 5:12) and profanation (Ex. 31:14; Ezek. 20:13; 22:8; 23:28) associated with sabbath expresses its removal from the secular round of activities including making a living. What might be called the ontological character of sabbath was conferred by God himself at creation (Gen. 2:3). For the community to sanctify sabbath means to acknowledge that character and embody its acknowledgment in observance of the sabbath law. While sabbath was certainly an ancient institution, the origins of which have been the object of inconclusive speculation, it seems to have achieved what we might call confessional status only from the time of the exile. According to Isa. 56:1–8 its observance is practically synonymous with fidelity to the covenant. It is therefore less surprising than it might seem that Nehemiah, following Ezek. 20 and the late passage in Jer. 17:19–27, should attribute the present unsatisfactory state of the people, namely, subjection to a foreign power (cf. Ezra 9:13; Neh. 9:26–27), to nonobservance of the sabbath law throughout Israel's history.

[19] As noted earlier, the city gate structure would have included rooms opening onto a plaza which, on account of the constant traffic, was an ideal place for vendors. One might compare the situation which obtains today at the Damascus Gate of the Old City. Characteristically, Nehemiah at once took measures to ensure that his decision was obeyed. He stationed his personal militia (his *n^e'ārîm,* see on 4:10 [16]) to prevent traders from entering from Friday to Saturday at sundown. Since, however, the gates would be closed after dark anyway, we must suppose that they were not opened until Sunday morning.

[20–22] Deprived of the space inside the gate for setting up shop, the more persevering of the vendors camped out overnight just outside the wall in the hope of either smuggling their wares into the city or doing business with those who were coming and going through the night, presumably by means of a postern gate of some kind. Threatened with violence, they eventually withdrew. Since the guard duty assigned to his militia was clearly an interim measure, it only remained to set up a more permanent arrangement to prevent a recurrence of the abuse. Several commentators have found the appointment of Levites as city gatekeepers to be historically implausible, and have therefore bracketed the sentence as an insert from the hand of C or of an editor with similar ideas. While the regular duty of the Levitical gatekeepers was to guard the entrance to the temple, the preservation of the sanctity of sabbath was an equally pressing religious task calling for a ritual of purification (cf. Ezra 6:20; Neh. 12:30). Hence the assignment of this duty to Levites was a natural extension of their regular tasks. We may, in fact, observe how the sanctity of the temple is being increasingly predicated of the city enclosed by its wall (cf. 11:1; Isa. 52:1; Joel 4:17 [3:17]), a theologoumenon which will be taken up to and well beyond its logical conclusions in the Temple Scroll from Qumran.

On the final brief prayer see at 13:14.

Nehemiah's Anti-Assimilationist Policy (Neh. 13:23–31)

R. J. Coggins, *Samaritans and Jews,* Atlanta, 1975, 93–100; M. Fishbane, *Biblical Interpretation in Ancient Israel,* 123–129; K. Galling, "Bagoas und Esra," *Studien,* 149–184; H. G. Kippenberg, *Garizim und Synagoge,* Berlin, 1971, 50–57; R. Marcus, "Josephus on the Samaritan Schism," *Josephus* VI (Loeb Classical Library), Cambridge, Mass., 1978, 498–511; S. Mowinckel, *Studien* II, 104–118; H. H. Rowley, "The Samaritan Schism in Legend and History," in B. W. Anderson and W. Harrelson (eds.), *Israel's Prophetic Heritage,* New York, 1962, 208–222; "Sanballat and the Samaritan Temple," *BJRL* 38, 1955/56, 166–198 (= Rowley, *Men of God,* London and Edinburgh, 1963, 246–276); E. Ullendorf, "C'est de l'hébreu pour moi!" *JSS* 13, 1968, 125–135; H. G. M. Williamson, "The Historical Value of Josephus' *Jewish Antiquities* xi.297–301," *JTS* n.s. 28, 1977, 49–66.

13:23 Also in those days I saw that some Jews had married Ashdodite, Ammonite, and Moabite women.[a] [24]Half their children spoke the language of Ashdod, or that of the respective nations,[b] and were unable to speak Hebrew.[c] [25]I remonstrated with them, cursing them, striking some of their men and pulling out their hair.

I made them take an oath in the name of God: "You shall not give your daughters to their sons in marriage, nor shall you take wives [d] from among their daughters for your sons or for yourselves. [26]Was it not on account of such women [e] that Solomon king of Israel sinned? Among the many nations there was no king like him, and he was beloved of God, who made him king over all Israel. Yet foreign women led even him into sin. [27]Shall we then follow your example [f] and do all this great evil, breaking faith with our God by marrying foreign women?"

[28]Now one of the sons of Joiada, son of Eliashib the high priest, was the son-in-law of Sanballat the Horonite, so I banished him from my presence.

[29]Remember them, O my God, for having defiled the priesthood and the covenant of the priests and Levites. [g]

[30]So I purified them from everything foreign, and established the services of the priests and Levites with the duties proper to each. I also arranged for the wood offering at fixed times and for first-fruits. [31]Remember this, O my God, in my favor.

a. Lack of the conjunction before "Ammonite and Moabite," together with the word order in the following verse (see note b), suggests a gloss (see Hölscher 1923, 561; et al.).
b. MT $v^e kil^e \check{s}\hat{o}n$ 'am $v\bar{a}$'$\bar{a}m$, lit., "and according to the language of a people and a people," absent from LXX, should follow "the language of Ashdod" instead of coming at the end of the sentence as in MT. It may therefore be a gloss added to include Ammonites and Moabites (see Mowinckel, *Studien* II, 41; Kellermann 1967, 53; Williamson 1986, 393).
c. Lit., "the language of Judah" ($y^e h\hat{u}d\hat{i}t$); see commentary.
d. "wives" supplied.
e. Lit., "on account of these."
f. If $ni\check{s}ma$' is first-person pl. imperfect Qal, the literal translation would be "shall we listen to you . . . ?" But it could also be third-person masc. sing. perfect Niphal, meaning something like, "and, with respect to you, should it be a thing heard of . . . ," which, however, is much less natural.
g. MT has "the covenant of the priesthood $(hakk^e hunn\bar{a}h)$ and the Levites." If this reading is retained, $v^e hal^e viyyim$ would almost certainly have been added. But it seems preferable to follow L, Syr., Eth., Arab. in reading $hakk\bar{o}h^a n\hat{i}m$, in which case allusion to Levites may still be a later addition (Mowinckel, *Studien* II, 41; Kellermann 1967, 54), perhaps occasioned by the reference to the "covenant of Levi" at Deut. 33:9 and Mal. 2:4, 8.

The passage which follows, parallel with 13:15–22 as we have seen, deals with two specific incidents linked by the theme of ritual ethnicity. Both are excerpted from the NM, though there may have been some abridgment, especially in the very succinct account of foreign marriage involving the high priestly family. The final prayer for remembrance is preceded by a summary of the cultic reforms dealt with in 12:44–13:14, together with the wood offering and firstfruits, stipulated in the covenant (10:35–36 [34–35]). There is a distinct possibility that this final summary—following "I purified them from everything foreign"—has been added by a well-meaning scholiast, thereby concluding Nehemiah's career on a note almost as anticlimactic as that of Ezra.

[13:23–24] The unacceptable marriages which came to Nehemiah's attention cannot be used as an argument for Nehemiah's chronological priority over Ezra. If the incidents reported came toward the end of his administration, about a quarter of a century would have passed since Ezra's arrival, long enough for recidivism of this kind to have developed, even assuming Ezra's measures to have been an unqualified success. The first incident arose out of an encounter, in Jerusalem or elsewhere, with Jews who had married women from the province of Ashdod in the coastal region to the west and southwest (see 4:1 [7]). In view of the dominant influence of the mother during the formative years, it is not surprising that many of the children spoke her language, though why the other half did not remains unexplained. There have been several guesses, all inconclusive, as to the language in question: a residue of the Philistine language—about which, unfortunately, we know next to nothing; an Aramaic dialect; perhaps even Phoenician, given the political and commercial Phoenician presence in the coastal area. Ullendorf's suggestion that *'ašdôdît* was simply a current designation for any unintelligible foreign language (as in our expression, "It's all Greek to me") is attractive but overlooks the actual issue, which is Jewish-Ashdodite marriages. What was really at stake was not so much speaking a foreign language as the inability to speak Hebrew ("the language of Judah"; see 2 Kings 18:26, 28; 2 Chron. 32:8; Isa. 36:11, 13). Language has always been an important ingredient of national identity: whether Gaelic in Ireland or Welsh in Wales or, more to the point, Hebrew during the Bar-Kokhba rebellion and in Israel in the modern period. This particular incident shows that Hebrew was still spoken in spite of the prevalence of Aramaic, which must have been *de rigueur* for anyone aspiring to a professional career. It also illustrates the important and easily neglected point that Nehemiah's religious measures were part and parcel of a larger objective, namely, the survival of a *people*.

[25–27] Nehemiah's reaction cannot be construed as taking legal action against them (Fensham 1982, 267) or having recourse to torture (Smith 1971, 135), which would hardly include pulling out hair. While it may simply reproduce a conventional expression of public humiliation (cf. Isa. 50:6), it matches other indications of an impulsive and even intemperate nature. This was the kind of man he was.

The wording of the oath is based on Deut. 7:3, the most quoted text in the book, but adapted to the context. In other words, it is couched in the oath form and transposed from the second person singular to the second person plural. It also applies the prohibition not just to their sons but to themselves (as at Ezra 9:2), though this would be implied in the general prohibition with which the text referred to begins ("you shall not intermarry with them"). The prohibition applies equally to both sexes. The motive clause in Deut. 7:3, which speaks in general of the religious implications of marrying foreign women, is displaced by the example of Solomon in 1 Kings 11:1–2. The Deuteronomic character of this text is at once evident in its quoting or paraphrasing the law of Deut. 7:3 and the motive clause following; that is, it applies scripture to a particular instance. It might easily be overlooked that the first four nations supplying wives to Solomon are precisely those subject to an absolute (Moab, Ammon) or qualified (Edom, Egypt) exclusion from the community in the law of Deut. 23:4–9 [3–8]. The illustration is therefore more than a routine use of prophetic-homiletic invective. It is a deliberate and specific application to the contemporary situation of a text which, in all probability, is itself worded to recall the law in Deut. 23. What is notable here is the exegesis of a scripture still in the process of formation, and that in the interests of a particular ideology. And since we may be sure that those who did not share Nehemiah's anti-assimilationist views also had their "scriptural" arguments, though for obvious reasons they have not been preserved, what we are witnessing is a conflict of interpretations, applying authoritative texts in different and mutually exclusive ways to the solution of current problems. Other Second Temple texts, e.g., Isa. 56:1–8 and Ruth, confirm the impression that by this time the interpretation of texts was an essential factor in the struggle for normative self-definition.

The point of the illustration would have been immediately obvious. If Solomon, beloved of God (indicated by his personal name Jedidiah, 2 Sam. 12:24–25), was not exempt from the disastrous religious consequences of foreign marriages, how could Nehemiah's contemporaries hope to be so?

[28–29] The incident which follows, and the prayer or imprecation with which it concludes, illustrate the conflict between the governor and his predominantly lay supporters on the one hand and the
upper-level clergy on the other. Eliashib was the high priest contemporary with Nehemiah (3:1, 20–21; 12:10, 22), and he was succeeded
in office by Jehoiada/Joiada (12:10–11, 22), though it is unclear to
which of the two the designation "high priest" used here applies. One
of Jehoiada's sons, other than the Jonathan and Johanan of Neh.
12:11, 22 (*pace* Galling, 164–165), had married into Sanballat's family, for which he was expelled from the province by Nehemiah (cf.
Ezra 7:26; 10:8) and presumably retired to Samaria. As sparse as our
information is, it reveals a network of relationships cemented by
mariages de convenance between the Sanballats, Tobiads, and important elements of the lay and clerical aristocracy in Jerusalem (cf.
6:17–19; 13:4).

A very similar story is told by Josephus about a certain Manasseh,
brother of the high priest Jaddua, who married Nikaso, daughter of
Sanballat, was for that reason expelled by the Jerusalem elders and
began a new career as high priest of the Samaritan temple built
expressly for him by Sanballat on Mount Gerizim (*Ant.* 11.302–312).
Josephus places this incident at the time of Darius III and Alexander, but there are good reasons for believing that it is a garbled and
tendentious retelling of Neh. 13:28, especially since Josephus evidently identified his Sanballat with the opponent of Nehemiah (11.
302) and omits mention of the expulsion in his account of Nehemiah's administration. Whether anything can be salvaged from it for
historical reconstruction is doubtful. Nikaso may pass, but Manasseh
is suspect since Samaritan tradition knows of no high priest of that
name. The role of the elders might fit in with other indications of a
version of events in which Nehemiah does not figure (e.g., 3:1–32,
the building of the wall). On the whole, however, it would be prudent
to leave it out of account in reconstructing events during Nehemiah's
administration.

The prayer, offered in the spirit of the imprecation psalms, is
directed against a plurality; certainly the high priestly family, possibly a larger group of opponents in the clerical establishment. The
legal basis for the condemnation is the ordinance in the Holiness
Code (H) that the high priest must marry a native woman (Lev.
21:13–15). The language is reminiscent of the strongly worded condemnation of the priesthood in Malachi (2:1–9) for having corrupted
the covenant of Levi (Deut. 33:9). The antisacerdotal diatribe of this
prophet cannot be far removed in time from Nehemiah. On the basis
of Neh. 13:29 one might be permitted the guess—and it would be no

more than that—that the promised messenger of the covenant who will appear in the temple, purify the priesthood, and reform the sacrificial system is not Ezra (as certain rabbis argued) but Nehemiah. In this as in other respects Malachi at least represents positions very close to if not identical with those of Nehemiah.

[30–31] The conclusion of this section, and of the book, will inevitably leave the reader disappointed, though abrupt endings are not so unusual in the Hebrew Bible (e.g., Isaiah; Jonah). The purification from everything foreign takes the reader back to 13:3 *(kol-nēkār . . . kol-'ēreb)* and thus serves to impose a certain unity on the intervening narrative. With the final prayer to be remembered it may have formed the original ending to the NM. Another reference to Nehemiah's cultic reforms (12:44–47; 13:10–14) is not expected at this point, especially when linked with the wood offering "at fixed times" (cf. 10:35 [34]; Ezra 10:14) and firstfruits. It is therefore possible that a later and not entirely felicitous insertion has been made by an editor anxious to attribute these measures, detailed in the covenant document, to Nehemiah.